CAN'T *Slow* DOWN

ALSO BY MICHAELANGELO MATOS

The Underground Is Massive:
How Electronic Dance Music Conquered America

CAN'T *Slow* DOWN

HOW 1984 BECAME
POP'S BLOCKBUSTER YEAR

MICHAELANGELO MATOS

hachette
BOOKS
NEW YORK

Cover design by Nick Bilardello
Cover photographs: Prince © Steve Skjold/Alamy Stock Photo; Madonna © ZUMA Press, Inc./ Alamy Stock Photo; Michael Jackson © KMazur/Getty Images
Cover copyright © 2020 by Hachette Book Group, Inc.

Hachette Books
Hachette Book Group
1290 Avenue of the Americas
New York, NY 10104
HachetteBooks.com
Twitter.com/HachetteBooks
Instagram.com/HachetteBooks

First Edition: December 2020

Published by Hachette Books, an imprint of Perseus Books, LLC, a subsidiary of Hachette Book Group, Inc. The Hachette Books name and logo is a trademark of the Hachette Book Group.

The Hachette Speakers Bureau provides a wide range of authors for speaking events. To find out more, go to www.hachettespeakersbureau.com or call (866) 376-6591.

The publisher is not responsible for websites (or their content) that are not owned by the publisher.

Print book interior design by Linda Mark

Library of Congress Control Number 2020946920

ISBNs: 978-0-306-90337-3 (hardcover); 978-0-306-90335-9 (e-book)

Printed in the United States of America

LSC-C

Printing 1, 2020

CONTENTS

INTRODUCTION

ABOUT TWO-THIRDS OF THE WAY THROUGH WRITING THIS BOOK, I WAS taking a car home while listening to a Jack station, the driver's choice. Shortly after Phil Collins's "In the Air Tonight" (with the last thirty seconds cut off—*boo*) gave way to the Bangles' "Walk Like an Egyptian," the driver said, "I'm from the eighties." Me too, I said—big-time.

One of my cherished early memories of being a pop fan—an afternoon I've long recalled as having sealed my fate as one—was in the summer of 1984, when I was nine. I was being forced to clean my room, a task I took to with great indolence. I wasn't allowed out until it was done. I turned on the radio, toggling between two Top 40 stations, skipping past commercials, and for about three or four hours, I waited until one of them played a song I disliked. It had to happen—the radio *always* played songs I disliked. But it didn't. After a couple of hours I realized, *I should be recording this*, and took out a cheap C-60. The first song on after I hit RECORD was Patty Smyth and Scandal's "The Warrior," with its "bang-bang" chorus. I had a busted air rifle I tried to "bang-bang" along to the song with, but it wouldn't load twice in time, alas.

Growing up in the Twin Cities at the height of *Purple Rain* mania—and being a Prince fan and a pop fan since memory—made 1984 an acutely exciting period. A few years later, as I began seriously investigating rock and pop history, reading books and old magazines and newspapers, it came to light that I wasn't alone—a number of rock critics and historians considered it a peak year then and afterward. In particular, Dave Marsh's *The Heart of Rock & Soul: The 1,001 Greatest Singles Ever Made*, in 1989, championed '84 as the year of an "American explosion . . . the greatest group of American pop singles of the decade." I'd been right that day in my room.

Then the nineties happened, and for many young rock fans coming of age, it seemed urgent to discard anything that had the mark of the eighties upon it. Gated drums, brassy synthesizers, canted keyboard–bass lines—the coked-up sonic hallmarks of the Reagan decade were suddenly, desperately uncool. I once met someone at a party who insisted that Prince had never made rock music because, and I quote, "It doesn't sound like the Pixies."

But it wasn't just that music had changed. So had the business of it. Part of what made 1984 seem so future-forward was the fresh background of the business nearly having sunk five years before. It's hard not to hear that new-found confidence in the music itself. It was the most jam-packed pop radio year since the mid-sixties, and just as fertile underground: hip-hop and dance music, punk and new wave, artists from Africa and Jamaica, reissues and box sets, all flourished in 1984. The mode as well as the music changed. It was the year cassettes outsold vinyl LPs for the first time, and the year the Compact Disc (always capitalized—it was a *trademarked brand name*, remember) began making serious commercial inroads, not to mention the year the first CD was manufactured in America.

Every city in the world has something happening every week called "Eighties Night." Michael Jackson and Prince, particularly in the wake of their passing, have acquired the mythical resonance of Elvis, the Beatles, and Bob Dylan. Madonna is still a major pop idol, one of the acknowledged forebears of modern music.

Yet the pop of 1984 was nowhere near as anodyne as people appear to think. Pop culture was a moral battleground during the *Stranger Things* years. Prince and Madonna—even the publicly squeaky-clean Michael Jackson—were seen as sexual deviants to a populace far closer to pre-sixties innocence than we see today.

The era's collective tale seems to exist only in pieces. For a musical period whose popularity has never waned—particularly with a younger generation that venerates the decade's pop in much the way kids in the eighties themselves often looked to the sixties with longing—there's been surprisingly little written about eighties pop, per se. Apparently, everyone who loved music but hated the radio in the eighties was so worked up over it that they all wrote books. The titles on indie rock, hip-hop, postpunk, acid house, Goth, new wave, and a nonstop torrent of punk micro-histories have created a lopsided effect: we now know far more about eighties music outside the mainstream than anything *in* that mainstream—unless we read a raft of individual artist bios.

This brings us to methodology. Whereas my previous book, *The Underground Is Massive*, was built on more than three hundred interviews, *Can't Slow Down* is drawn primarily from archival material. It's strange how under-covered this period of pop has been, considering the sheer overload of frankly amazing source material on it. I read a lot of books and magazines (physical and digital), raided the shelves of a number of public and personal libraries, combed through oral history transcripts from two major music museums, and spent a lot of time googling things.

One of my favorite stories from the research came from that August, when a San Diego rock station, XHZ-FM (Z90.3), suddenly had its plug pulled—the station's Mexican owner, Victor Diaz, revoked his contract with his American operators over low ratings. He enlisted his teenage sons, instead, to select the new playlist. The station's program director complained to *Billboard* that Diaz had "sent us a letter last week informing us that he was going to take over the programming. The next day, his wife walked into the studio with a box of singles and told our announcers to insert these records—mainly American Top 40 hits that didn't fit in at all with our programming—every fifteen minutes."

Pop music is easier to create, record, and disseminate than ever. But in 1984, it felt like the brass ring. There are a lot of chart placements mentioned in this book. My intention is to demonstrate why a heavily commercial era in pop music mattered; gauging its popularity serves a necessary contextual purpose.

That's one of the main things that changed—in rock culture, the pop charts stopped mattering so much during the seventies, when much of the music's leading edge was seen as in the LP cuts played on album-oriented rock (AOR) stations, rather than the singles on pop radio. This critical line held sway for many years, but in more recent years, music writing has shown a greater appreciation for the pleasures and craft of mainstream pop of that (and any) era. Our Pixies fan above might not have been able to hear these things as well a couple of decades ago, when we had that conversation, but her present-day equivalent is much more likely to.

Another change was that, when Marsh wrote his singles book, the music business's regained bullishness still carried a charge only five years after the business had nearly sunk itself. In the early 2000s, even with Napster having already begun its termite work, the biz had been so extravagantly successful for so long that a once-crippling downturn amounted to a blip.

In a way, 1984 is the last year of the old world—as David Hepworth pointed out, both the hole in the ozone layer and acid rain were discovered in 1985. But 1984 was also a decisive year for technology, both in and around the music world. (Chapter 2 looks closely at some of those changes.) That November, the biz tip sheet *Radio & Records* ran an interview with Quincy Jones, who'd produced *Thriller* and had one of the savviest and most varied careers in show business. "I've seen the changes go from mono to stereo to quad," he said. "One thing that's bothered me for thirty-four years is the archaic record distribution system. With 250, 260 million people in this country, it's outrageous to get excited about one million albums." Instead, Jones proposed an "Avon kind of system":

> JONES: With computers around now, it would be very easy to get musical profiles of people's likes and dislikes. . . . Maybe using TV to make impulse buying more accessible to more people . . . the screen lists whatever you're listening to. . . . You say "I like that" and look at the information on the screen. Then you hit one or two buttons that ask for your purchase selection and credit card number . . . something in that direction.
>
> *R&R*: That would be a great way to chart sales electronically.
>
> JONES: Right. And it could be possible in five years for you to have no inventory in your house. No records, tapes, anything. If you had access to a satellite, a code book/catalog, and a television set, you could punch up anything you wanted anytime. . . . And you could really target the music because you don't always want to hear a whole album. So you're programming several hours of music from this vast catalog in the sky. That would be incredible. You'd have access to anything out there that's current and have an intelligent way to catalog it.

That vision was truer than most of us could have guessed. In 2020, music is available any way you care to hear it, but in 1984 its level of omnipresence was new. The model of Michael Jackson's *Thriller* as a "tentpole" album, spinning off hits—in the way a tentpole movie franchises sequels—became the music business's standard operating procedure.

If "The Golden Age of Corporate Synergy" is a little much for you to swallow, I can't blame you. What's striking is just how vibrant it all sounded— genres that, for years, hadn't spoken to each other on the air suddenly were in conversation again. "Our audience is completely mixed, seven to seventy, black to yellow, and everything in-between," Roy Hay of Culture Club said in 1998, after they reunited. "I can't think of many bands who have that."

Downloading, then streaming, allowed the tribalism surrounding genres to become an afterthought—straight-up pop included. "Pop just means shit that went out and got popular," Kanye West said in 2003. "That don't mean 'Backstreet Boys.' I think a lot of people like old Madonna songs. Not everyone sits around watching *Scarface* over and over 'til they got gassed up to go to the club and try to kill somebody."

It's not a coincidence that he picked an artist and a film that both emerged in 1983 but blew up in 1984 (she on MTV, it on cable). That's also true of much in the book. It is not doctrinaire about release dates; plenty of pre- and post-1984 music comes into discussion where and when necessary, and in a few places where it seemed mete, I tie up a loose end past the book's conclusion. But for the most part, the trajectories it traces end when it does.

The reason it ends when it does is simple: The later eighties sucked. When people think of the era's clichés—boxy shoulder pads, hair only a stylist could love, Patrick Nagel, the period's patented studio trickery—the playful, fun examples invariably come from the decade's first half and the rigid, formulaic ones from the second. "You can divide the eighties into pre– and post–Live Aid," Marco Pirroni, the guitarist for Adam and the Ants, said in 2007. "After Live Aid it was all over." As an accompanist of the act who bit it harder than anyone that day, Pirroni knows it—and the eighties—better than most.

WPLJ-FM,

NEW YORK CITY

August 7, 1983

"IT'S EIGHT O'CLOCK ON **WPLJ,** NEW YORK—TIME FOR A SPECIAL EDI-tion of *Let's Hear It*, with our program director, Larry Berger."

For six years, *Let's Hear It* had aired on New York's FM rock leader at 10:00 p.m. on Sundays, to help fulfill the station's public affairs programming re-quirements and to bridge its music with an eleven o'clock talk block. It also helped "create the feeling of accessibility to the station," says Berger. "There was always some kind of crank call."

Berger had joined WPLJ in 1974, and under him it became an AOR (album-oriented rock) powerhouse. But it was also among the first stations in America to play Barry Manilow's "Mandy," a ballad as soft as a dead mango. "WPLJ was quite an unusual AOR station in the seventies in that it was pretty broad," says Berger. "The main crux of the station was rock and roll." Along with format staples—Led Zeppelin, the Who, Rolling Stones, Lynyrd Skynyrd—he says, "We played everything from Simon and Garfunkel and John Denver to Earth, Wind & Fire, Marvin Gaye, Stevie Wonder, even Barry White."

Only a few years before Berger joined WPLJ, that would have been busi-ness as usual: Top 40 radio played everything popular. But by the mid-seventies, the Top 40 audience had begun to subdivide. AOR had begun the shift, early in the decade; by the middle, adult contemporary (A/C) had lured away adults who liked ballads by playing *only* ballads. In the summer of 1978, the New York Top 40 WKTU went all-disco and took away the audience of the city's premiere black station, WBLS, helmed by the legendary Frankie Crocker. "It happened overnight," says Berger. "They went from a one-point-something to an 11.2. It sucked audience from everywhere."

That stratification meant that by 1979, WPLJ had to rock, or else. "We became more narrowly focused than we had been before," says Berger. "That seemed like the right thing to do for a while." On air, Berger said that in the late seventies, the station was "playing a lot of heavy metal. These were the years when WPLJ [had its] lowest ratings in at least recent history." By 1980, he added, "We played only records by white people with long hair who played electric guitars."

Rock and roll had once signified racial inclusion, but by 1980, *Billboard* would run a cover story that began, "Has AOR radio become lily-white?" Clearly, it had—and it was bad for business. "Within a year," he says, "it became clear to me that this wasn't going to work in the long term." The baby boomers were growing up and taking their demographic skew with them. By 1982, Americans' median age was thirty-one; sticking with a narrow young-male market, AOR had painted itself into a corner. "The twelve-to-twenty-four demos will shrink by about one-third in this decade," noted a Seattle program director (PD) that year, predicting that rather than two or three AORs per market, by the end of the eighties there would be only one.

Meanwhile, Top 40 became inundated with mush, via either adult baby food like Air Supply or rockers scoring with "a soft mid-tempo ballad," per *Billboard* in 1981, "as REO Speedwagon, Styx, and Journey have recently done." Bands like those were dubbed "corporate rock": Asia, Boston, Kansas, all wielding acres of echo to bitchin' guitar leads and a soaring, soothing ocean of suboperatic power ballads. That, rather than the rockers, was what you heard on pop radio in the early eighties.

These new radio formats reflected an increasing reliance on consulting firms to tell stations what to play. One leading firm was Burkhart/Abrams/Michaels/Douglas, whose cofounder Lee Abrams had codified the AOR format in 1971. WPLJ did its own research and found, too, that listeners were far more comfortable with familiar music. By 1983, the percentage of new music WPLJ played had slid, over four years, from 70 percent to 30 percent. "It happened gradually," says Berger. "By 1982, it was becoming very difficult to find enough current, appropriate songs that would appeal to the rock coalition."

The very idea of a "rock coalition" seemed to be disappearing. "On the sixties' Top 40 radio, it was possible to hear Sam and Dave, Otis Redding, the Beatles, the Four Tops, and Bob Dylan all in the space of an hour," *Time*'s Jay Cocks wrote in 1982. Neil Bogart, who ran Boardwalk Records and had one of that year's biggest number ones with Joan Jett's "I Love Rock and Roll," told Cocks, "They play music for the fourteen-to-eighteen audience, the thirty-to-thirty-five, the fifty-to-sixty, or for white, black, Chicano. And only two out of five stations are willing to play new records."

RUMORS OF THE RECORD BUSINESS'S IMPENDING INSOLVENCY BEGAN BUZZ-ing in the summer of 1979. "The sales of musical product are apparently way off from this time last year, and no improvement is expected in the foreseeable future," reported *Trouser Press* that September. "On a rough guess, one executive used 20 percent as an estimate of how much the reduction amounts to." In fact, record sales would fall 11 percent that year.

There was a general recession on in the United States at the time—but after World War II, record sales had kept rising even in bad times. Music, the prevailing wisdom went, was recession-proof. No longer. What made it worse was that the slump was directly preceded by the blockbuster sales of the *Saturday Night Fever* and *Grease* soundtracks, which, as one biz reporter noted, "shattered sales records to imply that commercial music would continue its sixties and seventies market expansion with redoubled momentum. Instead, time has caught up with the world of gold and platinum. . . . The glory days are over."

Much of the blame for this was placed squarely on disco, whose popularity had inspired the major labels to issue a glut of dance twelve-inches that the public didn't want. The sales returns, representing money lost on the label's part, did a lot to feed the 1979 crisis. "We wanted to work with a white artist so people could stop tagging us as black producers or disco producers," Nile Rodgers of Chic told *Billboard* in December 1979. "You can't make any money with that label." In the early eighties, fewer people would call it *disco* and they began instead to call it *dance music*.

A similar thing happened with Top 40 radio. That phrase had become so unfashionable that a new term emerged in the trade magazine *Radio & Records*: contemporary hits radio, or CHR.

Things became dire in 1981. That August, Paul McCartney, one of the few commercial sure bets left, finished *Tug of War*—his first album since John Lennon's death, a highly awaited reunion with Beatles producer George Martin—but didn't release it till the spring of 1982. "One of the reasons was the market," Martin said. "The record business was at such a low ebb." That November, Russ Solomon, president of the retail giant Tower Records, told *BusinessWeek*, "This is just not a growth industry now."

Nineteen eighty-two was even worse. The major labels were hemorrhaging money; CBS Records was forced to lay off three hundred employees that August. "The number of albums certified platinum in 1982 was down 11 percent from '81 totals, while gold albums were off an even more pronounced 20 percent," *Billboard* reported.

Yet there were glimmers of optimism. Over Christmas of '82, the 140-store chain Record Bar wound up 16 percent ahead of the previous holiday. It was hardly the only retailer that season to sell more cassettes than LPs. And despite revenues being down 12 percent and earnings per share having fallen nearly two dollars in a year, CBS Records' fourth quarter of 1982 actually showed an 8 percent rise. Michael Jackson had done his job.

NORMALLY, QUINCY JONES RADIATED POSITIVITY, BUT EVEN HE WAS WOR-ried. In the studio producing Michael Jackson's second solo album for Epic, Jones said, "The record business is not what it was a couple of years ago, and if we get six million out of this, I'm gonna declare that a success."

Thriller was a success, all right—released at the end of November 1982, it was certified platinum the following January and ensconced at number one in February. No surprise: its predecessor, *Off the Wall*, released right as the 1979 record-biz recession was taking hold, had moved seven million. What you might not have expected was to see *Thriller* listed as the third-most-added title at AOR in the December 18 *Billboard*, below Sammy Hagar and Bob Seger.

Jackson and Jones had explicitly aimed to make *Thriller* an all-seasons blockbuster, full of surefire hits in all formats—and AOR was one of them. "I said at the time, 'I need a song like [the Knack's 1979 hit] "My Sharona"—we need a black version,'" Jones said. Michael went home and wrote "Beat It." To ram the song home, Jones cold-called Eddie Van Halen, the premiere guitar shredder of the age, and asked if he'd play a solo. Van Halen thought he was being crank-called, then said yes and refused payment.

The song's flat metallic boogie drew immediate notice. "'Beat It' is not just for kids, but for everybody," a PD from Minneapolis reported. "It started out eighteen to twenty-four, then built into all demos. Gets stronger and stronger every week." *Rolling Stone* reported that the song had been added to "about fifty AOR playlists." "Beat It" would eventually reach number fourteen on *Billboard*'s Rock Tracks chart.

WPLJ was one of the AORs that programmed "Beat It"—on, says Berger, "a trial-balloon basis." They'd done the same at the beginning of 1983 with another rock song by a black artist, Prince's "Little Red Corvette." But Prince was a known shredder; Michael Jackson rocking out was something else, especially to the AOR audience. "On our call-out research, first week, extreme negatives—people *hated* it," says Berger. "We continued to play it. By the second week, it started to move into the middle. By the third week they *loved* it. I knew something was up if this was acceptable to our rock and roll sample base."

In 1996, Berger described the initial audience response in a different way. "If there was a lawn at 1330 Avenue of the Americas," he told *Billboard*, "they would have burned a cross."

After launching on August 1, 1981, MTV had played, during its first eighteen months, a whopping total of 24 videos by black artists, out of 750. MTV's head, Bob Pittman, made the same kind of excuses as his radio peers. "I'm tired of all this 'racist' stuff," he griped. "Why doesn't anyone ever talk about the barriers we *have* broken down? Like between punk or new wave and mainstream rock?"

That mattered, because MTV sold records. One Tulsa retailer told *Billboard*, "I had fifteen copies of the Buggles LP sitting in a bin for eight months"; within weeks of the network's launch—first video: the Buggles' "Video Killed the Radio Star"—they'd disappeared. "The average MTV viewer last year bought nine albums," Les Garland, MTV's executive vice president of programming, boasted in 1983. "The national average is about seven, but the MTV viewers bought nine. And of the nine they bought, four of them were purchased as a direct result of having been seen on MTV. That's almost 50 percent."

Michael Jackson wanted those numbers too. His managers Freddy DeMann and Ron Weisner delivered the clip for *Thriller*'s second single, "Billie Jean," to the network by hand. This is the point where everybody stops agreeing.

Weisner recalled that MTV declined it, then changed its mind after the intervention of CBS Records' president, Walter Yetnikoff, and chairman, William S. Paley. Yetnikoff recalled it much the same way, as did MTV video jockeys (VJs) Mark Goodman and Martha Quinn; the latter recalled being told, with a chuckle, "Yeah, but we can't play this."

On the other hand, Les Garland said in 2015, "There was never any sort of a threat from anybody—from Walter or anybody else. . . . We really believed—unanimously—that it was groundbreaking, and probably the best video anyone in the room had ever seen to that date." Of course MTV would play it: "There was never a question, ever." A spokesperson for Warner Amex, MTV's owners, told *Billboard*, "The only 'Pressure' they've ever given us is Billy Joel's."

Once the stylish blue noir of the "Billie Jean" clip made it to MTV, it never left. Jackson was breaking two color barriers at once, with two very different recordings: the disco pulse and chicken-pickin' guitar break of "Billie Jean" were as "urban" (a radio-biz code word for "black") as the stiff beats and Eddie Van Halen power-tool impersonations of "Beat It" were "rock." While "Billie Jean" made it into MTV's rotation, a producer at Bob Giraldi Productions, then working on *Thriller*'s second video, told *Billboard*, "We've been guaranteed that 'Beat It' will be shown on MTV."

On March 25, 1983, the rest of Jackson's stars aligned. He'd had to be convinced by Berry Gordy himself to participate in a Jackson 5 reunion at the Pasadena Civic Center for a show, filmed for prime-time TV, celebrating Motown Records' twenty-fifth anniversary. Jackson's condition was that he'd get to perform "Billie Jean" as well as a J5 medley—the only non-Motown song of the three-hour program.

Jackson often talked about being transformed during performance, but postmedley, when he announced, "But especially, I like . . . the new songs," he accompanied it with a sneer that sent a shock wave through the 2,965-seat Civic Center. Wearing a single white rhinestone-studded glove that flashed in the spotlight—a moving, gesturing disco ball—Michael cocked his black fedora, thrust his hips and knees, and began miming to the record of "Billie Jean." Weeks before anyone could see it on television, *Rolling Stone* reported, "He showed off moves that owed as much to street 'break' dancing as to traditional Motown choreography: stop-on-a-dime spins, some astonishing backward walks." Michael had learned the move, which he dubbed the Moonwalk, from ex–*Soul Train* dancer and Shalamar member Jeffrey Daniel; he ended it here by hopping on his toes and freezing. This was a tough crowd of showbiz lifers, and they went berserk. Backstage, Richard Pryor went up to Jackson and said, "That was the greatest performance I've ever seen."

Together, the *Motown 25* special and MTV pushed Jackson's album into the sun. "*Thriller* had already sold about three million copies before any of the videos got on MTV," publicist Susan Blond said. "But *after* MTV, we were selling two hundred thousand copies of it a week, and we ended up selling six million more copies." By summer's end, *Rolling Stone* would predict, a little wide-eyed, that *Thriller*'s sales "may end up going as high as 12 million worldwide."

ONE WAY LARRY BERGER DID RESEARCH WAS TO VISIT ANOTHER MARKET and "sit in a hotel and monitor other rock stations," he says. In mid-1982, he did this in Philadelphia, intending to pay attention to a pair of AORs. "But I found myself gravitating to the Top 40 station there, WCAU-FM," says Berger. "They were playing what was called the Hot Hits format, created by a consultant named Mike Joseph out of Connecticut. The music they were playing was just terrific. There was a song they were playing on hot rotation, every seventy minutes, called 'Forget Me Nots' by Patrice Rushen. I would tune back to them to hear it when it came on."

Berger suddenly realized that something was changing: "The music was getting better. Top 40 had gone through the early eighties [playing] a lot of soft music, more Adult Contemporary than Top 40. But I knew it was out there."

Rushen's supple R&B groove—danceable and melodic but leaner than overblown late-seventies disco—and others like it, by Rick James, Prince, and the S.O.S. Band, weren't the only exciting new things happening. "In 1981–82 there was an influx of very pop-sounding, mostly British artists: Joe Jackson, Men at Work from Australia, Elvis Costello," says Berger. "There was less music like Supertramp and Asia. This music that was coming out was very poppy sounding; it lacked, in many cases, an upfront electric guitar."

But new wave polarized the WPLJ audience too much. "The people who liked new wave hated Led Zeppelin and the Who," says Berger. "People who liked heavy metal hated everything except heavy metal."

Late in 1982, another company made overtures to hire Berger away from WPLJ to start a new Top 40 station in New York. (Berger declines to specify which company.) "It got pretty serious, but they could not get it approved by their corporate bigwigs, so they didn't do it." By then, he says, "Every broad-caster in New York knew there was an opening for a Top 40 on FM."

FOR THE TIME BEING, WPLJ KEPT ON PLAYING OLD MUSIC. THAT'S WHAT AOR stations had been doing for half a decade by 1982, and the reason for that was Lee Abrams.

Growing up in Chicago, Abrams obsessively analyzed radio station play-lists. He'd barely hit puberty when he decided he could program rock radio better than anyone else. The late sixties was the era of free-form FM radio—broadcasting in stereo, full of stoned-out DJs playing what, to Abrams, sounded like "bullshit": "You'd hear twenty minutes of Ravi Shankar, some bluegrass, a little jazz, and I just wanted to hear some good Cream, Yes, and all that." In 1971, Abrams designed the SuperStars format to eliminate such frippery—the true beginning of AOR.

In the late seventies, AOR—hence, much of America—had shown little taste for punk or new wave, with a handful of exceptions, such as Blondie and the Cars. ("Punks" killed each other with ice picks, like on *Quincy*. Didn't they?) A few crucial stations embraced new wave, notably Los Angeles's KROQ and WLIR in Long Island. (Abrams consulted for the latter, which utilized a new wavier format dubbed SuperStars II.) But the folks who preferred the old stuff, ad infinitum, outnumbered them.

The weather, though, was changing by the mid-eighties. As 1983 began, Abrams suddenly switched tack for the eighty SuperStars stations his firm con-sulted. "In 1977, I felt no regrets about our stations being oldies-oriented, but the music has changed, and so must we," he told *Radio & Records*. "We have become our own worst enemy. . . . Now, finally, some of those great AOR stan-dards seem to have burned out. . . . The final indicator that we were off-target was looking at the top ten of national sales charts and seeing bands like the Clash, Men at Work, Stray Cats, and Joe Jackson. A year ago, when these were new records, we were unconvinced they would work for us. But they are unde-niably happening, and it's time for us to reflect it."

"We're changing from an industrial base to a technological one, and such changes always bring about turmoil," a PD in Baltimore said. "I think the new music reflects that."

The term *new music* was fast entering the American radio lexicon. During *Billboard*'s Radio Programming Convention in Pasadena in January of '83, a session called "State of Popular Music," the magazine reported, "pointed to an emergence of post–new wave pop—the melding of electronic rock, disco, soul, and pop, often lumped together under a 'new music' tag—as a most prominent indicator of [the] change" that was beginning to occur.

Just days earlier, Abrams had delivered his edict. "We're de-emphasizing the oldies," he told a gathering of fifty AOR clients. Instead of playing up to 80 percent familiar hits and album tracks, Abrams now counseled a 70–30 mix of new hits and old favorites. In place of inactive seventies icons like Thin Lizzy and—gulp—Led Zeppelin, programmers were encouraged to empha-size new bands, most British, most tried and tested on MTV: Men at Work, Missing Persons, Thomas Dolby, Pretenders, Joe Jackson, Duran Duran, the Psychedelic Furs.

"In their hearts, I believe most of our programmers feel the same way we do: that it's time for such a change," Abrams said. "The only hurdle they must get over is the feeling of, 'How can we drop [Aerosmith's] "Dream On"?' Well, it's time to."

Abrams's new edict was the talk of Pasadena. For many of the five hundred programmers in attendance, it was a come-to-Jesus moment; *Billboard* com-pared it to "a group of sinners confessing together." Dave Logan, the PD for KFOG-FM, San Francisco, spoke for many: "We were lulled into a false sense of security. We've got to change our way of thinking."

John Gorman, PD of Cleveland AOR powerhouse WMMS-FM, was even more succinct. "There's been a reversal," he told *Rolling Stone*. "Top 40 has be-come the adventurous format."

ON THURSDAY, JUNE 23, 1983, LARRY BERGER WENT TO THE OFFICE OF WPLJ's general manager, Joe Parish, to deliver the bad news. It was time for the station's quarterly budget meeting, and Berger had been projecting the station's ratings for the next eighteen months so the sales department could figure out its revenues. Nothing he saw looked favorable. "I'm going to have to project downward," Berger told his boss.

AOR numbers had been plummeting around the country, sometimes by a lot: in mid-1982, Boston's WCOZ-FM fell from a 12.6 audience share to a 4.7 share; Detroit's WLLZ-FM slipped from 9.2 to 4.7; San Jose's KOME-FM, from 6.8 to 3.8. One PD said that women were "by and large a lost cause for AOR." And women were what Berger was after—specifically, women aged twenty-five to forty-four—to go with WPLJ's large audience of teens and eighteen-to-twenty-fours. Adult women were a prime demographic. "The amount you can charge for a spot, the national advertisers who would be interested, is far greater than what we had," says Berger. And the "new music" they were slipping in was starting to work.

So Berger loosed his pitch to revamp WPLJ as "an adult-oriented Top 40 station: 80 percent adults—eighteen and older—and 20 percent teenagers." The station's general sales manager, says Berger, "nearly had a coronary. In the summertime—and this was mid-June—we had pre-booked a whole shit-load of youth-oriented business: soft drinks, beer, concerts. He was a little bit disturbed."

Nevertheless, they went with it. Most of the DJs had Top 40 experience and were ready to adjust their on-air styles. "I spent the weekend at home sketching out lists—music lists, rotations," says Berger. "As a rock station, we were repeating the most popular songs every eight hours; as a Top 40 station we'd repeat them a lot more [often] than that.

"They were taking a risk here. Everybody knew that. It's one thing to change the format of a station that's in the toilet; there's nothing to be lost. We were the top rock station in the market. In our final book as a rock station we had a 4.1 ratings share of audience. It was a very successful operation."

WPLJ's record library was still missing a large number of Top 40 titles—the album-oriented rock station had no 45s at all. "I had to buy the disc jockeys a lot of records," says Berger. "An independent record promoter, Herb Rosen, went to one-stops and bought a bunch of records for me. We needed 'Celebration' by Kool & the Gang, a lot of stuff we didn't have. Herbie must've bought fifty or more singles." The A rotation that summer included the Police's "Every Breath You Take," Donna Summer's "She Works Hard for the Money," Kajagoogoo's "Too Shy," Eurythmics' "Sweet Dreams (Are Made of This)," and Michael Sembello's "Maniac," from the *Flashdance* soundtrack.

WPLJ's new format debuted on June 30, 1983, at 4:00 a.m.—only the station hadn't informed anyone they were doing it. "It was very half-assed, I must admit," says Berger. "One of the compromises was to make a gradual transition. If you're going to change the format of a radio station, you either blow it up, fire everybody, or read the telephone book for three days—do some kind of stunt thing. We just slid it in with most of the same disc jockeys and different music." That morning, he says, "I remember sitting in my office listening to 'Wanna Be Startin' Somethin'' by Michael Jackson on what had been a rock station—for many years, a successful rock station—and thinking to myself, 'What the fuck am I doing? Have we lost our minds?'"

"Some of the letters, frankly, I can't read on the air because they're so wild."

It had been five weeks since the changeover, and it had exercised a number of WPLJ's listeners. A number had written in—that's why *Let's Hear It* with Larry Berger was on during prime time, so he could read and respond to some of their letters. He received between fifty and a hundred complaints in total.

"Some of them," he said on-air, "have racial overtones." Over and over, the letters mentioned "disco," and the way some of them did it made it plain that they were using that word in place of an epithet. This night, he ignored the phones.

Berger began with a potted overview of WPLJ's programming history from the late sixties forward. "A couple of months ago, we [found] that . . . the average year in music represented on WPLJ was 1971," Berger said. "We also find a lot of new, exciting, vibrant popular music surrounding us. We find ourselves struggling to play it or not to play it." Ultimately, he concluded, "We just felt that we could not continue to play so much of the old music over and over and over again and still, in a year from now, continue to be in business."

Several listeners disagreed. The first letter Berger read was dated July 28 and came from a listener in Bay Ridge:

It's Thursday at 6 p.m. and I am currently listening to the putrid disco song "Maniac" from the *Flashdance* soundtrack. Before this song you played [Irene Cara's] "Fame," which until recently you never once played on your once rock-oriented station. My friends, what has happened over the last few months? Upon hearing Michael Jackson's hit songs on your station, I had first thought that my stereo indicator was broken. But lo and behold, my once favorite rock was, for some reason or another, playing disco songs. Let's face it, folks, your new sound just is, in fact, just disco music. . . . So why are you playing this junk? I don't know of any *red-blooded* Bay Ridge rockers who are enthused at this point in time about WPLJ, the once-great rock station. [my emphasis]

The belligerent, wounded tone typified these letters. This was the part of the rock audience sometimes referred to in radio circles as "earthdogs"—

working-class male listeners, largely suburban or outer-borough. John Gorman of Cleveland's WMMS once described them as the station's "juvenile, dumb, or stoned-out callers," adding: "Get a higher class of listener on-air." They wanted to rock, period. Some of them wrote with real feeling:

> You have a lot of nerve playing that kind of music and saying that's what we want to hear. You think people don't listen to rock and roll anymore? Well, you're wrong. WPLJ used to be number one when it played rock. We had to put up with that new wave [*blank*] because all the stations were playing it. There was no choice. So what if new wave is becoming popular? You played rock, so why should you care? Don't you think it is good anymore? Or are you just doing it for the money?

Another letter demanded to know "Which one is rock and which one is disco?" next to two boxes, marked "Beat It" by Michael Jackson and "War Pigs" by Black Sabbath. "I don't think either of them is disco," Berger responded. "I suppose that 'War Pigs' is rock. But we've never played it on WPLJ as long as I've been here." The station had never played much heavy metal. "We always received telephone calls—for *years* on this program—saying, 'How come you only play one Ozzy Osbourne record?' or 'How come you don't play Def Leppard?'"

One missive demanded WPLJ play more "kick-ass rock and roll like Led Zeppelin, AC/DC, Ozzy, Black Sabbath, Pink Floyd, Aerosmith, Queen, Kiss, April Wine, BTO, Bad Company, Blackfoot, Girlschool, Hot Tuna, Iron Maiden, Saxon, Ted Nugent, UFO—" only for Berger to cut the letter off. "I don't remember the last time we played UFO," he said. "I don't think we ever played a Saxon record or Ted Nugent; I *know* we never played Iron Maiden records."

Oh, and by the way: "The station in Boston, Massachusetts, that created the term 'Kick-Ass Rock and Roll'—that [slogan] didn't start here—is now playing the same music that we are."

These were the children of AOR's increased bleaching of rock and roll's legacy. To them rock and roll wasn't racially diverse, the way it had been to its original fans; it was racially narrow, the way AOR radio had made it, and they preferred it to stay that way.

WPLJ's fans weren't the transition's only critics. Lee Abrams called it "one of the classic stupid moves in the history of radio. They had it all: they had consistently high numbers, they were making a ton, and all of a sudden, they threw it all away." In suburban Secaucus, New Jersey, another PD just settling into his new job would lob a fusillade of abuse at both WPLJ and Berger, on air and off, that lasted for years, to the latter's bemusement.*

Over an organ fanfare, his volume and pitch rising in intensity, Scott Shannon signed on at 6:00 a.m. August 2 and announced: "As the New York City area wakes up to a wonderful day, little do they know a new era is about to begin in New York radio. Up on the ol' gorilla belly there's a brand-new transmitter. We call it the Flamethrower. Ladies and gentlemen, Z100 has arrived!" Then, cut in from a secondary source: "EEEEGAH!"

Soon enough, gaseous-sounding processed voices: "Hit radio—Z100!" A jingle—a device AOR had explicitly dismissed from the rock radio arsenal, now given pride of place again. "I want you to take your radio knob and crank it up nice and loud and welcome Z100!" Shannon practically screamed. "The Flamethrower's on!" The riff of Survivor's "Eye of the Tiger" surged forward. "It's time to wake up!"

WHTZ, previously a jazz station at 100.3 FM, was the property of Malrite Communications, which owned Cleveland's WMMS. "When they applied for the call letters, we thought there was going to be a rock station going on," says Berger. Nevertheless, it was hardly an industry secret: there it was on the front of *Radio & Records'* July 1 issue. "Now!" a deep-voiced announcer told us over sci-fi space blips in one jingle. "There's a new way to spell hits."

Shannon's presentational style was a direct throwback to pre–psychedelic sixties hit radio: "high energy and fast talk, contests and requests—interspersed with all the hits, all the time," as *New York* put it. "We just dedicated ourselves to serving the listeners, not just of the five boroughs, but Long Island, New Jersey, and Connecticut," Shannon said. "No one had done that before."

The key was offering something the radio audience hadn't encountered in nearly a generation. Z100 wasn't an AOR-gone-CHR that largely retained the laid-back atmosphere of the former. Z100 was in-your-ear silliness full of fake commercials ("This is a test," followed by science questions) and loose, lowbrow group banter in much the manner Shannon had perfected for five years prior in Tampa, where he'd taken Q105 to the highest audience share of any US station. That group and this were dubbed the "Morning Zoo," the banter

---

* "I would hear about it from salesmen coming in from Long Island or New Jersey more often than I would hear it myself," says Berger. "I don't know what his motivation was."

and taped bits occasionally daubed with monkey chatter, just in case. "I can't blame Lee Abrams for taking people's money, but he's programming the entire country from Atlanta," Shannon told *Rolling Stone* of the wave of AORs turning CHR. "And one day he wakes up and tells everybody he was wrong!"

On air and off, Shannon brashly promised to take the station "from worst to first." Amazingly, he did just that. "In the spring of 1983 WHTZ posted a .0," noted *Radio & Records*. "Summer '83 saw WHTZ rise to a competitive 2.0, followed by the miraculous fall '83 rise to number one with a 6.2." By contrast, the summer 1983 Arbitron book found WPLJ's share dropping from 4.1 to 3.5. The dip was temporary, says Berger: "By the fall of 1983 we went into the 4s, and we went up from there." But it wasn't nearly enough. Z100 would stay on top of New York's radio ratings for years, and WPLJ would never return.

SUPREME COURT,
WASHINGTON, DC
January 17, 1984

THE SUPREME COURT'S RULING ON THE SONY BETAMAX CASE CAME AL-most exactly a year after it had first gone to trial, on January 18, 1983.

In 1975, the Japanese electronics giant Sony had introduced the Betamax videocassette recorder to the US market, and before the year was out, MCA Inc./Universal City Studios and Walt Disney Productions filed a federal copyright theft suit; Sony prevailed. Then, in October 1981, the US Court of Appeals reversed that ruling, claiming Sony and its ad agency, Doyle Dane Bernbach, were liable for "contributory infringement" of copyright laws. This embold-ened MCA/Universal to open suit "against sixteen additional ad agencies, including many of the biggest shops in the country, and their VCR marketer clients," *Advertising Age* reported.

For the networks, video's sticking point was that viewers could now fast-forward through the commercials. In 1983, an executive from General Foods, one of network TV's largest advertisers, told an industry conference, "We pay more every year for network time. Fewer viewers are delivered. Add to this picture the increasing loss of viewers at the commercial break, and you begin to wonder at what point television [advertising] is no longer worth the price."

The music business was equally up in arms over home recording. Shortly after the Court of Appeals reversal, on November 1, 1981, the British Phonographic Industry (BPI) unveiled a new slogan: "Home Taping Is Killing Music." The following spring, the Recording Industry Association of America (RIAA), along with fifteen other organizations, formed a lobbying group called the Coalition to Save America's Music. "Their goal," as *Trouser Press* described it, was "an across the board surcharge on blank tape and recording equipment." Congress, having yet to decide on passing this new bill or not, appeared to be waiting out the Supreme Court ruling.

The reasoning for this so-called tape tax had come from the RIAA's Stan Gortikov. In 1981, he said, "Our industry sold the equivalent of 475 million albums. But at the same time, about 455 million albums were home-taped. So for about every album we sold, one was taped. One for one! In our hen-house, the poachers now almost out-number the chickens." This figure was widely disputed—in 1982, the *Village Voice* reported, "blank tape sales were barely half" of the RIAA's figures.

But all these arguments became moot on January 17, 1984, when the Supreme Court reversed the October 1981 ruling, deciding in favor of Sony. "Time-shifting"—the practice of recording a program to watch it later—"does not constitute contributory infringement if the product is widely used for legit-imate, unobjectionable purposes," Justice John Paul Stevens wrote in his major-ity decision. The majority was slim, five to four, and the dissenting opinion, by Justice Harry A. Blackmun, was sharply critical. The decision, he wrote, "risks eroding the very basis of copyright law by depriving writers of control over their works and consequently of their incentive to create."

The record business at large was outraged. A *Cash Box* editorial sternly admonished: "Copyright infringement has traditionally been viewed as a white-collar crime, but the laws are too gentlemanly and too lax. It's time for us to seek new legislation that will give us protection." The country music business, which relied heavily on cassette sales, was keenly against the deci-sion. "We know that a great percentage of our sales are lost to home taping," a Warner Bros. Nashville VP said. "All one has to do is go out and talk to con-sumers and they openly admit that they receive home taped albums and they pass on home taped albums to friends."

Retailers saw things differently. "I'm dancing in the streets!" Tower Re-cords' Russ Solomon whooped. "It was absolutely correct, the only decision they could have come up with." He was still itchy that Congress might pass home taping legislation: "I'm hopeful that they'll be wise enough to see that . . . the growth of the retail video industry will prove to be extremely profitable to the studio."

Tom Shales, the *Washington Post*'s TV critic, celebrated the Supreme Court's verdict in a column that began, "One small step for man, one giant kick in Big Brother's pants." Congress was no longer interested in passing a tape tax, and while the biz continued to fume, any worry over home taping's legality was effectively moot.

BETAMAX ITSELF WAS ON THE WAY OUT BY THE TIME ITS CASE WAS WON. America had spoken in numbers, and it wanted VHS—larger and clunkier than Betamax, but with longer running times for recording. Americans, yet again, preferred convenience to quality.

Videocassette recorders were moving at speed: two million Americans had purchased them in 1982, and twice that many again in 1983. By early '84, estimates were that a VCR would be in 20 percent of US households by the end of the year, and in one-third of them by 1986.

Many other home electronics were starting to become noticeably smaller around this time. A January 1983 *Billboard* report from that month's Consumer Electronics Show (CES) in Las Vegas had made special note of the effects on consumer goods the recently developed microprocessor chip was beginning to have:

> Microprocessors have made possible a whole range of automatic dialing telephones and remote wireless telephones. The Watchman hand-held television set and a whole range of small TVs and AM/FM and short-wave radios have been reduced in size with new technology "chips" sets. The complete redesign of television set circuitry is taking place, using computer circuits built around microprocessors. Video accessories like home [sub]titlers, effects generators, and miniature cameras all owe their lightweight and numerous features to the use of super "chips" that think.

The microprocessor chip was key to the personal computers that were flooding the market and that would dominate the 1984 Winter CES in Las

Vegas that January, one week prior to the Betamax decision. It was the largest CES to date, drawing sixty-six thousand.

Cunningly, Apple Computer, the second-biggest computing outfit in the States after IBM, took a small, twenty-by-twenty booth rather than its customary large one. This was a feint, followed by a giant right hook. Two weeks after CES, Apple rolled out its most ambitious computer yet, the Macintosh. It, too, was small: $13.6 \times 9.6 \times 10.9$ inches, weighing sixteen and a half pounds, its 9-inch monochrome screen glowing white.

Macintosh was intended for homes, not just businesses, and it retailed for $2,500. With a $20 million ad budget, $100 million in development costs, and another $20 million to build a new factory just to make this one computer, everything rode on it. "If Mac's sales are just average," Apple's cofounder, Steve Jobs, said, "then our vision of the world is significantly wrong."

Apple's business environment was new and different, too. In 1984, the yuppie (the term derived from the initials of "young urban professional") was fast becoming a new kind of all-American mythos: overachieving, health-conscious, and constantly combining work and leisure. "The Yuppie work style demands that a considerable portion of each day be spent socializing," *Success!* magazine reported in November 1984. Apple took this casualness to a crunchy Cali extreme. "The Mac team alone spends a hundred thousand dollars on fresh juice per year," *Playboy* noted. One young employee compared it to "an endless cocktail party, with chips and software instead of drinks."

SHORTLY BEFORE THE BETAMAX VERDICT, STAN CORNYN, THE SENIOR VP of Warner Bros. Music, wrote a *Variety* editorial that sounded a plea for "a union between hardware and software": "We in the U.S. record industry have spent a great deal of time in the past few years doing battle with Japanese hardware manufacturers over the issues of copyright and home taping. Why must the razors be fighting the blades?" Cornyn had a vision of the Third World, in the parlance of the times, as "a vast new market for us, developed cooperatively by hardware and software people working hand in hand."

This was a more sanguine scenario than his colleagues foresaw. "We can't afford to rely on our hopes," RCA Records president Bob Summer wrote on the same newsprint page as Cornyn. "We must fashion the future of the entertainment industry as a harmony of interests that works to the benefit of all."

Summer took particular delight in a new object also on display at the Winter CES, as it had been three years running: the Compact Disc.*

Developed by the Japanese, this five-inch aluminum disc promised a revolution in sound quality, in storability, in space saving, and potentially in creativity. A vinyl LP could hold, at most, an hour of sound, but the Compact Disc held seventy-four minutes. Just as attractive were its technical aspects. "Because the player is digital, it can be programmed easily to repeat or skip selections," *BusinessWeek* reported. Summer called it "a marvel" and wondered, "How will this new product be received? Is it to be a lending library of perfect master quality copies? I hope not. *Our product is for sale.*" [Italics in original.]

WHAT WAS MOST NEWSWORTHY ABOUT COMPACT DISCS AT THE '84 WINter CES was their prices. "Throughout the show, speculation ran wild over how low prices would go this year," *Rolling Stone* reported. "The final consensus was that players will be selling for well under $400—and could approach $300—by midyear."

Even with prices falling, CD players were still a little too high-end for record retailers branching into electronics. "The personal cassette systems in the $20 to $30 range are especially hot for us," a Camelot Records VP said that June, adding, "I think all the publicity the break dancing phenomenon has received is really helping there." (See Chapter 9.)

Yet demand was picking up. By March, over eight hundred Compact Discs were available domestically, with projections of more than two thousand by year's end. At the top of '84, RCA announced that Eurythmics' second album, *Touch*, would be released as an LP and a CD *at the same time*. This had never happened before—the closest anyone had previously come was *What's New*, Linda Ronstadt's 1983 collaboration with big-band maestro Nelson Riddle, whose Compact Disc had tailed the LP by a mere three weeks. PolyGram head Jan Timmer declared bluntly, "The black disc will be dead by 1989."

ONE OF THE KEY SELLING POINTS OF THE CD WAS ITS ALLEGED INDEstructibility. This was a myth, as many bored kids over the years would figure

---

* Long before it fell into common use, the term *Compact Disc* was a copyrighted trademark, and therefore capitalized for much of the period covered here. Hence this book capitalizes it also.

out, and its willful promulgation infuriated some of the people who worked on the technology. "We should not put emphasis on the fact it will last forever because it will not last forever," an engineer in Philips's Holland office said. "We should put emphasis on the quality of sound and ease of handling."

That sound quality was another major selling point. Explaining the difference between the LP and CD versions of classical pianist Bruno Walter, CBS's classical producer Andy Kazdin said, "It will be like hearing the tapes that Walter's recording engineer heard, without the limitations and distortions of the old pressing process." As a result, the CD was usually priced in the twenty-dollar range—at a time when LPs still cost less than ten dollars. The marketing VP of a San Francisco chain called CD buyers "sophisticated": "Do you cut the price on fine wine?"

Record company people, especially Americans, did not take kindly to being coaxed into investing their rapidly dwindling dollars into a brand-new format when people weren't even buying the *old* format anymore. Nor did they particularly trust Philips, which stood to earn money even if its fellow labels lost it. That company's Robert Huber refused to budge: "We're talking real innovation," he insisted. "The compact disc's future is secure. The only question is whether you will join the future."

One exec eager to sign on was Walter Yetnikoff, who ran CBS Records in New York—which had partnered with Sony to make CDs. As part of the deal, Sony agreed to purchase CBS's disused cassette-making plant in Terre Haute, Indiana, to manufacture the new discs. To *Billboard*, Yetnikoff had pointed to the facility's demise as one of the keys to CBS's dismal 1982 earnings, adding that the Compact Disc "could be one of the things to save this industry. There's a lot of money behind this configuration—these aren't two-bit companies involved in the launch of the format—and I'm getting the initial feeling that the format's introduction may be better than expected." But even CBS had only a handful of titles available on Compact Disc by 1984.

The best-selling recorded-music format in early 1984 wasn't a disc at all. In September 1983, prerecorded cassettes outsold LPs for the first time. Tapes were now the primary means by which people listened to music in both the United States and the UK; British tape sales went up nearly 20 percent in 1983. Island founder-president Chris Blackwell had gotten up the noses of his peers by offering titles on extra-long cassettes: the entire album on side A, side B blank for the listener's home-taping purposes.

Certain genres, like country and hard rock, did especially well on cassette: by late '83, Def Leppard's *Pyromania* was selling six-to-four cassettes over LPs, the same ratio at which Nashville did business. That October, a shop opened in Atlantic City—an outpost of Record World, ironically—that featured only two hundred vinyl titles versus seven thousand on cassette.

CONVERTING ANALOG TAPE TO DIGITAL FILES WAS A TIME-CONSUMING process in 1984. The expedient thing, then, was to record straight to digital. Here was the microchip coming to the fore of pop, as recording tech grew more sophisticated. Take the Solid State Logic (SSL) console, a widely adopted all-digital mixing board.

"Everything was automated," says Tom Silverman, the founder of Tommy Boy Records, one of the era's important hip-hop labels, of the SSL. "It was really a game-changer because you could do recalls. But it also was a cheater. If you could fix it in the mix and you could do things later, it means you don't have to get it right. And once the SSL came, you could go back and do it again. So you could work on the same mix for months. You'd just do a recall, and you'd bring in all the other stuff. It changed the way records sounded."

Not everyone fell in line right away. In 1982, Todd Rundgren rejected digital recording as "too much trouble—it's too expensive." Glyn Johns, who'd worked with Led Zeppelin, the Who, and the Rolling Stones, insisted he would record only on sixteen-track tape—"Nobody, in my opinion, needs to use twenty-four tracks"—and added that the move toward digital recording seemed to be driven by the equipment manufacturers, not the artists or producers: "I think a lot of people . . . are very easily led by the nose by a flashing light or a pretty thing or something with a lot of knobs on it."

But for others, the chance to keep working till a track was perfect was too good to resist. Lindsey Buckingham of Fleetwood Mac had long been a studio rat; in 1984, his second solo LP, *Go Insane*, was made largely with a Fairlight CMI (short for Computer Musical Instrument), the first keyboard-based digital sampler, with a green-screen monitor as well as a keyboard and bank of ready-to-use sounds. "For someone who considers himself a colorist, which I do, the number of colors was just increased radically," Buckingham told *Billboard*.

"You didn't really sample with it—it was more like [using] what was there," explains record producer Arthur Baker, who used the Fairlight on "Planet Rock," a 1982 rap twelve-inch by Afrika Bambaataa and Soulsonic Force, released on Tommy Boy, that remains one of the decade's most influential records. The Fairlight made it easier to recycle elements wholesale from one recording to another. Baker's coproducer John Robie overdubbed a "groovy, weird, African" clavinet part onto "Planet Rock" that Baker took off that record and later made into the foundation of another record from 1982, Planet Patrol's "Play at Your Own Risk."

THE MOST DIFFICULT THING ABOUT SYNTHESIZERS HAD ALWAYS BEEN GET-ting them to sync up together correctly. In 1971, when Stevie Wonder hooked up with the British synthesists Robert Margouleff and Malcolm Cecil, their custom-built synth bank TONTO (The Original New Timbral Orchestra), which patched together more than a dozen synthesizers, took up an entire room. A decade later, the toy manufacturer Mattel could market Synsonics, a cheap, programmable drum machine intended for the kids' market. But synchronizing patterns on, say, a Juno synthesizer and a Linn drum machine was still a pain in the ass.

That changed in January 1983, when Roland announced a new system called MIDI: Musical Instrument Digital Interface, which, per *Billboard*, "establishes a universal standard of interface for synthesizers, electronic musical instruments, and computers." Roland president Tom Beckmen said, "The basic premise behind MIDI is to allow keyboards, synthesizers, sequencers, drum machines, computers, and many other instruments to communicate through a common data line." Additionally, the company had shared the interface with its rivals; Yamaha, Korg, Kawai, and Sequential Circuits had all signed on.

At the National Association of Music Merchants (NAMM) Convention in Anaheim in January 1984, MIDI was "the lead story," according to Jock Baird of *Musician*. "The liberation of the keyboard player into pure orchestration and arrangement was won in a walk," he wrote, and noted that "there were literally hundreds of independent software writers combing the hall and congregating at the booth of the International MIDI Association, a grassroots garage software information clearinghouse."

The rise of MIDI was directly linked to the rise of the personal computer—an IBM or Apple II was usually the conduit between synthesizers, drum machines, and sequencers—the latter, academic Richard J. Ripani wrote, "allow a complex mix of parts to be created, stored electronically, and used to trigger any number of keyboards or other electronic instruments."

MIDI spread through the digital instrument field like a brush fire. So did, through 1983, built-in polyphonic sequencers on synthesizers. (Early synthesizers tended to emit only one particular tone—monophonic—while the likes of TONTO offered a vastly expanded, and expandable, timbral palette: polyphonic.) "Since last summer, keyboard players have come to expect the pair of features as standard, even on budget synths," a *Melody Maker* staffer wrote in a February 1984 gear review. "Now, no one wants to be without the all important MIDI link, nor the ability to compose and memorize snatches of chords, bass lines, or riffs in a sequencer chip."

When Roland updated its Juno 60 synthesizer, first marketed in 1982, to a Juno 106 in 1984—its buzzy analog sound like thick, tough plastic, suitably spacey and inorganic for the *Space Invaders* era—another *Maker* reviewer summed up its virtues: "One hundred and twenty-eight memories instead of sixty-four, MIDI instead of DCB . . . lighter styling and most importantly, cheaper. I don't need to tell you how good it is—it's so easy, the cat could use it."

NEWSWEEK: "BRITAIN ROCKS AMERICA—AGAIN"

January 23, 1984

THE FRONT OF *NEWSWEEK*'S JANUARY 23, 1984, ISSUE IS ONE OF THE MOST boldly colorful magazine covers ever published. Staring out from a riot of hues are Annie Lennox of Eurythmics and Boy George of Culture Club, below the headline: BRITAIN ROCKS AMERICA—AGAIN. Against a blobby backdrop of lavender, blue, yellow, and pink, Lennox's bright orange hair—and George's shirt and bow tie, in a determined three-pattern clash—thicken the visual noise.

"The extent of the new British beachhead was revealed on July 16, 1983, when eighteen singles of British origin appeared in the American Top 40, eclipsing the previous record, set on June 19, 1965," Jim Miller, the magazine's pop music critic, wrote. Seven were in the top ten. The Police's "Every Breath You Take," number one for eight weeks total, was followed by Eddy Grant's "Electric Avenue" (two), the Kinks' "Come Dancing" (six), Kajagoogoo's "Too Shy" (seven), Madness's "Our House" (eight), Duran Duran's "Is There Something I Should Know" (nine), and Culture Club's "Time (Clock of the Heart)" at ten. They were the face of this Second British Invasion.

Miller's editor, Charles Michener, had suggested the assignment, and Miller readily agreed. "I spent nearly two weeks on the ground in early December," he says. Culture Club and Eurythmics were his focus from the beginning. He also hit the London clubs, where much of the current pop scene had germinated, and interviewed Malcolm McLaren, the former Sex Pistols manager/provocateur who was now having hits under his own name; the BBC Radio DJ John Peel; and Geoff Travis of Rough Trade Records, the hugely influential independent label and distributor.

Miller also bought a lot of British music magazines. There were many to choose from: five weeklies (*New Musical Express* [*NME*], *Melody Maker*, *Sounds*, *Record Mirror*, and *No. 1*), the biweekly *Smash Hits*—the most successful title by far—and the monthlies *The Face*, *Blitz*, and *Flexipop*. There was also a substratum of titles aimed, says Miller, "at sub-adolescents, a huge demographic by then both in the UK and US." One of the latter contained the image *Newsweek* put on its front cover.

The image initially met resistance when Miller suggested it: "The art department declared that *Newsweek* never ran an image of two people on a cover: it was one person, or an action scene." When a solo shot of Boy George replaced it, the new editor in chief "dithered and stammered and finally vetoed the image, saying words to the effect that he couldn't be the first editor of *Newsweek* to put a transvestite on its cover," says Miller.

The august newsweekly got a lot of flak from its readers for featuring such silliness. "Really, are Boy George and Annie Lennox the best *Newsweek* has to offer?" a Michigander wrote. "If so, I suggest you leave the cover blank!"

This scene fascinated Miller, but like many of his colleagues, he was also deeply skeptical. His report finished: "So roll over, America. Forget about nostalgia for the earnest pop optimism of the sixties and face the era of cramped hopes and wild style. Here comes the rock and roll of 1984."

"The kicker of the piece was definitely not meant to be straightforward, it was an allusion to Orwell," says Miller, adding: "The allusion wasn't intended as a judgment against pop music, per se, which I have always adored. It was more a reference to the super artificiality and self-consciousness that had beset pop music aimed at teens and sub-teens."

Miller, a late-thirties family man, was increasingly disenchanted with the charts, as were many of his peers reared on sixties rock. "The cynicism I felt by then was one reason I got out of the rock-crit business as soon as I possibly could," he says. The *Newsweek* feature alluded to that, too: "It is ironic to watch these older fans grimace at the new bands," Miller wrote. "But the kids love it—after all, irritating parents has always been a prime function of rock."

BORN GEORGE O'DOWD, THE MIDDLE CHILD OF A LARGE IRISH CATHOLIC family (five boys, one girl) in Eltham, Boy George had become London's echt club kid in the late seventies. "Before I started Culture Club, I didn't have any money whatsoever, so I thought, 'Well, I'll have to become very well known so that I can chat my way into everything for free,'" he said when the band's second album, *Colour by Numbers*, was released in October 1983. "So I went out of my way to be the most outrageous person in the world. I'm quite tame now compared to what I used to be like."

Still, he felt compelled to clarify his intent on US television. "What I do is not drag," he told Joan Rivers in the fall of 1983, when he first appeared on *The Tonight Show*. "I don't ever go out looking ordinary. . . . I didn't conjure up this image for the stage. I'm not like Kiss or David Bowie. I don't make excuses for the way I look. I've been doing it a long, long time."

Tall and thickly built, George appeared cuddly onstage and on TV but was imposing in person: "He's built like a boxer," the head of Virgin Records' promo team said. George's unapologetically sharp tongue had sparked feuds well prior to his forming a group. Once Culture Club became successful, his calculatedly outrageous appearance made trouble worldwide. The band was refused permission to tour the Soviet Union because the Kremlin considered him a corrupting influence on the nation's youth. In Nice, a French airport official refused him entry for three hours: "You must understand I am only carrying out orders. In France, immigration officials do not allow in transvestites. I have to follow rules."

His entrée into the glamorous life came from working the coatroom at Blitz, a club night at the Roxy in Covent Garden that launched much of the Second British Invasion. There, George would supplement his tips: "I used to be the biggest handbag thief in London," he said. Soon he was nursing showbiz ambitions: "I thought, if Johnny Rotten's a singer, so am I."

After a very brief stint fronting Bow Wow Wow, George met the fledgling bassist Mikey Craig while deejaying at Planets, in Piccadilly. Craig had seen George's picture in the papers and introduced himself. Next came Jon Moss, who'd briefly played drums with the Clash but soon left for political reasons: "It seemed like empty sloganeering to me, and I just ended up arguing with them." Guitarist Roy Hay, a hairdresser from Essex, came last. "I knew when I met George that we might not be successful, but we would get noticed," Hay said.

George and Jon had the same basic vision for the band—something more fun than the dark, droning underground rock that had come in the wake of

Joy Division. Culture Club would wholly embrace mass appeal. "I don't believe in the generation gap, which is why a lot of housewives in England buy our records," George said. "I'd rather have Frank Sinatra's fans than Siouxie Banshee's."

Vocally, he said, "I didn't want to be another Bryan Ferry or Bowie. I didn't want to be another great white hope with an angular voice going, 'Ooh-woo-woo!' in a really affected way. I'm not interested in that crap. They may be good entertainers, but they're not good singers, and being a good singer is really my main thing."

CULTURE CLUB'S DETERMINATION TO MAKE, AND BE, *POP* RUBBED A LOT OF old-school rock fans the wrong way, as did a lot of other Second British Invasion bands. "Listening these days to the new pop tarts, I'm continuously struck by the overwhelming absence of those primitive qualities I first associated with rock and roll," *Melody Maker* editor Allan Jones wrote in 1982. "Virtually unanimously, the new pop tarts are neatly turned, clean, and tidy; mostly polished, they're never ruffled." Profiling the Birmingham quintet Duran Duran, *Rolling Stone* lamented: "Whatever happened to the idea that rock and roll was supposed to be subversive?"

But many in Britain thought nothing of the sort. "The [UK] 'rock' press is becoming redundant because 'rock' is a dirty word," Steve Taylor wrote in 1982. "The music it denotes and the attitudes that go with it, such as a morbid fascination with lengthy expositions of the innermost thoughts of the most banal musicians, are well on the way out." Punk had been the great leveler, Paul Morley of the *New Musical Express* (*NME*) wrote—"never necessarily anti-technique or willfully, consciously crude, but simply about *change*. The New Pop developed naturally out of the punk assault."

The "New Pop" was Morley's coinage for a gaggle of brightly colored, unabashedly hooky onetime punks who'd decided to go for the main chance while still utilizing what they'd learned in the DIY trenches. "The eighties," Boy George said, "was really a lot of kids who left punk when it became establishment, when it became a student thing."

Punk's handshake deals and DIY enterprise showed a different methodology than the exploitative contracts that frequently bound rock stars to unscrupulous labels and managers. "The way in which punk opened up the music industry, the way in which it made business accessible to musicians, somehow—it was possible for musicians to participate in the business side of their careers after punk," Dave Rimmer, then a staff writer for *Smash Hits*, later said.

The first to make the switch was Adam Ant, born Stuart Goddard, who in 1980 reinvented himself from a failed punk to a successful teen idol, using David Bowie as his exemplar for pop stardom as role-play. He decided against trying to appeal to the *NME*: "The serious rock press has never sold a record for me," he said. "If you're going to be exploited and you're in the music industry, you should at least be holding the reins."

Instead, he went for the teen market, just as the tide of the British pop press was shifting. The "inkies"—as the broadsheets *NME*, *Melody Maker*, and *Sounds* were dubbed—were losing ground to *Smash Hits*, whose glossy paper, full-color photos, printed song lyrics, and cheerfully sly editorial bent both gloried in pop's plastic coating and undercut it with aplomb. Adam and the Ants scored seven UK top tens in 1980–1981, two of them number ones. Moreover, as Simon Frith noted, in 1981 Adam "shifted as many posters and magazines as records." They looked great in *Smash Hits*.

Far from musos, New Pop groups were barely seen as musicians— deliberately so. "The greatest skills of the New Pop stars are reserved for the sales campaigns—the commercial process itself has become the canvas on which they play their artistic games," Frith noted.

Blitz was the place where the Second British Invasion's cockatoo-like visual sensibility took flight. Promoted by Rusty Egan, with DJ Steve Strange, also lead singer of the group Visage (which hit in 1980 with "Fade to Grey"), Blitz began in 1979.

As the nicknames the UK press gave its clientele indicate—"the New Dandies," "Peacock Punk," "the Look Bands," "the Futurists," most infamously "the Cult with No Name"—Blitz was a place to be *seen*. "Blitz took up the gauntlet thrown down by the punks and turned it into an all-pervasive camp—whether as a way of looking at things or a way of wearing your clothes," Jon Savage wrote. Strange's pseudo-Elizabethan costumes, in particular, inspired the most lasting description of the Blitz scene's collective look: "the New Romantics."

Between work in the Blitz coatroom and at a Carnaby Street clothes stall, Boy George thrived. "He was like the pied piper; fifty kids would follow him around," Egan said. In 1977, the UK punk zine *Sniffin' Glue* had published an illustration of the guitar chords A, E, and G, captioned: "This is a chord. This is another. This is a third. *Now form a band.*" Two years later, Blitz said, in effect: "Here is a look. Here is another. Here is a third. *Now be a star.*"

Blitz, as one habitué put it, was one of "the first clubs run for kids by kids." When Spandau Ballet, all five members of which were Blitz regulars, played its first show there, it didn't bother advertising it. "There wasn't any need to," the band's guitarist and songwriter Gary Kemp said. "You only advertise if you can't get people to come. Our shows were an extension of Blitz." Another reason, Kemp said, was that "we thought the music press were too rockist, so we went straight to the nationals."

Blitz's musical policy was anything but rockist—the soundtrack, regular David Johnson wrote, was "hard-edged European disco, synth-led, but bass-heavy: German sounds such as Kraftwerk and Gina X, Giorgio Moroder, dissonant no wave on the Zé label, and always Bowie." That menu, not three-chord punk, provided the New Pop's musical blueprint.

AMERICA'S SECOND BRITISH INVASION BEGAN IN EARNEST IN MID-1982, when the Human League's "Don't You Want Me"—a UK number one the previous Christmas—topped the US charts. Like Adam Ant, the Human League was a New Pop archetype, starting out by making abrasive electronic postpunk before splitting. Martyn Ware and Ian Craig Marsh formed Heaven 17; Philip Oakey kept the Human League name and recruited a pair of untested vocalists, Susan Anne Sulley and Joanne Catherall, at a Sheffield disco—before he heard them sing, naturally. "We want to be like ABBA or Donna Summer," Oakey explained. The girls figured it for a laugh: "It was an opportunity to take a few weeks off school," Catherall said.

Instead, *Dare*, the Human League's 1981 album, yielded four top ten UK hits—"Don't You Want Me" was the fourth—and set up daunting expectations. Following up *Dare* didn't just mean zigzagging in yet another direction; by definition, it couldn't. "The problem with having a number one," Sulley said years later, "is the only thing you can do is have another number one."

It didn't help that *Dare*'s producer, Martin Rushent, jumped ship during the follow-up's sessions. "We relied on him like a dad," Oakey admitted. "He filled in all the bits we couldn't do." Chris Thomas, then working on the third Pretenders album, took over but exited within months, as studio bills piled up; eventually Hugh Padgham replaced him. "At that point there were more tapes than people," Sulley said. (Thomas, Padgham, and the Human League shared production credit.)

Hysteria was released on May 7, 1984; *Smash Hits* called it a "plodding, second-rate *Dare*." It moved away from its predecessor's all-synth sound, and the band began to look different, as well. An American reporter compared the black-leather-jacketed Oakey, his hair long and his face covered in stubble, to "a refugee from the Ramones fallen on bad times." Oakey admitted, "I wouldn't mind looking like somebody from the Ramones."

A lot of New Pop performers wouldn't have minded being mistaken for rockers right then. Another Sheffield group, ABC, who'd supported 1982's lush *The Lexicon of Love* with a sixteen-piece orchestra, including six string players ("Even the roadies are in tuxedos," *Musician* noted), came back at the end of '83 with a pointedly sour follow-up, *Beauty Stab*, that cut back on the strings and emphasized squalling guitars. It belly-flopped. A joke Oakey once made to a visiting writer from *Musician*—"You're in the wrong dressing room. We're not musicians"—didn't seem quite so funny.

THE SECOND BRITISH INVASION'S MID-JULY 1983 BONANZA WAS FOL-lowed, as *Radio & Records* editor Ken Barnes put it, by "a general slide." By mid-January, right ahead of the *Newsweek* issue, *R&R*'s Contemporary Hits Radio Top 40 featured thirteen UK hits; *Billboard*'s list was similarly proportioned. The drop-off gave Barnes an opening: "So if there's a new British Invasion, it's already lost almost 40 percent of its CHR [contemporary hits radio] impact in six months. That's not to deny the remarkable achievements of British artists in 1983, or to say that further fluctuations won't follow. But as of now the invasion appears to have encountered substantial resistance."

That was already happening in the UK. "By early 1983 there was already a dawning suspicion that things had gone awry," Simon Reynolds wrote in *Rip It Up and Start Again*. "The bright sparks . . . were being gradually displaced by opportunists who weren't as ideas or ideals driven."

But even if the inkies disliked it, back home, the New Pop band's clear, visible roots were in punk. Not so in America. To the US rock press, these were—*sneer*—boy bands. This wasn't the glittery exhaust of the equally neon but respectably raucous Sex Pistols; it was a dumb plastic update of the Bay City Rollers.

For many critics in the United States and UK alike, the New Pop's most insidious aspect was its conservatism. It wasn't just musical differences that made

Jon Moss leave the Clash: "Jon was a staunch Tory. 'Thatcher, bloody brilliant,'" Boy George wrote. The oleaginous lead singer of Spandau Ballet, Tony Hadley, was a vocal fan of Thatcher and has remained an active Conservative for decades. (Songwriter-guitarist Gary Kemp, by contrast, said, "I certainly wasn't a fan of Thatcher's politics.") Hell, even Ian Curtis of Joy Division had voted Tory in 1979.

And in mid-1983, John Taylor of Duran Duran told *Creem*, "I've never seen politics and rock music mix successfully. I can't stand politics, personally. I think it's incredibly boring. I'd rather write songs about parties. . . . All I know is that at least with Margaret Thatcher we pay less tax." Taylor would later backtrack, writing in his memoir: "We had no political agenda. We just went with the energy."

Duran Duran became the press's especial whipping boys, on both sides of the Atlantic. The *Washington Post* called them "the ultimate glossy pop confection that is better seen than heard." In the *Village Voice*, Ken Tucker wrote that Simon Le Bon—who had told *Rolling Stone* that he believed in "genetics and breeding"—"talks like a cross between Hitler and Thatcher."

There was plenty of sniping from their peers, as well. Philip Oakey of the Human League slagged them for "do[ing] things that we frankly felt too proud to do," such as appear in the million-selling preteen magazine *Jackie*, where "the basic message there is, you have got to find a boyfriend."

Duran Duran even became tax exiles—taking themselves out of Britain to prevent having to pay the bulk of their individual incomes in taxes—just like the seventies superstars (and regular targets of punk spite) Rod Stewart and the Rolling Stones. "I see no reason why, with a career that may at best last five years, I should give away 70 percent of the money I earn now," John Taylor told *Smash Hits*.

When Andy Taylor auditioned to join Duran Duran, he was told, "We're poseurs. We want a good-looking poseur band."

"Good," the guitarist responded, "because I like dressing up and I love wearing makeup."

Duran Duran was a "Blitz band" from a different Blitz. Guitarist (soon bassist) John Taylor and keyboardist Nick Rhodes started the group while working at Birmingham's Rum Runner, Rhodes as a DJ spinning a similar mix to Steve Strange's. The Rum Runner's sibling owners became the band's managers.

Taylor and Rhodes began with the idea to crossbreed the Sex Pistols and Chic, Rhodes told *Rolling Stone*, "two and a half years *before* Duran Duran." Drummer Roger Taylor and singer Simon Le Bon finished the lineup. (All three Taylors are unrelated.)

Early on, the group set some modest goals: "To headline shows at Hammersmith Odeon by '82, Wembley by '83, and New York's Madison Square Garden by '84," John wrote. "It was a plan that seemed perfectly achievable."

They happily "jumped on the bandwagon" of the newly dubbed New Romantics, Le Bon said. "But after a month or two, we had to get out of that New Romantic thing, because the frilly shirts looked really stupid." John would later say, "We're sort of the Roy Lichtenstein of pop music, blatant and colorful."

Just as alarming to the American rock radio and press were the band's musical references. "Talk to Duran Duran about their influences, and you won't hear a standard roll call of dusky icons like the Rolling Stones or even the Beatles," *Rolling Stone* gasped. Their roll call, instead, was Roxy Music, David Bowie, Cockney Rebel, and Sparks—only one of whom, Bowie, was anything like a real star in the States, and whose popularity level had only recently approached Duran Duran's.

Many British bands found the sheer amount of glad-handing and roadwork required to break the States forbidding, but Duran Duran was game, even if American radio was a tough sell. "We'd go to . . . like, Pittsburgh and the local guy would take us to two or three radio stations," John said. "The only reason they were speaking to us, or even shaking our hands, is that they thought, 'Hey, *Kenny Rogers* might be breezing in here with the same Capitol rep this time next week, and he might not bring Kenny along unless we see these schmucks.'" They also toured assiduously. "We can actually *play*," John said. "I think that counts for a lot."

That said, no band was ever dubbed an "MTV band" or "video band" as often as Duran Duran, and none more correctly. "Video to us is like stereo was to Pink Floyd," Rhodes said. "It was new, it was just happening. And we saw we could do a lot with it."

Of course they could—Duran Duran was a good-looking poseur band that liked dressing up and loved wearing makeup. "In Britain we have these chocolates called Quality Street, and the selling line is 'Every one is someone's favorite,'" John said. "We're a bit like that."

Duran Duran were teen idols who liked, and saw nothing wrong with, being teen idols. "I've got two sisters, aged thirteen and fifteen, and they're just the same about pop music as I was at that age," Andy Taylor said in 1982. "Posters on the wall, off to see Adam; their appreciation is exactly the same as mine used to be."

Still, even Duran Duran wondered about their own videos' pomp: "We're a fucking rock band," Andy muttered after catching a stomach bug during the Sri Lankan shooting of the gleefully incoherent clip for "Hungry Like the Wolf," from the band's second album, *Rio* (1982). "What the fuck were we doing out there prancing about on elephants?"

The band released its third album, *Seven and the Ragged Tiger*, in October of 1983. The accompanying tour was sponsored by Coke, and it was fueled by coke. "I crossed a line when I started getting high onstage," John Taylor wrote in his memoir. "I had always remained sober for the duration of the show, as I wanted to give my best and did not want to compromise my talent so publicly. But now I couldn't wait for the performances to end. I wanted to take back control of my life, and getting high felt like that."

Duran Duran played a sold-out Madison Square Garden on March 19, 1984. The band members flew their parents to New York for the occasion—all those Taylors! Also backstage was the band's new friend Nile Rodgers. He and drummer Tony Thompson of the disco band Chic had been formative heroes of the Durans, and the black New Yorkers dug them back. Nile introduced John to the young woman whose second album he was producing. "She was tiny and didn't seem to give two fucks about me," John Taylor wrote. "That was the most vivid impression I had about meeting Madonna."

DURAN DURAN FRETTED THEY WEREN'T TAKEN SERIOUSLY AS MUSICIANS. Not Eurythmics, who were the most traditionally talented of the Second British Invasion. Singer Annie Lennox was, per Miller, "a stunning hybrid of Joan Baez and Aretha Franklin." And a reporter from *Musician* was suitably impressed by guitarist Dave Stewart's axemanship during sound check in San Francisco: "An incredible variety of music flowed from his fingers as he checked effects settings and monitor levels. Blues slide work. Richard Thompson's 'Calvary Cross.' Funky rhythm riffs. Some classical finger picking."

Annie and Dave met in 1976 in Hempstead. He was the hippie veteran of several nothing groups; she was a waitress who'd attended London's Royal Academy of Music only to spit out the classics: "I hated it. I spent three dreadful years there trying to figure a way out." Instantly, Dave proposed. Then she auditioned for his new band at her place. "From that minute on, we lived to-gether for about four years," Stewart said. "That next day Annie said, 'You don't know me but I can go strange.' I said, 'Oh yeah, I go strange as well.'"

Their new band, the Tourists, slogged through the latter half of the decade, scoring a couple of top ten UK hits, including a cover of Dusty Springfield's "I Only Want to Be with You." When the band ended in 1980, Lennox rebelled against her girlie Tourists image: "I had to get rid of that poppy Annie Lennox, the strain was unbearable. So I killed her." Lennox cut her hair close to the scalp after an audience member tore off her wig during a performance. When rumors began that Lennox was in fact a man, she began wearing suits and ties: "To be neither male nor female widens your scope," she said.

Lennox and Stewart became Eurythmics and recorded a debut, *In the Garden*, with the krautrock production pioneer Conny Plank. It tanked, so Stewart went to the bank. "I dressed up like a businessman—I had a briefcase and everything," he said. "I told him that Annie and I were going to do something absolutely amazing and that the bank should invest in us. I made the point that most bands spent thirty thousand pounds just recording one album, but that we could buy the equipment we needed for seven thousand and then make all the albums we wanted." He got the loan. "Often we had to wait for the timber factory downstairs to turn off their machinery before we could record vocals," Stewart said.

Their biggest hit was largely improvised on the spot. Lennox and Stewart were at an impasse, bickering. "And he said, 'Okay, fine, you don't mind if I go ahead and program the drum computer then, do you?'" Lennox recalled. "It sounded so good that in the end I couldn't resist it. I sat down behind the synthesizer and *fam!*, the riff came." Only later did Lennox overdub the "Hold your head up / Keep your head up" bridge; the rest of the words came out in one continuous take.

By the time the *Sweet Dreams* album was released, Lennox and Stewart were still musical partners but no longer a couple. "RCA offered that if Dave and I got married they'd hire a ship and fly journalists to it for a huge reception," Lennox said. "We considered getting married and starting divorce proceedings next day but it didn't seem worth it."

On the same page in the January 14, 1984, issue of *Melody Maker* that re-ported that Lennox's "voice was beginning to deteriorate towards the end of the band's recent UK tour" sat an item that summed up the way New Pop was shooing out "old" postpunk heroes of less than a decade's vintage. The title was

"Wally of the Week: Bob Geldof." It mocked the Boomtown Rats leader for "prancing around in thermal underwear like a caged monkey" on the TV show *Give Us a Clue*: "We do remember, though, that he once wrote a rather fine song called 'Lookin' After No. 1.' Even at the expense of self-respect, Bob?"

"FILM OF MARGARET THATCHER SMILING AS DOLE QUEUES GET BIGGER; animate her so that she's singing the song."

This was part of Stewart's original treatment for the "Sweet Dreams" video, which went unused. Compare that mild rebuke with another, following the October 12, 1984, Irish Republican Army (IRA) bombing of a Brighton hotel targeting the prime minister and her cabinet but killing five others instead: "The sorrow of the IRA Brighton bombing is that Thatcher escaped unscathed." This statement came from Morrissey, the lead singer of the Manchester quartet the Smiths, and it wasn't the only obstinate or attention-getting thing about him.

Like the New Popsters, Steven Patrick Morrissey had emerged from punk, briefly fronting second-stringers Ed Banger and the Nosebleeds ("Ain't Bin to No Music School"). He was a fanatic reader of the UK music press and one of its most singular correspondents: "Indubitably, Buzzcocks will hardly figure strongly—or even weakly—in the *NME* poll," he wrote the weekly, before concluding his pitch: "But for now, they are the best kick-ass rock band in the country. Go and see them first and then you may have the audacity to contradict me, you stupid sluts."

Like the Velvet Underground and Jonathan Richman before him, Morrissey was an oppositional pop star—except in the UK he was bigger than either; he actually *was* a pop star. A number of rock musicians had been vegetarians, notably Paul McCartney, but few were as snidely self-righteous about it as Morrissey. Long-faced and pompadour-headed, Morrissey wore hearing aids and cardigans and thick-rimmed glasses, styling as bookish, dowdy, a wallflower, but doing it with the foppish flair of a dandy. He was deliberately, provocatively fey, and he wrote lyrics clearly intended to be read as much as sung. Not that Morrissey could sing much—but the clear passion of his faint voice turned yet another defect into a lance. "We're so uncool," the Smiths' guitarist Johnny Marr boasted, "we're the fucking coolest."

Bassist Andy Rourke and drummer Mike Joyce possessed seemingly effortless rhythmic telepathy, and Johnny Marr was the glue, emitting hooks like he was pouring milk. But you were instantly for or against Morrissey. The figure he cut was literary, not musical: "Books were always more important to me than music," he told *Musician*. On another occasion, he sniffed, "I find most people in the music business are still morbidly macho. . . . I think we need more brains in popular music."

Modesty was not Morrissey's strong suit. "I couldn't imagine how things would be if we weren't here," he told one interviewer. To *Rolling Stone*, he lamented, "I can't think of anybody I'd cross the street to see. Just to see modern music in its present state is like seeing a kitten dying." He told *Creem*, "We're the most important band in Britain right now. I mean, how could you even compare us to, say, the Police? . . . Our music is the music that's needed in England now—and even more so in America."

Indeed, America was just about primed for a guitar band in the post-Beatles mode that took rock seriously instead of pranced around it in funny clothes and willful color schemes. (Not to mention those synthesizers—an instrument the Smiths refused to touch.) And even groups on small labels, such as Rough Trade, the Smiths' imprint, were getting the opportunity to break the States. Not that Morrissey cared. "Where America's concerned, I don't wish to go door-to-door," he told Roy Trakin. "I refuse to take the long route that seems to have destroyed so many others. I want it the easy way. I won't go to America unless we're really wanted there. If the record can be listened to over there, then that should be enough." Such thinking, Trakin wrote, "suggest[s] a bunch of nouveau hippies whose non-image will leave them lost in the land of *Entertainment Tonight*."

Britain was another story: *The Smiths* debuted at number two in the UK, and in May they'd reach the national top ten for the first and only time with the most aptly titled song of Morrissey's life, "Heaven Knows I'm Miserable Now."

The "indie" ideal that the Smiths on Rough Trade emblemized was another remnant of punk that no longer quite resembled its old self. New Pop stars had left behind the handshake deals of the indie labels for the bigger ones their bigger-sounding music could nab. What dominated the mid-eighties UK indie charts were gauzy dreamscape-makers like the Cocteau Twins and This Mortal Coil, both on the cultish 4AD label; punk flag-flyers of varying levels of political seriousness, the apogee being the anarchist collective Crass; and industrial noise makers such as Test Dept. and the notorious Einstürzende Neubauten.

"Einstürzende play hydraulic drills, concrete mixers, springs, sheets of metal, industrial containers, buzz saws—all found urban materials," Merle Ginsberg wrote in the *Village Voice*. "Live, this music is physically devastating, as it was on two occasions at Danceteria last week. But it confuses people about how they're *supposed* to respond to it."

At least one audience had some ideas how to respond to Neubauten. In early January, at the London gallery the ICA, a performance by the group along with guests from London band the Bic devolved into a riot. "Before anyone knew what was happening, concert-goers were pulling anything and everything closer to them," *NME* staffer Cynthia Rose wrote in a column for the US rock mag *Creem*. "This included the ICA's giant electrical generator—which was ripped right out of the wall—to become the object of a tug-of-war between the terrified staff and their guests."

"When the [ICA staff] brought the concerto to a premature close, a hardcore of thirty or so spectators refused to leave the hall," Chris Bohn reported in the *NME*. "To persuade the 'band' to continue they hurled debris at the back of the stage and staff clearing the hall. Damage to bodies and the building was, surprisingly, minimal." The stunt only enhanced the reputation of a band that, as Rose noted, had "managed to violently polarize just about all the listeners in the UK's rock population towards either total espousal or heartfelt hatred." Like a far more sonically extreme Smiths, Neubauten's "customized industrial steel drum kit gave the British synthoscape a kick in the teeth it heartily deserved," Rose wrote.

ON MAY 6, 1983, THE SMITHS HAD OPENED FOR GOTH ROCKERS THE Sisters of Mercy at the University of London Union. John Walters, who'd recently rejoined *The John Peel Show* as producer, was in the audience; soon after, the band was offered a Peel Session—a three-hour studio taping of (typically) four new songs with minimal overdubbing, to be played exclusively on Peel's show.

Peel championed the Smiths so ardently—he'd played the session version of "This Charming Man" three times before the commercial recording was issued—that he became central to their narrative. He'd done that for a lot of artists: Jimi Hendrix, David Bowie, Rod Stewart, and T. Rex, just for starters. No broadcaster was more critical to punk's impact in Britain.

For an indie band in 1984, Peel's enthusiasm was tantamount to knight-hood. As Ken Garner, author of the book *The Peel Sessions*, put it: "The Peel Sessions of 1978–1981 permanently changed bands' perspective on worthwhile musical ambitions. From now on, a Peel Session became as much a career am-bition in itself as a means to advancement." Many of these came from bands in small towns; by late 1978, David Cavanagh wrote, Peel had the power to "spark an entire regional scene merely by playing one song."

On January 2, Peel played a record by another band he'd helped push forth, giving them their first session in November 1982—a Liverpool group called Frankie Goes to Hollywood. In October 1983, the quintet had issued this record, titled "Relax," on ZTT, the new imprint cofounded by producer Trevor Horn, his wife and manager Jill Sinclair, and former *NME* writer Paul Morley. The twelve-inch had an enormously thick, viscid sound, to match its subject matter.

Led by the flamboyantly gay and out William Holly Johnson (blond, sleek) and Paul Rutherford (brunet, mustached), and backed by a trio of straight male instrumentalists—Peter Gill, Mark O'Toole, and Brian Nash—Frankie Goes to Hollywood were, the *NME* panted, "a scorching leather-bound ver-sion of the lifestyle [Johnson and] Rutherford led." As one excited but intimi-dated A&R man (the liaison between band and label; it stands for Artists and Repertoire) after another stopped short of an offer, the band appeared on *The Tube*, BBC TV's mid-eighties new band showcase. That performance had led to the ZTT signing. And when "Relax" began slipping down the UK chart before reaching the Top 40, despite ZTT having sunk a hundred thousand quid into it, *The Tube* put Frankie back on for its Christmas show. That's when "Relax" took flight.

Then Mike Read, Radio 1's breakfast DJ for three years in January, played "Relax." The BBC had already played "Relax" more than seventy times; this time, though, Read pulled the record off midway through and announced on-air that he wouldn't play it again, thanks to the sexually suggestive lyrics: "Re-lax, don't do it / Till you wanna come!" On the following Sunday's Top 40 show, Simon Bates finished playing the week's number seven hit, the Culture Club ballad "Victims," then said a quick, "And at number six, 'Relax' by Frankie Goes to Hollywood, and at number five"—and went right into Paul Young's "Love of the Common People." A de facto ban was in effect.

Or was it? "There's no one person at the BBC who can ban this record," a station rep told *Melody Maker*, adding, weakly, "There was so much new material in the Top 40 that there wasn't space to include it." This was followed days later by a statement from *Top of the Pops* (*TOTP*) producer Michael Hurll: "In common with Radio 1, BBC TV believes that the lyrics of this song are sexually explicit and not suitable for viewing in family viewing time."

"And if you're thinking of flicking through your back issues of *Smash Hits* to check out what's so controversial about the lyric, don't bother," the nation's top pop magazine told its readers. "We decided weeks ago not to print it because we thought it was a bit rude."

"I HATED PUNK," TREVOR HORN TOLD SIMON REYNOLDS. HE WAS SO un-punk that in 1979—after he'd teamed up with Geoff Downes under the moniker the Buggles, and made "Video Killed the Radio Star," which sold five million copies before becoming the first-ever video shown on MTV—he and Downes joined the most un-punk band of all time, Yes. He regretted it the first night out, hours before taking the stage of Madison Square Garden, before twenty thousand persnickety longhairs expecting him to measure up to the departed Jon Anderson *or else*. "I remember thinking—how could I ever be worried about making a record again, or getting a mix right, after something as truly horrific as this?" Horn said.

Post-Yes, Horn decided to start producing pop. His first project was "this little MOR [middle of the road] group named Dollar." His first major statement was ABC's lush, devastated *The Lexicon of Love* in 1982. "It's like Bob Dylan, but it's disco music instead of an acoustic guitar," Horn told his uncomprehending peers. "The guy's actually writing about what he really feels, but the record's going to be played in a dance club, so it's gonna have a function." Malcolm McLaren hired Horn to make the first McLaren artist LP, *Duck Rock*, in 1983; McLaren was so persuasive he even charmed Trevor's wife and manager Jill Sinclair, who loathed punk even more than her husband. The album was a proto-sampling global-fusion let's-exploit-everyone classic—a process Horn likened to "knitting fog."

In late 1983, four years after joining Yes, Horn produced their comeback album and its number one hit, "Owner of a Lonely Heart." Wait—hadn't Yes split? They had: Horn initially went to work for a band called Cinema—long-standing Yes-men Chris Squire (bass) and Alan White (drums) with a newly rejoined early member Tony Kaye (keyboards) and newcomer Trevor Rabin on guitar. Horn took the assignment, he said, "to see if I could do an

AOR thing, if I could manage to get inside that AOR format and pervert it from within," he said. One of Rabin's songs, "Owner of a Lonely Heart," began with a drenched power chord that was intended entirely as a piss-take of airbrushed AOR. "It was imperative, coming back after such a load of shit, that Yes have a single. I would have killed to get that," Horn said.

Cinema's debut album was about 80 percent done when Horn decided he wasn't certain of Rabin's lead singing. Squire "just threw this out one night— 'Let's get Jon Anderson back'—and it sort of freaked everyone out." When Anderson arrived, he said, "I enjoyed it right away. [Squire] said, 'Why don't you sing on it?' I said, 'Well, if I sing on it, we're going to be back into the Yes groove.' And he said, 'That's obvious.'" Yet even with Anderson's stratospheric vocals and a tricky stop-start structure, "Owner of a Lonely Heart" was in fact a dance-rock number that hit big in the clubs. "Anyone can make the-wall stuff," Horn said. "The challenge is to make off-the-wall stuff that sells."

And no one managed the trick like Horn did. Yes's *90125* album sold a million and a half copies in its first three weeks; by March it had moved 2.5 million—the best-selling Yes album by far—in addition to million-or-more sales for "Video Killed the Radio Star," ABC's *The Lexicon of Love, Duck Rock*, and in the UK, "Relax." The latter was the UK's number one on January 22, the day before "Owner" topped the US chart. The week *Newsweek* covered a British Invasion, Horn had the top singles in both the United States and the UK with wildly different records by wildly different artists.

"Relax," in Frankie Goes to Hollywood's repertoire from the start, attracted Horn immediately. "I'm sure I'm not denigrating it in any way by saying that it was an advertising jingle, and a brilliant one," he said. It wasn't hard to tie that in with the band's obvious appeal. "They want to be loved; and they want to have as much sex as they possibly can with as many people as they can," Horn said. "They are the first group I've ever known that when they get fan-mail they don't write back, they phone up."

ZTT had come to be after Horn began palling around with Morley, the New Pop's chief theorist, who had singled out Horn's work for especial praise in the *NME*. The producer made the critic part of his new label's creative core.

Frankie Goes to Hollywood knew Morley prior to working with him as well. ("We used to hate him, to be quite honest," Holly Johnson told the *NME*.) The band took a very low advance to join ZTT: "When you're working with someone like Trevor Horn you don't mind making sacrifices," Johnson said.

Guitarist Brian Nash put it even more succinctly: "People say, 'Oh they couldn't do it without Trevor Horn.' Why should we? We're both quite happy."

In fact, Trevor Horn actually *had* done it largely without them. Frankie had played on the original version of "Relax." But they were out of the studio the day Horn suddenly changed the entire thing. "With 'Relax' we did a complete swerve," Horn said. "It was around lunchtime on a Wednesday, and we had worked for two weeks on a version on which the band had played, but it wasn't really happening for me. It was neither the band playing live nor a good sequenced version. . . . [I] said, 'This isn't working. We've got to start again.' It was just one of those things; the guys weren't there. Then by the end of that Wednesday we had completely rerecorded the track. It all happened in the space of fourteen hours."

The resultant stomp was concentrated and hard, a mile from the airy *Lexicon of Love* or the freeze-frame jump cuts of "Owner of a Lonely Heart," not to mention the hip-hop beat-boxing of the McLaren hit "Buffalo Gals." Horn had reinvented himself as the ultimate baron of dance floor sleaze. The lyrics were transparently about holding off an orgasm; the video was explicitly about gay sex. The uproar sent the record, already selling strongly, into overdrive. "Mike Read?" Frankie's lead singer Holly Johnson said. "I thought, *Thank you, Mike Read.*"

SUNSET STRIP,
HOLLYWOOD
February 25, 1984

LIKE A LOT OF NEW YORKERS, TOM WERMAN SAW LOS ANGELES AS THE Promised Land. In the mid-seventies he was an Epic Records A&R man, signing Ted Nugent, one of seventies rock's most consistent concert draws, and the redoubtable Cheap Trick. The latter band first brought Werman out west, to make their second LP, *In Color*, at Burbank's Kendun Recorders in 1977. A year later he made the move.

Werman was boggled by the ease of making records in Los Angeles: "In New York the entertainment business—it exists, but it's hardly paramount, hardly a big deal. And in LA, that's all there is, really. It's the number one industry. I said, 'Jeez, if I'm going to make records for a living, I'd better live there.' CBS, they paid for the whole thing. It was great."

Along with Elektra, Atlantic, Capitol, Columbia, and RCA, Epic's West Coast office was a short distance from the Sunset Strip—the stretch of Sunset Boulevard in West Hollywood from Doheny to Fairfax—which in the sixties had been Los Angeles's primary rock and roll launching pad. In the seventies, the action moved to the Troubadour, Werman's favorite area bar. "People like the Eagles used to hang out there before they were the Eagles," he says. But by the early eighties, the Strip's clubs were happening again: the Starwood, Gazzarri's, the Roxy, and the Whisky a Go Go.

Werman arrived in LA just as the kind of hard rock he specialized in was beginning to achieve fissure, thanks to the self-titled debut album by four wild-asses who'd come up through the clubs—first in their hometown of Pasadena, then at Gazzarri's, just off North Weatherly Drive. Though they'd graduated almost immediately to playing arenas, the Strip's clubs would remain Van Halen's playhouse.

That wasn't the way Tom Werman rolled—he was too much the professional. Werman preferred industry showcases put on by bands aiming for the big time: "I would go right up to the VIP section—it was better than being down on the floor, in the mosh pit. I saw a lot of Mötley Crüe's shows in town."

Mötley Crüe was the most popular of the bands following in Van Halen's footsteps. They dressed like they sounded: loud and skimpy. Most of the new Sunset Strip bands dressed like it was Halloween every day. These rockers were there to be *seen*, not just heard. "There was a ton of activity on that part of the Strip, and it was quite concentrated, in a very, very confined area," says Werman.

When Werman had signed Ted Nugent in 1975, he remembers, "The kids that came in were literally head-to-toe in denim and motorcycle boots. That was the look." It was the look that defined what was called "heavy metal" in the mid-seventies—hard, blues-based rock that, sartorially at least, felt defiantly down-market. "Ten years later, you wouldn't see any denim," Werman remembers of the crazily ascendant Sunset Strip of 1984. "It went from denim to spangles."

In June of **1984,** Werner told *Billboard* that the metal market was "glutted." "I'd be foolish to look for heavy metal right now," he said. "We're loaded with it. The record companies have gone overboard the same way they did with 'skinny tie groups' in the wake of the Knack."

For heavy metallers, 1979 had been the year heavy metal got its mojo back. But for the biz, 1979 was the year of *Get the Knack*, an instant smash, going gold (half a million sold) in a mere thirteen days. Better yet, it cost only $18,000 to make, compared to the million-dollars-plus of a Fleetwood Mac or Eagles album—right when instant blockbusters were suddenly less than sure things.

The Knack, too, was a Sunset Strip band—they'd debuted at the Whisky in 1978—and their sudden ascendancy meant A&R people were sprinting toward anything that could be reasonably dubbed "new wave." Naturally, this gave the

Sunset Strip heavy metal school license to deride anything connected to new wave. "You know, once they signed Van Halen, they slammed the door on metal," Rudy Sarzo, the bassist for another Sunset Strip band, Quiet Riot, said. "Unless you were a band that was new wave or punk that showcased locally at the Starwood or the Whisky or the Roxy, the record company didn't care [in Los Angeles]."

But few of the post-Knack major-label signings—the Records, 20/20, Rubinoos, Bram Tchaikovsky—did much chart-wise; the Knack itself was kaput by the end of 1981. By contrast, Werman told *Billboard*, "Heavy metal and hard rock have always sold; it's the most stable commodity in the music industry."

The tipping point came during day two of the 1983 US Festival, the second and last Memorial Day Weekend gathering sponsored by Apple cofounder Steve Wozniak. Sunday was Heavy Metal Day, and it drew 330,000—three-quarters of the number that Saturday (New Wave Day) and Monday (Rock Day) had *combined*.

Not content with mere symbolism, the simmering tension between new wave and heavy metal was made highly explicit in the form of a tiff between Sunday's headliners, Van Halen, and Saturday's, the Clash. (David Bowie topped the Monday bill.) Van Halen earned $1.5 million for this one gig, by some distance the biggest single-performance fee in rock history. "God decided to pay us off in one game," David Lee Roth cracked backstage.

Onstage, a completely trashed Roth got in the loudest of a weekend's worth of licks against the British punks. Having come on two hours late, in the midst of a show full of forgotten lyrics, at one point Roth slugged down a hefty volume of Jack Daniel's. "I just want you to know," he slurred at the audience, "that the only band that puts iced tea in a Jack Daniel's bottle . . . is *the Clash, baybee!*" The crowd roared.

EDWARD VAN HALEN AND DAVID LEE ROTH WERE TWO SHOWBOATS sharing the same vessel. Between them, bassist Michael Anthony recalled, "Usually it's whoever threw the most punches won." Roth once typified the band as "one big long argument, man."

Van Halen was the most California band imaginable—they came across like the impossible dream was their natural inheritance. Lots of scrawny, funny-looking dudes took up the guitar because mastering it meant women would flock to them, but what gave the members of Van Halen their edge is that they'd probably have gotten laid anyway. "Van Halen smacked of enthusiasm.

It has to do with smiles," David Lee Roth told *Creem* in 1984. To *Billboard* at the end of that tumultuous year, Roth said, "I sell big smiles. Here, have one."

The Van Halen family moved to America from their native Holland in February 1962, when Edward was seven and Alex nearly nine. Their father, Jan, *Rolling Stone* wrote, "was a Dutch resistance fighter who was captured by the Nazis and forced to tour Germany playing in a band." The family arrived in Southern California, living together in a single room in a shared house with two other families. Their mother, Eugenia, got a job as a maid; Jan did similar work while continuing to play music. "He had to walk six miles every morning to wash dishes to pay the rent," Edward recalled. "He didn't even know the language! That taught me that no matter what happens, if you got the will you can do anything you want, anything."

Despite Eugenia's hopes, the boys inherited their dad's habits. "My dad was one of the baddest clarinet players of his time," Edward boasted. "He was so hot—unbelievably. And he had tone. My dad is the person who would cut school and smoke cigarettes, and my mom would be the cheerleader. Complete opposites—the conservative and the screw-up. If you sat there and talked to my dad, he'd make you roll over and laugh. He's just like me and Al—sixteen years old."

Edward began as a drummer, Alex on guitar, but when Alex began practicing his brother's drums while Ed was on his paper route, they decided to switch for real. "Alex is better technically at music than the rest of us combined," Roth once said. "Plus he's got near-perfect pitch. You can play him a song on the radio, and he'll tell you what key it's in."

Edward, meanwhile, could mimic any guitarist he heard. At Pasadena City College, he and Roth shared music classes, and at the end of one, the students had to perform a song. "Edward played acoustic guitar, and did the Blind Faith tune 'Can't Find My Way Home.' He played the guitar exactly like it was on the record. It was very impressive," Roth wrote in his memoir. "I sang 'Go Away, Little Girl,' the Donny Osmond version."

FROM HIS THREE-PART NAME TO HIS ONE-TRACK MIND, DAVID LEE ROTH was born to the stage. He was born in Bloomington, Indiana; his father, grandfather, and several uncles were surgeons (his father, an ophthalmologist). Little Dave loved to read, so he learned to shoplift books. He wooed girls and joked around during class and participated in lots of fights. The family member who completely *got* Dave was uncle Manny Roth, owner-operator of the folk club Café Wha? on MacDougal Street in New York, where Bob Dylan first performed after arriving in 1961. "New York certainly reflects the dinner table I grew up with," Roth said. "Obviously it encouraged me."

Roth was trying his act out cross-country long before Van Halen's first tour. "My family moved around a lot because my daddy was in medical school," Roth said. "I went to high school starting in Massachusetts and then transferred over to Pasadena, California." There, in 1970, when he was sixteen, Roth was bused to a majority-black high school. "I went to junior high and high schools that were 95 percent black and Spanish-speaking. I can gang-sign the whole alphabet," he said.

Instantly, he loved rock and roll, but he kept tabs on R&B and disco: "I was on the floor of Studio 54 probably a hundred times," he said. This was always going to clash with Edward, who loved "blues," but just meant Cream, and who in 2015 told an interviewer that the most recent album he'd purchased was Peter Gabriel's *So*, from 1986. Roth, on the other hand, "listen[ed] constantly," he said. "I have no particular taste in music whatsoever."

Roth and the Van Halens had connected through the backyard party circuit in and around Pasadena, with its plethora of "upper-middle-class daddies": "You would visit the kid who was now living in the[ir parents'] guest house, by the little kidney-shaped pool," Roth wrote. "His parents would ultimately go on some kind of a vacation and you would have a party." He auditioned for Mammoth, Ed and Alex's group, and flunked, so he started the Red Ball Jets, who became the Van Halens' chief rivals.

Instrumentally, it wasn't even close—but Red Ball Jets' singer was a show of his own even then. Swiveling his hips like a pole dancer, Roth moved, in Mikal Gilmore's words, like "a carnal gymnast." Years later, watching a pair of women bump and grind on a banquet table backstage in Detroit, Roth told Gilmore, "Lost denizens of the night. Man, I relate to them heavily."

Roth eventually jettisoned the Jets to join the Van Halens. The brothers wanted to call the band Rat Salade; Roth insisted they name it after themselves. "I felt the name Van Halen was like the name Santana," Dave said. "I didn't like the idea at first," Edward admitted, "but now I have to admit it sounds powerful—like a German nuclear bomb."

The final Van Halen lineup was completed in 1974 by bassist Mike Sobolewski—himself the son of a musician, a trumpeter for forties swing hitmaker Kay Kyser—who in 1978, for their first album, legally changed his name to Michael Anthony. "The first show I played with the band, I was wearing gold lamé pants and vest, and Ed was wearing silver lamé," Anthony recalled. "I mean, this is a backyard party in Pasadena." Eventually, they left the more flamboyant outfits to Roth. "Around the time we auditioned to play Gazzarri's on the Sunset Strip, I got some platforms and nearly broke my ankles," Edward said.

Van Halen became the de facto house band at Gazzarri's in 1976. There, Ed began doing a two-handed exercise that J. D. Considine described as "the hammer-on and pull-off—a technique in which instead of plucking the note with a pick, the first note is sounded by hitting the string very hard at the fret, then plucking the string with that finger to sound a second, lower note." Finger-tapping, or "tapping," in shorthand, was merely one of an armful of techniques Ed had taught himself. Alex had to tell him to turn around onstage whenever he did it: "These bastards are going to rip you off blind."

After Gazzarri's, the band began gigging at the Starwood, in Hollywood. There in 1977, Warner Bros. A&R man and producer Ted Templeman first caught Van Halen. "They just floored me," he said. "David Roth came across as the most convincing thing I'd seen in rock and roll theater since Jim Morrison, but mainly it was Eddie who impressed me. . . . I think he's the best guitar player alive, and I've listened extensively to George Benson, Django Reinhardt, Tal Farlow, Charlie Christian, Jim Hall, and Jimi Hendrix. Eddie can play thirty-second-note melodic lines with a complexity that rivals Bach, and I haven't heard *anybody* who can phrase like him since Charlie Parker."

While recording the first Van Halen album, Templeman heard Edward practicing his tapping, asked what it was, and put it on their debut album under the title "Eruption." Consisting of "shimmering arpeggiated figures that sounded more like a Bach harpsichord than rock guitar," as Considine wrote, "Eruption" spawned an instant flurry of imitators. "I did not take it as flattery," Edward said.

The two main figures' differences were plain. Roth *read*—and Edward hated books. ("But you're really articulate," a reporter insisted. "You see?" Edward replied. "I don't even know what that means.") When J. D. Considine—one of the few rock critics to take Van Halen's music as seriously as his colleagues did Roth's sexual threat—told Edward that he'd spoken with Roth the night before the interview they were concluding, Ed responded, "You actually listened to him?"

Van Halen didn't popularize heavy metal in America by themselves, but they did the most to make it broadly acceptable. Especially on MTV, the silly shtick of the band's performance clips brought them across even better than the hits. "The sense of humor was there in the songs, but you had to pay attention," MTV VJ Mark Goodman said of Van Halen. "The videos hit you over the head with it."

Nonetheless, CHR, like society, was ambivalent about metal. A summer '84 survey in *Radio & Records* reveals stations' skittishness. In Hartford, an assistant PD reported, "While people over twenty years old may tolerate an occasional metal hit by Ratt or Twisted Sister, an hour of nonstop metal is enough to send them screaming into the night."

A Denver ad director for the Budget Records & Tapes chain said, "AORs are basically chicken about metal. Everybody's playing Ratt and Twisted Sister and maybe Helix, but not much else." One of the city's rock station music directors pled, "We can't have all three AORs here blasting away at once."

VAN HALEN PUT A COVER SONG ON EVERY ALBUM, AND IT WAS STARTING to make Ed itch. On 1982's *Diver Down*, Ted Templeman—who'd forged a strong bond with Roth in the studio—insisted Edward, who composed all the band's originals (Roth wrote lyrics), leave off a Minimoog original in favor of a version of Martha and the Vandellas' "Dancing in the Streets," a minor Top 40 hit.

The guitarist began building a home studio he dubbed 5150—LA police code for a mentally disturbed suspect. "The whole reason I built this studio," he said years later, "was to shove it up Templeman's ass." For the first time, a Van Halen album would be entirely originals.

The first thing Ed recorded was a keyboard riff he'd come up with one album earlier. On the demo, his wife, Valerie Bertinelli, could be heard in the background, yelling, "Shut up!" Both Templeman and Roth ("Keyboards in our band? No way") rejected it at first but changed their minds; Templeman would eventually call the track "perfect": "I played it for the people at Warner Bros., just the track, there wasn't a song, it was just his synthesizer part. And everybody at Warners flipped out and we went in and cut the track the same way, almost identical."

Roth tended to drive around while writing lyrics, but he'd gotten the idea for this song while watching television: "There was some stud on top of the Arco Tower who was ready to punch out early. And there was a crowd of people down thirty-five stories on the street and it occurred to me there's always at least one schmoe in the crowd who says: 'Go ahead and jump.' So I wrote that down because I guess I was the schmoe in that case. But it turned out much more positive than that."

"'Jump,'" wrote J. D. Considine, "is not exactly the kind of song you'd expect from Van Halen: the main synthesizer figure uses suspended chords and a pedal-point bass in a manner more suited to Asia." On February 28, 1984, two months after its release, "Jump" became Van Halen's first number one pop hit—and the first heavy metal song to mount the Hot 100. It didn't just cross over from AOR to pop, either. In the *Village Voice*, critic Greg Tate referred to Van Halen's hit as "that Prince clone 'Jump.'" Even *Billboard*'s dance music columnist Brian Chin paid his respects: "Van Halen's 'Jump' really does belong on the Dance/Disco Top 80, although it isn't."

Roth liked the company at the top of the charts. "The world's Top 40 is like an audio shot in the arm for everybody," he said. "We're all different and we're all being consumed by the radio for no other reason than we're all a hundred and twenty-eight beats a minute and damn good looking." But that kind of acclaim meant little to Ed. "I read reviews of 'Jump' or people tell me 'Hey, that's a great pop tune!' Kiss my ass! It ain't a pop tune, it's just goddamn, downright music. . . . We're not heavy metal. I'm a *musician*."

VAN HALEN HAD HEAVY METAL'S FIRST NUMBER ONE SINGLE, BUT NOT ITS first number one album. That honor belonged to one of the group's longtime Sunset Strip rivals, Quiet Riot—whose big crossover came thanks to a cover version of Slade's 1973 British hit "Cum on Feel the Noize."

Like every Los Angeles hard rock band in Van Halen's wake, Quiet Riot's Randy Rhoads was a shredding lead guitarist with a pronounced classical influence. The flamboyant-loudmouth front man was Kevin DuBrow, whom *Rolling Stone* described as having "a laugh like a gaggle of honking geese" and the ability to "talk uninterruptedly for something like a week."

In the fall of 1979, Ozzy Osbourne hired Randy Rhoads for his new solo band. Rhoads cowrote *Blizzard of Ozz* (1980) and *Diary of a Madman* (1981), the albums that—along with urinating at the Alamo and biting the heads off bats and doves—reestablished the former Black Sabbath lead singer as metal's foremost personality. For a spell, Quiet Riot soldiered on under the name DuBrow, but it took until 1982 before Pasha, a CBS subsidiary, brought Quiet Riot on board. Bassist Rudy Sarzo had returned to the fold full-time that September; he too had gone off with Ozzy for a spell, before a plane crash killed Rhoads.

At Pasha, and with a new guitarist, Carlos Cavazo, Quiet Riot resisted the suggestion of their producer, Spencer Proffer, that they cover "Cum on Feel the Noize." They'd barely rehearsed it when Proffer called for it in the studio. To DuBrow's dismay, the band floored it straight through—the finished track took three takes. "He finally just said, 'It's just another song,' and he sang it and sang it great," drummer Frankie Banali said.

Metal Health, the band's debut, was released in March of 1983, followed immediately by heavy roadwork. This was a necessity—radio didn't touch this stuff. "Heavy metal bands are always bigger than their airplay," Quiet Riot's booking agent said.

But the band helped reverse that. Their album and first single, "Metal Health (Bang Your Head)," rose steadily on the rock radio charts through the summer. Quiet Riot opened for ZZ Top in June; in July they played at the foot of a Eugene, Oregon, stadium bill, below Loverboy, Triumph, Joan Jett, and Night Ranger. Then, the first week of August, MTV added "Cum on Feel the Noize" to its rotation. On September 17, "Noize" entered the Hot 100 at number ninety-two, leapfrogging up to number five on November 26—the same week *Metal Health* hit number one on the LP chart, eight months after its release. When Quiet Riot returned home near the end of January from a ten-month, 182-show tour, the album had sold 4.5 million copies.

That steady climb, though, meant Quiet Riot was expected to craft another smash—immediately. *Condition Critical*, released in July 1984, was an archetypal botched follow-up. DuBrow later said the band was "trying to repeat the same formula twice, and it didn't work. . . . We shouldn't have gone into the studio at that time. We weren't ready. We didn't have the songs." Critic Jon Young was more succinct: "Their own anthems stink."

BUT QUIET RIOT WASN'T THE BIGGEST METAL BAND OF '83. THAT WAS Def Leppard, a Sheffield quintet so populist they made Quiet Riot sound like Pere Ubu. Though plenty of the British heavy metal bands that shared their time with Def Leppard—Iron Maiden, Judas Priest, Motörhead—wrote politically and socially critical lyrics, Def Lep's guitarist Steve Clark told *Rolling Stone*, "Kids don't want to go to work all day and then hear somebody raving about living on the dole. . . . [The Clash] might do nine songs that are political, but they're always gonna do one for the radio. We don't. We just do ten for the radio, 'cause we just do it for the entertainment value."

Pyromania, released in January of 1983, was the band's third album, and the chewiest yet. This was in large part thanks to its producer, Robert John "Mutt" Lange. "His idea for the band was that we would be a cross between AC/DC and Queen but more raw," lead guitarist Phil Collen wrote. "Mutt told us, 'Def Leppard will be all about great pop songs that resonate with the punk ethos. We won't have lovely harmonies like Styx or Foreigner. Our vocals will be more like a screaming chant, which will set them apart.'"

What really set *Pyromania* apart, though, was the sheer heft of the album's mix. "There's synthesizer all over the Def Leppard and Mötley Crüe records," Werman told *Billboard*. "You can't hear it, but it helped the sound." Biggest of all were *Pyromania*'s drums—built from samples from the Fairlight CMI (Computer Musical Instrument), the first widely used digital sampler, rather than band drummer Rick Allen on every track.

"Mutt's whole thing was, 'Kids these days don't want to hear honky little snare drums,'" Mike Shipley, Lange's engineer on the *Pyromania* sessions, said. "'They're all out watching *Star Wars* and having visual experiences, so let's make records like that.'" *Pyromania* was made, he added, by "working eighteen-hour days, seven days a week, for that whole record. . . . I'm surprised we ever got it finished, because the tape literally fell to pieces."

Pyromania would be certified six times platinum in the United States in October of 1984. It spun off multiple Top 40 hits ("Photograph," "Rock of Ages," "Foolin'") and became ubiquitous in America's cars. "There are a lot of kids out there racing around in cars," one retailer said, "and they're listening to hard rock on their car tape players."

Def Leppard didn't do nearly so well in the UK. "Britain has always looked for something new, something fresh, something different, something contemporary, something inventive, and North America has always gone very 'steady as she goes,'" David Bates, the A&R man who signed Def Leppard to its first deal with Phonogram, said. In Britain, he added, "the hair bands . . . didn't register. Bon Jovi was truly the odd one out."

John Bongiovi was the son of a pair of former marines who'd grown up in Sayreville, New Jersey, idolizing Bruce Springsteen. His cousin Tony Bongiovi, who'd produced the Ramones and Talking Heads, got John a gofer job at his Manhattan recording studio. John cut a demo there—a tune with a nagging hook called "Runaway"—that got nos down the line in both New York and Los

Angeles. He had better luck with WAPP-FM in Long Island, which accepted the demo as part of a contest for local bands. That song, recorded by John with help from synthesizer player David Rashbaum, was included on a station-sponsored compilation LP, *New York Rocks 1983*, and picked up airplay on other stations owned by the Doubleday Broadcasting Company. From there the song attracted the attention of Polygram Records.

"I felt he had an unbelievable burning desire to be huge," Polygram A&R man Derek Shulman said. To prove it, the twenty-year-old Anglicized his surname and shaved his first: he was now Jon Bon Jovi, leader of the band Bon Jovi—time to assemble it. His first member would be Rashbaum, who sheared his surname to become David Bryan. Jon signed the deal solo; from day one, the band members have been employees.

With its insistent keyboard hook, "Runaway" felt like power pop or even new wave. Discussing possible bands to open for on tour, Bon Jovi told his new manager, Doc McGhee, "I think we should go out with the Cars and Bryan Adams." McGhee replied, "No, we're going to go out with the Scorpions and Kiss, and that's going to be more of a loyal rock audience and not a pop audience."

On April 21, 1984, "Runaway" peaked on the Hot 100 at number thirty-nine. *Bon Jovi* sold 350,000 copies. It also made a lot of people wonder: If this candy-ass was "heavy metal," what *was* heavy metal, anyway? Leather and Satan had long been a way of selling pop: even ex-punk Billy Idol was styling himself closer to metal now (though the tune of his fall '84 hit "Flesh for Fantasy" was, as *Smash Hits* pointed out, "lifted almost wholesale" from Simple Minds' "Up on the Catwalk"). "Like Loverboy, Bon Jovi coats its hard-rock bottom with the smooth, melodic veneer essential for radio play," the *Washington Post* opined. "But the band's brand of antiseptic hard rock only makes you want to cheer on all the more the undiluted heavy rockers like Mötley Crüe."

WHEN ASKED IF JUDAS PRIEST MIGHT BE OPEN TO INCLUDING SYNTHESIZER solos on Priest records, the band's guitarist, K. K. Downing, was succinct: "I don't like any of that shit." His co-guitarist Glenn Tipton would elaborate: "Van Halen, and I'm sure they'd be the first to admit it, aren't a heavy metal band. They're a pop-rock band, and there's nothing wrong with that; I think they're great. But we are heavy metal and there's no way we'd stray from those margins. Otherwise, we'd have already done it."

Edward Van Halen agreed. "When I think of heavy metal," he said, "I think of Judas Priest."

Though the first version of the band had formed in Birmingham in 1969, the same time and place Black Sabbath took off, Judas Priest wouldn't become fully defined until 1974, when Tipton joined Downing on the band's front line. They got some US rock airplay thanks to (what's this?) a cover of Joan Baez's "Diamonds and Rust" in 1977; the live *Unleashed in the East* (1979) was their first platinum LP. Then in 1980, the bluntly definitive *British Steel* eased up on the classical frippery and emphasized hooky catchphrases ("Living After Midnight," "Breaking the Law") and put Priest at the top of heavy metal's class.

Rob Halford's stage wear—leather bondage gear, no more or less—would be particularly influential on the new wave of British heavy metal (NWOBHM), the school Priest helped sire. It also nodded toward the gay S&M underground, though Halford himself wouldn't come out publicly until 1998. "I couldn't figure out what to wear. How do I dress with the music that sounds this way?" Halford told *The Advocate* that year. "So I said, 'OK, I'm a gay man, and I'm into leather and that sexual side of the leather world—and I'm gonna bring that onto the stage.' So I came onstage wearing the leather stuff and the motorcycle, and for the first time I felt like, *God, this feels so good. This feels so right.* . . . [And] nobody seemed to have a problem with it, and everybody was crazy for it, so we kept doing it."

In a much more code-aware era, we can see just how close to the surface this stuff was. Among the song titles on the sweeping *Defenders of the Faith*—released simultaneously with Van Halen's *1984*—were "Jawbreaker," "Rock Hard Ride Free," "Love Bites," "Eat Me Alive." When *Creem* asked Halford about the latter's lyric, "I'm gonna force you to eat me at gunpoint," the singer dissolved in laughter: "It's tongue in cheek." "Whose tongue in whose cheek, we won't venture to guess," the correspondent noted.

The rest of Priest's stage show was similarly over-the-top—the show behind *Defenders* featured the "Metallian": "A twenty-foot-high aluminum gargoyle who holds the drum kit in its left claw. Fog wafts across the stage as the Metallian's vari-light eyes scan the audience," Considine reported. "When we use those props, people see them and they say, 'Oh, what is this?'" Halford told him. "But when they suddenly connect with the props, it's a total unification, music and material object working together."

The same principle applied to Priest's nearest contemporaries, Iron Maiden. In the fall of '84, the band began a thirteen-month world tour for their new album *Powerslave* with shows in Poland, Hungary, and Yugoslavia. Typically, when Western bands played Eastern Europe with the Cold War at its height in the mid-eighties, they brought the minimum of gear. Not Maiden— four semis of stage gear, forty thousand watts of sound, and seven hundred lights made the trip.

At the center of the stage show, and of the sleeves of Iron Maiden's releases, was the band's mascot, Eddie, originally a screaming skull mask with wispy long hair that morphed in appearance to suit the band's projects. On the *Powerslave* tour, that meant taking the guise of a sculpted Egyptian sphinx shooting sparks from his eyes. As singer Bruce Dickinson insisted, "How can a band be pompous when Eddie lumbers on stage dressed as the Mummy?"

Iron Maiden's founder, songwriter, and bassist Steve Harris described the NWOBHM as "heavy metal bands with punk attitudes." Another crucial influence on it was Motörhead, which bassist-roarer Ian "Lemmy" Kilmister had formed after being kicked out of the psychedelic rockers Hawkwind. Where Maiden and Priest were near operatic in scope and themes, Lemmy was blunt as dirt, an unrepentant speed-head with a smart, nasty, brutish wit. But Motörhead was beginning to mellow a bit. Shortly before the release of 1983's *Another Perfect Day*, drummer Phil "Philthy Animal" Taylor said, "Before, our records were like being punched in the teeth. Now it's like being punched in the teeth with an apology afterwards."

By March of 1984, Lemmy had kicked out the other members and hired three more, turning Motörhead from a trio into a quartet. New guitarist Phil Campbell exulted: "It's great to be back on the folk circuit." That August they released a new single, "Killed by Death," ahead of a double-LP overview, *No Remorse*. Reviewing the collection, *Melody Maker* noted the way that Kilmister's feral charm, and the band's uncompromising throttle, had shifted opinions over time: "Ageless, trend-free, and packing nothing but choice decibels, Motörhead emerged in the middle of the seventies . . . and soon were dubbed 'the worst band in the world.' Somehow, critical revulsion did a U-turn. Suddenly, loud, ugly, violent, and sexist Motörhead were endowed with inverted chic, an aura of metaphorical significance, instant legend. Lemmy became a Chap."

On December 2, the band secured their legend by playing a show at the Variety Theatre in Cleveland, where "the volume was so loud that it brought the plaster down from the ceiling," the *Plain Dealer* reported. At 130 decibels,

Motörhead broke the Who's world record of 128 dB eight years earlier. "It was wild seeing them playing as plaster was coming down," one eyewitness said.

FOR AMERICAN KIDS WHO DOTED ON THE NWOBHM, IT WASN'T A MATter of simply going to the record store. Many of the bands hadn't been signed, and their demos became hotly sought items among tape traders. With MTV's exposure to the bigger bands beginning to dilute the crowds at shows, these diehards would form heavy metal's new vanguard.

One of them was Lars Ulrich—born and raised in Copenhagen, the son of tennis pro and jazz fanatic Torben Ulrich; Lars's godfather was the saxophonist Dexter Gordon. They moved to the United States in the summer of 1980 so the seventeen-year-old could become a tennis player himself. Instead, Lars, who'd been a metal fan since seeing Deep Purple at age nine, became so obsessed with the NWOBHM that he flew to London in the summer of '81 to see Motörhead, Saxon, and Tygers of Pan Tang, spending a month on Diamond Head's couch.

Back in LA, Ulrich began playing drums with a guitarist he'd met through an ad in *The Recycler*. James Hetfield wasn't as knowledgeable about the NWOBHM as Ulrich, but they clicked immediately: "Hetfield felt like an American version of myself, a little bit more introverted, but he was interested in the music that I played him and he had a very easy time interpreting it."

A year later, Hetfield and Ulrich and a revolving cast of players—including guitarist Dave Mustaine, who later founded and led Megadeth—were hawking a demo called *No Life 'til Leather*. Ulrich knew his fellow tape traders would hip one another to it if they liked it enough—like a British indie band wishing nothing more than to be played by John Peel, the circuit was as far as Ulrich figured to go. But as Metallica's lineup solidified—Cliff Burton had joined on bass, Kirk Hammett replaced Mustaine on guitar—so did its material.

While the punk rock underground was noted for its indie-label ingenuity, the same thing was happening with heavy metal. New Jersey's Megaforce, New York's Mongol Horde, LA's Metal Blade, and San Francisco's Shrapnel were rewriting the genre's rulebooks. "These labels have already proved to be the spawning grounds for such artists as Mötley Crüe, which went from Enigma, distributors of Metal Blade, to Elektra; and Queensryche, which comes on the LP chart this week at 182 as an EMI America release after first being distributed by Mongol Horde," *Billboard* reported in September 1983. "Before Mötley Crüe signed with Elektra, they sold 60,000 records." A year later, the same paper reported, "Metal Blade's 'speed metal' act Slayer has sold 50,000 copies of the year-old album *Show No Mercy*."

Similar things were happening with Metallica—there was a near-instant groundswell for their second album on the mom-and-pop Megaforce, *Ride the Lightning*, released in July 1984. On August 3, Metallica stole the bill from openers Anthrax and headliners Raven at New York's Roseland Ballroom. An Elektra Records A&R man, Michael Alago, came backstage and asked the band to meet at his office the next day, where he greeted them with "beer and Chinese food." Metallica signed to Elektra without telling Megaforce's owners; they agreed to give Elektra Metallica's newly issued second album, *Ride the Lightning*, once Megaforce had cleared seventy-five thousand sales on its own. Metallica was on Elektra in two months.

THAT SUMMER, A COUPLE OF STATION MANAGERS FROM MONROE, LOUISIana, wrote a letter to *Billboard*. "We were shocked by the inside back cover of the July 7 issue. The ad for the new Dio album was sickening," they said. The full-page spot for *The Last in Line* had featured a horned wolf's-head monster with glowing red eyes and its index and pinkie fingers extended. The writers fumed that it wasn't "right for record companies, rock artists or trade publications to push Satanic messages on us. The demonic figure towering above the masses with both hands brandishing the symbol of Satanic worship was one of the most graphic examples we have seen."

Heavy metal got up the noses of a lot of fundamentalist preachers who had been burning rock records since the fifties. In 1979, a pair of minister brothers, Steve and Jim Peters of the Zion Christian Life Center in St. Paul, Minnesota, had heard another preacher, Craig Harrington, inveighing against rock lyrics. "We had a very small church at that point, maybe a hundred," says Steve Peters. "The kids in my youth group were really on fire for God. They wanted to live closer for God. A lot of them had already told me they wanted to get rid of those records. They started turning in thousands of dollars' worth of music and drug paraphernalia before we ever talked."

When the Peters brothers decided to set the castoffs ablaze, they invited local news media. (Steve Peters cites Acts 19:19, King James Version: "Many of them also which used curious arts brought their books together, and burned them before all men.") All four local stations' news crews showed up. A cameraman told Steve, "You did a great media event." Peters asked, "What's a media event?" The cameraman explained: "You did it at night, and you used fire. Cameras are attracted to fire."

Soon the Peters were attracting international television, including appearances on *Nightline* and *Good Morning America*. Their timing was perfect. The eighties saw the rise of several made-for-TV ministers, from Jim and Tammy Faye Bakker to Pat Robertson, fundamentalists operating from a conviction that popular culture was a modern-day Gomorrah, a jungle of sin from which children required protection.

As critic Mick Farren wrote in *Creem* magazine: "Clearly, any parents who were raised on *A Hard Day's Night* and *Woodstock* but missed out on everything between *Ziggy Stardust* and Judas Priest are going to be a trifle concerned should they happen to catch, say, the video for Twisted Sister's 'We're Not Gonna Take It' . . . Crosby, Stills & Nash just got stoned. They didn't want to push daddy through a wall."

But the Peters brothers sold merchandise just like any heavy metal band: audiocassettes, videotapes, bumper stickers, even muscle shirts. In 1984, they published *Why Knock Rock?*—their first title from the St. Paul publisher Bethany House, after a couple of self-published books—in which the authors referred to themselves as "The Giant Killers," little Davids taking on the Goliath of the record business. The book includes a petition, ready-made for the reader to send to Congress or the Federal Communications Commission (FCC), with calls to ban "indecent, obscene, or profane" records.

But the Peters brothers were having the opposite effect for many—making illicit records seem cool. They insisted that certain rock records employed "backward masking," literally recording something in reverse to subliminally instill evil messages in their songs. Their campaign against backward masking led some bands to start doing it, just to needle them. Besides, being called to the carpet on nightly news shows was a great sales aid. As one metal musician told *Billboard*, "A lot of people watch Ted Koppel. So if they tell their kids, 'You're not buying that album,' the kids will go out and buy it."

Twisted Sister was the band that pushed Daddy through the wall. It'd been around since the early seventies, the spotlight firmly on lead yeller Dee Snider's pugnacious vowels, his enormous sculpted blond frizz, and his slasher-flick glam-wrestler outfits. The rest of the band, as Charles M. Young put it, "look[ed] like the Green Bay Packers on Halloween."

They packed 'em in on Long Island but meant bubkes elsewhere. "We made a standing offer to any A&R person that we would ride them out to the Island in a limo, treat them to dinner and drive them home, if they would just come see the band," Dee Snider said. "Two people took us up on it. Two." Years later, guitarist Jay Jay French recalled being told, "'Your image is ridiculous, it'll never sell in Dubuque.' Well, when we played Dubuque, it was a hit! So *fuck you*, we knew we could sell in Dubuque."

Despite their raunchiness, Twisted Sister were lifers, not partiers. Shortly after they signed to Atlantic Records in the mid-eighties, VP Phil Carson was "particularly surprised when one of the band's main concerns was if there was a gym close to the recording studio," Snider wrote. "He said most bands wanted to know how close the nearest bar was." They also shied away from some of the genre's usual lyrical fallbacks. "We don't want to alienate women," Snider told *Billboard*, "and we don't think everyone can sink their teeth into black magic and demons."

Tom Werman recalls when Atlantic president Doug Morris called to ask him to produce Twisted Sister. "He said, 'I have a band that's doing quite well in Europe but they can't get arrested here. And you are the only guy I know who can make a hit record with this band,'" he says. "When a record company president calls you at home, you listen. He said, 'I want you to do me a favor and do this record.'"

Stay Hungry, Twisted Sister's second album, was released in May 1984. "It was a very difficult album to do," says Werman. "I enjoyed the people in the band. I found Dee to be a little difficult and very defensive, very cautious, guarded. And then after the album was over, he sat through all the mixes, which I did routinely. I always insisted that a member of the group, or a designated guy, approve the mixes before I turned them in to the label. I never mixed an album without the band hearing it first. Dee Snider sat through all the mixes and approved them, and then the day he left the studio, he started badmouthing me so fiercely, I was just totally dumbfounded. He wrote a book: 'I firmly believe that Tom Werman singlehandedly ruined our record,' which incidentally sold five million copies."

There were lighter moments, says Werman. "Dee and I were both very big *Animal House* fans, and we used to quote Neidermeyer: 'A pledge pin on your uniform? You're worthless and weak. Now drop and give me twenty.' So obviously, Dee had that concept in mind before they made the videos."

Modeled on Slade ("*All of my anthems are,*" Snider clarified in his memoir), "We're Not Gonna Take It" builds on its irresistible shouted hook with a clip in which a white suburban preadolescent everykid wreaks Wile E. Coyote/ Roadrunner-style revenge on his dad, played by Mark Metcalf, who'd portrayed Neidermeyer in *Animal House*. (The clip's roughhousing became something of a blueprint, as well, for the 1990 blockbuster kids' movie *Home Alone*.)

That October 6, Snider was arrested in Amarillo, Texas, for cursing onstage; he was released on seventy-five dollars bail. At the next show, Snider wrote, "the police were there in force with complaint forms already filled out to arrest me the minute I spewed one word of profanity." He got around it by having the audience say "fuck" for him, while he substituted the mayor's name, though the next city had already canceled the show when word of the arrest got out.

SHOWS CANCELED OVER PERFORMER CONDUCT WERE A WAY OF LIFE IN heavy metal, especially for Ozzy Osbourne. Through the seventies with Black Sabbath, he'd more or less invented worshiping the dark side, or pretending to, as a viable rock and roll career. In February of 1983, the Catholic Youth Center in Scranton, Pennsylvania, reneged on a verbal agreement to host an Ozzy show after some four thousand tickets had already been sold. The center's director stopped the show after learning of Osbourne's "satanical worship, desecration of a monument, and cruelty to animals."

The first part was debatable, unless you took everything Ozzy did onstage seriously, up to and including having "a tray of drinks delivered . . . by a henchman clad in full medieval armor," as *Smash Hits* reported. Besides, Ozzy insisted any devilry was purely in fun. "I'm a Christian guy, in my own way," he told *Creem* in 1984. "Do you have to go around with the Bible and shove it down people's throats to be a Christian? I don't believe it—I believe Christianity's within you." As for the monument—well, yes, Ozzy did in fact urinate at the Alamo. And the animals? Well . . .

In 1981, Ozzy bit a dove's head off—already dead, according to him—at a meeting with CBS in Los Angeles. In January 1982, onstage in Des Moines, Iowa, a kid in the audience threw a bat onstage, and Ozzy, thinking it was a rubber toy, chomped down; to his surprise, the bat chomped back. "I didn't feel too clever after the bat incident," he later said. "I mean the rabies shot wasn't exactly a bundle of fun . . . it was like someone sticking a golf ball in your bum.

This stuff they injected was thick, like Three-in-One oil. The cure was worse than the problem."

Then there was the incident with the plane. It wasn't Ozzy's fault, he wasn't even involved except as an after-the-fact witness; in fact it had shattered him. But it was indicative of the chaos that pervaded his life, and heavy metal as a whole.

Two months after the bat incident, on March 19, 1982, Ozzy and his band—including ex–Quiet Riot guitarist Randy Rhoads, who'd cowritten his comebacks, *Blizzard of Ozz* (1980) and *Diary of a Madman* (1981)—had stopped in Leesburg, Florida. Rhoads's articulated buzz saw spray was at the center of "Crazy Train," which went top ten on *Billboard*'s rock radio chart. In Leesburg, the tour bus driver, who had a suspended pilot's license, took a Beechcraft Bonanza up twice, the second time with Rhoads and a makeup artist. That time, he decided to repeatedly "buzz" the tour bus—and the third time, one of the plane's wings snapped against the bus's roof. The plane spun out, landed on a large home, and burst into flames. Rhoads had to be identified by his dental records.

MÖTLEY CRÜE, THE SUNSET STRIP'S SECOND MOST NOTORIOUS PARTY band, hit the road with Ozzy in November of 1983. "It was a full-on fight to see who would top each other, on stage and off," Crüe bassist Nikki Sixx said. "We would set ourselves on fire, literally. Our egos and drug abuse were absolutely out of control. It was a wonderful time."

Mötley Crüe had been the find of a young go-getter named Tom Zutaut, who saw the band at the Whisky a Go Go. In addition to noticing five hundred teenagers screaming their heads off, Zutaut found the band's bassist-ringleader, who went as Nikki Sixx, "so intense it seemed like he would be in the streets killing somebody if he wasn't playing bass."

Elektra had been recently dormant of hits. Tom Werman worked there doing A&R in 1982 when he hired Zutaut as his assistant; the latter got Mötley Crüe onto the label. Werman left after a few months. "I couldn't deal with the new boss, same as the old boss," says Werman. "But when I left, they said, 'Would you like to sign a production deal with us and make three records for us?' Mötley Crüe was the first record I made after I left."

Werman had heard their independent debut, *Too Fast for Love*. "I didn't love it. I was a very neat producer. I liked timing, I liked tuning, I liked good pitch, all those things. And they were a little on the sloppy side. But [Zutaut] hammered on me and said, 'You're the guy. You need to do this next record. You'd be a great producer for them.' So I met with them in my office. There were no shenanigans. They sat on the floor and leaned back against the couch and the cabinets. Nikki was frosty and guarded, because they had had a really bad experience with their first manager. They didn't like suits. And Tommy [Lee, drummer] said, 'Listen, guys, if this guy's going to produce our record, then we ought to listen to him.' And I thought, 'Whoa boy, that's a gift. Thank you.' Then I went to see them, probably at the Whisky, and that was that."

Shout at the Devil was, says Werman, "a pretty fast album, aside from Nikki's bass tracks. Tommy's superb in the studio; he's one or two takes. Nikki, it was tough with him, because he wasn't a great bass player at the time, and he had broken his shoulder in a car crash, of course. He ran into a utility pole on Coldwater Canyon. I guess he was driving a little sports car. That was a tough one. Vince [Neil, vocals] was very . . . he took a long time.

"Nikki was the brains. He and Tommy were the drivers of the band. He and Tommy wrote almost all the music. I would say the other two guys were hired hands."

Mötley Crüe angered sixties-bred liberals as much as conservatives. One critic wrote, "I'm struck far less by the implied Satanism than by a brutalized consciousness romanticizing its own lack of hope," and called heavy metal "as reactionary a strand as popular music has ever produced. It's the spiritual godchild of the Reagan era, facing up to a complex world and responding with a long leap backward into machismo, sexism, militarism, and bigotry."

Phonogram A&R man Jerry Jaffe had a different idea, telling *Billboard*, "In the same way that [teen-sexploitation movie] *Porky's* made money, a record company can make money on Mötley Crüe."

"SORRY," NIKKI SIXX TOLD AN INTERVIEWER IN THE SUMMER OF 1985 after putting them on hold for several minutes, "I lost my drugs."

Born Frank Feranna, Sixx had played with the Strip band London alongside Lizzie Grey before forming Mötley Crüe with Tommy Lee in early 1981. The first time he met Lee, Sixx said, they "looked at each other and it was like, 'Hey, what kind of hair dye do you use?' 'What kind do *you* use?'"

They recruited Mick Mars (Bob Deal) from a Top 40 band called Vendetta and Vince Neil (surname Wharton) from another called Rock Candy. The umlauts, Neil said, came about because "we wanted to have a worldly vibe, even though we'd never been outside of L.A." That unworldliness didn't stop Sixx from telling the youth of America, "You might as well learn about sex from Mötley Crüe than your parents because it's a *lot more interesting.*"

The band stayed on tour for some thirteen months beginning with the Ozzy jaunt. At the time Sixx was dating Anna Spheeris Fox, the seventeen-year-old daughter of documentary filmmaker Penelope Spheeris (the *Decline of the Western World* series). "He told everyone I was fifteen, what a perv," Anna said years later. "He wrote a song about it ['All in the Name of . . .'], it's on the *Girls, Girls, Girls* album, it's ridiculous."

All that calculated outrage paid off in spades when the May 1984 issue of *Esquire* appeared on stands. Therein, "American Beat" columnist Bob Greene, traveling in Texas listening to a San Antonio rock station, learned of a promotion: "What would you do to meet the Crüe?" Greene asked to see, and quote, the letters the station received. One sixteen-year-old girl wrote in with an elaborate BDSM scenario with herself in charge:

> First, I would tie you up, spread-eagle and naked, with leather straps. Then I'd shave all the hair off of your chest, and if I should nick you I'll suck up all the blood as it slowly trickles over your body. . . . Then when you are screaming for mercy and begging for more, telling me how you want it all, I'll slam the spiked heel of my right leather boot into your navel, call you a very naughty boy, and laugh as I slowly walk away, telling you I'm just not that kind of girl.

When Greene spoke with her, she admitted, "I didn't let my boyfriend read it before I sent it in. It would make him wonder what he didn't know about me." Even more alarmingly to Greene, the girl's mother had delivered the letter for her: "I guess I was shocked in a way, but I'm sure she didn't mean anything by it. She's a very Christian girl."

SHRINE AUDITORIUM,
LOS ANGELES
February 28, 1984

LIVE FROM THE SHRINE AUDITORIUM IN LOS ANGELES, CALIFORNIA, IT'S the twenty-sixth annual Grammy Awards with your host, John Denver!

Denver: "The big words this last year were video . . . Boy George . . . and Michael . . . ?"

Audience: "JACKSON!"

As the audience shouted the answer, the camera cut to Jackson, in his Rhinestone General getup, moving one seat over. That's where the camera was.

STURDY, EFFICIENT, UNFLAPPABLE, AND BEATIFIC, JOHN DENVER WAS hosting his fifth Grammy Awards telecast. Though his run of huge, gooey hits had ended before the seventies were out, he remained a top live draw. The previous summer, in the middle of a concert-biz drought, he'd sold out Red Rocks, the amphitheater near his home in Denver.

Though he was open to all manner of technology—he'd gotten his pilot's license in 1974, in the midst of becoming one of the richest men in music—Denver also had a deeply old-fashioned image and wore it with a Hollywood gleam. (He became a busy actor in the eighties.) As such, he was the soul of the biz as represented by the National Academy of Recording Arts and Sciences

(NARAS), the body that voted on the Grammy Awards—which, in the 2000s, would simplify its label to the Recording Academy.

Not long before the Grammys, Denver had severed ties with his manager, Jerry Weintraub, with whom he'd signed in the late sixties, shortly after leaving the Chad Mitchell Trio. That summer, Weintraub, a lifelong Democrat, would announce that he was planning to vote to reelect Ronald Reagan. He wasn't alone. The Reagan Democrat would become one of the decisive factors of the 1984 presidential election, and the music business had more than a few.

The 1984 Grammys would be John Denver's last as host, but he went out on a (Rocky Mountain) high: the event attracted the largest Grammy television audience ever, 43.8 million people, a number it wouldn't come near again until 2012.

"SHE'S ALREADY WON FOR BEST INSPIRATIONAL PERFORMANCE TONIGHT . . ."

In 1984, *disco* was still a word that dare not speak its name and the woman who'd been named "Queen of Disco" had spent most of the early part of that decade going through the professional wringer. "When disco started to die or fall from fashion, I was already in another world; soundtracks, for one," Donna Summer's producer Giorgio Moroder said. (He would be nominated that night for coproducing the *Flashdance* soundtrack, up for Album of the Year.) "It was, however, really bad for Donna, because she was labeled—as if she couldn't do anything else, which couldn't have been further from the truth."

She'd tried. Still working with Moroder and lyricist Pete Bellotte, with a splash Summer left her label, Casablanca, which was drowning in red ink, for Asylum Records founder David Geffen's new, self-named imprint; her first album for it, *The Wanderer* (1980), moved into straighter rock and new wave terrain. But neither the title track nor "Cold Love," both fairly savvy new wave cops, did much on the radio.

In addition to Summer, the Village People, and Parliament, Casablanca's roster included Kiss, whose popularity led them, in 1978, to insist the label let each member release a solo album. "Basically, we weren't given a choice," says Larry Harris, then Casablanca's vice president. "It was, 'The band's gonna break up, and the only way we can think of keeping them together is these solo albums. It'll buy us time.' We didn't think it was a good idea."

It wasn't. Two million unsold Kiss solo LPs were returned, and many thousands of them landed in cutout bins—the mark of death for a thriving act. By

1979, Casablanca went under in a blaze of coke-fueled overspending—just like the rest of the biz, but more so. By the mid-eighties, Kiss, who'd gotten famous by wearing Kabuki makeup and fronting a pyrotechnics-heavy stage show, had stopped wearing face paint. ("Why did we take the makeup off?" bassist Gene Simmons taunted. "We didn't want to copy Mötley Crüe!") Neil Bogart, Casablanca's founder, would go on to found another label, Boardwalk; when Bogart died of cancer in 1982, one of its releases, Joan Jett and the Blackhearts' "I Love Rock and Roll," was in the midst of a long streak at number one in America.

Disco had gone back underground to the gay clubs—in particular, a synthed-up variant called Hi-NRG, whose roots were in Summer's robo-disco landmark "I Feel Love" (1977). But not everyone liked what they were hearing. At the New York gay club the Saint in 1983, the young music journalist Barry Walters "hated" hearing "So Many Men." "It felt like an unintentional commentary on gay men's predicament at the time," Walters said. "This was before we knew what safe sex was; we just knew that many of the people who were the most promiscuous were among the first to die, and the willful denial in that record terrified me."

A lot of people were terrified right about then. Ever since AIDS (acquired immunodeficiency syndrome) had become public knowledge in July of 1981, it seemed unknowable and unstoppable. In June 1983, *New York* magazine reported, "The number of cases is doubling every six months. As of May, there were 722 cases in this city. In two years, that number might reach into the thousands. . . . A recent count showed that 72 percent of the victims were male homosexuals. Another 17 percent were intravenous-drug users. . . . Other victims include 25 city youngsters who apparently had infected mothers, eleven women who had sexual relations with members of a risk group, and ten people who received transfusions of blood that may have been tainted."

A lot of what disco had celebrated—the sexual liberation of gay men, in particular—was snafuing horribly. Robust young men didn't suddenly die from AIDS; they wasted away over months and years, and because the disease was so new it was impossible to determine just how long one might live with it. For the people who had it, and their loved ones, it was a round-the-clock horror show.

In New York, the playwright Larry Kramer, concerned as soon as word of the disease got out, organized a meeting of eighty men to listen to Dr. Alvin E. Friedman-Kien of New York University. "[He] told us in no uncertain terms exactly what was happening," Kramer said. "There were a lot of nasty questions put to the doctor at that meeting. There were a lot of people who said, 'How can you make all these assumptions on the basis of so few cases? How can you expect a whole community to stop fucking?' No virus had been discovered yet, so people could say that he had no evidence on which to base his opinions."

The month of the Grammys, a battle was drawn between the owners of San Francisco's bathhouses and the medical community dealing with a surfeit of new AIDS cases every week. Dr. Marc Conant of University of California, San Francisco, wanted the bathhouses to close of their own accord. This barely registered with the owners, one of whom told a local doctor, "We're both in it for the same thing: money. We make money at one end when they come to the baths. You make money from them on the other end when they come here." The doctor was aghast.

This was the environment into which Donna Summer had become a born-again Christian—and, the rumors persisted, uttered anti-gay slurs. Summer, for the record, denied this: in her memoir, she wrote, "To me it had always seemed pointless to dignify rumors with a public response, and so my inclination was to ignore the false allegations." Nevertheless, after Summer died, Moroder told a reporter, "Donna . . . really did not like gays—her attitude was sometimes difficult in the eighties."

Summer needed a makeover. Quincy Jones came aboard, but the self-titled Summer LP that ensued was hampered by her condition: "I was tired and cranky and pregnant," she wrote. David Geffen had asked Bruce Springsteen to write a song for his new signing. He auditioned "Protection" for Summer on her couch. There were hopes that the song would break the AOR color barrier, but nothing much happened. "It takes more than Springsteen's name and his guitar to get Donna Summer on AOR," a radio tip sheet editor told *Rolling Stone*.

Recording *Donna Summer* went so far past schedule that it cut into Jones's next project, *Thriller*. But nothing on it stuck, and Summer still owed an album to Polygram, Casablanca's corporate owner. For that, she worked with Michael Omartian and came up with a single after observing a restroom attendant asleep on the job: "I came to find out later that she had a good day job at Cedars-Sinai as a lab technician. She made a good living, but with no husband and a son she was putting through college, she had taken on this second job."

"She Works Hard for the Money," issued on Mercury, became a surprise hit—number one R&B, number three pop—which complicated Summer's relationship with both Polygram, which was "upset because I was back on top and they had let me out of my contract," and Geffen, which was "upset because I had a hit with my old label. They felt I should have saved that material for them."

Summer was on her way to the Grammys when she "got stuck in a mile-long line of stretch limos. I was dressed in full costume, ready for the show, and getting very, very impatient." She stopped off at a McDonald's to use the restroom. The diners cheered after seeing her in the waitress costume from the album's cover. Funnily enough, the female dance troupe that accompanied her onstage were gotten up more or less as the Village People—hard hat, cop, sailor, and at the back a woman in a towering feathered headdress. And behind them all, on the giant screen, in perfect sync with the stage performance, the video.

"Mr. Bob Dylan and Mr. Stevie Wonder!"

These two were a comedy team. When Dylan tried to open the envelope, Wonder mock-snarled, "Gimme that!" The card was in braille as well as in type, and they announced it together: "'Every Breath You Take' by the Police—Sting, songwriter." As the orchestra's horns played the song's melody as a fanfare, Dylan said, "He couldn't make it here tonight. He's touring."

The Police were finishing a three-date run in Australia and New Zealand—and that, more or less, would be the end. That spring, *DownBeat* had asked the band's drummer, Stewart Copeland, "The Police was originally your band. Do you resent Sting becoming the focal point?" Copeland snapped, "It still is my band."

Copeland's father was a CIA man, and the subsequent musical ventures of Stewart and his older brothers Ian and Miles would pay tongue-in-cheek tribute to law enforcement. (In addition to Stewart drumming for the Police, Ian would form Federal Booking International—FBI—and Miles, the eldest, founded the International Records Syndicate—IRS.)

"One of the Copelands' favorite family stories concerns a time when they claim that their father helped to provoke a military coup in Syria by creating a terrorist incident in 1949," noted a *Maclean's* profile of the Police. "He hired a gang of hoodlums to shoot up his house in Damascus. On the night of the mock raid he sent his pregnant wife and five-year-old, Miles, into the mountains to stay with friends. But the provocateurs took their instructions literally and used live ammunition instead of blanks. A bullet-ridden Persian carpet is now displayed as a treasured family heirloom at Miles III's home in London's St. John's Wood."

All three Copeland brothers were living in England in the mid-seventies, with Stewart playing drums with prog-rockers Curved Air. When punk came in, he teamed up with Newcastle bassist and singer Gordon Sumner, nicknamed Sting, from jazz-rockers Last Exit to try the new style on; they were soon joined by Andy Summers, a fellow Northerner a decade their senior who'd hung with Clapton and Page in sixties London.

"The Police was a catalyst to throw away all the influences," Summers said. "Instead of that kind of three-chord power blast, I went the other way with it. I found that what I could do with the guitar was kind of drift and float around Sting's vocal lines. Rather than a wall-of-sound, it was much more like a light, floating thing."

After finishing their debut album, *Outlandos d'Amour*, in 1978, the Police toured North America with no financial or publicity support from its record company, A&M Records, playing twenty-three bars in a van and sleeping three to a room. It saved them from label debt and got the ball rolling. "We played the Last Chance in Poughkeepsie, and the only people in the place were a disc jockey and a journalist," Stewart said in 1981. "It was a Monday night and it was freezing so everyone stayed home to watch the football game, apparently. We went out into the audience and talked to them for a while, watched the game on television, then jumped on stage and did our set. It was strange. We introduced the members of the audience to each other. We had come nine thousand miles from home and made twelve dollars. But, hey, we got three encores."

Shortly after the tour, in February 1979, A&M released the Police's first US single, "Roxanne," inspired by Sting's stroll through Paris's red-light district. It peaked at number thirty-two in April and got heavy AOR play. Sting's most un-punk-like voice—a warm, high, slightly phlegmatic warble with a steel center that could belt rockers and croon slow ones with equal facility—made the band easy on ears that had been reared on sixties rock.

Though Sting protested that the song was actually a modified tango, the beat of "Roxanne" was so close to reggae that it would be covered by a number of Jamaican artists. "It takes two to tango, and three to reggae," Stewart said. "Reggae [is] an interactive form; no one instrument by itself can play it." Titling the Police's second LP *Reggatta de Blanc* (1979) made the link explicit. And the Police kept finding new ways to sound exotically white. On 1980's *Zenyatta Mondatta*, they tried on ska ("Canary in a Coalmine" and "Man in a Suitcase") and Middle Eastern sonorities (Summers's instrumental "Behind My Camel"), as well as the compact funk jam "Voices Inside My Head"—a black radio hit in Detroit, played with gusto by cult DJ the Electrifying Mojo.

Zenyatta was heavily informed by the band's early 1980 tour of the Near and Far East—part of 130 dates the band played that year, spread from January through December. "One aspect of the Police that has allowed them to survive a trans-oceanic search for fame and fortune is a sense of humor nearly as dry as the Kalahari," *Trouser Press* noted in 1981. "When a journalist asked about their intermixing of musical styles, Copeland replied, 'We've been cross-pollinating all over America.' Sting has explained his unusual nickname thusly: 'I'm from a very poor family. We could only afford one name.' Why did the band play Bangkok and Istanbul? 'We've already been to Cleveland,' Summers once answered. 'Besides, they've probably got some interesting ethnic music we can rip off.'"

The Copeland brothers were hardly typical music biz liberals—Stewart described himself as "a raving capitalist." Sting, meantime, had ties to British Marxism. "Sting and I would argue about politics, and I would lay waste to his flimsy arguments," Copeland said.

Sting, meantime, wasn't all that impressed by his fellow rock stars. "I think the Clash have fourteen-year-old intellects," he said. "Musically, I think they're very good; I do like them. But the political posturing is laughable. They talk about Marxism; they haven't the faintest idea of what Karl Marx is all about." When asked by *Creem* to clarify "the difference between the Clash being 'fourteen-year-olds' and you telling me the world stinks," Sting laughed at his own rejoinder: "I'm *fifteen* years old."

Needless to say, these guys got along just great. "It's not an easy relationship, by any means," Sting said after *Synchronicity*'s release. "We're three highly autonomous individuals, and a band is an artificial alliance most of the time. . . . None of us is easy to work with. It's not all buddy-buddy, and never was." How did the group make decisions? the interviewer asked, and Sting answered, "Violence." He wasn't kidding any more than Van Halen was.

The December 1982 sessions for *Synchronicity* were incredibly tense—each member tracked his contribution in a different room. "The drums sounded so much better in that dining area," engineer Hugh Padgham said. "So this setup worked both sonically and for social reasons."

The worst conflagration between Copeland and Sting came during the recording of their biggest song. When Sting played "Every Breath You Take"—a creepy love song by a controlling stalker—to the woman he'd written it about, she was, he later said, "both flattered and horrified." He had to tell Stewart to play only the groove, not embellish. "It was really difficult," Padgham recalled. "I remember calling my manager, Dennis [Muirhead], and telling him 'I can't handle this,' and I also remember quite clearly working full-on for ten days in Montserrat and having nothing on tape that was playable."

Eventually, Copeland capitulated, particularly once Summers replaced the demo's organ part with a simply played, sharply echoed plucked guitar part that provided the "updated fifties atmosphere we were really looking for, a futuristic fifties sound," as Summers described it. On June 4, *Billboard* reported that "Every Breath You Take" had been added to the playlists of 110 CHR stations—more than double Duran Duran's "Is There Something I Should Know?" at a time when the Durans could have gone gold singing the alphabet. Furthermore, "Every Breath" leapt to the top of *Radio & Records'* AOR chart in three weeks. It was also climbing the A/C chart. The Police had fulfilled the post-*Thriller* maxim of the album as multiformat hit machine with finesse. In some shops, *Synchronicity* outsold *Thriller*.

The Police's twenty-seven-city North American tour of 1983 grossed some $8 million. The band did a lot of press for it, and their impending breakup came up constantly. "This band *could* end tomorrow," Sting said. "That gives me a sense of freedom." So did the acting he'd been doing—that summer, Sting appeared in the $50 million adaptation of Frank Herbert's science fiction classic *Dune*, produced by Dino De Laurentiis and shot in Mexico by director David Lynch. He was also shopping around an adapted screenplay of the Mervyn Peake trilogy *Gormenghast*.

And every night on that last, teeth-gritting tour together, Sting could glance over at the drums and see the message Stewart Copeland had written on them for only the singer to see: "FUCK . . . OFF . . . YOU . . . CUNT."

"WE NOW HAVE A NEW KIND OF ROCK THAT STIRS THE SENSES VISUALLY AS well as audibly."

Up for Best New Artist, Big Country was a Scottish postpunk band with a guitar sound that evoked bagpipes—an easy hook for journalists and a distinctive sound qua sound. As the band performed "In a Big Country" (number three rock, number seventeen pop), local affiliates ran this chyron: "CBS News estimates that Sen. Gary Hart will win the Democratic Primary in New

Hampshire, where the polls are now closed. Details from Dan Rather in New Hampshire later."

Big Country's leader, Stuart Adamson—formerly of the Skids, whose "Into the Valley" was one of the great punk one-shots in 1979—had a porcupine-like haircut, clean and short around the back and sides but spiky everywhere else. Sting had it too; so did Bono, the singer from the Irish band U2. This 'do would later be dubbed the "mullet."

Nominated for Best New Artist and Best Rock Performance by a Duo or Group with Vocal and losing both, Big Country's appearance on the broadcast was both forward-thinking and grasping at straws. The Grammys needed a performance from a new British band because 1983 was the year of new British bands. Punk had been abrasive, and the Grammys did not deal well with abrasion. From the Clash to Public Image Ltd., none of those bands would be nominated for anything. (The Clash's first Grammy nod came in 2003, when the documentary *Westway to the World* won for Best Music Film.) The Police were touring; U2 wouldn't be on NARAS's radar for another four years. Big Country, bless 'em, were the best the Grammys could do.

WHEN CULTURE CLUB GOT TO A STUDIO AT TWO IN THE MORNING IN London to transmit live, via satellite, to Los Angeles (and the world), they discovered there were only two chairs. One was for Boy George; the other was for Joan Rivers, who'd hosted George's American chat-show debut in the fall of '83—she was, at that point, the permanent fill-in host for *The Tonight Show*'s Johnny Carson—and nothing for the other members of Culture Club. "The band were understandably distressed," Boy George wrote.

Culture Club was there to read the RIAA rules with Rivers—and to stick around, because, you know, they had trophies waiting for them, for Best New Artist. For the read, the band was shoehorned into the frame. This was fast becoming their way of life.

"You look like Grace Jones—on steroids," George told Joan.

"And you look like Brooke Shields—on steroids," she responded.

Steroids were in the news: In 1983, the Pan Am Games in Caracas found steroids on enough US and Latin American competitors that the organizing committee stripped twenty-three medals, including eleven gold. During the summer of '84, three athletes (from Sweden, Lebanon, and Algeria) would have their Olympic medals taken away after they each failed a drug test. Later, Dr. Robert

Kerr of Toronto testified "that he had provided anabolic steroids for about twenty athletes who won medals" that summer, the *New York Times* reported.

THE POLICE WEREN'T THE ONLY NOMINATED STARS TO SKIP THE CEREMONY. David Bowie, for example, was at home in Switzerland, recuperating from the tour behind *Let's Dance*, up for Album of the Year alongside *Thriller*, *Synchronicity*, *Flashdance*, and Billy Joel's *An Innocent Man*. The latter, written in eight weeks and inspired by Joel meeting his new wife, supermodel Christie Brinkley, was a tribute to pre-Beatles rock and roll, in particular girl groups and the Four Seasons, and yielded a handful of MTV hits, notably the Ed Sullivan–styled "Tell Her About It," as well as the glorious a cappella "The Longest Time," the finest single Joel ever made.

Bowie's album was its own sort of throwback. On *Let's Dance*, he took cues from the first wave of fifties rockers—Little Richard, Gene Vincent, the Isley Brothers, Chuck Berry—and wrote, in the words of Bowie chronicler Chris O'Leary, "public songs—exhortations, common causes—keeping his lines (relatively) simple, writing words meant to be sung back at him."

The messages would be the opposite of the late-seventies work that left him, at the end of his 1976 tour behind *Station to Station*, feeling "empty, drained, and rotting inside." Rehabbed chemically and reoriented artistically in Berlin in *Station*'s aftermath, Bowie produced some of his greatest and most audacious work in *Low*, *"Heroes"* (both 1977), and *Lodger* (1979), but those albums' demeanor had been harrowed, their synth-heavy sound deliberately alien.

Having divorced his first wife, Angela, in 1980, Bowie had relocated to Switzerland and taken custody of his son, Joe (birth name Zowie), and took his new responsibilities seriously. "I would never have thought it possible, but for me the one most enjoyable and hope-giving quality of my life over the past four or five years is my son," he said, crediting fatherhood for making him "consider how important life is, and how important it is for him."

Let's Dance, then, embraced a straightforward-for-Bowie positivity. "I don't think I would want to continue performing anymore if I didn't think I could do something hopeful and helpful with my music, both for myself and my audience," he said. Bowie wanted "very organic, basic instrumentation . . . [that] doesn't say anything other than it comes from a hybrid of white and black culture," he told *NME*. "If you use the synthesizer it means this particular thing; that I'm part of this angular society."

To ensure hits, Bowie enlisted Nile Rodgers to produce *Let's Dance*—a sharply intuitive leap of faith, considering that Rodgers, guitarist-songwriter-producer of disco hit-makers Chic, himself was coming off a commercial slump that had followed disco's "death." The two had met in late 1982 at a New York after-hours bar.

When Rodgers flew to Switzerland to discuss the project, Bowie played him a dolorous song called "Let's Dance" on a twelve-string acoustic. "Man, it must be fantastic to be white," Rodgers told Bowie. "Where I come from, if you write a song called 'Let's Dance,' and no one wants to dance, you're gonna get killed. It's got to be *incredible*."

That winter they camped out at New York's Power Station studio and cut the album in less than a month. The album's booming sound, particularly the boxy drums—which, as Rodgers told an audience at the 2010 Pop Conference in Seattle, was inspired by the third Peter Gabriel album—would define mid-eighties pop much the way Chic's "Dance, Dance, Dance" did the late seventies.

The Power Station had been built by engineer Tony Bongiovi (the cousin of Jon Bon Jovi) to enhance the "live" sound missing from the drily recorded seventies rock albums that isolated each instrument, without reverb. As O'Leary points out, "It didn't really turn out that way—many Eighties records sound far less 'live' today than their seventies counterparts."

"TO ANNOUNCE THIS YEAR'S PRODUCER OF THE YEAR IS LAST YEAR'S PROducer of the Year—ladies and gentlemen, Toto!"

Five nondescript-looking guys in tuxes announced one nominee apiece. One person was actually nominated twice: Quincy Jones by himself, for producing James Ingram's *It's Your Night*, and Jones with Michael Jackson; the latter was credited as coproducer of the four *Thriller* songs he'd written. A year earlier, Toto had accepted Grammy after Grammy—six in total, including Album (*Toto IV*) and Record of the Year ("Rosanna"). The big winners, Quincy and Jackson, hugged the members of Toto, all of whom played on *Thriller*—and plenty of other albums, because the band's members were all highly in demand as session men.

Thriller was the culmination of Toto's heavily worked LA session style, a hallmark of both black and white pop in the seventies and eighties. This smoothly played stuff was, as Mark Rowland and Nelson George noted in *Musician*, "the only black musical style that consistently dented white Top 40 radio" in this period. The obverse was also true:

> The Doobie Brothers and the Eagles, who started as rockers and country rockers respectively, were recording in a "beige" style, similar to [Earth, Wind & Fire] and the Commodores, before their demise. Even Toto, the quintessential L.A. studio group, appears regularly on sessions of top L.A.-based black stars—including, of course, Michael Jackson. None of which should surprise. L.A. is the official capital of the entertainment industry and its commercial standards must reflect that fact. Since provincialism and eccentricity simply won't sell in Middle America, edges must be rounded and homogenized, and if that sometimes makes the L.A. sound seem less a conduit than a Cuisinart, so be it.

Toto outtakes, keyboardist David Paich noted, went "on Michael Jackson albums. . . . Steve [Porcaro, the band's other keyboardist] had this song 'Human Nature' and he brought it to Toto, but we said, 'We can't use it right now. We're into songs right for stadium rock situations.' And sure enough, I turn on my TV and there's Michael Jackson singing 'Human Nature' in a stadium. It backfired on us."

By the 1984 Grammys, Toto's day as a major band was basically over. The critics who'd called the band names—*Rolling Stone* had memorably compared the sound of *Toto IV* to "a Velveeta-orange leisure suit"—had nothing to do with it. Guitarist Steve Lukather would refer to Toto's prime problem as "the MTV horrific years, where they tried to dress you up like a fuckin' clown, you know? You know, when I came up, I didn't realize you had to be an actor too." But Michael Jackson did.

"THE MAIN JOB OF THE PRODUCER," JONES SAID AT THE PODIUM, "IS TO produce, and see that everything works. And we'd like to thank the people that make this work." He pulled out a folded-up sheet of paper from inside his jacket. "We'd like to thank Paul McCartney, Eddie Van Halen, Vincent Price, [engineers] Bruce Swedien, Humberto Gatica, Donn Landee; sixty-two musicians, the best in the world; twenty-two of the best singers in the world; the voters of NARAS, Epic Records, the disc jockeys, Freddy DeMann, Ron Weisner; the songwriters, without whom we couldn't fly: Rod Temperton, Michael Jackson,

James Ingram"—a pause; the young girls in the auditorium's balcony squealed at the very mention of Michael's name. Michael grinned, relishing it.

Jones went on: "Steve Porcaro. John Bettis. My wife, who chose to take care of me rather than pursue her own career"—Quincy giggles—"and our family and I love her. And Michael Jackson." Shrieks up. "And his beautiful family, and I also want to thank him for coproducing three of the sides [an old-fashioned term for a single track] on the album.

"And," Quincy added, "one of the greatest entertainers of the twentieth century." They embrace. Cut to a tight close-up of Peggy Lipton Jones, the woman who put her career on hold so her husband could make the biggest album ever. She smiled savvily. They'd divorce six years later.

Other people getting credit for his work seemed to gnaw at Michael at the time—understandable for a young man who'd been carrying his family on his back since kindergarten. His suspicion even extended to his strongest musical ally. Though Jackson received credit as *Thriller*'s coproducer, CBS president Walter Yetnikoff alleged that Michael called him the night before the Grammys to insist that Jones "shouldn't get a Grammy for producing the record, I produced it . . . go to the Grammys, tell them to take Quincy's nomination off, I want to be the only one getting the Grammy for producing the record." Walter responded, "Go to the goddamn Grammys, Michael, and act like you're happy."

You might have figured that *Thriller*'s becoming the most ubiquitous piece of music ever recorded would soothe young Michael's emotions. Not entirely. Three weeks prior to the Grammys, on February 7, the *Guinness Book of World Records* threw a party for a thousand guests at New York's Museum of Natural History, where Michael was the guest of honor. The occasion was *Thriller*'s inclusion in the year's edition as the best-selling solo LP ever—twenty-three million copies. "For the first time in my entire career," Michael said, "I feel like I've accomplished something."

"MAGAZINES THINK WE'RE A GREAT FASHION GROUP, BUT WE'RE NOT," DAVE Stewart told the *Washington Post*. Actually, almost no one thought Stewart was in any way fashionable, and his Grammy getup told you why: black jeans and gold spangled shirt, like a bearded *Solid Gold* dancer playing guitar. *Melody Maker*'s report from a January show in Frankfurt noted Stewart's "preposterous hunting coat," while the *Village Voice* dubbed him "the still-suffering victim of psychedelia."

Annie Lennox was a *whole* different story. Two weeks earlier, she'd attended a Music Therapy luncheon held by the producers of BBC Radio 1, gotten up in the exact opposite of her butchy Eurythmics role—miniskirt, wig, fake eyelashes—with much the same sense of ironic play. "I looked like a groupie, because I was *being* a groupie," she said a year later. "All these men were patting me on the head saying, 'Oh, your hair is so beautiful.' Really! I looked the epitome of a prostitute and they were leering and winking." Seated next to a Radio 1 exec, she finally had enough and gave him a piece of her mind. "So the head of promotion took her out of this huge event, saying, 'You can't do that,'" an onlooker said.

When the camera hit Lennox on Grammy night, everything had changed again. Instead of, per the *Voice*, "a second- or third-generation Bowie clone," she now resembled the singer Bowie shared a birthday with, Elvis Presley. Black pompadour, mutton-chop sideburns, black suit with open-collared black shirt, black shoes: it was a deliberate provocation. "There had been a lot of talk about sexual ambiguity that year, so we decided it would be perfect to kind of put it back in their faces. . . . 'You want me to be a gender bender? Here I am,'" Lennox said.

They hadn't told anyone, including the show's producer, Ken Ehrlich. "He melted," Lennox said. "He went right down on his knees, in the middle of all this mayhem." Laughing, Ehrlich proceeded to shoot Lennox straight on.

Lennox's drag confused many viewers, who only knew the redhead from the video—as *Spin* would later note, "90 percent of Middle America didn't catch on." But in one fell swoop, she'd done something nobody else had managed to for nearly two years—stolen the show from Michael Jackson.

"YOU KNOW, CYNDI, I REALLY LOVE YOUR RECORD—'GIRLS JUST WANT to Have Fun.'"

Rodney Dangerfield is the old lech, Cyndi Lauper the cartoony new wave feminist—two loudly dressed showbiz figures each playing to broad type. Rodney in a plaid suit jacket; Cyndi, a riot of gold lamé, with blood-orange hair, wide yellow bracelets, and lace gloves. She pouts, in full comic swing; they're playing a vaudeville routine expertly: he wants it, she doesn't.

Rodney was on the Grammy stage three years earlier, when his *No Respect* LP won Best Comedy Recording. An old-fashioned comic updating age-old Borscht Belt shtick for the hard-R cable nation, Dangerfield was born Jacob

Cohen in Suffolk County, New York. He'd been through a number of professional aliases before landing on the one that brought him the kind of fame and fortune his entire down-in-the-mouth persona was built to repudiate. Two weeks later, onstage in Washington, DC, Dangerfield would snap: "My wife believes in oral sex. All I hear is 'Fuck you.'"

Rodney and Cyndi are giving away Best New Artist—this is one of those cheat moments the Grammys allow themselves, because it's obvious that Lauper will be nominated in this category next year. Her roundelay with Dangerfield is proof of why. She's indefatigable and unflappable. Thirty years old, her persona entirely self-constructed, her speaking voice a Noo Yawk squeak, her singing voice the size of a volcano, Cyndi Lauper was a pro. Of course the Grammys loved her. Of course America did.

Born in Queens in 1953, Lauper attended St. Mary Gate of Heaven Catholic Academy until third grade. "They asked me to leave because my parents got divorced and they didn't want that type of person in their school," Lauper recalled. "So then I went to a special Catholic school that took kids from divorced homes but I got thrown out of there because I asked the nuns a very risqué question that I should not have asked. Then I went to about four different high schools and hated them all."

Cathy Gallo raised Cyndi and her brother and sister by working as a waitress. "I'd see her come home dead tired after twelve or thirteen hours of work so that she could feed us," Lauper told *New York*. "I saw her suffer an enormous amount, and I was angry." Obsessed with the Beatles as soon as they landed at JFK, Lauper wrote her first songs when she was eleven. Her mother remarried, and by the time Cyndi was seventeen she'd moved out to escape her new stepfather's unwanted attentions.

With a few abortive school stints behind her, Lauper worked retail and sang covers in a band. In her memoir, Lauper describes being gang-raped by members of one of those groups: "I told the other guys in the band and they didn't believe me. And after that, if you can believe it, I still stayed with the band because I refused to let them break me."

In 1978, at twenty-five, she formed the band Blue Angel, a local club favorite that released a 1980 debut the press liked—*Rolling Stone* compared them to "the Crystals with punk hair and Fender guitars"—and no one else knew existed.

Following Blue Angel's breakup, Lauper met a former singer named Dave Wolff at a holiday party. "He was trying to pick up another girl," Lauper told *Interview*. "He was just starting a management company. And I was a singer trying to get another record deal." The two lived together before deciding to make it a business arrangement as well: "As I was looking for managers, he'd tell me, 'Ask them this and ask them that.' I would always bring it home anyway, so he just said, 'Forget it. Let's just work together' . . . he helped me make what I do creatively commercial. I couldn't do that. It's hard to do that."

Lauper's stylistic choices were showing up in other places as well, not least in a downtown disco singer named Madonna. *Creem*'s Laura Fissinger dubbed Lauper's loopy fashion sense "a sort of MTV Bernadette Peters with cupid's bow mouth and big blue eyes and punked-out orange hair." "Serious and silly on top of each other, that's how I am," Lauper told Fissinger. "I like things that really sneak and say something while you're busy laughing."

For her solo debut, *She's So Unusual*, Lauper said she wanted "to make a record where people could really feel who I am. I wanted to cover the spectrum of my emotions." This she did with originals like the deeply compassionate "Time After Time" and the slyly pervy "She Bop," as well as some expertly chosen covers. The album opened with a powerful version of "Money Changes Everything," by the Atlanta new wavers the Brains, a cult hit on college radio in 1979, which Lauper and the studio band—a Philadelphia outfit called the Hooters—attacked like the Clash. And her version of Prince's "When You Were Mine," from 1980's *Dirty Mind*, utilized an arrangement that played as homage to the techier groove Prince cultivated on *1999* (1982).

The big one, though, was "Girls Just Want to Have Fun," written by Robert Hazard. When producer Rick Chertoff played Lauper Robert Hazard's original "Girls Just Want to Have Fun," she said, "It was basically a very chauvinistic song. [But Chertoff] said, 'But wait, think about what it *could* mean.'" Amending the lyrics to come from a woman's perspective rather than a man's helped refocus the song and gave Lauper room to sound delighted. (Lauper thanked Hazard in *She's So Unusual*'s credits "for letting me change your song.")

She'd begun to conceptualize the video before the album was completed; in late August 1983, she sat down with Wolff, Portrait president Lenny Petze, and Epic product manager Dan Beck and outlined it: "Just a logical thing suggested by the title and lyrics—you know, girls wanting to have fun, and maybe having a hard time doing it. But not heavy; keep it fun."

To play Lauper's father, Wolff called in the professional-wrestler-turned-manager Captain Lou Albano, whom they'd met on a flight. With the strange shtick of sticking rubber bands into his beard (he was a tough guy, all right—

ouch), Albano managed the rock band NRBQ. On set, he and Lauper got along swimmingly: "Oh, Lou, you're such a natural," she told him. "Hey, kid, can I adopt you?" he responded.

"Girls"—and, in the months following the Grammys, "Time After Time," with a more straightforwardly dramatic (and charmingly klutzy) video in which Cyndi leaves Wolff, playing her small-town boyfriend—made Lauper a hit, and not just with young rockers. "You know when I was surprised? When I saw *little* kids at the concert. That shook me up," she said. "And you know when I really flipped out? When I saw grandmothers, mothers and their kids, with their hair shaved back on the side, and even the grandmother had a little pink something in her hair. That was the weirdest thing, seeing all three generations, and that's when I thought I did something really good."

"SAY SOMETHING; SAY SOMETHING."

Joan Rivers was stage-whispering into Boy George's ear in the London studio. Culture Club had just won Best New Artist. Soon the drummer Jon Moss got down to business—he was the band's manager. What wasn't known widely yet in the States, but was already common gossip in Britain, was that Moss was also Boy George's lover, and had been for some time.

"In Britain," Mary Harron wrote in 1988, Boy George "retained a disturbing quality, redolent of London nightlife, transvestism, and the gay art and fashion world." By contrast, she added, "in America, where he reached audiences through a series of playful videos, George was seen as a kind of benign extraterrestrial, a pop E.T."

Moss was adamant that he wasn't gay, which hurt George's feelings. "When a man says he's straight, while humping another man, it means one of two things: you're unique, or he can't deal with his sexuality," George wrote.

Their differences often turned physical. Moss broke his finger twice during altercations with George, once on a tour bus, once at a hotel in Munich, where they were to appear on TV. The drummer from Nena, the German new wavers who'd crossed over to the US charts in 1984 with the bouncy apocalypse number "99 Red Balloons," played in Moss's stead.

Culture Club was becoming terribly overexposed. "Virgin wanted any old press," George wrote, adding: "It wasn't about money—I would have been happy for my face to appear on a toilet seat, as long as it was a good picture and the right toilet seat."

It was well past three in the morning by the time Culture Club accepted their Best New Artist Grammy, a lot to ask even of veteran London nightclubbers on a Sunday in 1984. Bassist Mikey Craig put his head into the frame and thanked the band's American label, Epic Records. Roy Hay, wearing a new set of blond dreadlock weaves the lead singer had insisted would jazz up his appearance, thanked the rest of the band. Then came a pause, during which the gears in George's head turned almost visibly, before he took his turn.

"Thank you, America. You've got—you've got taste, style and you know a good drag queen when you see one."

Frank DiLeo, Epic's head of promotions, the man whose fervent belief had turned "Do You Really Want to Hurt Me" into a US hit, was said to have dropped his cigar.

The director, in a moment of semiotic genius, cut to the country-gospel family group the Gatlin Brothers Band in the auditorium audience. They looked puzzled.

At first, George didn't quite understand what he'd said. "In America, 'drag' has different connotations," he said. "The English have a tradition of drag: look at our judges and priests! So it's ingrained into our culture whereas America was founded by Puritans. So, for them 'drag' means 'homosexual.' . . . The knock-on effect of that is that whenever I go to America the drag queens come up to me and hug me."

When the cameras went off, George's bandmates made their displeasure known; George's appearance courted controversy without half trying already. And there was still more to do—much more. There was a spring tour of America to come. There was another album to write and record. "There was never any time to stop and breathe," George wrote.

"FOR ALBUM OF THE YEAR, THE AWARDS GO TO THE ARTIST AND ALBUM producer."

The Beach Boys were at the podium. Two months earlier, founding drummer-singer Dennis Wilson had drowned in Marina del Rey; as many pointed out, he'd been the only Beach Boy who surfed. When Dennis died, his blood alcohol level was 0.26, double the legal limit. "When you're sixteen years old and you're literally handed millions of dollars, you get crazy," frequent Beach Boys session drummer Hal Blaine said of him. The Wilsons' imbroglios could make the Jacksons seem serene.

But the Beach Boys seem nonchalant as they announce the Album of the Year nominees—apart, of course, from the spacey Brian. "There's no winner!" he barks upon opening the envelope; "Awww," the band responds in unison (not harmony). "*Thriller!*" Brian yells. He knew the joy of writing songs that everyone wants to sing, and the darkness that can accompany it.

This time, Michael calls up "the best president of any record company, Walter Yetnikoff—where are you? Come up here, Walter!" They embrace, and the bearded exec sonorously announces that *Thriller* is, officially, "the biggest-selling album in the history of music." He did it so Michael and Quincy didn't have to. A coarse loudmouth who'd do the yelling was just what Michael needed. That summer, Yetnikoff would tell *Billboard* that Michael "would be totally qualified to run a record company if he so desired."

Back on the microphone, Michael tips his hat to Jackie Wilson, who'd died the month before. "He's not with us anymore, but Jackie, where you are, I'd like to say I love you and thank you so much." Wilson had been one of R&B's most electrifying performers in the fifties and sixties, first as Clyde McPhatter's successor as lead singer of the Dominoes. In 1958, Wilson met another Detroit native, Berry Gordy, and recorded his song "Lonely Teardrops," Wilson's first solo hit. But Wilson was on Brunswick Records, a Chicago label whose owners favored middle-of-the-road pop treatments over the tougher, more soulful sound that Gordy would take to the bank with Motown.

On September 29, 1975, Wilson suffered a heart attack while performing "Lonely Teardrops" at the Latin Casino in Cherry Hill, New Jersey. In a coma for a year, Wilson incurred brain damage that kept him living in nursing homes until his death on January 21. Michael Jackson had watched Jackie Wilson intently as a child, vowing to match his impossibly lithe physical grace—and not replicate his lack of power over his own career and fate.

"HE PERFORMED WITH THE CHICAGO SYMPHONY WHEN HE WAS ONLY eleven years old."

By contrast, Herbie Hancock was forty-three when he performed on the Grammys for the first time. Prior to 1984, he'd been nominated nine times—and this was the second time he was up for three prizes. In 1975, Hancock had been nominated for Pop Instrumental Performance (*Head Hunters*), Instrumental Composition ("Chameleon"), and Original Score (*Death Wish*). None of those categories contained the word *jazz*.

For many, neither did "Rockit," the song he performed that night. It was contemporary dance music, festooned with the scratches of a rising style, hip-hop, with stage accoutrements taken from a video in which Hancock barely appeared—all the better to get it onto MTV.

Hancock had released his first album, *Takin' Off*, in 1962. It featured "Watermelon Man," a song Mongo Santamaría took into the top ten a year later—the first of Hancock's many crossover hits. He joined the Miles Davis Quintet in 1963 and for five years helped drive the decade's most acclaimed jazz band.

Like Davis, Hancock felt the lure of funk in the early seventies. The trigger was Sly and the Family Stone's 1969 single "Thank You (Falettinme Be Mice Elf Agin)." "It just went to my core," Hancock said. "I didn't know what he was doing, I mean, I heard the chorus but, how could he think of that? I was afraid that that was something I couldn't do. And here I am, I call myself a musician. It bothered me."

Hancock's deep dive came up with 1973's *Head Hunters*. "When I did *Head Hunters* I was not trying to make a jazz record," Hancock said. "And it came out sounding different from anything I could think of at the time. But I still wasn't satisfied because in the back of my head I wanted to make a funk record."

Hancock became a divisive figure in jazz. Some hard-liners accused him of "just tryin' to make some money," to which Hancock responded: "I'm not just trying to make money. I'm doing this kind of music because I like it. It's part of my musical development. And in order for me to be really honest with myself, I don't want to ignore these urges."

Hancock understood pop even if he didn't always pull it off. "One thing about pop music that I've discovered is that playing something that's familiar or playing the same solo you played before has no negative connotations whatsoever," he said. "What's negative is if it doesn't sound, each time, like it's the first time you played it. . . . [The] lesson was to try to learn to play something without change, and have it sound fresh and meaningful."

Hancock was an avowed futurist, and not just musically. By 1984, he owned eight Apple computers and kept up with his road manager using electronic mail. But he kept his hand in straight jazz—in the late seventies he began touring with his former bandmates in the classic Miles Davis Quintet, with trumpeter Freddie Hubbard in Davis's place, as V.S.O.P. Quintet. Hancock also produced the 1982 debut by the hotshot New Orleans trumpeter Wynton Marsalis. "Columbia wanted him to do a pop-jazz record a la Tom Browne," Hancock said. "I knew it would be a mistake."

For his 1983 LP *Future Shock*, Hancock enlisted a pair of New York producer-bandleaders, Bill Laswell and Michael Beinhorn of the conglomerate outfit Material, who'd worked with everyone from Ornette Coleman to Nile Rodgers prior to connecting with Hancock. "For people who like 'out' music, we're communicating with those people, and people who like dance music, we're communicating with those people, and the only difference there is the number of people, because obviously there are more people who are in than out," Laswell said.

Laswell had been immediately attracted to hip-hop: "I always approach it as sort of a collage system," he said. That's what Hancock liked about it as well. When Laswell and Beinhorn sent him the track that became "Rockit," Hancock said, "Those guys had read my mind."

The scratch at the record's center came from Grandmixer D.ST (Derek Showard, who in 1989 changed his handle to DXT), one of the earliest adapters of New York's hip-hop DJ style, extending drum breaks by switching between two copies on a pair of turntables even before Grand Wizzard Theodore introduced scratching as the style's vital technique. He recorded for the New York indie label Celluloid Records, for which Laswell was a quasi-in-house producer.

On the "Rockit" session, Laswell played bass, Beinhorn programmed the drum machines, Daniel Ponce played percussion, and D.ST rubbed the needle against another Celluloid title, "Change the Beat," by a New York graffiti artist and social connector named Fab 5 Freddy (Fred Braithwaite). The phrase D.ST was scratching, "Ah, this stuff is really fresh," came from the artist manager Roger Trilling at the beginning of "Change."

This sort of noisy, unmelodic, repetitive stuff largely repelled the traditional R&B business. "You're not going to get on Johnny Carson doing hip-hop," a black A&R person told *Cash Box* in June 1984. "You're going to have to do standards and stuff, and I'd like to see black musicians and black artists go toward that."

Vibrant and unmistakably musical, "Rockit" was one of the first dominoes to fall in changing that perception. D.ST's scratches were fluid and on point. Hancock knew he had a hit, and he wanted it on MTV. He'd picked the video's directors, Godley and Crème, best known for their avant-garde visual approach, in part to sidestep race. "They said they wanted to do the most unusual video they've done," Hancock said, "and they did it, too."

Godley and Crème enlisted the animatronic robots of London sculptor Jim Whiting to perform break-dancing moves—that was certainly unusual. So was the fact that the record's performer barely appeared in it: Hancock cameos on a TV screen. "I have no proof that MTV had a racist policy," he told *Rolling Stone*. "But I didn't want to take any chances." Now, these robots could render this very black and brown dancing style *literally raceless*. Though the record stalled at seventy-one pop (number six black, number one dance), it was indeed an MTV smash.

The robots were out in force for Hancock's Grammy rendition of "Rockit"— the clear favorite for R&B Instrumental, with that category announced following the performance. D.ST was particularly joyous to watch, and his scratches, which elongate the word "Fresh," were deft and near-offhanded. The many kids who began experimenting with their families' stereos, and wrecking the turntables' styluses, were less successful. But a number would become hip-hop DJs themselves, notably future turntablist scratching heroes QBert and Mix Master Mike.

This performance would turn "Change the Beat" from a New York obscurity (even by the standards of the mostly homespun labels putting out rap records in 1982) into a scratch DJ staple. Soon that *"fr-fr-fr-fresh"* was everywhere in hip-hop—in 1984 alone, Davy DMX's "One for the Treble (Fresh)" and UTFO's "Roxanne Roxanne" featured it, as did "Surgery," a fast electro number by a nineteen-year-old Los Angeles DJ calling himself Dr. Dre, and it has continued to echo out from there.

In his white jeans, black leather jacket, red handkerchief around his neck (see also Prince on the cover of *Dirty Mind*), and of course his keytar and big grin, Hancock was crossover's triumphant embodiment. He looked a little silly, sure. He also looked like he was on top of the world. Minutes later, picking up his first-ever Grammy Award, he thanked "the whole industry for letting me do my thing."

"You're a whole new generation, you're lovin' what you do . . ."

We have arrived at the world premiere of the Pepsi commercial, featuring the Jacksons, that Michael's scalp had suffered to make. The ad began backstage at, what do you know, the Shrine Auditorium, with close-ups of Jackie, Jermaine, Marlon, Randy, and Tito's faces as their stage makeup was topped off, they put on sequined jackets, and Michael's stand-in's sequined shoulders cut dramatic angles. (In a sign of his enthusiasm for the product at hand, Michael limited his exposure to a four-second close-up.) The brothers walked through a scrim of people backstage to the stage, but Michael entered through the audience's aisle, as if he were accepting a Grammy rather than performing a show. Seeing Michael stand dramatically at the top of a staircase, backlit by booming pyro, it was hard not to wince, even before anyone saw the actual footage of Michael's hair catching fire.

Jackson attended the Grammys wearing a hairpiece. He was beleaguered in other ways as well. *Thriller* was sweet vindication that he didn't need the family who'd surrounded him, cocooned him nearly, his entire life and career. But the accident had come about because that family had insisted he do yet another tour with them—one that Pepsi would sponsor. The Jacksons—just what the world had been waiting for! Especially with Jermaine back in the fold! Wait—were those crickets? Or was it just Joseph, the Jackson patriarch, bending the room's atmosphere with a furrow of his eyebrows?

The ads were not supposed to be public knowledge—they were intended as surprise spots for the Grammys. Bob Giraldi, who'd directed Michael's "Beat It" video, was at the helm. The song was "You're a Whole New Generation," a Pepsi slogan Michael had draped over the tune of "Billie Jean." They were doing the sixth take at half past six when Michael, atop a staircase, stood next to a magnesium flash bomb that exploded roughly two feet from his head. Several people—including Jermaine, standing just a few feet away—initially thought Michael had been shot.

Jackson was rushed to Cedars-Sinai Medical Center; following treatment, he was transferred to the burn unit at Brotman Memorial Hospital. (He'd visited the latter twice before to cheer up the kids.) There, he watched *Close Encounters of the Third Kind* on the VCR and took his first painkiller, a Dilaudid. Nearly alone among those near his level of fame, Michael had never before taken a narcotic.

"PLEASE WELCOME MENUDO!"

Five Puerto Rican teenagers wearing white suits onstage in perfect formation, Menudo wasn't so much a boy band as a boy *brand*. The managers owned the name; if a boy got too old, he was replaced. This revolving door incubated future stars. Ricky Martin, who joined in 1983, would be on the ground floor of the next concerted biz effort to cross Latin music over into the mainstream after the mid-eighties' during the late nineties as a solo artist.

Martin was turned down three times before being accepted: "The fourth time, they just told me, 'You are the new Menudo. Tomorrow you're on a plane to Orlando. Maybe you're not the best singer or dancer, but you wanted it so bad. That's why you became a Menudo.'"

The group's appearance wasn't just a shrewd gambit to give Michael Jackson and Quincy Jones a proper lead-in for their inevitable victory for Best Children's Album. It was also the Grammys' way of welcoming Latin music into the fold—the 1984 awards were the first to include *any* Latin music categories. Jose Feliciano, Tito Puente, and an up-and-coming LA band called Los Lobos had picked up their trophies earlier. (The Grammys wouldn't award any reggae prizes until 1985.)

It wasn't just the Grammys. Prior to late 1983, when RCA started a Latin distribution division and signed Menudo, not one US major label had a Latin music division.

In 1984, as ever, there was no one kind of "Latin music." Salsa, for example—though the Fania All Stars made four Columbia LPs, most of that style's giants recorded for the small New York indie Fania Records. Menudo—along with a middle-aged crooner named Julio Iglesias—seemed set to change that.

Two weeks prior to the Grammys, Menudo had caused pandemonium at Radio City Music Hall. On February 13, a day ahead of the group's Valentine's Day opening of their ten-day engagement, the fans, mostly female and Hispanic, crowded the doors so that police were brought in. *Variety* compared it to "the days when Frank Sinatra attracted hordes of bobbysoxers to the Paramount." Teen fans "stood guard at the Plaza and at Radio City [and] camped throughout the day at the Roosevelt Hotel, where the group is staying. The police also had to be called in there to maintain order."

RCA's Latin division—which in 1984 would also sign up salsa bandleader Willie Colón—left little to chance with Menudo, but the group's US bow, *Reaching Out*, released January 1984, stiffed, peaking at number 108. No matter—the group was already cleaning up on merchandise. Soon kids could watch Menudo through their View-Masters, plastic 3D viewers showing images on flimsy cardboard discs. View-Master had already cleared $1.5 million on Jackson product during 1984's first quarter. At Grammy time, negotiations were ongoing with Culture Club, Quiet Riot, Adam Ant, and Van Halen.

MICHAEL DOTED ON KIDS, QUITE PUBLICLY. IN THE SHRINE AUDIENCE, TO Michael's left—with Brooke Shields on the right—was Emmanuel Lewis, the pint-sized twelve-year-old star of ABC's *Webster*, a family sitcom that essentially cloned NBC's kiddie breakout hit *Diff'rent Strokes*, starring Gary Coleman. No one was publicly questioning Michael's motives for being around those kids yet—that wouldn't surface for a decade. Michael was a showbiz kid and liked being around others. He'd give Lewis piggyback rides, carrying him around the Hayvenhurst estate, playing cops and robbers like kids half Lewis's age and a fifth of Michael's. What's a little eccentricity from the world's biggest star?

Soon Michael and Quincy rose to accept Best Children's Album, not for *Thriller*, but for the *E.T.—The Extra-Terrestrial* storybook album, which Jackson narrated. "Of all the awards I've gotten, I'm most proud of this one, honestly, because I think children are a great inspiration, and this album is not for children, it's for everyone," he said.

"IT IS RARE FOR AN ARTIST TO HAVE BOTH JAZZ AND CLASSICAL ALBUMS released in the same year."

Near the end of 1984, Herbie Hancock would sit across from Wynton Marsalis, the young trumpeter he'd kept away from corporate meddling, and explained why he didn't appear in his own clip for "Rockit."

"It's not important to me," Hancock insisted. "Why should I have to be in my own video?" Wynton winced.

> HERBIE: Anyway, if it was true that MTV was racist . . .
>
> WYNTON: It was true. You don't have to say "if."
>
> HERBIE: I have never claimed that to be true.
>
> WYNTON: I'll say it.

The exchange was not unlike a post-bop version of Alex P. Keaton, the Reaganite teenager played by Michael J. Fox on the NBC sitcom *Family Ties*, which debuted in 1982, at intellectual odds with his groovy hippie parents. Like Keaton, Wynton Marsalis represented an age-reversed generation gap. Herbie Hancock's throwing in with the young hip-hop generation was significantly different from jazz's conservative post-seventies direction, as exemplified by Marsalis.

Wynton had come from a long line of players. Ellis Marsalis, his father, was a jazz pianist who played with Al Hirt, a white trumpeter popular with New Orleans tourists in the sixties and seventies. Hirt gave Wynton his first horn when he was six. The oldest of Ellis's sons, Branford, played saxophone in Wynton's quintet. (The others who played at the Grammys were pianist Kenny Kirkland, bassist Charnett Moffett, and drummer Jeff Watts.) "I don't have him in the band because he's my brother," Wynton assured *DownBeat* in 1982. "I use him because I like the way he plays."

The teenaged Wynton became "obsessed" with jazz under the spell of the Miles Davis mid-sixties quintet that Hancock had anchored. He was also exploring classical music. "I got into it because I dug the music," Wynton said. "Plus, I had always heard that black people couldn't play classical. That's bullshit—music is music. That's some hip shit, too." He moved to New York in 1979. Branford soon followed him, having had his own epiphany to Cannonball Adderley's *In the Land of Hi-Fi*, poring over the leader's solos.

Wynton had made the decision to join Art Blakey's Jazz Messengers after their father had told him, "If you don't play with Art Blakey, I'll break your neck." On the road, Blakey gave the young Marsalis some advice: "The only thing you can take to the cemetery is respect. An armored car will never follow a hearse."

Wynton signed to Columbia at age nineteen, and he moved units: *Wynton Marsalis* sold two hundred thousand copies, *Think of One* more than three hundred thousand. This was a rarity at a time when a jazz best seller might move forty thousand copies.

The A&R man who'd signed Marsalis, George Butler, spent eight months convincing Masterworks to record the wunderkind as a classical player. "I wore them down with memos," he said. He moved units there, too: Marsalis's classical debut, *Haydn/Hummel/L. Mozart: Trumpet Concertos*, sold two hundred thousand copies, held the top of *Billboard*'s classical chart for more than six months.

Butler was clear on where he wanted this young man to go. "I wanted to sign him because I knew this was an extraordinary person who would be an excellent role model for the young," Butler said. Marsalis appeared on *The Tonight Show* in 1981, before the debut's release, and was anointed by guest host Bill Cosby—the ablest pitchman in America at that point, and an unparalleled power broker in black America (allegations of his serial sexual assaults, over many years, took decades to surface)—as "the young man I want my daughter to marry."

Marsalis had already received a Grammy for Best Instrumental Soloist, Performance (with Orchestra) (for *Haydn: Trumpet Concerto in E Flat*) prior to his taking the stage at the Shrine. The performance would be a rarity: Marsalis got eight minutes—an eternity in Grammy time—to play pieces from both LPs. He opened with a Hummel concerto—lively and colorful and rhythmically dexterous, nothing stuffy about it. Four minutes later, his quintet replaced the orchestral players and kicked into "Knozz-Moe-King" from *Think of One*—knotty, dense, swift, thrilling, and absolutely in fealty to mid-sixties Miles, whose elegant manner he aspired to both sartorially and in brooking no bullshit as a tastemaker.

When Joe Williams and Ernestine Anderson announced Wynton's name while reading the Best Jazz Instrumental Performance, Soloist nominees, the program cut to the trumpeter backstage. Marsalis wiggled his eyebrows and kissy-faced the camera, irresistibly cocky. When he won, he reentered the stage with trumpet in hand and finished his acceptance speech with: "And last, but certainly, certainly not least, I would like to thank all the great masters of American music: Charlie Parker, Louis Armstrong, Thelonious Monk. All the guys who set a precedent in Western art and gave an art form to the American people that cannot be limited by enforced trends or bad taste." Huge grin. "Thank you very much!"

Naturally, many people thought the last comment was directed at Hancock. "I wasn't even thinking about that," Wynton claimed, while Herbie responded, "That never dawned on me."

For many, Marsalis's performance and acceptance speech were "a shot of adrenaline for jazz." "I was on the phone calling my friends about it," young vibraphonist Jay Hoggard said. "I had a phone in each hand. It was unprecedented. . . . This wasn't a jazz club. It was the Grammys, and Wynton and his quintet were playing our music. It was an inspiration to me."

Wynton's older brother, on the other hand, was ready to stake his own claim—a far pop-friendlier one. On Branford's list of 1984 favorites for *Musician* magazine were LPs by Old and New Dreams, Art Blakey & the Jazz Messengers, and Wynton's quintet, as well as from Midnight Star, Prince and the Revolution, and Talking Heads, with all his favorite songs either pop or R&B. Branford told an interviewer that his differences in taste with his brother weren't down to Branford "being more open; it's just that [Wynton is] kind of set in his ways."

". . . PRINCE, FOR '1999' . . ."

The only performer nominated for Pop Male Vocal not to show up on this night, making it to the ceremony a grand total of zero times, is Prince. Perhaps this is for the best. Two years earlier, he'd shown up to the Minnesota Black Music Awards and accepted a trophy by asking, "When do they give the award for best ass?"

When Michael won Pop Male Vocal for *Thriller*, he said, "When something like this happens, you want those who are very dear to you up here with ya—my sisters La Toya and Janet, please come up." La Toya wore a glittering headband and a teal one-shoulder dress with a similar gold epaulet to Michael's—very Wonder Woman. Janet was in a boxy red suit and bow tie.

Michael often used those two as his proxies during interviews—they'd repeat the question a journalist had asked, and he'd whisper his answer to them to give to the perplexed reporter. "Michael told me when you hear bad things about yourself, just put your energies into something else; it's no good crying about it," Janet told *Interview*. "Just put it into your music—it'll make you stronger." The Jacksons were a competitive family, however loving, and Janet was no different, telling Michael after *Thriller* hit: "God, you make me sick. I wish that was my album."

"My mother and father were with us all the way," Michael continued from the podium. "My mother's like me, she won't come up." Mother Katherine gets a close-up anyway. "I'd like to thank all my brothers, who I love dearly—including Jermaine." Nice qualification; nothing odd there. Finally, Michael's oldest sister, Rebbie, joined them. Michael also thanked Steven Spielberg (he'd forgotten to earlier) and "Quincy's wife, Peggy Jones—she was a great help on the *E.T.* album." And then he moved in for the kill:

"I made a deal with myself that if I won one more award, which is this award—which is seven, which is a record—I would take off my glasses." Stands up, huge roar, turns back—golly, *really*? You *like* me? Shucks—and then puts a finger up: "I don't want to take them off, really, but . . ." Stands back up, ready for the wave. Finally, he informs us that his good friend Katharine Hepburn *insisted* he take his glasses off. A brief hello from Michael's preternaturally wary eyes; the requisite fan shrieks; a swift departure from the stage.

The plummy adult contemporary singers Melissa Manchester and Julio Iglesias read the nominees for the night's final category, Record of the Year, without bed music—a silence that, planned or not, jumped the tension on what amounted to a coronation. Manchester pronounced Irene Cara's "What a Feeling?" like a confused person asking directions. Soon enough, "Beat It" won. "I love all the girls in the balcony," Michael began. They loved him back louder than ever.

After he and Q ran through their regular lists, Michael also made sure to thank Lionel Richie. "I've known him ever since I was ten years old." Lionel, in the audience, pushes his hands down: *Not so loud*, a good comedic gesture for someone even more anxious than Michael to win one of these things. He'd been nominated some eighteen times prior to the 1983 Grammys, including seven the previous year, and whiffed them all. And finally: "I'd like once again to thank Quincy Jones and the fans in the balcony."

MTV AIRPLAY HAD SENT *THRILLER'S* SALES SOARING TO TWO HUNDRED thousand copies a week. The Grammys reached far more people and produced an even more frenzied reaction, with the album shifting over a million copies *per week* following the ceremony.

Three days after the show, on February 28, the independent label Scotti Brothers Records released "Eat It," by "Weird Al" Yankovic—the nerdy accordion player's parody of the Grammys' Record of the Year. It followed Yankovic's tradition, beginning with "Ricky," an *I Love Lucy*–themed variation on Toni Basil's "Mickey," which had peaked at number sixty-three.

In 1983, Yankovic began working with guitarist-producer Rick Derringer, who'd made definitive rock anthems in the mid-sixties (the McCoys' "Hang On Sloopy") and seventies ("Rock and Roll, Hoochie Coo"). Their collaboration spanned the eighties. *In 3-D*, Yankovic's 1984 album, featured ridiculous takeoffs of the Police ("King of Pain" became the salesman's lament "King of Suede") and Greg Kihn ("I Lost on Jeopardy," an improvement on Kihn's "Jeopardy"). And, of course, of Michael Jackson, who proved surprisingly easy to deal with. "He's got a long chain of command, but Michael has the last word and it finally had to come to him," Yankovic said. "I was delighted to find that he had a sense of humor."

On "Eat It," Derringer re-created Eddie Van Halen's guitar solo by slowing the tape down to learn it. The video was equally meticulous. It cost nearly $40,000 to make—high-end for Yankovic, largely because they shot it on film so it would look like Jackson's video. On the set, Yankovic said, "We had a videotape and monitor on stage and we'd freeze a scene from 'Beat It' and the set people would duplicate it." Not only did Jackson enjoy Weird Al's parody, he made a decent chunk of change from it: such was the hunger for anything Michael-related, "Eat It" made the top twenty.

6

CASTRO THEATRE,
April 24, 1984

Rock singers didn't sing about stockbrokers sympathetically until David Byrne came along. By 1984, the stockbroker had become a kind of culture hero, and Byrne was on his way there as well.

Talking Heads—Byrne on rhythm guitar and vocals, bassist Tina Weymouth, drummer Chris Frantz (her husband), and, from 1977, keyboardist and guitarist Jerry Harrison—was part of the late-seventies CBGB's era. CBGB was a dive bar in New York's Bowery that nurtured many of the decade's key punk and new wave bands, including Blondie, Television, the Ramones, the Patti Smith Group, Richard Hell and the Voidoids, Johnny Thunders's Heartbreakers. Of them, Talking Heads seemed least on the surface like "punk." That was why, in the mid-eighties, it appeared to be the one with the most enduring shelf life.

That didn't mean they were cuddly. In 1986, looking back at some early Heads performances, Byrne was struck by "how really strange we were. . . . The music had this disturbing hue to it." Byrne would later refer to his early lyrics as "my slightly removed 'anthropologist from Mars' view of human relationships."

That detachment could seem terminal. "With David it's all or nothing—total aggression or total meekness," bassist Tina Weymouth said. "So I always tried to act like a very gentle older sister with him. I could yell at Chris, but I

92

could never yell at David." In the summer of '84, Frantz said, "Talking Heads still enjoy playing with each other. But if something came up that destroyed it or made it impossible, there are alternatives."

The increasing perception of Talking Heads was that it was merely the David Byrne Show. That wasn't about to lessen after the San Francisco International Film Festival in April 1984. The final night, a Tuesday, featured the premiere of *Stop Making Sense*, a documentary of the Heads live in concert, filmed over three nights in Hollywood the previous December. "Finally, people can see David Byrne up close, and that's really the thing—he really holds up to the magnifying glass," the film's producer, Gary Goetzman, told *Cash Box*.

Directed by cult director Jonathan Demme—seven years away from a Best Picture Oscar for *The Silence of the Lambs*—*Stop Making Sense* was a rarity, concentrating near entirely on the performance, rather than cutting back and forth from the stage to the crowd. The shots were sustained and consistently well framed—not the sort of on-the-fly, up-the-nostril concert doc that briefly flourished after *Woodstock*. All 1,560 tickets to the Castro Theatre sold out a week before the screening; scalpers were selling them for up to twenty bucks a head.

At the theater together to introduce the film were Byrne, Demme, Harrison, Goetzman, and Lynn Mabry, one of the Heads' backing singers—but no Chris or Tina. "We've never seen this before, either," Demme admitted.

Somewhere along the movie's sixth number, "Burning Down the House"—a top ten hit the previous summer, the Heads' biggest yet—the Castro Theatre began not to burn but to shake. Up in the projection room, the manager was trying to stop the movie—the theater was sixty-two years old and had been declared a historic landmark in 1976. *Tell them to sit down!* Eventually, the manager relented, and the filmgoers kept boogying in the aisles till the end of the film.

Still widely regarded as the greatest rock and roll performance film, *Stop Making Sense* made Talking Heads stars on their own terms. That's the way Byrne liked it. The night after *Sense* premiered, he was in Minneapolis, where the Walker Art Center was premiering *The Knee Plays*, his collaboration with the experimental New York theater director Robert Wilson. The other Talking Heads were nowhere to be seen.

SEYMOUR STEIN CONSIDERED THE WORD *PUNK*—ORIGINALLY A GAY MALE slur—a commercial block. In October 1977, Stein's label, Sire Records, took out a full-page label ad in the American underground rock magazine *Trouser Press* with the headline DON'T CALL IT PUNK. Below it were new Sire LPs by Richard Hell and the Voidoids, Talking Heads, Dead Boys, and Australians the Saints. This music, Stein insisted in an open letter to FM radio programmers, should be called "new wave": "The term 'punk' is as offensive as 'race' and 'hillbilly' were when they were used to describe 'rhythm and blues' and 'country and western' music thirty years ago."

Very few commercial stations were interested in punk during the late seventies, though. The CBGB band to make the first serious dent in the national consciousness was Blondie, whose disco stab "Heart of Glass" hit number one in early 1979, the first of several.

But Blondie had dissolved in 1982; Television had done the same in 1978. Richard Hell, of the Voidoids, and Patti Smith had both retired from music. All four would make music again, but not until the nineties. In 1984, Johnny Thunders brought out a newly refurbished version of his 1977 album with the Heartbreakers, *L.A.M.F.*, but was by this point a professional junkie as much as musician. (He died in 1991.) Alan Vega of Suicide was making downbeat electro-rockabilly on his own for a small audience.

Sire's bellwether act, the Ramones, would reestablish themselves in 1984 by embracing hardcore and synthesizers with the critical smash *Too Tough to Die*, released that October. But as had been the case from the beginning, press plaudits guaranteed nothing: the Ramones still toured in a van, as they would to the end of their days.

Byrne and company were the only members of the CBGB first generation to make it to 1984 not simply intact (the Ramones were on their third drummer in a decade) but having achieved mass success. Blondie had broken through to Middle America through the discos, and so, in a different way, did Talking Heads, whose powerful grooves were staples of the rising number of "rock discos" opening around the country through the early eighties. Even prior to their expansion as a live group from a quartet to a ten-piece, half–African American live unit in 1980, Talking Heads had been not so much the era's great white funk band as its whitest great funk band.

Among other things, Talking Heads made a performance of its own whiteness. At CBGB, a scuzzy rocker bar where long hair, black leather jackets, and Converse All-Stars ruled, Talking Heads took the stage with their hair chopped short, wearing Izods—like preppies, the most un–rock and roll thing imaginable. (The band's short hair also had utility value. "This was right when Martin

Scorsese's *Taxi Driver* came out," Weymouth said, "and I had to cut off all my hair to avoid being propositioned by pimps on my way to CBGB's.")

By the eighties, "punk" had gone from connoting disparate bands to signifying something far narrower and more violent. CBGB was making its bones on the Plasmatics, led by Wendy O. Williams, who sang "punk" (later, "metal") songs when not destroying large machinery with a chain saw. ("It's the spaghetti in the face principle," Plasmatics manager Rod Swenson declaimed.)

Beginning in 1982, CBGB hosted hardcore matinees every Sunday afternoon. Even in a scene where fistfights were common coin, New York hardcore had a rep for being filled with knuckleheads. One hardcore musician recalled a mid-eighties Agnostic Front show at CB's where another scene regular "took this bottle and smashed it over [a] guy's head and cracked it open" as he was filing out.

THE WIDER US ECONOMIC RECOVERY OF 1983–1984—NOT JUST IN THE record business—was a late-coming mirror of what Wall Street had started doing a year earlier. "At a time when unemployment and corporate bankruptcies have reached postwar highs, the stock market is in the midst of its most explosive rally since the 1930s," *BusinessWeek* reported in October 1982. "Propelled by frantic trading of record-shattering volume, the Dow Jones industrial average has soared 30 percent since mid-August . . . [and is] in the neighborhood of its long-standing peak of 1051.70." That the Dow was over a thousand was said to be "psychologically important."

The traders making these big-payoff investments were themselves becoming public personalities. In February 1984, *Newsweek* ran a story titled "The Celebrity Stockbrokers," which estimated that the number of Wall Street traders had "swelled to about seventy thousand—a 45 percent leap during the last three years." In Merrill Lynch's DC office, brokers earned an average of $150,000 in annual commissions, and "even a rookie broker can earn more than half that amount in his first year." Many successful brokers sidelined into the self-help guru market, raking in fees from lunchtime seminars for newbies needing stock tips, while the brokerage houses quietly overlooked potential ethical improprieties for the "blatant publicity grabbers" whose commissions could bring in up to $4 million a year.

Wall Street's surge played into the New York real estate boom of the mid-eighties. Left to its own devices for most of the sixties and seventies by city officials, Lower Manhattan became a haven for artists, who could rent large lofts cheaply, even if it meant going without water or electricity on weekends and dodging criminals on the streets. That began to change once art collecting—what veteran collector Eugene Schwartz called "the only socially commendable form of greed"—became the eighties nouveaux riches' favorite new pastime.

In July 1984, *Rolling Stone* began serializing a new novel by Tom Wolfe. In *The Bonfire of the Vanities*, Wolfe made Sherman McCoy, his hapless antihero—or, really, nonhero—a stockbroker. "A friend of mine set up a meeting with me with four young Wall Street guys, and this one lunch really opened my eyes to what was going on [down] on Wall Street. It was a real boom time," Wolfe said. (After biweekly installments in *Rolling Stone*, Wolfe rewrote the book and published it in 1987.)

That real estate boom created a raft of new problems. Much of the Lower East Side was purged of its drug trade after Mayor Ed Koch launched Operation Pressure Point in 1983 (the heroin and cocaine dealers and their clients mostly went across the river to Brooklyn). Many of the people beginning to gentrify the area were Sherman McCoy prototypes. The neurotic workaholic achievers Byrne had long sung about were now a sociological phenomenon.

But the area's bad habits lingered. "In the early eighties," Tom Feiling wrote in his book *Cocaine Nation*, "Wall Street executives, most of whom had no history of drug or psychiatric problems, started to show up at drug treatment clinics asking for help in overcoming their cocaine habits, only to be turned away on the grounds that cocaine wasn't addictive."

CHRIS FRANTZ AND TINA WEYMOUTH BOTH CAME FROM MILITARY FAMI-lies and met at the Rhode Island School of Design (RISD) in 1971. (Each would earn a Bachelor of Fine Arts in painting.) Weymouth was canny and voluble; she'd spent time in France as well as the United States. "It makes a big difference in what you know you can do in life if experience has taught you that you can live anywhere," she said. Frantz, who'd played drums since he was ten, was laid-back and genial. Theirs was a classic personality yin-yang. They married in 1977 and remain so.

At age three, Byrne had emigrated to the United States from Scotland, settling in Baltimore. Near-pathologically shy well into Talking Heads' career, Byrne found being onstage liberating: "I decided that making my art in public . . . was a way of reaching out and communicating when ordinary chitchat was not comfortable for me." He spent some time busking in Berkeley, California, before heading to RISD.

He dropped out after a year, but while there he embarked on a number of performance-art pieces, such as the one where he shaved onstage, sans mirror or shaving cream, rampantly bloodletting. "David would do anything to get attention," Weymouth remembered. "He'd do anything on a dare. He'd go to a party wearing a red taffeta dress."

Byrne and Frantz started their first garage rock band, the Artistics, in late 1973. The outgoing drummer recruited the other members; he also suggested the group try Al Green's "Love and Happiness" as well as the usual Lou Reed songs and "96 Tears." The band also regularly went disco dancing in Providence: "Somehow, to us, this club music didn't seem antithetical to the rock we were playing and listening to," Byrne recalled. "Dancing was fun, too."

David would arrive in New York first, sleeping on the floor of fellow artist Jamie Dalglish's Bond Street loft. Chris and Tina, staying at her brother's place in Long Island City, soon joined them at CBGB to see the new bands. "We started Talking Heads because we thought we'd never be happy in life until we gave rock a shot, a serious try," Frantz said.

Tina joined them, she later admitted, "only to please Chris. I figured I would leave as soon as they found a real bass player." They opened for the Ramones in June 1975. Immediately afterward, Johnny Thunders of the New York Dolls and Heartbreakers, approached the band, pointed to Tina and her bass, and asked, "Are you guys a feminist band?" In August, the *Village Voice* put them on the cover.

Byrne would call Talking Heads' early gigs "less a band than an outline for a band. . . . It was a performance defined by negatives." They called attention to their distance from rock norms, from the stark white lights on their stark white self-presentation to having a woman onstage playing an instrument—still shockingly rare in 1975—and their early bio's assertion that "The image we present along with our songs is what we are really like."

Shortly after the band signed to Sire in 1977, they hired Jerry Harrison, who'd been in the Modern Lovers. The new guy was impressed with his bandmates' professionalism, a rarity in rock. "I always felt that the Modern Lovers' problems were half 'Who's going to do the dishes?' and stuff," Harrison said. "One thing about this band, everyone was more likely to do the dishes."

Brian Eno, who produced Talking Heads' three 1978 to 1980 albums (Tony Bongiovi did their debut, *Talking Heads: 77*), told NPR, "The first time I ever met Talking Heads, I played them a record by Fela Kuti. I thought that was just the most exciting music going on at the time. . . . I said to the band that this was what I thought the future of music was, actually."

That fascination bore fruit on *Remain in Light* (1980). The album was an explosion: four chattering instruments crisscrossing unto climax were now suddenly sextupled. "We built up twenty-four tracks of knotty interwoven parts," Byrne wrote, "and by switching groups of them on and off, we could create sections that might work in place of conventional verses and choruses." Byrne's pinched WASP persona had suddenly reversed course. The cynic who yawned, "I wouldn't live there if you paid me to," on "The Big Country" (from *More Songs About Buildings and Food*, 1978) was now pushing ever outward.

Byrne deliberately opened his language on *Remain*. These lyrics were newly communal without falling into good-time hippie cliché. He followed the chorus exhalation of "All I want is to breathe," in "Born Under Punches," with "Won't you breathe with me?"—from the harried straight arrow to the pan-universalist seeing endless splendor in the ever-deepening urban panorama. "The world don't lie / She's gonna open our eyes up" goes the refrain of the exhilarating "The Great Curve." And on the single "Once in a Lifetime," he contrasted a portrait of yuppie anomie ("This is not my beautiful house. . . . This is not my beautiful wife!") with the all-embracing "Time isn't holding us / Time isn't after us."

When Eno and the Heads recorded *Remain in Light* at Compass Point Studios in the Bahamas, they went in empty-handed, jamming out riffs, pinpointing parts, building up the whole. But on the LP's first pressing, Byrne and Eno were listed as the writers of the album all five had put serious creative work into. (Eno wrote the chorus melody for "Once in a Lifetime.") "We raised a stink about it and David took the blame," Weymouth said. "About two years later I found out Eno pushed him to do it."

The press release raised even more eyebrows. In it, Byrne and Eno included a *bibliography*, unheard of for a rock record in 1980, full of books like John Miller Chernoff's ethnographic landmark *African Rhythm and African Sensibility*. "I wanted to have more interesting interviews," Byrne said. "It was my way of saying, 'These are the things I want to talk about.'" Weymouth was incensed: "I didn't read those books!"

Remain in Light was nevertheless a breakthrough, particularly when the band presented it in concert—the lineup expanded to ten pieces. Harrison had done most of the recruiting and got the legendary funk keyboardist Bernie Worrell, late of Parliament-Funkadelic, and bassist Busta Jones, who wound up dominating the low end for the band's 1980–1981 tours. "When Busta was in the group it was a lot of fun, but it was also like two kings in one palace," Weymouth said. "It just didn't work out that well."

The band took 1981 off from working together. Byrne scored a Twyla Tharp dance piece, Harrison made a solo LP, but the married rhythm section went out to Compass Point Studio in the Bahamas and recorded a loose, straight funk album with a handful of helpmates, including Tina's three sisters singing harmony. "Tom Tom Club was intended solely to support me and Chris—to put food on the table," Weymouth said. "We had no money, and we decided to work up our own songs instead of accepting the session work we were being offered."

The smallest-budgeted, most efficiently done, and, quite on purpose, least cerebral of the Heads' solo works of 1981, *Tom Tom Club* was by far the most successful, thanks to the blipping synth riff and elastic bottom of "Genius of Love." It became a hit twelve-inch single—after Sire had to be strong-armed into releasing "Wordy Rappinghood," *Tom Tom Club*'s first single, in that format—and subsequently one of the most widely utilized riffs in hip-hop. Chris and Tina even made their *own* rap version, "Yella!!," credited to Mr. Yellow.

The fifth Heads album began on even ground. "We never said 'the band's breaking up' to each other," Weymouth said. "The problem went away because Eno went away." The multilayered grooves from *Remain in Light*, however, remained—this time looser and deliberately more playful than ever. Byrne had sung nonsense syllables to get his melodies down: hence deliberately silly song titles like "Making Flippy Floppy" and "Girlfriend Is Better." *Speaking in Tongues* was Talking Heads for normal people. Its classic isn't one of the dance numbers but the lilting finale, "This Must Be the Place (Naïve Melody)," a (gasp!) love song written both obliquely and with real feeling.

Still, Byrne admitted that one of the reasons the Heads kept moving funk-ward was in the hope of getting on R&B radio, "because white radio doesn't play us anymore, they stopped a couple years ago." Byrne even played guitar on a gospel-funk cover of *Speaking*'s "Slippery People" by the Staple Singers—produced by Gary Goetzman. "It's nothing but a gospel song talking about church people," Roebuck "Pops" Staples told *Cash Box*.

THE OVERSIZED SUIT BYRNE WORE AT THE CLIMAX OF THE SHOWS ON THE *Speaking in Tongues* tour had come about after Talking Heads had toured the Far East. In Japan, Byrne attended numerous types of traditional theater and was struck by the "highly stylized" costuming and performance style of Kabuki, Noh, and Bunraku. Over dinner in Tokyo, designer Jurgen Lehl told Byrne that "everything on stage needs to be bigger." Byrne drew a Noh-style oversized business suit on a napkin: "This wasn't exactly what he meant; he meant gesture, expression, voice. But I applied it to clothing as well."

Equally inspired by the way Balinese gamelan orchestra performances made "no attempt to formally separate the ritual and the show from the audience," Byrne "decided to make the show completely transparent," he wrote.

The *Speaking in Tongues* shows enacted a dramatization of the band's evolution. Byrne walked onto a bare stage and performed "Psycho Killer" with an acoustic guitar and a boom box—a giant radio the size of a briefcase, playing a cassette of a drum machine beat. Then Weymouth joined for the second number, "Heaven," while Lynn Mabry sang harmony offstage. Behind them the drum risers came together, with Frantz bounding out for a brisk run through "Thank You for Sending Me an Angel." Harrison's rig was readied for him as he joined on second guitar for "Found a Job." All the gear was on rolling platforms wheeled out from the wings. After that, the full ensemble in joyously high form.

Everyone was satisfied with what they were doing onstage. "It was a very transcendent experience, every night, that tour," Frantz said. At the end of August, Demme saw the *Speaking in Tongues* tour, at Hollywood's Greek Theater, and wanted to film it. Byrne already had the same idea: "I realized the show was 'cinematic' and that it sort of had a narrative arc. It might work on film, or so I believed."

The day before the shoot, backing singer Ednah Holt showed up with her long hair cut into a buzz. "I freaked out—hair whipping was a big part of the show—so I paid for her to get a weave immediately," Byrne said. "It took her many, many hours, poor girl, but it worked."

Demme had been directing a comedy-drama about wartime working women titled *Swing Shift*, which had turned into a power struggle with the star, Goldie Hawn, and the studio, Paramount. Demme was forced to do reshoots he didn't want to include during the days of the Heads shows—then go to the Pantages and supervise another seven-camera shoot.

The film's director of photography, Jordan Cronenweth, had also shot *Altered States* and *Blade Runner*, not to mention the Beatles in *A Hard Day's Night* and *Help!* "My main idea there was, you can't compete with a live concert, except in one way—you can get the audience up on stage," Demme said. "You can get the movie audience really intimate with the artists."

Stop Making Sense took its time from San Francisco International Film Festival (SFIFF) to wide release, opening early in New York and LA, with plans for a general release on October 15. But at the end of the summer, *Variety* reported that the general opening had been moved up to October 1, the better to chime with the September 10 issue of the soundtrack. The soundtrack never made the Top 40 but remained on the Billboard 200 for a solid two years, becoming the band's best seller. The big-suited Byrne would become a kind of yuppie icon. That fall, Rich Hall parodied him on *Saturday Night Live.* "It was a combination of feeling very strange and being flattered," Byrne said of the bit. "But it makes me think that I should probably stop doing that."

Stop Making Sense also, as he'd hoped, gave Byrne an entrée into filmmaking. By summer, he was slated to direct and act in his own movie, being cowritten by Pulitzer Prize–winning playwright Beth Henley (*Crimes of the Heart*). "The other Heads will also appear and sing in the pic, per Byrne, but they will not perform together as a band," *Variety* reported. The Robert Wilson collaboration was iced after financing got cut, but Byrne's intellectual stock was rising. Within a year, he was on the cover of *Current Biography* and profiled in the *New York Times Magazine* as part of a series called "The Creative Mind"—under the headline "David Byrne: Thinking Man's Rock Star."

SHORTLY AFTER *STOP MAKING SENSE* WAS FILMED, THE RECORD-BIZ TRADE magazine *Cash Box* ran a guide to the forthcoming year in music-related film. It would be the busiest in years. That spring, two titles stood out: Rob Reiner's heavy metal satire, *This Is Spinal Tap*, and *Repo Man*, "a story about a Southern California punker who becomes the sidekick of a car repossessor." Both were made cheaply: *Spinal Tap* for $2.2 million, *Repo Man* for $1.5 million—and the latter film's director, Alex Cox, would later claim, "Even making *Repo Man* for $1.5 million seemed like a waste of money to me."

This Is Spinal Tap had come from a quartet of comedy pros: director Reiner, best known as Meathead from the hit seventies sitcom *All in the Family*, Michael McKean (Lenny on *Laverne & Shirley*), Christopher Guest (*National Lampoon's Lemmings*), and Harry Shearer (*Saturday Night Live*). McKean (imperious blond lead singer David St. Hubbins), Guest (nitwit lead guitarist Nigel Tufnel), and

Shearer (mutton-chopped bassist Derek Smalls) were also musicians, and they wrote and performed all of Spinal Tap's music as well. The film savaged nearly every rock and roll style to emerge since the Beatles' ascension: folk rock, flower power, and of course heavy metal.

The movie, a trim ninety-three minutes, had been edited down from fifty hours of footage, though there was a strict historical breakdown of the characters' relationships to one another—the four had written out a seventeen-year band history to improvise from. "We tried to make it as accurate as possible, to keep it as close to the bone as we could," Reiner said.

One of *Spinal Tap*'s prime influences was "The Troggs Tapes," a spellbinding twelve-minute recording, made in 1970 and bootlegged for years, of interband bickering between the members of the group famous for "Wild Thing." ("It's a fucking number one! It is!" snarls singer Reg Presley as the group struggles through an unrehearsed number: "But it fucking well won't be unless we spend a little bit of fucking thought and imagination to make it fucking number one!") In January 1984, the British label DJM (for Dick James Music—the Beatles' publisher) issued an EP with "The Troggs Tapes" on the B side of three of the group's hits, including "Wild Thing." "Unprintable! Uncensored! Unleashed! Outlawed for over ten years" trumpeted an ad in *Melody Maker*.

Anyway, what happened in *Spinal Tap*—which *Melody Maker* described as "a kind of Greatest Hits of Rock Idiocy"—wasn't *that* crazy compared to what routinely happened in rock and roll. The film's drummer number two, Eric "Stumpy Joe" Childs, may have died after choking on someone else's vomit, Reiner told *Musician*, "but how weird is this Dennis Wilson incident? How weird is the death of a guy in Marina del Rey, drowning while he's scrounging around for lawn chairs at the bottom of an empty ship? You can't make that up." Metal musicians loved it: Scorpions' Rudolf Schenker called it "delightful," though Kiss's Paul Stanley averred: "It's not anywhere near as funny as the real thing."

Initially, the movie's luck was no better than the band's. "We were chased out of theaters—not because people weren't coming to see the movie, but because we were distributed by a company that was in the process of going bankrupt," Shearer said. "The company we were being distributed by said, 'We'll be in Chapter 11 by Christmas.'"

Home video gave *Spinal Tap* a durable afterlife, and did the same with *Repo Man*. The latter's director, Alex Cox, was an Englishman who'd gone to UCLA's film school on a Fulbright Scholarship; he first encountered punk in 1978 Los Angeles. (Tito Larriva and Steve Hufsteter of the Plugz, one of the scene's key bands, composed *Repo Man*'s score.) "Just by chance, I knew this fellow who was a car repossessor," Cox said. "It has sort of an emblematic quality, doesn't it? A symbolic quality about what the repo man does: He's the criminal of capitalism."

Starring Emilio Estevez—son of the actor Martin Sheen—and the eccentric character actor Harry Dean Stanton as apprentice and veteran repo men, respectively, *Repo Man* was pulp fiction supreme, but the movie did little at the box office—only after it moved to cable and video, and its soundtrack album sold fifty thousand copies on its own, was the studio forced to give it a wider release.

It helped that the *Repo Man* soundtrack functioned as a user's guide to LA punk and hardcore: Black Flag, Suicidal Tendencies, and Fear all appeared with definitive tracks. It was released on MCA, meaning you could actually find it in any shop—something that could not be said for those bands' own albums, all on independent labels. But the film and soundtrack's cultural cachet didn't necessarily help at the box office: though the movie, as Cox put it, has been "endlessly imitated," it took until 1999 for *Repo Man* to break even.

A NUMBER ONE SINGLE IS A GOOD PLACE TO ADVERTISE YOUR FORTHCOM-ing film. Shortly before the opening of *Saturday Night Fever* in 1977, "Staying Alive" took off like a shot. The Bee Gees had a number one single and album, with the soundtrack, before the movie had even opened—and their ballad from the film, "How Deep Is Your Love," had been a number one earlier than that. This would be the formula for the mega-soundtracks to come, starting with *Flashdance* (1983), a (cough) drama about an exotic dancer who works days as a welder that teased the film with Irene Cara's title song in a deliberately similar manner.

The result was a sensation—by the end of 1983, *Flashdance* had grossed $100 million at the box office, and the soundtrack sold five million before the year was through, plus a pair of number one singles. Even Bill Oakes, the head of RSO Films, which produced the movie, was forced to admit, "If you continue to go further in the direction of *Flashdance*, you end up with a film with no characters and hardly any dialogue." Yet it was clearly what the MTV-bred audience went for. "When the teen market finds a music film it likes," noted the *Washington Post*, "the soundtrack album sells like white wine at a singles bar."

A *Flashdance*-style reverse-engineered mega-soundtrack was the course Paramount took with *Footloose*—instead of a girl struggling in the big city, a boy doing the same in the sticks, via the same method, dancing. Dean Pitchford, who'd been lyricist for both *Flashdance* and *Fame* (Irene Cara's first major title-song hit), wrote *Footloose*'s script and cowrote its songs. It was, he said, "a rock video in reverse. The idea was to mold the music to fit the visual images."

By the time *Footloose* opened in February of 1984, Columbia had already issued three singles, including Kenny Loggins's obnoxiously cheery number one title tune. (Loggins was Pitchford's first choice: "It felt to me he was the voice of the country, America," he said.) "The first video, consisting of nothing but film footage, got 'Footloose' in heavy MTV rotation so quickly that the movie's star, Kevin Bacon, was mobbed by teenage girls at *sneak previews*," Marianne Meyer wrote.

She added: "The film opened simultaneously in 1,340 theatres nationwide— a tactic employed when a studio wants to generate quick opening-weekend sales before the reviews take hold. (*Footloose* made back its $8 million budget the first weekend.)" Prior to this point in American film, a wide opening was considered a desperate measure, rather than the only way to do business at that level.

The movie was balderdash—Kevin Bacon was a rebellious city kid stuck in the sticks with a crush on the daughter of the preacher (John Lithgow) who, yes, bans the town from dancing. *Footloose* grossed over $80 million at the box office, while the soundtrack knocked *Thriller* off the top for ten weeks and generated a second number one, Deniece Williams's "Let's Hear It for the Boy." Shalamar's "Dancing in the Sheets" was also a hit, reaching number seventeen on the pop chart—and peaking at eighteen R&B.

Both Williams and Shalamar had spent years before *Footloose* headlining for black audiences without crossing over to pop. Shalamar had been a studio moniker before it was a group, first appearing on LPs of discofied Motown covers. But under the tutelage of producer Leon Sylvers, the eldest of the post-Jacksons R&B family group the Sylvers, the Shalamar lineup solidified into the trio of *Soul Train* dancers Jodi Watley and Jeffrey Daniels and the Akron-bred lead singer Howard Hewett, and they began spinning out R&B hits.

Make that Black hits. "Black" was the new name of *Billboard*'s R&B chart— which had also gone under "Soul" and, in the forties, the "Harlem Hit Parade." The renaming was prompted by the magazine's columnist Nelson George as an affirmation (e.g., "Black Is Beautiful"); over time it's often been read differently, as a mere update to a far older biz term, "race records" (also initially an affirmation, as in "race man"—someone working for the good of the race). Either way, it was an audacious flag to plant during this moment of high crossover.

Like much post-disco R&B, Shalamar's records were modern and clean; as George put it, they "synthesize the rock-funk of Prince, Michael Jackson, and Thomas Dolby into a crossover style." But it took a wholesale appropriation of new wave sound of the late-1983 single "Dead Giveaway" to break pop.

Meanwhile, the trio was fracturing. Shalamar had become unexpectedly large in the UK on the heels of 1982's *Friends*, nudged along by Daniels's sudden new wave makeover, as George wrote: "Gone was his H-bomb Afro, replaced by straightened hair on his right side and a partially shaved scalp on the left." But the shift left a lot of their original fans feeling alienated. "We got flak from some people in the black community about it," Hewett said, adding: "Everything must change."

Daniels had decided to stay put in London after filming the video for "Dead Giveaway" there, and by the end of 1983, both he and Watley officially left the group. But in spring 1984, two new Shalamar tracks appeared on soundtracks—"Dancing in the Sheets" and "Deadline USA," the latter on *DC Cab*, a flop comedy starring *The A-Team*'s ultra-macho Mr. T—both recorded by Hewett, who retained rights to the name and who soon recruited a new lineup that included guitarist Micki Free, who'd played lead on "Dancing in the Sheets."

That November, as Shalamar prepared to release its rock-heavy new album, *Heartbreak*, Free said, "I think black audiences are ready for what we're doing." Britain was, anyway—the single "Amnesia" was added to the playlist for Capital Radio's *Heavy Metal Hour*.

The producer of "Amnesia" was George Duke, a jazz-funk keyboardist who'd worked with Frank Zappa and had become a go-to R&B hit-maker as the eighties dawned. Duke also produced the other big crossover number on the *Footloose* soundtrack, Williams's bouncy "Let's Hear It for the Boy." *Sepia* had labeled her "R&B's reigning female vocalist" in 1980, but Niecy wasn't a dance floor diva; her top ten pop hits prior to *Footloose* had been schmaltz—"Too Much, Too Little, Too Late," a duet with Johnny Mathis, and her fluttering remake of the Royalettes' "It's Gonna Take a Miracle." Williams was already in her mid-thirties by the time *Footloose* came along.

She'd first worked with Duke in 1983. When Pitchford and Tom Snow, the songwriters, brought them the winsome trifle they'd earmarked for her,

Duke said, "I sort of looked at Niecy and said 'I'm not so sure about this one.' But she loved it, and really wanted to do it. I said 'What *am* I going to do with this song?'" Eventually, he recruited Latin percussionist Paulinho da Costa to emphasize the quirks in the track's groove.

Raised Pentecostal in Michael Jackson's hometown of Gary, Indiana, Williams actually saw herself in the film—specifically, in the female lead, the preacher's rebellious daughter: "In the sort of church I attended girls couldn't wear make-up or short dresses or trousers. You couldn't go to films or dances even. As I was one of their biggest gospel singers, they felt it was my destiny in life to sing gospel music so a lot of people were very upset with me when I wanted to sing R&B and pop. They didn't appreciate it at all."

THE NUMBER ONE SONG IN AMERICA THE WEEK *STOP MAKING SENSE* DE-buted also came from a soundtrack. As did Yes, drummer-singer Phil Collins had come out of UK prog rock to conquer the post-MTV charts; his band Genesis, formed in 1967, was still a going concern. Collins's solo "Against All Odds (Take a Look at Me Now)" wasn't even from a hit movie—the song hasn't just lasted longer in the public imagination than the Jeff Bridges–Rachel Ward–James Woods love triangle in *Against All Odds* but also eclipsed the movie from the word *go*.

Against All Odds was the work of director Taylor Hackford, whose *An Officer and a Gentleman* had been an Oscar-winning hit in 1982. "He has a great awareness of the record business," a Columbia exec exulted. "It's almost impossible to put together a soundtrack like *Against All Odds* if you have a director who has no understanding or consciousness of the record industry." (Three years later, Hackford would direct the classic documentary *Chuck Berry—Hail! Hail! Rock and Roll*.)

Collins had left the song off his solo debut, *Face Value* (1981), he said, "because I had one too many ballads, and that was my least favorite. . . . I don't know what would have happened to it if Taylor Hackford hadn't got in touch." Crunched for time, Collins enlisted Arif Mardin to produce it for him: "We did it on two days off, one in New York and one in L.A. To me, it was such a different way of working that I never took it seriously." Hackford became salty that Collins kept singing "against the odds" instead of "all" ("It just tripped off the tongue easier," Collins later said), prompting him to throw in a titular "all" at the song's climax for appearance's sake.

The video, festooned with movie footage, amounted to a trailer interspersed with a medium shot of Collins lip-syncing and recorded on a studio set built to "match the scenes from the film," a Columbia VP said. But it did nothing to help the movie itself, which was largely out of theaters by the time the song reached number one. A *Variety* report on the film added this crucial parenthetical: "(Collins does not appear in *Against All Odds*.)"

ISLAND RECORDS,
LONDON
May 8, 1984

DAVE ROBINSON HAD HIS WORK CUT OUT FOR HIM WHEN HE JOINED IS-
land Records. For one thing, Island had nothing in the bank. Robinson had
founded the punk and new wave label Stiff Records in 1976 and had run it with
brisk efficiency. Chris Blackwell, on the other hand, was as permanently spliffed
out as many of the hippie rockers and ganja-soaked reggae stars whose music
he issued.

Island had broken reggae in America, thanks to the soundtrack of 1972's
The Harder They Come, and the label had made a star out of Bob Marley, who'd
initially signed with the wildly talented trio the Wailers, alongside Bunny Liv-
ingstone (later Bunny Wailer) and Peter Tosh. The latter pair went on to successful solo careers after their mid-seventies split, both recording, initially at
least, for Island.

The Wailers then became the name of Marley's backing band—until, in
the fall of 1980, Marley was diagnosed with melanoma and given three weeks
to live. He made it eight months, but the cancer spread to his lungs; he died on
May 11, 1981, at only thirty-six years old.

Robinson was shocked to find that Marley had never issued a million-
selling LP. The right compilation, he figured, would mint badly needed money
for Island. Over summer 1983, Robinson had taken a bunch of Marley cassettes

with him on holiday: "I started figuring out what sort of a compilation would make sense," he said. "My vision of Bob from a marketing point of view was to sell him to the white world."

Robinson's Marley collection, then, would "stay out of the more political songs. The fact is that he was a great pop songwriter, and he had a way of putting deep meaning into very innocent terms and very simple terms. . . . I thought there would be a huge market for it."

Legend was launched in Britain with a campaign of TV ads, and the results were immediate. Two weeks after its May 19 release it was on top of the UK album chart, staying there an amazing fourteen weeks. America waited until early August to issue it, but soon enough, *Legend* became a perennial best seller, the *Kind of Blue* of reggae—the one album of its type that everyone knows and owns.

PERENNIAL OR NOT, *LEGEND* GENERATED A NEAR-INSTANT PROFIT. REISSUES and compilation LPs of back catalog, Joe Polidor, head of marketing for Polygram in Nashville, told *Billboard*, "are profitable even though the margin is tight. The cost comes primarily from remastering, recoupling cuts, and maybe new artwork. These packages have unlimited shelf life once they're released."

It took the 1979 crash for easy reissue profits to be taken seriously, as a Chrysalis marketer said, "When things were steamrolling along and people were having a lot of hits, there wasn't much time spent thinking, 'How can we eke more dollars out of old material?'" MCA was tanking nearly everywhere else in 1982, but that year it earned nearly $20 million in reissue and catalog sales.

Still, the majors' primary interest was in "seeing what's in their own catalog and just selling that," Rhino Records cofounder Richard Foos said in the summer of 1984. "It leaves a gap for someone to come in and seriously preserve the history of rock and roll."

West Germany and the UK had been doing it for years. In the mid-seventies, Richard Weize founded Bear Family Records in 1975, issuing exhaustive, deeply annotated multi-LP box-set career overviews of blues, country, and early rock and roll. The year 1984 saw the most ambitious Bear Family package to date: honky-tonk paragon Lefty Frizzell's fourteen-LP *His Life—His Music*, covering his entire career, from 1950 to 1974 (Frizzell died in 1975).

Two London labels were equally important. Charly had begun in 1974 with a heavy emphasis on Sun Records' fifties rockabilly catalog. In 1984, Charly issued the nine-LP *Sun Records: The Blues Years, 1950–1956*. It didn't sell a lot of copies—around ten thousand per title—but, as its managing director, Joop Visser, said, "I don't think the majors, with their hit orientation, are geared for that patience. But what we do *is* a source of income for them, and they're recognizing it more and more."

In the late seventies, Ace Records established itself as the UK's other model gatekeeper of older rock and soul. In 1984, Ace licensed the holdings of two crucial early rock and roll labels: Laurie Records, which included the Dion and the Belmonts catalog, and Specialty Records, home of Little Richard. For many old-guard rock and roll businessmen, their holdings were just old and in the way. Laurie's tape librarian told Ace cofounder Roger Armstrong of the masters, "I've been tripping over them for the last 20 years."

As with Ace Records, the American label Rhino Records spun off from a shop—near the UCLA campus in Westwood, founded by Foos in 1973. The store's remit was the same kind of studied irreverence that was fueling the era's comedy boom; the shop's promos included Hassle the Salesmen Day, Jewish Day (featuring free corned-beef sandwiches and yarmulkes), and, on Thanksgiving, a forty-cents-a-pound sale of their "turkey" albums.

The earliest titles on the Rhino label were novelties, but soon it was diving into the vaults, with an air of wit, such as the green vinyl turtle-shaped EP by the Turtles and a compilation titled *The World's Worst Records*, packaged with a vomit bag.

In May 1984, *Rolling Stone* dubbed Rhino "probably the most intelligent re-packager of the music of the fifties and sixties in the world, and certainly the most off-the-wall label in the business." By then it'd put out then-definitive surf, girl group, bubblegum, and garage rock collections, as well as titles by Love and the Bobby Fuller Four; many of the compilations were cross-licensed from multiple labels, something most reissuers didn't bother trying.

Rhino also distributed the San Francisco R&B reissue label Solid Smoke, which released twenty titles in 1984. (The success of the Motown-heavy soundtrack for the 1983 film *The Big Chill* undoubtedly contributed to the demand.) Many were licensed from the catalogs of independent R&B labels such as Chicago's Vee-Jay Records (Gene Chandler, the Spaniels, the El Dorados) and Detroit producer Ollie McLaughlin (a pair of *Detroit Gold* collections). Even for knowledgeable listeners, much of it was genuinely new music.

The most important Solid Smoke titles came from James Brown. In spring 1984, Solid Smoke issued parts one and two of *The Federal Years*, separately sold overviews of Brown's earliest recordings. These weren't hits, but they were crucial to understanding the evolution of a great artist. And almost none of them had been in print since they were first released.

This was true for many of this era's reissues. "For the first time in decades, you can obtain the original 'I Put a Spell on You' by Screamin' Jay Hawkins or Bob Wills' 'Cotton Eyed Joe' without paying collectors' prices," *Rolling Stone* reported in 1983. To have this music available in convenient LP form, rather than scattered across seven-inches of variable rarity, was revelatory.

Brown, in particular, was being served well by both an indie label and the major he'd once been signed to. In 1984, Polydor released two volumes of *The James Brown Story*, volumes one (*Ain't That a Groove: 1966–1969*) and two (*Doing It to Death: 1970–1973*). Brown's impact on the R&B, funk, and rap of the mid-eighties was already manifest; hearing his work all together like this made it plain even to longtime (white) fans just how important it was. Critic Robert Christgau noted in the *Village Voice* that December that this slew of reissues was the place "to start convincing yourself that JB belongs in the pantheon with Elvis and the Beatles"— at a time when, in rock critic circles, this was not yet a foregone conclusion.

THE ROCK BIZ'S LONG-STANDING DIRECTIVE TO *SELL TO TEENAGERS*, SEEN AS the music's natural constituency, was beginning to change shape. That October, RCA Records intended to rebrand Elvis Presley through a "teen-directed compilation" called *Rocker*. But according to RCA's research, Elvis's core audience was far older (mid-thirties to mid-fifties), more female (68 percent), "a country or adult contemporary radio listener, and a fan of *Dallas* and the *National Enquirer*," *Variety* reported.

More and more, Presley's listeners were more apt to buy an expensive box set than a new hit single. In September, RCA issued *Elvis—A Golden Celebration*, a six-LP overview of what critic Dave Marsh termed "the loose booty from an amazing career: the complete 1956 TV appearances, spread over four sides; a side of Sun session outtakes; a revelatory live performance at the 1956 Mississippi-Alabama Fair and Dairy Show; material from his 1968 'comeback' TV special." Marsh called it "a triumph from start to finish."

And *Elvis—A Golden Celebration* sold, peaking at number eighty in *Billboard* the following February. Elvis was big business. His Memphis mansion

Graceland, which had opened to the public as a museum in 1982, was attracting half a million visitors annually, generating about $4.5 million a year in revenue.

Much of *A Golden Celebration* had been discovered when RCA's A&R woman Joan Deary went to Graceland while it was closed for business and discovered some twenty-nine tape reels, as well as Elvis's personal collection of record lacquers and test pressings. Everything went into a brand-new suitcase Deary wouldn't let out of her sight; she flew back to Los Angeles with it as her carry-on. The majors were learning that the musical past had significant, even priceless, value.

THE SUCCESS OF BOB MARLEY'S *LEGEND* WAS A MIXED TRIUMPH FOR JA-maican music as a whole. In the UK and especially in the United States, reggae had always occupied a rather small niche even at the height of Marley's living success. For much of that audience, Marley *was* reggae—without him, there was no need to bother.

Rather than a thriving, if small, part of a typical major-label roster, reggae artists in America began to be handled by smaller, specialist labels, many with roots in folk (Rounder, Shanachie) or blues (Nighthawk Records). "My contact with white and black audiences indicates that in fact it is roots reggae's unique character and sound that appeals to an audience, not that it may be similar to something they already know," Nighthawk head Bob Schoenfeld told *Cash Box*.

There were, however, plenty of successful reggae *songs* in the late seventies and early eighties by non-Jamaican artists: the Police's "Roxanne," Men at Work's "Down Under," Blondie's cover of the Paragons' "The Tide Is High," Stevie Wonder's "Master Blaster (Jammin')," Culture Club's "Do You Really Want to Hurt Me," Musical Youth's "Pass the Dutchie" (British teen siblings transposing the subject of the Mighty Diamonds' "Pass the Cutchie" from weed to cookware).

"The music is getting out," a former Island Records VP said of reggae. "Black artists just aren't getting the credit."

In Jamaica, roots reggae was old hat by the time of Marley's death. There, the sound of the eighties was dancehall, which was far heavier on synthesizers and *slack* (dirty) lyrics, particularly from deejays (the talker on the mike as opposed to the person playing the records, who's the *selector*).

The name had long been in use for the outdoor, record-driven parties that had been part of Jamaica's urban scene for decades, but the term came to wider use in 1983, when promoter Michael Thompson threw a rammed jam called Dancehall '83 at a drive-in cinema. The headliners included the ribald likes of Charlie Chaplin, General Trees, and dancehall's breakout star, the twenty-three-year-old albino deejay Yellowman (Winston Foster). "The name 'dancehall' started popping up on several shows and dance posters," wrote reggae historians Kevin O'Brien Chang and Wayne Chen. "Because deejay songs virtually ruled the dancehalls, the music played there became known as 'dancehall.' Soon *dancehall* no longer meant a place where dances were held, but rather the dominant music form of the day, be it deejays or singers on a popular rhythm."

Less rock-like and far less overtly political than roots reggae, dancehall held less sway for foreign (particularly white) audiences than in Kingston. Yellowman's full-on embrace of slackness helped him rule 1984 with two of the year's biggest Jamaican records, "Belly Move" and "Zungguzungguguzungguzeng." Those suggestive tracks were deeply offensive to reggae fans hungry for the next Bob Marley.

Not that he cared. Like many a young star feeling his oats, Yellowman took his newfound sex appeal in a kind of dumbfounded stride. "I found out the women like it very much when you talk about dem, y'know?" he told a *Creem* reporter at a New York club, while sitting between a pair of female fans.

LOOKING FOR THE "NEXT BOB MARLEY" BECAME AS MUCH A RECORD-BIZ pastime as finding new Bob Dylans had once been. Any nonwhite, non-US/UK singer-songwriter with some political bent could be assured of being handed the mantle, at least for a while.

The Panamanian salsa singer-songwriter Rubén Blades did not call himself a political singer. "A political singer sings to an ideology," he explained in 1984. "I write city songs about people whose lives are affected by political circumstances."

Born in Panama City in 1948, Blades was seduced by rock and roll in 1956 and subsequently swept up by Beatlemania. The rioting in the Canal Zone on January 9, 1964, that left twenty-one Panamanians dead and nearly five hundred wounded over Canal Zone Americans refusing to fly the Panamanian flag (the law was for both flags to be flown) shook up many of the fifteen-year-old Blades's generation; for his part, he fervently reembraced Latin music, refusing to sing in English.

It took years for Blades to be signed as a leader. "You have to remember, I was writing at the time when there were about seventeen Latin American dictatorships," he said. "So some of these executives would look at the lyrics and start saying, 'This guy is obviously a leftist. Why is he writing about these things?'"

Moving to New York in 1969, Blades advanced from Fania Records' mailroom to singing in the band of one of the label's prime movers, Ray Barretto. In 1977, Blades switched to Willie Colón's band—daunting, because he was replacing the beloved Héctor Lavoe. But Blades's social realism was a complete turnaround that yielded three albums that sold big, in particular *Siembra*, which, Dave Marsh wrote, "sold somewhere between three hundred thousand and one million copies (Blades and Fania are suing each other over royalty payments) in a market where forty thousand units is a hit."

In 1984, Blades jumped to Elektra, a Warner Bros. subsidiary. "A lot of the major labels are looking at salsa now," Blades's old partner Willie Colón said. "The numbers look interesting to them. . . . It's been permeating jingles. All of the rock bands have congas and Latin percussion. It's been seeping in slowly, but the American non-Spanish-speaking public is ready."

Elektra didn't bank the house on Blades's debut for it, *Buscando America*: the album initially shipped a mere ten thousand copies. Festooning it with, you guessed it, synthesizers, Blades was reaching out to the Anglo audience—the "rock-oriented record buyer for whom his salsa-derived pop is a logical choice after the Clash, Bob Marley, or the Police," as *Billboard* put it—an audience that wouldn't fully materialize for years, until the nineties' rise of *rock en español*.

Blades had an astoundingly busy 1984: that fall, he entered Harvard Law School, receiving his master's the following June, with a thesis on law and justice through history. He was already talking about eventually returning to Panama to run for, yep, president. "I needed the degree," he explained, "to reestablish my credentials as a professional." (He eventually ran in 1994, losing to Ernesto Pérez Balladares.)

If that weren't enough, Blades also spent part of 1984 making his first movie. *Crossover Dreams*, directed by Leon Ichaso, would premiere at the Museum of Modern Art in March of 1985, as part of the New Directors/New Films Festival, and it opened wide that August. Blades complained about the movie scripts he'd been receiving: "In half, they want me to play a Colombian coke dealer. In the other half, they want me to play a Cuban coke dealer. . . . Doesn't anybody want me to play a lawyer?"

CHRIS BLACKWELL FOUND HIS NEXT BOB MARLEY IN AFRICA. ISLAND HAD first dipped its toe into African pop in October 1981, with the release of *Sound d'Afrique*, a compilation of tracks from the stable of International Salsa Musique, featuring artists from West and Central Africa, followed a year later by *Sound d'Afrique II: Soukous*. And in 1982, Blackwell announced Island's first African signing: King Sunny Adé and His African Beats, a large Nigerian juju unit with a supple, mellifluous, stimulating groove.

This move puzzled many: beyond Nigeria, few had heard of Adé, a guitarist-singer-bandleader born into royalty in Ordo. Still, between 1982 and 1984, he made a trio of LPs—*Juju Music*, *Synchro System*, and *Aura*—for the Island subsidiary Mango that grafted ever more blatantly Western touches onto his bedrock Nigerian groove to inch it into the US/UK mainstream.

A French music journalist turned record producer, Martin Meissonnier had groomed Adé for stardom. Meissonnier was also managing another popular, and very different, Nigerian bandleader-singer, Fela Kuti, at the time when he was stuck in Lagos traffic and heard "incredible pedal steel guitar solos screaming out from a big sound system." Meissonnier said, "I went down to ask who was performing that music and I went to meet him right away."

By then, Adé had already recorded some four dozen LPs. Adding pedal steel to an already guitar-heavy ensemble took Adé's sound out of this world, just one of its many canny aural bridges between deep tradition and the present day. *Juju Music*, Adé's first album for Mango, was, as Meissonnier called it, "re-record[ings of] some of the greatest hits tunes of Sunny that could suit a world audience . . . recorded in two days only."

Issued to rapturous praise in the fall of 1982, *Juju Music* placed a surprising fourth in the annual *Village Voice* rock critics' poll. In February 1983, the eighteen-piece African Beats made its first US tour. Paul Rhodes Trautman, a New Yorker with a day job as an X-ray technician, was the promoter. In the early eighties he managed downtown New Yorker John Lurie's Lounge Lizards and trumpeter-composer Jon Hassell.

"The hip crowd was ready for it, because of what was going on in England with Adam Ant," Trautman says. Ant's musical hook was a rhythm derived from the Central African nation of Burundi. "Ethnic tones were creeping into postpunk," says Trautman. In addition to Ant and Talking Heads' *Remain in Light* was Malcolm McLaren, whose 1983 album *Duck Rock* had featured the British hit "Soweto," the first track many outside the country had heard of South African pop. But South Africa's racist apartheid regime had prevented a lot of people from hearing the Zulu jive that "Soweto" swiped wholesale—the UN Special Committee Against Apartheid had called for a cultural boycott in December 1980.

Though Adé had played in the United States in 1975, he hadn't done a full tour. "There was a desire for it to work," says Trautman. "It had the right amount of African elements there that people wanted. The market didn't know they wanted Sunny Adé, but if you knew where the market was, you knew that Sunny Adé was who they wanted."

Adé's US shows would last anywhere from ninety minutes to three hours—a pittance compared to the eight-hour performances the African Beats were used to playing in Adé's Ariya club. A *New York Times* rave by critic Robert Palmer helped the box office in other cities: "We pulled a lot of money out of UC Berkeley," says Trautman.

Still, on that tour, Trautman told *Billboard*, the African Beats played "for expenses." The LP's lack of radio play didn't help—Chicago and Boston were about the only cities that played *Juju Music*; Boston's mayor, Kevin White, made Adé an honorary citizen there the day of the African Beats' February 5 performance. Nevertheless, the album had managed to sell fifty thousand copies due to critical acclaim and word of mouth. "We think it's the coming thing, this kind of third world music," an Island VP said. "We're starting with a zero base, after all."

The follow-up, provisionally titled *Two Thousand Adé*, was sanely renamed *Synchro System*. There was more automation on this album than on any of Adé's to date. *Synchro System*, adjudged *Musician*, "fully integrates electronics into his ensemble, uniting organic African rhythms with electronic textures in order to make African music competitive with state-of-the-art synth/pop/funk dance music."

There were even more machines on the summer 1984 follow-up, *Aura*. Adé's deepest reach into the US market was through the burgeoning post–disco club market, where DJs worked them into increasingly beat-matched sets. In particular, Sunny's "365 Is My Number/The Message," from *Juju Music*, had become a standard at the Loft, the foundational New York disco, a private party hosted by David Mancuso, who'd been schooling the city's club DJs since 1970.

In July 1984, the South African saxophonist Hugh Masekela's "Don't Go Lose It Baby" peaked at number two on *Billboard*'s dance chart. Masekela's producer Stewart Levine had told him, "Hugh, let's make one they're going to dance to in New York City." Masekela even performed a good-natured rap.

Aura, too, took in hip-hop's influence, and the artist saw it not simply as an experiment but as a principled one. "Adé strives to compromise the format of his music without compromising the style," *DownBeat* wrote. "He says that he won't use horns because that's Afro-beat, not juju, and he won't use reggae rhythms because that's African reggae, not juju."

That summer, Adé and the Beats hit the United States again, this time co-billed with fellow Island-ers Black Uhuru, a roots reggae trio with a cult following. Trautman had been ousted in favor of FBI, Ian Copeland's Police-flush agency. "With all these people, at some point they'll say, 'We need a commercial agency,'" says Trautman. "Island had got a hold of him and tried to convert him into a pop star. What seemed natural became too staged—they were trying to turn him into more of an American, British rock type. There was an unnatural quality to it. It's like they put cement shoes on him. There's a spiritual aspect in Yoruba music and African music in general. You lose that. That's the quality that people are getting. They were no longer being transported."

At the Greek Theatre in LA, *Variety* noted that Adé's ensemble was "more reminiscent this time out of the Talking Heads and other such progressive rock types who've assimilated Third World musical and rhythmic influences into their contempo dance-rock sound." The journal wrinkled its nose at the "soul revue-type emcee, in full Nigerian robes, who whipped up the crowd pre-show and pre-encores in decidedly familiar ways." Sunny's co-headliners would do a little better in the short term. In January 1985, Black Uhuru would have a new LP in the stores—*Reggae Greats*, part of a new series of compilations on Mango, sixteen in total, four per month starting in October, that showcased Island Records' Jamaican catalog. It had worked once. This time, Blackwell took the credit in the trades.

THE 13TH ANNUAL INTERNATIONAL COUNTRY MUSIC FAN FAIR,
NASHVILLE
June 4-10, 1984

"WILLIE WAS NOT . . . IS NOT . . . AND WILL NOT BE SIGNING AUTOGRAPHS at the CBS booth."

You can't blame anyone for being confused. Just minutes earlier, the same voice boomed over the same PA system to the same teeming crowd that Willie Nelson was, in fact, sitting at the CBS Records booth with pen in hand, waiting to meet and greet his fans. There was no shortage of other stars at the Tennessee State Fairgrounds, but Willie was, without a doubt, the biggest country music star in America that year. In 1984, he released three studio albums, and by the time of his nonappearance at Nashville's International Country Music Fan Fair, he had already scored the year's top country hit, per *Billboard*: "To All the Girls I've Loved Before," the most unlikely duet of the eighties.

"To All the Girls" had actually been Willie's idea—he'd heard Julio Iglesias on the radio in London and his wife thought they'd sound good together. He agreed. "I phoned [manager] Mark Rothbaum," Nelson said, "and said, 'Try to find out who Julio Iglesias is and see if he wants to cut a record with me.' Mark found Julio in Los Angeles. Julio said, sure, he'd like to do a song with me. I didn't know Julio was selling more records at that time than anybody in the world." Of course not.

"To All the Girls" was released as a single the month of the Grammys and took off like a rocket, but the prime had been pumped the previous October, when Nelson, resplendent in long red braids, red bandanna, T-shirt, and jeans, premiered the song on the Country Music Association Awards with the tuxedoed Iglesias. Julio, meanwhile, had no English-language LP at the ready, which from the retailers' point of view was a massive fuckup: The single was outselling Willie's album (which didn't contain the song) two-to-one. Willie Nelson wasn't selling "To All the Girls"—Julio Iglesias was. *1100 Bel Air Place* finally appeared in August 1984.

Iglesias was as much a figure out of old-Hollywood-on-TV as Ronald Reagan—his theme song was "Begin the Beguine," a World War II–era standard. Iglesias appealed to a similar demographic as Ronald Reagan—older women who liked being crooned to by a smoothie in a suit.

There was nothing sudden about Iglesias's break into the American market. In March 1983, he'd played dates in New York and Los Angeles to great fanfare. At LA's Universal Amphitheatre, booking agent Larry Vallon had suggested booking Iglesias months before only to be asked in return, "Do you want to keep working here?" Vallon was unfazed: "Although he was not well known in the Anglo world, this town has a 40 percent Hispanic population and it was for damn sure that they knew who he was."

In 1984 all manner of crossover was on the mind of everyone in all manner of pop. Willie was a master of it and had been for some time. In the seventies he'd co-drafted the blueprint for country crossing over to the rock audience by playing by the latter's rules, just as he now did with pop.

Nelson began in the fifties as a songwriter and turned performer in the mid-sixties, abandoning Nashville for Austin and signing with Atlantic Records in 1971. He cut *Shotgun Willie* in two days and watched it outsell his entire previous catalog in half a year. By 1974, he closed out his Atlantic deal with *Phases and Stages*, which sold four hundred thousand copies at a time when a Nashville album was lucky to reach the high five figures. A year later, on Columbia, *Red Headed Stranger* went gold; within a month, so did *Wanted: The Outlaws*, a compilation put together by RCA of old tracks from Willie, Waylon Jennings, Jessi Colter, and Tompall Glaser. The collection's title would retroactively brand the entire scene.

By 1984, Willie had pulled off the most unheard-of type of crossover—completely ubiquitous, yet so subtle that no one minded. Permanently Zen or permanently stoned—it's a sliding scale with Willie, as are all things. "What I always liked to do was be the guitar player," he told an interviewer. "Somewhere along the way, I started being the singer. I'm not sure how that happened. I think one night the front man didn't show up, and I wound up fronting the band and doing the singing. And I don't know if that was really the best day of my life."

Nelson worked his casualness like a runway walker works a pair of pumps. He was the wise man next door, doing business as one of the ten highest-paid performers in Las Vegas. When Brenda Lee came knocking on Willie's door in '84 looking for something personal she could auction off for charity at that year's Fan Fair, she got a pair of sneakers and one of his famous red bandannas. It was certainly preferable to country comedian Jerry Clower's contribution that year: a chain saw.

"To All the Girls" was one of the mid-eighties' ubiquitous country duets. In 1983, Kenny Rogers and Dolly Parton's "Islands in the Stream" had been one of only two 45s to go platinum in the United States—one million sales. The song had been written by the Bee Gees; prior to it, Rogers had hit number one country by covering Bob Seger's "We've Got Tonight" as a duet with the Scottish soft-pop singer Sheena Easton.

Dolly, like Kenny, had also gone pop, moving to LA and becoming a movie star. Before June was finished, her film career would suffer its first real dent, with the release of *Rhinestone*, a fiasco that *Billboard*'s "Nashville Scene" columnist Kip Kirby lamented "could set the image of country music—not to mention the South—back ten years," under the headline: "Dolly, How Could You?"

But Dolly was omnipresent the week of Fan Fair, which ran June 4 to 10. On June 1, the Country Music Hall of Fame and Museum opened a five-part exhibit of artifacts from throughout Parton's career, from a 1946 photo of her birthplace in Sevierville, Tennessee, to the actual coat of many colors her mother made for her as a child, costumes from her movies, and over two hundred wigs.

Dolly was hardly alone in putting her life on display that week. Monday, June 4, saw the grand opening of Bill Monroe's Bluegrass Hall of Fame and Museum. "They worked right up to the last minute to get this finished for Fan

Fair, they sure did," Monroe told *The Tennessean*. "I'm very pleased." The next day, six names were added to the Walkway of Stars at the Country Music Hall of Fame and Museum, with the crowd beside themselves over the Oak Ridge Boys. And on Thursday, June 7, Barbara Mandrell would spend the day with her fans at *her* new museum, Barbara Mandrell Country.

It had been a slow climb from the 1972 opening of Opryland, which by 1984 was drawing two million people a year. "Subsequently Opryland begat the Opryland Hotel," wrote *Nashville!* magazine's Miriam Pace that June. "The hotel begat the lucrative convention business; the convention begat the current hotel/motel boom on Briley Parkway (where eight new operations have been planned in the past three years) . . . [and] the multiple births of acres of 'entertainment complexes' in the area: [Conway] Twitty City and Music Village (a hundred-million-dollar development of star museums and homes on one hundred and thirty acres in Hendersonville), the Cajun's Wharf Music Complex (a seventeen-acre, eight million dollar development on Cowen Street), and Country Music World (four hundred thirty-five acres around Foxland Hall in Gallatin)."

By the mid-eighties, tourism was Nashville's largest of what Pace referred to as "the offshoot industries spawned by country music": "During 1982, 7.4 million people dropped in on our city." Don Belcher, director of research for the Nashville Area Chamber of Commerce, said, "We've got millions of people who come to this city each year just begging us to take their money. All they ask is that maybe we smile back at them." Fan Fair only had a fraction of that, but they counted. Terry Clements, Metro director of tourism, told the *Nashville Banner* that the entire city would "reap the harvest" from Fan Fair. He elaborated: "The money tourists spent this week will be turned over many times in the coming weeks."

Fan Fair had begun as the offshoot of the International Fan Club Organization (IFCO), the brainchild of three sisters from Colorado, Loudilla, Loretta, and Kay Johnson. Loudilla, the eldest, had joined the George Jones Fan Club in 1960; the three of them, after watching him perform in Colorado Springs, drove to a radio station two hours from their home where he was spinning records, including Loretta Lynn's "Honky Tonk Girl," made for the small Zero label while Lynn was still living in Washington State. Loretta Johnson, because she shared her name, was the first to write Lynn; by 1963, she'd started a Lynn fan club. The IFCO followed in 1965; by 1984 it was overseeing over 250 country music fan clubs around the world.

Fan Fair was founded in part to maintain crowd control for more biz-oriented events in Nashville. "So many fans were coming to the annual disc-jockey convention we hold each year in October that we had to do something," Loretta Lynn explained. At the 1971 edition of the DJ confab, Country Music Association (CMA) suits began planning the first Fan Fair. Loudilla told them, "If you want to load people on buses and show them Webb Pierce's swimming pool, forget it, because that's not what we're after. We want fans to be involved and not just come down and buy tickets." She later reasoned, "A fan club is the best promotional tool an artist can have. It provides a kind of support that an artist can't buy. All fan club members ask for is a thank you here or there."

Fan Fair amplified that thank-you a thousand times. The Tennessee State Fairgrounds contained 660 booths. By late March, 200 of those booths had been claimed, while advance tickets were sufficiently up from 1983, which had drawn 17,000, that 2,000 additional seats were added to the grandstand.

Of course, there weren't 660 country music stars in the world in 1984—though Fan Fair's panoply of live shows did include an international showcase featuring groups from Norway, South Africa, England, Canada, Polynesia, Czechoslovakia, New Zealand, and West Germany, along with American ring-ers the Jordanaires. One reporter recalled watching performers who were "not-too-well-known outside of their neighborhood, sometimes ask passers-by if they would like an autograph."

Nonetheless, the atmosphere was convivial. "Something like Fan Fair would be almost impossible with any other kind of music," said Gus Hardin, who issued her second LP on RCA that year and scored a top ten hit in duet with Earl Thomas Conley. "There is no rudeness as there would be if this was a rock and roll gathering. Lord, I wouldn't come within three miles of something like that."

For some people it was a lovefest in more ways than metaphor. On Tues-day, June 5, country musicians Charly McClain and Wayne Massey announced their engagement at Fan Fair. Two days later, Edith Newsmen and B. W. Sipes of Albuquerque actually got married in booth 431, which belonged to singer Billy Blanton. The Reverend Jimmie Snow officiated. "Their first gift was a red bandana from Boxcar Willie," *The Tennessean* reported. "The bride wore it on her leg for the service." Just as Reverend Snow let the bride and groom kiss, the loudspeakers squawked, "Brenda Lee is now signing autographs in the MCA Records booth."

ONE OF THE RISING ACTS PLAYING FAN FAIR THAT YEAR WAS A MOTHER—
daughter duo, the latter of whom had garnered many flattering comparisons to
Brenda Lee. This often came from people who hadn't been sold on the idea that
Wynonna, the daughter, needed any help from Naomi, her mother. But the latter's drive and ambition were remarkable even in a city of nonstop hustle, and
once Naomi realized she could harmonize with the daughter, who inevitably
outmatched her in talent, she began to sell them as a throwback duo, decades
before that word took any root in the culture.

The Judds fought horribly and seldom minced words. "My mother is the
kind of person that feels the need to develop her own reality to spare her from
the heartache of the truth," Wynonna would later tell Bruce Feiler. "For in-
stance, her dad was an alcoholic. He would be sitting there at the kitchen table
with the newspaper drinking a Coke and they would be walking out the door
going to church. She thought it was because he was just so exhausted from
working the night before. That was her reality."

Wy's reality wasn't much better or different for a long time. Like her mom,
she changed names for showbiz: Wynonna's birth name was Christina. Naomi
was born Diana Judd; she became pregnant in high school, but didn't tell her
daughter who her real father was until she was in her thirties. When they
moved—along with the younger daughter, Ashley—back to Kentucky from
California into a no-electricity, no-phone cabin in 1975, it was a shock to the
girls. It was here that Wynonna got serious about music, and where Naomi
began singing along with her elder daughter.

Naomi, a nurse, passed their demo to one of her patients, producer Brent
Maher. When he finally played it, Naomi said, "he just about had to pull over to
the side of the road to try to figure out what the deal was because one minute
there was a Bonnie Raitt song and another would be something like an An-
drews Sisters song and then there would be an old Appalachian song." This was
almost certainly an embellishment, but it was also an apt parsing of the group's
unique style, and of what a surprise they were, coming along at the height of
country's MOR crossover. "Their background has traditional roots, but Wynonna's role models were not traditional people," Joe Galante, the head of RCA
Nashville, their label, said in 1985.

Traditional was a word that came up a lot in talk about country music during
this era. "One of the chief concerns of those who enjoy traditional country is
that the modernization of the form has fostered changes in the instruments

used in country recording," wrote John Lomax III in *Country Music U.S.A.*, published in 1985. "The steel guitar, staple of the sound during earlier years, has all but disappeared, replaced by various keyboards and even synthesizers. The distinctive sound of the Dobro has also been all but dismissed from country sessions, and the role of acoustic guitars has likewise diminished."

One exec in particular seemed a harbinger of that change: Jimmy Bowen, who took over MCA Nashville in mid-1984, came aboard to replace the courtly Jim Foglesong, who dusted himself off and took a job running Capitol's Nashville division. "I left one company on a Friday and went to work on Monday with the other company," Foglesong said.

Bowen had come from the pop world but brushed off accusations of being a ruthless crossover magnate. He had been so impressed with Reba McEntire upon meeting her that he not only didn't drop her (his first idea) but also let her switch producers and take charge of the song selection. Released that October, *My Kind of Country* put all the chips on the old stuff and paid off. "Western swing, that's my roots, that's my heritage," said McEntire. "The old Ray Price songs are something I'll never get away from. . . . But it seemed like when I did *My Kind of Country*, nobody was doing that kind of thing, and it really did feel like country music was slipping away."

Reba was becoming a personality, but not yet a superstar, and something similar applied to her labelmate George Strait, whose back-to-basics style and stock stillness onstage made him a throwback as a type as well as a musician. Bowen was a lot less politic when he described it: "There are young women attracted to George Strait. Once they get there, they don't care what kind of music he happens to be doing. It's just a fact of life. Some young people are attracted by the way George Strait looks and then fall in love with country music."

But fewer of them were falling for it through pop crossovers. "There are no pop [crossover] records coming out national[ly]," Joe Galante said. "There hasn't been a pop record since . . . 'Islands in the Stream.'" Since then, he continued, "there are probably half a dozen records that have crossed over to AC, and that's not pop enough for me to say that we're making pop music."

Bowen had a theory as to why. In the early eighties, he said, "pop music became very stale; the albums were . . . not that good, actually, and pop music sales fell dramatically. . . . When that happened, country music filled those slots on the AC [adult contemporary] radio stations and in the racks where we sell seventy percent of our records and cassettes today. Now, when pop music got its act back together . . . they simply pushed us back off of those racks. . . .

People who sold fifty thousand started selling a hundred fifty thousand–two hundred thousand. They are back to fifty, sixty, seventy thousand now because the outlets are gone."

YET THE SHOWSTOPPER AT FAN FAIR WASN'T A NUMBER ONE COUNTRY hit. That may be surprising, considering that it's never gone anywhere, culturally speaking—certainly, it's far more familiar to a noncountry audience than all but a handful of the year's actual country number ones. Naturally, it came from Las Vegas.

Lee Greenwood had been a card dealer in Vegas as well as a singer, and Sin City is where he learned how to survive in a cutthroat business. "I'm quick to do things because in Vegas you had to be quick or you would get buried," he told *Music City News*. "You had to be a hustler to get the next job." Yet "quick" is not how you'd describe Lee Greenwood's music—as David Gates put it, "Greenwood's repertoire ranges from soft rock to soft country." This was a winning formula for a time when pop radio was being paced by Kenny Rogers and Air Supply: it won him two consecutive CMA Male Vocalist of the Year awards.

Four months prior to Fan Fair, Greenwood had the best week of his career: winning a country male vocalist Grammy for his "I.O.U.," being nominated for two CMA awards, watching his single "Going, Going, Gone" hit number one country, and accepting a gold record for his album *Somebody's Gonna Love You*. A trade ad for Greenwood's 1982 LP *Inside and Out* proclaimed, "We should have called his first album *Lee Greenwood's Greatest Hits!!*"

"Lee is not, certainly, a country singer in the tradition of country singers," said Jim Foglesong, who signed Greenwood, "but yet [his] demo that he had indicated . . . a kind of a country-pop sound. I loved his phrasing and the quality of his voice." When Foglesong listened to the demo for a song called "It Turns Me Inside Out," he heard "totally middle-of-the-road pop music that we wouldn't have a chance with at radio, and I don't think the pop department would be excited about them either because they were too slick and lush-sounding . . . we had a lot of trouble getting country radio to go on it, because they felt it was pretty pop. And we weren't able to get much pop." One day his wife came home and asked, "Is Lee Greenfield on your label?" One of her tennis partners had been singing the song off-court.

One thing made Greenwood different from Air Supply, though. Following, in Tom Roland's words, a "wave of patriotism that followed when a Soviet plane downed a South Korean flight on September 1, 1983, killing 269 people," Greenwood penned a master class in broad-chested, play-to-the-balcony bathos and began singing it to his audiences, who flipped. When his producer Jerry Crutchfield told Foglesong about it, he was skeptical: major labels didn't like releasing political songs. Foglesong's response was "Anything that's getting that kind of a response we need to get on tape, and then we'll figure out something to do with it."

"God Bless the U.S.A." only reached number seven country, but it would become, as Foglesong put it, "one of the most lucrative songs that's been written in the last twenty-five years . . . in many places it's played a lot more than the national anthem now. Ronald Reagan, every time he did anything, every time George [H. W.] Bush did anything, you'd hear 'God Bless the U.S.A.' . . . It's been a huge sheet-music seller, band arrangements, choral arrangements."

Greenwood's was the song of the moment that Fan Fair. An unintentional response to Bruce Springsteen's "Born in the U.S.A.," the title track of an album also released that week, "God Bless" was the song a lot of people thought that Springsteen's song was, except it wasn't. On Monday the fourth, at the eighteenth annual Music City News Country Awards, Greenwood brought down the Grand Ole Opry House with his new song, whose standing O, the *Banner* reported, "[left] little doubt that Greenwood now takes his place as a star in a star-laden field." When he won Male Vocalist of the Year, he said, "This is the ultimate compliment. I had no idea we'd win this kind of award performing. I don't think of myself as a singer. I'm a songwriter." Let the record show that "God Bless the U.S.A." was Greenwood's first self-penned single.

Fan Fair was something like Greenwood's coronation. That Friday morning, he participated in the Nashville Songwriters Association International show, and the night before, on Thursday, Greenwood had climaxed Fan Fair's MCA Records showcase. Here, Reba McEntire and George Strait were the openers—the insurgent New Traditionalists warming up the crowd for a performer for whom Vegas was a starting, not end, point. Barbara Mandrell showed up as Greenwood's surprise guest; they had recently cut a duets album together. And eighteen thousand people stood and stayed standing the minute "God Bless the U.S.A." began, as Robert K. Oermann put it, "as though it were a new national anthem. Greenwood made his grand exit holding aloft a giant stars-and-stripes."

Having a roster that veered from Greenwood to Reba or Strait was what Jimmy Bowen thought of as the right balance. "For the future, I think there has to be a balance also," he said. "I'm not trying to go out and sign the rock and roll–country artists of the future, although I'm going to sign a couple, and if I find another pure traditional artist who's exceptionally good, [I'll] sign them same day. It doesn't matter. The other day we picked up the option on a new act who some people think isn't country and some people think is country, and picked up the option on Bill Monroe the same day. What the hell's the difference? It's a business."

WPIX CHANNEL 11,
NEW YORK CITY
June 29, 1984

THE OPENING SHOT OF THE FIRST AND ONLY EPISODE OF *GRAFFITI ROCK* was of an Enjoy record being scratched. Like many of the earliest New York hip-hop labels, by the time the show—an attempt to make a hip-hop *Soul Train*—was filmed, Enjoy's output had nearly ground to a halt.

Graffiti Rock was shot in the winter of 1984 at a studio on 114th Street in East Harlem, not far from Bobby's Records, the shop Enjoy founder Bobby Robinson had founded in 1947, next to the Apollo Theater on 125th Street. He became the neighborhood's canniest record man, his opinion sought out by numerous R&B indie labels—including, in the fifties, such imprints as Fire and Fury, issuing sides by stars like Elmore James, Lee Dorsey, Gladys Knight and the Pips, and King Curtis. But Robinson's were largely on ice by the late sixties.

Then, in October 1979, the Englewood, New Jersey, label Sugar Hill Records released "Rapper's Delight," by the Sugar Hill Gang—a twelve-inch by a trio nobody had heard of: three guys reciting (not singing) rhymes over a neighborhood funk band covering Chic's "Good Times." "Rapper's Delight," Robinson recalled, was "such a phenomenal smash, I figured that rather than search for more conventional artists, I'd go with what was right under my nose." Quickly, he revived Enjoy and issued a trio of genre-defining early twelve-inches—"Rappin' and Rockin' the House," by the Funky Four Plus

One; Grandmaster Flash and the Furious Five's "Superrappin'"; and Spoonie Gee's "Love Rap" backed with (b/w) the Treacherous Three's "The New Rap Language"—by early 1980.

By the time DJ Jimmie Jazz rubbed an Enjoy label back and forth on one of his paired Technics 1200 turntables in a tightly framed opening shot, the label was slowing down again. In 1984, Enjoy put a couple new twelve-inches out, among them "Just Having Fun," by someone then calling himself Dougé Fresh. A year later, he'd change it to Doug E. Fresh and, with the Get Fresh Crew—including a young British-born MC named Slick Rick—make the classic "The Show"/"La-Di-Da-Di," whose showbiz-savvy style would pivot hip-hop yet another step away from the days when Enjoy Records ruled the roost. No pop music style of the eighties mutated faster than hip-hop.

GRAFFITI ROCK'S COPRODUCER, CREATOR, AND HOST, MICHAEL HOLMAN had been the first to use the term "hip-hop" in print. It ran in his interview of Afrika Bambaataa, the Bronx gang leader turned DJ and recording artist, for the *East Village Eye* in January 1982.

Along with DJs Kool Herc—who'd more or less invented it—and Grandmaster Flash, Bambaataa was one of hip-hop's primary architects; the music's entire up-from-poverty story was irresistible to the press and helped make hip-hop a critics' favorite long before the general public caught on.

Holman was an army brat who'd spent most of his childhood in Europe, moved to California at age eleven, and spent junior high and high school in Los Angeles and San Francisco; in the latter city, he became a dancer for local art rockers the Tubes. Holman moved to New York in 1978 and spent a year working for Chemical Bank, but got sidetracked by his fascination with subway graffiti, then efflorescent throughout the city's lines. Taking the 1 to work, Holman recalls, "I'd see these trains rolling with these top-to-bottom burners. I've always been an artist, and I was watching these things go by, thinking, 'This is amazing!' No one else was paying attention, while I was in glee."

Holman quickly ingratiated himself into the bustling downtown art scene, forming the band Gray with Jean-Michel Basquiat in 1979 and cold-calling Fab 5 Freddy (Fred Braithwaite), a fine artist who'd been making social headway within the art, punk rock, and uptown DJ scenes. Moreover, he was helping to commingle them, most famously in the video for Blondie's "Rapture," a number one hit in 1981 that name-checked Grandmaster Flash, the Bronx DJ who worked with the MC crew the Furious Five. But despite being asked, Flash didn't appear in Blondie's video—he simply didn't believe it was real—so Basquiat appeared in his stead.

Soon Holman invited Freddy's crew to show at a party in the art space Canal Zone. "To me, it was the first time that the downtown and uptown scene came together," Holman told *Wax Poetics*. "You had elements of hip-hop and then the downtown kids. I'd say hip-hop, as a culture, could easily not have happened if it wasn't for the downtown art scene embracing uptown culture and promoting it in venues downtown."

In 1982, Holman brought Malcolm McLaren, in full New Romantic regalia, up to see Bambaataa spin at the Bronx River Community Center, leading the British manager/producer/flimflam man to hire Holman to put together a representative package of what he was seeing—the breaking, the spinning, the graffiti—to open for Bow Wow Wow at the Ritz. Soon after, Holman began working with Ruza Blue, a British punk promoter who'd moved to New York, to put on hip-hop club nights—first at Negril, just off Sixth Avenue below Houston, and then in Midtown at the Roxy, a roller-skating palace. A configuration of these events would tour Europe in 1982 as well, helping spread hip-hop globally—assisted by Bambaataa and the Soul Sonic Force's huge hit "Planet Rock" that year.

For his part, Holman wanted to introduce this stuff to folks stuck at home. "There was a slot open on Manhattan Cable Network," he says. He had just stopped promoting with Ruza Blue at Negril: "She went off to do the Roxy and I went off to do television."

THE NEW DOWNTOWN CONNECTIONS FORGED IN **1982** WERE STRENGTHened when, on July 1, Grandmaster Flash and the Furious Five released "The Message," a song they had to be talked into releasing under their name. The DJ the group named itself for, after all, had nothing to do with it—the song had been written primarily by percussionist Ed Fletcher, and the song's lyrical climax, by Melle Mel, was an exact duplicate of his verse from the 1979 single "Superrappin'." The song only reached sixty-two on the Hot 100, but its then-shocking imagery, as well as the sizzling rhythm track, gave the group enormous credibility.

Then, in late 1983, came "White Lines (Don't Don't Do It)," an anti-cocaine song, right in line with his group's recent penchant for, you know, "message songs." Only this wasn't Grandmaster Flash and the Furious Five—this was credited to Grandmaster and Melle Mel, and was, more or less, Mel's solo debut. The song was *seductive*—despite the fact that he was decrying cocaine in its frighteningly popular new rock form, quickly becoming known as crack, Mel would be in thrall to the stuff himself not long after recording it.

Worse, "White Lines" had, it seemed, swiped the musical bed from "Cavern," a track by downtown New York postpunk minimalists Liquid Liquid that had been issued on the small label 99 Records, operated by Ed Bahlman out of a downtown shop of the same name. A lawsuit between the two labels dragged out for eighteen months before 99's finances gave out.

Then the Furious Five's lead rapper decided to skip the ampersand and dub himself Grandmaster Melle Mel. Flash took action: in late February 1984, the DJ, along with Furious Five members Rahiem (Guy Todd Williams) and Kidd Creole (Nathaniel Glover, Melle Mel's brother), filed to dissolve their recording contract with Sugar Hill Records, their management contract with Sylvia Inc. Management, owned by Sugar Hill founder Sylvia Robinson (no relation to Joe), and take back the stage name Flash had originated—a name, the label insisted, was "a generic street term meaning 'disc jockey'"—and for $5 million in actual and punitive damages. "If you got five pockets," Flash said of Robinson, "she had a hand in every pocket."

The federal court ruled in favor of Flash, who got to keep his moniker, sever his ties with the company, and receive a thorough accounting. Sugar Hill got to use "grandmaster" as long as it was paired with a "name that does not sound like 'flash,'" as well as the "Furious Five" name. Within a month, Grandmaster Flash signed with Elektra. Soon, the newly official "Grandmaster" Melle Mel took his reconstituted Furious Five to play shows in London. *Melody Maker* panned their "glib, show-biz style of presentation," including utilizing a "backing track by the Art of Noise only to exalt the crowd to accompany it with 'De Camptown Races.'"

That summer, Melle Mel scored a title hit from the soundtrack to the best financed and promoted of the flurry of breakdance-exploitation movies released that year. Sylvia Robinson sent off a tart telegram to the nation's radio stations: "We would like to request at this time that *all disc jockeys* refrain from announcing 'Grandmaster Flash' as the artist of 'Beat Street [Breakdown].' The artists are 'Grandmaster Melle Mel & the Furious Five.' By the DJ's announcing the wrong artist, this is causing the group tremendous damage."

But the real damage was coming from elsewhere. That fall, Sugar Hill released *Grandmaster Melle Mel and the Furious Five*, the new group's "debut." The tell came on "The Truth," in which Melle Mel dissed Run-D.M.C., the top-billed guests on *Graffiti Rock* and the rap group that had taken the mantle from Mel's crew: "I always wear black and I always will / 'Cause I'm dressin' [*beat*] for your funer-ill!" It was too little, too late. Not long after the 99 suit ended, Sugar Hill itself would go bankrupt in late 1985.

HOLMAN WANTED "A STRONG HIP-HOP CROWD" FOR HIS DANCERS: "70 percent black, 20 percent Latino, maybe 10 percent white, and real kids from the street." But when he'd ask kids at the Roxy to come audition, none of them took it seriously: "It was unbelievable to them there could be a hip-hop TV show, so people wouldn't show up for casting." There was also pressure from the show's producers to rejigger the dancers' racial ratio, which Holman reluctantly did.

As host, Holman was game but clearly green. Today, he regrets not having asked Fab 5 Freddy to host instead—they'd worked together in cable access. But his cohosts had unimpeachable cred: Kool Moe Dee and Special K of the Treacherous Three. The third, LA Sunshine, had just left the group prior to the show's taping.

Born Mohandas Dewese, Kool Moe Dee ran the group with an iron fist, and he was shown a rare level of respect by his peers. He was also a renowned battle king who took all comers to the mat. In December 1981, he went up against the Bronx-born Zulu Nation MC Busy Bee in a battle at Harlem World, on 125th Street. "Kool said, 'Take that *burrgidy-burrgidy bum* shit out of here,'" the Bronx-born rapper Fat Joe recalled. "Busy was the crowd pleaser back then, and Kool roasted him."

Looking back, Holman wishes he'd asked the Treacherous Two to perform. "I also would have had them dressed differently." Kool Moe Dee and Special K (Kevin Keaton) arrived in freshly made leather getups. "The street kids, getting to be on TV, they ironically bent over backwards to look like what they thought successful out-of-town bands looked like," says Holman. "I remember being in the green room—I had just flown in from France, for the

Beat Street premiere at Cannes—and they're dressed like that. I said, 'Why are you dressed like Labelle or Earth, Wind & Fire?'"

France wasn't the only global hip-hop scene sprouting up. That April, Tim Westwood, a columnist for the British magazine *Blues and Soul*, started the first UK all-hip-hop show for London pirate radio station LWR Radio 92.5 FM, soon moving the music into the city's nightspots. "First rap club was the Language Lab—late on a Monday night in a strip club upstairs in Soho's Meard Street," Westwood wrote. "There was always an overlap of the MC's starting and the strippers finishing."

No American city outside of New York took to hip-hop more readily than Los Angeles. The emphasis in LA was on slick, synthesized grooves—not just the locally made records on the Solar label, or produced by Quincy Jones, but George Clinton's P-Funk army. LA's biggest DJ crew even called themselves Uncle Jamm's Army, after a 1979 Funkadelic album, *Uncle Jam Wants You*.

"IF YOU THINK THIS DANCING'S FRESH, I'VE GOT SOMETHING THAT'S gonna blow your mind."

On the show, Holman introduced the New York City Breakers, a break-dancing troupe in skintight red bodysuits. Holman was their manager; he'd assembled them by "cannibalizing other crews," he says. Immediately, Holman was booking them onto TV newsmagazine shows—*PM Magazine, Ripley's Believe It or Not!*—and filming their segments himself.

"Break dancing was the loss leader of hip-hop; it's what got it on the air," says Holman. "Before it was, 'Why is somebody playing a record? Why is somebody reading a poem?' But somebody spinning on their head? *That* was new. Break dancing kicked the door open for hip-hop."

To the wider world, spinning on one's head barely seemed aerodynamically possible. But this type of dancing had been around. Working in New York in 1979, Joni Mitchell chanced upon a street crowd, as she told *Rolling Stone*: "When we get up on it, it's a group of black men surrounding two small black boys. It's about midnight, and two boys are dancing this very robot-like mime dance. One of the guys in the crowd slaps his leg and says, 'Isn't that something, I thought *tap dancing* was gone forever.'"

The New York City Breakers had names that described their moves: Mr. Wave slid his limbs and torso so quickly and liquidly that he made some of his colleagues seem faintly marionette-like. Glide Master spun his entire body on the axis of his left hand; you wouldn't want to be within ten feet of his circumference. Guess what Flip Rock did? At the end, several Breakers did, indeed, spin on their heads.

The Breakers were in high demand during 1984. "One of my dancers was actually doing a McDonald's commercial and dancing on *Graffiti Rock* at the same time," says Holman. "Break dancing was already in commercials by then." This, of course, became a talking point with sponsors: "As any smart producer would do, you try to use every angle you can to get people to invest their money."

And 1984 was, as *Melody Maker* put it, "the year when big money got hip to hip-hop." Rapping, scratching, graffiti, break dancing—the music's four elements, per Holman and Bambaataa—sold designer jeans, margarine, and Puma sneakers, not to mention both McDonald's *and* Burger King. There was a raft of instructional books and, especially, home videos for the at-home break dancer, released by everybody from Warner Home Video (*Let's Break: A Visual Guide to Breakdancing*) to K-tel (*Breakdance*).

To some people, this stuff was a little *too* popular. In LA's Westwood, the LAPD issued jaywalking tickets to more than 150 teenagers for breaking the 10:00 p.m. curfew after crowds gathered on the street to watch breakers do their thing. The dancers, said the cops, were "creating obstacles on the sidewalk."

Naturally, one of 1984's biggest rap crossover hits was explicitly about dancing: the stutter-bass electro classic "Jam on It," by Newcleus, a Brooklyn family group. "Jam on It" depicted an intergalactic dance throwdown between lead rapper Cozmo D "from outer space" (Ben Cenac) and no less than Superman: "We rocked his butt / With a twelve-inch cut / Called 'Disco Kryptonite.'" It reached number fifty-six pop that summer.

On *Graffiti Rock*, the New York City Breakers dance not to Newcleus, but to "Play at Your Own Risk," by Planet Patrol—a black male vocal quartet backed up by "Planet Rock" producers Arthur Baker and John Robie. The song was two years old by the time the show aired—an eternity for hip-hop, where the music seemed to change completely every few months. Indeed, by the time *Graffiti Rock* aired, most of the music on it would seem old hat to hip-hop's core audience.

THREE WEEKS BEFORE *GRAFFITI ROCK*'S AIRDATE, A MOVIE THAT HOLMAN, the New York City Breakers, and the Treacherous Three were all involved with opened in theaters. *Beat Street*—Holman was the film's associate producer, the others among its performers—heralded a slew of break-dancing-themed movies released that year.

It had begun in November 1983, with the wide release of Charlie Ahearn's *Wild Style*. Shot in 1982 for $200,000, *Wild Style* was a fairly upbeat musical fantasy that featured performances from a number of hip-hop's biggest names, including a showcase of Grandmaster Flash cutting it up on the wheels of steel.

Wild Style became a cult favorite, but it might have gone further commercially had it emphasized break dancing. (The title refers to graffiti.) Nevertheless, *Wild Style*'s release spread break dancing off-screen: in Washington, DC, for the film's January 1984 premiere there, the 9:30 Club hosted a breakers' contest judged by Fab 5 Freddy and graffiti artist Lady Pink (Sandra Fabara).

"What they do here that's unique is they combine the electric boogie with the breaking," Braithwaite told the *Washington Post*. "In New York, they keep it separate. . . . The kids who are probably the best have a little martial arts, that's the basis of it. All that floor work—the kids in New York picked it up from kung fu flicks and gymnastics."

A native of Bedford-Stuyvesant, Brooklyn, Braithwaite was hugely ambitious and equally suave. His godfather was Max Roach; his dad had been in the room when Malcolm X was murdered. Fred could ingratiate himself easily into any situation and made it his business to know everyone. He was alive to graffiti's vibrant possibilities. In 1980, he covered a subway car top to bottom in Campbell's soup cans, an homage to Warhol that made the line connecting subway art and pop art—and, ergo, high art—resoundingly clear. "I wanted to make sure that we weren't perceived as folk artists," Braithwaite said.

Shortly after *Wild Style*'s official opening, in December 1983, New York's WABC-TV aired *The Big Break Dance Contest*. Six hundred contestants were whittled down to the winner, Leslie Uggams informed us, of "twenty-five hundred dollars in cash, an appearance on *New York Hot Tracks* [WABC's video show], and a role in the new feature film, *Beat Street*."

Beat Street had begun as a three-page treatment drafted in 1982 by Steven Hager, a New York journalist who'd written the *Village Voice*'s first hip-hop cover story. Hager involved his friend, the producer Arthur Baker, who'd produced Afrika Bambaataa's "Looking for the Perfect Beat"—the screenplay's original title. "I was part of the package," says Baker. "I had five percent of the movie."

(Baker's share would eventually be lost in the shuffle after Orion was sold to MGM.)

But for a project like this one to get anywhere, it needed to be attached to a *name*. Harry Belafonte was that name. He'd been a hit-maker in the fifties, helping break calypso in the United States; his 1957 single "Banana Boat Song (Day-O)" had been as big as Elvis Presley's "Jailhouse Rock." Belafonte was a political heavyweight, on the civil rights movement's front lines, a confidant of both Dr. King and Fidel Castro. But although Belafonte had been involved, uncredited, behind the scenes of several of his movies, *Beat Street* was the first picture he produced.

Belafonte's assistant gave a friend of Hager's the treatment. "She thought this might be important," Hager told writer Ron Hart. "Harry knew absolutely nothing about hip-hop." The studio, Orion Pictures, had the script rewritten. "It should have been just about street kids in the Bronx and nothing else," Holman said. "Instead you had this boring modern dance scenario."

After a week of filming, the original director, Andrew Davis, who'd done most of the script rewrites, was out. "They didn't want it to be an unrealistic, Hollywood kind of film, and they didn't want the kids to be alienated by someone who didn't understand the culture," Davis's replacement, Stan Lathan, told the *New York Times*. Lathan was black, certainly an advantage here, but he was best known for directing episodes of *Cagney and Lacey*, and it showed.

Belafonte had told *New York* he hoped *Beat Street* would "prove that blacks can make 'bankable' films, and that hip-hop will communicate to a mass audience the strength of black culture in America." This was important, because in 1984, despite blindingly obvious evidence to the contrary all around, it was still ingrained record-business wisdom that what appealed to blacks didn't appeal to whites. But hip-hop was close to the opposite—not only did white fans love rap but also many blacks hated it, particularly within the record biz. And Belafonte was careful to toe the line. "If this film and soundtrack are successful, it will give rise to the courage that this industry needs to take bigger and bigger steps," Belafonte said. "Yet for it to achieve its goals, it must be economically viable."

Beat Street took its marketing cues from *Flashdance*-style tie-ins—even before it opened, Cotillion Records, which handled the soundtrack, was already talking about issuing "possibly three volumes." (There wound up being two.) Grandmaster Melle Mel and the Furious Five's "Beat Street Breakdown," an Atlantic rep boasted, was "the epitome of rap records." Maybe in a different year it could have been.

HARRY BELAFONTE'S GOOD INTENTIONS HAD LITTLE TO DO WITH 1984'S run of breakdanceploitation flicks. Take *Breakin'*, a purely mercenary enterprise that was conceived, written, financed, produced, shot, edited, and exhibiting within two months, because the brass at Cannon Films—whose biggest draw was the cheeseball action star Chuck Norris—saw the hubbub over *Beat Street* and decided to get the jump on it.

Breakin' barely had a plot: "Two blacks and the token white girl dancing their way to the top of Reagan's recession-hit America," *Melody Maker* surmised, adding: "Oh really?" There was barely time to come up with one. *Breakin'* began shooting March 1. On March 20, Russ Regan, a Polydor executive who had overseen the *Flashdance* soundtrack, was hired to coordinate the soundtrack; the movie was in theaters on May 4. "It is one of the fastest-made successful films ever produced in Hollywood," Regan said.

The point, of course, was the soundtrack. Regan had attempted to sign *Beat Street* but got outbid by Atlantic. "But in March, a friend from Cannon Films called me up," Regan said. "His breakdancing movie was about half-shot. I saw about twelve minutes of footage and it convinced me. It was low-budget, but I felt that the first film out there that had any kind of credibility would be a success." He also admitted, "I didn't get tuned into it until my fourteen-year-old son started taking breakdancing lessons. That convinced me right there."

Breakin' was made for $2 million, as opposed to *Beat Street*'s $10 million (and *Wild Style*'s two hundred grand), and opened in more than one thousand theaters. It grossed some $13 million its opening weekend. The *Beat Street* soundtrack, for its part, went gold. "I made a lot of money," says Arthur Baker. But the *Breakin'* soundtrack went platinum in six weeks, and would sell some three million copies. "Harry was really disappointed that *Breakin'* beat *Street* to the market," Holman recalled. "I remember seeing *Breakin'* and thinking it was a really horrible film. It made the talented artists in that film look really stupid." Tom Silverman agrees. "*Breakin'* was very West Coast," he says. "That really wasn't a hip-hop thing."

On September 28, New World Pictures issued *Body Rock*, a Latino version of the template, directed by music video maker Marcelo Epstein and starring Lorenzo Lamas, star of the prime-time soap *Falcon Crest*, as Chilly, leader of the rap and break-dancing crew, the, uh, Body Rocks. Lamas received a nomination for a Golden Raspberry Award for worst actor in a motion picture; he lost to Sylvester Stallone in *Rhinestone*.

December 21 saw the release of the sequel, legendary for its title alone, *Breakin' 2: Electric Boogaloo*. Shooting began July 16: "The title song and many of the tunes for the new soundtrack have already been chosen," *Cash Box* reported shortly beforehand.

"TWO YEARS AGO, A FRIEND OF MINE / ASKED ME TO SAY SOME MC rhymes . . ."

Joseph Simmons, better known as Run, standing left on the *Graffiti Rock* stage, rhymes staccato—not in the orotund, vowel-stretching manner of Melle Mel, but leaner, more purely shadowboxing with the beat, which is a drum machine blasting away, and nothing else. It serves notice that hip-hop's rules, yet again, had changed.

To Run's right is his rhyming partner Darryl McDaniels—D.M.C.—and behind them is Jason Mizell—Jam Master Jay. All are naturals onstage. Mizell doesn't have to do anything much beyond make the records do what they're supposed to—his scratching puts Jimmie Jazz's wobbly turntable work into relief as stark as the beat—but his unselfconscious crowd hyping and watchful eyes make him as magnetic as the two in front. Standing on a small elevated platform together doesn't give Run and D.M.C. much room to move, but they use the space deftly, weaving around each other like seasoned sparring partners. The smile D.M.C. flashes after inserting a perfectly timed "Run Love!" between Run's first two verses is as contagious as the music.

Black-clad black everymen with block-rocking skills, Run-D.M.C. is in fighting form, absolutely electrifying. Their power is that they don't have to show off; such is their youthful confidence in their mastery. It seems they're holding back a little, the kind of ineffable cool that hip-hop seemed to have in abundance.

Then it's D.M.C.'s turn. He gets a close-up for his verse:

> *I'm D.M.C. in the place to be*
> *And I go to St. John's University*
> *And since kindergarten I acquired the knowledge*
> *And after twelfth grade I went straight to college*

You can hear, in the background here, some noise beginning around the word *University*, gaining in depth and volume through the third line and into the fourth. It's the sound of men hollering their approval of a stone classic verse, and though it remains in the background, it flavors the moment indelibly.

"Their performance on *Graffiti Rock* is the best performance they ever did on TV," says Holman proudly. "They're ambitious but they're not overdoing it. The new jacks were coming from Queens. Run-D.M.C., being more suburban blacks in New York—not from Brooklyn, not from the Bronx—were trying to look like street kids from the Bronx."

Both Run and D.M.C. were still in college: Run studied mortuary science (an uncle's profession) at La Guardia Community College, with D.M.C. studying business management at St. John's. Barely out of high school, they were hip-hop lifers. Run started rapping in 1977, age twelve, with the leg up that his older brother Russell was the biggest rap promoter in New York. Within a year, Joey was performing regularly, as the "Son of Kurtis Blow"; Russell was also Blow's manager.

The siblings had shared an upstairs bedroom in their Queens home. Russell was a bored smart kid, selling weed and taking acid; he briefly joined the Seven Immortals gang, dropping out after a fellow member was killed. He enrolled in Harlem's City College in fall 1975, but it was short-lived—Russell was too busy partying.

Then he got religion—at a party, naturally. In 1977, at the Charles Gallery in Harlem, Russell watched Eddie Cheba get on the microphone and exhort the audience, as a DJ cut up a pair of copies of Parliament's "Flash Light." Soon Russell was throwing these kinds of parties himself, turning Bronx rap acts like Grandmaster Flash and the Furious Five into Queens regulars. He helped mold his friend Curtis Walker into a rapper, with a new name, Kurtis Blow, inspired by Eddie Cheba. The writer Nelson George called Russell, in these years, "the only guy on the rap scene who seemed to have any long term goals."

By November 1978, when he turned fourteen, Joey was making thirty-five dollars a show. His fame was small-time even on this small circuit, but it impressed his best friend nevertheless. Darryl McDaniels discovered rap in the spring of 1978; he tried to emulate Flash's scratching on the family record player. Within days, his older brother Alford had added a second turntable and cheap mixer, enabling Darryl to DJ in earnest.

D.M.C. obsessed over one tape of an MC battle—the Cold Crush Brothers versus the Fantastic Five at Harlem World, where the crews got busy over a break by a group he'd eventually come to identify as Toys in the Attic. (That was the Aerosmith album the break came from: "Walk This Way.") He was particularly inspired by the way Cold Crush traded off not only on each line but word by word within lines. When Run saw D's notebook filled with rhymes—the best he'd seen—he recruited him as his partner.

Despite Run's proximity to action's center, Russell drew the line at recording his kid brother and his new partner: "It's too hard. It's too aggressive. It's not commercial." Run took his frustrations out on other rappers—battling anyone who'd let him, nearly always winning. Run and D were also starting to disdain the softer R&B material so many rappers were saddled with. "We didn't want to do what the Sugar Hill Gang was doing or take a typical hot R&B record and rap over it," D.M.C. said. "We didn't want to take anything that was familiar to regular black radio and make a record over it."

Their DJ came aboard at the end of 1982. Jason Mizell had moved to Hollis from Brooklyn at age ten, in 1975, and quickly became a natural leader and troublemaker alike—among his high school associates was a group of kids who robbed houses in Jamaica Estates, and one night he was arrested as an accessory. After four days in Spofford juvenile home, Mizell, surprised that it hadn't been a charnel house, told his mother on the drive home, "I had a lot fun, Mom." She burst into tears; an instantly remorseful Jay resolved to change his ways.

Mizell dropped out of high school and earned his GED while he helped take care of his ailing father at home. (Jesse Mizell died in October 1982.) Run had wanted Jay to DJ for him and D, and when his schedule opened up again, Mizell surprised them by agreeing. Jay's rep had other benefits as well. The clubs were rough—Russell, Kurtis, and Run once walked into an armed robbery after a show, the three of them ducking under cars to escape gunfire. As Run-D.M.C. biographer Ronin Ro noted, "Jay knew many drug lords from Queens who partied at the club, so once the drug lords saw Jay was with Run-D.M.C., the drug lords would protect Jay *and* the group."

ASIDE FROM A HANDFUL OF CASSETTE RECORDINGS OF LIVE PERFORMANCES issued on twelve-inch, nobody had really attempted to re-create the sound of the actual parties—rhyming over DJs mixing and scratching records in real time—since rap hit record in 1979. (The "Adventures of Grandmaster Flash on the Wheels of Steel," from 1981, was the DJ's seven-minute cut-up routine, performed live, but featuring no rapping.) That changed with Run-D.M.C.'s first single, in 1983.

It helped that Run-D.M.C. were in the studio with a seasoned pro. Larry Smith, a studio bassist, stripped the beat to almost nothing—a spacey, endlessly blasting-off variation on "Planet Rock." Though the record involved guitars, basses, keyboards, and percussion all played live, the DMX drum machine battered through absolutely everything. And when Smith allowed the rappers to rap their way, rather than mimic Kurtis Blow or Melle Mel, the track ignited.

The A side, "It's Like That," was a post-"Message" catalog of urban ills, but the duo's joyous performance and Smith's punishing percussion were like stark black and white compared to the colorful electro of the Furious Five's record. The B side was even starker. "Sucker MC's"—the song they performed on *Graffiti Rock*—featured Run taking down a titular character who'd been aping his style. When D.M.C. rapped his verse in the studio, he said, "Russell was like, *oh* shit." During the mixdown, Russell took the drums away from D's opening lines, inserting scratches from Davy DMX, Kurtis Blow's former DJ. The entire song took eight hours, start to finish.

This, Russell knew, was a hit. None of the major labels he took it to agreed, so he wound up at Profile Records, founded in 1981 by Steve Plotnicki and Cory Robbins to release dance twelve-inches. When Russell took Robbins a tape labeled "Runde MC," Robbins played it in his car and couldn't get it out of his head. The renamed Run-D.M.C. signed to Profile for three grand. The twelve-inch was issued in May 1983, and by summer, it was moving ten thousand copies per week. Jay's all-black, leather-suited look became the group's, on Russell's orders.

They began doing one-nighters all over the country. That December, Run-D.M.C. made their Minneapolis debut at the club First Avenue, three months before the release of their self-titled debut album. The trio received $1,150 to appear on a Wednesday night. Their to-the-point rider indicated either inexperience or the awfulness of venues they had already played: "Professional sound system, including voice monitoring equipment. Professional lighting with at least one spotlight for center stage. . . . Liquid refreshment made available and readily accessible."

"I had to leave town that night, but I did sound check with them," says Paul Spangrud, a First Avenue DJ for three decades. "A lot of feedback came through that hollow stage. You had to tippy-toe when you had DJs up there—the records would skip all the time." Just to be safe, Jam Master Jay spun the show with his turntables hung from the ceiling. But breaking out beyond the coasts would take some time still. Chrissie Dunlap, a First Avenue employee during the eighties, recalls a mere sixty-four people showing up. "Rap music was a new thing," she says. "We bombed on that show, and we should not have, because that was a great fucking show."

Russell was reluctant to make a full album on the group: "Rap albums don't sell," he told Robbins. This one did: *Run-D.M.C.*, released in March 1984, was certified gold by December. Only three hip-hop discs had done so prior, all of them singles (Kurtis Blow's "The Breaks," Blondie's "Rapture," Afrika Bambaataa's "Planet Rock").

Run-D.M.C. wasn't the first hip-hop album, but it was the first one that sounded like a *hip-hop* album—no cheesy rock covers, no drippy crossover ballads. The Queens trio made hip-hop's flamboyantly leather-suited front tier look suddenly, badly dated. Run-D.M.C. had done well on *Soul Train* that June—a show whose host, Don Cornelius, made no secret of his distaste for this music. But with the album's single, "Rock Box," featuring snarling guitar work from Eddie Martinez (who'd played with Blondie on its 1982 tour, its last until the late nineties), ensconced in the R&B chart (number twenty-two the week of the show), Cornelius had little choice but to present them.

Critics loved *Run-D.M.C.*—its starkness spoke to the rock-trained ear. *Musician* enthused, "When punkers tried to snatch rock back from middle-American complacency and return it to amateurs, they failed because the music still needed instruments and sound systems. All rap requires is two guys in an alley."

"Rock Box" was the first video Profile ever produced. Featuring Larry "Bud" Melman (Calvert DeForest), the annoying-old-man character from *Late Night with David Letterman*, and a "Rock and Roll Hall of Fame" a full two years before the inauguration of the real one in Cleveland, "Rock Box" became an MTV favorite, despite its low budget—$27,000—and the fact that, you know, black people had made it.

"THERE ARE TWO OTHER FRESH MCS IN THE HOUSE."

The crowd's "ooohhh!"s sound real—there was clearly a lot of energy in the room surrounding this battle between *Graffiti Rock*'s hosts and its biggest guests. Backstage, Holman recalls, Jam Master Jay approached Kool Moe Dee as both fan and confidant: Could he please lay back? "Jay was like, 'Don't really battle them, they're just getting on their feet and you'll destroy them on television.' Moe Dee was the battle destroyer," says Holman. "But they knew that, they were good sports, and they took it easy on them."

The difference was immediately noticeable. It wasn't just the sharp contrast of Treacherous Two's white designer leather (and Kool Moe Dee's oversize ski-mask shades) with Run-D.M.C.'s signature basic black. In performance, the old schoolers lay back, the new schoolers punched through the fourth wall. (Jam Master Jay cut the records for this battle—no way were they leaving that job to Jimmie Jazz.) D.M.C. went last—and though it had been polite till then, he used the placement to his advantage: when Special K did his second verse, he stumbled ever so slightly, and his anodyne boasting lit a match under D.: "I love to perform, but I'm not a ham," he hollers—and his eyes go sideways enough to implicate just who he might think *is* one.

We cut back to a two-shot of Kool Moe Dee and Special K; they rap us out to the break. "If you think that was a battle—huh, that was light," Special K promises. But their era was vanishing even as they stood on camera.

"IF YOU THINK THAT LOOKS FRESH, I'VE GOT SOMETHING THAT LOOKS *REAL* good."

Brenda Shannon Greene, working under her middle name, performed her second single, "Give Me Tonight," with tinsel in her hair, wearing a lipstick-red unitard, shoulder- and belly-less, and a sweet smile; she even gamely lip-synched to the sound of her own voice being chopped up and pitch-shifted or going through echo. A New York City Breaker approximated his limbs disintegrating in front of her as the song finished.

Holman had put Shannon on *Graffiti Rock* reluctantly. "I had to make a lot of compromises with the dance crowd—we needed to have an artist in there that's not hip-hop," he says. "She was cool—it didn't spoil the party that much." In 1984, most music bizzers saw things in reverse—at that point, hip-hop was considered a specialist form of dance music. Shannon's model was familiar from disco, an act, often a front for a studio project, that issues a twelve-inch single that explodes in the clubs and then works its way onto radio.

Shannon was a bookkeeper who'd studied music and trained with Andrew Frierson of the Metropolitan Opera. "I wanted to stay jazz," she said, "but I love pop most of all." In September 1983 she was hired to sing a demo titled "Let the Music Play," produced by Mark Liggett, a staff producer at the New York dance indie Emergency Records. "I liked the beat, melody and rhythm, but didn't think it was a smash, to tell the truth," Shannon told *Cash Box*. "It surprised me, too. I thought it was just another dance song."

"Let the Music Play" was, in a sense, *the* dance song, running at a brisk 116 beats per minute (BPM). "Rock Box," on the other hand, was a mere 100. Hip-hop was slowing down, getting heavier—its aesthetic priorities were shifting away from dance music's. Get too slick and suddenly you were suspect. And much of the new dance music was *entirely* slick, deliberately so.

"Let the Music Play" jumped to number one on the club chart so quickly that Mirage, an Atco/Atlantic subsidiary, rushed out a seven-inch that October to facilitate radio play. By February it was in the top ten and number two R&B. Shannon's *Let the Music Play* album stayed in the charts for half a year and yielded another R&B top ten (and dance chart number one) with early 1984's "Give Me Tonight." "Plans are to release, drip-drip-drip *Thriller* style, each of the album's seven songs as singles," *Creem* reported. They stopped at three.

"AND IT WAS THE HIP-HOP KIDS WHO MADE THIS SHOW / AND IF YOU LIKE what you saw, just let us know."

As the assembled guests surrounded Holman, Kool Moe Dee looked perturbed behind the shades; Special K, like he couldn't wait to depart the whole silly business. Run-D.M.C., though, held a pose—the rappers' hands, over their heads, touching and Jam Master Jay crouching below them—and didn't budge.

When *Graffiti Rock* premiered that summer, it received a write-up in the *New York Times*: "It presents hip-hop as one big party—that is, hip-hop with its anger and hard-hitting protests softened. . . . *Graffiti Rock*, which is clearly a pilot for a series, is ready to capitalize on it." Though Holman's hustle had gotten the pilot made, turning it into a series was something else.

"Up to that time, creating the New York City Breakers, all I was getting was yeses," says Holman. "We were golden. So I was cocky about *Graffiti Rock* making it." The show had gotten yeses from major sponsors: Coca-Cola and the US Army. "We ended up getting really good ratings, eighty-eight markets around the country, all kinds of great feedback, and when we went to NATPE to sell it"—that is, to the National Association of Television Program Executives convention, in Las Vegas—"we had a rude awakening."

Holman himself didn't attend the convention—the show's investors did. He explains: "You have to sell your show regionally to syndicated markets all over the country, and when you build up enough of a critical mass of middle-class white Republican family-man station managers, you have some advertising muscle, and the station managers were all like, 'Well, we already have *Soul Train*.' Don Cornelius didn't even *like* hip-hop. Also: 'This is a fad—this isn't even going to be around in a year, and I'm not going to be stuck with egg on my face.'

"But then we did get a bite from the LA syndicator: 'We'll buy if Chicago buys.' Chicago: 'We'll buy if New York buys.'" But the deals looked shady, so the show's investors balked. Holman had hoped *Graffiti Rock* might make him a hip-hop mogul. "I would have had antitrust lawsuits against me, because I was going to start my own label," he says. "But profiting off it was never where my smarts were. I wasn't a New Yorker, really. The kids who made that happen? They were New York kids. Kids in New York are hustlers." Two of the biggest would meet at the *Graffiti Rock* after-party.

"RIGHT OFF EIGHTH AVE ON TWENTY-NINTH STREET, IN CHELSEA, IN one of these fashion showrooms that was being tricked out as a pop-up party," says Holman. Russell Simmons, of course, had negotiated Run-D.M.C.'s appearance. "I knew Russell mostly as a fellow impresario. He was from Queens; he was running in different circles than I was." The other guy was an even more distant acquaintance, there as a friend of Kool Moe Dee and Special K.

Rick Rubin was a white twenty-one-year-old who lived a walk away in the dorms at New York University (NYU), where he ostensibly studied film. Raised on Long Island, Rubin dressed like a Ramone and had produced a record for T La Rock and Jazzy Jay called "It's Yours" that had been screaming out of New York speakers all summer long. Kool Moe Dee was Rubin's rapper, but they were under contract to Sugar Hill, which wasn't looking for an outside producer, much less a white one. Besides, Rubin thought Sugar Hill's formula sucked.

Rubin instead worked with Special K's brother, T La Rock (Terry Keaton), who rapped his sibling's lyrics for a track Rubin had concocted. A squadron of the rappers' pals made the trip to a Queens studio where Rubin had previously recorded his punk band, Hose. "It was forty-five dollars an hour, and we made 'It's Yours' in, like, three hours," Rubin recalled.

"It's Yours" was loud, raucous, and, Russell declared, "the blackest hip-hop record that's ever been." At the *Graffiti Rock* after-party, Russell asked Jazzy Jay how he'd made it. When the DJ introduced Russell Simmons to Rubin, the manager did a double take, which Rubin accepted in stride. "Russ's name was on all these records: Jimmy Spicer, Run-D.M.C., Kurtis Blow! I was excited to meet him," Rubin said. "He couldn't believe that I made 'It's Yours.' . . . Russell was dressed like a substitute teacher, in a sports jacket with elbow patches, and penny loafers. Drinking screwdrivers. I remember he was really funny and fun to talk to. Full of energy. I really liked him."

Russell and Rick were yin and yang. Both rebelled against their suburban upbringings by embracing the most city-identified music yet invented. Both were charming wild cards with definite, even ornery opinions. Both knew what a rap record was supposed to sound like, and it wasn't Sugar Hill.

Rubin had spent high school looking down on the AOR warhorses his classmates loved—a stance that took a one-eighty when he hit college. But in addition to punk rock, he loved James Brown and other hard funk. When his black classmates began listening to park-jam tapes, he paid attention. "It felt like black punk rock," he said.

Enrolled at NYU, Rubin began going to Negril's Wheels of Steel nights and couldn't believe the difference—this stuff was *way* better live. "The experience that I had going to hip-hop clubs, which was the greatest experience, wasn't being equaled by the records I could buy. No one was really making down-and-dirty hip-hop records," he said. "'Sucker MC's' was the first track I had heard that reflected what goes on in the club."

Rubin decided to get involved in hip-hop at a point, he said, when "there were no white people involved in any way, shape, or form." Nevertheless, he added, "I felt like the music made a kinship that transcended skin color. Everyone was a fan. It was a shared passion."

Sarcastic, hyper, and entitled, Rubin fit right into the burgeoning gaggle gathered at 1133 Broadway, the address of Rush Productions. There, Simmons presided over a management company (as of September 1984, he handled "twelve rap acts signed to eight labels," according to *Billboard*) as well as Simmons's production work. "No management companies understood this music, so they came to me because of the success we had with Kurtis Blow," he said. "Besides, we'd worked with most of these acts in the days before they made records."

Many of the people Russell was bringing into the fold were curious journalists. One of his early partnerships had been with Robert "Rocky" Ford, a *Billboard* staffer who helped write and produce Kurtis Blow's early records. In 1984, Russell hired Bill Adler, who'd profiled Blow for the *Daily News* in 1980, as Rush Productions' publicist. When Bill Stephney first began talking to Russell on the phone, when Stephney was writing for the new wave magazine *New York Rocker*, both men thought the other was white. "Of course, this is typical of the strangeness that became the culture of Def Jam," Stephney said.

It only got stranger when the Beastie Boys arrived. Mike D (Michael Diamond), Ad-Rock (Adam Horovitz), and MCA (Adam Yauch) had met in the hardcore punk scene; the Beastie Boys were initially a hardcore band. But all three latched onto hip-hop immediately. "We'd sit around with my little RadioShack tape recorder," Kate Schellenbach, the Beastie Boys' first drummer, recalled. "Yauch would rap over [the Sugar Hill Gang's] 'Apache.' He had the deepest voice, so he was the most believable."

In 1983, the Beasties went to record some new punk songs at a friend's studio. "We were listening, and it was, like, 'This sucks. We should do some other stuff,'" Horovitz recalled. In the impeccable logic of wiseassed teenagers, they decided to record a prank call to an ice creamery and put it over a quasi-funk beat and guitar lick. "Cooky Puss" is, at best, juvenile: "Bitch, I'll kick your ass!" the squeaky-voiced Horovitz croaks after the Carvel clerk hangs up on him again. An equally preposterous dancehall takeoff, "Beastie Revolution," was on the B side.

Yet the twelve-inch made fans of serious hip-hoppers. "Not only did we get 'Cooky Puss' at [Adelphi University radio station] WBAU, but the whole crew of us was heavily into it," Stephney said. When British Airways used a portion of "Beastie Revolution" without permission, the Beasties sued them and won $40,000. The trio moved into a loft on Chrystie Street, above a Chinese-owned sweatshop. Now the party could *really* begin.

"American hardcore became too much the same," Diamond said. "It was almost like a uniform—you had a leather jacket and blue jeans and what we always liked about punk rock was that things were always changing and always different. As soon as we all heard rap music, especially once rap records started to come out, we would just memorize every word. Why not try doing it for real?"

Horovitz had gotten tight with Rubin, attending the "It's Yours" session and hanging out in Rubin's NYU dorm room, which was also the first headquarters of Rubin's fledgling label, Def Jam. Rubin was the Beasties' original DJ—not because he could scratch worth a damn, but because he was cool. (And because he had money. As Cey Adams, Rush's art director, noted, "Rick picking up the tab played a big part in us hanging out with him.")

Rubin's pitched obnoxiousness began rubbing off on Mike and the Adams (and pushed Schellenbach out). "Rick was this larger-than-life character—loud, confident, and very animated, funny," Horovitz said. "He was very into that early eighties, Captain Lou Albano wrestler thing—a lot of crazy, yelled speeches, really hyped up."

Simmons found the Beasties similarly irresistible. "Russell was talking about getting a white rap group together very, very early on," Kurtis Blow songwriter J. B. Moore said. "He could smell how big that was going to be and he was actively looking." Russell's wild-man mien, in turn, deeply impressed the Beasties: "This guy would be out drinking, like, twelve screwdrivers and going to three clubs every night," Mike D said.

There is literally no other way the Beastie Boys would have had a serious hip-hop career, because in this era they inspired a common reaction among their black peers—namely, *You've got to be kidding*. "The first time I met 'em, they all three came in, and I thought I was on *Candid Camera* or something," D.M.C. said. "But the thing about 'em was that they were so real. It wasn't like a bunch of white guys faking just to be down with hip-hoppers or just trying to play a role. I respected that a lot." The Beasties, by all accounts, deftly navigated their role. "They were incredibly deferential to Run-D.M.C.," Stephney said. "It's like they knew what the pecking order was."

During the summer of 1984, Horovitz bunked in Rubin's ten-foot-square cinderblock DJ-booth-with-bed. With the success of "It's Yours," demo tapes began arriving at 5 University Place. One particularly persistent kid from Queens called Rubin "every day for, like, two weeks," the kid later said. Rubin didn't play the demo, but Horovitz did, and he flipped, so Rubin invited James Todd Smith down to the dorm. Smith's double take matched Russell's: "I thought you were black," he stammered. "Cool," Rubin replied. Together they made a new song, "I Need a Beat." The teenage rhymer had no shortage of effrontery, boasting: "They hear me, they fear me, they hear me, they fear me / I'm improving the conditions of the rap industry."

As a young teen, Smith had asked his grandparents for a motorcycle; they instead gifted him two turntables and a mixer. He'd taken his rhymes seriously ever since he began writing them at age nine. "If you can write a song about it, you can write a rap about it," he insisted in 1985. "Rapping is just another vocal style. Some rap songs are so mellow Frank Sinatra could sing them."

Smith's rap moniker had been a mouthful in more ways than one: Ladies Love Cool James. Rubin helped him shorten it to L.L. Cool J. Rubin then asked

Simmons for advice. Simmons suggested selling the record to Profile, which set Rubin off—Simmons complained *constantly* about Profile. Finally, he blurted: "Why don't we just do it ourselves?" Simmons balked: he had a deal cooking with Mercury. "This is separate," Rubin insisted. Besides, he intended to do all the work himself: "You just be my partner." Simmons had a legal partnership drafted, threw a thousand dollars into the pot, and agreed to let Rush Productions assume booking, management, and PR duties for all the label's acts.

Within months, "I Need a Beat" sold a hundred thousand copies on Rubin and Simmons's new venture, Def Jam Recordings—with barely any airplay or promotion. "He delivers his raps in an unsyncopated monotone, without shouting, boasting, or use of any gimmicks," critic John Leland noted. "He's an *intellectual*." The kid's ego was already the size of a tank. The first time he met Russell Simmons, L.L. said, "I want to make records like Run." "Do you like them?" Simmons asked. L.L. responded: "They're selling." A year later, preparing to release his first album, L.L. would tell the *Daily News*, "I'd like to play the Meadowlands on a stage that's three stories high. Or the Superdome. Look out, Bruce!"

ARROWHEAD STADIUM,
KANSAS CITY, MISSOURI
July 6, 1984

WHEN HE WAS EIGHTEEN, MICHAEL JACKSON ANSWERED A QUESTIONNAIRE for *Rock & Soul* magazine. It asked, *What do you like most about your work?* "Learning," Michael wrote. *What do you dislike about your work?* "Arguing." *Do you have a nickname?* "Nose"—and next to it, the word crossed out, "niger" [*sic*].

Michael had gotten the nickname "Big Nose" from his father. To Joseph, it was important that none of his kids' heads get bigger than the others'. This was the sort of military training that—as he said, and some of them parroted—kept them off the streets and out of trouble. But giving your most sensitive child the most demeaning nickname you can think of about the thing he's most ashamed of is, above everything, a species of abuse.

The Jacksons' tight familial cocoon in Gary had turned out to be good practice for being on Motown. Ever since they'd signed with the label in 1969, Motown made sure the young performers' lives were intensely stage-managed. Even after they left Motown, in 1976, for CBS Records, the Jacksons would shield themselves from any but the puffiest of press inquiries. In particular, much of the African American popular press—in particular, Johnson Publishing titles such as *Ebony* and *Jet*—was happy to run virtual press releases on the family in exchange for access. *Ebony*'s "interview" with Michael in the May 1984 issue was so skimpy that it quoted his horoscope.

Maintaining the Jacksons' public image was paramount for all concerned. In 1981, during an interview with the Jacksons for the *NME*, Michael threw a tizzy when the paper's photographer appeared to take some shots: "Oh come on, look, the only thing is we don't like the way covers come out because they're not what we like them to be. How come . . . I mean, we don't have makeup on!"

"HOW BIG IS MICHAEL JACKSON?" *ROLLING STONE* ASKED IN THE GRAMMY Awards' aftermath. "Add up all the copies of David Bowie's *Let's Dance*, the Police's *Synchronicity*, the Rolling Stones' *Undercover*, Culture Club's *Colour by Numbers*, Quiet Riot's *Metal Health*, and Duran Duran's *Seven and the Ragged Tiger* that have been sold in the US. A lot of records, right? Now double that figure. That's how big Michael Jackson is."

A month prior to the Grammys, the *Guinness Book of World Records* had, as the *Washington Post* put it, "stopped the presses for the 1984 edition to make certain [Jackson's] accomplishments are listed"—*Thriller* as the all-time best-selling album, at twenty-three million, and the first album to yield six top ten singles. Naturally, Michael was scheduled to receive the first copy off the presses.

He had intended to take 1984 off. He wanted to make movies, and his big closing gambit of '83 seemed like a perfect career bridge. The video for "Thriller"— the album's seventh and final top ten single—had been a way to try to squeeze every commercial drop from its album, and it had succeeded handsomely, not least in spinning off *Making Michael Jackson's "Thriller,"* an hour-long video documentary that, by fall, sold eight hundred thousand copies worldwide.

The video itself was fourteen minutes long and directed by John Landis, specifically requested by Michael after seeing Landis's *An American Werewolf in London*. In the *Village Voice*, J. Hoberman noted, "Although 'Thriller' is no more misogynist than the average horror film, you can bet that if Jackson's date/ victim were white instead of black, the video could never be aired."

Yet there was Michael with Brooke Shields as his date—to the Grammys, to the American Music Awards before that, and to the Museum of Natural History for the *Guinness Book* ceremony. Even for Michael, that last one had been odd. It had cost CBS $1.4 million to put on. Some fifteen hundred fans lined up along Central Park West, but Michael came out only briefly. "Jackson wore no hat," the *Post* noted. "For guests who watched him on stage, it was impossible to see the scalp burn that has been described as large as the hole in a forty-five-rpm record." A letter from President Reagan was read: "Dear Michael: I was pleased to learn that you were not seriously hurt in your recent accident. I know from experience that these things can happen on the set. . . . You've gained quite a number of fans along the road since 'I Want You Back,' and Nancy and I are among them."

Michael's taste in companions did not please everyone. One Baltimorean wrote an angry letter to *Ebony* in 1983, after Jackson had discussed dating Tatum O'Neal and Brooke Shields: "All your article on Michael Jackson did for me was turn my stomach. Why is it that his interviews consist of his bragging about his White girlfriends? If Michael is showing Black kids that success and Whiteness go hand in hand, he's a sorry example for them."

IN **1980,** FOLLOWING AN ONSTAGE TUMBLE THAT BROKE HIS NOSE, Michael had the first of many plastic surgeries. (The first operation had accidentally obstructed his breathing, so a second one followed to correct it.) The results pleased Michael, who'd come to dislike his own appearance. When he went vegetarian, he dropped to a slim, sinewy 120 pounds. After sweeping the Grammys, he got a third nose job. He wanted it to look, he told his doctor, more like Diana Ross's.

Ross had been Michael's mentor. She hadn't "discovered" him—that had been another Motown PR ruse. (Gladys Knight had first recommended the Jackson boys to Motown, and Bobby Taylor of the Vancouvers got them their label audition.) But after Berry Gordy moved the Jackson family to Los Angeles, Diana, in essence, gave Michael hauteur lessons. She taught him to conduct himself as a star—to carry himself at a slight remove from the world.

In 1978, Michael worked with Diana on his first movie, *The Wiz*, the Sidney Lumet–directed adaptation of the Broadway musical, which reset *The Wizard of Oz* in Harlem. (He also met Quincy Jones, who was scoring the film, on that set.) It led to other offers, many of which came from Broadway, to which Michael's agility seemed perfectly tailored. But the roles weren't what he wanted—he wasn't going to play a gay dancer in *A Chorus Line*, not with all the rumors swirling around that Michael himself was homosexual. "Michael isn't gay," his mother Katherine assured *Time* magazine in March of 1984. "It's against his religion."

A lot of things were against his religion. Like his mother and his sisters Rebbie and La Toya, Michael was a devout Jehovah's Witness. He attended his local Kingdom Hall four times a week with Katherine, as well as continuing to go door to door to spread the word, even after *Thriller* had made him as recognizable as anyone on the planet. So Michael began dressing in costume—fake facial hair, hat-and-wig combos, glasses, a fat suit.

But Michael's circumstances weren't normal. Jehovah's Witnesses were expected to engage solely in p-in-v sexual intercourse, within the bounds of matrimony. Homosexuality is also forbidden—not simply in real life but in the mind, since the tenet of the religion is that Jehovah can see into the believer's heart. Moreover, the only way a Witness is supposed to interact with anyone outside the sect is while converting them—a big reason the Jackson family remained sheltered even as they reached and passed voting age. Almost nobody Michael worked with—none of the *Off the Wall* or *Thriller* personnel, most of his family, his old-Hollywood friends—was a Witness.

Michael's dancing also came under fire for its overt sexuality. So did his wearing makeup onstage—and off. In 1984, Michael was diagnosed with vitiligo, which causes patches of the skin to lose their melanin, causing the skin to blotch; makeup evened it out. (It would be another decade before Michael divulged this, during a televised interview with Oprah Winfrey.)

But the biggest issue the Witnesses had was the "Thriller" video. By turning into a zombie werewolf and leading a group of the undead in a climactic dance routine, Jackson had crossed the line into what the Witnesses called "spiritism"—glorifying the occult. The church objected so strongly that it threatened to excommunicate its most famous member. "That would kill him if that ever happened," an unnamed intimate told *Smash Hits*, "because only at home and at church is he treated like a normal person."

Days before the video was delivered to MTV, Jackson tried to have his lawyer, John Branca, destroy the negatives, before Branca suggested he include a disclaimer at the video's beginning. John Landis wrote the note ("Due to my strong personal convictions, I wish to stress that this film in no way endorses a belief in the occult"), and Michael signed it. "I'll never do a video like that again," he promised the Witness magazine *Awake!*

WHEN THE JACKSON 5 MOVED FROM MOTOWN TO CBS IN THE MID-seventies, Jermaine stayed behind. He'd married Hazel Gordy, Berry's daughter, and kept going as a solo act; the youngest brother, Randy, joined in his stead as the group became the Jacksons. Now, all six brothers were going to share one stage for the first time. They announced it at Tavern on the Green, on Central Park West, on November 30, 1983.

They arrived in coordinated styles: outsized, colorful, heavily contoured jackets in varsity or, in Michael's case, military style, as well as matching aviator shades, the freshest of looks at the time. (Pink and pale pastel purple was a typical color combo.) And then the boxing promoter Don King, who was promoting their tour, proceeded to talk . . . about Don King.

King had been Joseph's idea, not Michael's. This was the sort of decision-making that had prompted Michael to fire his father as his manager, even as he remained the other brothers'. Michael had long been a boardroom adept, overseeing a rapidly expanding array of nonperformance interests. He was buying up publishing catalogs—his friend Paul McCartney had been doing it for years. Be the best by learning from the best—that was his motto.

It was abundantly clear to anyone outside the family unit that Michael had thoroughly eclipsed the rest of them. The most recent Jacksons album, *Triumph* (1980), had sold a million copies. *Thriller* did twenty-three times that. When Michael's lawyer, John Branca, suggested that the proper payback for *Thriller* was for CBS to eventually hand Jackson ownership of his own master tapes, Walter Yetnikoff obliged—nearly unheard-of in the mid-eighties major-label record business.

Joseph hadn't even told Michael he was shopping a Jacksons tour before he began discussing it with promoters—before the *Motown 25* special had even aired. He was in financial straits. Apart from Jermaine, so were Michael's brothers. They weren't making money, just spending it. They, too, needed a windfall. Who better to provide them one than their son and brother, the biggest star on earth?

Joseph could make water curdle. When Cecil Holmes, who cofounded Casablanca Records, offered the Jacksons a $250,000 check to handle the tour, Joseph ripped it up and tossed it at Holmes's feet in front of the entire family, telling him, "Are you kidding me? We're not going to be undersold like this!"

The boxing promoter Don King was Joseph's kind of guy. The two had met when the elder Jackson attended a Las Vegas press party for one of King's matches. "I found him extremely impressive," Joseph said.

King came from a hard background, having served four years in prison for killing a man in Cleveland during a street fight in 1967 (the governor of Ohio would later pardon him). After he got into the boxing biz, he became a font of noisy, nonstop self-congratulation. That, along with his flamboyant troll-doll coiffure, which he compared to Samson's ("My hair gives me an aura of invincibility," he told *Sepia* in 1981), obscured his often-brilliant deals.

He'd promoted the Thrilla in Manila—the third Muhammad Ali–Joe Frazier fight in the Philippines, in the fall of 1975—with a pay-per-view audience of over a billion. King was an outsized personality in a field where loudness counted. You had to hold your own if you were to handle an Ali. But the soft-spoken Jacksons weren't Ali, particularly not Michael.

At Tavern on the Green, King nattered on about the Thrilla in Manila—"The wrong *Thriller*," as Branca later put it. Michael was already incensed that King was on board, comparing the situation to "get[ting] on a plane with a pilot that never flew before." But King had come to Hayvenhurst with a check for half a million dollars apiece for his brothers. So, Michael was outvoted. In the group, everybody's vote counted once, not twenty-three times the others'.

Michael certainly didn't need the money. His royalty rate was higher than anyone else's—around $2.10 per album sold; *Thriller* had earned him in the area of $50 million by spring of '84. Michael went along at the behest of Katherine. He couldn't bear to disappoint his mother.

Michael wasn't likely to talk much anyway—he never did at these things—but at Tavern on the Green, almost none of the Jacksons got a word in. Unless Michael absolutely had to, he didn't deal with the press at all anymore. The fact that he didn't just seemed to feed his popularity.

Soft drinks are as dependent on young buyers as pop music is. Pepsi was locked in deadly competition with the behemoth Coca-Cola for the youth dollar. US soda sales were worth $20 billion by 1983, with Coke still owning the market; Pepsi did better only in supermarkets. But in 1977, Pepsi had launched the "Pepsi Challenge," a head-to-head taste test and PR gimmick, and found most people liked its taste better than Coke's, and the younger brand began to gain on the giant.

Coke's solution turned out to be diet soda—something Pepsi had been selling since 1964. Diet Coke didn't appear until July 1982—one month after the Coca-Cola Company had acquired Columbia Pictures for $750 million. Diet Coke was seen as something of a risk—it was only the second drink ever to feature the company's sacrosanct script logo—but both gambles paid off: Diet

Coke was America's best-selling soft drink within a year, and Columbia's stock, previously selling at $41.75, jumped more than twenty dollars when the Coke buyout was announced.

That wasn't the only change happening: in early May of 1983, Pepsi decided to allow up to 50 percent high-fructose corn syrup in its drinks, letting its bottlers make the product far more cheaply—something Coke had been doing for years.

Another thing Coke had been doing for years was targeting African American consumers. During the sixties, the company had run a series of radio jingles featuring well-known rock and soul stars, including the first recorded duet by Ray Charles and Aretha Franklin. These ads sounded like the artists' hits until, inevitably, they veered into the "Things Go Better with Coca-Cola" jingle. In addition, Coke spent the seventies and eighties signing celebrity pitchers such as Bill Cosby, Julius (Dr. J) Erving of the Philadelphia 76ers, and Vanessa Williams, elected the first black Miss America in September 1983. By mid-1984, the black consumer market in the United States was estimated to be between $160 and $200 million.

Pepsi needed to leapfrog the competition right when Don King came a-knockin', dangling the as-yet-unsigned Jacksons, with the further enticement that Coca-Cola had also expressed interest. King hadn't even spoken with Coke, but Pepsi took it. The agreed amount was $5 million, the largest amount any pop star—sorry, pop *group*—had ever earned from a corporate sponsor.

"This is an area where consumers respond to promotion," Allen Rosenshine, chairman of BBDO, Pepsi's ad agency, told *New York*. "So there's considerable switching back and forth between Coke and Pepsi. It's irrelevant whether Michael Jackson drinks Pepsi or Duran Duran drinks Coke. This isn't testimonial advertising where we suggest he drinks this, and therefore so should you. This is lifestyle advertising."

For rockers of the hippie era, accepting corporate sponsorship messed badly with the idea, however suspect, that rock and roll was a site of autonomous creativity. But that had begun to shift in the mid-seventies, when Jay Coleman formed Rockbill, a company that put bands together with corporations. "It took me about five years to persuade the ad community that rock and roll was kosher," Coleman said. Corporations, he explained, were "nervous about getting too close to a band because of the whole image of music and counterculture. The band[s], meanwhile, [were] nervous about getting too close to a company because they didn't want to commercialize themselves or sell out."

That began changing after the 1979 slump. Labels cut down drastically on tour support, forcing bands to find other ways to get and stay on the road. Speaking to *Advertising Age* in 1981, Coleman credited the sudden corporate prominence of "the Woodstock generation"—yuppies with dollars to spend—for these campaigns' success.

That year, Rockbill sired a deal for Jovan to sponsor the Rolling Stones' US trek for their 1981 album, *Tattoo You*. (In addition, the Stones had secured backing from TDK cassettes in Germany and Piaggio motor scooters in Italy.) "While the Stones themselves will not endorse Jovan products," *Ad Age* reported, "the fragrance marketer will handle all promotion and has the right to advertise the concerts with the phrase, 'Jovan presents the Rolling Stones.'" The musk makers had ponied up a cool million for the privilege.

By 1984, rock tour sponsorships had become the norm. In spring, Pepsi made another, even bigger deal with Lionel Richie: $8 million for a TV special and two concert tours, plus Richie's appearance in a series of television ads. Coke sponsored tours by Duran Duran and Julio Iglesias. "Now the only big rock stars who aren't interested in such support are Bruce Springsteen and Billy Joel," Coleman told *New York*. "Woodstock could never have had a corporate sponsor fourteen years ago. Woodstock 1984 probably would have."

With banners onstage bearing the sponsors' name, this sort of advertising wasn't simply a distraction. It was becoming insidious. Some companies were beginning to insert their products directly into films and TV shows, thanks to a firm called Prime Time Promotions; the foremost example was *E.T.*'s use of Reese's Pieces. "The payoff is down the road with a thing like this," an executive from BASF (a building-materials manufacturer) told *Billboard* as he awaited two upcoming movies his products had been put into: *Ghostbusters* and *Gremlins*.

PEPSI'S $5 MILLION FOR THE JACKSONS WAS CONTINGENT ON THE BROTHERS' willingness to do a pair of TV ads for the soda. That had ended less than well. Additionally, it transpired that Quaker Oats, whose products Michael would, in fact, ingest, had been ready to pay the Jacksons 40 percent more than Pepsi—except King had jumped the gun by giving the soda an exclusive, rather than adopting multiple sponsors. When the family found out, King's star drooped further in the Jacksonian skies.

In the early months of 1984, it became clearer that King had no idea how to organize a music tour, let alone one as complicated as a Jacksons performance,

with its state-of-the-art staging. When Michael discovered King's criminal record, the promoter's days were numbered. King soon received a memo—later
leaked to *Rolling Stone*—instructing him, among other things, "not to communicate with anyone on Michael Jackson's behalf without prior permission."

Michael had an idea for the tour's name: The Final Curtain. Instead, his
brothers went with Victory—also the title of the next Jacksons album, due
out to coincide with the tour. They'd chosen the name before nearly anything
had been recorded. As it transpired, *Victory*—unlike its predecessors *Destiny*
and *Triumph*—was less a group album than a series of Jackson-brother solo
recordings.

Also, *whose* victory? At Tavern on the Green, Marlon explained: "The tour
name means that the brothers are getting together once again to unite, and
we're real close with each other, and [to] show the world that we can make
everybody happy." Would that be everybody in the world, or everybody in the
Jacksons?

Something else announced at Tavern was guaranteed to make a lot of people very unhappy: Tickets would be $28, plus a $2 service and handling fee,
each—and available only in blocks of four, sold solely by mail order. You had to
invest $120 (the equivalent at this writing is $290) just to get one ticket. "Tickets
are being sold on a lottery basis," *Smash Hits* noted. "Losers will not be notified
and will have to wait up to two months to get their money back. During which
time it'll be in the Jacksons' bank account earning interest. All sounds like a bit
of a swizzle."

The biggest rock act of the time, the Rolling Stones, charged only $16 a
ticket, thanks to the Jovan deal. The Philadelphia soul-rock duo Daryl Hall and
John Oates had been working with sponsors since the late seventies. "It helps
us keep ticket prices down," Hall told the *New York Times*. "If you keep prices
down, people will come out to see you."

There was none of that coming from the Jacksons. Their new engagement with Pepsi *and* a ticket price nearly twice that of the Stones' meant they
profiteered coming and going. The victory they were announcing had more
in common with the cutthroat, winner-take-all Wall Street ethos sired by Rea-
ganomics than with the genuine excitement worked up by *Thriller*. Michael
had conquered the world; now, it seemed, everyone attached to him, or able to
attach to him, was staging a raid on the profits.

The Jacksons didn't understand what the big deal was. "Nobody talked
about Julio Iglesias at fifty-five dollars, Frank Sinatra at a hundred dollars, or

Bette Midler's forty-five-dollar ticket prices," Marlon claimed. People *did*, though—and noted, every time, that Iglesias, Sinatra, and Midler played for decidedly adult audiences. The Jacksons' constituency, not just Michael's, was seen as teenagers, particularly the underprivileged kids who were being priced out.

By spring, King had been replaced—first by the Rhode Island promoter Frank Russo, who'd worked on tours for Diana Ross and Earth, Wind & Fire. King received 3 percent to take a back seat. This wouldn't stop King from later boasting to *Billboard*, "Who else could have organized this tour and brought in a partner to put up a $40 million guarantee? No one." *Rolling Stone* reported that one promoter was referring to Victory as "the Nitro Tour: At any moment, the whole thing could blow up."

Airtight security was absolutely crucial. With the Who's concert in Cincinnati in December 1979, which resulted in the death of eleven fans when concertgoers stampeded the doors, and Diana Ross's Central Park concert in July 1983, when more than eighty arrests were made, big rock shows were seen as genuine security risks. The Victory Tour's coordinator, Larry Larson, whose prior experience had been as the manager of soft-rock soundtrack king Kenny Loggins, told *Rolling Stone*, "The Jacksons do not have a history of creating riots." The reporter pointed out that, in 1981, the Jacksons' Madison Square Garden appearance had included dozens of arrests for kids snatching chains on the premises.

DESPITE HAVING PUT ON SOME CONCERTS IN COLLEGE, CHUCK SULLIVAN wasn't any more a concert promoter than King was. The Boston-based Sullivan's family owned the New England Patriots and the team's venue, Foxboro Stadium. Still, Sullivan arranged a $12.5 million loan and put up the stadium as collateral so he could get on board as the Victory Tour's new promoter following Frank Russo's departure.

Sullivan tried to quell criticisms of the ticket prices frustrating Jackson's younger, darker fans, promising to reserve "four hundred tickets [from] each stadium show for underprivileged children." But he also had to push the tour's opener back, from June 22 to June 30. The original plan to kick off at the 23,600-seat Rupp Arena in Lexington, Kentucky, fell through because Rupp's management wanted the venue to sell its own tickets. They weren't alone.

Tricks that worked in the NFL fell flat with a touring group. Sullivan asked to get the Jacksons' hotel rooms all for free, a tactic commonplace for the Super

Bowl. Here it received a swift, public backlash. "If I make all the concessions they're asking me to make, I'm going to lose money on the show and the taxpayers of this state are going to have to subsidize it," the Louisiana Superdome's general manager told *Billboard*. "Initially, they asked for a complete waiver of taxes and zero rent. . . . As long as the Jacksons have been in the concert business, I don't understand why they suddenly have to do something that's such a deviation from the standard."

Then the ultimate embarrassment: On June 20, Foxboro's board of selectmen denied the Jacksons the right to stage a concert in their town. The Victory Tour's promoter couldn't even book the show into the stadium he owned—or reap profits that once seemed surefire but that appeared to be vanishing by the day. Soon, Sullivan was renegotiating his contract: the Jacksons would now receive 75 percent of ticket price, not 85 percent; and he relieved himself of the burden of paying the Jacksons twenty-one dollars per unsold seat. This became a cudgel for Sullivan's rivals, notably King.

A number of other African American promoters were exercised over the white arriviste Sullivan becoming the Victory Tour's face. The Reverend Al Sharpton eventually met with the Jacksons and got them to agree to co-promote in larger cities with a number of black promoters. Sharpton was already in the midst of boycotting Lionel Richie, whose spring 1984 tour had only four dates, of forty, co-promoted by black promoters. Many had been incensed by Richie's blithe rebuttal that they "have got to understand . . . that artists want the best, and the best doesn't necessarily mean color."

"Comments like these anger black promoters, who complain that when black artists become bankable commodities they hire white managers who in turn use only white agents and promoters to book their shows," *Black Enterprise* noted. "This is a particularly volatile issue because black promoters feel they take the early risks and losses to nurture talents like Richie and Michael Jackson until they reach superstardom."

IN THE SEPTEMBER 22 ISSUE OF *CASH BOX*, SIX RECORDS BY VARIOUS JACK-sons sat in the R&B top fifty. (In line with *Billboard*'s recently renamed Black chart, *Cash Box*'s list was dubbed Black Contemporary.) Michael was on three of them, two by the Jacksons: "Torture," a duet with Jermaine, written by Jackie, and "State of Shock," a duet with Mick Jagger (numbers eighteen and nineteen, respectively); and oldest sister Rebbie's "Centipede," which Michael wrote and sang on (number forty-eight). In addition to "Torture," Jermaine's own "Dynamite," from his self-titled solo debut for Arista Records, was at number thirteen. And two Jackson sisters also made the list: Janet's "Don't Stand Another Chance" (produced by Marlon) and La Toya's "Hot Potato," at twenty-five and forty-seven, respectively.

It could have been seven. The hot track on *Jermaine Jackson* had been another Michael duet, "Tell Me I'm Not Dreamin'," which was getting big airplay. But it wasn't released as a single—CBS had blocked it. They were following Michael's orders. Arista's workaround was to press an airplay-only, promo-only three-song EP. Some copies of the promo were destroyed to prevent them from reaching the secondhand market. Still, "Tell Me" wound up topping the *Billboard* dance charts as an album cut.

These weren't the only records by other people that Michael was appearing on in 1984. The year began with Michael at number one with "Say Say Say," a duet with his old friend Paul McCartney. In January, Motown released a record by Berry Gordy's son, Kennedy—Michael's in-law, thanks to Jermaine and Hazel—who called himself Rockwell. He played the Jackson family his demo for a new wave synth number about paranoia called "Somebody's Watching Me." Michael, who had already written many hit songs on this very topic, loved it, committing to sing backup on the spot. So did Jermaine, but fewer people noticed.

"Somebody's Watching Me" reached number two that spring. Motown denied Michael was even on it. This was rich, considering that on May 15, it issued *Farewell My Summer Love 1984*, an LP's worth of unissued Michael vocals from 1973 given new instrumental tracks to lend them a "contemporary" patina. They didn't forget to credit him that time.

The biggest of the Jacksons' hits, "State of Shock," was, to be horribly obvious about it, "Beat It II: Electric Guitar Boogaloo." This was a classic backroom team-up: Jackson and Mick Jagger shared a lawyer, Branca, and the Rolling Stones had cost CBS Records a reported $28 million for four albums. But *Undercover*, in 1983, was the first new Stones album since *Sticky Fingers* in 1971 not to reach number one in America (it stalled at four). And "State of Shock" was nowhere as electrifying as its title. It shot out of the cannon, moving a million copies within a month. Yet its popularity was fleeting and hollow—everything *Thriller* wasn't.

As far as CBS was concerned, *Victory* was the follow-up to *Thriller*. The label shipped two million copies opening week, but the album landed with a thud. "There's no direction, no fire," *Smash Hits* complained of the album's "comfy and rather dull pop. . . . It must have been a nightmare putting this together." Critic Vince Aletti's review finished witheringly: "What more could you want? Don't ask."

Perhaps the last word came from, once again, "Weird Al" Yankovic. On September 3, Yankovic hosted "AL-TV," a spoof special on MTV, and introduced a "video" for "State of Shock" (no official clip existed)—a single camera shot of Epic Records executive Harvey Leeds sitting at his desk, tunelessly yammering the riff: "Da-da-da-*dahhh* . . . You talkin' to me good—da-dat, da-da-da-da / Ya know ya like ya should—da-dat, da-da-da-da." Its dead-eyed artlessness was an inbuilt critique of the record's own.

THE OTHER BIG EVENT IN KANSAS CITY THE FIRST WEEK OF JULY WAS THE Diamond Jubilee Convention put on by the National Association for the Advancement of Colored People (NAACP). The civil rights organization's seventy-fifth anniversary took place July 2 to 5. Among other events, the gathering included a "March to Bury Voter Apathy," which stretched for fifteen miles. Speaking to the assembled, Kansas senator Robert Dole "suggested that Black America is a challenge for the Republican Party, and that this is an untapped resource," the NAACP magazine *The Crisis* reported.

Another comment suggested why. Peter W. Rodino Jr., the chairman of the House Judiciary Committee, said, "Under Mr. Reagan's leadership, billions and billions of dollars have been slashed from what I call 'People Programs': employment and job training, Aid to Families with Dependent Children, Medicaid, food stamps, community development, block grants, housing, education, and child care for single-parent families. There can be no doubt about it . . . civil rights are under siege . . . and they have been under siege since the earliest days of this Administration."

This was not the only place where anti-Reagan sentiment showed its head that week—far from it. The NAACP's executive director, Benjamin L. Hooks, seethed that Reagan's idea of "what America ought to be . . . is so far from what it is and so deadly to what black people have to have that I cannot think of anything worse than that."

All three frontrunners for the Democratic Party presidential nomination, to be decided in less than two weeks at the Democratic National Convention in San Francisco, came to the Diamond Jubilee: Walter Mondale, Gary Hart, and Rev. Jesse Jackson. Mondale, the former VP from Minnesota and the likely choice for the nomination, warned: "Don't let Mr. Reagan get his hands on the Supreme Court." Hart, the senator from Colorado, "came from nowhere in 1984 to stalemate Walter Mondale and overturn the aging Democratic establishment in the process," as the *New York Times* put it.

The biggest response, though, went to the Reverend Jackson. "There is the liberal, who wants to put one foot in the past and one foot toward progress," he said. "Blacks cannot be liberals, we must be progressives." The night of his speech, the NAACP received more than $30,000 in donations.

Michael and Tito Jackson made it out to the conference's final night, where Hooks presented them with the Dr. H. Claude Hudson Medal of Freedom, which honored "the ideals of family unity and togetherness." They also announced the Jacksons would be honorary chairmen of the NAACP's youth voter drive. The booth at the first show registered 350 people.

Michael, though, wasn't saying anything bad about Ronald Reagan. On May 14, Michael had visited the White House, where he was honored for donating "Beat It" to a national anti-drunk-driving campaign. President Reagan thanked him "for the example that you've given to the millions of young Americans who look up to you . . . your success is an American dream come true." Commentators compared it to Elvis Presley visiting Richard Nixon in the Oval Office.

Michael made another public appearance on July 5, this one at the Westin Crown Center Hotel. He called a press conference—there happened to be five hundred or so reporters in the city that weekend. First, Michael announced he was donating his entire share of the Pepsi money to charity at the Victory Tour's end, adding that he'd intended to do so as soon as the tour's plans began. Additionally, the mail-order system would be ended "as soon as possible, so that no one will pay money unless they get a ticket." The room full of reporters hummed approvingly.

In particular, Michael said, "The other day I got a letter from a girl in Texas named LaDonna Jones," which had spurred his decision. Though the letter was addressed to him, Michael "received" it the same way the rest of the country did: when the *Dallas Morning News* ran the letter on July 1 and the wire services picked it up.

Jones was an eleven-year-old from Lewisville, Texas, who'd babysat and done chores to save money to see Jackson perform, until the four-ticket pricing scheme thwarted her plans. "I've always believed you to be a person of feeling up until now," she wrote. "I'm so disappointed in you. How could you of all people be so selfish? Is your appearance here in Texas Stadium only for the rich?" It was like Michael had been slapped in the face with a rhinestone glove.

After less than five minutes on the dais, Michael directed questions to his manager Frank DiLeo. With this, Jackson made it clear that he saw the Victory Tour as an obligation. One last time, for the family, the greatest entertainer on earth was going to grit his teeth and get it over with.

THE TEMPERATURE REACHED THE HIGH NINETIES IN KANSAS CITY THE weekend of the Victory Tour's opening, though the world's greatest entertainer refused to air-condition his hotel room—it hurt his voice. The heat reflected the atmosphere. Kansas City's city limits housed only about a half million people, but the Victory opener had generated more press requests than the most recent Super Bowl. The municipality expected to gross $10 million from the shows, $500,000 of it through state and local taxes and usage fees.

Nelson George, there on dual assignment for *Billboard* and the *Village Voice*, called the scene around the Westin "a carnival," with the parking lot a veritable tailgater full of families and fanatics: "Rumors were rife: Michael was too sick to perform; Michael hated his brothers so much he wouldn't go onstage; counterfeit tickets had flooded the market." Vendors sold shoddy secondhand merch throughout the parking lot—even in the hotel's gift shop. For $7.95, a white glove dotted with a few rhinestone studs could be yours. The Glove, it was called, with the tagline at the bottom: "You just can't BEAT IT."

There was Michael merchandise everywhere, not just in Kansas City. That year, LJN Toys manufactured a Michael doll with six separate outfits (the "Grammy Award," "American Music Award," "Beat It," "Thriller," "Motown 25," and "Human Nature"). Jackson had negotiated one-quarter of the dolls' profits, netting over $4 million that year alone. ("Contrary to popular belief, however, when you wind up the doll it does not walk backwards," *Cash Box* ribbed.) He was cracking down, too—in 1984, a pair of Jackson-affiliated companies filed a $50 million civil suit against bootleg manufacturers. On opening night evening, federal marshals seized more than two thousand unauthorized Michael T-shirts from the Arrowhead Stadium parking lot.

Often with Michael, "best" simply meant "most." Victory was the first concert tour to travel with its own power source. The set weighed 375 tons, contained a series of hydraulic elevators, run by pressurized fluid, and required a crew of 240 a full five days to erect; two hundred pounds of dry ice was utilized. But the extra-large stage meant an extra-large problem—to house it, stadiums needed to remove seats, meaning the promoter, Sullivan, was on the hook for the difference. The operation was losing a million dollars a week.

The month of June was particularly nerve-wracking. "Each brother had a lawyer, an adviser, an accountant. Sometimes it became trying to get everything settled," DiLeo said.

The Jacksons had begun rehearsing at Zoetrope Studios, in San Francisco, owned by Francis Ford Coppola, prior to moving into dress rehearsals in Birmingham. By the time they got to Alabama, Michael's five feet nine inches had dropped from 120 to 105 pounds; he was living on nuts and herbs. Reportedly, they rehearsed the show nearly eighty times.

Like the Jacksons, Kansas City was ultra-prepared. More than five hundred police and security were added, as well as seventy handheld metal detectors. ("That's unconstitutional, you know," writer Dave Marsh noted of being frisked with the latter.) It cost Sullivan five times the amount he'd have spent on security for a football game.

"I DON'T THINK THE BLACK COMMUNITY IN KANSAS CITY WILL SEND A hundred and twenty dollars to New York City for six weeks to see anyone," one ticket-biz honcho told *Billboard* in the lead-up to the Victory Tour. Nevertheless, many of the reporters sent there noted that Kansas City was also the headquarters of Hallmark Cards. The lead was nearly too easy: the biggest black act in the land would kick off their tour in the home of homilies to white-bread gentility.

But inside the stadium on opening night, a curious thing was occurring: *nothing*. This wasn't the rambunctious drunken bonhomie of young yuppies at a Stones show or the youthful exuberance threatening to spill over of a teen-aged Jacksons crowd. This was, as critic Greil Marcus put it on *Nightline* that night, "perhaps the oldest and youngest audience I've ever seen at a rock and roll concert. It's a family audience; it's a Fourth of July picnic; it's a church social. It's a quiet, placid, sociable crowd—lots of little kids, lots of people in their forties and fifties."

The word Marcus was too polite to use was *whitest*. Writing about it afterward, he estimated the "composition of the audience [at] perhaps 5 percent black in a 30 percent black city." *Nightline* had flown him to Kansas City to cover the show, or at least the half hour he could see before being called on camera. And this was what he and nearly five hundred cops had shown up for—a family night out.

The evening opened with Randy Jackson pulling a sword from a stone to defeat a gaggle of menacing Muppets and ended with "a fireworks display that's straight out of Disneyland," as *Billboard* put it. For most of the crowd, as George wrote in the *Voice*, this show was "like going to the Ice Capades."

"Who's Michael Jackson, Mommy?" a five-year-old girl seated behind Marcus asked. "He's a singer, darling," her mother said, "and don't kick the gentleman's chair."

Attending the Victory Tour was a way for upper-middle-class white people to display their wealth—LaDonna Jones had nailed it.

Backstage presided a pair of Jehovah's Witnesses, on the tour to keep their eyes on Michael. "Thriller" never made it onto a Victory Tour set list—and neither did any of the songs from *Victory* itself. The only new songs on the set list belonged to *Thriller*. Besides the new stage and special effects, the show was basically the same as the *Triumph* tour three years earlier. Of course, it hardly mattered: the vast majority of the audience hadn't seen the Jacksons in 1981—or ever.

Despite the hoopla over the six-Jackson lineup, only five lined the front of the stage in Kansas City. Early in the show, Jackie Jackson waved from the back. He was on a pair of crutches. On June 21, the Jacksons announced that their oldest brother would sit out at least half the tour because of a knee injury. He'd been hit by a car: Jackie's wife, rumor had it, had done the honors after finding out he was having an affair with a young Los Angeles Lakers cheerleader named Paula Abdul, who in short order became the choreographer of both the video for the Jackie-written Jacksons single "Torture" and the Victory Tour itself. Despite the injury, Jackie still received his tour percentage.

For the seventh song, Jermaine began playing a familiar bass riff. For once, it wasn't his younger brother's song but his own—"Let's Get Serious," a 1980 R&B number one written and produced for Jermaine by Stevie Wonder.

"You think you can come back and put your songs anywhere in the show?" Marlon mock-admonished his brother. "It just doesn't work that way." Stagily, Jermaine threatened to quit; "I've heard that before!" Michael responded, before giving Jermaine the floor. It was, *Billboard* wrote, "So obviously scripted as to be painful."

Jermaine performed three songs in a medley: "Serious," "You Like Me, Don't You?" (later replaced by "Dynamite," from his new album), and finally a duet with Michael on "Tell Me I'm Not Dreaming." Michael announced, "We're gonna give you the old stuff!" Following a Jackson 5 medley, everyone taking a line or two on "The Love You Save," he announced, "You got it the old-fashioned way!" and segued right into his solo "Rock with You." And that was the end of the others—just as everyone had no doubt hoped, this was essentially a Michael Jackson solo tour. He'd designed the stage and he called the shots.

By the way, you couldn't find a Pepsi on the premises. Arrowhead Stadium's existing contract with Coca-Cola was ironclad.

MANY CRITICS FOUND OPENING NIGHT OF THE VICTORY TOUR ANTISEPTIC. George in the *Voice* called it a "glorified rehearsal"; his *Billboard* colleague Paul Grein thought the show "seamless and precise, but dishearteningly stiff," and added: "Michael Jackson is coming off the most phenomenally successful year any performer has had since Elvis and the Beatles. Would it be asking too much for him to take a few seconds and give us some sense of what it's meant to him?"

The second show, on July 7, was much better received. Yet everyone found it downright strange not to hear *anything* from the LP that had given the tour its name. "They're buying the *Victory* album even though the Jacksons didn't play any of the music from it," a Kansas City Musicland store manager told *Billboard*.

The Arrowhead Stadium stand was, a Kansas City Chiefs executive admitted, "a limited financial success. We knew that going into it, and it wasn't strictly a business decision. The amount of national and international attention that Kansas City received was worth it. You can't buy that kind of publicity." At one meeting a few weeks into the tour, one of the Jackson brothers brought up the audience's unexpected paleness during a meeting: "Everyone seemed baffled," tour publicist Howard Bloom said.

But that—and thirty dollars—was the price of crossover. A Dallas promoter not working on the Victory Tour got straight to the point: "The Jackson concert is now a white show," he said, "and they're a white group."

MANN'S CHINESE THEATRE,
HOLLYWOOD
July 26, 1984

A WEEK AFTER THE KANSAS CITY OPENER, LADONNA JONES WAS BACK-stage with the Jacksons at Texas Stadium.

Jones's open letter had gotten so much attention that her appearance at the first night of three in Dallas became a mini-media event unto itself. It wasn't what the shy eleven-year-old had been after, but who could turn down four free tickets and a limo ride to the biggest show of the year? After meeting Michael backstage, she got an autograph and a peck on the cheek; back at her seat, she said, "It felt like my legs were going to give out. It was so weird." Soon she was being asked for autographs herself.

LaDonna Jones wasn't the only one arriving to Texas Stadium in a limousine. All of the city's 320 chauffeured limos were booked solid that weekend. This sort of flaunting of wealth was becoming a kind of spectator sport. That spring, the Australian producer-host Robin Leach started a syndicated TV show for just these sorts of displays titled *Lifestyles of the Rich and Famous*.

The tour's opening-weekend glitches were smoothing, but things were growing genuinely dangerous. Three days before the Jacksons' July 21 Gator Bowl opener in Jacksonville, Florida, James Huberty, a forty-one-year-old from San Diego who had sent messages threatening the Jacksons, entered a local McDonald's carrying three guns—a shotgun and a pair of 9 mm machine guns—and spent seventy-seven minutes opening fire on everyone in the building. He killed twenty-one people and injured nineteen others before being felled by a police sniper.

At the time, this was the largest mass murder in American history. "Understandably, everyone was freaking out as the San Diego incident played itself out on television," Jermaine wrote. In Jacksonville the weekend after Dallas, the brothers' already-taxed security detail had to clear every room they went into, with the help of a fire marshal, local police, and trained dogs.

One of Edward Van Halen's promises to Michael was that he'd perform "Beat It" with him onstage, and he made good on it at Texas Stadium. "In Dallas, the humidity was so bad that I was taking oxygen behind the stage and my legs were getting weak," Marlon later said. But Eddie was game, zooming his fingertips along the fretboard during the break to a thunderous ovation.

Another shredder showed up to Dallas one night later. Watching from a tower on July 14 was a small group from Minneapolis: tour manager Alan Leeds, lighting director Roy Bennett, a handful of security guards, percussionist Jerome Benton of the Time, and the guest of honor, Prince.

Prince was well regarded within the Jackson camp. "That cat is really talented," Quincy Jones told *Musician* shortly before he began recording *Thriller*. "When I met Stevie [Wonder] at age fifteen there was never any doubt what he was going to be. . . . I think Prince has it too."

And Prince held Michael in rare regard. "Quite honestly, in real life, there was always artistic competitiveness [between Jackson and Prince], but they never had a harsh word to say about each other. *Ever*," Albert Magnoli, the director of Prince's film debut, *Purple Rain*, later said. "Never did Prince say one word of negativity about Michael in my presence, and he had every opportunity to. He grew up watching Michael Jackson, and he honored Michael Jackson."

Both men were fiercely competitive—with everyone else in pop, and especially with one another—and it had showed its face the previous summer. On August 20, 1983, Prince and Jackson had, quite by accident, appeared on the same stage together in Los Angeles, at the Beverly Theater, during a James Brown show. Brown spotted Jackson in the audience and called him up. Michael was game, but he whispered to JB, who was soon calling for Prince to join them.

What followed was a genuinely awkward moment. Rather than falling in with James and the band, as Michael had, Prince tried to take over—preening, leading the audience in a clap-along, playing some tentative guitar. None of it caught flame. "He just kind of choked in a really weird way," his collaborator and paramour Jill Jones said. Prince had a way of shrinking when the spotlight wasn't to his liking.

PRINCE HAD BEEN A PRODIGY. HIS FATHER, PIANIST AND COMPOSER JOHN L. Nelson, played with, and named his son after, the Prince Rogers Trio; his mother, Mattie, was a singer. Picking out the "Batman Theme" by ear at age seven, Prince approached music as a tradesman rather than a consumer—it was something he did, not just something he listened to—not to mention that, as he told *Rolling Stone* in 1981: "I didn't really have a record player when I was growing up, and I never got a chance to check out Hendrix and the rest of them because they were dead by the time I was really getting serious."

His parents divorced right around the time Prince hit puberty; he ping-ponged between them before moving in with Bernadette Anderson, the mother of his best friend Andre, né Andre Cymone. Prince's volcanic drive manifested early: he taught himself more than two dozen instruments before he finished high school and took classes on the business of music to ready himself for the paperwork to come. Even then, Prince acutely understood how small Minneapolis was. "We basically got all the new music and dances three months late, so I just decided that I was gonna do my own thing. Otherwise, when we did split Minneapolis, we were gonna be way behind and dated."

The scene around Prince during high school was fertile: his classmates, bandmates, and rivals included future Time members Jimmy "Jam" Harris, Terry Lewis, Morris Day, and Garry "Jellybean" Johnson, as well as singers Alexander O'Neal and Cynthia Johnson (the voice of Lipps Inc.'s "Funkytown"), and bassist Cymone. Notably, everyone in this scene was as turned on to white rock as black funk, in part because of their open tastes and in part because of how minuscule was Minneapolis's African American population; the 1980 census put the Twin Cities' black population at 2.4 percent.

"The predominance of German and Nordic elements may well make it the most homogeneous major urban area in the country," local journalist Steve Perry wrote in 1988. Terry Lewis, a Northside bass player, would tell Martin Keller in 1984, "To an extent the music we're making today is the result of white rock and roll radio and black music station static. None of our radio stations would come in as good as the mainstream stations. You could hear the beat and the rest was noise."

Prince caught the attention of British-born Chris Moon, who owned a local recording studio, while recording demos with his band, Champagne. Moon, in his mid-twenties, invited the teenager to cowrite songs on a fifty-fifty split. "Moon . . . chose Prince for reasons that turned out richly ironic," Perry wrote in 1986. "Quite simply, he liked Prince because he played his guitar well and didn't seem to have much of an ego."

The high school kid began taking more and more charge in the sessions, learning to use the recording console as well as gaining valuable experience and ease in overdubbing his instrumental parts, and one of his collaborations with Moon, "Soft and Wet," was key to his emerging style. "I told him, 'I think we've got your marketing strategy worked out and a song to go with it,'" Moon told Perry. "'We'll have thousands of thirteen and fourteen year old girls going crazy over you.' He smiled for once. He liked the idea."

By 1977, at age nineteen, Prince had signed a contract with Warner Bros. Records that allowed him to produce his own recordings—an unprecedented move, but no one could argue with the kid's skills. Recording next door at Sausalito's Record Plant, members of Santana got excited at the prodigy whose sheer chops sent any reservations out the door, while the band's teen-age percussionist, Sheila Escovedo, would reencounter him on and off over the years; in her memoir, *The Beat of My Own Drum*, she recounted taping Prince's poster to the wall above her waterbed before even putting the needle down on his debut.

WHEN KEYBOARDIST MATT FINK—WHO'D GROWN UP IN ST. LOUIS PARK alongside the Rivkin brothers, Bobby, later Prince's drummer Bobby Z, and David, later his engineer David Z—first heard Prince's demo tape, he was especially impressed by the keyboard playing. "Whatever he did on it was really good—*really* good," Fink says. "Especially the solo on the song 'Soft and Wet'— pretty impressive for a kid that age, improvising a solo like that on the synthesizer. You just didn't hear a lot of that."

Fink joined Prince's first band after the release of *For You*. "It was becoming more common for keyboardists to have at least one synthesizer in their arsenal," he says. Flush with big money from his major-label deal, Prince had stocked up on instruments. "He had all this state-of-the-art gear when I went into that audition," says Fink. Among these were a "real Clavinet" (see the main riff of Stevie Wonder's "Superstition") and a Fender Rhodes piano (prominent in the soft, glowing sound of Roberta Flack's early work), as well as an ARP Pro Soloist, with which he'd taken the solo of "Soft and Wet." Later, when Fink took a wowing and zapping solo on "Head," on Prince's third album, 1980's *Dirty Mind*, he'd play the ARP Omni 2.

For years, Prince had played with junior high and high school classmates from Minneapolis's Northside. The talent pool was deep: Prince could have picked anyone. He went with a deliberate mix—male, female, black, white, an admixture modeled on Sly & the Family Stone.

The night of the band's non-Minneapolis debut at the Roxy in West Hollywood on November 26, 1979, Prince turned to his band and gave a little speech. "Prince had a talk with us—inspiration would flow on the fly," remembers guitarist Dez Dickerson, who played in the group from 1978 to 1983. "He said, 'I want each member of this band to have their own persona. I'm going to personify sex in every possible way.'" This was a bold choice for someone groomed to be a black teen idol.

After spending half a year making *For You*, Prince resolved to work faster, embrace spontaneity, stop being a fussbudget; *Prince*, from 1979, was done in six weeks. He scored a number eleven hit that summer with "I Wanna Be Your Lover." But when he appeared on *American Bandstand*, he mostly just smirked at Dick Clark.

It was a sign: Prince was rebellious. He cranked his guitar in concert—not just on "Bambi," *Prince*'s screaming plea to a lesbian that "It's better with a man," but on *everything*. In February 1980, the *Soho Daily News* wrote of his show at the Bottom Line: "Judging by the [second] album, you'd never know that Prince is anything but a rock dilettante. In concert, it's clearly his lifeline."

Not long after finishing *Prince*, he and the band cut a heavy rock album under the name the Rebels that was never released. Dickerson says Prince found inspiration in new wave and "the New Romantic thing"—UK bands like Spandau Ballet and Duran Duran, who were played at the downtown Minneapolis club Sam's. "We needed to be a little edgy to capture the essence of the time," Cymone said, citing Sid Vicious and "even groups like Blondie."

In the spring of 1980, Prince and his band—Dickerson, Cymone, Fink, Chapman, and drummer Bobby Z (Rivkin)—spent nine weeks on the road opening for Rick James, sparking one of R&B's most storied rivalries. James accused Prince of "copping my licks" throughout the tour and boasted in his memoir *Glow*, published posthumously, about the birthday party where he grabbed teetotaler Prince "by the back of his hair and poured cognac down his throat." Clearly, the headliner was touchy that the opener was, by many accounts, upstaging him every night.

Prince's arsenal included a new song the band had been working out at club dates prior to the James tour: "Head," in which he sings about interrupting a wedding when the bride fellates him *right there* and ditches her fiancé for Prince. Even the band was taken aback by the lyrics: "It was definitely, like, 'OK, I guess we're going there!'" recalls Dickerson.

Of course, for Prince—who would become famous for cultivating dozens of women as collaborators, muses, and lovers—pioneering a hypersexual persona was no mere academic exercise. Whomever he might have been romantically connected with at the time, he made certain to give the song a realistic charge by making out with Chapman every night as they performed it. She left his employ at the end of the tour and was replaced by Los Angeles native Lisa Coleman. "I think it may have gotten to be a bit too much for Gayle," says Cymone. When Chapman left in 1980, Prince told her of her replacement: "She's amazing, she can play her ass off, but she can't sing like you."

The daughter of Gary L. Coleman, a top LA session musician percussionist, Coleman's audition for Prince lasted some three hours—she'd opened with some Mozart. They were instantly simpatico. "There was something about Lisa's sound as a keyboard player, particularly on acoustic piano, that Prince was very fond of and found hard to duplicate himself," Prince's tour manager Alan Leeds said.

After the James tour wrapped, Prince returned home to Minnesota, rented a house in suburban Wayzata (near Lake Minnetonka—yes, the real one), and outfitted the basement with a sixteen-track studio that Warner Bros. paid for. "Nobody knew what was going on, and I became totally engulfed in it," he told *Rolling Stone* of these home sessions. "It really felt like me for once."

As in the past, Prince mostly recorded alone, but the band was starting to put its stamp on the new material. A keyboard line that Fink jammed out during a rehearsal provided the seed for "Dirty Mind"; Prince brought him over to cut the track and had a completed song by morning. Coleman's classical and jazz colorings eventually would have an outsized impact on Prince's music, and that summer she murmured a spoken vocal on "Head."

When manager Steve Fargnoli presented his artist's new album to the label, as he told the *Los Angeles Times*, "Warner Bros., understandably, didn't know how to react. The last record had sold almost a million, and they expected something with the same sound." Dickerson recalls that Warner was "scared to death. I remember being in L.A. shooting videos, and the execs pulled up and took Prince on a long ride, on a break, to talk about the record. They thought they were signing the new Stevie Wonder. They didn't know they were getting a cross between Stevie Wonder and Johnny Rotten." But when top Warner executives Mo Ostin, Lenny Waronker, and Russ Thyret backed Prince, the company fell in line.

The first part of the *Dirty Mind* tour was rocky, and the album's lack of radio play translated into sluggish sales. On December 9, 1980, the night after John Lennon's murder, the band played the Ritz in New York. The club was only half-full, though the audience included Andy Warhol. But the album got rave reviews, placing ninth in the *Village Voice*'s annual critics' poll that ran in early February 1981. That was followed shortly by *Rolling Stone*'s four-and-a-half-star review. "The LP might just as accurately have been called *Prince Confronts the Moral Majority*," Ken Tucker wrote.

That excitement fed directly into the second leg of the tour, which kicked off with a packed hometown gig at Sam's on March 9, 1981. Warner Bros. A&R man Ted Cohen had flown into the Twin Cities to join the tour. "Prince was intimidating, even at the beginning," remembers Cohen. "He was so quiet, so mysterious. Not rude—just not somebody you sat and shot the shit with. Prince was the first artist I was ever sent on the road with [where we had] the understanding that he would never do an interview, an appearance, a meet-and-greet, photos, or handshakes."

The music was more than enough. At the Rainbow in Denver on March 26, a mob of teenage girls surrounded the band's trailer, and fans chased its car through the city's streets. Prince's persona—and his sound—had taken on a life of their own.

ALMOST ALONE IN MINNEAPOLIS, FIRST AVENUE WAS A DOWNTOWN VENUE that didn't discriminate when it came to booking acts. It had opened in 1970 as the Depot, closed after a year, then spent the seventies as part of a national disco chain, Uncle Sam's. But it was reborn at the turn of the eighties as Sam's—a new wave club with a wide booking policy and dance nights featuring DJs playing the same kind of mix that Prince was. One of the club's cofounders, Allan Fingerhut, used to allow Prince in as a teenager to see shows featuring black bands, which were unusual for the time: "If you were a black band in the 1970s . . . you couldn't play the downtown clubs," Jimmy Jam said. "It was never said, but we knew what the score was."

Prince's March 1981 headlining debut was the stuff of instant legend. "That first Prince show was one of the best shows I ever saw," says the club's DJ, Kevin Cole, who mixed sound that night. "You could see him connecting. I got a sense that he felt like, 'This is my audience.'"

Cole also worked alongside Jimmy Jam at a record store downtown near both First Avenue—which changed its name from Sam's at the end of 1981—and the Fox Trap, a black club where Jam was a DJ. Jam was one of the Twin Cities' most plugged-in and well-liked musical figures. One Friday afternoon in April 1981, Jam told Cole, "Prince is having us over to the studio to record some demos." That weekend, Jam and most of his Flyte Tyme bandmates, minus O'Neal, cut the reconfigured and renamed Time's self-titled debut with former Prince drummer Morris Day on lead vocals. Warner Bros. released it that July.

Dressed in vintage-shop zoot suits, the Time came off onstage, quite deliberately, as the black id to Prince's ego. "One of the things we learned from Prince is he would record everything looking at the sound meter and every track would always be in the red, meaning that it was being recorded too loud," Time keyboardist Jimmy Jam said. "Prince's theory was, if you put a little distortion on things, it sounded louder because your ear thinks when it hears distortion that something is loud." In 1985, Jam told *Billboard*, "Prince is the Minneapolis sound. People like us, Vanity, the Time—we're all sort of like his children."

The Time's tightly choreographed show was unveiled at Sam's on October 7, 1981; the near-sellout earned the band $1,500, with 75 percent of the tickets purchased at the door. By staying put in the Twin Cities, Prince installed a goodly amount of hometown pride among his protégés. "The only thing we intend on coming into Los Angeles for is to master the product—and pick up the check," Jimmy Jam told *Billboard*.

But Jam and the Time's bassist, Terry Lewis, were already looking beyond that. They began writing and producing their own songs in 1982, starting with Klymaxx's "Wild Girls." By early 1983, Prince fired the pair for missing a Time concert because of a snowstorm while working with the S.O.S. Band, and they decided to go all in as writer-producers.

PRINCE'S RISE CAME AT THE SAME TIME AS A NEW DARK AGE OF R&B crossover. *Billboard*'s year-end 1981 singles list featured only eight black records in the Top 40—half of what had been there just two years earlier.

"The record industry provides probably the strangest example of segregation since South African apartheid—a frequent, unspoken separation of blacks and whites that subtly and insidiously damages our industry," Prince's publicist Howard Bloom wrote in an August 1981 *Billboard* commentary. He added: "If a black act's record is rock & roll and belongs on AOR radio, that's too bad. The black special markets department drops the record because it's not appropriate to black radio. And the white AOR and pop departments generally refuse to touch the record because of the color of the artist who made it."

Bloom was ready to put his ideals into action, writing in a memo to Prince's then-manager Steve Fargnoli, "I'd suggest booking him two dates in each market: a date as a second act on the bill to a major black headliner like Cameo, Parliament, etc., and a date at the local new wave dance club. . . . Neither date will conflict with the other." He added: "Ads in publications like the *Prairie Sun*, *Night Rocker News*, and *Oasis de Neon* are dirt cheap, and they reach a staunch record-and-ticket buying audience."

BIZARRELY FOR AN AVOWEDLY ANTIWAR LIBERTINE PROVOCATEUR, PRINCE was quoted as being pro-Reagan. He liked the president's machismo. Nevertheless, Prince's entire career was predicated on tweaking the Moral Majority. The latter had played a significant role in Reagan's 1980 election.

Initially, the Reverend Donald Wildmon, a pastor of a six-hundred-member church near Memphis, formed the Coalition for Better Television (CBTV), with the help of fellow conservative activist Rev. Jerry Falwell. "I also knew that the concern regarding TV was not confined to the 'fundamentalist Religious New Right,'" Wildmon said. "There's a lot of broad-section people who share this concern. Why not make them a part of the coalition, why not bring them in, broaden your base, get more numbers and be that much more effective?"

Their brief was to boycott advertisers who sponsored programs that offended them. Among these were such prime-time hits as *Dallas*, *Three's Company*, and *M*A*S*H*—shows dealing with adult sexuality in however juvenile a manner. "They agreed to come around. We'll see if they [do]," Wildmon said. "If not, we'll boycott. Our patience is not inexhaustible."

Among the offensive programming these conservative groups targeted were advertisements for Planned Parenthood. In the fall of 1981, thirteen New York City radio stations (including all three owned by the major broadcasting networks—ABC, CBS, and NBC) rejected spots telling listeners that Senator Alphonse D'Amato was "in favor of outlawing abortion. Let him know you think abortion is something personal. Not political."

Prince's hometown also had its share of conservative activists. One man was pushing the Northwestern Bell Telephone Company to purge the large display ads for massage parlors, escort services, saunas, and modeling services from the Yellow Pages. When it did, in 1982, a spokesman for Bell insisted, "It was our decision alone."

IN 1981, PRINCE GOT THE CALL TO OPEN FOR THE ROLLING STONES AT the Los Angeles Coliseum. This was a rare opportunity—in front of ninety thousand people—for an early coronation.

Prince was allotted thirty minutes at the foot of a bill that also included George Thorogood and the J. Geils Band. "Mick Jagger was a big fan," says Fink. "They wanted to help us reach a bigger audience. And we were just suddenly being thrown into a stadium show. It's afternoon, we get onstage, and immediately we're met with consternation. People were flipping us the bird, they started throwing food, they started throwing bottles, cups, anything. It got a little dangerous there because a bottle missed Prince's head by [holds fingers apart] that much."

The rattled singer flew home to Minneapolis that night. Jagger called and talked him into returning to LA, telling him, "Just weather the storm. Just get out there, show them who you are, be tough, don't back down. Just watch so you don't have to dodge anything."

"Next time, same thing happens and we have to deal with it," says Fink. "Prince manages to keep his composure. We don't *finish* the set, but we manage to get through at least twenty minutes. The stage is covered in debris. And Prince after that said, 'I refuse to be subjected to this kind of abuse.'" He would never open for anyone else again.

MICHAEL JACKSON WAS THE AVALANCHE, BUT PRINCE WAS THE TEST CASE in breaking AOR and MTV's color line. The two-LP *1999*, full of long, creatively unfurling dance tracks, played as homage to the twelve-inch singles that were dominating pop's creative edge, from British synth acts like New Order and Depeche Mode to New York post-disco labels like West End and Prelude and the first flourishing of recorded hip-hop. But Prince also had his eye on the rock and roll big-time. The title track of *1999* was a party-hearty chant in the face of the apocalypse, while "Little Red Corvette" smirked like Chuck Berry and rocked out like Bruce Springsteen, complete with wheezing organ and handclaps.

Rock radio noticed, though the spread took a while. The first week of January 1983, *Billboard* reported that a key Denver AOR station was rebelling against his format by programming "1999." "Programmers may have a problem with black artists, but the audience certainly can't see what color they are," John Bradley, program director for KBCO-FM, said. "It reminds me of so many other techno artists who are white and are getting airplay. I'd hardly call '1999' a black record." Nevertheless, it only reached number forty-four.

Then "Little Red Corvette" reached number six in May 1983. "Finally . . . the one radio has been waiting for!" said a trade ad—meaning rock and pop, not just R&B, radio. The *1999* tour, recalls Fink, played "arenas, twelve-to-fifteen-thousand seaters—or more, depending on the city."

REVIEWING PRINCE AT THE MET CENTER ON MARCH 15, 1983, *City Pages'* Martin Keller wrote, "After seeing him perform with such mature swagger and soulfulness, my only question is, 'When will Prince make his first movie?'" By then, Prince had been collecting ideas in a purple notebook for a film—not a video but a movie, for a performer with only one top ten hit to his credit at the time. His managers were charged with getting him a motion picture deal or else he wouldn't re-sign with them. Eventually, against long odds, they did.

"He sat me down for breakfast personally and went, 'We're going to make a movie,'" says Fink. "I just went, 'Really? Cool! Are you serious?' I thought, 'This guy has never acted. What's he thinking?' But I believed he could pull it off, because I knew his personality and that he was really actually quite a chameleon."

The summer of 1983, Prince's openers from the *1999* tour, the Time and another new Prince-sired act, Vanity 6, led by the singer's real-life girlfriend Vanity (Denise Matthews), began learning new songs for the movie at a warehouse on Highway 7. They also took acting and dance lessons, the latter courtesy of the

Minnesota Dance Theatre, led by Loyce Houlton. Prince agreed to play a benefit show for them at First Avenue on August 3, where the dance troupe performed four numbers, including a dance to Prince's "DMSR," choreographed by Houlton—the first time for ballet on the First Avenue stage. Tickets were $25, and the show sold out well in advance, raising some $23,000 for Houlton's group.

Two incidental expenses from the benefit's paperwork stand out: a dozen tambourines for Prince to toss to the audience, totaling $127; and $35 to the City of Minneapolis to use "the curb lane of the street, 200 linear feet in front of Sam's [sic] . . . for filming purposes." There sat a recording truck from New York studio the Record Plant. "They had everything set up," recalls Paul Spangrud, a First Avenue DJ. "They were there at eight a.m., loading in. They brought in tons of extra PA. Prince spent a *lot* of time on sound checks."

The club's video-making side enterprise, AVE Productions, filmed a number of the club's shows, including the benefit. A lot of AVE footage did not survive a major club cleanup around 2010: "It was all down in the basement, basically moldering," says Corrigan. "We needed the space." At least one thing did survive: the performance of the full, unedited version of "Purple Rain," which pops up on YouTube every few months. (First Avenue's DJs also recorded several concerts: "We had microphones hung from the ceiling in the Mainroom that you couldn't see unless you specifically looked for them," says Spangrud.)

"Purple Rain" was one of several new songs premiered at the benefit.[*] Along with a medley of "I Would Die 4 U" and "Baby I'm a Star," the show on August 3, 1983, would provide the source recordings for the final three songs on Prince's next album—the soundtrack to the movie that Prince was about to start filming in his hometown—and at his home club.

A LETTER OF INTENT DATED SEPTEMBER 22, 1983, WAS SENT FROM MANagement firm Cavallo, Ruffalo & Fargnoli to First Avenue. It offered $100,000 to use the Mainroom between November 26 and December 20, "for dressing, filming, and strike during our filming of *Purple Rain*." The Entry would stay open. "Every effort will be made by my company to employ as many of your personnel as may wish to work in our film, so as to ease their fears of employment," wrote the production manager.

---

* The file for this historic show is one of the period's most complete, including an extensive guest list with many of Prince's friends and family—but the name that stands out (and is crossed off, meaning he showed up) is R.E.M.'s Peter Buck.

"Almost every single person that worked [at the club], even up in the office, was in it," says Chrissie Dunlap, an employee at the time. A club employee became the star's stand-in after the first one violated the set's strict confidentiality by talking to *City Pages*. Prince went even further with photographer Daniel Corrigan, who shot frequently at the club. "I was not allowed in the building," says Corrigan. "I was the only one specifically banned from First Avenue for the entire filming of *Purple Rain*. There was a no-photograph rule. He's always been twitchy about photos."

McClellan's handwritten notes, taken during a prospective meeting with Cavallo, Ruffalo & Fargnoli, Prince's management team, about using First Avenue as the shooting site, are large and all-caps, in black Sharpie. The phrases that stand out are "THE NEGATE [*sic*] ASPECT OF" and "THE MANNER IN WHICH THE CLUB IS PORTRAYED IN RESPECT TO INDIVIDUALS." "That's the point of contention," recalls Dunlap. "Steve had slowly built up this club, then Prince makes one movie [and] now is getting all the credit—he did not want Prince to take that away. He must have known what was going to come, because it did come."

In her living room, Dunlap pulls out Albert Magnoli's shooting script for *Purple Rain*, dated November 30–December 1. "[It was] on one of the bar tables, so I took it. It's early, too—with Vanity. Then she and Prince broke up, so that was the end of that."

Cole, who missed the job call and wasn't in the picture, hung out regularly nonetheless. "I recall them filming concert scenes at eight in the morning, full volume, with the room packed out with [extras]," he says. "It was so loud and so powerful, and to see Prince looking like he's playing along, and it seeming like a real live performance, the emotional quality behind songs like 'Purple Rain' was just stunning. Nothing about it felt like he was lip-synching or air-guitaring. They were feeling it, and the audience was feeling it." The staff was also abuzz. "I remember hearing stories about getting paid a hundred dollars to go buy a sandwich," says Cole.

Maggie MacPherson, an eighties staffer, told Seattle's Museum of Pop Culture: "Almost every night when they would get done filming they would have these little cast parties, and Prince would jump up onstage and play acoustic, and everyone else would grab an instrument."

The stage also received a parting gift. "First Avenue had shitty lighting prior to *Purple Rain*," says former employee Rod Smith. "They actually put in the patch bay and the dimmer packs."

Culture Club, 1984. At that year's Grammy Awards, Boy George went from America's sweetheart to a pariah when he quipped that the nation "know[s] a good drag queen when you see one." From left: Jon Moss, Roy Hay, Boy George, Mikey Craig. (DAVE HOGAN/ HULTON ARCHIVE/GETTY IMAGES)

Andy Taylor and Simon Le Bon of Duran Duran tool around New York, 1984, the year they could have gone gold singing the alphabet. Within a year, Duran was split apart, and Le Bon and Taylor each in different groups. (DENIS O'REGAN / GETTY IMAGES)

David Lee Roth and Edward Van Halen ham it up at Nassau Coliseum on April 14, 1984. Van Halen's singer and guitarist were two showboats sharing the same vessel, but over the course of their biggest year, the two of them grew completely estranged. (LARRY BUSACCA / WIREIMAGE)

Twisted Sister lead singer Dee Snider performing in Illinois on August 8, 1984. A clean-living Christian, Snider would offer the sharpest direct retort to the PMRC during a testy Congressional hearing on "porn rock" in 1985. (Paul Natkin/Getty Images)

Vince Neil and Ozzy Osbourne commiserate during a post-concert party at the New York nightclub Limelight. Neil's band, Mötley Crüe, and Osbourne toured together in late 1983. "It was a full-on fight to see who would top each other, onstage and off," Crüe bassist Nikki Sixx said. (RON GALELLA / RON GALELLA COLLECTION VIA GETTY IMAGES)

Michael Jackson and Quincy Jones backstage at the 26th Annual Grammy Awards at the Shrine Auditorium, February 28, 1984, in Los Angeles. That night, *Thriller* swept the awards, with Michael taking home a record eight trophies. That summer, he'd grit his teeth and hit the road one last time with his family. (BOB RIHA JR. / GETTY IMAGES)

Cyndi Lauper and Rodney Dangerfield backstage at the Grammys, where they presented Best New Artist together. Lauper would win the award herself a year later; Dangerfield had already taken a comedy Grammy home a few years earlier.
(Frank Edwards/Fotos International/Getty Images)

Eurythmics—Dave Stewart and a very Elvis'ed-up Annie Lennox—did the near-impossible and stole the 26th Annual Grammy Awards out from under Michael Jackson—even if, as one writer put it, "90 percent of Middle America didn't get" that Lennox was performing in male drag. (Bob Riha Jr. / Getty Images)

Herbie Hancock shows off his first-ever Grammy after twelve nominations, for Best R&B Instrumental, "Rockit." His performance of the song on the telecast, with DJ DXT on the wheels of steel, is the first time most Americans saw a live hip-hop DJ scratching on TV. (BOB RIHA JR. / GETTY IMAGES)

David Byrne onstage with Talking Heads, January 29, 1984. The band's concert film, *Stop Making Sense*, directed by Jonathan Demme and premiered that April at the San Francisco International Film Festival, was a critical and box office success, its soundtrack the Heads' most successful album, with Byrne becoming a Yuppie icon. (GERI ALAN FOKKEMA/FAIRFAX MEDIA VIS GETTY IMAGES)

Run-D.M.C. onstage in 1984—from left, Run (Joseph Simmons), D.M.C. (Darryl McDaniels), and Jam Master Jay (Jason Mizell). Dressing in basic black instead of tailored leather suits, stripping the music from disco boogie to minimalist drum machines, and moving rapping cadences from orotund to plainspoken, the trio rendered nearly all hip-hop before it irrelevant. (RAYMOND BOYD/MICHAEL OCHS ARCHIVES)

Prince in Hollywood for the premiere of *Purple Rain*, July 26, 1984. The movie and its soundtrack vaulted him to the top of the world during pop's most dizzying year, but Prince was already bored with his juggernaut. (Ron Galella, Ltd./Ron Galella Collection via Getty Images)

R.E.M. backstage at the Aragon Ballroom, Chicago, July 7, 1984—from left, Bill Berry, Michael Stipe, Mike Mills, and Peter Buck. Their second album, *Reckoning*, put them firmly in the front of a burgeoning, and musically diverse, American rock underground. "We didn't distinguish between Metallica and the Violent Femmes," one booker recalled. "If they were on an independent label, if they were doing it on their own, they were the same." (PAUL NATKIN/GETTY IMAGES)

Henry Rollins of Black Flag at Perkins Park, May 5, 1984. The hardcore pioneers began leaning toward heavy metal by 1984, but either way, Southern California cops hated them: "We always felt a lot safer out of town," said founding guitarist Greg Ginn. (IRIS SCHNEIDER/LOS ANGELES TIMES VIA GETTY IMAGES)

Madonna and Jellybean Benitez at the opening of the New York video club Private Eyes, July 1984. He was the first "superstar DJ," and his remixes of her singles became huge pop hits—the first from a working club DJ. She was fast becoming one of the most famous people in the world, unable to finish filming *Desperately Seeking Susan* on the New York streets that summer without requiring crowd control. (DAVID McGOUGH/DMI/THE LIFE PICTURES COLLECTION VIA GETTY IMAGES)

ZZ Top backstage at the MTV Video Music Awards, Radio City Music Hall, September 14, 1984—from left, Frank Beard, Billy Gibbons, and Dusty Hill. A blues-rock band who made hay with synthesizers, these Texans were surprise MTV favorites. The first time Beard saw the network, he and his wife "must have stayed up five hours thinking, 'Jesus, this is a long show.'" (THE LIFE PICTURE COLLECTION VIA GETTY IMAGES)

Bruce Springsteen in Philadelphia, September 19, 1984. That week, thanks to the popularity of his ambiguous anthem, "Born in the U.S.A.," both U.S. presidential candidates, incumbent Republican Ronald Reagan and Democrat Walter Mondale, had claimed that Springsteen had endorsed them both, when in fact he hadn't endorsed anyone. (DAVID GAHR/GETTY IMAGES)

Lionel Richie on closing night of the Los Angeles Olympics, August 12, 1984. He'd left the Commodores for a solo career marked by eagerness to please and a commitment to crossover, most notably onto country radio. Not pictured: two hundred breakdancers. (KEYSTONE/HULTON ARCHIVE/GETTY IMAGES)

Phil Collins at Wembley Stadium during Live Aid, July 13, 1985. The poet laureate of eighties divorce pop, Collins would overshoot his own charisma by half that day, performing multiple times each in London and Philadelphia with *very* mixed results. (Popperfoto via Getty Images)

The new face of British pop royalty at Live Aid. Bottom right, Bob Geldof whispers to Prince Charles, while in the center, David Bowie commiserates with Brian May and Roger Taylor behind Princess Diana. (Dave Hogan/Hulton Archive/Getty Images)

Though any film set can be full of tedium, the club was essentially going twenty-four-seven, and it was well fueled. "There was a lot of cocaine being done during that movie," says Spangrud. "Morris Day did most of it, I think." This was hardly a new development at First Avenue: Rod Smith quips that AVE Productions, unlike many such companies, "wasn't a front for a coke dealer; it was more like a front for a coke *den*."

"MUSIC IS LIKE A NEWSPAPER TO HIM," ALAN LEEDS SAID OF PRINCE IN 1998, "and his attitude is, 'What's the point of reading last week's paper?'"

In 1983 and 1984 alone, Prince, solo and with collaborators, recorded six full LPs that were released in 1984–1985, two his own—*Purple Rain* and *Around the World in a Day*—along with releases by his protégé acts, Sheila E., the Time, Apollonia 6, and the Family. He also wrote songs he gave to others, including Sheena Easton's "Sugar Walls" and the Bangles' "Manic Monday," and played synthesizer, uncredited, on Stevie Nicks's "Stand Back." All three were sizable hits. Several more tracks from this era would eventually appear on albums by Prince and others.

This prolific output spilled over into a bevy of B sides. Throughout the eighties, the flip side was where Prince put not merely leftovers but companions, fraternal twins, and commentary on the A tracks, and half the fun was discovering which it was each time. Arguably Prince's two best songs of 1984 were B sides. "When Doves Cry" excited enough attention by itself: the track had no bass line, which, along with its psychologically acute lyrics ("Maybe I'm just like my father—too bold"), gave it a starkness that punched through the airwaves. But its flip, the lustrous "17 Days," may well be Prince's catchiest song. The four-steps-down-then-back-up-and-repeat melody (shared by the verse and chorus—the bridge is spoken), the octave-gliding low end (*there's* that bass line missing from "Doves"), and Prince's openly pleading vocal make it one of his most endearing. Nah: Prince already had his album's "rain" song, so he gave the fans an Easter egg.

"Erotic City" was so hot that even radio couldn't avoid it, though one particular word of the chorus caused some problems. Did Prince and Sheila E. sing "We could funk until the dawn," or something racier and less FCC-regulations-friendly? Las Vegas station KLUC-FM was fined $2,000 for playing the song, with, in *Billboard*'s words, "at least sixteen apparent uses" of the F-word.

"Because it was not worked as the A-side of a single, 'Erotic City' never qualified to chart in *Billboard*," the report continued. "But at airplay-driven publications, it was playlisted by approximately 25 percent of the black radio reporters, probably a much lower number than those that actually played the song. It also received airplay at a number of major-market pop stations." In her memoir, Sheila E. claims they're singing "funk."

Before filming began, Prince gave Albert Magnoli, the film's young first-time director, some one hundred songs from his already teeming backlog to choose from—one of them, "Baby I'm a Star," had first been demoed in 1981. "He loved every one of them, but he loved them equally," Magnoli later said. "He had written them in the moment and wasn't going to say that 'number ninety-six is more special to me than number ten, the one you selected.'"

Issuing the soundtrack as a single LP—when there was such an abundance of material, and when the double LP *1999* had just done so well—was a conscious choice, Bob Cavallo, one of Prince's managers, told *Billboard*: "It seemed obvious that we could reach more people if the price were lower." A Warner sales VP said, "To us, this would still be a Prince album without the movie."

While filming the notorious "Lake Minnetonka" scene (Apollonia jumps into the lake in her skivvies only to be told it wasn't the lake he'd been talking about), actress Patricia Kotero nearly froze to death—it was getting to winter in Minnesota. "I jumped in and, basically, there was a little sheet of ice, and that was the very first take," she later said. "When I came out, I was supposed to have dialogue and I lost it—I was completely in a state of shock because it was colder than I ever imagined. Hypothermia was setting in." She was swaddled in blankets as soon as she left the water and refused to do it again. "She jumped into a lake in Minneapolis and jumped out in Los Angeles," Magnoli said.

MORRIS DAY FELT, REASONABLY, THAT HE WAS AS RESPONSIBLE FOR THE success of *Purple Rain* as a film as the boss. He'd stolen every scene he was in with his raffish comic timing. Prince, meanwhile, had been displeased by Morris's on-set behavior; Day, in turn, still fumed over Prince firing Jam and Lewis that spring.

Even Prince had to be feeling some humility for that. In February 1984, Jam and Lewis had their first R&B number one as a writer-producer team, Cheryl Lynn's "Encore." Thanks largely to the patronage of Clarence Avant, the founder of the CBS-distributed R&B label Tabu Records, Jam and Lewis worked with a wide array of R&B talent, mostly women: Lynn, Gladys Knight and the Pips, Patti Austin, Thelma Houston, the female-fronted Italian studio outfit Change, and of course the S.O.S. Band, featuring Mary Davis's electric-current trill.

Another Jam-Lewis artist, LA newcomer and Tabu artist Cherrelle Norton—billed first name only—got the writer-producers' special treatment when they relocated her project from LA to Minneapolis. "The studio we worked at was like a house on one side and a studio on the other, and it was so comfortable—it was like I was at home, working in my basement," she said.

Jimmy and Terry were hardly the only Time men seeking their own fortunes. Jesse Johnson, who'd cowritten the Time's hits "Jungle Love" and "The Bird," both featured in the film, had worked on *Dream Street*, the second album by Michael Jackson's little sister Janet. Andre Cymone had a solo deal and put together a familiarly "6"-y group called the Girls.

By the time of the *Purple Rain* premiere, at Mann's Chinese Theatre in Los Angeles on July 26, Morris Day joined their ranks: he'd quit the Time and he had a new manager, Sandy Gallin, who'd steered Dolly Parton to crossover visibility. He'd left Minneapolis near the beginning of the year and relocated to Santa Monica, near the beach. "Why pay taxes to a town that won't support you?" Day sniffed. "They never played our records."

Now, though, thanks to the movie, *Ice Cream Castles* handily outsold each previous Time release. The act Prince had put together to cater to R&B fans was now a pop act. Or were one.

WITH ITS TENDRILS IN ALL FORMS OF SHOWBIZ, WARNER BROS. put together a guest list for the Mann's premiere that looked like an episode of *Entertainment Tonight*. A great number of Prince's colleagues appeared, from Stevie Nicks and Lindsey Buckingham of Fleetwood Mac to Talking Heads and "Weird Al" Yankovic. So did a number of actors, including soap opera star Morgan Fairchild—whose husband had been a tech on the film crew; she'd joined him in Minneapolis—and Christopher Reeve, who played Superman in the movie franchise.

Some of the VIPs on offer had been long-standing fans. John Cougar Mellencamp, a rock journeyman who'd hit his stride as a hit-maker starting with 1982's *American Fool*, was such a Prince fan that he'd stopped a show in Tulsa to play "Little Red Corvette" to the audience on a boom box he held up to the microphone. Mellencamp liked to make a show of abjuring the swells, so he arrived in plain street clothes and skipped VIP for the ticket-holder line.

Another long-standing admirer went in via the red carpet and stopped to chat with Mark Goodman. Eddie Murphy seemed to regard the VJ faintly as a child when he asked why Murphy was a Prince fan: "Because Prince is *bad*." Why else would Murphy have named his HBO stand-up special *Delirious*, after the top ten hit from *1999*? He elaborated: "I'm a Prince groupie. I loved the movie. I think the man's a genius." Would he, as he had told *Rolling Stone*, still want to switch places with Prince? "No. I've got too much money now."

Like the teenaged Prince playing covers on Minneapolis's Northside, Murphy had cut his stage teeth telling Richard Pryor jokes at age fifteen in Long Island. In 1980, he got onto *Saturday Night Live* as a featured player and quickly outclassed everyone else who took the stage with him.

Murphy was particularly attuned to using popular musicians as source material, similar to John Belushi before him. Over four years on the show, Murphy cemented into the comedy pantheon his versions of James Brown, Little Richard, Michael Jackson, and Stevie Wonder (alongside Joe Piscopo's Frank Sinatra and, once, the actual Stevie Wonder), along with Clarence "the Fifth Beatle" Brown.

In the blockbuster summer of 1984, Murphy was stuck in an unmoving tank of a comedy called *Best Defense*. "I knew the script for *Best Defense* was horrible, but I got talked into the movie by Paramount [Pictures]," Murphy said. "They started offering me all of this money. I was twenty-one years old. I said to hell with it and went for it. It was a mistake, but we all make mistakes in our careers." The movie did so badly, Murphy would recount in his December 1984 *SNL* monologue, that he was reduced to accepting a hosting gig on the old show his popularity had long since outgrown. His next movie, complete with a hit soundtrack, would rectify that.

Prince, of course, arrived to the premiere in a purple limo, brandishing a purple orchid, and was hustled into the theater by security. When the entourage briskly bypassed MTV's Mark Goodman, not to mention autograph-seeking fans, the crowd erupted in boos—a bad sign of things to come. But Goodman blew it off, saying over the PA: "Don't feel bad. He doesn't talk to anyone."

En route to the theater, Prince sat with Alan Leeds, who'd also worked as a tour manager for James Brown and Kiss. Nearing their destination, Prince's bodyguard, Big Chick Huntsberry, reported to the boss that the premiere had incurred a two-block traffic jam. "At that point Prince suddenly lost it," Leeds said. "'He suddenly gripped my hand in a desperate vise and his voice broke . . . like a petrified ten-year-old. . . . [I] said calmly, 'He said we're going to have a day to be proud of and it's going to be fun. Now let me get to the theater and I'll meet you there.' It was . . . probably the only moment through the whole, tedious making of the movie that he showed any doubt or vulnerability."

Huntsberry was a shield Prince could erect against the world. "Once the movie was done being filmed, I saw a big change—almost like he was mentally going into this superstar mode, and really converting into something I didn't recognize," says Fink. "And he really did it quickly. Because he didn't want his picture taken anymore, and he made it very clear that if you take his picture you get in trouble. He'd [Huntsberry] grab your film and destroy it."

Standing six foot six with the physique of a wrestler, as well as an enormous salt-and-pepper beard, Huntsberry had joined Prince on tour in 1981; he was part of the security detail at the infamous Rolling Stones show that year. Huntsberry moved his family to Minnesota in 1982. The two became close; Prince attended July 4 picnics at the Huntsberry home, and Chick's eldest daughter would eventually work as Prince's personal assistant. His presence became ubiquitous by the time of the 1999 tour. It was then, Fink recalls, that "Prince was leaning toward" becoming generally inaccessible: "But he was more accessible to me—I could talk to him still on more of a friendships basis, not boss–employee relationship. As time went on, it became more like that."

Having built a juggernaut, Prince was nevertheless surprised when he was confronted with the results. "The first time I realized what was happening was the day of the *Purple Rain* premiere. There's a picture of me from then, and my eyes are just glazed over. I had just got out of a purple limousine, and I looked up and saw this huge image of myself. At that moment I realized the whole world is an illusion," he said.

During the screening, the early scene when Prince is lectured by First Avenue manager Billy Sparks—"Your music doesn't make sense to anyone but yourself"—a woman in the audience yelled, "It does to me." Another: "I love you!" A third: "I love you more."

Still, Warner was so nervous about the movie that the press didn't see it until a week before the premiere—and the Mann's gala was a mere day ahead of the general release. Warner needn't have worried—even the dourer notices were complimentary of Prince's onstage magnetism, and there were many positive reviews, most famously Mikal Gilmore of the *Los Angeles Herald Examiner* dubbing it "the *Citizen Kane* of rock movies." A more balanced viewpoint came from *Billboard*'s Nelson George: "Compared to *Beat Street* and *Breakin'*, both shot on equally thin budgets, this looks like a Stanley Kubrick film."

But Prince's mind, as seemingly ever, was elsewhere. He spent much of July in the studio working on the debut album of the group Prince had hand-picked to take up where the defunct Time left off. This was the Family. The co-lead vocalists were Susannah Melvoin, Wendy's twin sister and the woman for whom he'd written the pained *Purple Rain* highlight "The Beautiful Ones," and the just-out-of-high-school Paul Peterson, who, despite being from the south Minneapolis suburb of Richfield, was nicknamed "St. Paul." In Prince's immortal phrase, to engineer David Rivkin, "We've got to go after some of that Duran Duran money."

ON THE EVENING OF JULY 28, 1984, KEVIN COLE WAS LOADING A BAND into the 7th Street Entry's stage door when a man from Detroit pulled up in a Cadillac. "I'm the first guy he sees," says Cole. "He pops out, holding a cassette in his hand, and goes, 'Where's Billy Sparks?'" He was looking for the "manager" of the club, as depicted in *Purple Rain*, which had opened the night before in nine hundred theaters. "He saw the movie and drove to First Ave. *the next day*," says Cole. (The movie's "Billy Sparks" was actually played by a concert promoter named Billy Sparks—who, ironically, was from Detroit.)

The film's impact was forecast when its first single, "When Doves Cry," reached number one a few weeks earlier. It would become the year's biggest hit, while the *Purple Rain* soundtrack topped the album chart for six months. A young audience that had already made hits of music-driven movies from *Flashdance* and *Footloose* to *Breakin'* and Talking Heads' art-house smash *Stop Making Sense* ran to see the most head-turning pop star this side of Michael Jackson do his thing on a big screen. "People really resonated with the story," says Cole. "And the time was right for a new sound."

Prince had kept his visibility high at the club all summer. On June 7, his twenty-sixth birthday, Prince played an exclusive concert for First Avenue members only, the set full of rare and unissued material. "I brought him a strawberry shortcake, his favorite thing," says Dunlap. "Somebody ate it, but probably not Prince. I don't think he really eats." He came back on August 14, in the midst of *Purple Rain* fever, when 1,616 fans got an embryonic tour set: *1999*'s three biggest singles plus seven from *Purple Rain*.

That September, a young woman in DC sent the club a letter addressed to "Mr. Stark"—that is, Billy Sparks. "I plan to move to Minneapolis in the near future but would like to secure a job before moving," it begins. "Would you consider interviewing me for a position?" Soon she reveals her hand: "I'm sure that you realize I am definitely a PRINCE fan. I know you and he are very close friends and I hoped you would convey my message to him. . . . Is it possible that he needs someone to answer his mail?"

"Prince was getting all the credit for what Steve felt he had built," says Dunlap. "The rumors were, 'That's Prince's club.' And Steve would be like—[*imitates steam coming out of ears*]—because that was his whole identity." McClellan had particular scorn for the William Morris agents suddenly leaving him messages. "*Purple Rain* had to come out before they finally decided I was an OK venue," he says. "It changed the club from a real music crowd to a lot of tourists."

"For a couple of years, there were people wearing purple trench coats with studs on them from Germany," says Cole. "They thought everybody at the club looked like that all the time." On the other hand, after five years of just scraping by, the boost in revenue was more than welcome. "Jack [Meyers, the club's accountant] said up until *Purple Rain*, he didn't think we were going to make it," says McClellan.

MATTER NO. 9,
CHICAGO, ILLINOIS
July–August 1984

"SUBSCRIBE!"

The header above the third page of the ninth issue of *Matter*, the bimonthly underground rock fanzine from Chicago, trumpeted its own virtues thusly: "Yeah, we never thought we'd make it this long either."

When Northwestern University undergrad Elizabeth Phillip met fellow student Steve Albini in 1980, she told him she "wanted to start an R.E.M. fanzine," Albini recalled. "But she had collected around her a bunch of other people who weren't necessarily that monomaniacal about R.E.M."

R.E.M. wasn't mentioned on the front of *Matter*'s July–August 1984 issue, but the band pervaded the magazine anyway. On the inside cover lay a full-page ad for the band's second album, *Reckoning*, trumpeting the fact that the first, *Murmur*, had nabbed both Album of the Year and Best New Artist of 1983 from *Rolling Stone* magazine's critics.

Reckoning—only "$5.99 for the month of June" at ten Chicagoland shops—ended with "Little America," whose key line was "Jefferson, I think we're lost." As fans knew, the band's manager Jefferson Holt, did most of the driving on tour. The song's title was a simple, eloquent term for what R.E.M. and its fans personified—a self-made community, spread out in pockets around the country, dedicated to bands that had also come up through postpunk DIY networks but didn't necessarily sound like "punk."

In the back of the magazine was "New Matter," in which a dozen contributors weighed in on new releases. The cross talk was oft contentious—typical of the scene's discourse. This issue led off with *Reckoning*, released back in April. Gerard Cosloy, the nineteen-year-old college radio DJ from Boston who edited his own zine, *Conflict*, thought that *Reckoning* was "miles sharper than *Murmur*," even if the band was "still a trifle too bohemian-college student for me. The singer wears blankets, the guitar player has purple shoes—I mean, Jesus Christ, don't these guys know they're role models?" At the opposite end was Albini, who'd become one of Chicago postpunk's most outspoken figures. Albini thought *Reckoning* was "incredibly boring, ordinary pop," declaring that the band "blew their wad with 'Radio Free Europe'"—R.E.M.'s very first single, from 1981.

The same July *Matter* no. 9 was on the stands, two bands—San Pedro's Minutemen, a trio that played an unorthodox variation on Gang of Four's tense funk-punk but could also sound like a clock unwinding, and Minneapolis–St. Paul's Hüsker Dü, who sounded like a damn tornado—simultaneously released double LPs on SST Records, the standard-bearer for the American underground. Hüsker Dü was on the cover of *Matter* that month, standing on a road, three scruffy, indifferently dressed white guys whose nonchalant appearance was somewhat at odds with the band's overpowering sound, which resembled a riot in progress.

STEVE ALBINI WAS A MISSOULA, MONTANA, NATIVE WHO'D MOVED TO Chicago to study journalism at Northwestern University. He began playing bass for short-lived postpunk Stations, and their rhythm box made an impression on him. "[It] was the first time I realized that the drum machine could have its own personality—it could be a strong voice in the band," he said. The first band in town he really fell for was Naked Raygun. They had a big impact on the music Albini began to make as Big Black, particularly once Raygun's vocalist Jeff Pezzati (playing bass here) and guitarist Santiago Durango joined the band. The band's other major member was "Roland," aka the cheap Roland TR-606 Albini had purchased after leaving Stations.

Albini's persona—both on record and in his scorched-earth columns in *Matter*—was extremely confrontational. Take his sophomoric race-baiting: He nearly gave Big Black's second EP, late 1983's *Bulldozer*, the title *Hey Nigger*, insisting to a *Matter* interviewer that "Anyone stupid enough to be offended by that title is part of the problem. . . . It's better to be confrontational about things like this. Of course I think judging people by the color of their skin is absurd." His bandmates—and everybody else he spoke to—forced him to change the title. Later, when Albini named a project Rapeman, London's Rough Trade shop refused to carry it because of its offensive name.

The early Naked Raygun shows that Albini had caught were incredibly mutable: "They were a million things at once and they were doing all of them well," Albini said. But by 1984, Raygun's membership had changed almost completely, with only vocalist Jeff Pezzati remaining from the original lineup, and they began playing the hardcore that was burning through the scene.

Released in the summer of 1984, *Throb Throb*'s ambition isn't as breathtaking as Hüsker Dü's *Zen Arcade*. But Raygun's album nevertheless occupies its hardcore-centric dual lane with aplomb. "Only in America" is one of the era's great anthems, even if only a few thousand people total knew it at the time—the upbeat two-four rhythm and sardonically peppy sax riff give its speed-beat a surprising swing, just what Pezzati's call-and-response of "Eat your own weight in salt (only in America!)" needs to go down. The album is witty elsewhere, too, not just in following "Libido" with "No Sex," but in Camilo Gonzalez's strutting, jazzy bass breakdown on the former.

Prior to *Throb Throb*, which was issued on Homestead Records (so was *Racer-X*), Naked Raygun had put out an EP and seven-inch on Ruthless Records, the label cofounded by fellow Chicago punks the Effigies—who, by '84, had also grown restless with the increasing dogma of the political punk scene. "That whole axis of *Maximumrocknroll* bands—they're absolute destruction, tear down this system. Where's the alternative?" vocalist John Kedzy griped that year to a zine, adding: "I've got a lot to bitch about, everyone does, but that's not the reason we're in a band."

Nor was it just philosophy that increasingly marked the Effigies out from their local peers. Their 1981 EP *Haunted Town*, wrote *Matter*'s Lee Sustar, had a "significance [that] has become clear only in recent months as the various 'post-hardcore' bands search for something new and flirt with—guess what—heavy metal." Kedzy told Sustar that Earl "Oil" Letiecq's shredding tone "does make us sound different. . . . Sometimes we have to yell at him about those guitar solos." By 1984, Kedzy would tell another interviewer, "I'd say I'm a lot happier with the metal side than the punk," adding: "We're not a hardcore band. . . . If we're punks in anything, it's in spirit. And that's about it."

THE GRASSROOTS TOURING CIRCUIT FOR INDEPENDENT AMERICAN ROCK bands was just beginning to cohere in 1981. "Booking was like being an explorer," says Jefferson Holt, who managed R.E.M. at the time. "Punk" of whatever stripe was still viewed with extreme suspicion by Middle America. "The people who were running discos and blues clubs just didn't get it," says Holt. "I remember us playing this cavernous place in Cherry Hill, New Jersey. [The promoter], a young Italian American guy, took me back to this room, and there were all these older guys. I felt like I had walked into a Scorsese movie. There was nothing to be afraid of, really, but we were the aliens."

"Alien" is precisely how R.E.M. felt when they pulled into Minneapolis on the freezing afternoon of Thursday, November 26, 1981. Holt was behind the wheel; the gig paid $300, a kingly sum for a group whose members were on a strict $2 per diem. A blizzard was underway, and the venue where R.E.M. was to play—the 7th Street Entry, the 225-capacity side room of Sam's, as First Avenue was then called—was still closed when they arrived. So was nearly everything else—it was Thanksgiving. "The only place open was a Greek restaurant," says Holt. "There was a Greyhound sign spinning around. It was like an Edward Hopper painting. We were . . . *concerned* is an understatement. We didn't know who was going to turn up for an unknown band on Thanksgiving night."

Not many: Steve McClellan, the general manager, moved the show from the Entry to Sam's Mainroom. He later estimated the night's attendance as eighty-eight people—in a room that held twelve hundred. "Bands don't like playing to that emptiness," says Holt. "But because of the enthusiasm of the people that came out, it was one of the best shows that they ever did."

R.E.M. would appear at the venue twice the following year: On April 26, 1982, they drew 347 people. Then 942 came out to see them on September 22, a month after the release of their first EP, *Chronic Town*, a sign of the band's rapid ascendancy in the consciousness of America's burgeoning indie rock subculture, and its small but mighty mushrooming in size.

The club would become a hub in the firmament. "The American indie scene . . . was very connected nationally," says Julie Farman, the mid-eighties talent booker at the Boston club the Rathskeller, or the Rat. "We all knew each other. Everybody supported each other." Additionally, she adds, "we didn't distinguish between Metallica and the Violent Femmes. If they were on an independent label, if they were doing it on their own, they were the same."

IN 1984, BILL BERRY WAS FLABBERGASTED TO REALIZE THAT ATHENS, Georgia, an hour outside of Atlanta, had become home to thirty-five rock bands. When Berry began writing songs and playing drums for his band, R.E.M., Athens had only a handful of groups. "Largely, it's just the chemistry of a lot of kids together in one place," bassist Mike Mills would write. "But that's true for any college town; some more than others." And R.E.M. were ambassadors of a utopian mythos of an America full of rockin' college towns, all networked together, as much as they were of their own music.

Naturally, this critics' band started in a record store. Peter Buck was a dropout from Emory University working at the Wuxtry record shop in Athens. (Well into the eighties, Buck would work there when not on tour, taking his pay in records.) In 1979, Buck met Michael Stipe, an army brat born in Decatur who'd grown up all over the middle United States as well as West Germany. He'd sung in a couple of bands before meeting Buck, and his instrument was instantly unique—a reedy keen when declaiming, a throaty moan while crooning.

Bassist Mike Mills and drummer Bill Berry had gone to school together. Initially suspicious of one another—Bill the burnout, Mike the nerd—when they showed up to the same band audition in their teens, they clicked instantly. By senior year, they made sixty bucks a show playing "country clubs, weddings, and the like."

The four members of R.E.M. rehearsed and wrote constantly. "We'd take any date that anyone offered for any amount of money," Buck said. Everyone had ideas. The four-way writing credits the band adopted—inspired by Lennon–McCartney's agreement, and in a band full of songwriters—was a stroke of genius.

It took some time for the band's style to come into focus. "The early songs were all really skeletal and the lyrics were like simple pictures, but after about a year I got really bored with that," Stipe said. "So I started experimenting with lyrics that didn't make exact linear sense, and it's just gone from there."

"YOU CAN'T ESCAPE HISTORY," BUCK SAID IN 1984. "THAT WAS THE ONLY thing that I thought was wrong with the punk thing that excited everybody in '76–'77: It basically backed itself into a corner because it was so nihilistic. 'OK, all the past is gone. We're starting over fresh.' Well, really, there's not much you can do that hasn't been at least hinted in rock 'n' roll. . . . That leaves PIL [Public Image Ltd] climbing higher and higher up a tree and sawing the limbs as they go."

But what if you could escape the *present*? That's what R.E.M. seemed to do, and not just because their ringing sound—Buck's rudimentary but sturdy hooks, Berry's propulsive snare-hat work, Mills confidently running the board on bass—was so reminiscent of sixties folk rock and garage bands. Even more than their throwback vibe, R.E.M. lived up to its namesake, the rapid-eye movement that leads to vivid dreams, and the reason for that was Stipe's singing.

Slurring the lyrics was a rock and roll tradition, from Fats Domino to Mick Jagger, that was steeped in the blues. But Stipe wasn't a blues singer, and R.E.M. wasn't a blues band. His marble-mouthing fit the band's nervous energy, but it was also a way of hiding in plain sight.

One key difference between postpunk in the United States and in the UK was in how each treated queerness. Boy George and Frankie had to do fan dances, but they still signified with a wink. In US indie circles, things were closer to don't ask, don't tell. If you already knew, or found out, great; if you didn't know, also fine.

On Stipe's first visit to New York, he "saw the first billboard about AIDS," as he told Christopher Bolland:

It was like, "Holy shit. This is for real." It was scary. Suddenly there were all these people who were available to me—men and women— and I was really having fun. But then there came responsibility and feeling afraid and being afraid to get tested, because you couldn't get tested anonymously. It was so fucked up. . . . I came out of the free-swinging sixties and seventies. It was free love, baby. That was it. We had very liberal sex-ed classes in 1973, a yearlong environmental science class, and then Women's Lib and Gay Liberation. So it's insane to go from that to Reagan and AIDS. It was like, "What happened? Where's my future?" Our generation was supposed to be about trying to deal with nuclear concerns and environmental disasters. Suddenly, Reagan is in office, I'm 21 years old, and you can die from fucking.

Indie rock bands with queer members, like R.E.M. (Stipe) and Hüsker Dü (Bob Mould and Grant Hart), operated off-radar enough—and in a scene so adamantly *about the music*—that few people wrote, or necessarily cared, about their sex lives, not that it was anybody else's business anyway. But it was also very likely a matter of safety that R.E.M. never announced, or discussed in interviews, Stipe's sexuality.

Stipe was forthcoming about this in later years, but it wasn't until 1994 that either he or Mould stated their sexuality in print. Stipe certainly did his share of hinting at it, particularly on *Reckoning*'s fourth song, "Pretty Persuasion": "He's got pretty persuasion / She's got pretty persuasion / Goddamn your confusion."

WHEN R.E.M. SIGNED TO IRS RECORDS IN 1982, THEY TURNED DOWN some major-label offers in order to keep all the decision-making power. IRS head Miles Copeland described them as "a good, tight little business. They lived within their means and cut the cloth based on what they were going to generate, which is how you're supposed to run a business."

Yet they were willing to play the game a little bit. In August 1983, R.E.M. played five dates opening for the Police on the East Coast, for a total of 110,000 people; Buck called it "the most wretched and abysmal experience of our lives." That June, they taped an appearance on the TV special *Rock of the Eighties*, at the Palace in Hollywood, which also featured Jason and the Scorchers, Nona Hendryx, and Simple Minds, all performing on a rotating stage. They even appeared on *Solid Gold Hits*, miming the song "So. Central Rain (I'm Sorry)."

For *Murmur*, issued in April 1983, "We wanted no lead guitar and no heavy punk—just a fast, weird folk-rock record with tons of overdubs," Buck said. The album was an immediate critical sensation: *CMJ* magazine's review concluded: "Suggested cuts: ALL." *Rolling Stone* called it "intelligent, enigmatic, deeply involving," while also noting an essential detachment: "In the end, though, what they're saying is less fascinating than how they say it."

Or where they said it from: scenes full of bands like R.E.M. were popping up seemingly everywhere in the country—even a sleepy college town like Athens or a midsized city such as Minneapolis. *Especially* those places, it seemed.

Many of these bands lived on the road, adhering to an old-fashioned work ethic—and, it was strongly implied, an all-American one. This was a critical aspect of the very American year that was 1984, one as much part of the US indie scene's self-identity as it was stadium rock's. "Essentially, we make records to get gigs, which is still what we enjoy most," Berry said that year.

Following up *Murmur* was a snap—R.E.M. had such a surfeit of material that Buck wanted to make it a double LP, only to be voted down. *Reckoning,* released in April 1984, is a whole lot looser than *Murmur*—Buck said it "was mixed and recorded, I figure, in a total of twelve days, including a half day off for going to a movie." Berry noted, "We wanted to record as far as possible with all of us, including Michael, playing and singing at the same time."

Buck was particularly proud of "So. Central Rain": "It's one of the first ones that Michael captured that elliptical way of writing that still managed to say something specific and tangible." It also showed how savvy the band was about selling itself. When Stipe refused to lip-synch for the "So. Central Rain" video, IRS rep Altomare recalled: "We did major publicity to promote the fact that we had this really cool band that was breaking tradition by not lip-synching."

GRANTZBERG VERNON HART WAS BORN MARCH 18, 1961, THE YOUNGEST of three children, to working-class parents in South St. Paul. "I'd always been able to monkey around on a piano that we had in the basement, like so many other suburban families," Hart said. He was ten when his brother died in a car accident. "A very close friend of the family approached me and my brother and said that we each had to take on half of my brother's work. For me that was the music aspects of my brother's life. He was a drummer."

As a teenager, Grant began hanging out at Melody Lane, a record store in Signal Hills Mall in St. Paul, and becoming friendly with the staff. So did another budding St. Paul musician, bassist Greg Norton. By the fall of 1978, Norton and Hart were going to punk shows at the Longhorn Bar in downtown Minneapolis, and so was a newcomer to town from upstate New York. Bob Mould had moved to St. Paul to attend Macalester College. He'd been listening to and playing music from childhood. Hearing the Ramones' first album at sixteen "sealed the deal for what I wanted to do with my life," he says.

Shortly after enrolling at Macalester in the fall of 1978, Mould went to the Longhorn to see the Suicide Commandos. "It was the first time I'd been in a punk rock club in the Twin Cities; first time I'd been in a punk rock club," he says. "And it was just crazy—go in those big doors and you take those few steps down, and I was just like, 'Wow, this is home for me; I'll be here every weekend.'"

Near the Macalester campus was the record shop Cheapo, where Hart had begun working. "There was this half a PA out in front of this record store, and I think it might've been playing Pere Ubu, *The Modern Dance*," Mould said. "I just went in and there's this sort of hippie-looking, barefoot guy in there like, 'What's up?' I said I liked the choice of music, and we got to talking. He was like, 'I play drums. I play keyboard. I play everything.' I said, 'I play guitar.'"

Hart brought Norton in on bass, and the three of them bonded by seeing the Ramones open for Foreigner at the St. Paul Civic Center. In March 1979, they played a quartet gig with a coworker at a St. Paul bar. After that, they were a trio. The name Hüsker Dü came from a children's game; Norton had suggested it at a rehearsal for a laugh, then again later in earnest. "Number one, it's foreign," says Norton. "We could use umlauts. It means, 'Do you remember?'—as in, 'Do you remember when rock and roll was good?'"

"I THINK WE'RE MAKING INROADS TO CHANGING PEOPLE BECAUSE WE'RE getting the mainstream to see us," Bob Mould told *Matter* in its Hüsker Dü cover story. He added: "It doesn't take a lot of balls to play in front of your friends for three years."

That DIY spirit propelled Hüsker Dü's early-and-often touring. They began meeting out-of-town bands coming through town—first at the Longhorn, then First Avenue. Touring together were two hardcore bands from Vancouver, DOA and the Subhumans, who came bearing information: "We opened up for them, and they're like, 'Hey, if you guys ever want to come west you've got contacts. We'll do whatever we can to help you get gigs,'" says Norton.

Vancouver was the north star of a West Coast touring strip cobbled together all the way down to Orange County, where SST Records was located. Hüsker Dü made contact with the label's founder, Greg Ginn, and his crew on its first road trip, in March of 1981, when they drove out to play Oz in Chicago.

"Oz was one of those classic punk clubs where basically somebody found an abandoned building and was like, 'Let's put in a bar and sell booze and have punk bands play,'" says Norton. "'And we don't need working toilets.' The guy that ran the Oz was like, 'Black Flag is coming to town. Why don't you guys play the after-party?' So we're like, 'Yeah, we'd love to.'"

When Hüsker Dü went to San Francisco, they crashed with Jello Biafra of the Dead Kennedys—on the verge of releasing *In God We Trust, Inc.*—for a month. Jello Biafra had been a fan of the PiL-like ominousness of their first seven-inch, "Statues" b/w "Amusement." But the band had changed course. "They were at that point a hardcore band, although they'd come to that kind of galloping hardcore style that they have on *Land Speed Record* independently of what was going on in Southern California or Washington, DC—and Dead Kennedys," says Biafra.

One thing that distinguished Hüsker Dü from its hardcore contemporaries was that for all the songs' rage, they seldom picked obvious political targets— specifically, Ronald Reagan. Reagan's easy victory over Jimmy Carter in November 1980 prompted Claude Bessy, the LA punk singer and writer (under the name Kickboy Face) for *Slash* magazine, to depart for the UK the same month. Hüsker Dü had a more classically midwestern fatalism, which pervaded their most political early song, the 1982 single "In a Free Land": "Why bother spending time / Reading up on things? / Everybody's an authority / In a free land."

When Hüsker Dü returned to the Twin Cities, they cut their debut, *Land Speed Record*, live at the 7th Street Entry. Months of roadwork had led them to play blindingly fast and tight. In Chicago, with the band on the bill with Black Flag, lead singer Henry Rollins said, "It was heading in a direction—they morphed into the more melodic, more tunefully ambitious Hüsker Dü."

Mould recalls the atmosphere around SST HQ as "family": "It was like a commune. We slept in the office. I slept under Henry's desk. Greg Ginn's mom would bring a block of cheese over. We'd go get chili cheese fries once a day. That was our allotment of money for food. It was great."

SST finally signed on for Hüsker Dü's third major release, a seven-song EP titled *Metal Circus* that cemented the band's rep: Gerard Cosloy named it the best release of 1983 in *Conflict*. The opening song, "Real World," was, as SST's Joe Carducci put it, "a song about pulling away from the political *Maximumrocknroll* kind of limitations." *Metal Circus* also signaled Hart's emergence as a songwriter on par with Mould—in particular, the harrowing "Diane," based on the true story of a waitress who'd been raped and murdered, told from the killer's POV.

Rollins recalls the band's redoubled fire in 1983. "We [Black Flag] were doing shows up the coast, and it was Santa Barbara, I think, and Bill Stevenson, Black Flag's drummer, and I were watching Hüsker Dü play, realizing we have to go on after their set. And we're just watching them, and we simultaneously look at each other, like: 'What are we going to do?' Because they were just so good. You better have eaten your Wheaties that morning."

OVER IN ST. PAUL, A COUPLE OF GRANT HART'S FRIENDS HAD PURCHASED a deconsecrated church where the Hüsker Dü drummer slept in a tent, and his band began to rehearse. While Mould was a speed-head for much of this period, Hart and Norton were ingesting far more colorful substances—psilocybin and LSD. "After a while, I felt a contact high—I could see it in the air," Mould wrote in his memoir.

"[We were] writing all the time and probably taking a fair amount of speed and drinking a lot," Mould recalled. "Everything was firing on all cylinders. We couldn't tour enough. We were always on the road. We were living in that van. We were building a following.

"We were friends with R.E.M., so we were playing a lot in Athens and hanging out down there. I would go down there for a week at a time and stay with [Michael] Stipe until he got sick of me, and then I'd go stay with Peter [Buck]. It was in full bloom. Everybody was going crazy, just loving being on the road, and just writing all the time—writing songs at sound check, writing songs in an alley after sound check, writing most of the words for *Zen Arcade* sleeping in the back of that van."

The band began discussing how the material might be shaped into an arc. "We talked about it in the van," says Mould. "We started to see similarities with the songs because it was the first time the three of us were dealing with being adults. It was like wait, we are the product of our respective parents and—whether it's coming from abusive childhood, violent childhood, broken homes—that's where those themes—it just all started to come to the surface for the first time. . . . We knew what the songs were about and we started to create storyboards to tie everything together."

In late October 1983, the trio headed to Redondo Beach, California, the home of its label, SST Records. The session started late, and the band, which had been sipping meth-laced coffee for hours, attacked its first song, a warm-up cover of the Byrds' "Eight Miles High," like a rabid timber wolf. Then it recorded and mixed its twenty-three-song opus in three days. When labelmates the Minutemen heard about it, they, too, decided to make a double LP, and SST opted to issue them simultaneously. In April 1984, Hüsker Dü put out "Eight Miles High" on a seven-inch and blew a hole in the universe. The album that followed, *Zen Arcade*, would be just as overwhelming—and seventeen times as long.

"They would come into SST and argue and drink coffee and then fight and get into the van and work on songs and take walks to get away from each other," Rollins recalls of the album's making. "They were just kind of slammed together and then they'd explode apart, and have written three more songs.

"And that's what led to *Double Nickels on the Dime* by the Minutemen, who said, 'If Hüsker Dü gets a double album, then we're going to do a double album.' And SST went, 'Uh, okay.' They were writing songs in the day and going in and recording them that night. I'd never been around a band that wrote it at noon and recorded at ten p.m."

To the label's surprise, both albums sold out of their initial shipment of five thousand copies, and there was a delay on the next one. Ray Farrell, who joined SST Records in 1985, recalls, "When I started, the *Zen Arcade* album was in a situation where we were running out of money because the distributors weren't paying us. But there would be cases where we'd be back-ordered and we'd be waiting for money and we wouldn't have it and of course the band could say, 'This is crazy. We can't find our records in stores.'"

Major label AOR scouts were starting to show up at shows. Terry Katzman, the band's longtime soundman, recalled, "They were already thinking, 'How can we move on?'"

"SWIMMING IN THE MAINSTREAM / IS SUCH A LAME DREAM."

Black Flag had been laying low for two years because of lawsuits over the 1981 album *Damaged* when, at the end of 1983, Rollins made a promise. In 1984, he said, "Black Flag's going to tour a lot and put out a lot of records. We are a live touring band, and this sitting-at-home shit is not happening."

Delays had been an unfortunate hallmark of Black Flag's career. Though the band had actually begun in Hermosa Beach in 1977, it wasn't until 1979 that they gigged in Los Angeles. That February, they released *Nervous Breakdown*— four songs, five minutes, seven inches of vinyl, and a revolution enjoined. This is where hardcore begins.

The band's spray-painting of its instantly iconic four-bar logo—designed by Ginn's brother, the artist Raymond Pettibon—all around LA and Orange County aroused the ire of local police, and Pettibon's subsequent artwork on a sticker advertising the song "Police Story" fanned the flames: it depicted a cop with a gun held in his mouth, with its unseen holder saying, "Make me come, faggot!"

"To this day," *Option* reported in 1985, "the L.A.P.D. orders extra patrols, summons police helicopters and harasses fans at Black Flag's hometown gigs, having never forgotten nor forgiven the anti-cop sentiments the band expressed early in their career." Ginn recalled: "It got to where we would rent a hall and the cops would be there before the crowd." That was a big reason that Black Flag toured so much. "We always felt a lot safer out of town," Ginn said.

In 1978, Black Flag felt themselves ready to take on the world. They'd signed a deal with another local label that, Ginn said, "flaked out, and I just thought, I'll figure out how to do it. In order to survive and not just sit and practice, we've had to take the business on ourselves." Hence Ginn's formation of SST Records out of DIY necessity.

In summer 1981, Black Flag added new vocalist Rollins (born Henry Garfield) from Washington, DC. He'd been brought up in the District—his liberal mom divorced his strict conservative father and raised him alone on a government job. "My mom was working for Humphrey's election campaign in '68, so we were a politically motivated little household," Rollins said. "By the time I was like second or third grade it was 1968, and it was racially intense. The hood of my mom's VW, we had a dent from where a mace canister bounced off."

Rollins first began performing by subbing for the lead singer of the Teen Idles, whose bassist and drummer, Ian MacKaye and Jeff Nelson, started the label Dischord to issue the band's *Minor Disturbance* EP. Teen Idles split in late 1980, and MacKaye (now on vocals) and Nelson formed Minor Threat, whose fearsome sound and stringently ascetic "straight-edge" philosophy—no drugs, alcohol, or (good luck, kids) sex—would have an equally outsized impact on hardcore as Black Flag (who were, quite adamantly, *not* straight-edge).

With Rollins on board, Black Flag's shows took on a new intensity. Bruce Pavitt, in Seattle's *The Rocket*, called Rollins "a monster performer—spilling sweat, swaying, bending, thrusting, with hippie hair and tattoos, combining the raw sex of Elvis or James Brown with the psychotic edge of Charlie Manson."

Weeks after Rollins joining, Black Flag was signed to Unicorn, a subsidiary of MCA Records. The band recorded *Damaged*, which moved into heavier guitar, slower tempos, and longer songs—"Damaged I," the album's finale, lasted nearly four minutes!—as well as Rollins's pitiless-bordering-on-absurdist self-abnegation at the front.

But MCA balked—they wouldn't touch the album after distribution head Al Bergamo told the *Los Angeles Times* that he considered its contents "anti-parent." SST took over distribution, moving some eighty thousand copies of the album, but the band soon sued to get off Unicorn, thanks to a contract mandating that one hundred thousand copies of the album needed to be sold before the label owed the band any royalties. Only after Unicorn went bankrupt was Black Flag able to release new music again. Pavitt reported in the March 1984 *Rocket* that *My War* would be the "first in a series of four LPs to be released this year" by the band.

By 1984, Greg Ginn was the only original member left in Black Flag. Little wonder—he was a martinet, mandating practice every day. Founding bassist Chuck Dukowski left the band before *My War*'s recording, though he continued to manage the band and was SST's co-owner until 1989. (The album was recorded as a trio, Ginn doubling on guitar and bass, with Bill Stevenson on drums and Rollins singing.) Rollins later claimed that Dukowski was "vibed out" of the band; Dukowski later explained that he'd written *My War*'s marinating-in-hostility title song ("You say that you're my friend / But you're one of them") "about Greg Ginn." Ginn himself just shrugged: "Whenever the band changed, I took it as a new band."

By that summer, Black Flag had a new bassist—Kira Roessler, later a sound effects editor who won an Academy Award for her work on *Mad Max: Fury Road* (2015). Her first album with the band was an oddball: *Family Man*, released in September, featured Roessler and Stevenson on the B side only—all instrumental, no Rollins, whose spoken pieces occupied the A. (He was becoming active in Los Angeles–area reading nights involving other musicians.) That year, Black Flag played a series of instrumental-only gigs. These were not well received: one critic compared these vocal-free sets to being doused with "raw sewage."

The four-album cycle was completed in December, with two simultaneous releases, à la *Zen/Double*. On *Slip It In*, Roessler added some welcome counterpoint to the title track, which was not titled "The Joy of Sex" for a reason. The rest of *Slip It In* sounded even more like metal than *My War*. The cassette-only *Live '84*, recorded in San Francisco that August, amounted to housecleaning. Within two years, the band would be finished; decades later, nearly everyone involved with Black Flag would disown Ginn, including his brother Raymond Pettibon.

"MAKE NO MISTAKE, THE MINUTEMEN WRITE TUNES," MATTER'S GLEN Sarvady wrote. "But they don't bother padding them. If there's thirty-five seconds of melody there, the song will end in thirty-five seconds."

Minutemen—guitarist-vocalist D. Boon, bassist-vocalist Mike Watt, drummer George Hurley—had formed in San Pedro, thirty miles from Hollywood, responding as much to heavily deconstructed UK postpunk bands such as Wire and Gang of Four as to hardcore. Minutemen recordings were a big bear hug of all things off-center. Boon's guitar skronked like a spring snapping from sustained tension, Watt zagged under D.'s zigs, and Hurley marched imperturbably through. They never sounded the same way twice.

Boon and Watt had been childhood friends, going to see arena rock shows until punk turned their heads around. When Hurley met them, he "was nineteen and working as a truck unloader" and befriended Watt at a drunken party. Watt talked Hurley into playing with them. Within a year, they were the Minutemen—the ultimate hardcore moniker, since hardcore songs were all about a minute long.

But hardcore was strict, and the Minutemen were anything but. "The incredible thing is that even though the cuts are often shorter than 60 seconds, each is still a complete song," critic John Leland wrote of 1983's *Buzz or Howl Under the Influence of Heat*. "This EP's eight songs all sound entirely different from each other."

Double Nickels on the Dime was the right salvo at the right time. Leland called it "the punk answer to *Blonde on Blonde*. . . . Given this much material, the Minutemen's idiosyncratic fragments, like Bob Dylan's, add up to a richly coherent whole. And who but the Minutemen could cover songs by both Van Halen and Steely Dan?" In fact, David Lee Roth was, on the sly, helping fund a Los Angeles after-hours bar called Zero Club, where he became friends with a number of punk figures, including Watt and Rollins; the latter would ghostwrite Roth's 1998 memoir, *Crazy from the Heat*.

IF BLACK FLAG'S AUDIENCES DIDN'T QUITE GET THEIR PLAYING HARD ROCK instead of hardcore, they *really* didn't get the opening band. If Minutemen were art weirdoes, Phoenix, Arizona's Meat Puppets—brothers Curt and Cris Kirkwood on guitar and bass, both singing, and drummer Derrick Bostrom—were that most sixties and un-punk of things: hippies. "We liked the Grateful Dead," Curt said. "We didn't want to sound like the Dead, but we definitely wanted to play at parties where people were getting high. . . . We thought punk rock was the new psychedelia."

This stance, needless to say, divided the *Matter* staff—Albini and two others hated the band's April-released *Meat Puppets II* ("This would only be any good at all if I liked Beefheart and smoked pot," Albini wrote. "And I don't"), but the other reviewers were all rapt. "Comparisons be damned," Blake Gumprecht wrote, wondering: "Is there such a thing as accidental brilliance?"

The band had released its first album on SST in 1982—a twenty-two-minute hardcore jamboree that, SST's Joe Carducci recalled, was made with the band "on mushrooms, so you couldn't talk to them. . . . [And] they couldn't play together, so the amps had to be pointed at the drums, so you could move the faders all you wanted and nothing changed. It was just ready-mixed."

But that Deadhead vibe came through loud and clear on the second album. Recorded in spring of 1983 but held back for a full year, *Meat Puppets II* was cloud-dust psychedelia—Curt's phantasmagorical solo in "Split Myself in Two" gave the speedy song its otherworldly touch—atop the wooziest twang imaginable. Curt Kirkwood wrote a raft of classics—though it would take another ten years for the wider world to hear them, when Nirvana brought the Kirkwoods out to perform "Plateau," "Oh, Me," and "Lake of Fire" with them on *MTV Unplugged*.

By 1984, "the country thing" was all over American indie. "A variety of bands, mostly from L.A., have adopted a rootsier, country feel," Pavitt wrote at the end of the year, naming Rank & File, Jason and the Scorchers, Blood on the Saddle, Tex and the Horseheads, Green on Red, True West, the Long Ryders, the Last Roundup, and Meat Puppets. Hell, even the Replacements, a bunch of flannel-clad punk jokers from Minneapolis, had gone faux-country, a little, on the 1983 album *Hootenanny*.

Page 7 of *Matter* no. 9 featured a write-up on the Last Roundup: "Four people onstage are trading off on banjo, pedal steel, standup bass, washboard, mandolin, and acoustic guitar . . . [and] the singer's fine country drawl." The band had originated when "Michael McMahon, his sister Amy, and friend Garth Powell became disenchanted with the punk/new wave movement" in 1982. Last Roundup, *Matter* noted, do not "*ever* sound like the middle-of-the-road stuff [on] WHN, New York's country music station." Similarly, Pavitt wrote of Blood on the Saddle's self-titled album on New Alliance: "This is pure spurs and barbed wire–rippin' cowpunk."

The term "cowpunk" itself was just the latest coinage in a sweep of them. Just like "rock" had a decade earlier, "punk" was bisecting like crazy. Tangents became wholesale approaches. In 1984, Manhattan's CBGB—which had incubated New York punk in the mid-seventies and hardcore at its all-ages Sunday matinees during the eighties—began holding semi-regular "Country Sundays" series, featuring bands like Last Roundup.

It was all part of a general reclaiming of "Americanness" within the indie realm. A number of groups in LA spearheaded a roots-oriented approach, steeped in hard country and pre-rock R&B played at punk velocity—the Blasters, the Gun Club, and New York transplants the Cramps. "The Blasters had a huge influence on us," John Doe of Los Angeles's X said.

In July 1983, X put a song called "I Must Not Think Bad Thoughts" on their fourth album, *More Fun in the New World*—their second for Elektra. The song was a protest of US foreign policy, but it also threw in some shots at what they called "Glitter-disco-synthesizer night school," protesting further: "But what about the Minutemen, Flesh Eaters, DOA, Big Boys, and the Black Flag?"

Even if X's innate artiness essentially guaranteed they'd never break big in Middle America, their frustration wasn't entirely mislaid. "Groups like Blondie, the Pretenders, Devo, and the Go-Go's had all cracked the Billboard's Hot 100, but somehow we were still stuck in dirty rock clubs," Doe would write. The strain began to show up in Doe's and co-lead singer Exene Cervenka's marriage: "Exene began to feel bullied by my constant work ethic and stifled by our constant 'John and Exene' identity, losing her sense of self."

And by 1984, the world had changed for all four of the bands Doe mentioned. Blondie was finished; Devo's sixth album, *Shout*, released in '84, tanked. The Pretenders were around, but only in the wake of the overdose deaths, less than a year apart, of the band's guitarist James Honeyman-Scott and bassist Pete Farndon. Singer-songwriter-guitarist Chrissie Hynde and drummer Martin Chambers hired replacements and pressed on.

Then there were the Go-Go's, X's LA peers, who'd skyrocketed with their 1981 debut—their success had directly enabled R.E.M.'s, who signed to IRS Records a year later—and who were working, partying, and fighting constantly by their third album, *Talk Show*, released in March 1984. The ebullient "Head Over Heels" reached number eleven. But guitarist-songwriter Jane Wiedlin was sick of her bandmates' drug use and furious over the money, and left the group after they finished promoting the album that fall. Afterward, she went to see *This Is Spinal Tap* and wept. The Go-Go's called it quits early in 1985.

X's signing to Elektra had made them an easy target for abuse from their peers. The worst of it came from Slash's founder, Bob Biggs, who went so far as to write an editorial in *Billboard* that July that barely tried disguising his dismay over losing his prize "Band 'Z.'" "I've got three other friends that I didn't want to betray," Cervenka said of such cavils.

At her suggestion, the band made a single-only cover of the Troggs' mid-sixties garage rock standard "Wild Thing." It was their first release without Ray Manzarek, the Doors keyboardist who'd produced their first four LPs. Those records, even fans noted, sounded nowhere near as powerful as X did onstage.

To try to get "Wild Thing" on the radio, X agreed to work with Michael Wagener, a German-born heavy metal producer who piled on the overdubs— he "triple, quadruple, octuple tracked" Billy Zoom's guitars, Doe wrote, while DJ Bonebrake's drums "sounded like they came from the far side of an airplane hangar. . . . We were all seduced." Lots of old fans weren't: Cosloy suggested it might be "the worst record of the year," alongside the Fleshtones' "American Beat '84," another clomping America(na)-first anthem.

As if to atone for such naked careerism, X began leaning more and more into roots music. Cervenka, Doe, and drummer Bonebrake, plus the Blasters' Dave Alvin and Bill Bateman on guitar and bass, formed a side group called the Knitters, frequently opening X's shows with acoustic covers of folk and country oldies.

"IF YOU ARE A CHICANO AND YOU GOT MARRIED BETWEEN 1973 AND 1980," Louie Perez, the drummer for Los Lobos, told biographer Chris Morris, "we probably played your wedding."

Formed in 1973 on the Eastside of LA, Los Lobos had begun playing the traditional Mexican music of their parents' generation, scouring thrift shops for authentic instruments. They'd also earned a rep as the area's killer wedding band. They'd play wherever there was work: "We were playing in a restaurant for two, three years, just background music," guitarist-singer Cesar Rosas said, "and we got tired of it." They, too, cranked out a loud version of "Wild Thing" and lost the gig.

Los Lobos could, and did, play anything—and anywhere. In May of 1980, they accepted a gig opening for Public Image Ltd. at Olympic Auditorium—a pure stunt, but one with repercussions. Los Lobos played a folkloric set and were pelted: "We hadn't even got to the middle of the first song when the entire audience went nuts and started throwing everything they could get their hands on," Perez wrote. But rather than be put off, the band's interest was piqued, particularly after they began listening to the Blasters' first album. Soon Los Lobos were opening for the Blasters at the Whisky a Go Go.

Los Lobos' command of a myriad of styles attracted instant notice. *DownBeat* noted their "skirling norteno accordion, country-swing pedal steel swells, Charlie Christian–to-rockabilly guitar figures, strong and individualized voices, and dance beats from south of the border."

When Los Lobos signed to the LA punk indie label Slash, they debuted with an EP, . . . *And a Time to Dance*. It gave the band time to cook up a rock-solid bunch of songs—in particular, "A Matter of Time," cowritten by Perez and the band's other guitarist-singer, David Hidalgo, about a Mexican man who heads to the United States looking for work so he can send back for his wife and kids. This was not a topic anyone in rock and roll had written about, one long overdue. Their full debut, *How Will the Wolf Survive?*, was released to rapturous reviews in October 1984.

NOT EVERYBODY IN THE UNDERGROUND LOOKED ASKANCE AT MAJOR-LABEL deals. "We were grooming [the Replacements] and hoping they would go to a major label," Twin/Tone cofounder Chris Osgood said. "We saw ourselves as a minor league, trying to develop talent." There was certainly a groundswell: The 'Mats handily outdrew Hüsker Dü. Between 1982 and 1986, the latter's average local show attendance hovered between four and six hundred. By contrast, on December 26, 1984, the Replacements brought in over fifteen hundred.

"We're more conscious of trying to become a national label instead of a little regional independent," the band's manager Peter Jesperson told *City Pages* as 1984 dawned. The Replacements, he promised, had the goods: "We're making a hit right now, boy. That sucker's gonna be a monster!" The title of Paul Westerberg's song summed up the tenor of things: "I Will Dare." Released as a twelve-inch single, the song featured a sandpapery Westerberg flirting shamelessly over a bright beat, bouncy riff, and zippy solo played by R.E.M.'s Peter Buck. It hit college radio that fall like a pipe bomb.

The first time the Irish postpunks U2 played Minneapolis—at First Avenue—Westerberg had gone along with Jesperson and watched the band run through its biggest hit, "I Will Follow," twice. With a mixture of inspiration and bemusement that would become his calling card, Westerberg then went off and wrote an answer song. Soon his band, the Replacements, were performing "Kids Don't Follow," along with a torrent of other similarly snotty material.

Westerberg had handed Jesperson a tape at Oar Folk two years earlier, hoping to get a Longhorn gig. Jesperson flipped; he was telling friends, quite seriously, that they were "the greatest thing since the Rolling Stones." Not everyone agreed. Daniel Corrigan, the club's longtime photographer, adds, "I remember watching one of their drunken shows where I just thought, *This isn't artistic; this is stupid.*"

Jesperson's immediate and intensive championing of the Replacements put the band on a lot of local side-eye lists, but even when they got shit-faced and played joke covers—which they did a lot—their cocky exuberance was hard to resist. Even Corrigan admired it at times; he recalls seeing guitarist Bob Stinson hock a loogie onto the ceiling of the Entry dressing room and then just walk away. "It's going to come down eventually, right?" Corrigan says with a laugh. "Whenever I was in the room [with Bob] I'd always check the ceiling, just to see what was up there."

In October 1984, the month they released *Let It Be*, the Replacements' bassist Tommy Stinson would turn eighteen. They had a routine: If a show seemed right from jump, they were the best band you saw in your life. If it didn't, they torpedoed it, on purpose, to test the audience's patience. "Anything we can do, we'll do badly, that's our motto," Westerberg told a Wichita college radio DJ in 1983.

Years later, Westerberg would admit, "We were either going to be the greatest band on earth or the worst. Settling for just being a good band was not an option. People like to see human error when it's honest. When people see you swing and miss, they start to root for you."

Let It Be reached number one on fifty-five college radio stations. The album displayed the band doing everything it did, very well. "We're Comin' Out" was ramalama punk raucousness, an opportunity for Bob to spit fire from his axe. The slow shuffle "Androgynous," meanwhile, offered a slightly bemused ("Something meets boy, and something meets girl") but empathetic take on the folks who would eventually be called simply trans. And "Unsatisfied" and "Sixteen Blue," the latter written for his teenage bassist, were heartrending teen angst that stopped short of self-pity—very Minnesotan.

When the group went to New York that December, their own faces greeted them from every newsstand in the city. The Replacements were on the cover of the *Village Voice*, the feature written by reporter RJ Smith. "It was pretty overwhelming," Jesperson recalled, "considering I'd usually be with one or two or three of them." On that trip, they played two shows. The first one, with the press assembled, sucked. At the second one, Seymour Stein of Sire Records showed up. He promised to sign the band before they returned home from the tour.

NEW MUSIC SEMINAR,
NEW YORK CITY
August 6–8, 1984

ON JANUARY 28, 1984, *CASH BOX* PROUDLY ANNOUNCED "THE INDUSTRY'S first weekly trade chart for twelve-inch records based on sales and club play." The top thirty was led by Shannon's "Let the Music Play," still burning up the clubs of '83 on its way to pop success in '84; at number three was "Hard Times," the follow-up to Run-D.M.C.'s out-of-box smash "It's Like That" b/w "Sucker MC's." But the second spot seemed, at best, an outlier: Yes's "Owner of a Lonely Heart," which *Cash Box* described as "a rocker with just enough of a beat to cut it in the clubs. After all of the supposed antagonism between the disco and rock camps, the dance music banner appears to be the one everyone can rally under."

Cash Box counted about two-thirds of the chart being "funk and R&B-oriented." But that included the German George Kranz's "Trommeltanz (Din Da Da)" (number ten), as well as R&B from Cheryl Lynn ("Encore," seven), Patti La-Belle ("If Only You Knew," twenty-four), and Melba Moore ("Keepin' My Lover Satisfied," thirty). If pop radio was enacting a fantasy of a racial, sexual, and social integration that seemed to be running in the opposite direction of Reagan's increasingly separatist early eighties, it was only catching up with the clubs.

The big new club sound of '84 was Hi-NRG, which pointed straight back to disco. Essentially an update on the synth-led sound of composer Patrick

Cowley's production work for Sylvester, it also looked ahead to the proudly artificial sounds to come in house, techno, R&B, and pop. The name came from Evelyn Thomas's "High Energy," a record that "brought the over-mixed 'thump' back with a vengeance," as *Billboard* noted. This instantly iconic gay-club anthem would reach the US Hot 100's lower reaches in September 1984.

Sadly, Cowley didn't live to see his pioneering work gain traction. He died in November 1982 of what one writer termed, simply, "cancer." Soon it had a definitive name. "By '84, the music industry was being ravaged by AIDS, especially the core of the dance music industry," says Tommy Boy Records founder Tom Silverman. "It was gay initially—that's what built the dance music business." And Hi-NRG was a specifically gay style. Not everybody was ready to come right out and admit this. One bizzer insisted to *Smash Hits* that Hi-NRG "is not gay music," since its plaints about unreliable men were sung by women: "If it was a man singing I'd see your point." The magazine noted: "As he speaks, a coy smile spreads slowly across his face."

Soon after "High Energy" made its impact, the production team of Stock Aitken Waterman (SAW) upped the ante. Mike Stock, the trio's idea man, wanted to make "technologically brilliant" records, modeled on Motown, and when he heard Hi-NRG, he decided: "I knew I could give them exactly what they wanted, with quality."

Their first salvo of '84 was a taunt: "You Think You're a Man," a British top twenty for Divine, the American drag star of John Waters's underground films. When the gothy-trashy Liverpool quartet Dead or Alive approached SAW, Pete Waterman recalled, "Pete Burns had actually said, 'Make me sound like Divine!'" The result, "You Spin Me Round (Like a Record)," reached number one in the UK in March 1985 and remains a dance floor go-to, not to mention a karaoke one. SAW would dominate the rest of the eighties: thirteen number ones, thirty-five million sold.

Reactions to this stuff in big macho America were decidedly mixed. That December, a radio tip sheet said that the London synth-pop trio Bronski Beat's "Smalltown Boy"—singer Jimmy Somerville's autobiographical tale of a young gay man's coming out to, and subsequent rejection by, his family and city—"weaves a touching tale." Two weeks later, the same publication trashed Bronski Beat's album, *The Age of Consent*, in decidedly homophobic terms: "This English trio of limp-wristed boys are among the leading gay wavers in their home country. . . . It's a shame that some wonderful music must be so lyrically radical."

IF ANYONE DEFINED THE TWELVE-INCH AS THE SITE OF AGGRESSIVE EXPER-
imentation that still went pop, it was Trevor Horn. After the producer's simultaneous number ones in the United States (Yes's "Owner of a Lonely Heart")
and the UK (Frankie Goes to Hollywood's "Relax") in January, he saw "Relax"
reenter the chart and peak at number two in July, with its follow-up, "Two
Tribes," at number one. By the end of the summer, Frankie Goes to Hollywood
was estimated to have sold between five and six million records—the vast majority on twelve-inches. The band hadn't even released an album yet.

On August 6, Horn delivered the keynote address at the New Music Seminar (NMS). That morning, New York mayor Ed Koch declared it the city's
official "New Music Week," an honor essentially bestowed at the recipients'
request: "Our PR company just went to the city and asked for it," says Tom
Silverman, who cofounded the NMS.

It wasn't an altogether unreasonable ask. The NMS had grown out of a
small, scratchy start in 1980 to become the premiere US music biz confab: the
1984 edition had a paid attendance of thirty-eight hundred. Silverman, who ran
the rap label Tommy Boy Records, had hit pay dirt in 1982 with "Planet Rock,"
by Afrika Bambaataa and the Soul Sonic Force, which ushered in the next three
years' worth of jittery electro-funk. Bambaataa was a marquee participant in
the '84 NMS.

Silverman's partners in the NMS were Mark Josephson, who'd cofounded
the college radio trade sheet *Rockpool*, and Joel Webber of the dance label
Uproar. In addition to publishing, Rockpool was also a record pool that "distributed records to DJs that specialized in danceable rock," says Silverman.

Rock discos aimed at the postpunk diaspora picked up in the United States
through the early eighties. When Rockpool began, Josephson said, "Most of
our DJs were actually anti-mix; they used no cue-phone and jammed records
together. . . . Rock DJs choose shorter mixes, so you hear about twelve songs or
three, four, five sets an hour in a rock club." Note the word *set*. A DJ's job was
to play at a club all night long—not a "headlining" set of an hour or two, but
for up to twelve hours a go. John "Jellybean" Benitez of New York's Fun House
played eleven. "I'm in and out of a peak all night. Now I sometimes let the record end, play a sound effect and go into another trip," he said.

By 1984, pop producers were increasingly adopting dance production tricks:
metronomic rhythms that made beat matching easier for DJs, bass and drums
to the fore, lots of echo intended to be heard whipping around the cavernous
spaces of clubs like King Street's Paradise Garage, where DJ Larry Levan reigned

supreme. François Kevorkian, a DJ and remixer who'd gotten his start in New York clubs in 1977—and who in 1983 did a twelve-inch remix for, of all people, those luddites the Smiths—told author Tim Lawrence that "all the DJs from those rock clubs started going to the Garage every week" because "they all had to hear what Larry was playing."

Frankie Crocker of WBLS, New York's leading black music station, would hang in the DJ booth with his good friend Levan and put the biggest jams on-air. When *Billboard* dance editor Brian Chin wrote in June that Strafe's "Set It Off"—a hypnotic, minimalist, low-budget dance track from Brooklynite Steve Standard, featuring a slurping hi-hat pattern programmed on an 808—had been "making some substantial neighborhood noise here in New York, in the same way unusual cuts by Peech Boys and Loose Joints have," he meant that Levan was playing them at the Garage. "Set It Off" went on to be one of the most heavily sampled tracks of the eighties.

For Josephson, the clubs becoming an incubator for pop success was sweet vindication. "Many veterans of the new wave scene are now expressing disappointment that radio, Rockpool and other elements of the infrastructure have gone 'mainstream,'" he wrote in a *Billboard* op-ed timed to the '84 seminar. "This is a grave misreading. . . . Rock's left wing has not moved to the center. It is the center and right wing elements that have moved to the left."

"By 1984," says Silverman, "people were seeing a lot of records that were breaking from the clubs." Shannon's "Let the Music Play," a twelve-inch from October '83 that reached the pop top ten in February 1984, was the announcement of freestyle, a Latin hip-hop hybrid that would emerge as a major late-eighties pop style. "Record companies were starting to say, 'How do we get through to this audience?' The New Music Seminar was looking at the music industry from the perception of DJs," says Silverman. "We put together panels about every part of the business, but we loaded the panels with people with DJ sensibilities. The wave that we were riding was the growth in DJ culture."

Just as long as nobody called it "disco." "The business had been growing, and 1979 was a real down year. And they were looking for a scapegoat, and they blamed it on disco," says Silverman. Just as the term *new wave* coded as *please, not punk*, the new term everyone used was much simpler, more elastic: *dance music*. Another, much shorter-lived term made plain the record business's desire to assert a new clubland hegemony: DOR, for "dance-oriented rock."

The New York club that first embraced this hybrid ethos was Hurrah, near Lincoln Center. Just as importantly, it was the first New York club to install a giant video screen, with Mudd Club and others following suit. By 1984, video clubs defined the new nightscape. "System installers are working around the clock to meet the demand for hardware as venues from hotels and restaurants to old disco dance clubs are adding the latest technology in hopes of reviving their business," *Billboard* reported. One Denver club nearly doubled its attendance after switching emphasis from live bands to video. Gay clubs, in particular, adapted to video quickly: San Francisco's Midnight Sun, in the Castro; LA's Revolver; Chicago's Berlin and Sidetracks.

The video club ur-model, though, was Danceteria—which, *Billboard* noted, "provides four floors of entertainment including a concert room, a video lounge, a dance floor, and a private lounge for special events. Integrating the modern art world of graffiti artists like Keith Haring to abstract painters and sculptors involves a segment of the population [that] needs an outlet to showcase their work."

Danceteria was the favorite spot of Arthur Baker, who'd coproduced "Planet Rock" and had a dizzyingly busy 1984. "It was open every night," says Baker. "I'd leave the studio and go down to Danceteria and just hang out. It was over four floors. That was an amazing club. When I worked with Jeff Beck, I brought him to Danceteria. I wasn't going to bring him to the Fun House. Danceteria has the rock element. It was more of a social place, though the music was amazing—Mark Kamins and Johnny Dynell and Freddy Bastone all DJed there. And it was a really good place for me to test my records. I'd bring my stuff to Mark and he would immediately put it on. At that time, I was remixing rock records to make them danceable. That was the perfect testing for me. They were made for Danceteria for sure."

Specifically, Baker was remixing Cyndi Lauper and Bruce Springsteen; the latter attended an overdubbing session for one of the remixes. "The A/C went out," Baker says. "It was a really hot summer night. Springsteen's like, 'Oh man, let me go get a case of beer.' He got a case of beer, hung with us." Baker's first assignment (of three) for Springsteen was to rework "Dancing in the Dark," the single that Bruce had tested out at Club Xanadu in Asbury Park that spring. He wanted to make sure the crowd would dance to it.

Because of the major labels' newfound interest in twelve-inches, they began crowding the indie labels, who'd nurtured the format, out of shelf space in stores—a hotly contested state of affairs at the New Music Seminar. "When we do something, the majors let us do it, get the kinks out, and then come up with the big money," said Adam Levy of Sunnyview Records, which struck gold in 1984 with Newcleus's electro-rap classic "Jam on It." At one NMS panel, a Capitol Records executive said that his label wished to "leave the lion's share of the twelve-inch market to the indies," which earned him the vocal approval of co-panelist Cory Robbins of Profile Records, Run-D.M.C.'s label.

HIT RECORDS MAY HAVE BROKEN IN THE CLUBS WITH GREATER FREQUENCY, but they still had to prove themselves on the radio. A pair of panels on the NMS's final day—"The Future of Pop Radio" in the morning, "Charting the Hits" in the afternoon—were the confab's first attempt to address mainstream radio. The results were mixed—as *Radio & Records* editor Ken Barnes, a panelist on "Charting the Hits," noted: "Some of the NMS people want to tear down the established music biz structure, and others want to build an alternative system that will allow them to operate profitably without using the mainstream. But another big chunk are chiefly concerned with how to break into the mainstream, now that so many others have done it."

One panelist for "The Future of Pop Radio" was Larry Berger of New York's WPLJ. "Admittedly, we don't break a lot of records at WPLJ because I want to play the hits, not force what we think are the hits down their throats," he told the crowd of about 250. Each new contemporary hits radio station per market meant that the programming tended to become tighter, trimmer, more careful—safer, just the reason that listeners had turned to CHR after tuning out AOR. Nonetheless, Berger said, "As long as hit radio continues to follow popular music, black or white, fast or slow," it would remain profitable.

Still, the fissure between the NMS's majority-indie crowd and the more established business troubled Barnes. "For years, I've heard people bitch about radio—how it's impossible to 'beat the system,' how programmers won't play new acts, how conservative and stodgy and behind the times radio stations are," he wrote. "With the glittering array of programmers showcased on NMS's radio panels, you'd think it would be the perfect chance for the disaffected 'outsider' types—artists, alternative radio people, independent label folks—to air their grievances and stimulate a healthy exchange of views. . . . But the 'new music contingent' wasn't there, the element of difference, [so] the dialogue between the sometimes-naive creative element and the sometimes-myopic professional crowd didn't come about, and that's a shame."

EVEN IF HE PREFERRED DANCETERIA, THE ICONIC IMAGE OF ARTHUR Baker hustling a new track out for a preview play takes place at a different club: Midtown's Fun House. That's where Baker and the members of New Order go in the video for "Confusion," to hand over the reel-to-reel master for Jellybean Benitez to test out on the floor.

Guitarist Bernard Sumner (then billing himself Albrecht), bassist Peter Hook, and drummer Stephen Morris had been three-quarters of Joy Division, the Manchester postpunk band whose vocalist, Ian Curtis, had hanged himself in his home on May 18, 1980. Morris's girlfriend Gillian Gilbert stepped in on keyboards and Sumner became the singer; they called themselves New Order. Their New York visit occurred that fall: they and Anthony Wilson of Factory Records, their label, spent a number of nights clubbing at Hurrah and Danceteria. Returning home to Manchester, they built their own version, the Haçienda, the following year.

With "Blue Monday" and the LP *Power, Corruption & Lies* (to which the song was appended in later editions), both in spring 1983, they dove into dance music headfirst. "Blue Monday" became a British "Planet Rock"—completely ubiquitous. It became the best-selling twelve-inch in history—and because "Blue Monday" was packaged so elaborately, like a floppy disk, its costs overran any profits; New Order was losing money on every record sold. By the time they found out, it had sold a quarter of a million copies.

"Confusion" was made specifically for the Fun House floor. If dance music had a first "superstar DJ," it was Jellybean Benitez. A South Bronx native born in 1958, Benitez had gotten his start at Hurrah and spun at Studio 54 before landing his storied mid-eighties residency at the west-side skating palace, the Fun House, which held twenty-five hundred. There, Benitez spun records in a DJ booth that resided in the mouth of a fourteen-foot sculpture of a clown's face. From April 1981 to June 1984, Benitez not only built his own following but also crafted his own unique style, cementing the Fun House's place as one of New York's legendary clubs.

"It was crazy," Benitez told *The Fader*. "You have to imagine that the place was packed with kids dancing until well after the sun came up, and they danced to everything—I mean everything. They had to; most of them were underage, so they couldn't go anywhere else."

In June 1984, Benitez left the Fun House to do studio work full-time. He'd become an in-demand remixer, not least because of his work with the woman he was dating. When Jellybean remixed Madonna's "Holiday" and watched it reach number sixteen, it was, *Billboard* pointed out, "the first Top 40 pop single to be produced by a working club DJ." He also remixed the follow-ups "Lucky Star" and "Borderline," both pop top tens, as well as the title track from Madonna's second album, *Like a Virgin*, which spent six weeks at number one starting that December.

Jellybean and Madonna proved a mercurial combination. "We get on fine, unless we have problems at home. You can't bring them into the studio," Madonna told *No. 1*. For his part, Benitez told *Rolling Stone*: "We both started to move at the same pace. My career has exploded within the industry, and hers has exploded on a consumer basis. We're both very career oriented, very goal oriented." By the NMS, though, things were becoming visibly rocky between them. "We have a very volatile relationship," Madonna said. "We hear each other's name much too much."

Despite her rising fame, Madonna was every bit the club habitué of anybody on the scene. That May, she sang a new song she'd just recorded for her second album, "Dress You Up," for Keith Haring's twenty-sixth birthday party at the Paradise Garage. She and Jellybean attended the opening of Private Eyes on July 17; on August 4, the duo attended the Jacksons' Victory Tour at Madison Square Garden, taking pictures backstage with the brothers. That spring, she enthused, "Saturday nights at the Roxy are great now. I go to the Fun House, too," noting that she did so "when I'm around weekends and I'm not too tired."

Cash Box called Madonna's success an example of "the co-opting of the dance scene . . . come full circle." Sire's Seymour Stein found his biggest catch ever because she was working with (and dating, prior to Jellybean) Danceteria's Mark Kamins, whom Stein admired: "He already had a sound." Though he was impressed with her forthrightness, Stein wrote, "there was no reason to believe I was looking at a female Elvis." Indeed, his boss at Warner Bros., Mo Ostin, initially refused to sign off on Madonna, figuring her music, Stein wrote, as "a downtown dance experiment . . . pointless twelve-inch bullshit." Stein quickly learned better: "Madonna was always the smartest person in the room, even when she wasn't physically there."

NEW YORK WASN'T THE ONLY CITY WHOSE CLUBS WERE DETERMINING THE future of pop. In June of 1984, the city of Chicago hosted a pair of gatherings that emphasized the bright digital future of music. Early that month at the Westin Hotel-O'Hare, some one thousand engineers from around the world attended the International Conference on Consumer Electronics to hear over a hundred presentations on the latest in computer, video, and communications gear.

Two weeks later, McCormick Place hosted the largest edition yet of the National Association of Music Merchants (NAMM) International Music and Sound Expo, an instrument dealers' exhibition featuring 437 booths—up 10 percent over the previous year—whose panels included "The Use of Computers in Music Education," "Computer Bits That Don't Bite," and "Selling Digital Keyboard Technology in the Eighties." Machines blanketed the year, but in Chicago's punk and dance undergrounds, drum machines and synthesizers were used not for big-bucks sheen but as DIY tools. (See also Chapter 12.)

Though New York is where the model of Danceteria became broadly influential, the very first rock disco opened in Chicago, in 1978, with DJ nights at the Lincoln Park gay bar La Mere Vipere. Club DJs and DIY punks commingled closely in Chicago, thanks in good part to the Lincoln Park record shop Wax Trax!, whose co-owner Jim Nash had issued one of Chicago's earliest punk titles in 1981 (Strike Under's *Immediate Action* EP) but struck oil a year later with "Cold Life," by local dance-oriented industrial act Ministry, which sold ten thousand copies and got the band briefly signed to Arista. In 1984, Nash told *Billboard* that "Cold Life" still sold "about a hundred copies a month."

That year, Wax Trax! licensed twelve-inches from England (A Popular History of Signs) and Israel (Minimal Compact), right on the heels of a successful signing from Belgium, another industrial-dance act named Front 242, with 1983's *Endless Riddance* EP. Nash further told *Billboard* that he intended Wax Trax! to remain "on a smaller level, so we can really give our artists the right attention. I'd be happy to sell twenty-five to fifty thousand copies of any of our product."

The de facto showplace for the emerging Wax Trax! sound was Medusa's, a teen disco at 3257 North Sheffield that Dave Shelton—nicknamed "Medusa" for his thick blond curls—opened in October 1983. On September 28, 1984, Front 242 made their US debut at Medusa's, a week after a Ministry appearance there. The club's third floor contained a "video room," with large screens onto which VJ Joe Michelli would project both rock videos and random graphics to accompany DJ selections and beanbags to sit on and watch it all if you didn't feel like dancing. With a pair of local UHF stations scoring big ratings with clips—*Music Video 60*, on WPWR (channel 60), and the all-video (at least until summer) WFBN (channel 66)—there was a corresponding leap in local sales for Cyndi Lauper and Billy Joel titles in the heavily black South and West Side neighborhoods. "A lot of accounts are selling pop product that doesn't get played on [top urban stations] WGCI and WBMX," the head buyer of local distributor Colorite told *Billboard*.

The Wax Trax! aesthetic didn't just appeal to the predominantly white suburban crowd at Medusa's. A black South Side teenager named Vince Lawrence had been impressed by "Primental," from the first Ministry twelve-inch. "I just loved that record because every single sound in it was clearly a synthesizer," says Lawrence. "I was like, 'I'm going to make records like that one day.' I was listening to new bands like New Order and Frankie Goes to Hollywood at that point, and the end of the new wave scene and the beginnings of the industrial scene, that was where I wanted to be."

Lawrence had made a couple of heavily new wavy records under the name Z-Factor for his dad's label, Mitchbal Records, issuing the twelve-inch "Fast Cars" in 1983. He was also spinning records around town, one of a number of young black DJs who were taking their cues from a New York transplant named Frankie Knuckles, who'd made his name at a spot called the Warehouse—a nonalcoholic "juice bar" for black and gay clientele. Lawrence went there the first time around the time of "Fast Cars": "It had a mystique about it," he told Jacob Arnold. "I heard Frankie Knuckles spin and heard the music at those parties, it was just so seamless and so physical due to the size of the sound system. . . . That drove us to want to make different records—more records, and get better."

Knuckles had come up in the world of disco's New York beginnings—a regular at the Loft, in charge of spiking the Gallery's punch bowl with LSD, and finally a resident at the Continental Baths. He moved to the Midwest in 1977 at the behest of Warehouse owner Robert Williams, wowing the after-midnight crowd with twelve-hour sessions of not just disco and R&B but also rock and new wave, particularly synth-heavy European titles, as well as his own specially made edits—or just back-and-forth turntable work—of tracks that extended-extended-extended the breakdown till it milked a dancer's resistance dry. (A Chicagoan from the era once recalled a Warehouse night when Frankie played First Choice's Salsoul classic "Doctor Love" for half an hour.) By '83 he was ensconced in a new place, the Power Plant, and using a drum machine he'd picked up from a Detroit kid named Derrick May, who'd started coming to Chicago to visit his mom but wound up making the four-hour drive nearly every weekend just to experience Frankie driving the floor.

Knuckles's DJ style had spread throughout town, and it even had a name. Driving through the South Side in 1981, Lawrence saw a sign at a bar: "We play house music." *What's that?* he wondered. His friend told him: "It's that shit you be playing down at the Warehouse." There was even a section of a local shop called Importes Etc. with "House Music" as a header. The term was being used on the radio, thanks to the "Hot Mix 5" DJs spinning Saturday nights on WBMX-FM, traveling all around town. Chicago native and writer Jane Lerner recalls that by 1985, at her Wisconsin summer camp, "Some kids kept talking about house music: 'J-j-j-jack the house!'—upper-middle-class white kids."

But the core of house music's young fandom came from the black neighborhoods. They'd congregate on Saturday afternoons at a South Side Catholic prep called Mendel High School, which regularly threw teen dances featuring local house DJs. "No one was upper class in the Chicago house scene," says Charles Little II, who regularly attended the Mendel parties. "It was all black and it was all gay. It was all street. You got guys in there dancing to house music, spinning around looking like ballet dancers. But when you look at the guy, he's got gang tattoos all up and down his arms. He's ripped, and he will beat your ass. They're ready to fight."

Mendel High hosted every local house DJ of note: Knuckles, Ron Hardy of the Muzic Box (Robert Williams's new club after Frankie went on his own), Farley Keith of the Hot Mix 5 and his roommate Steve "Silk" Hurley (who'd planned to change his name in 1984 to "Jackmaster" Silk, only for Keith to preempt him by announcing on-air that he was now Farley "Jackmaster" Funk), and the members of a conglomerate known as the Chosen Few, headed by future A&R man Wayne Williams (who would later sign, among others, his homeboy R. Kelly).

Another member of the Chosen Few was Wayne's stepbrother Jesse Saunders, who'd been making longer versions of his favorite dance tracks with a tape deck's Pause button. "I'd extend the drum break and the intro parts, the musical parts where it would just break down with the bass or maybe just one little line where she's singing and that was it," Saunders said. "I'd take these parts and I'd put them in between others, extend them and make a remix out of it. The twelve-inch versions of any of these songs, which they would call disco versions, were more or less taking the musical bed, extending it in the front so the intro was longer . . . [but] there were no real breakdowns."

By the mid-eighties, Saunders was beginning to salt his mixes with "more electronic-sounding things: European import records and things like Men Without Hats' 'Safety Dance,' new wave-ish types of records: B-52's' 'Mesopotamia,' a little reggae." He had a residency at the Playground, playing to "fifteen hundred to two thousand kids a night—and not only just from the South Side, now, we're getting from all over Chicago." One night, WBMX's Kenny "Jammin'" Jason was playing a guest set at the Playground and brought in a Casio keyboard to accompany himself. "I ran out and bought one of those and started fooling around with it, and I start playing myself in a set," Saunders said. "Right after that I had a drum machine, a TR-606 by Roland. And I would program drum patterns in there and I'd mix in and out of the drum patterns. . . . I was like, 'I want to make a record now.'"

Saunders was Vince Lawrence's best friend, and he'd joined Z-Factor for a track called "Fantasy," sung by a Warehouse regular named "Screamin'" Rachael Cain. Many of the track's elements were recycled for Saunders's solo debut, "On and On"—by acclaim, the first-ever Chicago house record, manufactured at the city's only pressing plant, Precision Record Labs on the Near Northwest Side, which had opened on January 1, 1984, in the wake of the December '83 closing of Musical Products. Precision worked fast: "If a guy brought in a tape I tried to have a record out within a week," president Larry Sherman said. "I was buying a record on a Monday, cutting it Monday night, Tuesday it was in the tank, Tuesday night I had a test pressing. If the thing sounded OK, Tuesday afternoon I was in the print shop making the labels. Monday it was a new release."

Despite Precision's promise that "All LPs are pressed on virgin vinyl," Sherman was notorious for recycling old records—among them, a ton of returned copies of the soundtrack to Robert Stigwood's *Sgt. Pepper's Lonely Hearts Club Band* movie, a notorious stink bomb. By '84 they'd need the extra material, because "On and On" didn't just sell in the thousands but also kick-started a ton of newly minted producers. "That was the single most important record to me of the twentieth century, because it let the non-musician know that he could make music," Marshall Jefferson, who began recording in 1984, said. "It was the revolution, man. Everybody and their brother, their aunt, their uncle, started making music after that."

Lawrence, Saunders, and their friend Duane Buford began a label called Jes' Say to put "On and On" out, but as they began bringing in more similarly styled tracks made with cheap and castoff equipment such as the Roland TB-303 bass synthesizer—intended primarily for timekeeping and discontinued in '84, it provided the b-line of "On and On"—they struck up a deal with Precision's master. "I approached Larry and said, 'Hey, we have records that are hot, [but] we can really only afford to press one at a time. If you press the records, we can split the money,'" says Lawrence. They began working together to create a new label: Trax Records, beginning in early '85 with Le' Noiz's "Wanna Dance?" The B side's title echoed the answer Chicago and the world would give over the next few years: "Certainly."

"THE MOST FAMOUS PANEL IN THE HISTORY OF THE NEW MUSIC SEMI-nar," as Silverman describes it, took place at 5:15 Tuesday afternoon in the hotel's main ballroom and drew a crowd of more than twenty-five hundred. The lineup was formidable, a mix of cult figures, serious up-and-comers, and legends. In alphabetical order: Afrika Bambaataa, James Brown, George Clinton, Joe Ely, Robert Görl (D.A.F.), Nona Hendryx, Andy "Coati Mundi" Hernandez (Kid Creole and the Coconuts), Debora Iyall (Romeo Void), Madonna, John Oates, Lou Reed, Fred Schneider (B-52's), and Peter Wolf.

The giant of giants liked to be called Mr. Brown. He'd been atop the R&B charts consistently from the late fifties until the mid-seventies, but his disco-assisted descent was swift and unforgiving. Like a lot of his peers, he soon found an appreciative new audience elsewhere. On July 12, 1982, appearing on *Late Night with David Letterman*, James Brown told the host, "I'm working the rock clubs . . . those kids, they never got to get into James Brown. And today, the new wave kids like James Brown, and it's a new day for America."

He wasn't alone. A number of older R&B acts were discovering the new wave club circuit as an alternative to the traditional black club circuit—in the parlance, the chitlin' circuit—and gaining an easy, young crossover audience at the same time. In early 1984, James Brown played First Avenue in Minneapolis. That night, as the crowd chanted "James Brown! James Brown!" he shook the assistant manager down for a thousand dollars cash before he'd get onstage. When he did, Prince, who was watching from the club's DJ booth, sneered: "He's too old."

Brown was sixty-one that year, but he was still giving everything he could onstage. He'd hit the new wave clubs just as punk's year zero had turned to a deep burrowing into the pop past, from Coventry's 2-Tone bands playing ska, or the Blasters in LA, mining postwar R&B.

But those worlds often clashed in close quarters. Steve McClellan, then First Avenue's general manager, recalls Brown's 1984 appearance as "one of the most disappointing shows of my entire life. He treated staff like shit, everybody like shit." JB's thousand-dollar demand was not uncommon among R&B performers dealing with new wave venues. "A lot of those old R&B guys did that," says McClellan. As Tom Silverman puts it, "I think he represented a class of people that was deeply suspicious because they had been discriminated against and/or ripped off all of their lives." Adds Chrissie Dunlap, who gave Brown his cash, "I could see all of that history and segregation and everything, and it came flooding back, leading me to say, 'OK, here's a thousand dollars,' because I just wanted him to get onstage and for the chanting to stop."

Brown's appearance at the New Music Seminar was his part for the record he'd made for Tommy Boy, a collaborative EP with the label's biggest act, Afrika Bambaataa, titled *Unity*. The soul titan was paid a rumored $30,000 for one day in the studio to record his part, as well as doing press for the release. *Unity* was finished in two days, video included.

No one referred to *Unity* as an EP back in 1984. Instead, Tommy Boy proffered it as a "mini-album." "If we'd just put it out as a twelve-inch, it would make it difficult to get it in racks, while as a mini-album, its chances of charting are increased," Silverman explained to *Billboard*.

Far from a fossil, James Brown considered himself "a contemporary artist." Certainly, his fingerprints were everywhere in the "new music" the Seminar championed. That September, *Billboard*'s Nelson George pointed out that "funk grooves have finally seeped into the mainstream, utilized by everybody from Duran Duran to Talking Heads to avant-garde jazzmen," and noted that Brown's "confident, uncompromising personality have made him an eighties media darling."

But Brown was increasingly out of step with the new generation he'd found the path for. Traveling in the South that summer, the British writer Cynthia Rose noted that "teens . . . regarded JB as a virtual has-been in black culture; one Mom said that her fifteen-year-old had 'even called him an Uncle Tom.'" And his bravado could become unmoored. In Canada a month before the NMS, he said, "I got too far ahead of the business and they stopped me. I never got cold, I was just too big for the business. . . . I was coming up with too many hits."

The Godfather had known his new DJ collaborator since the mid-seventies. "Bambaataa always came and talked to me at all the different shows," Brown told *Interview*. "He always said to me, 'We play your music. We believe in you.'"

The son of Bahamian and Jamaican parents, Bambaataa was raised in the southeast Bronx. A towering figure, he quickly became involved with the street gangs burgeoning in the Bronx. "I used to be in the Black Spades—the largest black gang in New York City," Bambaataa told *Melody Maker* in 1984. "There were divisions everywhere. My patch was the southeast Bronx. It wasn't just about fighting, though. We had chants and war cries which were taken from people like James Brown and Sly Stone."

Inspired by his mother, who had the biggest record collection in the neighborhood, Bambaataa began to DJ in 1970, eventually earning the sobriquet "Master of Records." In 1976, he threw his first block party, billed to Afrika Bambaataa and His Zulu Nation. He'd named his crew after a mid-sixties British war drama called *Zulu*, best known for a star-making performance by supporting actor Michael Caine. "I thought *Zulu* was a great movie," Bambaataa said, "because for once the black man was portrayed as brave and sensitive. The Zulus fought like warriors, but they also spared the British even though they could have wiped them out."

Bambaataa's DJ style was astoundingly eclectic. "Bambaataa played everything from Aerosmith to Sly Stone to the Beatles," Afrika Islam told Tim Lawrence. "I heard the Clash before I knew who they were, 'Trans Europe Express' before I even knew where Germany was. He would take thirteen cases of records with him, and he would play everything from soca to Fela Kuti and Miriam Makeba to the Rolling Stones to the Plasmatics. There was no limit."

This wasn't simply a statement of rhythmic thrills; it amounted to a restructured canon. "Flash and Bambaataa [were] taking records that fans would say are soul classics, taking records that most sane people say were trash and mixing them into something that was really new and exciting," David Toop, the author of 1984's *Rap Attack*, said.

(There was a seldom-discussed undercurrent to Bambaataa's kingpin status: "For years there were rumors both in local black communities in the Bronx and in the broader hip-hop community about Bambaataa being sexually involved with teenage boys," Dave Wedge wrote for *Noisey* in 2016, in a story featuring testimonials of three men who alleged that Bambaataa had molested them during the eighties—and allegations of many others. Bambaataa denied all charges.)

Bambaataa was the proselytizer of hip-hop as a culture with "four elements"—rapping, b-boying (dancing), graffiti, and DJing. And by bringing it downtown to the Roxy and other clubs, he was a crucial, conscious bridge to hip, white new wavers. "Hip-hop's something us downtown kids thought was going on uptown and we wanted to bring it downtown, but all these elements were all disparate elements," Michael Holman told Tim Lawrence. "Rappers didn't hang out with breakers and breakers didn't hang out with graffiti artists. Downtown kids created a subculture by mistake. We were toying with evolution."

Like another of his heroes, George Clinton, Bambaataa devised different aliases to sign records to different labels. "I had a separate deal for Jazzy Five as I did for Soul Sonic Force, and with Bambaataa solo, I made a separate deal," says Silverman. "He made another deal with EMI. He had a deal with Celluloid."

He would follow his tête-à-tête with Mr. Brown with that of another big figure. Bambaataa wrote the lyrics for "World Destruction" having been inspired by *The Man Who Saw Tomorrow*, a 1981 documentary, narrated by Orson Welles, about Nostradamus. He called producer Bill Laswell and said, "'I want to make this record with a heavy metal singer. Do you know Def Leppard?' I said, 'What about Johnny Rotten?'" The DJ quickly agreed. Bambaataa saw "World Destruction" as the yang to "Unity"'s yin: "With James Brown [it was], you know, peace, love, harmony, and havin' fun. And here's Johnny Rotten, he's supposed to be this crazy rock star who don't give a crap about nobody." Bambaataa had a good time with Johnny in the studio: "He was dancin' and gettin' down in the studio. . . . There's a track that nobody's heard when he's cursin' and everything," he said.

During the NMS panel, Bambaataa was composed and thoughtful, earning applause when he said, "If you're going to steal from somebody's culture, don't pay them a hundred dollars and send them off. But as long as [employing street dancers] helps people work and travel and see the world, then I'm all for it." Yet the uneasiness of his comradeship with Brown was evident—Bambaataa, typically a quiet, assumptive leader, mindfully played second fiddle to his mentor, to the degree that Silverman recalls, "Bambaataa—I forgot he was on the panel."

Mr. Brown stole the Artists' Panel with little effort. He promised that if he and Bambaataa ever toured together, "Tickets would be ninety-nine cents for kids." (In other words, he and Bambaataa were never going to tour together.) At one point, Brown took the time to boast about playing to 1.3 million people in

France, telling the throng, "That's more people than live in Atlanta, Georgia"—at a time when Atlanta's population was nearly twice that large.

During the audience Q&A, journalist Lee Ballinger asked about the Jacksons and the "responsibility of an artist to his fans"—was a good album or show the extent of it? No, said George Clinton, who called the ticket prices a rip-off. Brown hastily responded, "Let's not criticize the Jacksons. The price is too high, but you've got to understand that the Jacksons had no control over how the tour was organized and can't be blamed at all." "Bullshit," said another audience member; Brown was so offended he threatened to walk.

A friendlier question came from the audience: Would Mr. Brown oblige everyone with one of his patented screams? He would. That's when Brown's co-panelist and key acolyte, George Clinton, decided, as usual, to up the ante. "Do the splits, James," Clinton goaded. "Do the splits as well." Brown got onto the podium and did "a mean little shuffle and two full-length splits," Martin wrote, to a standing ovation. The Godfather then turned the request around. "James Brown said, 'George, get down and give me two,'" says Silverman. Clinton, in fact, responded with *three* splits. "Those were the things that made the panels—you just didn't know what was going to happen," says Silverman.

George Clinton had long been R&B's wild card. He'd been singing doo-wop from age fourteen and opened a barbershop in Plainfield, New Jersey—he'd eventually do Mr. Brown's hair, as Clinton reminded the Godfather at the NMS. After cycling through a Motown songwriting gig and some small label releases, the Parliaments eventually chucked the matching suits of the Motown age and went for the freaks. Rechristened Funkadelic, Clinton's band released a slew of LPs that emphasized instrumental freakiness and conceptual heft, as well as Clinton's increasingly baroque wordplay. "I like to get into all the extremes," Clinton said in 1976. "A lot of people fear certain emotions or the taboos we fuck around with. Why, sometimes, we try and scare the shit out of the audience."

By then he'd extended the idea into a dozen or so subgroups, offshoots, and sequels under the banner of P-Funk. Parliament LPs were heavier on horns and hooks than the spiky, guitar-driven Funkadelic albums, and they sold—on average 850,000 apiece. Several of Brown's disgruntled sidemen went to work for Clinton. Brown, of course, was all bravado about this, telling *Interview* shortly after the NMS, "The only thing [Clinton] did was pull a few of my musicians away. It was good for me. If they'd have stayed with me too long they'd have become stale. He just did me a favor."

But by the early eighties, Clinton was without a deal at all. During this period, he produced "about fifteen to seventeen albums" for various members of the P-Funk family. None was released at the time. One was with Sly Stone, with whom Clinton was arrested in a Denny's parking lot after police searched their car and found "vials of cocaine and the freebasing equipment on the front seat between the two men."

But in the fall of '82, Clinton signed to Capitol Records as a solo artist and released *Computer Games*, which blew up early in 1983 thanks to "Atomic Dog," whose spellbinding synth hook, courtesy of Junie Morrison, catapulted the track to the top of the R&B chart for a month that spring. But the song didn't even make the Hot 100 (stalling at number 101). And by the time of the NMS, Clinton was already having trouble with his Capitol deal—and still in thrall to the cocaine he'd be hooked on for decades.

ARTHUR BAKER WAS IN THE CROWD AT THE NMS ARTISTS' PANEL. HE had a connection with both Bambaataa, of course, and, in a more roundabout way, Peter Wolf, who'd left the hit-making blues-rockers J. Geils Band a year earlier and had just issued his solo debut, *Lights Out*, which Michael Jonzun had coproduced. Jonzun was Baker's old friend from Boston and a producer whose hot streak rivaled Baker's own.

Jonzun and his brother, Maurice Starr, produced "Showdown," a "battle record" between the Sugar Hill Gang and Grandmaster Flash and the Furious Five. (The latter won.) As the Jonzun Crew, Michael recorded "Pack Jam," a big club record in the "Planet Rock" mode, for Tommy Boy in 1982.

A *New York Times* feature about Jonzun and Starr had piqued Wolf's interest—Wolf prided himself on knowing every musician in Boston and didn't know *them*. He visited their studio, House of Hits, and he and Jonzun clicked. Wolf had written much of *Lights Out* for the J. Geils Band, but the band turned it away. After leaving the group, Wolf and Jonzun kept working on it, freely mixing rock with funk and taking heart from the radio.

Jonzun called Wolf "the easiest person I have ever produced"—especially compared to his biggest success thus far, the Roxbury teenagers of New Edition, whom his brother Maurice Starr had groomed for stardom. "They were really poor and trying to do something positive—that's what I dug," Jonzun told *Musician*. "But they couldn't sing, and I thought Maurice was really wasting his time. He worked on one song—"

"For a year," his brother Sonni, who'd also worked on the song, chimed in. "It took Ralph [Tresvant] all year to sing 'Candy Girl.'" Was this sour grapes? Y-y-you know it.

In 1982, New Edition—Bobby Brown, Ricky Bell, Michael Bivins, Ronnie DeVoe, and lead singer Ralph Tresvant—entered a talent show that Starr put on. He took the group—average age fourteen—into the studio to perform "Candy Girl," a bald rewrite of the Jackson 5's "ABC." Starr went to New York to shop the demo, staying with his old friend Baker, who'd moved to Brooklyn and started his own label, Streetwise. When Baker heard the much-rejected song, he made a deal on the spot.

"It was one of those situations in the eighties that happened a lot," says Baker. "A lot of labels would pick up records from the producers, and the producers would pay the acts, especially with dance music. He was pretty much ripping the group off, or not giving them much." How not much? "All I got was five hundred dollars and a VCR," Brown would later complain.

Nevertheless, after a year and a half on the road, instead of simply rolling over, New Edition acquired new management, which signed them to MCA Records without Maurice Starr's help. Then they sued to invalidate their contract, signed while underage, with Starr and Streetwise.

New Edition, their second LP and first for MCA, was, according to MCA VP Jheryl Busby, "selling about two hundred thousand [copies] a week, while we're moving fifty-five thousand singles a week. . . . The great thing about the single is its rapid crossover strength. The pop acceptance has been very encouraging."

MEMORIAL COLISEUM,
LOS ANGELES
August 12, 1984

THE FIRST LOS ANGELES OLYMPICS SINCE 1932 WAS ALSO THE FIRST Olympics—ever—to be broadcast fully in color. The opening ceremony for the Games of the XXIII Olympiad convened at the Los Angeles Memorial Coliseum on July 28. Inside were athletes from 140 countries—a record. But people had their minds on the fourteen missing, led in a boycott by the Soviet Union, including East Germany, Vietnam, Poland, Cuba, Hungary, Ethiopia, and Afghanistan. The USSR made its declaration on May 8, the same day Island Records released Bob Marley and the Wailers' *Legend*.

This was, in a sense, payback: in 1980, the United States and sixty-five other countries boycotted the Moscow summer games—the largest such move in history. The Soviets' statement on the matter cited the "anti-Olympian actions of the U.S. authorities and organizers of the Games. Chauvinistic sentiments and an anti-Soviet hysteria are being whipped up in the country."

They weren't wrong. Though Ronald Reagan was working toward nuclear de-escalation behind the scenes with Secretary of State George Shultz, he still breathed fire publicly in their direction. In March 1983, he referred to the Soviet Union as "an evil empire." By the middle of his second term, Reagan was in an arms-building race with the Soviets. "If a Third World War is not inevitable," one political reporter wrote, "it has become a real possibility."

That month, Reagan announced a new plan, the Strategic Defense Initiative (SDI), which used laser and particle beams launched into space to, the president said, "intercept and destroy [Soviet] strategic ballistic missiles before they reach our own soil or that of our allies." SDI earned a more lasting, and mocking, nickname: "Star Wars." One retired navy rear admiral denounced Reagan's announcement as "a propaganda ploy to sell the budget. It's as phony as a three-dollar bill."

But in January 1984, the president got on TV and conceded that diplomatic relations with Moscow could be improved, noting that European stockpiles of American missiles allowed the nation to negotiate from strength. The Kremlin wasn't buying it. In Stockholm, Soviet Foreign Minister Andrei Gromyko intended to leave his meeting with George Shultz as a standoff: he alerted TASS, the official Russian news agency, some three hours before his five-hour meeting was finished, that it had been one. Before the conference was out, Moscow hinted that the Soviet Union was likely to skip the Summer Olympics in Los Angeles.

It became more than a hint after Yuri Andropov died in the hospital on February 9, 1984, and was succeeded by Konstantin Chernenko as General Secretary of the Communist Party of the Soviet Union. According to Paul Ziffren, chairman of the board of directors of the Los Angeles Olympic Organizing Committee (LAOOC), "Chernenko was always Leonid Brezhnev's man. Brezhnev never forgave the United States for the '80 boycott."

THE LOS ANGELES OLYMPICS OF 1984 WERE THE MOST COST-CONSCIOUS in decades. They had to be—the Olympics' habit of losing money and eroding goodwill had been going on for a few years by then. The City of Montreal had racked up a billion-dollar debt after hosting the 1976 Games; Munich '72 had been the site of a terrorist attack. The City of Los Angeles had already written a charter promising not to, "directly or indirectly, appropriate or disburse" a cent to the 1984 Games.

The job of running the thing went to Peter V. Ueberroth, who'd built the second-largest travel agency in the United States from scratch. He was given a $510 million budget to work with: the "no-frill Games," as *Sports Illustrated* called them. Rather than constructing new stadiums and villages for the Olympics, per tradition, Ueberroth used existing facilities: the Coliseum for track, the Rose Bowl for soccer, the Forum for basketball. Athletes stayed at college dorms. One sportswriter called it "basically the Southern California Olympics.

They had the rowing up in the north, almost near Santa Barbara; they had the equestrian, basically, in San Diego. They really spread it out."

Ueberroth also negotiated the by-far-largest broadcasting deal for the Games ever, winning $225 million from ABC—nine times what it had paid for the Montreal Games eight years earlier. He also made sponsorship a premium rather than a free-for-all—the 1980 Winter Games, in Lake Placid, New York, had nearly four hundred sponsors. The 1984 LA Games would have around thirty, paying $4 million apiece, minimum. Fuji Photo Film ponied up $9 million.

There was a near snafu close to the start, when Olympics security director Ed Best informed producer David Wolper, "I don't think you can light the torch. . . . Because we have a bomb scare." The door holding the torch had been broken into by ABC technicians who needed to get to a piece of wiring, but a thorough inspection needed to be done to ensure the torch had not been compromised. "This was fifteen minutes before opening ceremonies, and I saw the bomb squad was scampering over the thing," Wolper recounted. Everything was fine by airtime.

The Olympics allowed Mayor Tom Bradley to give Police Commissioner Daryl Gates the go-ahead to clean up the streets on any pretext necessary. Thousands of people were jailed before and during the Games. Gates's hard-line tactics, dubbed "Operation Hammer," remained in place well after the Olympics left town, with police not just targeting known gang members but also harassing young black men generally. On the ABC broadcast, host Jim McKay extolled the presence of police helicopters at the Games; for many, they were constant reminders of extralegal surveillance.

Conversely, the number of police officers reassigned to Olympics duty from their regular beats meant a boost in gang activity. Both the Bloods and Crips, Los Angeles's two main gangs, spread in number and swelled in power. "After this summer, gang violence, instigated by turf battles over prime crack-dealing locations, grows noticeable even to those who only experience black and Hispanic L.A. via the Metro Section of the *Los Angeles Times*," Nelson George wrote.

With the Soviets out of the picture, American athletes cleaned up, taking 174 medals, 83 of them gold, compared to the runner-up, Romania, with 20 gold out of 53 medals total. A number of new stars emerged—track star Carl Lewis, with 4 gold medals; Mary Lou Retton, the first US gold gymnast ever; and, dominating an Olympic basketball team that also included future Hall of Famers Patrick Ewing, Michael Jordan, and Chris Mullin.

The Olympics were a nonstop show of patriotism, right from the start. The sight of people in the crowd literally wrapping themselves in American flags and chanting "U-S-A! U-S-A!" unnerved many of the foreigners present. *Sports Illustrated* columnist Frank Deford lamented: "God only knows what the 2.5 billion people around the globe who are watching the games will think of a vain America, so bountiful and strong, with every advantage, including the home court, reveling in the role of Goliath, gracelessly trumpeting its own good fortune while rudely dismissing its guests."

PETER AFTERMAN, A BAY AREA NIGHTCLUB BOOKER AND PROMOTER, WAS given the job of updating the staid Olympics soundtrack for 1984. His original plan had been to hire the Rolling Stones to perform in the Rose Bowl, only to run smack into the LAOOC. When he ran a list of the equipment necessary to amplify the Stones, someone from the board told him, "Gee, when I used to go to concerts in the fifties and saw Rick Nelson, he didn't need all this stuff."

"It was hard to explain to someone who isn't in the music business why a band would need a thirty-six or twenty-four channel mixer, or why different instruments need to be double or triple miked," Afterman told *BAM*.

The opening ceremonies made the Olympics' allegiances plain. Much of the opening extravaganza's soundtrack was provided by a gargantuan, eight-hundred-piece marching band. The marching band, as McKay put it, played "the music of America, from Dixieland to the Gershwins to the big bands"— and little beyond that, chronologically.

Still, about a half hour into the program, the marching band arrived in New Orleans. Cue "When the Saints Go Marching In." The special guest singer, Jennings notes, was "a woman whose career was in its twilight years when she wrote to the producer, David Wolper, and said, 'I want a chance to sing.'" McKay answered: "Meanwhile, the musical director had been saying he wanted to get somebody who sounded like Etta James. Suddenly, there she was."

There was nothing sudden about Etta James singing at the Olympics. A longtime Angeleno, James had first recorded at seventeen: her first record, "The Wallflower," was an R&B number one in 1955. Through the sixties, on Chess Records, she scored eleven more R&B top tens; conversely, the highest she got on the pop chart that decade was number twenty-three, with "Tell Mama" in 1967. (Her version of the Glenn Miller oldie "At Last," which reached number two R&B in 1960, and eventually became James's signature song, didn't even make the pop Top 40.)

In the early seventies, James's heroin addiction spiraled out of control. In mid-decade she landed in drug treatment for seventeen months—it was either that or prison.

Things had improved markedly by the beginning of 1984. She worked steadily at LA's Vine Street Lounge, "singing low and sultry for the wine-and-cheese set," but James—who could, and did, sing everything—"was ready to belt it out for the beer-and-pretzel crew."

That winter, James began singing the national anthem for the Los Angeles Rams at Memorial Stadium. When she met Mayor Bradley, she mentioned she wanted to sing at the Olympics. "A month or so later I got back a nice reply, saying he wasn't in charge of entertainment." David Wolper had, indeed, been trying to find "this one gal singing this song about a blind girl" ("I'd Rather Go Blind," 1961). When he caught wind of the letter, James was brought into rehearsals.

A lot of James's peers weren't so lucky. Many had signed penurious contracts to labels and managers who saw their careers in the short term. Richard W. Penniman, the performer better known as Little Richard, made a classic bad deal when he sold his songwriting catalog to Venice Music, the publishing arm of his label, Specialty Records, in 1959, for $11,000 cash, waiving his royalties. Richard entered the ministry full-time that year. Who was going to remember rock and roll in ten years?

On June 20, 1984, Little Richard filed suit against Specialty Records, its founder Art Rupe, and ATV Music Corp., which had purchased the Venice Music catalog in 1979. The figure in damages was quoted, variously, between $50 million (*Variety*) and $114 million (Associated Press).

Every Wednesday, Richard would picket the Los Angeles offices of ATV Publishing. That October, Rupe countersued Richard for $3 million on charges of slander after the singer told a radio host that Rupe had once said, "All that a black person needed is twelve thousand dollars a year, they didn't need any more." Richard's case was dismissed in federal court that December, but an appeal was settled privately in 1986.

The bad deals that had permeated black music were brought home with particular acuteness that summer with the death of blues singer Willie Mae "Big Mama" Thornton at age fifty-seven. Thornton had recorded the original version of "Hound Dog," though she didn't see very much money from it, even though, in the wake of Elvis Presley's smash hit cover of it, Thornton's version had been reissued and anthologized numerous times. Living in a boarding-house at the end of her life, Thornton's funeral nearly didn't happen for lack of funds.

"There are pirates all around, they've pirated all her music and she died without a penny. . . . It's an injustice," Etta James told *Cash Box*. She added, "You sit back and you look at television and you see the history of this and the history of that and Willie Mae's name never comes up. It's like they took a big eraser and scratched that part of history out."

IN THE AUGUST 25 ISSUE OF *BILLBOARD*, FOR THE FIRST TIME EVER, BLACK artists accounted for six of the top ten pop albums *and* singles. Prince's *Purple Rain* was in its fourth week at number one; Tina Turner's comeback album, *Private Dancer*, was fourth; the *Ghostbusters* soundtrack, anchored by Ray Parker Jr.'s smash title track, was sixth; the Jacksons' *Victory* was seventh, down from fourth, a bad sign after only six weeks; and the Pointer Sisters' *Break Out*, a late-'83 release now in its fortieth week on the *Billboard* 200.

The singles shook out similarly. The top four were all by black artists—in order: "Ghostbusters," Turner's "What's Love Got to Do with It," Richie's "Stuck on You," and "When Doves Cry"—with "State of Shock" seventh and MOR crooner Peabo Bryson's "If Ever You're in My Arms Again" tenth. Even two of the white acts on the list—Dan Hartman's "I Can Dream About You" and Cyndi Lauper's "She Bop"—had crossed over to R&B radio with their hits.

It wasn't simply pop radio that was treating black artists with newfound respect. Another chart in the August 25 *Billboard*, for adult contemporary, or A/C, also featured six high-placing records by black artists: Richie, Bryson, Turner, and Parker were all top ten, alongside a pair of duets: Julio Iglesias and Diana Ross's "All of You" and Teddy Pendergrass and Whitney Houston's "Hold Me."

This wasn't Lionel Richie's only crossover triumph that week. *Can't Slow Down* was still in the top ten in its forty-seventh week, and "Stuck on You" was number thirty country. *Country*. It would peak there at number twenty-four. And Richie was about to play his biggest gig ever: the Olympics.

CROSSING OVER TO POP VIA A/C HAD BEEN CENTRAL TO *THRILLER*'S success, thanks to "The Girl Is Mine." Especially as rap began moving in on R&B's young audience, black radio was retrenching in much the way AOR had done in punk's aftermath. In mid-1984, *Billboard* reported an "upswing in contemporary R&B ballads. Smooth, traditionally styled songs from Patti LaBelle, Bobby Womack, Luther Vandross and DeBarge provided a balance for stations, and also served as 'safe' records for Top 40 outlets with a healthy percentage of black listeners."

The Quiet Storm had been the title of a program on Washington, DC's groundbreaking WHUR-FM. Founded in 1971 on the Howard University campus, WHUR was originally a community station, heavy on African American news and politics, but moved into the straighter soul market by mid-decade. Sales manager Cathy Liggins (later Hughes) employed sophisticated psychographic research to create *The Quiet Storm*, hosted by the velvet-voiced Melvin Lindsey and named for a Smokey Robinson song that Hughes called "all subliminal suggestion about oral sex."

First aired in May 1976, *The Quiet Storm* went nightly in November 1977 and was number one in the market within a year. Soon other R&B stations were adopting the show's format wholesale, and by 1984 it was gaining momentum. Inner City Broadcasting, the wholly African American–owned media company that operated a number of radio stations throughout the United States, switched the format of its Los Angeles FM flagship, KUTE, to Quiet Storm shortly after Christmas of 1983; it had already converted Berkeley's KBLX to the format after purchasing it in 1979.

That July, *Radio & Records* published a recent fifteen-song playlist from WHUR's *The Quiet Storm*. Only two songs had reached the *Billboard* Top 40 (Joyce Kennedy and Jeffrey Osborne's "The Last Time I Made Love" and Diana Ross's two-year-old "Muscles," which Michael Jackson had written and produced). Furthermore, only six of the fifteen songs were from 1984—just as many selections predated 1980—and LP cuts were played as frequently as singles.

But in a sign of the era's cautiousness in the face of the crossover dollar, KUTE's announcement included the note: "Inner City officials do stress, however, that this isn't a Black format." Motown's president, Suzanne de Passe, told *Black Enterprise*, "I'm proud of the fact that we are a black-owned company, but that doesn't mean we are a black company. We are a corporation. . . . You don't get millions of dollars just from blacks."

Even LA's Solar Records, a black-pop standard-bearer since the late seventies, was looking to cross over. One of its key acts, Midnight Star, went on tour in 1983, and Solar president Ray Harris noted, "There were quite a few white folks as well as Chicanos. It was a nice ethnic balance."

Motown was holding tight to the middle of the road. In 1984, Motown was, per *Billboard*, the year's number three A/C label, achieving the placement with a mere nine records; fourth-place Warner Bros., by contrast, had twenty-one. Lionel Richie did the heavy lifting here, as well.

Marvin Gaye had helped make this high crossover moment as much as anyone. His seventies albums established him as R&B's premiere male stylist, a serious artist who sold to the white rock audience. Commercially, he'd stumbled badly at the end of the decade. By 1981, Motown had taken away his creative autonomy by seizing Marvin's tapes for his next LP, *In Our Lifetime?*, which was taking too long for the company's liking, and issuing the album minus the question mark, and his input.

Gaye had led a troubled life—mental health issues, long-standing cocaine addiction, suicidal tendencies. But after some time in Belgium, put up by a local promoter, where Gaye cleaned up, and after extricating himself from Motown, the singer signed with CBS Records in early 1982. "I deliberately set out to make the most commercial album that I could," he told *Jet*. Released that October, *Midnight Love* was platinum by December, and critics received it rapturously. The lead single, "Sexual Healing," topped the R&B chart for ten weeks, the longest run at the top since Ray Charles's "I Just Can't Stop Loving You" twenty years earlier. It was also number three pop—a dam-breaking moment for the de-whitification of the Hot 100.

The tour that followed, though, was a shambles. On the opening night of a sold-out eight-show run at Radio City Music Hall, Sheila E., Gaye's percussionist, recalled, the headliner "came to Radio City an hour and a half late, spaced out, and didn't even know where he was. He was yelling he couldn't stand the pressure, that he hated performing, just before the curtain went up."

When he returned to Los Angeles, he moved into a bedroom of the house at 2101 South Gramercy Place, a ten-minute drive to Memorial Coliseum, that he'd purchased for his parents during the mid-seventies. The atmosphere there grew toxic. Marvin's father, the Reverend Marvin Gay Sr., was constantly ripped on vodka and had long despised his son, a feeling the singer returned in kind.

Holed up in his room, watching porn, snorting an unending line of coke, having women over for the purpose of sexually brutalizing them, Gaye was chasing his demon's tail. "My son, my poor son, turned into a monster," his mother said.

On the warm morning of April 1, Marvin's father began yelling at his sainted mother, and Marvin physically intervened. "He kicked me everywhere he could kick me," Rev. Gay said. "He knocked me onto the bed and when I fell, my hand happened to feel the little gun under the pillow. . . . I thought it was loaded with blanks or BBs. I didn't know any bullets was in the gun." The gun was a .38. Rev. Gay shot his mentally ill son twice in the chest, sat down on a porch chair, tossed his gun to the lawn, and waited for the police to take him in. The Reverend was held on $100,000 bail. His wife paid it—"I still felt sorry for him, and I no longer saw any reason for him to suffer," she said—shortly after filing for divorce.

It was only proper that Marvin's voice was the first thing the gathered mourners heard—a tape of his performance of "The Star-Spangled Banner" at the 1983 NBA All-Star Game, that February 13, less than fourteen months before his death. When the backing track began—the beat from a Roland 808, with Gaye on keyboards and tour bandleader Gordon Banks on guitar—the Lakers' PA announcer, Lawrence Tanter, nearly panicked: "Ah, shit," he told *The Defeated*. "They've got the wrong tape. This is 'Sexual Healing.'"

The open-casket funeral on April 5 at Forest Lawn Memorial Park in Glendale lasted seventy-five minutes and was attended by five hundred mourners. Another ten thousand fans passed through to view the body, with another ten to twenty thousand turned away. Little Richard sang a hymn, followed by Gaye's touring band performing an overture of his hits. Comedian and activist Dick Gregory—whom Gaye had pulled a no-show on a year earlier, when Gregory had proposed a retreat in Cape Cod—gave a eulogy. "If Marvin Sr. were here I would tell him I love him. We hear about tragedy but I've prayed enough with you all to know you can handle this," Gregory said.

Smokey Robinson and Stevie Wonder each spoke after Gregory. Both men had taken Gaye's lead in expanding their musical palettes beyond the diamond-hard three-minute Motown hit formula. "Marvin was the person who encouraged me that the music I had within me, I must feel free to let come out," Wonder said.

Robinson's *A Quiet Storm* was the 1975 LP that named the WHUR show and subsequent format. But following the success of 1981's number one

R&B ballad, "Being with You"—also top five pop and A/C—Robinson had also gotten hooked on cocaine. He wouldn't be free of the habit for another two years after the funeral.

UNBEKNOWNST TO GAYE, HE WASN'T THE FIRST CHOICE TO SING THE ALL-Star Game anthem that year. Lionel Richie was. Their images couldn't have been further apart. In 1984, Richie said, "I think that there is, uh, a group of people out there who, in this day and age, just want to be left alone. They think the world is going a little bit too fast." Pause. "Those are the people I wanna sell to."

A native of Alabama who'd grown up on the Tuskegee Institute campus, Richie told *Ebony* he'd been recruited into an R&B band that made him famous simply because he owned a saxophone. "What they didn't realize," he said conspiratorially, "was that I had brought the instrument to school in order to learn it; and it took them two years to find out that I had no training on the sax." Public pronouncements like this—broad, slick, hokey—were right in line with the songs that made Richie's fortune.

The young Lionel could play piano by ear. He'd also been an altar boy at his Episcopal church, and even had considered the priesthood. Richie was part of the upper middle class, and excellence was expected of him. His grandparents lived in a house on the Tuskegee Institute campus that the institute's founder, Booker T. Washington, had sold them for a dollar as a wedding gift.

Richie's relative isolation on the campus gave him an air of naivete. "Lionel does live in another world," his wife Brenda said. (They'd met at Tuskegee as students.) "You have to be naive to a certain extent, you have to be unaware of some things, you have to live in the sort of world he lives in to create the way he does."

Lionel's storybook marriage to Brenda, almost too good to be true, was central to his appeal. Brenda accompanied Lionel on Commodores tours; when he worked outside the group for the first time, she took on the title of Lionel's production assistant. At a public appearance in 1984, Brenda's closeness to her husband led an onlooker to observe, "That's a clever sister." When someone asked if the onlooker would have moved on Lionel were Brenda not there, she responded, "Most definitely."

Nobody in Richie's position could be a complete innocent. In his memoir, producer David Foster, one of the people who worked on *Can't Slow Down*, recalled telephoning Richie's house one morning and having to play along with a shaken Brenda. Lionel had told her Foster "had had a heart attack, and that Lionel had spent the night next to my bed at Cedars-Sinai, practically holding my hand. I don't know where Lionel had spent the night, and I don't know if he ever cheated on his wife, but he was a smart guy, and you'd think he could have come up with a more viable alibi."

FROM THE BEGINNING OF THEIR CAREER, THE COMMODORES HAD BEEN managed by Benny Ashburn, who kept everyone's heads level. "The thing was to pick the best songs from each person that would make that album stand up and be real strong when you put the whole package together," co-lead singer Walter "Clyde" Orange said. "It was always a fight, but the fight came for the seventh and eighth song because that meant somebody was going to have two songs on the album. And [that] kept you razor sharp . . . it was a competition."

The Commodores had signed with Motown and released their 1974 LP, *Machine Gun*, to gold sales. They quickly became the slickest R&B hit-makers of the seventies, combining hard funk like "Machine Gun" with Richie's cream-centered ballads for a commercial ace in the hole. The first to catch fire, from *Movin' On* (1975), was "Sweet Love," which was, as Nelson George put it, "as sentimental and courtly as roses on the first date." "Easy," "Sail On," and "Three Times a Lady" had enormous appeal to older pop fans. Lionel made the middle of the road sound very comfortable indeed.

"Three Times a Lady," in particular, was so slow and careworn it practically sounded elderly. "With 'Three Times a Lady,' we knew we were in deep water because there were no waltzes being played in the seventies," Commodores producer James Anthony Carmichael said. "So when you come along with a song in three-quarter time, you had better have spent a long time thinking about it." It hit number one in June of 1978, selling two million copies in America. When both "Sail On" and "Easy" broke out in similar fashion in 1979, the colt broke the stable.

Kenny Rogers, too, knew the middle of the road. The silver-haired country-pop crooner was a sales colossus during this era, receiving at least one platinum album per year between 1978 and 1984, with eleven total by December of '84, the most of any artist at the time. "The Commodores have done what I tried to do," Rogers said. "They haven't limited themselves to any one area." In Dave

Marsh's words, Richie wrote "not just country songs but countrypolitan ones." So Kenny asked Lionel to write one for him.

"Lady" spent six weeks at number one near the end of 1980. "I feel like I've opened a door for other black artists who're interested in country music even though I got negative reactions from black stations," he said a year later. Richie then produced Rogers's *Share Your Love* LP in 1981. "I feel very good about this album," Lionel said. "I'm sure we'll get at least four singles."

Rogers's manager, Ken Kragen, was now handling Richie's solo career. Polygram asked for a theme to their teen romance film, *Endless Love*, starring Brooke Shields; Richie gave them a Commodores reject, fibbing later that he'd made it up on the spot for the execs. Berry Gordy took one listen and demanded Motown release it, not Polygram. He got his way. Good thing: "Endless Love" spent nine weeks at number one, was nominated for an Oscar, and made Richie the hottest writer-producer on the market.

At first, Richie denied he was leaving the Commodores: "I considered myself a quarterback. If I won it was because the team did it." But the strain was too much for anyone to bear. "I thought I could keep it at *we* instead of *I*, but that was Fantasyland," Richie admitted.

The final blow had come in August 1982, when Benny Ashburn died of a heart attack. William King called his loss "more of a blow to the Commodores than if Richie had quit twenty times." He added: "The greatest thing that happened is that we broke up without a fight."

The severely cautious first solo LP, *Lionel Richie*, was, Richie said, intended "to make sure that the people who followed me through 'Sweet Love' and 'Endless Love' knew that it was the same guy." It sold four million copies; one reviewer called it "the musical equivalent of shaking hands and kissing babies."

In the post-*Thriller* manner, *Can't Slow Down* was intended to cross over as Lionel had never crossed before. Richie was now upping the tempo and aiming for the kids. "All Night Long (All Night)" featured a lithe groove heavily marked by Caribbean rhythms but still squarely in an American pocket—propulsive enough for the clubs, mellow enough for A/C. The follow-up, "Running with the Night," was Lionel's rock move, with a squalling guitar solo by Toto's Steve Lukather, who'd also played on "Beat It," and did well on AOR.

The video for "All Night Long," naturally, featured break dancers. ("We're seeing breakdance appeal in the suburbs," the PD of an urban station in Boston reported.) An increasing number of veteran R&B acts were having break dancing pushed into their videos, as in Gladys Knight's "Save the Overtime for Me," directed by Kenny Ortega. "Nice choreography, great to see breakdancers and all—but it has *nothing* to do with the song," video maker Alvin Hartley complained, adding, "I would've had Gladys sitting at home, calling her girlfriends, playing solitaire like it says in the song—doing things real people do to pass the time waiting for their loved one. Things people can *relate* to."

At least the "All Night Long" clip didn't worry itself with a story line. That was reserved for "Hello," another number one, and the meatiest ballad Lionel had written since "Easy." The instantly infamous video for "Hello" featured a blind sculptor making a likeness of her teacher, played by Richie. A UK critic called the "Hello" clip "vile," an example of "those who prettify and idealize things they know nothing about in order to push products, while at the same time feeling noble about their 'service' to the underprivileged."

The public, of course, begged to differ. "It started as a Lionel Richie album," trumpeted a 1984 *Billboard* ad, "and became A GREATEST HITS ALBUM."

Lionel hit the road almost immediately upon the release of *Can't Slow Down*. Long stiff onstage, Richie was now, as one reviewer put it, "energetic, loose, mobile." He made sure this fall–winter run of shows were up-tempo—he even cut his signature, "Three Times a Lady," from the set, condensed "Still" to a single minute, and performed "Sail On" faster than the record. Throughout the tour, Richie's camp offered tickets to radio programmers in all formats.

His appearance at Nashville's Municipal Auditorium on May 22, to a crowd of ten thousand, was a near coronation. Nashville, of course, was very much Lionel's turf—Kenny Rogers had seen to that—but even prior to "Lady," Motown had successfully pitched "Sail On" to country radio in 1979. Country stations were even responsive to "Hello," from *Can't Slow Down*—despite the record's largely covert sense of twang (mainly in its silky acoustic guitar solo).

"We heard that stations were saying that if Motown would get behind Lionel, he could get country airplay," Motown PR man Don Wright told *Billboard*. "We realize we were too late with 'Hello.' This time, we aren't going to leave our promotion team stranded."

With the next single, Motown was ready, and so was country radio. At Music City's stalwart AM station, WSM, the call-in responses to "Stuck on You"—from young women, especially—were overwhelmingly positive. "It's a great country record," a Montgomery, Alabama, programmer told *Billboard*. "If Conway or T.G. or Ronnie McDowell had it out, I think every country station would be on it. Country radio is going to have to be more open-minded if we're going to compete in our markets. This is the kind of record you can do it with."

Early on at Municipal Auditorium, Larry and Steve Gatlin of the Gatlin Brothers joined Richie onstage. The Gatlins were Nashville's mainstream personified—they'd been nominated for three country group performance Grammys in the previous five years, and the Academy of Country Music Awards had named Larry Male Vocalist of the Year for 1979. "The Gatlins walked out carrying a 'cowboy outfit' only a dimestore cowboy would be caught in," the *Banner* reported. "The glittering black and silver outfit was donated by Richie to a local wax museum to go on permanent display."

The two Nashville dailies' concert reviews demonstrated a distinctly old-world approach to the show's racial dynamics. *The Tennessean* noted approvingly that Richie "drew applause when he spoke simply but eloquently about brotherhood and learning to live together," and added that although "it was mainly young whites" who'd gone to see Richie, "this was hardly your 'ghetto get-down' event." Equally dubiously, the *Banner* opined, "If Democratic presidential hopeful Jesse Jackson had the 'rainbow coalition' that packed Municipal for Richie, he'd be in the White House in November."

Richie was notably generous with his stage time. His opener in Nashville, Tina Turner, got fifty minutes, rather than the half hour a typical arena warm-up act received, and he brought her back out to sing "Hot Legs" during his set, before the two of them settled into a duet of "Three Times a Lady," brought back for the 1984 shows.

On an earlier tour leg, the Pointer Sisters had opened. They'd also crossed over from R&B to country—in 1975, their "Fairytale" had won a country vocal group Grammy Award. In 1978, the Pointers had teamed up with producer Richard Perry, who'd helmed hits for Carly Simon and Ringo Starr, and went to number two pop (fourteen R&B) with a Bruce Springsteen cover, "Fire." On the fall 1983 *Break Out*, Perry and the group perfected a slick mix of bouncy pop ("Jump [For My Love]") and new wavy funk ("Automatic"). In October 1984, *Break Out* would earn the Pointer Sisters their first platinum album.

"And now, to give voice to what we all feel about the athletes—Mr. Lionel Richie!"

The Summer Olympics' closing ceremony began with an "alien landing," with a replica of the mothership from *Close Encounters of the Third Kind*'s climax, minus the awe.

After a couple of minutes' worth of laser foofaraw, an illuminated center stage revealed Lionel Richie—as *Billboard* noted, the "only entertainer to appear in the games' spectacular closing ceremonies." Accompanying him were two hundred break dancers, choreographed by Damita Jo Freeman, a former *Soul Train* dancer and Richie's tour choreographer.

Many people would be taping these Olympics, and Richie's closing night performance in particular. The first six months of 1984 saw VCR sales jump 84 percent from the previous year; projection TVs were also up, nearly 40 percent over 1983. Along with recorded music—according to National Association of Recording Merchandisers (NARM), 1984's first six months had outearned those of 1983 by 17 percent—entertainment sales weren't merely leaping but somersaulting. By contrast, ABC, which had signed on to broadcast the Olympics in expectation of making $100 million in ad revenue, found its profits "largely evaporated because of increased production costs," as *Forbes* reported, in part because of disappointing ratings for the Winter Games.

On ABC, an announcer promised that Richie would "be singing 'All Night Long' with special lyrics for these Olympics." Her co-anchor responded, "That's the name of the tune, and it may be the circumstance as well, the way things are going." The "special lyrics" were along the benign lines of: "Captured all our hearts, they captured the world / Saw the face of brotherhood on every boy and girl."

"I know I speak on behalf of all the people in America—and the world!" Richie was now stepping in place, sweeping his arm. He'd never been an elegant mover. "When I say how proud we are for these fine two weeks these wonderful people have given us tonight."

Everything was delivered in the manner, not of a preacher, but of a game show host. In white trousers and a dark blue blazer, Richie was amiability personified. After the song's first chorus, Lionel led the break dancers onto the stage; they too are wearing white, with Freeman, the choreographer, in a red tutu, dancing by herself while the others mostly pop and lock, the robo-funky standing moves.

Freeman recruited from a number of local breaking crews—they were in high supply—including the Majestic Visual Break Dancers, a crew affiliated with the Watts-Willowbrook Boys Club (later Boys and Girls Club) in LA, whose members included the young actor Cuba Gooding Jr. "We were the group of kids who would put a piece of cardboard down and a boom box radio, and we would practice our moves out in front of storefronts and get change from passersby. And that's how we'd eat," Gooding later said. The group was allowed to practice as long as they brought, and did, their homework there.

Despite Ueberroth's much-bruited thrift in putting the games on, the closing number spared no expense. The stage cost half a million dollars and required two hundred people to put it together. Richie would later describe the performance this way: "I left the house, went and ran around this field for twenty minutes, got back in the car and left the stadium."

In sports and politics alike, the United States increasingly defaulted to Hollywood. Not always, though. The unraveling of Lionel and Brenda Richie's storybook marriage began at the Olympics, when Lionel met a comely eighteen-year-old dancer named Diane Alexander, who would eventually become Richie's second wife—after Brenda, in 1988, caught the two of them together in Alexander's apartment and flew into a rage that ended with Brenda being arrested for assault and battery. The middle of the road gets rough sometimes.

15

RADIO CITY MUSIC HALL,

NEW YORK CITY

September 14, 1984

ACCORDING TO DIRECTOR JULIEN TEMPLE, THE MUSIC VIDEO BUSINESS IN 1984 was "an industry in search of an identity." That February, *Billboard* reported that MTV was in talks with several record labels to negotiate payments for limited exclusivity deals on video clips—enough time to cripple any other network or video program attempting to get traction on a new hit.

In June, MTV announced it had signed such deals with CBS, RCA, MCA, and Geffen. "There are no provisions for giving any of the exclusivity income to the artists at this time," one report went. Within two months, the Justice Department's antitrust division opened an investigation; and on September 19, Discovery Music Network, a fledgling all-video cable channel due to premiere in January of 1985, filed an antitrust suit against MTV that also listed five labels—RCA, MCA, CBS, Geffen, and Elektra/Asylum—not as defendants but as "co-conspirators" in "contributing to the 'monopolization' of music video programming by MTV," *Billboard* reported.

Discovery Music Network wasn't MTV's only newly minted competition. In the summer of 1984, Ted Turner, the cable giant behind CNN (Cable News Network)—which launched in 1980, reaching thirteen million households and growing 50 percent annually by 1982—announced Music Video Network (MVN), to debut December 5. Then he moved the date up, to October 26.

MTV had a right to be nervous. The model for Turner's channel was *Night Tracks*, which TBS broadcast overnight every weekend. In many ways better than MTV, with a far wider and broader music mix—Prince, Barry Manilow, Ronnie Milsap, Twisted Sister, Devo, and New Edition might all share a single segment—plus no VJs mugging on camera, *Night Tracks* was perfect for the music fan who just wanted to immerse.

Talk was afoot at the New Music Seminar about the new station. "If he says he's going to do it, he'll do it, period," one of Turner's new hires avowed during a panel. "He's got the money—he's got hundreds of millions of dollars." He also owned a transponder on Satcom IIIR, the satellite at which the largest number of cable systems' dishes aimed; turning on a sister, all-music station to TBS, Turner's basic-cable mainstay, would be a snap.

No one knew that MTV could use some competition better than MTV did—so it was launching its own sister station, Video Hits One (VH-1), on January 1, 1985.

In October 1984, the Festival International du Video Clip de Saint-Tropez, France, was attended by some 2,000 people, 360 of them press. Videos blanketed the bars, clubs, and the giant Diamond Vision projection screen at the harbor's entrance, viewable all over the city. The aimless event would underline the fact that, aside from the odd *Making of "Thriller"*-style fluke, nobody was going to make a killing in music home video sales.

Right on cue, two members of Duran Duran arrived aboard a "huge white motor-yacht in the most prominent position in the harbor," *Melody Maker* editor Adam Sweeting noted. "[Simon] Le Bon had told me that the Durans had just dropped in to St. Tropez for a quick look, which was of course completely untrue since they had a packed schedule of interviews arranged."

Sweeting described the awards ceremony as "chaos"—the winners were to be announced at 4:00 p.m., only for them to be rescheduled for 9:30: "In the end, it sort of leaked out by word of mouth that the Best Video award had gone to the Cars for 'You Might Think.'"

NOT EVERYBODY HAD CABLE IN 1984, THOUGH—INDEED, MOST OF AMERica still didn't. According to a report in a mid-December *Billboard*, only "about 41 percent of American homes now subscribe." But music video shows sprung up like weeds in MTV's wake. By 1983 that included long-standing syndicated titles like *Soul Train*, *American Bandstand*, *Solid Gold*, and *American Top 10*, as well as the fledgling likes of *Radio 1990* (a *Night Flight* knockoff hosted by rock journalist Lisa Robinson) and *We're Dancin'* (pseudo-*Bandstand* from *AT10* producers). Of a dozen likely new shows, not one outlasted the calendar year.

NBC had spent years in the ratings toilet before Brandon Tartikoff took over as head of programming in 1981 at age thirty-two, and he capitalized on MTV's popularity by green-lighting Dick Ebersol's *Friday Night Videos* in the summer of 1983, to occupy the 11:30 post-news slot in place of a Johnny Carson rerun. It did so well that rumors ran that NBC was looking to rerun it on Saturday mornings.

Not so NBC's new Saturday-evening hit. The oft-reported sound bite that Tartikoff "scribbled [a] note to a producer that said simply, 'MTV Cops,'" as the *New York Times* put it, was an exaggeration—show creator Anthony Yerkovich, who'd also created NBC's hit police show *Hill Street Blues*, was already at work on a script titled *Gold Coast*. But "MTV Cops" was still right when *Miami Vice* premiered on September 16.

"*Miami Vice* is about colors and shapes in violent motion, a kind of rock video for the bloodshot eye," John Leonard wrote in *New York*. Alongside the pastel-heavy visual palette—producer Michael Mann had specified that the show avoid earth tones—this was the first US prime-time fiction program with a wall-to-wall *soundtrack*. Not counting Jan Hammer's title theme, a number one in 1985, the two-hour pilot featured six fully licensed rock and R&B hits—the Rolling Stones' "Miss You," from 1978, was the oldest. The most notable was Phil Collins's "In the Air Tonight," a 1981 single that reached number three in his native UK and received renewed airplay in fall '84.

In February 1985, *Miami Vice* would build an episode around Glenn Frey's "Smuggler's Blues," including a guest-starring turn by Frey himself, and featured Collins acting in another episode that December. Frey's song played right into the show's cocaine-cowboy story lines. "There is a fascinating amount of service industries that revolve around the drug trade—money laundering, bail bondsmen, attorneys who service drug smugglers," Yerkovich said, calling it "free enterprise gone berserk."

IF NBC COULD BITE MTV'S STYLE, THE VIDEO NETWORK COULD DO THE same—by programming sports, for example, or, at least, sports entertainment.

That July 23, MTV aired *The Brawl to End It All*, a production of the World Wrestling Federation (WWF), featuring a match from Madison Square Garden between female wrestlers Wendy Richter and the Fabulous Moolah (the latter won)—though the fighters themselves were less the point than their managers—Captain Lou Albano and Cyndi Lauper. MTV followed the match with the premiere of Lauper's newest video, "She Bop."

It was yet another crossover entrée. After Albano had appeared in the "Girls Just Want to Have Fun" video, Lauper and Wolff decided to utilize him further. Eventually, the WWF's leader, Vince McMahon, had Lauper promote wrestling on Johnny Carson. The Portrait Records staff kept up the ruse (or, in wrestling talk, kayfabe). "I said that even though we were going to fight, I still wanted to promote women's lib somehow," Lauper wrote.

For years, pro wrestling had been heavily regional. Then, McMahon brought his son into the business in 1971 to replace a promoter in Bangor, Maine. Vince Jr. knew television was key, so he began putting his matches on then-nascent pay-per-view cable, greatly increasing their audience. At the end of 1983, McMahon signed the six-foot-eight wrestler Hulk Hogan, a balding blond Florida native with a drooping mustache and preening ringside manner. Vince Jr. flew to Minneapolis and laid out his vision: "I'm gonna take over this business. I have plans to change the wrestling business and make you the biggest star in the world." On January 23, 1984, Hogan beat the Iron Sheik—a Persian American villain whose persona played on Carter-era tensions between the United States and Iran's Ayatollah Khomeini—at Madison Square Garden. The WWF had claimed the entire United States as its territory. Seven months later, at *The Brawl to End It All*, Hogan beat Seattle wrestler Greg Valentine to retain the WWF World Championship title.

That May, USA Network began airing the WWF every week as *Tuesday Night Titans*, where it became so popular that it was soon airing on Fridays as simply *TNT*. "A wrestler might do anything on *TNT*: sing, dance, or perhaps do a rapturous monologue on his racial background," the Minneapolis–St. Paul *City Pages* noted. "Something akin to MTV video pops up on *TNT* regularly, manic soap operas featuring wrestlers. The fans might be treated to Jesse 'The Body' [Ventura] singing 'My Body Rules.'" Yes, the future Minnesota governor.

DURING THE SUMMER OF **1983**, MTV FINALLY BEGAN TO ATTRACT MAJOR advertising. Its audience was at fifteen million people, and its Nielsen ratings determined, as Michael Shore wrote, that it "had the highest twenty-four-hour rating of any basic cable service." Within a year, MTV was making a million dollars a week in ad revenue.

An ever-increasing amount of TV advertising looked like MTV; in the spring of 1984, an ad agency, Doyle Dane Bernbach, brought out a video for the Alan Parsons Project, "Don't Answer Me," "featuring cel animation super-imposed over 3-D sets," one biz reporter noted. When Warner Amex offered 5.125 million shares of MTV stock in August, it was estimated that 60 percent of the stock was snapped up by large group investors.

If Ted Turner still thought he was going to make money off music videos, he was mistaken. Turner played the Moral Majority card—huffing to *Rolling Stone*, "MTV's definitely a bad influence. My wife used the word 'satanic' to describe it"—and trumpeting his Cable Music Channel as a refuge from filth. But CMC misreported its initial subscriber base by more than two million—and because of restrictions on Turner Broadcasting's credit, it was "prohibited from losing more than $1.5 million in 1984, $7.5 million in '85, and $5 million in '86 on CMC," *Billboard* reported. The CMC went off the air on November 30, a month after it launched. The other new MTV wannabe, Discovery Music Network, had a twelve-million-viewer base ready for its January launch. But it didn't last much longer than Turner's venture.

MTV's original five VJs—Nina Blackwood, Mark Goodman, Alan Hunter, J. J. Jackson, and Martha Quinn—had become as ubiquitous as the rock stars they presented. That summer, when they were informed that the network was planning an awards show, live from Radio City Music Hall, they were dumb-founded to find they had been confined to a single award giveaway and one introduction. The hosts would be Bette Midler and Dan Aykroyd—*real* stars, *real* entertainers. "We were the faces of the channel the rest of the year—and then on this night, we weren't cool enough," Blackwood said. "We sat in the audience, watching something that we weren't really part of."

The VJs were, the network brass knew, replaceable. The channel itself was the star. The network began specializing in outrageous giveaways to viewers who entered contests via postcard. That July's stunt took the cake: MTV gave away a house—a pink house in Bloomington, Illinois, to tie in with Indiana na-tive John Cougar Mellencamp's "Pink Houses," a number eight pop hit earlier in the year. The winner also received "five hundred cases of Hawaiian Punch, a pink Jeep CJ7, a widescreen TV, and a Pioneer stereo."

But more and more, some artists simply *did not like* MTV and were beginning to say so. The loudest was Joe Jackson, a British singer-songwriter on A&M. "I'd like to explain my decision not to make a promo video, and to voice an opinion on the current 'video revolution,'" he began a *Billboard* editorial that June. He added: "Voicing these opinions to various people in the music business, I've met with some surprisingly nervous reactions. . . . Many people agree with me, but are afraid to buck the system and maybe make less money."

THE VIDEO MUSIC AWARDS (VMAS) WERE ANNOUNCED IN JANUARY 1984. "We see the awards show especially as expanding the concept of music video as an art form," MTV president Bob Pittman told *Billboard*. "The general spirit of awards shows will be left intact, but our approach will be more in keeping with the rock and roll audience."

Though Madonna's self-titled debut album had spun out hits for a year, she'd open the show with a brand-new song, "Like a Virgin," the title track of her second LP, which had been done for months, as Sire waited for the *Madonna* string to end. She'd wanted to sing the song to a white Bengal tiger, as she had in the video she'd already shot in Venice, Italy, but the network said no to having a wild animal onstage. Instead, Madonna came out of a seventeen-foot-tall wedding cake, clad in a bridal gown, and descended a staircase.

During a rehearsal the day before the performance, some MTV brass saw the singer practice her moves. Under the wedding dress she had on a matching white bustier. Mid-performance, as she crawled along the stage floor, one of the singer's breasts fell out of her top. Live on television, as she headed down the ladder, Madonna's boob didn't break free—her shoe did. She kicked the other one off and accidentally flashed her underwear on camera. It caused a firestorm. The *Los Angeles Times'* Robert Hilburn wrote that during the VMAs Madonna "prowled about the stage so suggestively in her Hollywood Boulevard lingerie that parents must have thought their kids were watching an adult channel."

At first, Arthur Baker thought "her career was over, that she had simply lost the plot," because the act came across as underwhelming to an audience of music-biz pros. But it came across loud and clear to the home viewers. "It was the performance that made her career," Baker told Madonna biographer Andrew Morton.

MADONNA'S FATHER CONSIDERED PERFORMING "IMMODEST" AND TOLD her so repeatedly. "There were talent shows in high school, and I'd perform in them every year, and I'd do one outrageous thing after another," she said. "My father would sit and be horrified. One time I put a bikini on and painted my body with fluorescent paint. I painted weird designs all over my body and danced to a Who song with black lights flashing and the lights off."

They lived in Bay City, Michigan. Madonna Louise Veronica Ciccone was the fourth of six kids; her dad worked at Chrysler Auto as an engineer. "He never wanted me to be a dancer or a singer, because he came to America poor and lived in a Pittsburgh ghetto," she said. "He wanted me to study law." When she was six, Madonna's mother, for whom she was named, died of cancer.

She knew her own power early: "From when I was very young, I just knew that being a girl and being charming in a feminine sort of way could get me a lot of things, and I milked it for everything I could." Her rebellious streak widened after her father married a housekeeper. "We had to start calling her Mom, and it was really hard," she said.

In high school, she "enjoyed athletics but hated the mentality of the jocks. And I hated the lazy, spaced out potheads." The same for the latter's music, in diametric opposition to Madonna's. "When I was growing up, my older brothers were into hard rock and I hated it," she said. "And they would purposely scratch the needle across my pop records, like my 'Incense and Peppermints' record [by the Strawberry Alarm Clock], and they would tell me it was trash. Then they'd put on something like Mahavishnu Orchestra."

As a teenager, Madonna studied ballet and befriended her instructor: "He's the one who really inspired me. He kept saying, 'You're different' and 'You're beautiful.'" She credited him with "my introduction to glamour and sophistication. . . . He used to take me to all the gay discotheques in downtown Detroit. . . . He was constantly putting all that stuff about New York in my ear. I was hesitant, and my father and everyone was against it, but he really said, 'Go for it.'"

Her father kept asking when she was going to come back and go to the University of Michigan; she had, after all, won a four-year scholarship there. Instead, Madonna left for New York in 1978, at seventeen. She was thrilled to live on Avenue B—a white girl like her didn't belong there, but she wasn't scared. Among other jobs, she modeled nude for art classes. "You got paid ten dollars an hour versus a dollar-fifty at Burger King," she said.

She arrived in New York right as punk, disco, and hip-hop were beginning to mingle in the clubs and became a regular at the Roxy when Afrika Bambaataa spun there. She refused to stay in one box—she would be an exhibitionist and a feminist, a white girl who flaunted black and Latin style, a Catholic who sang explicitly and unashamedly about sex.

Right down to dubious/exciting racial subtexts played to the fore, the comparisons of the young Madonna to Mick Jagger were not idle. Both played the heartbreaker on record with real feeling plus an air of cavalier entitlement. And their role as whites utterly indebted to black music, but expressing no guilt or shame in their borrowings, was irksome at times, thrilling at others, deeply complicated always.

She caught a break in 1979 when she got work as a dancer, then backing vocalist, for the French disco singer Patrick Hernandez, who'd had a hit with "Born to Be Alive." Hernandez's management moved Madonna to Paris, and she hated it: they gave her spending money but nothing to *do*. "I was just too smart for that," she said.

Returning to New York, she soon moved into the basement of a synagogue with the musician brothers Eddie and Dan Gilroy; she dated the latter. The Gilroys had a studio stocked with instruments. "He stuck a guitar in my hand and tuned it to an open chord so that I could strum," she said. "That really clicked something off in my brain." For ten months, Madonna woodshedded.

She first played drums in the Gilroys' band, the Breakfast Club, and was soon leading her own outfit, Emmy, singing and playing guitar. She called an old friend, Steven Bray, whom she'd met at a disco near the University of Michigan—the band needed a drummer. He showed up a week later. "He was a lifesaver," Madonna said. "I wasn't a good enough musician to be screaming at the band about how badly they were playing."

Blondie, the Police, and the Pretenders were among the band's models. They never found a decent guitarist. Later on, Bray was playing with a different band, and Madonna spent a year living, incognito, in their rehearsal space. "It didn't have a bathtub, I bathed in the sink," she said. "I slept curled around amplifiers in a sleeping bag. I wore the same thing every day."

Bray had been an R&B drummer when he met (and briefly dated) Madonna, and that was the direction of the new material they were writing together. After she gave Danceteria's DJ Mark Kamins her demo, they began dating. Her demo knocked him out as well. "He took me around to record companies and Sire offered me the best deal right away," she said.

Madonna's first twelve-inch, "Everybody," appeared in 1982 and did not feature a picture of the artist. Sire first marketed her, if not as black, then also not precisely as white, either. "Many are surprised to learn she's not black but a green-eyed white blonde fireplug with a teen London/Bronx look," said one early profile. In August 1984, *Billboard*'s Nelson George was moved to include *Madonna* in a roundup of R&B albums with remarkable chart longevity, alongside Luther Vandross, the Pointer Sisters, and Patti LaBelle. In short, she spent 1984 crossing over from R&B to pop, just like Michael Jackson and Lionel Richie and Prince.

"Everybody" led to some "track dates"—where a disco singer belts live over a recording of the hit(s). "You get paid thousands of dollars, which didn't make sense to me because when I was in a band I got paid nothing," she said. "With my dance training I thought, why not make a dance scenario out of it?"

Released in September 1983, "Holiday" came in the wake of any number of other records exactly like it, cosmetically speaking—bouncy disco tracks with an au courant synth overlay and lyrics that affirmed positivity in the face of, well, reality. But the husky catch in Madonna's voice, the hunger for the good life and good times she's singing about—the lust in it—sold the record's pretty lies, gave them weight. This was dance music made by somebody who clearly loved dancing to music just like it.

RUBBER BRACELETS, HAIR TIED BACK WITH TIGHTS, THE INFAMOUS **BOY TOY** belt buckle—Madonna had become as notorious for her style as her music. She would soon tire greatly of being asked if she, herself, was, indeed, per her buckle, a Boy Toy, and she would explain, each iteration more impatiently curt than the last, that it had been her graffiti handle and was a joke, and then she'd be asked if she were aware that, by proxy, she was recommending that young girls everywhere also be boy toys.

Pop being pop, Madonna and Cyndi Lauper were pitted against one another—the two high-pitched New York singers who dressed funny. One newspaper took a poll and found more women liked Lauper and more men liked Madonna. "I guess that means *I'm* ugly," Lauper replied, noting: "In the beginning, [I said], 'Hey, listen here, I'm a feminist, pal. I burnt my bra when

I was fourteen. Don't give me that sexist crap.' But then, wouldn't you know, here comes a woman, who feels sexual, and they have to give her some *more* sexist crap. The same women who complain about her being sexual probably own tons of Rolling Stones records, tons of Prince albums."

Madonna's first three clips were all straightforward performance pieces, and neither "Everybody" nor "Burning Up" received much attention. "Holiday" did, but it broke through in clubs, then on radio, not through MTV. "I'm desperate to start my second LP, but because of 'Holiday,' I'll have to wait," she mused in February. It wouldn't be until the promo for *Madonna's* fourth single, shot in Los Angeles early that month, that she could seriously be considered a "video artist."

"Borderline" featured Madonna dancing, but her moves enacted part of a scenario. The "plot" was interchangeable with the era's break-dancing flicks: street dancer Madonna, a white girl among Latinx breakers, is torn between her Hispanic beau and the preppie photographer in a baggy jacket with large eighties shoulder blades who turns her into a fashion model. Her bleached hair shows its roots. She wears a black Keith Haring print skirt. Her eye commands the camera. *Madonna* was generating hits, but Madonna had arrived.

The title of "Borderline" clearly referred to something musical *and* racial. "Art and music can never be too permissive, especially if they act as an alternative to the reactionary attitudes of people like Reagan and the Moral Majority," she told the UK pop magazine *No. 1*. Sire followed it up with "Lucky Star," in which she danced with a couple of backups again. "None of the dancing was planned—I just did it," she said.

Early in August, when the Jacksons came to New York, Madonna became "a constant presence backstage at Madison Square Garden and the Helmsley Palace," Jermaine wrote. "At first, she . . . seemed like more of a VIP fan than a fellow artist as she moved between rooms at the hotel, being social, spending most of her time with Michael and Randy. . . . Not only did she end up being managed by the Jacksons' management, Weisner and De Mann, she would recruit our keyboard player, Pat Leonard, as her musical director and our drummer Jonathan Moffett for her Virgin Tour."

It's a wonder Madonna had time to schmooze with anyone. She spent summer 1984 shooting a co-lead role in *Desperately Seeking Susan*. The director, Susan Seidelman, had made *Smithereens* (1982), an art-house hit filled with downtown New York figures like Richard Hell, Amos Poe, and Cookie Mueller, for less than $100,000. Madonna's costar was Rosanna Arquette, who'd garnered raves for her work on the TV movie *The Executioner's Song* and in John Sayles's indie film *Baby, It's You*.

Arquette played Roberta Glass, the bored New Jersey housewife who follows an obsession with a series of personal ads involving Susan, a free-spirited urban sprite living largely on her wits. Seidelman wanted Madonna specifically to play Susan. Madonna showed up for her screen test in a taxi she couldn't pay for and stuck the director for the fare. "It was exactly what Susan would have done," Seidelman said.

Seidelman was impressed by Madonna's rigorous taking to the task. "When there was a 6 a.m. call, the rest of us would have to be rousted out of bed," Seidelman said. "The driver assigned to Madonna would pick her up at a health club every morning where she'd already done fifty laps by six a.m."

But Madonna's fame grew with stunning rapidity through summer 1984. "On the first day, when Madonna walked down the street, only a few people turned their heads," Seidelman said. "By the last week of shooting, *Like a Virgin* had dropped and we needed security." Her costar suddenly had to play second fiddle. Seidelman said, "Rosanna was very upset."

THAT MARCH, MADONNA AND NILE RODGERS ATTENDED THE DURAN Duran show at Madison Square Garden together. They were nearly finished with *Madonna*'s follow-up, *Like a Virgin*, though nobody would hear it for months.

Rodgers had first seen Madonna opening for the disco singer Jenny Burton in the summer of 1983. "The very first night I met her, I thought that she was going to be the biggest star of all time," Rodgers recalled twenty years later. "Black groups, which had traditionally done all the choreography, our lives changed when we became the self-contained band, like the Chambers Brothers and Sly and the Family Stone. . . . I hadn't seen choreography in music [again] until that night."

He went on: "I remembered the truth about pop music is that when white artists capture the essence of black music and do it from the heart, and it's right, it's bigger than anything. . . . So when Madonna came out and she was dancing, every black artist, even the hip-hoppers, were standing there looking at her going, oh my god, check this out. And now it's as common as the sun rising in the east."

Rodgers watched the Video Music Awards at the Power Station in Midtown, where he was working on the first solo album by Mick Jagger of the Rolling Stones, who had pretaped his appearance on the show, just like his friend David Bowie. There were deadlines to make.

JUST BEFORE THE SHOW BEGAN, A NERVOUS MARTHA QUINN TOLD THE Radio City audience that she "felt like she was at a bar mitzvah." Outside, *Creem* reported, were "mobs of fans" along Fifty-First Street. The largely dressy event was costly: $100 for an orchestra seat, $17.50 for a balcony seat. One writer said, "The MTV Video Music Awards are apparently going to be with us for awhile as a once-a-year embarrassing reminder of just what kind of scary monster the pop music scene is turning into."

The night's biggest winner wasn't Michael Jackson's "Thriller." Instead, the Cars' "You Might Think" took home Video of the Year—it also did so in Saint-Tropez. The clip was a major technological breakthrough—one of the first to be entirely animated by computer.

"Thriller" didn't go home empty: it won Best Overall Performance in a Video, Best Choreography, for Michael Peters, and the Viewer's Choice Award. When Peters went up, he thanked each of the video's dancers by name, "because no one ever does it," he said. Michael wasn't there; accepting his awards for him was Diana Ross.

Van Halen also won thrice that night: "Jump" received Best Group Video, Best Stage Performance in a Video, and Best Overall Performance in a Video—all for a clip that cost $600 and was made with a single 16 mm camera. The album *1984* went through the roof, selling four million copies by October. The band's new echelon of success emboldened their singer to start thinking big. "I feel absolutely no responsibility whatsoever to the fans of Van Halen," Roth said. "You start trying to please everybody, you please no one. . . . I'm not changing shit! It's me!"

Van Halen was now the rock establishment. Roth and Edward Van Halen appeared in the video for "L.A. Is My Lady," the title song from Frank Sinatra's well-publicized 1984 comeback. (Ed had previously worked with the album's producer, Quincy Jones.) Diamond Dave was becoming a talk show fixture. For the 1984 tour, Roth began traveling in a separate tour bus from the rest of the band.

THE VMAs' SECOND PERFORMER WAS ROD STEWART. HE DID "INFATUA-tion," a top ten hit that summer, his first in a while. Ever since "Da Ya Think I'm Sexy?"—his massive disco number one in 1978—Stewart's image as a hard rocker had been tarnished, and he himself admitted to "a loss of focus at that time—say 1979 to 1981. I'm not entirely sure what the root causes were, but I suspect that too many late nights, too much partying, too much booze, and a few too many dabs of recreational cocaine might have had something to do with it."

Unlike many of his boomer peers, making videos didn't bother Stewart—he saw nothing wrong with writing a song and conceiving of its video simul-taneously, and said so on *Entertainment This Week*. He'd already been under fire from his fellow artists for violating the cultural boycott of South Africa's racist apartheid state by performing at the segregated casino resort of Sun City in the summer of 1983, only to announce in December of '84 that he'd be returning the following February.

At Radio City, his vivacity onstage overtook even the crowd's skeptics: "Stewart, perhaps, was the most welcome surprise of the night, turning in the kind of professional yet enthusiastic performance I honestly believed he'd never be able to pull off," *Creem* reported. In his band, for the first time in over a decade, was Ron Wood, his old guitarist in the Faces. At the VMAs, the two of them gave Quincy Jones his Special Recognition Award, only to enact what *Cash Box* called a "giggling-church-boys routine during Jones' speech," refusing to leave the stage while the gentleman accepted his award.

THOUGH HE WAS THE UNDISPUTED PREDECESSOR FOR THE NEW POP'S stylistic shenanigans, David Bowie was disdainful of London's trendsetting pop fashionmongers. He had a particular distaste for the FRANKIE SAYS T-shirt: "God, I hate those damn things. . . . That's why I had my Ernie character in 'Blue Jean' wearing a RELAX T-shirt!"

"Blue Jean" was the first single from Bowie's fifteenth studio album, *Tonight*, released ten days after the VMAs. Largely a covers album—three from Iggy Pop, who cowrote two new ones, and one each from Chuck Jackson and the Beach Boys (a truly grisly "God Only Knows")—*Tonight* was, as Bowie chronicler Chris O'Leary put it, "among the least-loved number-one records of its era."

As he did many things, Bowie seemed to know this in advance. "I wanted to keep my hand in, so to speak, and go back in the studio—but I didn't really feel as if I had enough new things of my own because of the tour," he explained to

NME in 1984. "I can't write on tour, and there wasn't really enough preparation afterwards to write anything that I felt was really worth putting down." The success of *Let's Dance* meant that EMI wanted new product, fast, and Bowie felt obliged to deliver.

For the "Blue Jean" video, Bowie was compelled to "Thriller" things up: "Jazzin' for Blue Jean," as it was retitled, was a twenty-minute mini-film, directed by Julian Temple. In it, he performed the song in a video-within-a-video, as Screamin' Lord Byron, his face and hair covered in translucent paint. "I wish I'd thought of this in '74," Bowie said on the set, drolly. He simultaneously filmed a "live" version of the song for the VMAs—through the looking glass yet again.

TWO WEEKS BEFORE THE VMAS, TINA TURNER SAID A FINAL GOODBYE TO her old life. On August 27, she performed at a McDonald's corporate gathering in Ottawa, a show scheduled well before it was clear that she really was having a comeback. "What's Love Got to Do with It" had hit number one, but she was legally bound to fourteen shows for the burger chain. "Ottawa was the fourteenth and last of them, and the tech crew and the six-man band were audibly relieved," *Rolling Stone* reported.

Eight years earlier, on the weekend of the Bicentennial, Tina's husband, Ike, backhanded her one time too many in a limo headed to the Hilton hotel in Dallas at the start of a tour. When Ike finally fell asleep at the hotel, Tina put a cape over her clothes, a wrap on her head, sunglasses over her swollen eyes, grabbed her toiletries, and hid in a nearby alley until 9:00 p.m.—showtime. She then ran to a Ramada Inn, where the manager gave her the best suite; she paid him back for it two years later.

Even before the divorce was finalized, Turner was in the hole financially—leaving the tour on opening night made her liable for the promoters' losses. Rhonda Graam, who'd been Ike and Tina's business manager, got her doing TV: *Hollywood Squares, Donny & Marie, Dinah!* "She was on food stamps and I was getting unemployment every two weeks, and between checks we'd charge things on my credit cards," Graam says in *I, Tina*. The divorce was finalized March 29, 1978.

Turner would stay on the road nine to ten months a year for seven years, initially with a cabaret-styled act—tuxes, dancers, "Disco Inferno." This was not what she truly wanted to be doing: as she would tell *Musician* magazine's

Mark Rowland in 1984, "I *am* rock and roll." In 1986, she explained to Rowland why she'd nixed a producer's suggestion of adding a gospel choir to a song: "Because I don't want to go to church. . . . I enjoy the fun of *not* being that serious." Plus cabaret paid the bills, which tripled after the IRS touched her up for back taxes.

But the way forward came in 1979, when she appeared on an Olivia Newton-John TV special. Turner wound up working with the host's Australian manager, Roger Davies, a fan since 1966, like so many other non-Americans, after Turner shouted down the Wall of Sound on the Phil Spector–produced "River Deep—Mountain High."

Surveying Turner's show, with its costumes by Bob Mackie and its residencies in Tahoe, Roger Davies waited a year to finally tell Tina what she needed to hear, backstage in Bangkok in late autumn 1980: "You have to fire everybody." Her no-B.S. response: "Well, if that's what we need to do."

The new band—guitarist James Ralston, bassist Bob Feit, and drummer Jack Bruno—was built around remaining pianist Kenny Moore, who would become the singer's onstage foil, alongside two new dancers, Ann Behringer and former Ikette Edna Lejeune Richardson. The band wasn't virtuosic, just tight and flashy and sympathetic. Tina Turner still put on a hell of a show. Davies's job was to make everybody notice.

In summer 1981, Davies booked Turner at the Ritz, then New York's major new wave showcase. It was Tina's first New York appearance in a decade, and Jerry Brandt, the club's owner, went all out, taking a full-page ad in the *Voice* and selling out three shows. She returned for two more nights, September 30 and October 1; Rod Stewart turned up at the latter, and two nights later brought Tina onto *Saturday Night Live* with him to perform "Hot Legs," one of her recent show openers. A month after that, Tina and her band opened for the Rolling Stones at the Brendan Byrne Arena in East Rutherford, New Jersey.

Before the year was over, Turner would make a record to shift the tide. In 1982, the British synthesizer players Martyn Ware and Ian Craig Marsh had already formed not one but two of the era's key acts: the Human League, which they left to Phil Oakey, then Heaven 17, with vocalist Glenn Gregory, whose 1981 debut *Penthouse and Pavement* had been a British hit. "Synthesizers always sounded good no matter how badly you played them," Ware would explain in 1985, adding: "We are not in the time of the sixties rock group anymore."

Ware and Marsh were preparing a new project as the British Electronic Foundation, featuring an armload of guest vocalists. Turner and Davies flew first-class to England for a $2,000 fee, only for Tina to balk when she found out she was to sing the Temptations' "Ball of Confusion," a song she was completely unfamiliar with. But she was persuaded to take a shot, and nailed her vocal.

By the time she played the Ritz the following September, she'd signed to Capitol Records, but an EMI executive had tried cutting her out of the deal. Then, on the night of the show, another Capitol executive called Davies: Could they please have sixty-three spots on the guest list? David Bowie was in town and he was going to see her, so they all thought they'd tag along. They were *her* record label now, too, right? "They all came down: the executives, the A&R guys, the people from International," said Davies. It set the table for a new consideration of Turner's future.

Davies wanted Capitol to reunite her with Heaven 17. She wanted to rock; Martyn Ware would respond, "Look, there's no point in phoning us unless you want to do a soul number because that's our fascination. We know it's strange because you've already done it all, but it's also the right time commercially." Resigned, Tina consented to the Al Green song they'd played her—that one she didn't mind so much.

She knocked out her version of "Let's Stay Together" in one take. "It's more respectful than radical: she follows Green's lead on key phrasings, misses his slyness, can't get near his sweetness, but more than makes up for this, word by word, with her urgency and passion," Vince Aletti wrote in the *Village Voice*. It hit the British top five, sold 250,000 copies, and in America eventually went top five R&B and top thirty pop.

In February of 1984, Capitol sent out a new bio. It began: "Tina Turner is a show business phenomenon!" It ended by promising a new album in the spring. She had two weeks to make it.

She cut it in London because she'd already booked a sold-out British tour. Clearly, they got her and America didn't. Davies cast his net and landed stars. Mark Knopfler had a song left over from the last Dire Straits album that he'd felt wrong about issuing with a man singing it called "Private Dancer"; the band's other members backed Tina singing it. Because they needed a lead guitarist, Davies tried Jeff Beck. "When Tina Turner's name came up, I would have *bicycled* to wherever she wanted me to play," Beck told *Musician*.

Rupert Hine, who'd worked with the Fixx, whose sound was pitched between old AOR and new MTV, produced a version of "Better Be Good to Me," an obscure song by obscure New York rockers Spider. Hine brought in his girlfriend, the lyricist Jeanette Obstoj, who interviewed Tina and turned it into a song called "I Might Have Been Queen." Another song from the British Electric Foundation (BEF) sessions, David Bowie's "1984," was added to the stack. Davies also called an old Australian he knew named Terry Britten, formerly of the Twilights, who brought two tracks, "Show Some Respect," and a cowrite with Graham Lyle, "What's Love Got to Do with It"—a little off-brand for Tina, maybe, but she could do *something* with it. Or maybe not: "I hate it, it's just not my kind of song," she told her manager. Nevertheless, she agreed to meet the songwriter four days later, and after some rewriting, she got it down in "two or three" takes.

The whole album, named *Private Dancer* after the Knopfler song, was completed by the end of April. Tina would hit the road again, this time bringing keyboardist Alan Clark and guitarist Hal Lindes, both of Dire Straits, with her for the summer as the opening act, beginning May 15, for Lionel Richie.

"It was real hard being on stage by myself at first," she told *Ebony*, "because Lionel's crowd is not my crowd. Plus, it was brand new material, and the only thing they wanted to hear was 'Nutbush City Limits,' 'Let's Stay Together,' and 'Proud Mary.'" Tina was playing mellower than she ever had. Part of it was an oft-stated desire to be heard *as a singer* rather than a showgirl with pipes.

It didn't take long for the Lionel Richie audiences to acclimate to Turner. Even Tina liked "What's Love Got to Do with It" now: "Oh, is *that* how it sounds on the radio?" she said.

SHORTLY BEFORE ZZ TOP PERFORMED ITS HIT "LEGS," WHICH WON THE group one of two Moonmen that night, the patrons in the front rows of Radio City Music Hall were handed fake beards and sunglasses to don. Not everyone cooperated: Grace Slick of Jefferson Starship, who'd been onstage earlier in the evening, co-presenting Best New Artist in a Video to Eurythmics, shoved the whiskers up her dress.

Rockers from the sixties and early seventies had a hard fight staying relevant in the eighties. Slick knew it better than most. That June, Paul Kantner, the only other member of the original Airplane left in the band, had departed Jefferson Starship in the middle of a tour. A month after the VMAs, Kantner would sue the group over the name. By the following March, the band would have no more claim to either "Jefferson" or "Airplane" without consent from all five original members.

Thus, with only Slick as the remaining link to the band's sixties heyday, came the moniker Starship. They would launch a fusillade of grotesque hits beginning in 1985 with "We Built This City," sung largely by the oleaginous Mickey Thomas. Slick retired from performing in 1989—old people, she said, didn't belong on rock and roll stages.

Far from being stymied by MTV, ZZ Top rode it for everything they could—both visually and by adopting its sonic trappings. The band had been fans from the beginning. "First time I saw it, it was late at night and [my wife] Debbie and I were in bed," drummer Frank Beard told *Creem*. "We saw a band come on and play a song and then another band and then another band and we thought it was a new show we'd never seen before. We must have stayed up five hours thinking, Jesus, this is a long show."

Guitarist Billy Gibbons was the son of the conductor of the Houston Philharmonic and became a blues fanatic listening to border radio in the fifties. He eventually led the sixties garage punks the Moving Sidewalks, who'd toured with Jimi Hendrix, who named Gibbons a favorite upcoming guitarist during an interview with Johnny Carson. Gibbons and bassist Dusty Hill formed the band in 1969; in 1970, Beard—the only member of the band, as was widely noted, without a beard (he sufficed with a long mustache before caving to the inevitable in 2013)—joined them.

ZZ Top jelled as a trio from the beginning. "None of us like organs. We don't like rhythm guitar players and we're not from the Southeast, so we don't need a second drummer," Beard explained.

They were good ol' boys—in December 1984 Hill was accidentally shot in the abdomen when his girlfriend was removing his boot, in which he kept his gun—who wrote Southern rock anthems that boogied hard and winked constantly: "Cheap Sunglasses," "Le Grange," the eternal "Tush."

For 1979's *Degüello*, they added a clavinet—the funky electric keyboard with a particularly clacking tonality—to a handful of songs; on the follow-up, *El Loco*, from 1981, they began working with synthesizers. It made sense—eschewing ballads, ZZ Top were a skintight rhythm machine. The blues had been the dance music of their youth, and the throb of the modern club floor, the place where synthesizers were most effectively being used, was the logical next step.

For their ninth LP, *Eliminator*, the band dove full on into synthesizers, sequencers, and drum machines. The grooves were constructed around disco pulses, using disco methodology, but the riffs still crunched. "The heaviness of the synthesizers created a nice platform that allowed the guitar to stand on its own," Gibbons said.

The platform that allowed *Eliminator* to stand out, though, was MTV. A trio of clips for the singles "Gimme All Your Lovin'," "Sharp Dressed Man," and "Legs," directed by Tim Newman, followed the same plot: ZZ Top would appear not as characters, but as avatars of the sort of sexually forthright, cheapo Americana lifestyle their lyrics espoused. The three of them, Beard flanked by those otherworldly beards, would magically give a dumbstruck young schmoe the keys—on a ring with the bright-gold ZZ Top logo—to a snazzy red top-down Caddy, out of which a bevy of scantily clad women would appear. Most rock videos aspired to porn. These were a lot funnier about it.

In 1983, ZZ Top outsold every other act on Warner Bros.; the album was still moving a hundred thousand copies a week in spring 1984, a year after its release. On the VMAs, the band performed "Sharp Dressed Man" in their custom Nudie suits, with Beard in particular sporting a truly luxuriant hairstyle not yet known as the mullet.

ZZ Top were on the left side of the stage, with a gargantuan lit-up MTV logo behind them; to the right was a reenactment of the video, with women in off-shoulder tops boogying around the band and the top-down cherry-colored Cadillac. The band didn't even pretend to be miming. At the end, the red-suited Beard jumped between the two guitarists, brandishing his drumsticks as the track battered away, untouched. ZZ Top was always in on the joke.

In July, *Billboard*'s dance columnist, Brian Chin, had reviewed a new Ray Parker Jr. twelve-inch. "Ghostbusters," Chin wrote, was "a bit of a step for him. The beat here is more rigid than the kind Raydio used to provide (not far from 'I Want a New Drug,' actually)."

Not far at all, and Huey Lewis, who'd cowritten the song with his lead guitarist Chris Hayes and took it to number six that winter with their band, the News, took action. On August 29, less than three weeks before the VMAs, they filed suit against Parker, claiming he ripped off their song, asking after all profits, plus $5 million in damages. Twenty years later, the producers of *Ghostbusters*, the movie for which Parker had made the theme song, admitted they'd used Lewis and the News' record as temp music, then lobbied unsuccessfully for the band to write a new theme. Lewis had declined. The suit was settled, quietly and out of court, within a year. The band's manager, Bob Brown, told the *San Francisco Chronicle*, "We got a major apology."

Part of the settlement was a gag rule: Neither party was to discuss the suit in subsequent interviews. In 2001, Lewis broke the rule, telling *Behind the Music*, VH-1's rock-doc cash cow, "The offensive part was not so much that Ray Parker Jr. had ripped this song off—they wanted our wave, and they wanted to buy it. . . . In the end, I suppose it was for sale, because, basically, they bought it." Parker would then sue Lewis back, for breaching the agreement. In 1984, the VMAs had both acts on, playing both songs, as if asking America to compare and contrast.

Both acts played straight to the middle of the road in their respective fields. Based in San Francisco, Huey Lewis was a raspy but limited bar-band singer and harmonica player whose band, the News, was R&B-inflected but with a slicker sound than the usual Springsteen clones; one critic described Lewis as sounding like "if Randy Newman could sing an eensy bit better."

The News signed to Chrysalis in 1980; their second LP, *Picture This* (1982), did OK thanks to "Do You Believe in Love"—upbeat corporate pop, written by super-producer Robert John "Mutt" Lange, every bit as machine-tooled as a Journey anthem, only with Lewis's Muppet-like yelp replacing Steve Perry's drama-king grandeur, a major improvement. Still, while on tour behind *Picture This*, "We could barely draw five hundred people in L.A.," Lewis said.

The third News album, *Sports*, applied the bright, bouncy lessons of "Do You Believe" as a first principle, even if the sport it looks like they played was mini-golf. It was a constant, consistent hit, and so were the singles from it, most of which reached number six. It makes sense: Huey Lewis and the News are a number six kind of band. Except on June 30, when *Sports* finally knocked *Thriller* off the top of the *Billboard* album chart—and not, as many had predicted, the Jacksons' *Victory*, which peaked at number four.

"I Want a New Drug" had been the second single from *Sports*, after "Heart and Soul," and by the time of the VMAs, the album was on its fourth hit, the doo-wop pastiche "If This Is It." But it was single three, "The Heart of Rock and Roll," that was most notable—it was the pop version of the indie-rock underground's America-first impulse, the same one that animated the Fleshtones' "American Beat '84," X's "I Must Not Think Bad Thoughts," and every Peter Buck interview. It was all rock and roll to Huey—a what-me-worry? outlook that neatly summed him up.

RAY PARKER CLOSED OUT THE VMAs: "I WANT A NEW DRUG" WAS NUM-
ber six, but "Ghostbusters" was number one—on the charts, at the box office,
you name it. The movie grossed $238 million in the United States alone. The
video piggybacked on the feature, both financially (the clip's budget was ab-
sorbed into the film's) and in its heavy absorption of its sequences, alongside
the cast and assorted random performers (including Chevy Chase, John Candy,
and Carly Simon) whose appearance, per one academic summary, "effectively
provided a sustained celebrity endorsement of the film."

It wasn't even Parker's most blatant steal that year. Early in 1984, Parker
reached number twelve pop with "I Still Can't Get Over Loving You," whose
lyrics quoted the Police's "Every Breath You Take." In addition to Lewis, more
than one observer noticed the resemblance between "Ghostbusters" and M's
1979 US number one/UK number two "Pop Muzik." *Creem*'s singles columnist,
Ken Barnes, dubbed Parker "the consummate riff burglar of his generation."

Clive Davis had initially signed Parker to Arista as part of Raydio in the
late seventies. Parker was then a mild-voiced session bassist, best known for
his work with Stevie Wonder. He'd begun writing hits for Chaka Khan, among
others, when Davis offered him an artist deal in 1977.

Parker initially hid behind the group named Raydio, enlisting the more traditionally piercing tenor Rodney Carmichael on vocals. On "Jack and Jill," top
ten pop in 1978, Carmichael wails while Parker murmurs. Within a few years,
Carmichael was gone. Parker kept murmuring. He perfected a role—the cutie-
pie horndog who, the times being what they were, just couldn't keep it in his
pants—and marketed it to an appreciable white buyership. Still, even when the
AOR-reaching "The Other Woman" (1982) hit number four pop, during the
pop charts' most crossover-unfriendly moment since the early fifties, the video
did not get on MTV—"Not because the song wasn't a hit," Davis said. "The
[clip's dancing] corpses weren't a problem, but Ray's white leading lady was."

THE VMAs MADE MONEY, NOT LEAST BECAUSE A TWO-HOUR VERSION WAS
syndicated to eighty-five markets. "A number of stations are playing the program twice," *Billboard* reported, "and almost all of them are airing the program
at least once in prime time."

Three weeks later, on October 6, Sire Records released *Like a Virgin*. The
same week, *Madonna* entered *Billboard*'s top ten and certified platinum, after
fifty-eight weeks on the chart. Many of the reviews were cautiously positive,

but Madonna's press was becoming noxious—in particular, an astoundingly sexist cover story on her in *Rolling Stone* that November. One critic noted, "In less than a year, she's garnered more negative press than any other musical act of the eighties."

But the line on Madonna was beginning to shift. When the Go-Go's Gina Schock told a journalist that Madonna made it hard to take female musicians seriously, but that she loved her album anyway, Madonna thought it was "pretty funny," but added: "I'm doing it because I like it."

CIVIC ARENA,
PITTSBURGH
September 21, 1984

On Monday, January 23, 1984, two members of the Essex-based anarchist-collective-cum-punk-band Crass walked into the London bureau of the Associated Press and admitted to audio forgery. Guitarists Andy Palmer and Pete Wright brought in a two-minute cassette of an audio collage they'd made of a phony conversation in which Ronald Reagan threatens Margaret Thatcher that he'd annihilate Europe "to see to it that the Soviet Union stays within its borders." It had taken some three months to assemble—on audio-tape, not reel-to-reel. As they explained to *Sounds*, "We wanted to precipitate a debate on the Falklands and nuclear weapons to damage Thatcher's position in the election."

The US State Department had included it in a report that September called "Soviet active measures." To discover it was a punk band's doing . . . made only too much sense, especially in the UK. Punk had been, among other things, a reaction to straitening social conditions and the rise of a hard-right political swing that, for many artists, portended fascism outright.

In September 1984, a UK retailer was convicted of an obscenity charge for selling punk records containing four-letter words, including two Dead Kennedys albums and the Crass single "Sheep Farming in the Falklands," a furious anti-Thatcher screed from the year before. "I don't think there is a major record company in the country that has not brought out a record with the offending four-letter word on it," Iain McNay of Cherry Red, the Dead Kennedys' UK distributor, told *Billboard*. "As things stand, Pink Floyd's *Dark Side of the Moon* would be rated obscene." But Pink Floyd had never perpetrated a hoax in the prime minister's name.

"VOTING FOR HER WAS LIKE BUYING A VERA LYNN LP, GETTING IT HOME and finding *Never Mind the Bollocks* inside the red, white, and blue sleeve," Julie Burchill wrote about Thatcher in 1988. Burchill had been one of the bellwethers of punk rock in the pages of *NME* during the late seventies—its most attention-getting, fearless critic. By the mid-eighties, she'd moved on to the style press, and her politics swerved rightward right along with England's.

Thatcher was a walking, breathing reaction to the mid-seventies malaise, the three-day-workweek days of incredible stress and repression. In October 1983, when the Canadian newsweekly *MacLean's* asked Thatcher whether she felt a responsibility to find more meaningful jobs for Britain's 1.2 million unemployed young people than service work at McDonald's and Disneyland, Thatcher snapped, "I cannot produce jobs that are fulfilling for everyone. No one in the world can." She added, "I am trying to redress the balance between the citizen and the state. Things got toppled far too much over toward the power of the state." Within months, Thatcher would use the power of the state to the exact opposite end.

The National Union of Mineworkers (NUM) had declared a strike in March 1984, after union president Arthur Scargill was "sent anonymously a copy of a secret plan prepared by NCB [National Coal Board] chiefs earmarking ninety-five pits for closure, with the loss of one hundred thousand miners' jobs"; the miners had successfully struck in 1972 and 1974, the latter having "brought down the Tory government in a general election," Scargill wrote. The NCB announced, first, the closure of five coal mines, then another twenty. "We realized that [these closures] had amounted to a declaration of war," Scargill wrote. "We could either surrender right now, or stand and fight."

Things came to a head on June 8, at the Orgreave coking plant near Yorkshire. Some eight thousand strikers were essentially led into an ambush. The police guided them to where nearly six thousand officers awaited, many in riot gear, about fifty on horseback, a number of others holding police dogs.

The officers leading the charge's intentions, in their words, were "incapac-itating" and "flushing out" demonstrators by leading the picketers toward "strike zones" where the police could attack. Ninety-five arrests were made, with injuries reported by fifty-one picketers and seventy-two police officers.

A number of musicians held concerts to benefit the striking miners, among them Crass. That July, exhausted from both the pressures of living communally and the backfire from Thatchergate, they split up following a miners' strike benefit gig in Aberdare, Wales.

Another was the London industrial band Test Dept., who made noise with found objects, à la Einstürzende Neubauten. Its first miners' benefit took place at the Albany Empire in southeast London. Test Dept.'s Paul Jamrozy recalled that someone "spotted these three old ladies and he was quite concerned about them because they were standing right by the bass bins. . . . At the end [he] went up to the old ladies and they said it was absolutely wonderful—they were all stone deaf and it was the first concert they'd been to where they could hear something."

ON JUNE 9, THE DAY AFTER THE BATTLE OF ORGREAVE, THATCHER MET with South African premier P. W. Botha. It prompted another mass protest—the PM was sitting with a monster, the head of the notoriously racist apartheid state. As Thatcher requested Botha withdraw from Namibia, per the UN Secu-rity Council's resolution, twenty-five thousand people were both blasting the record and group-singing the Special AKA's recent British top ten hit, "Nelson Mandela"—or, as it was titled in the United States, "Free Nelson Mandela"—for the leader of the African National Congress, a political party opposed to apart-heid, who'd been imprisoned for life in 1964.

The Special AKA—earlier, the Specials—were leaders of the knot of late-seventies Coventry bands that reached back a decade and a half to the sound of early Jamaican ska, the jumpier forerunner to reggae. Led by keyboardist and songwriter Jerry Dammers, the Specials' black-and-white uniforms and cover art for their classic self-titled debut was a signal of racial unity, stamped in place with their label name, 2-Tone.

In 1981, the Specials' three-man vocal front line—Terry Hall, Lynval Gold-ing, and Neville Staple—left the group and formed Fun Boy Three. Dammers rebuilt the band, hiring lead vocalists Stan Campbell and Rhoda Dakar; with the latter he made "The Boiler" in 1982, one of the most claustrophobic and genuinely frightening pop records ever—a depiction of a young woman, voiced by Dakar, being sexually assaulted. Dammers did not shy away from confronting social issues, nor did it feel exploitative when he did.

The Special AKA spent two years recording a third album. Dammers tried to appease all his bandmates by pursuing everyone's ideas and owed Chrysalis Records, the label, so much money that he was desperate for a hit single to pay off the studio costs. He brought Elvis Costello—who'd done the honors on *Specials*, their 1979 debut—back to produce them again after writing "Nelson Mandela." Costello agreed; the song, he wrote, was particularly gutsy considering that, at the time, "the British government was still referring to Nelson Mandela as 'a terrorist.'"

Costello had been having hits again himself—with topical songs, no less. In 1983, the year of Thatcher's reelection, he put out two singles as the Imposter. One was "Shipbuilding," which had already been a Top 40 UK hit for Robert Wyatt and went to number thirteen in Costello's new version. It was about the Falklands—shipbuilding was a dying industry briefly buoyed by wartime necessity, particularly in Costello's native Liverpool: "Fighting for dear life / When we could be diving for pearls." The other Imposter single, "Pills and Soap," snarled, the title phrase—"We're gonna melt them down for pills and soap"— curdling in the memory, the song seeming to look ahead to the time when the right wing, like the SS, might be experimenting with human victims.

Both songs appeared on the 1983 album *Punch the Clock*—which had yielded Costello's first-ever US hit, "Everyday I Write the Book." But after seven years of nonstop recording and touring, Costello was fried, a state reflected all too well by 1984's *Goodbye Cruel World*. Referring to his backing band the Attractions' staid "three-piece-suit-with-watch-and-chain arrangements," Greil Marcus wrote, "The music quietly settles on the tables and chairs, like dust." When the album was reissued with bonus material in the nineties, Costello began the liner notes: "Congratulations! You've just purchased our worst album."

The album contained "Peace in Our Time," a song Costello would later acknowledge had been a thin attempt at a "Shipbuilding" or "Pills and Soap" aimed at Ronald Reagan. He'd always written politically oriented material— his debut single, "Less Than Zero," had been a warning against fascism—but Costello's career was in a holding pattern. "A lot of the hit records of the time were not songs as I understood them, but shiny, open-ended sequences of music, mostly conjured up in the studio," he wrote. "I tried to go along with the plan for a while, but I felt like a blacksmith in a glass factory." And his life was in tatters: a chronic philanderer, he'd finally left his wife after a decade. After recording *Goodbye*, he toured solo. He couldn't afford to take the Attractions on the road—not that the band was on speaking terms, anyway.

IN SOUTH AFRICA, EVERY BLACK PERSON OVER SIXTEEN WAS REQUIRED BY law to carry their ID at all times. Failure to do so could result in arrest. Then again, so could just about anything.

Things were beginning to change, slowly, in the mid-eighties: black miners were allowed to unionize beginning in 1979. These unions "add[ed] to the blacks' leverage for nonwage demands, such as the freedom to live anywhere and the right to vote," *BusinessWeek* reported, quoting the chairman of Gold Fields of South Africa Limited: "There's always a danger that these unions will become politicized." All of which was just ducky to the Reagan administration.

One way musicians called attention to the situation involved saying no to bookings at the luxury casino-resort Sun City, which opened in 1979 and was located just northwest of South Africa, in the so-called free state of Bophuthatswana. This allowed artists to say that, technically, they hadn't performed *in* South Africa, which had been subject to an official United Nations cultural boycott since 1968. But the artists who played Sun City went onto the UN blacklist anyway.

That included black performers, who got invited as often as whites—how better to prove the South African government wasn't *really* racist? In 1983, the ribald southern soul belter Millie Jackson went. Previously unaware of the realities of apartheid, she became an "honorary white person." But even after she left the tour, Jackson's bookings suffered afterward. "The issue wasn't dying," her publicist told *Billboard* late in 1984. The chastened singer had to meet with a consortium of African ambassadors at the UN to get help removing her name from the blacklist.

Linda Ronstadt appeared at Sun City in May 1983, leading to an official UN denunciation. "The last place for a boycott is the arts," she insisted. "I just don't like being told you can't go somewhere. Like when they told Jane Fonda she couldn't go to North Vietnam. Of course she should have gone to North Vietnam." The *Rolling Stone* reporter she said this to wrung his hands: "The war in the jungles of Southeast Asia provoked a moral outcry in this country that helped to set the tone for a decade. And rock and roll added its loud voice to those protests. The music and the musicians seemed to have a moral dimension. But no more. Now rock and roll can be hired by apartheid."

Some recordings of black South African street music were getting into UK and US shops, starting with the compilation *Soweto*, which Rough Trade issued in 1982. "Rough Trade had a constitution and part of the constitution, apparently, said that Rough Trade supported the boycott of South African goods until South Africa was freed from the yoke of apartheid and Nelson Mandela was released," Rough Trade's Richard Boon said. "The problem wasn't the material, obviously, the problem was the handling of it." When Boon introduced Jumbo Vanrenen, a white South African expatriate, Boon said, "the entire room emptied—*everyone* got up and left." Eventually, Vanrenen and his partner Trevor Herman cut a deal with Virgin to distribute their new African label, Earthworks.

Out in New York during the spring of '84, Heidi Berg, a musician in the *Saturday Night Live* band, befriended Paul Simon through an introduction by her boss, the *SNL* producer Lorne Michaels. She played him the township jive that had been inspiring her—in particular, a cassette labeled "Accordion Jive Hits Vol. 2." Simon was curious—Why didn't Berg just fly down to South Africa and hire the musicians she was listening to? She scoffed: Who did she know in South Africa? Then Simon borrowed the cassette, and soon Berg received the news that he'd purchased the rights to one of the tape's songs, "Gumboots," to write a new song over. "Where's my end?" Berg cracked. Simon promptly ended the conversation.

PRESIDENT REAGAN WAS AT THE HEIGHT OF HIS POPULARITY ON AUGUST 11, 1984, when he sat down to do a radio speech. Into a microphone he didn't know was on, Reagan joked, "My fellow Americans, I'm pleased to tell you today that I've signed legislation that will outlaw Russia forever. We begin bombing in five minutes." Some reporters adjacent to the studio heard it, and there was a brief kerfuffle.

That live tape—with Reagan's voice played back every way possible over a skittering club beat—became the basis of a 1984 single that Talking Heads' Jerry Harrison made along with Bootsy Collins, the definitive bassist for both James Brown and P-Funk. "5 Minutes" was credited to Bonzo Goes to Washington. Collins, who'd been in Washington, DC, to speak with the US House of Representatives, drove all the way to Harrison's studio in Milwaukee and added his bass to the track, before driving back home to Cincinnati the next morning.

The New York dance indie Sleeping Bag issued it, and within three weeks it had sold out of its initial pressing.

A few musicians loved the guy, though. Mike Love of the Beach Boys was one. In April 1983, the US secretary of the interior, James Watt, had made a public statement about the Beach Boys' suitability to perform on the Washington Mall that Fourth of July—they played "hard rock" and "attracted the wrong element," which would "encourage drug abuse and alcoholism as was done in years past." Soon, Love received a phone call from Nancy Reagan to apologize for Watt's big mouth. Would he and his group like to play the White House?

Watt was out of the White House by October and the Beach Boys were back on the Lawn on July 4, 1984. The show was a revue—among the openers were the folk-pop America, the R&B O'Jays, and the country Hank Williams Jr.—something for everyone. Ringo Starr sat in on a Beatles mini-set. It was exactly the sort of family entertainment that Watt presumed it wasn't.

Despite Dennis Wilson's death—Carl dedicated "Good Vibrations" to him on the National Mall—the Beach Boys seemed more like family than they had in years. Brian Wilson, in particular, seemed in rude health again—his waist had shrunk from fifty-five inches to thirty-six, for starters. He'd begun seeing a radical therapist, Dr. Eugene Landy, whose intensive treatment—he had Wilson swimming a mile a day and was by his client's side near constantly—seemed to bring the once-bedbound Beach Boy back to the world. But Brian still seemed restless. In mid-August, he was arrested in Dallas while attending the Republican National Convention without authorization and released on a $200 bond. Brian's criminal trespass charge would be quietly dropped.

The turn that shocked people was when Neil Young announced that he, too, supported the president—not that Young, a Canadian citizen, could vote in America. Young had been the writer and lead singer on Crosby, Stills, Nash & Young's incendiary 1970 single "Ohio," with its excoriation of President Nixon's "tin soldiers." What was he doing backing a war hawk like Reagan? Young stood firm: "I do believe that Reagan's a good president and that he's a good man and I think he's a good leader."

Young was full of turnarounds in the eighties. He'd started off the decade with albums of, in order, hard rock (*Re-ac-tor*, 1981), synth-pop (!—*Trans*, 1982), rockabilly (!!—*Everybody's Rockin'*, 1983), and, with 1985's *Old Ways*, country. It was, as he said himself, "like a moth banging on a light bulb, this fast flitting from one thing to another. Not more change, but extreme change. There wasn't much relief—the change was obvious, then bang!—over here, bang!—

over there." His three kids with his wife, Pegi, all were born with disabilities—two sons had cerebral palsy, his daughter epilepsy. He was clearly preoccupied.

Young spent much of 1984 on the road with the International Harvesters, a consortium of Nashville studio veterans (such as pianist Hargus "Pig" Robbins), including several he'd worked with extensively, such as guitarist Ben Keith and bassist Tim Drummond. The International Harvesters' shows, though, were where Young's energy really came out—the live album *A Treasure*, recorded during the 1984–1985 tour, is far more vivid than *Old Ways*.

Young had joined the Geffen roster in 1981, and his new bosses did not appreciate his rapid changes of style. When Young gave the label *Old Ways* in 1984, they turned around and filed a lawsuit against him for making unrepresentative music, telling him, "We want Neil Young!" He explained, "That was confusing to me because I'd always thought that I *was* Neil Young. But it turns out that when I do certain things, I'm *not* Neil Young." The press had a field day, and the suit was quickly dropped.

ON THE COVER OF THE SEPTEMBER 3, 1984, ISSUE OF *BUSINESS WEEK*, Ronald Reagan sits atop a stallion, rearing onto its hind legs as the president raises a cowboy hat that dollar bills fall out of. "The Recovery Cheers the GOP," read the headline.

The movement toward deregulation had begun brewing in the seventies. "Conservative free-market economists allied with liberal consumer advocates like Ralph Nader to push back against federal regulations that had . . . actually benefited the regulated entities and stifled consumer choice," historians Kevin Kruse and Julian Zelizer wrote. The cable TV industry had sprung up as a result of these early deregulation efforts—Congress eased the restrictions of putting new networks on the air, and the FCC did the same.

By late 1983, the economy was more robust than it had been in a decade. "As deregulation takes hold, this $250 billion chunk of the American economy is experiencing a burst of competition—a spur that is encouraging innovation, increasing productivity, and reducing prices," *Business Week* reported in November 1983. "Long-distance airline fares, adjusted for inflation, have declined by almost 50 percent in the past seven years. Many trucking rates have skidded down 30 percent in real terms since 1980." An economist from the right-wing think tank the Brookings Institution crowed: "The net of deregulation is that we're much better off."

Reagan had little to worry about during the 1984 election. By the time of the Republican Party's convention in Dallas in August of that year, the results were in no serious doubt. "In sum, the president has precipitated a recovery that promises growth and prosperity," Michael Kramer had written in *New York*—a full year before the 1984 election. Even people who opposed every single item in Reagan's agenda found the man irresistible. As *New York Times* columnist James Reston put it, "He has a tendency to say the most hard-hearted things in the most lighthearted way."

BRUCE SPRINGSTEEN SAID THE MOST HARD-HEARTED THINGS IN THE MOST lighthearted ways. Prior to 1984, his biggest hit was a jolly-sounding tune about a man who abandons his family just because he feels like it. Springsteen had cut "Hungry Heart" early in 1979, over the torturously endless sessions for *The River*. As the studio fees hit seven figures, CBS Records president Walter Yetnikoff flew out to Los Angeles to have a little talk. "I said, 'Bruce, do you know who's paying for this record? It's not me. It's you. It's an advance against royalties—it's your money that you're spending,'" Yetnikoff told *Rolling Stone*. "His response was, 'How would you suggest I spend my money better than on my art?' You know what the answer to that is? Nothing."

Springsteen outworked nearly everyone in rock, to a frightening degree. A typical show lasted three hours. *The River* ate up an entire year in the studio and came out a double LP. When in doubt, just write and record dozens more songs, the Bruce Springsteen way.

With *The River* and "Hungry Heart" hits, he outdid himself by booking 140 shows behind them, starting in October 1980. When the tour ended and he came home in the middle of 1981, he realized, to his existential horror, that he had *absolutely nothing else in his life* than his music. It sent him into a tailspin, which went palpably into his next group of songs.

"That whole *Nebraska* album was just that isolation thing, and what it does to you," Springsteen said of his 1982 album. "The record was just basically about people being isolated from their jobs, from their friends, from their families, their mothers, just not feeling connected to anything that's going on. Your government. And when that happens, there's just a whole breakdown. When you lose that sense of community, there's some spiritual breakdown [that] occurs."

Nebraska wasn't merely an everyman portrait, the way the two albums before it had been—it had the aura, and backstory, of a found object, like a haunted-sounding blues record by performers nobody ever heard from again. He'd made a demo on a four-track recorder in his New Jersey bedroom—guitar, vocals, a little synthesizer—and the cassette endured every manner of stereotypical single-guy mishandling. When the E Street Band cut electric versions of these demos, something seemed missing. The tape had an irreducible purity that overrode its imperfections. The tape's mud had given it a resonance as well as an uncommon sense of intimacy. It made the jarring moments (cf. the screeches of "State Trooper") downright scary.

Nebraska went out as is. Wisely, Bruce decided not to tour behind it. Columbia took out ads echoing their mid-sixties "Nobody Sings Dylan Like Dylan" campaign, declaring: "Nobody But Springsteen Can Tell Stories Like These." Because, you could fill in for yourself, anybody else who tried to would have been dropped from the label *like that*.

Born in the U.S.A. didn't take a year to make, the way *The River* had. It took two—and when Springsteen refused to stop working, everyone else had to *keep* working. "One of the things that happens when you work for Bruce, you go down—as if in a submarine—for a period of time, and when you resurface, you realize that you've let the rest of your life go to seed," recording engineer Chuck Plotkin said. "Whenever I've finished working on a project, it takes six to eight weeks to regain my bearing. My tax returns are always late. I'm scrambling around trying to pay my bills."

This album was the "electric *Nebraska*," only with a lot more bounce. These songs were *poppy*, even more so than those on *The River*, and ready for large crowds to shout along with. The funniest was also the best—"Glory Days," a sardonic side-eye at nostalgia.

Springsteen first used synthesizers on *The River*'s "Drive All Night," but *Born in the U.S.A.* is where they began nudging into the arrangements regularly. "I think it originally started when I wanted to get a merry-go-round organ sound, like a roller rink," he told *Creem*. "That's the sound of 'Glory Days' and 'Working on the Highway.' It's that roller-skating sound. . . . When I did 'Born in the U.S.A.' we did it off the cuff, never taught it to the band. We went in and I said, 'Roy [Bittan], get this riff.' And he just pulled it out on the synthesizer. We played it two times and the second take is on the record."

The lyric was a Vietnam veteran's dead-end cry of anger, keynoting the desperation lying beneath the good times of Springsteen's characters. With his nods to big-picture American artists from John Steinbeck to Elvis Presley, Flannery O'Connor to James Brown, Springsteen was the conscious product of a shared cultural past. So was Ronald Reagan, but whereas the president offered a comforting vision of a past that never really existed, Springsteen probed rather than placated. But that was easy enough to lose sight of while the audience sang along: "BORN! In the U.S.A.!"

To casual listeners, that boot-stomping chorus might as well have been the same as its contemporaneous country cousin, Lee Greenwood's "God Bless the U.S.A." This was hardly the case: "It was a protest song," Springsteen wrote. He added: "The combination of its 'down' blues verses and its 'up' declarative choruses, its demand for the right of a 'critical' patriotic voice along with pride of birth, was too seemingly conflicting (or just a bother!) for some of its more carefree, less discerning listeners."

SPRINGSTEEN HAD FELT THE WAR CLOSE TO HOME—BART HAINES, THE drummer from his first band, was killed in action. "He left and he didn't come back," Springsteen said. "And the guys that did come back were not the same." Bruce himself had gotten a 4-F because of a motorcycle injury. "I remember being on that bus, me and a couple of guys in my band, and the rest of the bus was probably 60, 70 percent black guys from Asbury Park," he said. "And I remember thinking, like, what makes my life, or my friends' lives, more expendable than that of somebody who's going to school? It didn't seem right."

Born in 1949, Springsteen grew up in suburban Freehold, New Jersey, an Irish-Italian Catholic who spent most of his nights with his grandparents on his dad's side. His mother was a legal secretary, his father a stoic workingman. Springsteen would later write that his stage persona was his way of emulating his old man. The young Springsteen was picked on constantly in his hometown: when he crashed his motorcycle as a teenager, a local hospital had refused to treat him because of his long hair.

Many rock stars—many artists—react to such straitened surroundings by rejecting the trappings of their upbringings entirely. Springsteen did the opposite—he wanted in to the stability that surrounded him. "One of the things that was always on my mind to do was to maintain connections with the people I'd grown up with, and the sense of the community where I came from," he said. "That's why I stayed in New Jersey. . . . If the price of fame is that you have to be isolated from the people you write for, then that's too fuckin' high a price to pay."

He saw music the same way. "The subversiveness of the Top 40 radio can't be overestimated," he said. "I grew up on music that was popular; I sat in my bedroom and wrote the Top 20 down religiously every Wednesday night, cheering for my heroes and hissing the villains of the day. So I wanted to play in that arena."

After being hounded out of college, Springsteen briefly became a guitarist-for-hire on the Jersey Shore before starting his own band, Steel Mill, in 1969. After a brief sojourn to California—where his parents had moved—the group dissolved. After cycling through a succession of groups, he decided to work solo in 1972, and through his manager Mike Appel got an audition with CBS Records' John Hammond that May.

The first two albums Springsteen made for Columbia, *Greetings from Asbury Park, N.J.* and *The Wild, the Innocent & the E Street Shuffle* (both 1973), were word-drunk, carnivalesque depictions of Jersey Shore life. Springsteen paid clear debts to his rock and roll heroes—Dylan, the Rolling Stones, James Brown, Phil Spector, Roy Orbison—but wasn't a copycat. Both received good press; neither sold worth a damn.

What kept Springsteen going, in career terms, were his concerts. The group he'd put together, officially dubbed the E Street Band in late 1974, barnstormed small venues all along the East Coast, and his unbridled enthusiasm, his habit of stalking the entire stage and punctuating songs with lengthy, homey, funny banter and band intros, and the broad range of the music brought bigger crowds every time. His mission, he would explain, was "to get as close as possible to the audience. I'm not only in the show; I'm at the show."

One big fan was Jon Landau, *Rolling Stone*'s first reviews editor, then writing a column for Boston's *Real Paper*, an alternative newsweekly. Landau's favorable review was taped to the box office window at the club Charlie's Place the day Springsteen appeared. When the critic saw Bruce standing outside reading it, he introduced himself, and the two hit it off instantly. "When I was growing up we used to joke around and say, my school was like, 'What are you, some kind of smart guy?' And his school was like, 'What are you, some kind of dumb [BEEP]?'" he told a radio interviewer about Landau.

A few months later, after Springsteen played the larger Harvard Square Theater, opening for Bonnie Raitt, Landau wrote, "I have seen rock and roll future, and its name is Bruce Springsteen," a quote Springsteen's label seized upon. "I think what he was actually saying was that the music we were playing, me and the band, was a compilation of a lot of things," Springsteen said later. "Not just past influences but future. I think that was the intention of the line, but I guess somebody in the [Columbia Records] ad department was like, 'This is it!'"

A year later, Springsteen released his third album, *Born to Run*, an eight-song tapestry he'd finished after recruiting Landau as a coproducer; the critic wound up replacing Appel as Springsteen's manager as well. It went platinum—the first two hadn't come close—and Springsteen appeared on the covers of *Time* and *Newsweek* at the same time. "What frightened me about it was I started to get as much say and control of my life as I could, and that's what I felt slipping away," he said. "Something that makes money, all the sudden it's a different ballgame. You better get wise to it, or else you're going to get stomped on."

Billboard predicted that *Born in the U.S.A.* would have "a summer-long monopoly of the top spot" on the album chart. Then *Purple Rain* came along and dashed that dream, and "When Doves Cry" did the same with Springsteen's lead single, "Dancing in the Dark," which held at number two for four of the five weeks "Doves" topped the chart. Nevertheless, "Dark" made Bruce, at last, a pop star.

As with "Hungry Heart," "Dancing in the Dark" encased a fairly grim lyric in a candy-chewy tune. Its explicit subject was existential despair: "I'm just tired and bored with myself." It was the post-*River* crash turned into a pop anthem, with a celebratory-sounding chorus. What it celebrates is finally leaving the house. But the track's hook was the insinuating line played by Roy Bittan on the Yamaha CS-80 synthesizer.

"Jon [Landau] had been bothering me to write a single, which is something he rarely does," he explained in 1985. "But he did that day. And he wanted something direct. That seemed to be what he was hitting on me for at the time. I was angry. I had written a lot of songs and was kind of fed up with the whole thing. . . . So I picked up the guitar and I had this line: 'I get up in the morning and I ain't got nothing to say.' I had that line for quite a while. Then I said, well, I've got to be direct, this is about me. What do I do? 'I get up in the evening.' And that was it. The rest of the song popped out. I realized I'm bored, I'm tired, I'm sick of no action."

He wasn't the only one. Springsteen's close friend and longtime guitarist Steve Van Zandt was a key voice in Springsteen's inner circle, coproducing the albums along with Springsteen, Landau, and Plotkin. Van Zandt also spent much of the seventies as guitarist and primary songwriter for fellow Jersey Shore fa-vorites Southside Johnny and the Asbury Jukes and was leading his own band, Little Steven and the Disciples of Soul. Their debut, *Voice of America*, appeared one month prior to *Born in the U.S.A.*'s June release. ("When he's not bellowing, he's plodding," Robert Christgau wrote.) Shortly before the first Springsteen road show in three years touched ground in St. Paul, Minnesota, Van Zandt left the band under amicable terms; he'd reappear occasionally on the tour and appeared in a couple of the *U.S.A.* videos.

His replacement was Nils Lofgren, a DC-bred singer-songwriter with a sly, fluid guitar style. He'd just lost his recording contract, like Van Morrison and Bonnie Raitt recently had, and Bruce gave him an audition. "I got the job about four weeks from opening night, so there was no way I was going to assimilate the entire catalog in a month," Lofgren said. "I just did the best I could. There was a room in Bruce's home I moved into, and I just really banned all other music."

There was another newcomer as well—a backing singer named Patti Scialfa, who'd worked with a number of bands in New Jersey and New York and had known Springsteen for years. (She'd eventually marry him.) She'd had three days to prepare because Lofgren came down with laryngitis and couldn't sing. "As the first woman in the band, she sent shock waves through the troops, broke the boys' club, and everybody had to adjust, some more than others," Springsteen wrote. "The E Street Band carried its own muted misogyny (in-cluding my own), a very prevalent quality amongst rock groups of our genera-tion." This would be Springsteen's biggest tour by far: 156 shows, including his first time in arenas—the kind of places Springsteen had, a decade earlier, sworn never to play.

EVEN IN A PLACE GRIPPED BY *PURPLE RAIN* FEVER, THE TWIN CITIES WERE keyed up for the Springsteen tour opener in St. Paul on June 28. The show's security coordinator got excited after watching an afternoon rehearsal. "He's been running up and down the aisles, and I mean every aisle," he said. "The only other performer I know who does that is Neil Diamond."

The security head had another task that day—wrangling extras for the pre-concert shooting of a video for "Dancing in the Dark." "I cherry-picked about fifty people at a recent Rush concert . . . the sober ones," he said.

About two hundred showed up that afternoon, waiting on line for ninety minutes. The director was Brian De Palma, who largely made stylish suspense films, but no blood was shed in this clip: Bruce lip-synched to the song, then pulled up a young actress named Courteney Cox to dance with him. "He's abandoned, but she's self-conscious and mechanical," local newsweekly *City Pages* reported. "Springsteen seems frustrated by her lack of enthusiasm. Through the afternoon and into the evening, her dancing fails to improve."

The show itself was a glorified rehearsal: Lofgren messed up his first solo. They performed "Dancing in the Dark" twice during the show itself to ensure De Palma got everything he needed. The show quickly improved even if the outfits didn't. By the time they reached Pittsburgh for two nights in late September, the shows were long even by Springsteen standards—frequently as long as four hours.

These elongated evenings were part and parcel of Bruce's new look. He'd become a gym rat: "I was a big fan of meaningless, repetitive behavior," he told biographer Peter Ames Carlin. "And what's more meaningless than lifting a heavy object and then putting it down in the same place that you found it?" The cover shot of *Born in the U.S.A.* was another, um, turnaround. "We took a lot of different types of pictures, and in the end, the picture of my *ass* looked better than the picture of my *face*, so that's what went on the cover," he said.

Increasingly, AOR and CHR stations alike were competing for the Springsteen fan's ear. In LA that November, the Top 40 KIIS-FM, the city's biggest station, had "ruffled a few feathers the morning following the opening performance," when DJ Rick Dees told his audience "that Springsteen was still playing at the arena ('We heard he played long shows, but this is incredible') at 6:30 a.m. Dees conducted interviews with a KIIS reporter still at the scene, calling from a phone booth, crowd noise ever-present in the background. The Los Angeles Sports Arena reported over three hundred Springsteen fans trying to gain admittance that morning," reported *Cash Box*.

His drawing power even approached the Jacksons'. Bruce was selling out arenas on multiple nights—five in Philadelphia, seven in Los Angeles, ten at home in New Jersey's Meadowlands. New fans attracted to the new image were beginning to crowd in on the long-timers. Meatheads mistaking him for Meat Loaf was bad enough. But a gym bod? *Twelve-inch remixes? Bruce?*

"I would have regretted terribly if I felt like I had that opportunity and hadn't made the most of it," he later said. "It's not something I would particularly want to relive in the way that I did at that time, it's not something I would choose, but it was a laugh, it was at the right time for me—it was before I had my kids. I had a lot of experience and I was prepared for the things that happened." Well, maybe not one thing.

THOUGH HE UTILIZED THE AMERICAN FLAG AS A COVER AND STAGE BACKdrop during an election year, Springsteen had long kept his politics close to his newly expanded chest. "I'm registered, yeah," he told *Rolling Stone*. "I'm not registered as one party or another. I don't generally think along those lines. I find it very difficult to relate to the whole electoral system as it stands."

Indeed, he could send mixed signals. Springsteen played benefits like 1979's No Nukes, his songs were full of explicit social commentary, his entire act a tribute to the workingman and -woman. And some Vietnam veterans he'd met had inspired the title song of his new album. One of them, the peace activist Bobby Mueller, had been the first person Bruce played "Born in the U.S.A." for. "That was something," he said.

But songs like "The Promised Land," with their explicit adherence to old-fashioned values in the face of a changing world, were, however nuanced in the writing and despite Springsteen's affinities and alliances, easy to take as face-value conservatism.

In August of 1984, the *National Review* published a short editorial on, of all things, the current state of rock—the un-bylined writer cited high numbers for Reagan among those under thirty as evidence that "their music—rock, rap, and pop—has finally caught up with their conservative politics." The proof, among other examples, was Bruce Springsteen's "cowboy libertarianism," as heard on *Nebraska* (!) and *Born in the U.S.A.*

A month later, George F. Will, the nationally syndicated conservative columnist, saw Springsteen's show at the Capital Centre in a suburb of Washington, DC. Drummer Max Weinberg, who enjoyed watching Will and Sam Donaldson debate on television, had invited both, but only Will came. He left halfway through, but nevertheless wrote approvingly: "If all Americans—in labor and management—who make steel or cars or shoes or textiles made their products with as much energy and confidence as Springsteen and his merry band make music, there would be no need for Congress to be thinking about protectionism." "In other words," Springsteen biographer Dave Marsh retorted, "if you find slapping bumpers onto compact cars less fulfilling than singing rock and roll songs in front of adoring masses, fuck off."

Within hours, the White House requested Bruce's presence at Reagan's rally in Hammonton, New Jersey, scheduled a week later. Springsteen declined. On September 19, Reagan's speechwriters decided to invoke him anyway. At the Hammonton stop, Reagan stated: "All that we've done and all that we mean to do is to make this country freer still. America's future rests in a thousand dreams inside your hearts; it rests in the message of hope in songs of a man so many young Americans admire: New Jersey's own Bruce Springsteen. And helping you make those dreams come true is what this job of mine is all about."

Springsteen was furious. "It was part of a shopping list of things that needed to be done for the six o'clock news," he later said. "And I didn't want to be part of the shopping list, y'know? . . . Republicans at that time co-opted anything that was American. And my music had been American music. But I thought his policies were destructive. They contributed to the disparity in wealth that continues to this day. And it made me angry and made me think a lot harder about what I was doing and communicating." In his memoir, Springsteen pilloried "a Republican Party intent on co-opting a cow's ass if it has the Stars and Stripes tattooed on it."

On the way to Pittsburgh, Springsteen and Landau decided the time had come to say something. Pittsburgh was one of the cities hit hardest by Reagan's trickle-down economics. Twenty minutes into the show, Springsteen started talking.

"The President was mentioning my name the other day, and I kind of got to wondering what his favorite album must've been," he said. "I don't think it was the *Nebraska* album. I don't think he's been listening to this one," before launching into a ferocious acoustic version of "Johnny 99": "Ralph went out looking for a job but couldn't find none / He came home too drunk from mixing Tanqueray and wine / He got a gun, shot a night clerk / Now they call him Johnny 99." Nevertheless, the show review in the local *Post-Gazette* made no mention of the jab at the Reagan campaign.

Less than a week later, the same thing happened with the Democratic candidate, Walter Mondale. On October 1, in New Brunswick, Mondale declared, "Bruce may have been born to run, but he wasn't born yesterday." Fine. Then he quoted what Springsteen said onstage in Pittsburgh: "There's something really dangerous happening to us out here. We're slowly getting split into two Americas. Things are getting taken away from people who need them and being given to people who don't need them. And there's a promise being broken . . . that everyone was going to have an opportunity and the chance to live a life with some decency and some dignity and a chance for some self-respect." Mondale claimed Springsteen had written a letter containing that statement to himself: "That's the real Bruce Springsteen and he's for the Mondale–Ferraro ticket." Once again, the Springsteen camp had to clarify that Bruce was not endorsing any presidential candidate.

In September, the Hollywood Bowl hosted the first World Music Festival. The headliners included reggae giant Peter Tosh and the Trinidadian calypso king Mighty Sparrow. But the most hotly anticipated performer on the bill was the Nigerian bandleader, saxophonist, singer, and agitator Fela Kuti and his sixteen-piece band, the Egypt 80.

When he went to the Lagos airport, Fela claimed that he'd been asked for a "tip" (a bribe) by a customs agent and couldn't pay it because he'd brought British currency instead; he also said he'd declared the currency leaving the country, but the customs agent—the same one—suddenly couldn't locate the paperwork. Fela was arrested for currency violations, imprisoned for two days, and had his passport revoked. (The Egypt 80 was already in America, and Fela's son Femi played the band's scheduled US dates.)

After release, Fela gave a press conference, where, within minutes, *Melody Maker* reported, "the national security police broke up the meeting and arrested him." This time he was sentenced to five years. Reporter Randall Grass called the trial "Kafkaesque." Shortly thereafter, Fela was dropped from his label, EMI Records. Unbowed, in a prison interview with a French journalist, he said of Nigerian officials, "They know that my going to America would have exposed them more. They know my political views will destroy the image of this country."

Fela had been arrested numerous times. The Kalakuta Republic, as he'd renamed the two-story house in Lagos where his one-hundred-person entourage lived, was the site of violent police break-ins numerous times from the midseventies. Fela flaunted his polyamorous lifestyle (in 1978, he'd wed twenty-seven women, eventually divorcing them) and the bales of weed he was smoking, and he furthermore declared the Kalakuta Republic a sovereign nation, impervious to Nigerian law. Then he mocked the authorities on albums like *Expensive Shit* (1975—Fela swallowed a joint in front of the police, then, in prison, presented the authorities with someone else's feces for testing) and *Zombie* (1976—about policemen blindly taking orders, which started a "dance craze" in the process).

The most hideous arrest occurred in February 1977, when one thousand soldiers laid waste to the Kalakuta Republic—bombarding it with mortar shells, and beating, torturing, and raping everyone they could. Fela's mother, seventy-eight years old, was thrown out of a second-story window; she died in April 1978. In 1979, Fela brought a replica of his mother's coffin to the home of the head of the military junta, Olusegun Obasanjo, the topic of his 1981 album, *Coffin for Head of State*. Late that year, Fela was severely beaten and left for dead by the military.

The airport arrest in September of 1984 stopped Fela short of a hoped-for US breakthrough. That year, Capitol Records issued three Fela titles for the first time in the States, instantly doubling his discography here. Fela was to bring the tapes of a session he'd recorded in London with Dennis Bovell, the reggae producer, to New York for Bill Laswell, the coproducer of "Rockit," to remix.

"That should be put in your contract in future, that the artist should be in jail while you're doing the mixing," Laswell later said with a laugh. He added overdubs from drummer Sly Dunbar, keyboardist Bernie Worrell, and Senegalese hand drummer Aïyb Dieng: "It was a pretty bad recording of not so inspired music which we made an effort to make listenable." The result, *Army Arrangement*, was released in early 1985. Fela's arrest became integral to the album's marketing. The radio tip sheet *The Gavin Report* included a contact number "for more info (including Amnesty International's full report) on this fascinating dissident."

EMI RECORDS,
NEW YORK CITY
November 13, 1984

Lou Gramm, the lead singer of Foreigner, found his band's direction in 1984 "worrying." Foreigner had started off playing hard rock, but more and more, the band's founder, guitarist, and leader, Mick Jones, wanted "more ballads and less edge," Gramm complained in his memoir.

When Foreigner's bassist, Rick Wills, first heard the song Jones wanted as the first single from *Agent Provocateur*, their first LP since *4*, three years earlier, he dismissed it as "fluffy." But Jones insisted that "I Want to Know What Love Is," which featured a gospel choir, had to go first, despite Gramm pleading that they were "doing irreparable damage to our rock image."

"I certainly want to retain the rock image," Jones carefully told *Billboard* at the time. "We just put this out because the song was so strong, and because it was coming out at Christmas, and it had the right kind of mood."

For the rock press, the idea that Foreigner had a fan base seemed absurd on its face. The band epitomized "corporate rock," a term for bands whose line-ups, decisions, and direction were determined, even dictated, by managers and executives rather than the musicians, per se—and who marketed themselves via logos and iconography rather than through the performers' personalities.

This wasn't entirely fair to Foreigner: Jones, a British guitarist in New York, late of Spooky Tooth, assembled and determined the band's course. The band's members were also more apt to follow their muses—you didn't hear Journey or Asia bring Junior Walker aboard for some honking R&B sax on a sixties-soul pastiche like "Urgent," Foreigner's 1981 hit.

Nevertheless, Jones admitted, "I enjoy the anonymity." Indeed, everyone who wrote about Mick Jones from Foreigner took pains to point out that he wasn't the Mick Jones from the Clash. The latter may have been better known, but the former sold far more records. "I think we actually have an identity, which is being built slowly," Jones said. "It's not a flashy image that we have, but I like to think we're a group that people tend to take seriously."

But a number one hit had eluded them. "We've had number one albums, and we had number two singles," Jones said. Most frustrating had been "Waiting for a Girl Like You"—the "Dancing in the Dark" of 1981, stuck for ten tedious weeks at number two as Olivia Newton-John's "Physical" rode the new fitness craze to the top for the same stretch.

Foreigner spent a quarter of a year working with Trevor Horn only to scrap everything—Horn wanted to do "something nobody would expect me to do"; the band wanted someone who was keeping his eye on them, not on Frankie Goes to Hollywood. In came Alex Sadkin, who'd just produced the Thompson Twins' *Into the Gap*. The Thompsons had begun as avant-funk postpunkers, and much the way Horn had done with ABC, Sadkin steered them assuredly into the middle of the road. Released in February 1984, *Gap* would spin off a trio of UK hits, with "Hold Me Now" a US number three; the album went platinum in America. Tom Bailey, the Thompsons' lead singer, came along as well, providing a four-note synthesizer tag for "I Want to Know What Love Is."

When Jones told his fiancée the song's title, she snapped, "What do you mean you want to know what love is? We're about to get married." He's long disavowed the "power ballad" tag for both "Waiting" and "I Want to Know," calling them "tender and peaceful and minimalist for me." Indeed, "I Want to Know What Love Is" doesn't even have a guitar solo.

What makes it work is Gramm—whatever his reservations about the song, he sings as if for his life. On the second pre-chorus, there is a three-note "In my life" that he hammers downward the same way on each word; this isn't celebratory but a desperate lunge. Decades after it first appeared, it can be easy to take "I Want to Know What Love Is" for granted, to dismiss it as kitsch. But this record shocked people, and that moment is why.

The coda put it over the top: led by Jennifer Holliday, who'd starred in the Broadway hit *Dreamgirls* (she'd charted in 1982 with the musical's "And I Am

Telling You I'm Not Going"), the New Jersey Mass Choir enters. Foreigner had, after all, written a hymn. Black soul or gospel backing vocalists on white rock songs had become a rancid cliché by the mid-eighties, but this one flew. With thirty seconds left to play, Holliday steps out with a quick, pithy, "Only love is real" and brings the record to earth.

"I Want to Know What Love Is" was added to a record number of stations during its first week—two more than "State of Shock" had been. It debuted at number forty-five on *Billboard*'s Hot 100—very high for the era—and shot to number one in February, after only eight weeks, escorting "Like a Virgin" from the top. It even briefly charted R&B (eighty-five). *Agent Provocateur* sold three million copies and additionally yielded another top twenty hit with the rocker "That Was Yesterday."

"I Want to Know What Love Is" essentially led to the band's dissolution. In addition to directional disagreements, there was an authorship dispute—Gramm claimed he'd written about 40 percent of the song, while Jones countered that the singer had only 5 percent ("I'm being generous," he snapped). Gramm was gone by the end of the decade.

Foreigner may not have been as "corporate rock" as other bands, but it never hurts to please the boss. As *Agent Provocateur* was nearing completion, Ahmet Ertegun stopped by the studio to hear the rough mixes. Jones played "I Want to Know What Love Is" last. "Halfway through the song," Jones told David Fricke, "I looked over and there was a tear rolling down Ahmet's cheek. At that point I thought, 'Wow, I've done it, I've finally gotten through to him, to that heart inside there,' and I started crying. We were looking at each other, with tears streaming, and in that moment I felt, 'Oh my God—the thing I wanted to do, all through this association with him, has been to have some sort of reward like that.'"

"STADIUM ROCK IS A PHENOMENON THAT BELONGS ALMOST EXCLUSIVELY to the youth of America," one critic wrote in 1981. "The music is more than loud, it is earth shattering. The credo is have a good time, get drunk, get stoned, forget school and your parents. Stadium rock is a violent romance, and only the strong survive."

But power ballads belonged to *everyone*, not least the aging boomer demographic that still held tightly to rock, and to rock radio. Lighter-waving jams had gotten hard rock bands on pop radio since Aerosmith released "Dream

On" in 1973. Through the late seventies they'd helped push some of the hard-touring hard rockers into the pop mainstream—Styx with "Babe," Kiss with "Beth." And they were manna for bands moving from the album-focused seventies to the singles-oriented eighties. Take San Francisco's Journey, the ultimate corporate rock band.

Following the 1971 breakup of Santana's original lineup, that band's former road manager Walter "Herbie" Herbert reunited guitarist Neil Schon and keyboardist Gregg Rolie for something called the Golden Gate Rhythm Section. "I wanted to have a really high-end, together, state-of-the-art version of the Grateful Dead," Herbert said in 2001. (The band's cover illustrations, by Stanley Mouse, the Dead's longtime poster artist, made the link explicit.)

Following a name change to Journey, the band debuted on Columbia in 1975, playing flashy instrumental rock fusion. After a couple of years, as founding drummer Aynsley Dunbar put it, "We were told, 'Get a singer and some hit songs or you're off the label.'"

Late in 1977, Steve Perry joined the band. His vocal tone had the consistency of Miracle Whip, a match for his artistic sensibility. The first single he wrote with the band, "Lights," could have been a Madison Avenue commission; it would eventually become a staple of San Francisco Giants ball games. Journey was soon cutting TV ads for Budweiser—"It's the king of *beeaaaahs*," Perry wailed—and Nestlé candy bars. Schon insisted there was "nothing wrong with being commercial. It's just another way of getting a wider audience."

"Lights" only got to number sixty-eight, but the first Journey album with Perry, *Infinity* (1978), stayed on the chart for two years. The world's most brilliant semiotics major would throw her hands up at "Lovin', Touchin', Squeezin'," Journey's first real hit (number sixteen in 1979). Others threw up more than their hands. "I regret to announce the final appearance of the Journey Award for the worst album by a California band," Greil Marcus wrote. "Having released two LPs in 1981—*Captured* and *Escape*—Journey accomplished the astonishing feat of tying itself for the prize, which has therefore been retired for reasons of gross redundancy."

In 1982, the band signed off on *Journey Escape*, "the world's first rock and roll video game," which even featured a "cigar-chomping manager" modeled on Herbie Herbert. They kept pace sonically, too. The 1983 single "Separate Ways," from *Frontiers*, one radio exec told *Billboard*, had a "predominance of synthesizers, [which] is definitely new for them. That sort of directional change I like to see."

The *Frontiers* tour wore Perry, in particular, out. He'd been dealing with an ailing mother and a broken relationship and was ready to move on from the band. When the tour finished, he headed downstate to Los Angeles and, within a month, had written his first solo album. Released in June 1984, *Street Talk* featured a lighter touch than Journey's work—in particular, the single "Oh Sherrie," featured a genuinely funny MTV clip in which "Steve," the singer, walks off a silly pseudomedieval video set in order to just straightforwardly emote his love song to his girlfriend (Sherrie Swafford, who plays "herself"). Both the video and the song had a simple charm missing from the bulk of the Journey oeuvre.

A POWER BALLAD COULD CHANGE A BAND'S FORTUNES. NIGHT RANGER were San Francisco hard rockers who in 1984 rolled out their second LP, *Midnight Madness*, with "(You Can Still) Rock in America," complete with a pseudo–Van Halen finger-tapping solo and a giant US flag hung as a stage backdrop. The resemblance of the band's name to that of the David Hasselhoff kids' TV show *Knight Rider* led *Creem*'s correspondent to open a Night Ranger profile thus: "Let's get this straight. This article is NOT about a talking car."

But if you could still rock in America and miss the top fifty, as that song did, you could also turn around and power-ballad in America and reach number four, as Night Ranger did with the follow-up, that font of bitchin' bombast, "Sister Christian." The chorus's "motorin'! [*pause*] [*riff*]" moment almost didn't need the cinematic boost it received from *Boogie Nights* (1999), which featured it in its most memorable scene—it became a high-eighties totem the moment it was released.

The band filmed the video, with little prep time, at San Rafael High School. Shots of nuns roller-skating around the school turned viewers' heads. "Later, we got all these calls about it," drummer Kelly Keagy said—he'd written the song about his own sister, Christy (guitarist Jack Blades misheard him, leading to the title being changed to "Christian"). "One woman in Wisconsin said, 'Is this a song about nuns selling dope to school kids?' We said, 'Uh, sure.'"

A power ballad could *really* help older acts. Chicago stopped having hits in the late seventies and was dropped by Columbia in 1981. After changing management to Irving Azoff, they signed to the Azoff-helmed Warner Bros. subsidiary Full Moon and began working on *Chicago 16*. To help get them up to speed on the new era, the band worked with David Foster, who'd become a major player in 1979, after cowriting and playing keyboards on Earth, Wind & Fire's *I Am*, in particular the hit "After the Love Is Gone," a recording so vaporous that it sounded airbrushed. It won the Grammy for Best R&B Song.

Foster had his hands full—Chicago was bickering. Peter Cetera, who'd sung many of the band's hit ballads, was unhappy about staying in the group; two other players were deeply in thrall to cocaine. They soon got clean, but the whole band was straightened out by their new producer and new era. First came an edict from the top at Warner Bros.: *No more horns. Radio doesn't play them anymore.* "The feedback confused me," drummer Danny Seraphine wrote. "After all, we were a horn band!"

Foster was a kind of Dr. Phil of record making, the harbinger of another sort of doctor that would become ubiquitous across pop during the eighties— the song doctor, who would come in and touch up a band's desultory demo by pumping it full of commercial appeal, as if the latter were collagen. The name most often identified with this professional task was Desmond Child, who in 1984 was cowriting "Heaven's on Fire" for Kiss, perhaps, and not unusually, the most baldly formulaic song mentioned in this book.

The making of Chicago's *17* would be just as fraught as *16* had been— Foster made Seraphine play to a click track, and even tried replacing his work with Toto's Jeff Porcaro's. After threatening to break Foster's legs with a baseball bat, the drummer eventually learned to program the drum machines himself.

Released in May 1984, *Chicago 17*, another Cetera–Foster album in disguise, went six times platinum. After a flashy "rock" plod called "Stay the Night" stalled in the top twenty, did Chicago ever have a power ballad at the ready: "Hard Habit to Break" featured the kind of soaring chorus Cetera could sell a flamethrower in an icehouse with. What's more, the lyrics were timely. "I'm addicted to you!" Cetera and second vocalist Bill Champlin growled and mewled, the language of the twelve-step program retrofitted for A/C. Cetera went solo in 1985. Chicago found a replacement, like any good corporation.

CORPORATE ROCK EPITOMIZED WHAT ONE COLUMBIA RECORDS EXECUTIVE called the new "Madison Avenue approach to rock and roll." *Time*'s Jay Cocks summed up the critical view of this stuff: "It's no accident that these bland, faceless groups with no defined image, no personality, no boldness have the largest-selling albums. They're the easiest to sell."

In 1984, the RIAA estimated that rock, the general category, was responsible for one-third of all recordings sold that year. But the sixties and seventies artists who'd spearheaded rock's sales boom didn't move the same numbers as they once had. Many had signed contracts far more lucrative than their sales warranted.

John Sippel, a *Billboard* staffer and the former head of Mercury Records, told *Musician*: "A big star'll average two to three million per album; Geffen has to sell three-quarters of a million of Donna Summer's new record before they break even. Hell, CBS still hasn't broken even on the big Paul McCartney deal they signed a few years back. The companies just went out and gave the whole store away—literally. A&M gave George Harrison *ten percent of the whole company* back in '74, but they were smart enough to get out of that deal after only one album."

IF SEVENTIES-STYLE AOR HAD BEEN LEFT FOR DEAD AT THE BEGINNING OF 1983, by the fall of 1984 it was looking bullish again. That summer, Los Angeles's KLOS-FM, the city's top AOR, bumped from a 3.3 share up to a 3.9. A PD from Philadelphia noted, "You can't be an all-teen station and survive."

There were a lot of those stations. By the fall of 1984 there were four CHRs in New York. "Two of them didn't last very long," says Larry Berger with a laugh. WKTU had gone CHR, as had WAPP. "It was unsustainable. Those two were late to the game and didn't do it that well. I don't even remember what they sounded like."

The "stampede toward Top 40," as *Billboard* put it, was overwhelming the market. "Within five songs," a Houston programmer cautioned, "we're all in the same ballgame. You have to carefully know where you're going." And since many rock acts were crossing over to pop, A/C, and others, the differentiation between them began to blur. "One week in L.A., nine different stations were giving away Billy Joel concert tickets," said one radio exec. "That's just embarrassing."

But crossover was working for a lot of acts that might have, only a couple of years earlier, been relegated strictly to AOR. The former Babys front man John Waite scored his first and only number one hit on September 22, with "Missing You." Waite was opening for Missing Persons when "Missing You" (some consonance) hit the top. "The only silly moments were Waite's insistence on kneeling to perform his ballads, and the rock and roll cliché of stripping down to a muscle tee," *Billboard* noted of the Los Angeles show. "The only muscular thing about Waite is his larynx."

"I think you have to be excellent to get to number one," Waite said. "I think there's never been a bad song that's got to number one. You can't buy it." Oh, but you could! The major labels did heavy hiring of a handful of nationally based independent promoters, or "indies." About a dozen of them were known, informally, as the Network.

"Hiring the Network guys cost labels a bundle," Warner Bros. executive Stan Cornyn wrote. "Then two bundles. Then ten. . . . The Network worked. Payola was part of it. Program directors, some of them, got rewarded in cash, sometimes through pseudonym-registered post-office boxes. Whatever it took. Monthly birthday cards, whatever. Costs of Network services to record labels ran from CBS (the most thankful, spending over $10 million a year on Network consultants), down next to MCA, on down to the WCI labels (no purists we, at about $5 million a year). . . . The budget line item designated 'radio promotion' grew like a goiter, and just as visibly."

In the early eighties, the majors had attempted to stop using the indies; the effort lasted less than a year. Then, in September of 1984, a US House oversight and investigations subcommittee that had been convened to investigate independent promotion "found no evidence of payola," *Billboard* reported. The committee concluded: "We recommend no further action at this time in the absence of evidence of improper activity." It did, however, warn against "paper adds"—"the ethical limbo of stations' practice of falsely claiming to have added records to their playlists."

ONE ROCK RADIO DJ WAS EVEN LESS CONCERNED WITH PLAYLISTS THAN that. In January 1984, Randy Bongarten took over management of WNBC-FM in New York, and he made the fateful decision to tell the station's most popular new DJ, "Okay, do your act. Just be yourself."

Howard Stern was still playing records more than talking—but by spring, he was playing only four songs per hour and spending the rest of his airtime on the mike. "Yesterday on NBC Radio I played Led Zeppelin records because I'd decided I was going to play my own music for a day," Stern told *Cash Box* in March. "It was fabulous! We played all sixties stuff: Hendrix, the Who, Stones. That's what we wanted to do. Now, a lot of paranoid GMs would start worrying about, 'Oh my God, it's a Thursday, the day they mail out the diaries, etc. . . .' You don't worry about that kind of crap if you're really going to do personality radio."

Stern was so successful in 1984 that his contract was rewritten to double his salary at the beginning of 1985—only for Bongarten, now NBC Radio's president, to fire him at the end of that September. "Stern would joke about AIDS fears, Ethiopia, and Josef Mengele, and play the actual hotline message of the Ku Klux Klan," went a *New York* magazine profile. "The real mystery about Howard Stern, then, is not why he was fired but how he lasted at WNBC for as long as he did."

In addition to setting the tone for deliberately offensive drive-time hosts across the United States, Stern's March stunt also portended rock radio's next big shift. A number of individual stations were calling themselves "classic rock" by 1984, but much like "world music," the term wouldn't solidify fully into bizspeak for a couple more years. In the spring of 1985, the first issue of *Spin* magazine featured a full-page ad for Fort Lauderdale/Miami AOR WSHE featuring a hippie looking into the mirror and seeing a yuppie staring back under a headline, "You're never too old to rock and roll"; it would be reused for AOR ad campaigns around the country.

Fred Jacobs had begun working on the Classic Rock format in 1983. At first, he wrote, "I targeted 'dog FM stations'—total losers in medium and larger markets that were well out of the top twenty." The format debuted in the spring of 1985 on a tiny Class A FM in Charlotte, Michigan. It was a runaway success, with dozens of stations adopting the format by the fall of 1986. Classic Rock gave AOR a way to extricate itself from the present tense entirely.

TRY AS HE MIGHT, ROBERT PLANT *COULD NOT GET AWAY* FROM LED ZEP-pelin. Out on tour in 1983 behind a second solo LP, he was asked how he felt when he heard Zeppelin's "Stairway to Heaven" on the radio—not only did AOR still play it more than any other track, but as *Radio & Records* noted, "Top 40 stations . . . began playing it regularly as 'image gold' (records that lend the station a bit of AOR credibility) despite its length and its lack of single release."

Plant was stymied by that sort of staying power: "I've always been proud of the song—but I can't really relate to it at all now," he said. "I would prefer to listen to 'Kashmir' . . . or 'Trampled Under Foot,' or 'Achilles' Last Stand'—things that haven't become threadbare yet."

The people who didn't want to stop hearing it landed squarely in Led Zeppelin's demographic. By 1984, Americans aged twenty-five to thirty-nine outnumbered people in their forties to mid-fifties by 55 percent. And they had money. These were the people radio wanted to advertise to.

"The Baby Boomers are riding the crest of the technological revolution," *BusinessWeek* reported. "Their ability to use computers is giving them a significant advantage over many older managers." Please note—by "ability to use computers," the magazine didn't mean that boomers used computers better than their older colleagues. It meant that boomers knew how to use computers *at all*.

IN 1970, VAN MORRISON TOLD *ROLLING STONE*: "*ASTRAL WEEKS* IS THE kind of album . . . you know, Joe Smith [vice president of Warner Bros.] called me and said, 'We know what's going down with this album now. We're going to be selling it for another six years.'"

Things changed utterly by the mid-eighties. In 1983, after his album *Inarticulate Speech of the Heart* topped out at number 116 on the Billboard 200, Warner Bros. announced it was dropping Van Morrison, along with thirty other acts, from its roster—mainly singer-songwriters with long-term contracts and diminishing sales figures. Morrison was incensed at being included on that list— he later claimed he'd already left the company voluntarily.

Another of the dropped acts was Bonnie Raitt, who was notified by letter. "I don't think they maliciously said, 'Let's let her finish her album and get the tour all lined up and print the covers and hire the people to do the video and then drop her,'" she recalled. "But that's what they did. It was literally the day after I had finished mastering it." Eventually she'd recut half of it, and Warner released it in 1986 as *Nine Lives*; and that, it appeared, was that.

THE SIXTIES ROCK STARS THAT DID MAINTAIN RECORDING CONTRACTS DID so by dint of legend, not recent sales or expectations thereof. Bob Dylan spent summer 1984 generating income by touring Europe with Santana. He was clearly ill at ease with modern recording techniques. "You could be indoors for months—it's like working in a coalmine," he complained to one interviewer, telling another: "I'm just thankful I can play on stage and people come and see me. Because I couldn't make it otherwise, I mean if I went out to play and nobody showed up that would be the end of me. I wouldn't be making records, I'll tell you that. I only make records because people see me live. As long as they're coming along to see me live I'll just make more records."

Out in the Bay Area, the Grateful Dead didn't need to make records—they drew no matter what. By 1984, their ardent fan base, the Deadheads, had more going on than the Dead itself. It was a fallow era musically but a busy one in terms of infrastructure. In 1983 the Dead established an in-house mail-order ticket office, which would grow in sales from $24,500 in the first year to $115,000 in the second. Shakedown Street, the diehards' ragtag parking-lot marketplace of bongs and trinkets and grilled-cheese sandwiches and goo balls, was also solidifying.

Maybe most important was the Dead formally dedicating a "taper's section" for their weeklong run, beginning October 27, at the Berkeley Community Theater. "If somebody can find a use for music after it's been performed, fine," Jerry Garcia reasoned. "I used to be a bluegrass music freak, and I spent a lot of time taping bands. I loved being able to do it, and I loved having the tapes afterwards and being able to trade them around. I think that's healthy stuff."

But the Dead, as ever, existed in a bubble. That summer, Garcia's friend, the filmmaker Allan Arkush, played him the just-released "When Doves Cry." But the Prince single set him off: "There's no bass," he huffed. Arkush: "An earlier Jerry would have said, 'That's cool and interesting.' This Jerry said, 'That's wrong.' The walls were going up." At a disastrous 1984 recording session, with Garcia's playing increasingly erratic, a visiting Joan Baez, then dating the Dead's drummer Mickey Hart, asked, "What's going on?" Hart's response: "You're getting a contact *low*."

The Dead hadn't made a studio album in four years at that point; one wouldn't appear for another three. Nobody in 1984 could have guessed the good ol' Grateful Dead would conquer MTV in 1987 with "Touch of Grey," a song they'd started playing live in September 1982. Garcia's cowriter had recorded it for an unissued solo album. "Hunter sang 'Touch of Grey' as a sort of dry, satirical piece with an intimate feel, but I heard something else coming through it," Garcia explained. "'We will get by' said something to me, so I set it to play big. My version still has the ironic bite of the lyrics, but what comes across is a more celebratory quality."

They played the song nineteen times in 1984, and they placed it in the set list like it was already an anthem, even without a studio recording. On Halloween during the Berkeley Community Theater run, "Touch of Grey" opened the second set, and received a rousing cheer as soon as the opening chords appeared—and another as soon as the Dead creakily harmonized on

"I *will* get by." Well before an official section was installed, Deadheads had long traded show tapes. The tapers had made it a hit.

But burnout was running deep. Bill Kreutzmann, drummer, wrote of doing coke bumps onstage, in a bottle cap handed to him by the drum tech, in front of stadiums full of people—and having to tell Garcia, "Hey, Jerry, you're on stage!" while watching the guitarist "nodding off . . . unaware of what song he was playing even as his fingers picked out all the right notes." One Christmas, Jerry and his ex-wife Mountain Girl's daughter Annabelle, after spending Christmas with her family, told her mother, "God, wouldn't it have been nice if Dad had been here?" He was there—he just hadn't left his bedroom, or the Persian heroin that had hooked him.

Garcia would be arrested for possession in January 1985. A year later, David Crosby would begin a five-year sentence following a pair of 1982 arrests, for possession of cocaine, paraphernalia, and a concealed weapon (Crosby began carrying a .45 following John Lennon's murder). He plea-bargained into rehab in New Jersey and then left the hospital within two days—a pattern he'd repeat unto tedium over the decade's middle. Crosby was out on parole within six months.

LOU REED WAS DAVID CROSBY'S OPPOSITE NUMBER IN EVERY WAY APART from his avidity for pharmaceuticals. But after a speedy seventies, Reed began the long, difficult work of extricating himself from drugs and alcohol beginning in 1979. In classic tough-guy mode, "He did this on his own," Sylvia Ramos, to whom Reed was married from 1980 to 1994, would say.

Reed's new sobriety, as well as his marriage (conventionally straight, after decades of Reed's public and unapologetic queerness), was the grist for Reed's eighties triumvirate. *The Blue Mask* (1982), *Legendary Hearts* (1983), and, in summer 1984, *New Sensations*, featured the core band of guitarist Robert Quine, bassist Fernando Saunders, and drummer Fred Maher. (At least it did in the credits; Quine would complain of being mixed off the latter, especially.) But Reed's teetering walk was one a lot of other rock stars were beginning to take at the time.

It helped that the Velvet Underground, which Reed had led, was also getting its due. The Velvets had garnered their share of dismissals by the time Reed left in 1970. (The band limped on a few more years under the leadership of bassist Doug Yule.) By 1984, though, nobody could dismiss the Velvets anymore. They'd become as vital a link in the so-called new music as James Brown. Each Reed-led Velvets album had specific sets of aftereffects—a catalog that, in 1984 indie circles, was holy writ.

But Reed wanted hits, too—always. For *New Sensations*, *Musician* noted, "He's even making a video." Moreover, the album was his idea of a record for which one might make a video—a leap into the studio coal mine. He took heart from Art of Noise, clubland remixer Shep Pettibone, and the DJ mega-mixes on New York urban stations KISS and WKTU. Reed worked with producer John Jansen because, as he put it, "There's this great drum fill at the end of [Air Supply's] 'Making Love Out of Nothing at All'—he was involved with that. I liked the hugeness of his sound. So I got in touch with him."

In context, this, plus Maher's playing all the drum parts to a click track—no spontaneity!—was scandalous. But at least Reed was up-front about it. Most of his peers did much the same, in capitulation to label brass, the new era, or their own much-evident midlife crises.

THOUGH THE EAGLES' FINAL ALBUM, *LIVE*, CAME OUT IN **1980**, IT TOOK three more years for the band to announce it was done. This was despite the fact that both main Eagles, Don Henley and Glenn Frey, had released solo albums in 1982, to varying degrees of success: Henley with *I Can't Stand Still*, Frey with *No Fun Aloud*, both titles practically smothering you with their forced jollity.

In that time, their manager Irving Azoff had become chairman of MCA, or, as it was widely referred to at the time, the Music Cemetery of America. Azoff had made enemies during the Eagles' reign. "Irving's the kind of guy that walks in the room and says, 'Good morning,' and someone says, 'You're lying.' He can't help himself," Walter Yetnikoff of CBS Records told *Rolling Stone*. "And if you want to print it, I'll indemnify you."

Asylum Records, the singer-songwriter sanctuary founded by David Geffen, Azoff's onetime management partner, had issued both ex-Eagles' debuts. When Asylum was merged with Elektra Records in 1982, new management was determined to clean house. Frey fumed: "They had no sense of history and didn't care for the fact that the Eagles, Linda Ronstadt, Jackson Browne, and Joni Mitchell built that company."

But most of that gang wasn't looking too hot by the time *Thriller* hit. At the end of 1982, *Rolling Stone* named "California rock" one of the year's "Losers."

That was the situation when Frey turned in his follow-up—and the label rejected it. "They said it wasn't contemporary enough," Frey said. Soon, Azoff had taken Frey in at MCA—coincident with Frey and Muscle Shoals keyboardist Barry Beckett adding three songs: "We all decided it was time to write a couple of 'hits.'"

Like so many others of his generational cohort, Frey would lambast synthesizers and drum machines—"So concrete, so androgynous, and it's so dull and undynamic. That's what I miss out of all this synthesized music—it starts to lose dynamics"—then turn around in the same interview and admit, "I liked cutting with a drum machine and bringing the drums in after, 'cause real drummers get tired after about eight takes, and that's usually around the time the guitar players have figured out their parts."

It was that shibboleth, the "rock image." By the mid-eighties, along with many of his California-rock peers, such as Crosby, Stills & Nash and Chicago, Frey was getting much of his airplay on A/C, not AOR. When Frey was asked about having to "live down a perception of being this dewy-eyed tender type," he snapped, "You mean about me being perceived as [*sneers*] a balladeer?"

Like Frey, Henley was off Elektra-Asylum by the time 1984 rolled around—and on Geffen Records. "I was a little leery about signing with David," Henley said. "I still had some hard feelings and unpleasant memories. I was wary of him." Eventually, Geffen wooed Henley sufficiently for him to say yes: "Then he signed me to a shitty deal."

Henley, of course, grumbled about having to make a video for his new single in the first place. Most boomer rockers *did not understand* why they had to do anything of the sort—most videos, especially theirs, weren't getting on MTV anyway. But Henley's song was so strong—it really was better than anything the Eagles ever did—and the clip so arresting it was a fait accompli.

Shot by the French fashion photographer Jean-Baptiste Mondino, "The Boys of Summer" video looked like a black-and-white new wave classic rendered in modern terms. As a wounded youngster alternated with a yuppie in round-frame glasses and a carefree young couple running together on the beach looped endlessly on a giant-screen monitor in every room and/or at the pool, Henley intoned his words from the back of a truck touring the streets of LA, looking like he was on a day pass from the Hotel California.

Henley came up with the lyrics while driving up the Pacific Coast Highway, listening to the guitarist Danny Kortchmar's track: "I saw this brand new

Cadillac Seville and it had a big, green Deadhead sticker on it. The Cadillac is a symbol of the middle class American businessman, and I thought, 'Either this guy is a great eclectic or this is a sign unto me!'"

Still, their former band's shadow continued to loom over both. Frey said, "I think if the Eagles were to fart in a bag, the label would have tried to get a stereo mix and ask me what I wanted on the B-side."

The other titan of "California rock," Fleetwood Mac, was in remission, with all three of its singer-songwriters busy with solo work. Stevie Nicks's *The Wild Heart* (1983) had gone double platinum, confirming her as the band's star, as well as its prima donna—for Fleetwood Mac's 1982 tour, behind *Mirage*, Nicks would only rehearse the last ten days prior to the tour opener. Speaking to *Rolling Stone* in 1984, bandmate Christine McVie said, "Ten years ago, she really had her feet on the ground, along with a tremendous sense of humor, which she still has. But she seems to have developed her own fantasy world, somehow, which I'm not part of."

McVie released her solo debut in 1984, as did Lindsey Buckingham his second, *Go Insane*. But the member who made the most headlines was Mick Fleetwood, who on March 28 filed for personal bankruptcy, claiming assets of $2.4 million against debts of $3.7 million. "I had seen it coming, and denied it," he wrote.

ONE ATLANTIC RECORDS VP OPINED THAT "OVEREXPOSURE THROUGH video can kill an act quicker than anything." Just ask Billy Squier.

That July, Squier released his fourth album of workmanlike rock, *Signs of Life*, with the single "Rock Me Tonite" out in June. Capitol Records hired the choreographer Kenny Ortega to direct. Ortega "depict[ed] Squier cavorting in a high-tone bedroom scene, complete with satin sheets," as *Billboard* put it. It would occasion a very public case of gay panic—who did the media say "cavorted" in 1984 but male homosexuals?

"Rock Me Tonite" was actually Squier's biggest chart hit—number fifteen on the Hot 100. But the video, he would insist, had "fragmented my audience, especially males who relate to that tough side of me. I think it confused people who didn't know why this guy who they thought was so tough was in this nicely lit room dancing around and sleeping in satin sheets." His tour that summer, he added, sold only about 80 percent of the usual number of tickets.

LATE IN 1983, PAT BENATAR, WHO HAD SIGNED AN ABSURD DEAL WITH Chrysalis to deliver a new LP every nine months, did what a lot of musicians in her place did—she released a live album. Like many of these, Benatar's *Live from Earth* featured a pair of new studio recordings. In particular, she and Neil "Spyder" Giraldo, Benatar's guitarist, producer, and husband, had reworked a song called "Love Is a Battlefield" from a ballad to an up-tempo dance-rocker.

"[Giraldo] started fooling around with a brand-new drum machine and hearing Bo Diddley in his head," Benatar wrote in her memoir. The video, featuring the singer leading a group dance modeled on Michael Jackson's in "Beat It"—with the same director, Bob Giraldi—helped push the record into the US top five. Chrysalis had initially hated the track: "We were a 'rock' band. Anything that seemed to deviate from that wasn't acceptable," Benatar wrote.

The label was even less happy to discover that the singer was pregnant. "They wanted it to be a guarded secret," she wrote. "They didn't want any photos taken of me once I started to show, and they didn't want me talking about babies in interviews. And of course, they made it clear that they wanted me to go right back to my vixen self as soon as that baby was born and get right back on tour. No time off. Not during the pregnancy and not afterward. I guess they thought the audiences wouldn't notice that I was pregnant and that journalists wouldn't ask about it. I told them that they could kiss my ass."

This was all too typical—women rock stars ran the risk of getting fired over their pregnancies, while the men typically had their every indiscretion papered over in green. Benatar had been bolstered by the example of Chrissie Hynde, the leader of the Pretenders, who'd had her first child in 1983, six months ahead of Benatar. When she encountered Hynde backstage, Benatar asked, "How are you doing this?" Hynde responded by shaking her head: "I'm not doing it! I'm not doing it! I'm just trying to get through the day—every day." It wasn't what Benatar had hoped to hear—there was nothing easy about it—but it helped.

That summer, during a show in Long Island behind the third Pretenders album, *Learning to Crawl*, released in January, Hynde told the audience, "I want to congratulate Jim Kerr: He has just found out his wife is pregnant."

In a private ceremony in May, Hynde had married Kerr, the Scottish singer of the bombastic new wavers Simple Minds, shortly before their bands went on tour together. She'd been careful, as well, to keep her daughter Natalie—whose father was the Kinks' Ray Davies, with whom Hynde was involved for several years prior to Kerr—out of the papers.

Hynde had already been in them enough. In June 1982, the Pretenders' bassist, Pete Farndon, was fired over his drug abuse; two days later, the band's guitarist, James Honeyman-Scott, was dead of a cocaine overdose, and Farndon would shortly afterward drown in his own bathtub after taking heroin. "The doctors [had] told him, 'If you don't stop drinking, you'll kill yourself,' which was bad in a way because he did too much coke then," drummer Martin Chambers said of Honeyman-Scott. "Thank God he was asleep."

Hynde and Chambers rallied, bringing in replacement Pretenders Robbie McIntosh on guitar and Malcolm Foster on bass. "I suppose people could feel sorry for me, say 'Ah, look at the poor thing,'" Hynde told *Creem*. "But it's been just another year for me, really. If you can't handle a couple of deaths . . . that's just the art of living. The baby wore me out with the breast-feeding and everything, had me tired. But I'm never going to have a nervous breakdown. Sorry, it's just not in my Zodiac."

From its title forward, *Learning to Crawl* was explicitly about age, parenthood, and the long haul: "I'm not the kind I used to be / I've got a kid, I'm thirty-three, baby," she snarled on "Middle of the Road." Its reception was markedly different in the United States and the UK. American critics rained down plaudits: the album finished seventh in the annual *Village Voice* critics' poll, with *Rolling Stone* dubbing it "a triumph of art over adversity." The Brits found Hynde's AOR-ready constructs old hat, not least because "Hynde summarized her band's faceless vigor when she noted how a Pretenders record 'doesn't jar when it's played next to Foreigner or Styx,'" Richard Cook sniffed, while *Melody Maker* called it "About as interesting as a road map of Belgium." "As insults go," Hynde admitted, "that one's pretty funny."

In the summer of 1984, *Creem* sent writer Roy Trakin to New York to interview Daryl Hall and John Oates. He was warned: "They don't like to be called Hall & Oates," the duo's PR woman told him. "It's Daryl Hall and John Oates." Then, as a precaution, she yanked the advance cassette of their new album *Big Bam Boom* out of their car's cassette player, where it had already begun playing, and added "D-A-R-Y-L" and "J-O-H-N" above "Hall & Oates" on the tape's label—just in case.

Hall and Oates (sorry) had some hits in the seventies, but the avalanche came in 1980, right in the midst of the Hot 100's A/C quagmire. For a time, they were nearly the only reliably lively thing on the radio. The duo's early-eighties singles had a dryness that made the hooks leap out. And the grooves were slipperier than ever. "If we have a cause or a crusade," Oates said in 1982, "it's bridging the gap—moving away from black/white polarization and getting music itself back to the sensibilities of the late fifties and early sixties."

Hall could be quite windy. When a reporter asked if he considered himself a "pop" musician, he responded: "We're musicians who are using pop music to do something else, and you can look at our music and perceive it on different levels. . . . The subjects of our lyrics can be looked at in a lot of different ways. Pretty complex." Here was Oates's answer: "Once you have something good, you can repeat it. The problem is finding something good enough to repeat."

Released in October 1984, *Big Bam Boom* had an even R&B-heavier sound than usual—and the duo was confident it would only be an asset. They hired Arthur Baker to work on the mixes. Hall and Baker had coproduced Diana Ross's "Swept Away," which Hall had written.

Hall and Oates had purchased a Synclavier for help making the album, but it mostly went unused—for years. "It was the most expensive plant stand in the world," says Baker. "Literally no one used it. They ended up leaving it in the studio for, like, two years." But you can hear big tech all over *Big Bam Boom* anyway. It really is best reviewed by its title—the album's crash-bang screams mid-eighties.

The making of *Big Bam Boom* "was almost the peak of my cocaine frenzy," says Baker. "Compared to other people, I didn't do a lot, but I didn't need a lot. If I had an eighth of coke for a week, to me I did a lot. Daryl was more like Dad and the boss. The band—when we'd be in the studio when Daryl left, 'OK, we're gonna do drugs now.'" (Baker has been clean since 1987.)

How did Hall and Oates get along? "There weren't really disagreements in the studio," says Baker. "We'd be working together, and then John would leave and then Daryl would do what he wanted." For example, Oates had written a demo intended for the Stylistics, whom Baker had just signed to his label Streetwise. "He played it for me, and it was the song 'Out of Touch'—the full chorus, the full intro, no verses. And I go, 'John, that's a number one record.'" After Baker and Oates finished the track in the studio, the latter went to the Hamptons for the weekend, and Hall "goes into the control room and comes up with a fucking great melody. And I'm like, 'Uh-oh.' And then, of course, Daryl got to sing the lead."

When manager Tommy Mottola tried to have Baker tell Oates that another song of his, "Possession Obsession," should have Hall on lead vocal as well, the producer refused: "So he sang a lead—and end of story, it wasn't a hit. Daryl definitely had the good vocals. But they never fought in the studio, at least in front of me. John seemed to not be the alpha in the relationship. He seemed to let things slide."

IN ADDITION TO HALL & OATES' ALBUM, ARTHUR BAKER SPENT SOME time in 1984 working with Mick Jagger. Early in the year, he was tapped to remix the Rolling Stones' "Too Much Blood"—a twelve-minute experiment in dub echo and weird structure, with Jagger's ridiculous monologue, in the voice of a cannibal, its uneasy centerpiece. "That was the most coked-up record I've ever done, for sure," Baker recalls.

The Stones' deal in late 1983 had cost CBS's Walter Yetnikoff an alleged $28 million—$6 million apiece for four LPs, plus $4 million in publicity costs. A few years earlier, David Bowie would recall, Jagger had cried to him, "Am I gonna be saddled with the Rolling Stones for the rest of my life?" A deal like that made it seem certain. But Jagger was also itching to make his own name. "What constitutes a challenge for you at this point?" *Musician* magazine asked Mick Jagger. "It was a challenge just to get this frigging record finished," he responded. He wasn't joking, and the main reason was Keith Richards.

Jagger was constantly looking to push the edge of things. If anybody summed up slouching boomer rock conservatism, it was Keef. When *Musician* played him a weekly top ten in late 1983, he reserved some of his choicest words for the Stones' onetime opening act, Prince. "He's got a problem with his attitude and it comes across on record. . . . He's a prince who thinks he's a king already."

Jagger spent the fall of '84 working on his first solo LP, coproduced by Nile Rodgers and Bill Laswell. The singer called Baker back in to remix his "Just Another Night." "Or, as it should have been called, 'Just Another Nightmare,' because it was a fucking nightmare," says Baker. "He wasn't happy with his vocal. I have a good ear for pitch, and I had to tell Diana Ross and Daryl Hall they were out of tune. After that, you can tell anyone they're out of tune. When I worked with Dylan, of course, I had to just ignore that. You couldn't tell *him* he was out of tune."

THE PERSON WHO BROKE THE NEWS TO PAUL MCCARTNEY THAT HIS movie stunk was Gene Siskel, the cohost of the syndicated TV hit *At the Movies*. (The other cohost was Roger Ebert.) Siskel interviewed McCartney in his hotel room for the *Chicago Tribune*. "He asked me, 'What did you think?'" Siskel recalled. "Meeting Paul McCartney was very exciting for me, but I said, 'Well, you never lied to us. I can't lie to you. I thought it was terrible, everything about it.' He was shocked. He got very angry. He almost threw a glass of orange juice in my face."

McCartney had made some very badly reviewed music since the Beatles' 1970 breakup—*Red Rose Speedway*, from 1973, featuring "My Love," was near universally regarded as rancid—but he had never had his work attacked so loudly or visibly as with *Give My Regards to Broad Street*, the movie he wrote and starred in that year.

McCartney was, by some distance, the most bankable Beatle. By 1984, he was the only one still regularly making music. George Harrison was on an extended break from making albums; after *Gone Troppo*, in 1982, no one could be blamed for guessing he was in hiding. A year earlier, Ringo Starr couldn't even get a US or UK record deal for his latest album, *Old Wave*. Considering the sour raspberry Starr released in 1981, *Stop and Smell the Roses*, it was no wonder.

John Lennon, of course, was dead. That was actually a commercial advantage—it's the reason that, near 1984's start, Geffen Records released *Milk and Honey*, the follow-up to 1980's *Double Fantasy*, which was released two months before Lennon's murder. The dry wit of "Nobody Told Me" was good for a top ten US and UK hit. But *Melody Maker* wasn't alone in dismissing the LP as "merely the crumbs of the Lennon revival."

But McCartney had a bad 1984, right from the start. On January 15, Paul and his wife Linda were on vacation in Barbados when they were raided for marijuana possession and fined. Returned to London two days later, Linda was charged for possession *again* after more pot was found in her purse; she was released on bail.

In February, the tenth annual Beatlefest memorabilia convention took place in Secaucus, New Jersey. The Beatles had given it their blessing; less so, the Sotheby's auction of Beatles collectibles that took place at the end of August—350 items had gone to the tune of a quarter-million dollars. McCartney had, in fact, attempted to purchase a postcard he'd sent to Lennon, only to be outbid. "It's appalling to have to buy back your own used toilet paper," Paul said. When Ringo hosted *Saturday Night Live* that December, the cold open depicted him in his 1964 Edwardian collarless "Beatle suit," being auctioned off along with the Beatles' memorabilia, only to get no offers.

McCartney had long wanted to purchase Northern Songs, his and Lennon's old publishing company. "It's just a bit galling and absurd having to buy back, for millions, songs that John and I tossed off in an afternoon," he told *Time Out*. But Paul needed permission to record his old songs because he'd made a movie full of them.

Give My Regards to Broad Street was essentially a fable about the life of a rich rock star, from a script by a rich rock star. It concerned some missing master tapes, on whose locating the rich rock star's empire depends. It certainly echoed McCartney's own position vis-à-vis his song catalog—but it's a mistake to say the film was "about" that, or anything.

Broad Street was an early attempt at a jukebox musical, with the story line arranged around the songs; in a way, it's also a live-action equivalent of *Yellow Submarine*. When McCartney re-recorded his old material, he kept the original arrangements. Ringo Starr appeared in the movie, but he refused to play drums on any of the Beatles remakes.

The movie rolled out in October, and the notices were savage. *Billboard* shamed McCartney for exploiting his old work, comparing the movie to *Xanadu*, *Can't Stop the Music*, the Robert Stigwood version of *Sgt. Pepper's Lonely Hearts Club Band*, and that summer's *Hard to Hold*, a dud starring TV actor and rocker Rick Springfield—all musical flops.

On October 15, the day Paul and Linda McCartney arrived in New York to promote their failed movie, Charisma Records in the UK released *Valotte*, the first album from Julian Lennon. *Smash Hits* summed it up nicely: "The twenty-one-year-old Julian Lennon sounds like someone who wants to make *music* but isn't yet fully equipped to write *songs*." Three weeks later, while Paul sat for an interview on *Friday Night Videos* at the Carlyle Hotel, he ran into Julian Lennon, there for an interview himself, for the first time in a decade. The nerves showed on-air.

Two weeks later, near the end of *Broad Street*'s West End premiere screening, when a character on-screen said, "We've got the tapes," a shout came from the audience: "Thank God!" Paul McCartney was heckling himself.

SARM STUDIOS,
LONDON
November 25, 1984

THE **1984** *SMASH HITS* READERS' POLL MADE IT OFFICIAL—DURAN DURAN owned British pop. For the third year in a row, they were voted Best Group. Bassist John Taylor told the magazine, "I see Duran Duran as a group—it's our biggest strength—and winning the best group category means everything to me."

Seven and the Ragged Tiger won Best Album. "The Wild Boys," with its absurdly overscaled ten-minute clip, won Best Single. Drummer Roger Taylor—who seldom engaged the press in any manner—won Event of the Year for his wedding; keyboardist Nick Rhodes finished fourth, for his.

Rhodes tied the knot in August with Julie Ann Friedman, of Des Moines, Iowa, at the London registry, then hosted 219 guests at the Savoy while more than 400 fans stood outside. Everybody, including the guests, wore pink. Live flamingos were involved. The Friedmans were particularly pleased that their daughter's new husband was "a light drinker and not involved with drugs."

The drummer's nuptials took place in Naples on July 27. Roger and his bride, the dancer Giovanna Cantone, chartered a 727 to fly his band crew and mates and family to Italy. It was a church wedding followed by a boat ride around the bay. (John Taylor recalled that his father "got violently ill on the salmon mousse.") They avoided the hoi polloi by honeymooning in Egypt.

Maybe *Smash Hits* readers preferred Roger's to Nick's because it left more to the imagination. Both musicians were flummoxed at the result. "Event of the year? Was it? That's ridiculous," Roger said. Rhodes's plumage wilted: "It's a bit weird. I wonder why Roger's wedding got more votes than mine?" In the artists' lists that accompanied the poll, John Taylor's pick for Event of the Year was "Me and Simon not getting married," followed by an editor's note: "I didn't know they were engaged."

That summer, John Taylor finagled the band into recording the next James Bond film theme after meeting 007 producer Cubby Broccoli at a party for Wimbledon. The condition was that they work with John Barry, the series' theme composer, who did not cotton to these kids invading his turf, the truculent Rhodes in particular. John Taylor figured out a solution—he called Bernard Edwards, who came in and smoothed things out.

Duran Duran already had a working relationship with Edwards's old Chic confrere, Nile Rodgers; the latter had remixed "The Reflex" from *Seven and the Ragged Tiger*, and his heavy remodeling pushed the record to a transatlantic number one.

Around the same time, Andy Taylor and John began working on demos with Edwards and Chic drummer Tony Thompson in Paris. This would not be Duran Duran material but a new prospect entirely, completed after John sent the tracks to Robert Palmer and he accepted their offer. They were named the Power Station, after the New York studio where their album was cut. It was "the absolute acme of the recording industry in 1984," John wrote. "The Power Station had the best sound system of all. Urei speakers, monsters the size of a double bed. Plus, I'd never seen more drugs in my life. The access to cocaine was unlimited."

"THAT'S GOOD," GEORGE MICHAEL OF WHAM! TOLD *SMASH HITS* WHEN he heard that he'd been named number two male singer in the 1984 poll. "Second to Simon Le Bon. They've got such a strong following, that anything you come second in, it's almost like coming first."

Wham! was the number two group, "Careless Whisper" the number two single, followed by "Freedom" at four and "Wake Me Up Before You Go-Go" at eight. Michael was second Most Fanciable Male, after John Taylor, and he was the second-biggest Prat of the Year, after Boy George. "I don't really mind," he said. "I've been called Best Poseur, Best Wally this year. Prat's just another word."

Born Georgios Kyriacos Panayiotou in London in 1963, George Michael grew up in the suburb of Bushey and began dreaming of pop stardom at age seven. "It's not the something extra that makes a star—it's the something that's missing," Michael said in a 1989 *MTV Rockumentary*. "You know, it's an old story now, but it's true: I was fat, I was very unattractive [as an] adolescent—glasses, spots [*laughs*], all the best things. All my career I've tried to project myself in a sexual manner, that it must be trying to make up for something. And it's weird, because I know it's there; I know it's subconscious. And I don't see that person anymore in the mirror, but I know that deep inside, I'm still making up for that kid."

His transformation began when he met Andrew Ridgeley at age twelve. "The teacher ordered me to sit next to this horrible little boy, who then took charge of me," George said. Andrew was outgoing and always had friends around, and the two of them formed a short-lived ska outfit, the Executive, before becoming Wham!

In February 1982, Ridgeley played the Wham! demos to his friend Mark Dean, who ran the small Innervision Records, which had recently inked a distribution deal with CBS, who then signed them in March. Two songs stood out: "Wham! Rap," a cheeky hip-hop takeoff about living on the dole, and the ballad "Careless Whisper." "Wham! Rap" hit the UK top ten that November. The two of them shook their skinny little tushies on *Top of the Pops* and built a devoted teen-girl following.

The rock intelligentsia laughed, but Michael wore his teenybopper beefcake image proudly on his sleeve. "I think it's brilliant being overtly sexy, 'cause it irritates the hell out of everyone who doesn't like you and all the girls love it—right?—and all the blokes who like you think it's a laugh," he said.

After Wham!'s debut, *Fantastic*, which topped the 1983 *Smash Hits* albums poll, the duo sued to be let out of their Innervision Records contract, alleging it unfair. The legal haggling went on for six months before Wham! could sign with Epic—a long time away for a fickle fan base. "I think May [1984] is about as long as we could have left the single for," Michael said. "I think if we'd left it for another three or four months we'd be up the creek. We're lucky that nothing really new has happened."

In the UK, the single "Careless Whisper" went first—credited only to Michael, not Wham!, a clear market test. "I like to have a line or two that make your ears cock up when you hear them on the radio," Michael said of the song. "Like 'guilty feet ain't got no rhythm.' . . . How many people put a word like 'feet' in a love song? It's hardly a romantic word."

Michael knew exactly how much was riding on "Careless Whisper." He'd recorded a complete version in the United States, then threw it out and started over in London. Session man Steve Gregory played the song's key saxophone line. When Wham! appeared to perform the song on *Top of the Pops*, Michael insisted Gregory join them, and paid his airfare from France, where the horn player was on vacation. But George was hardly modest about it. "A lot of people . . . say, what a great sax solo. It's as if I had nothing to do with it," Michael huffed. "It's a great sax solo because I wrote it."

In America, Wham!'s early hits made little dent. That changed in November. "Wake Me Up Before You Go-Go," released concurrently in the United States and UK, hit number one in the States after only ten weeks on the charts. "If a bunch of ugly bastards had got up on stage and done 'Wake Me Up,' it would still have been a top-three record," Michael boasted.

"I JUST LIKE THE FACT THAT PEOPLE CAN BE BOTHERED TO PAY 16P TO TELL me I'm a prat—it just goes to show how important I am."

Prat of the Year was the only category of the poll in which Culture Club's standing improved over 1983, when Boy George was adjudged only the fifth-biggest prat. Best Group, Best Male Singer, Most Fanciable Male—down, down, down. "What? Paul Young came fourth?" George said when he found out who'd come ahead of him (fifth) in the latter category: "How can anyone who looks like a Cornish pasty beat me?"

When *Waking Up with the House on Fire* came in sixth on the album chart—*Colour by Numbers* was 1983's number two—Boy George said, "Again, considering all the bad press we've had with people trying to put the dampers on it, I think we've done surprisingly well. We must have some loyal fans." As for the band, George averred on *Donahue*, "A blowtorch couldn't separate us now."

If only. George had attempted to make touring free of distraction—no significant others, no drugs—and inevitably failed. Mikey Craig was busted at Heathrow in possession of hash oil, inside a new guitar he hadn't claimed at Customs. (He paid a fine and they didn't alert the press.)

And George had his own distractions. He fought constantly with Jon Moss. One bruiser involved the singer chucking "a family-sized Coca-Cola bottle" at the drummer's head. He was surprisingly unharmed and, according to George, "surprisingly forgiving."

But the band was increasingly taking a back seat to its front man's shenanigans. In June, George attended the unveiling of his own sculpture at Madame Tussaud's Wax Museum. On the Fourth of July, he appeared on *Face the Nation*. (The episode was about the "feminizing" of American culture.) He'd been offered his own TV talk show, but turned it down, he said, "because I think it's a mistake to be seen too much." It was already too late before the third Culture Club album was even out.

The album, *Waking Up with the House on Fire*, arrived in October. The title was the condition of George's life: "Being a pop star is like being thrown out of a window naked," he told *Smash Hits*. He'd later admit, "We were out of ideas and out of touch. . . . Songwriting had become secondary to our fabulous lifestyles."

The album's first single was "The War Song," George's retort to Frankie Goes to Hollywood's "Two Tribes." "Frankie's for kids who hate their parents, Culture Club are for little girls who've just discovered their freedom," he sneered. "Culture Club is intelligently rebellious." But even he had to admit that the lyrics ("War is stupid / And people are stupid") were "patronizing."

Waking Up with the House on Fire, Culture Club drummer Roy Hay said, was written in three weeks: "George was more interested in the artwork than the music."

BOY GEORGE'S OWN CHOICE FOR PRAT OF THE YEAR WAS HOLLY JOHNSON of Frankie Goes to Hollywood. They, too, did quite well with *Smash Hits* readers: *Welcome to the Pleasure Dome* number five album, "Two Tribes" and "Relax" among the top five singles, Frankie third-best group, Johnson ninth-best male singer. Frankie's Paul Rutherford named his Event of the Year: "Us not being able to get on the plane because our heads were too big."

George's vote helped make Johnson the eighth-placed Prat—directly below the BBC's Mike Read, who had inadvertently kicked off Frankie's huge year. "I actually get on well with Frankie," Read insisted. "And I did not ban 'Relax.' I only said I would not play it on my programme or the others I was involved with—*Top of the Pops, Saturday Superstore*, and *Pop Quiz*—because they're children's programs."

The Most Promising New Act was Julian Lennon. *Valotte* spotlighted his uncanny vocal resemblance to his father as well as arrangements that had nothing to do with most of the *Smash Hits* list. "He looks so 'rock and roll'!" Rutherford sneered, declaring the younger Lennon utterly passé. Frankie themselves mocked that sort of thing by donning leather jackets to perform Bruce Springsteen's "Born to Run" during their first-ever concert tour—in America, where nobody got the joke.

The plan, in Paul Morley's words, was "to kill them off completely." Here was a group whose public assault, from outrageous sleeve notes to bombarding tunes, was its sum total. Frankie was designed as a total pop explosion, an exploding trick—to disappear.

That had been Morley's idea, anyway. Going to North America wasn't. The band was eager to set things straight, as it were. "I know a lot of people think Frankie Goes to Hollywood is Holly and Paul, and the rest of us are a session band," drummer Peter Gill told *Billboard*. "We're not a session band. We're all musicians, and we all contribute."

Frankie was in full promotional gear, having "agreed to do literally hundreds of interviews, in-store, and television appearances." They began with four dates in Canada. The first US show, not by accident, was Washington, DC, on election night.

Ronald Reagan was reelected by a landslide: 525 Electoral College votes from forty-nine states; Walter Mondale won only in Minnesota, his home state, and in the District of Columbia. Despite Reagan's overwhelming victory, the Republican Party did not get a comprehensive rout. With ninety million voters, the largest turnout since 1964, the Senate retained its majority but slipped from 55 seats to 53, while the House of Representatives remained solidly Democratic, by roughly 70 seats. The White House chief of staff James Baker noted, "It will be very difficult to push some of the things that the president is going to want to push in Congress."

Among the many T-shirts on display at Frankie's American debut, one read FRANKIE SAY SHIT THE POLITICIAN. They misread the national mood. Britain was being torn apart by anger, by Thatcherism versus the miners. America was jubilant. Ronald Reagan was seen not as the enemy by a nation of recovering punks but as a conquering hero by pop fans.

Plenty of folks misread the group in kind. "Frankie Goes to Hollywood is supposed to be a rock band, not a disco cabaret act," one writer complained—wrong on both counts. One reviewer said Johnson "came across like Elvis Costello impersonating Peter Lorre half the time and Lorre impersonating Costello the rest of the time."

The band had some reason to be cocky: Their debut album had shipped 1.1 million copies in the UK, the largest prerelease sales yet. That wasn't counting the T-shirts. But Frankie Goes to Hollywood didn't own the rights to those T-shirts—and it added to their workload. "Suddenly people were looking to Frankie to come up with fashion as well as music," Frankie's manager Tony Pope said.

Despite a third UK number one early that December with "The Power of Love," a Frankie backlash was brewing. "I think it's garbage, total garbage," Mick Jagger said. "Onstage, it's the worst act I've seen. I went to see them at the Ritz. They were just terrible. And they know it." He added, "All the tracks were pre-recorded, so they weren't playing live. I mean, come on—these people didn't pay fifteen dollars just to hear a backing track. I think it's a joke."

BESIDES JULIAN LENNON, U2 WAS, BY SOME DISTANCE, THE MOST TRADI-tionally "rock" finisher in the *Smash Hits* poll. Their fourth album, *The Unforgettable Fire*, and its top three UK hit, "Pride (In the Name of Love)," both finished seventh, with U2 top ten in group, video, and male singer, as well.

They'd come out of the knot of bands loosely dubbed "big music," along with Big Country and Simple Minds, both from Scotland, and Liverpool's Echo and the Bunnymen—as well as the Alarm, from Wales, and fellow Dubliners the Waterboys, who'd named the style with their April 1984 single, "The Big Music." The songs were broad-shouldered, majestic, full of mossy romanticism—heavily Celtic in flavor, and in the case of the Alarm and U2, suffused with Christian symbolism. "We don't have blues scales engraved on our brains, unlike a lot of bands," Bono told *Trouser Press*.

U2's animating idea was that postpunk was, by rights, stadium music. "If we stay in small clubs, we'll develop small minds, and then we'll start making small music," Bono said. The band had been his creation in all ways but sonic. As the singer put it, "I never bought into the cliché: 'I'm the artist. Keep me away from the filthy lucre and the tawdry music-business world.' It's just complete horseshit."

They'd formed in 1976, while at Mount Temple Comprehensive School, in Dublin. Fourteen-year-old Larry Mullen Jr. had convened a jam session at his house. Adam Clayton showed up with his bass guitar perched on his shoulder, ready to go. Dave Evans had brought an acoustic guitar but played another attendee's electric. As one eyewitness recalled it, the singer, born Paul Hewson, "quickly took things over and began organizing everyone, playing little himself but expending considerable energy attempting to almost magically summon, cajole and exhort music from the others' instruments." Soon, Hewson became Bono Vox—pidgin Latin for "good voice"—and Dave Evans became the Edge.

By 1979, Bono figured the band was ready to become known. Still in high school, he went to London to hawk the band's demo directly to journalists at the inkies. "Usually they would say: 'Look, if I like it, give you a call back.' And I would interrupt: 'Well, then I'll call you in an hour.'"

A year later, U2 signed to Island Records. Shortly before the release of their debut album, *Boy*, in October 1980, the band visited America for the first time. The early tours were shoestring affairs—Island was still an indie, despite Warner Bros.' distribution. During one early US outing, their manager Paul McGuinness recalled, "We actually had run out of cash. We finished the tour on my American Express card, and when we got home I couldn't pay the bill and they took my card away."

But the band loved the States. "It's very hip to knock America and it really bugs me," Bono said. "We go back to England and people try to knock it." And parts of the States—college radio, in particular—loved the band's first US hit, the charging anthem "I Will Follow."

Bono, Edge, and Mullen were part of the Shalom Fellowship, a nondenominational Christian group. "They were devoted to the idea of Christ as a commitment to social justice, and having no possessions," Bono said, and both he and the Edge had considered leaving the band because of its teachings. Instead, they would quit the fellowship, though not religion itself. "I believe that Jesus is the Son of God," Bono said. "I do believe that, odd as it sounds."

The Edge pinpointed the beginning of his echo-heavy guitar style to the writing of "A Day Without Me." "Bono kept saying, 'I hear this echo thing, like the chord repeating.' So I said, I'd better get an echo unit for this single." It took a couple of tries to get one that worked: the Memory Man Deluxe, from Electro-Harmonix. "I mean, Electro-Harmonix made the cheapest and trashiest guitar things, but they always had great personality."

But for the band's third album, Bono asked the guitarist to stop echoing around and start slashing away. *War*, released in February 1983, was U2's most straightforwardly *rock* album yet—U2's "militant pacifism" at its most muscular.

Yet for all of *War*'s campaigning for Real Rock—the tour for it was dubbed "The War on Boring Music"—this was also the first U2 album on which drummer Mullen began playing to a metronome, or "click track." That precision tuning only made the record move more. On "Sunday, Bloody Sunday," Mullen fires his snares like artillery. "My year in the Post Office Workers Band finally paid off," he said.

For *War*, U2 shot a performance at Red Rocks, in Denver—a majestic outdoor arena perfectly suited to the band's dramatics. The weather was horrible—the rain was nonstop, the wind was heavy, and there had been flash flood warnings in the area—but the band pressed on. The video, titled *Under a Blood Red Sky*, became a key tool in selling the band to America: not only was U2 a *real rock band*, they rocked so hard *the weather couldn't stop them*.

This was not the time, Island Records felt, to bring in Brian Eno. As a producer, Eno wasn't interested in capturing a live band in action so much as molding the sound like clay. He'd pioneered "ambient music" on a series of seventies and early eighties albums—their slow-seeping effect had trickled down to the soft-focused "New Age" of Windham Hill Records, music Eno dismissed as having no "complexity to the emotion, and that complexity means that there has to be some darkness as well as all this lovely misty light. It doesn't hold your interest otherwise, it doesn't seem like anything real."

Eno had zero interest in contemporary rock—he listened to African music and gospel and made "ambient video installations." Why did U2 keep nagging him after he'd already told them no? Finally, he agreed to a meeting. Eno flew to Dublin and brought along his engineer, Daniel Lanois—"clearly with the intention of passing the gig to him," McGuinness noted. It didn't help when the band screened *Under a Blood Red Sky*, and Eno's "eyes glazed over," Bono said.

But Eno explained, "Once I'd met Bono I knew I had to work with him. I thought there was something about him—something that made the idea of spending time in a studio with him very interesting. . . . [U2] knew, I think, that I would encourage the 'new' side of them instead of harping on at the old." Recording began at Slane Castle.

The band had only three songs worked up before heading to Slane, one of them "Pride." "Bad" was about the heroin addiction eating through Dublin

City, including several of Bono's acquaintances. "When your friend becomes a junkie he ceases to be your friend; he'll steal from you, he'll fight you," he said. The band played the basic track live three times, Eno added a piano part, and he encouraged Bono's half-formed lyrics to stay as they were. "And I, like an idiot, went along with it, and so I never finished great songs like 'Bad,'" Bono later complained. It worked, though—the track sounded equally like U2 and Eno, endlessly cresting.

The album was completed at Windmill Lane Studios in Dublin—Slane's electricity was powered by the nearby River Boyne, and, as Slane's engineer Randy Ezratty put it, "When that stupid river started to run low, the voltage would go down and it would beat the crap out of my equipment. You could see the lights dimming on the gear and the power supplies fighting to stay alive, and I'd be going, 'Oh no!' . . . You had to be ready to go at all times regardless of what the river or the generator was providing."

Bono had begun writing "Pride" about Ronald Reagan. "It was originally meant as the sort of pride that won't back down, that wants to build nuclear arsenals," he said. "I was giving Reagan too much importance; then I thought, 'Martin Luther King, there's a man.'"

"Pride" went to a number three UK hit and number thirty-three on the Hot 100 (number two on the *Billboard*'s AOR airplay chart)—not as good as, say, Big Country's number seventeen "In a Big Country." Even so, "Pride" was U2's entrée to the big time. The fifteen- to twenty-thousand-seat venues they played in the States to support their fourth album were larger than they were playing in Europe. They adopted its title, *The Unforgettable Fire*, from a Chicago Peace Museum exhibition of paintings by survivors of the 1945 bombings of Hiroshima and Nagasaki.

Bono knew he couldn't leap from the rafters or wave a white flag onstage anymore. When a *Melody Maker* reporter charged that the latter was merely "pompous, signifying delusions of grandeur," Bono countered: "It came from the opposite emotion; it was done out of insecurity. A fear that the music would not stand on its own."

For that tour, the band would enlist London stylist Marion Smyth to help their onstage look. She told them to avoid, in Bono's phrase, "pop colors." In came the black, white, and olive drab era. "We were really trying to be a little bit looser and not quite so buttoned up to the neck and military-looking," Clayton said. "It was more Eastern European, something like that—refugee chic."

Bono began wearing leather pants and military boots—along with his puffed-out mullet, they gave him a Soldier of Peace mien he didn't need a white flag to accentuate.

LIKE BONO, PAUL WELLER WAS OBSESSED WITH HIS OWN CREDIBILITY. BY 1982, the Jam's fluid but limited formalism began butting against the edges of Weller's ambitions. "Town Called Malice" rode the bass line of the Supremes' "You Can't Hurry Love" (around the same time that Hall and Oates utilized it for "Maneater"), and the wah-wah guitar and horn funk of "Precious" signaled a songwriter moving away from three-chord, three-person rock, into R&B and jazz. Once free of the Jam, those were the areas he pursued. "I don't wanna play rock music or be involved in it anymore, because I don't think it progresses people anymore," he said. "It's just a load of big fucking empty words and theatrical gestures that do fuck-all, when it comes down to it."

Weller partnered up with Mick Talbot, the former keyboardist for Dexys Midnight Runners, and began recruiting from nearby. The Style Council's roughness onstage could make them seem like mere amateurs, as when a *Variety* reviewer saw them in LA and sneered, "jazz for people who don't like jazz, and smooth pop-soul and Latin-esque melodies for those who consider themselves too hip for Santana or Boz Scaggs."

In their first year together, the Style Council scored six UK top tens. But the Jam's core fans felt betrayed. Performing at New York's Savoy in the spring of 1984, Weller still had to endure audience calls for the Jam's songs. He remained adamant that "it isn't Paul Weller and some backing musicians," even though nobody in the audience was there to see anyone else. That lack of focus came across on *Café Bleu*, the Style Council's debut, released in March 1984.

Weller's communalism wasn't just for the stage. Though he'd told the *NME* in his first interview with it that he'd be voting for Thatcher, he recanted, and by 1984 he was one of British rock's most outspoken leftists. The Falklands War had turned him. He said of the PM, "She's not only doing her job badly, but she's calculating as well, and I find there's a real evil nature about the Tory party. . . . She's not just another dodgy politician."

That September, the Style Council co-headlined a miners' benefit at the Royal Festival Hall. The top-billed group was Wham! *"All of Wham!, that is—backing girls, brass section, keyboards, guitars—all miming,"* *Melody Maker* reported. The outspoken Weller had cocked his snoot at the group in print, telling *NME* of "Young Guns (Go for It!)": "Go for fucking what?"

Closing the Miners' Strike show was the London band Working Week. They'd originated not from jam sessions but out of club culture, inspired by Camden Town's Electric Ballroom, whose DJ Paul Murphy became the apostle to a heavily black audience. "It was almost entirely breakdancing in that hall. The jazz was a thousand mile-per-hour jazz, breakneck speed, or if not, intense all the same," the jazz-funk DJ Snowboy recalled.

At the Royal Festival Hall, Ben Watt and Tracey Thorn, the Hull-based couple who worked together as Everything But the Girl, joined Working Week onstage. EBTG's debut, *Eden*, had gone top thirty, thanks in part to their moving from the independent Cherry Red to Blanco Y Negro, a Warner Bros. subsidiary.

The band's breakout single, "Each and Every One," was a horn-led samba; along with the dulcet timbre of Thorn's voice, the comparisons to Astrud Gilberto arrived instantly. Thorn had been a member of the Marine Girls, Watt a solo singer-songwriter. "*Eden* came along when we were halfway through writing our solo albums and we just thought, 'If we bung these together now, we've got an album already,'" Thorn said. When Weller brought the two in to work on *Café Bleu*'s "The Paris Match," Watt recalled it as "quite an odd relationship, in a way," especially considering that EBTG had recorded its own debut a year before it came out: "And the Style Council were jumping all over it," Watt said.

They'd recorded *Eden* at the Power Plant, in Willesden, with the producer Robin Millar, who was also working in the same studio with another band mining similar terrain, Sade. "Quite often we would be doing sessions at the same time," Watt recalled. "We'd be downstairs in one studio and Sade would be upstairs in the other and Robin would be nipping between both of them."

Born in Ibadan, Nigeria, in 1959, Helen Folasade Adu was raised in Colchester, Essex, by her British mother, a nurse, who had separated from her Nigerian father, a lecturer, when Sade was four. "Her marriage had broken down and all her dreams were shattered," she said. "She was very unhappy. I've seen pictures of her when she first came to England and it's horrible."

Sade's good looks and uncluttered style could be forbidding, but her manner was forthright: "Charming she is, affected she isn't," *Melody Maker* noted. When her label tried to remove a scene in the extended video accompanying the twelve-inch version of the hit "Smooth Operator," depicting Sade getting out of the bed of the titular character "because they considered it wasn't my image," the singer refused to back down: "I spent the whole day screaming and ranting. The scene was left in the video."

Sade knew she wanted to be a singer from childhood. Her favorites included Ray Charles, Billie Holiday, Bill Withers, and Gil Scott-Heron. Holiday would become a point of contention, though, when she and Sade were lazily compared. "That's just chauvinism, I suppose. I'm a brown girl who wears her hair tied back, so compare her to another brown girl with her hair tied back," she snapped.

Sade had studied fashion at Saint Martin's School of Art and spent a year "making and selling one-offs, mainly to men," she said. The band Pride recruited her into the group. When the band's manager asked if she could sing, Sade responded, "Sure. And I can write songs, too." Pride had a sizable following and was soon devoting part of its show to a solo mini-set by Sade, backed by three of the band's members—saxophonist Stewart Matthewman, her cowriter; keyboardist Andrew Hale; and bassist Paul Denman—featuring her own material, including the onomatopoeic "Smooth Operator."

"Doing the small set was really satisfying but it was our own songs that caught my imagination," she said. "It also meant that the record companies were much more interested in us because we had original material."

DAVID FOSTER WASN'T THE ONLY DR. PHIL OF RECORD MAKING IN **1984**. Phil Collins was born in 1951 and grew up a child actor, with bit parts in *Chitty Chitty Bang Bang* and *A Hard Day's Night* and a stage turn in *Oliver!* He'd started playing drums when he was five. Bitten by the Beatles, he got serious about playing even as he was auditioning for roles. Then in 1970 he auditioned for Genesis. "We tried quite a few drummers, of which two or three were very good, but Phil told the best jokes," keyboardist Tony Banks said.

Even as prog-rockers in good standing, Genesis—featuring vocalist Peter Gabriel, bassist and guitarist Mike Rutherford, lead guitarist Steve Hackett, and keyboardist Tony Banks—appealed to a broad audience. "Younger fans who would never dream of stomaching two hours of Yes or ELP [Emerson, Lake & Palmer], for example, will queue to see Genesis, for though the music is often equally complex, the band go out of their way to make it as immediate and understandable as possible through theatrics, slides, and Peter Gabriel's quirky introductory stories," one UK rock mag reported in 1974.

When Gabriel left in 1975, Collins took the vocal chair. When guitarist Steve Hackett quit two years later, the remaining members titled their next LP . . . *And Then There Were Three* . . . "I remember I felt a bit of relief," Mike Rutherford said of Hackett's departure. "You feel strange when someone isn't as into it as you are."

The three-piece Genesis's music became less cluttered and more pop. Banks, Collins, and Rutherford were all recording solo as well as with the band. Starting with *Duke* (1980), Collins said, "We're channeling our individual songs into those outlets. Therefore, the purpose of the group now is a vehicle for us writing together. I come in with an idea, Tony and Mike come in with their ideas, and we write from scratch and compose a group tune, as it were."

Like fellow prog-gone-new-wavers such as Rush ("Tom Sawyer," 1981), Asia ("Heat of the Moment," 1982), and Yes ("Owner of a Lonely Heart"), Genesis got the most modernistic of sounds from the latest synthesizers and ladled them onto monster hooks. While touring Japan in the late seventies, Genesis were given brand-new Roland TR-808s, the synthesizer company's newest drum machines. Collins began collecting rhythm boxes. He used them as songwriting prompts. When Phil divorced his first wife in 1979, he found the songs pouring out. After Collins played *Duke* for Ahmet Ertegun, president of Genesis's label, Atlantic, he mentioned the demos he'd been working on. When he played them, Ertegun snapped to attention: "This is a record!"

Collins took the demos to Richard Branson's Townhouse studio in London and dumped his eight-track tapes onto the studio's sixteen-track. With engineer Hugh Padgham, he began overdubbing, using consoles built by Solid State Logic (SSL). The latter would soon dominate the field: "More producers and engineers were freelancers who moved among studios, as opposed to being on staff at just one studio," Greg Milner wrote. "With SSLs everywhere, you no longer needed to know the quirks and intricacies of a particular studio in order to use it." Even Neil Young was buying digital recording equipment. (He'd later change his mind.)

In 1980 Collins and Padgham made *Peter Gabriel*, the old Genesis singer's third solo LP (and the third titled *Peter Gabriel*). In particular, Collins's booming drum pattern on "Intruder" sounded like it was kicking up dust on Mars. "It sounds like synthesized drums, but they are just drums that were treated," Collins said. "Peter and I were literally mucking about with the sound of the drums. . . . At one point, when the compression was set up, I hit a snare, and it elongated the decay. . . . Basically, it's the 'In the Air Tonight' sound."

Glowering and synth-led, "In the Air Tonight," a British number two, was Collins's masterwork, a song about an ugly confrontation that builds a near unbearable tension that, three-quarters in, is wiped out thoroughly by a drum fill, captured the same way as on "Intruder." "We used to call it the facehugger," Collins said, "like the thing from *Alien*, 'Let's get the facehugger on this!' I remember playing 'In the Air Tonight' to Eric [Clapton]—it wasn't really his thing. But when the fill comes in he goes, 'What the *fuck* is *that*?!'"

In September 1981, seven months after *Face Value*'s release, Genesis issued *Abacab*, scoring a series of midsized hits. Collins's *Hello, I Must Be Going!* followed near the end of 1982. "If the first one was the divorce album, then this was the lawyers album," Collins said. Alongside the likes of "I Don't Care Anymore," the album also featured a note of stagy jollity with a cover of the Supremes' "You Can't Hurry Love" that went top ten in America and reached number one in the UK, propelling the album there as well.

A popular band and solo career would have kept a lot of people busy, but Phil Collins liked activity. In 1982, he produced *Something Going On*, the first solo LP by ABBA's Frida (Anni-Frid Lyngstad), then getting divorced from the group's co-songwriter-producer Benny Andersson; she'd identified heavily with Collins's first album, not to mention his drum sound, which propelled her "I Know There's Something Going On" to number thirteen in America that year. Phil Collins had become the poet laureate of eighties divorce pop.

Collins stayed busy whether it really made sense to or not. When Robert Plant asked him to play drums on his first two solo albums, how could he say no? When Plant subsequently asked Collins to tour with him in America in 1983, how could he say no? When Eric Clapton asked Collins to produce his new album in 1984, how could he say no? When, in summer 1984, the chance arose to produce a solo LP by former Earth, Wind & Fire singer Philip Bailey, how could he say no?

There was also another, self-titled Genesis album at the end of 1983. Its hit was "That's All," based on Banks's sprightly *Abbey Road*–esque piano riff. It became the band's first US top ten hit. By now, Phil Collins was *everywhere*.

"By the time February 1984 rolls around, I'm looking a bit greedy," Collins wrote. "Before Genesis have even finished our five-night stand at Birmingham's NEC, the last dates of a four-month tour spent mostly in North America, I've released a new solo single in the U.S. At least at home I do the decent thing—

'Against All Odds (Take a Look at Me Now)' isn't released in the UK until after the completion of the tour, at the end of March."

"Against All Odds" had been a 1979 demo Collins figured for a B side; he hadn't even played the unfinished song for Genesis. When the director Taylor Hackford asked for a new title song for his new love-triangle drama, *Against All Odds*, Collins took it out of mothballs and worked with producer Arif Mardin, who ladled on the strings. Collins handled the bathos. The record *soared*, sealed by a vocal whose passion is so obvious you either succumb or retreat. But he doesn't sell the forced inclusion of the actual words "against all odds," inserted on Hackford's dogged insistence, near the end—instead of "against the odds."

The Philip Bailey collaboration, *Chinese Wall*, arrived in the fall, with "Easy Lover," a duet, reaching the top five on the Hot 100, the R&B chart, *and* rock radio. No wonder: *Variety* called it "a rock cut with Phil Collins' style written all over it. In fact, since Collins' voice stands out more than Bailey's in the mix, it could almost be mistaken for a Genesis song."

PHIL COLLINS WAS EVERYWHERE IN THE FALL OF 1984, AND BOB GELDOF was nowhere. Geldof had been a journalist when he formed the Boomtown Rats in his hometown of Dublin in 1975. In August of 1977, the band's first hit, "Lookin' After No. 1," became the first punk single playlisted on the BBC.

The Rats were, for a short time, a reliable hit machine, scoring nine consecutive top fifteen hits by 1981. America barely registered them; their one semi-hit was "I Don't Like Mondays," inspired by Barbara Spencer, the teenaged San Diegan who'd opened fire on an elementary school with a .22-caliber rifle. In America, Geldof said, the song "was banned, effectively. We were threatened with lawsuits, and Columbia . . . withdrew the record on the first day of its release."

By 1982, the Rats' UK hit streak had run out. "A new lot of people came along to replace us—like Adam Ant," Geldof said. That year, he took his first movie role as "Pink," the title character of *Pink Floyd—The Wall*, the 1982 semi-animated adaptation of the band's album, a movie he would later call "silly." He spent early 1984 working on another film, *Number One*, for the director Les Blair.

But nobody figured Geldof would bother the charts again. The Boomtown Rats' manager greeted the news of their new album *In the Long Grass* by leaving the band's employ. That's where things were on the night of October 23, when

Geldof and his girlfriend, Paula Yates, the host of the BBC-TV rock show *The Tube*, watched a television special about the ongoing African famine.

IN 1983, THE UNITED NATIONS FOOD AND AGRICULTURE ORGANIZATION had issued a warning that twenty-two African nations would be facing starvation. By October 1984, a reported forty Ethiopians were dying per day— up from twenty per day in September. The aid that had been arriving was not enough and not on time: according to the UN, only about 43 percent of the amount of food aid pledged to Ethiopia arrived that August: 155,00 tons out of 354,000 pledged.

The BBC's Michael Buerk reported from northern Ethiopia, where famine had been underway for a year. For seven unblinking minutes, the devastation of the famine was put into plain view. Earlier, in July, ITV had aired another TV film, *Seeds of Despair*, which it repeated on October 24, the night after Buerk's report. It was the first time the needle moved on aid, according to an Oxfam report: "Once again it was the media, not the monitoring, that brought awareness."

Watching Buerk's report at home with Yates and their two-year-old daughter, Bob Geldof couldn't shake one image in particular.

> There were about ten thousand people there, starving people, and there was this woman—who I subsequently met—who had to pick three hundred people that she could feed. The three hundred were led behind a stone wall, and each was given a can of butter oil, because that's all there was to eat. And the ones who hadn't been picked stood up behind the waist-high wall and looked at them, without any rancor or envy, but with intense dignity. That waist-high wall was the difference between life and death. And I remember seeing one child just put her head against the wall, the flies buzzing around her eyes. That's what made me do it. That one image is what made me do the whole thing.

WHO COULD THINK ABOUT THE THIRD FLOP SINGLE AT A MOMENT LIKE this? Footage like Geldof had seen the night before was not remotely commonplace. That morning, Yates had put a note on the refrigerator: "Ethiopia. Everyone who visits this house from today onwards will be asked to give £5 until we have raised £200 for famine relief."

Geldof kept bringing up the idea of a benefit record, and everyone he said it to agreed. That included Yates. Was anyone on *The Tube* that week who might come aboard? Midge Ure from Ultravox—an old friend of the couple's—was. "Have you got a song?" Ure asked. They each brought fragments and pieced them together. Geldof wrote the lyrics for the full thing on the taxi ride to Ure's place. Ure suggested they raise the key, from A to C. The transition to the final chorus swiped a tune from Ultravox's "Hymn." *Voilà*.

Geldof's other friends—Simon Le Bon, Sting, Gary Kemp, Martyn Ware of Heaven 17—said yes, too. The day they finished the song, Geldof also got in touch with Eurythmics, Bananarama, Thompson Twins, Frankie Goes to Hollywood, Sade, the Human League, all of whom said no. But Culture Club, Wham!, Paul Young, and the Style Council, all reached that day, said yes. Momentum was gaining.

Weller, in particular, was a surprise. The Jam and the Boomtown Rats had sniped at one another after playing together at a Belgian festival. When Geldof called, Weller asked if the Rats would play a benefit for the striking miners. "I said, 'Piss off, I'm far too busy with this as it is,'" Geldof said. "And he says, 'There you are, nobody would do it for me because all the bands hate me so much.' I says, 'Well, Paul, for every one that hates you, there's four that hate me, so come on, let's do it!'"

It took a month for the song, the recording session, and the full guest list to fall into place. Geldof had managed to circumvent most of the attendant costs a record like this would normally incur. He got a freebie from Peter Blake, who'd designed the Beatles' *Sgt. Pepper's* cover. Production, manufacturing, and shipping of the disc would take one week instead of three, the length of a more customary rush job.

The lyrics, too, were rushed. Ure would later say, "[We] had to be brutal. We were looking at television pictures of children spending five minutes trying to stand up." Even so, the song contained a couple of outright whoppers. The very title question, "Do They Know It's Christmas?," earned side-eye ever since it was announced—of course they did, since most Ethiopians (and indeed Africans) were Christian. Another line, "And there will be no snow in Africa this Christmas," was easily refutable by any random photo of Kilimanjaro. But the bigger picture was the point. Geldof figured the single would make a million pounds. Then he could go back to his band, and back to his old life.

"IT'S CHRISTMAS TIME / THERE'S NO NEED TO BE AFRAID . . ."

The voice that opens "Do They Know It's Christmas?" is Paul Young's. The first two lines hadn't been intended for him; Geldof was hoping David Bowie, who'd turned down the session, might show up last minute anyway. Bowie had, as a consolation, recorded a message for the single's B side, as had Paul McCartney and Frankie Goes to Hollywood, among others. They left Spandau Ballet saxophonist Steve Norman's on the floor: "I'd like to say hi to all our fans in Ethiopia . . ."

Ure had recorded the basic tracks at home but brought in both Sting and John Taylor to play bass and Phil Collins on drums. "Geldof just says, 'Start here and play what you want,'" Collins wrote. "I do my drum track, and there's applause. I go into the control room and Midge says, 'That was great.' . . . That was it, one take."

"AND IN OUR WORLD OF PLENTY . . ."

The second lead singer on "Do They Know It's Christmas?" had been the last to arrive. In the middle of the previous night, Geldof had rung up Boy George at his New York hotel room. "Who's there?" George asked. "Every fucker but you," Geldof replied. "Get your ass on Concorde."

Everyone else had gotten to Sarm Studio—the ZTT Records building, run by Trevor Horn, in Basing Street, Notting Hill—by noon. They'd begun arriving around nine, to a blocked-off road festooned with police. Inside, seven camera crews—five British, two American—were setting up.

Things grew far more familiar between the musicians as the day went on. By the time Boy George walked in, things had reached an unheard-of comfort level among his pop brethren. "It was as if everybody had deflated their egos for the evening," he wrote. "It all seemed very natural. There was no banquet laid on for the stars, just cups of tea and coffee and bacon and cheese sandwiches."

George took advantage of the goodwill by quashing the still-simmering feud between himself and Duran Duran, squiring Simon Le Bon up the stairs for the flashbulbs and screaming fans outside.

Part of this comfort level was achieved by intoxication. Much of this was provided, legendarily, by Status Quo, the archetypal British boogie band of the seventies. "Everybody was just totally out of it and Rick [Parfitt] and I were the drug center," Quo's Francis Rossi said. "People were saying 'let's go and see Dr. Rossi and Dr. Parfitt, shall we?'"

"BUT SAY A PRAYER / PRAY FOR THE OTHER ONES . . ."

When George Michael had come aboard, he said, the recording "didn't seem a very big deal. I think most people that turned up that day were really surprised when they saw all the cameras and everything—I was."

He was also surprised that this would likely overtake his record that holiday. In February, he'd written the song "Last Christmas"—"And as far as I was concerned it was a number one," he said. "Then as Christmas approached, there weren't any novelty records out or anything, and I was thinking, 'I can't believe it. There's no real competition around.'" Then Geldof called.

At one point that day, Michael told a reporter that he'd thought was from *Smash Hits*, "This record might be number one at Christmas, but then again so might ours, but I don't care because I'm on both of them!" In his car shortly afterward, he heard those words played on the radio. "It sounded so flippant. I thought I'd instantly be made public enemy number one. I sat there, listening to it, in absolute terror. And I went back to the office the next day and said, 'I think we'd better give up on our number one.'"

"BUT WHEN YOU'RE HAVING FUN . . ."

All five members apiece of Duran Duran and Spandau Ballet had arrived together. The night before, they'd been out partying with Billy Idol in Dortmund, Germany, and took the morning plane, red-eyed, to make the session. Andy Taylor wore a hat and sunglasses "to hide how scruffy and hung-over I looked." Simon Le Bon was surprised to discover just how little he had to do. When Geldof had called, he'd suggested that Le Bon and Sting would be the singers—not a roundelay of every other star in and around London.

The full lineup of Band Aid included Sara Dallin, Siobhan Fahey, and Keren Woodward of the trio Bananarama; Martyn Ware and Glenn Gregory of Heaven 17; the other members of the Boomtown Rats and Ultravox; Marilyn;

and four African Americans—Jody Watley, who'd moved to London following Shalamar's breakup; and Robert "Kool" Bell, James "J. T." Taylor, and Dennis Thomas of American crossover R&B stars Kool & the Gang, who happened to be in London on tour. According to Geldof, when J. T. ("*the* voice") arrived, "suddenly nobody want[ed] to sing in front of him. Like, Bono and Weller are sort of really freaking out at having to sing with this guy there."

Spandau Ballet's Tony Hadley had actually been the first singer to go to the microphone alone that morning, asked to sing: "There's a world outside your window / And it's a world of dread and fear." Rise and shine!

". . . THE BITTER STING OF TEARS . . ."

He tried to say no. "Sting was moaning, 'Do I have to sing that?'" Geldof recalled. "I said, 'Yes, because it's just a coincidence that the word "sting" is in it.'"

Sting wasn't in the mood to argue. He'd had enough of that with his old band—well, the Police were officially still around. Either way, Sting's arrival had been the day's bellwether. "Right up until the last minute," Geldof said, "me and Midge were sort of panicking that nobody would turn up. We were just sitting there, really shitting ourselves and then in walked Sting, and it was like, 'Aw, good man yourself, Sting, we are going to be okay now!'"

While at the studio, Sting began chatting with Phil Collins, and the two got along smashingly, and the bassist accepted the drummer's invitation to do some singing on his third solo LP. Sting had already done a guest spot for Dire Straits' new album, *Brothers in Arms*—cawing "I want my MTV" for a song called "Money for Nothing." Sting would go uncredited on the LP. He was already planning his first solo album. He was going to hire jazz musicians.

"WELL, TONIGHT THANK GOD IT'S THEM INSTEAD OF YOU."

Bono didn't want to sing *that* line, either. When he was handed his solo lines, Bono protested, only for Geldof to bark: "This is not about what you want, OK? This is about what these people need."

Bono showed up with Adam Clayton, U2's bass player and also its truest partier. "I knew I was there to chaperone Bono and to contribute in any way I could," Clayton said. Until Le Bon approached him, the singer felt resolutely out of place. "Seriously, it was like a blow-drying convention," Bono said.

Ure would later justify the lyric: "[It's] not saying, 'Rather them than us.' We're saying how lucky we are that we don't have to deal with that kind of extreme poverty." To nail the line, Bono "kind of did an impersonation of Bruce Springsteen."

When he was finished, the Christian Bono teased the atheist Geldof: "Well, Bob, you've written your first hymn then, haven't ya?" The Boomtown Rat told him to fuck off.

"TODAY PROVED ONCE AND FOR ALL THAT POP MUSIC CAN STILL BE A force."

This was exactly the sort of sentiment *Smash Hits* had come along to *not* say. The magazine had spent its life span tweaking the pretensions of pop stars, championing heedless fun at the expense of hippiedom's and punk's seriousness. "To realize what made *Smash Hits* special, you have to be aware of the competition: *NME*, *Melody Maker*, and *Sounds*; weekly newspapers whose styles ranged from the faux intellectual to leaden music criticism," editor Neil Tennant would write. "In those days we used to call them 'rockist,' an ultimate term of abuse."

By 1984, Tennant was nurturing his own pop ambitions. He'd begun writing songs with his friend Chris Lowe, after they met at a hi-fi shop. On assignment in New York, Tennant brought their demo to the dance producer Bobby Orlando, who came to London two months later to record their best song, "West End Girls." "The Bobby O influence definitely focused us. We weren't just writing songs anymore," Tennant said.

It was apparent that the Pet Shop Boys would go places: John Taylor named them his Most Promising New Act for 1985 in *Smash Hits*.

WESTWOOD ONE,
CULVER CITY, CALIFORNIA
April 20, 1985

NINETEEN EIGHTY-FOUR'S ROBUST SALES FIGURES MADE IT OFFICIAL—THE music business was back in the rude health it had enjoyed for decades prior to the 1979 crash. "The number of platinum albums in 1984 jumped more than 20 percent over 1983 figures, while gold albums gained 16 percent," *Billboard* reported.

After a glorious summer and fall, there were worries—up till the last minute—that 1984's holiday season might not measure up. Didn't everybody already *have* all those blockbusters? Not on this new format, they didn't: "Record/tape retailers spelled Christmas with three C's: catalog, cassettes, and Compact Discs," *Billboard* reported. One California retailer reported that sales "were up 12 percent, and I think catalog sales had a lot to do with this because there were so few big, big albums."

The Compact Disc was becoming easier to play as well as to buy. In 1984, Sony had simultaneously introduced players for in-car and carry-around use. The latter was the Discman, a portable player that retailed for $299.95, the lowest price yet. Soon, players were being advertised for half that, while the once-twenty-dollar discs themselves were beginning to go for between thirteen and fifteen dollars. The silver discs had lost their members-only cachet. "It seemed there were a lot of kids buying CDs," a New York shop manager said. "The popular titles sold better than classical."

Despite the retailers' (and trades') worries, the end of 1984 produced its share of big hits. The most popular of these titles was Madonna's *Like a Virgin*. She'd already sold two million copies of her self-titled debut; it took less than six weeks for the follow-up to equal that number. A rep for the Atlanta chain Turtles noted, "When Madonna's newest was released simultaneously on CD and vinyl it just exploded."

Another late-'84 hit, released in December to accompany the film, was the soundtrack of *Beverly Hills Cop*, the Eddie Murphy box office smash. Murphy was a Detroit cop who goes comically rogue in LA to solve his best friend's murder, uncovering a cocaine-smuggling ring in the process. After *Miami Vice* laid out the blueprint, *Beverly Hills Cop* fully codified how screen entertainment of the post-MTV era would utilize rock and pop recordings—nonstop, as wallpaper.

Things were so bullish that the RIAA announced a new certification in December—"multiplatinum"—to honor titles that had cleared the two-million mark, just as platinum, instituted in 1976, was a way to differentiate million-sellers from half-a-million sellers (gold). The initial multiplatinum plaque was handed out for 106 titles—*Thriller* was certified at twenty million, Fleetwood Mac's *Rumours* at twelve million, *Saturday Night Fever* at eleven million. Still, it was hardly a complete tally, with *Boston*, *Off the Wall*, and the Eagles' *Hotel California* among the many missing. "Epic just wanted to certify what's out there now," an RIAA spokesman explained. "We had to ask them to do *Thriller*."

"Let's hope it won't be too long before a Compact Disc becomes part of the plaque, too!" *Billboard*'s editorial crowed. "Platinum alone may not be enough."

On New Year's Eve, David Lee Roth cohosted MTV's all-night special, live from Times Square, alongside VJ Martha Quinn. They presented the first airing of Roth's new solo video—a cover of the Beach Boys' "California Girls." Dubbing himself the "toastmaster general of the immoral majority," Roth had a message: "It's a good time to decide that you're going to be, a hot dog or a little wiener. I choose to remain a little wiener."

"California Girls" came from *Crazy from the Heat*, Roth's four-song solo debut. The entire EP was made up of cover versions: Van Halen had rejected the medley "Just a Gigolo/I Ain't Got Nobody," modeled on Louis Prima, for

1984. Before *Creem's* reporter even asked, Roth outlined it this way: "Let's pretend you and I were managers. Here we have a rock star. He's just got done selling eight million records. It's been his band's biggest year. His band's best year. They're writing better, they're playing better, they're more popular than ever. Posters of Dave in the bathtub, Dave on a boat, Dave in chains, it doesn't matter—Dave anywhere, it's worth five bucks."

This attitude was vainglorious even for Roth. Still, he consciously eliminated guitars from the EP's mix and made sure to praise his bandmate: "I've heard some great music coming out of Ed's studio," he told *Billboard*. But he added: "Since my very first days with the band eleven years ago, I have always had the feeling that one day I would wake up in a cold hotel, all the rooms would be empty, and I would be stuck by a phone with a busy signal. From the first day. Nothing has changed."

But everything had changed. "At first the *Crazy from the Heat* thing was great because Roth laid off of me a bit," Edward said a decade later. "Little did I know he was testing the waters." Having directed the band's—and his own—videos, Roth was attempting to become a filmmaker, with Van Halen rehearsals taking a back seat.

In the spring of 1985, Roth stormed out of a band meeting, telling the crew, "Well, guys, it's been nice knowing you." Edward was furious: "I felt like I'd put up with this guy's shit for all these years just for him to walk. . . . Then he called me up and asked me to go to his house and said he was going to make a *Crazy from the Heat* movie. . . . I cried, then I called my brother and told him the motherfucker quit."

Shortly after Roth's departure, Edward got a call from Sammy Hagar, the journeyman San Francisco AOR mainstay. Soon he was sitting in with the band. "We jammed, let the tape roll, noodled along, and it was just brilliant," Edward said. Many disagreed. One fan wrote that Hagar "shut the door on everything that Van Halen was about. Songs became about love and commitment, loyalty and service; nothing about indulgence, sex, and drugs. Hagar made the band grow up, and because of this, ensured that Van Halen would become humorless and irrelevant."

ANOTHER MULTIPLATINUM HEAVY METAL BAND'S FORTUNES TURNED THAT New Year's Eve. While driving in his hometown of Sheffield that night, Def Leppard's drummer, Rick Allen, crashed his Corvette Stingray with his girlfriend,

Miriam Barendsen, in the passenger seat. She wound up with a concussion and whiplash; he was thrown out of the vehicle and his left arm was severed completely, right below the shoulder.

"A nurse who lived nearby had been coming up the road, and incredibly, she happened to have a full cooler of ice that she was taking to a New Year's party," Def Leppard guitarist Phil Collen wrote. "A cop also stopped to help." Allen underwent a ten-hour operation to reattach the limb. Within days, it became infected and had to be re-amputated.

Allen wasn't a Sheffield resident—he'd lived in Amsterdam for a year. *Pyromania* made Def Leppard rich, and in the time-honored tradition of mega-selling British rockers like Rod Stewart and the Rolling Stones, the band's members became tax exiles, residing outside the UK to avoid a punitive tax rate of around 60 percent.

When Collen and Steve Clark, the band's other guitarist, finally visited the drummer in the hospital, they were prepared for the worst. Instead, Allen was beaming: he was going to relearn the drums, his left foot triggering electronic drums to substitute for his missing arm. He was already practicing on a pillow.

THE FINNISH GLAM-METAL BAND HANOI ROCKS HAD BEEN A SKYROCKET IN their home of Helsinki, but America was harder to ignite. But now they were on CBS, being produced by Bob Ezrin, who'd worked with Kiss, Alice Cooper, and Pink Floyd. *Two Steps from the Move* was their fifth album, but their first for the United States. "Their look seems tailor-made for MTV," *Creem* reported. "Hanoi Rocks could easily go all the way."

Early on the evening of December 8, 1984—a Saturday—Hanoi Rocks' drummer, Nicholas "Razzle" Dingley, rode shotgun in the 1972 Pantera driven by Mötley Crüe's lead singer, Vince Neil, to a liquor store in Redondo Beach. Neil was already loaded; going too fast, he missed a turn, lost control, and drove into an oncoming Volkswagen. The VWs twenty-year-old driver, Daniel Smithers, and his eighteen-year-old girlfriend, Lisa Hogan, sustained severe injuries; Hogan spent four weeks in a coma. Neil came out of it with minor injuries; Razzle died on the way to the hospital. Neil was released the next morning on $2,000 bail.

The accident spelled the end of Hanoi Rocks. "Our drummer died and the band wasn't prepared to go on," singer Michael Monroe said years later. It did not spell the end of Mötley Crüe—far from it.

That July, Neil pled guilty to drunk driving and voluntary manslaughter and received a thirty-day sentence, paying damages of $2.6 million and performing two hundred hours of community service. When Mötley Crüe returned to the road in summer 1985 they closed the shows with "Jailhouse Rock." "Don't drink and drive," Neil signed off.

Their third LP, *Theatre of Pain*, released in June 1985, "was a tough one," says producer Tom Werman.

They were doing more drugs then, and that was one of their heavier heroin times. When bands have a hit record, they go out on tour to support the record. There's a lot of demand for them. And the worst part is, when they come off the road to do the next record, the agents have already booked the next tour. And it's big. It's a lot of money. So there's a deadline.

They'll come in with songs that are not ready; they'll have more visitors in the studio. They're getting better drugs and more drugs. It's tough. A lot of stuff interferes with their creative process, if there is one.

I remember the session where Nikki came in with a big grocery bag full of candy bars, probably twenty-five of them. I wasn't aware at that time that junkies had a sugar thing. I looked at my engineer and I said, "What's that about?" And he said, "Dude, they're junkies." And I went, "Oh my god. They are?" I thought it was cocaine, and that was it. Cocaine was a party drug, but heroin? People died from heroin. It would never have occurred to me to take heroin, and I never saw them shooting up. Apparently they were snorting it. So they didn't do it in front of me, and if they did I probably thought it was coke. It doesn't sharpen your mind. We had a lot of stops and starts and re-dos on that album. We had finished a song, and Nikki came in one day and put down a piece of paper on the console and said, "Here are the words." And I said, "We already finished that." He had a completely different set of lyrics. That was a heroin moment.

It's great up to a point when a band are a bunch of bad boys and they misbehave, but when it gets to that point? Man, you're a jerk, you know? You got drunk, you got behind the wheel, and you killed somebody.

MICHAEL JACKSON RECEIVED SOME PULSE-QUICKENING NEWS IN SEPTEM-ber 1984. The ATV Music catalog—which contained the publishing copyrights for the Lennon-McCartney Beatles songs—was available for purchase.

Jackson had begun buying song-publishing rights three years earlier, when his friend Paul McCartney showed him a printed spreadsheet of his holdings and extolled catalogs as sound, solid investments. Soon, Michael owned the rights to the early-sixties Dion hits "Runaround Sue" and "The Wanderer" and kept his lawyer, John Branca, on the lookout for others.

McCartney—who owned the Buddy Holly catalog as well as several Broad-way hits—had spent 1981 trying to purchase ATV himself but was turned down. An attempt to partner with Yoko Ono for a $20 million bid went south: Yoko didn't want to deal with Paul. In 1982, the Australian mogul Robert Holmes à Court picked up ATV's parent company, Associated Communications Corpo-ration (ACC), for around $70 million. By 1984, ATV was on the block again; this time, Holmes à Court was asking $60 million.

"Michael Jackson appears the odds-on favorite to be the next owner of ATV Music, composed of the bulk of the Lennon/McCartney hits," *Billboard* reported in December. Jackson signed on the dotted line in May 1985, getting the ATV catalog for $47.5 million. McCartney was incensed—these were *his* songs. Not anymore.

THE VICTORY TOUR'S LAST STAND TOOK PLACE AT DODGER STADIUM from December 7 to 9, the second half of a six-show stand begun the previous weekend. The tour's LA dates were supposed to have taken place in Septem-ber, at the Forum, which seated about one-third as many as Dodger Stadium; the Forum, meanwhile, filed suit against the Jacksons just hours prior to their Dodger Stadium debut.

The Dodger Stadium shows themselves were on the verge of cancellation because of a pay dispute between the promoter, Chuck Sullivan, and the group, over the former's nonpayment of nearly $2 million in earnings from a pair of shows in Vancouver, British Columbia. Sullivan had asked the Jacksons to play the December 7 to 9 dates to make up for his losses in promoting the tour—he was initially on the hook for all unsold seats. The add-on shows were only three of the fifteen the Jacksons added altogether—the forty-date Victory Tour had ballooned to fifty-five to help Sullivan recover his losses.

It hardly mattered—Sullivan wound up taking a financial nosedive of some $8 million, and his family lost control of the New England Patriots and the Foxborough, Massachusetts, stadium in which they played. He'd also suffer a mild heart attack from the stress. By December, so much bad press had followed the Victory Tour that ticket sales tailed off; the Jacksons played their LA shows to houses with notably empty pockets of seats. *Cash Box* succinctly described Michael as "spending 1984 giving his family a yearlong Christmas present."

PRINCE SAILED INTO 1985 ON THE WAVE OF A TSUNAMI. *PURPLE RAIN* WAS a complete multimedia juggernaut: the year's eleventh-highest-grossing film, the LP atop the chart for half a year. The 160-store Record Bar reported that it was the chain's "biggest-selling record of all time outside of the Christmas season." When Warner Home Video released *Purple Rain* that fall, there were four hundred thousand advance orders.

That October, Chaka Khan's cover of "I Feel 4 U," originally on 1979's *Prince*, acted as a black music summit meeting: Stevie Wonder played harmonica, Melle Mel rapped. Not that Khan herself particularly liked it. "You know," she told *Smash Hits*, "for five years I have been going into the studio really working at creating masterpieces, mixing jazz and rock and funk. So now I do this song and put rapping on it to boot, which is really *the pits*. The lowest thing you can do from an artist's standpoint."

As if to prove this wrong, December saw the release of "Sugar Walls," by Sheena Easton—a Scottish pop star known for the anodyne likes of "Morning Train"—which Prince wrote and coproduced (with Greg Mathieson) under the tongue-in-cheek moniker Alexander Nevermind, the latest of his slew of aliases. With a title that explicitly described the interior lining of a woman's vagina, it was a little much even by Prince standards.

Tickets flew out the door for the *Purple Rain* tour. The six-month jaunt would sell a total of 1.7 million seats. The tour began November 4 at Detroit's Joe Louis Arena, the first of six sellout shows. Seven shows in Washington, DC, with a total of 130,000 seats, sold out in less than ten hours. Prince also capped ticket prices at twenty dollars apiece, a sharp retort to the Jacksons' thirty-dollar Victory Tour price.

The tour spent Christmas week in the Twin Cities, playing five nights at the St. Paul Civic Center. For the occasion, Minnesota governor Rudy Perpich declared it "Prince Week." "I'm supportive of the arts," Perpich told *Billboard*, "because I believe that it's art and artists that civilize society."

IN THE SPRING OF 1985, SUSAN BAKER, WHO WAS MARRIED TO THE TREA-sury secretary James A. Baker, had an alarming revelation. "Well, my husband was in government and we had lots of kids," she says. "The youngest was seven, and one day she just came to me and she said, 'Mommy, what's a virgin?' I said, 'What? Honey, why do you want to know that?' And she said, 'Well, Madonna was singing this song about "touched like a virgin for the very first time." What does it mean to be touched for the very first time?' And I just fell out; I thought, 'Oh my gosh, what is this?' I was really upset about it. I thought, 'These lyrics are just not appropriate for young kids. I just don't know why they're being broadcast all over.' And I talked to several friends who'd had sort of similar experiences. Parents would just say, 'Turn the music down.' They weren't listening to the lyrics."

Tipper Gore, who was married to Tennessee senator Al Gore, had her own experience with Prince's "Darling Nikki." She joined forces with Susan and a few other like-minded women and founded the Parents Music Resource Center—the PMRC.

A surprising number of women showed up to its first meeting. "One of the people that came was the wife of Eddie Fritts, who was the president of the National Association of Broadcasters," says Baker. "So he wrote a letter to eight hundred station owners, alerting them to concerned parents about porn rock"—the PMRC's term for any pop music that dealt with sex in a less than Christian manner.

Baker also admits: "We had a bunch of teenagers, and they said, 'Mom, what are you doing?' They thought we were nuts."

POP MUSIC'S AWARDS SEASON KICKED OFF ON JANUARY 28, 1985, WITH THE American Music Awards, which Lionel Richie once again hosted. A month ear-lier, *Billboard* had totted up 1984's top artists, and Richie had stood at the top—even over Prince, who was a nonfactor in A/C, which Richie dominated. Five of *Can't Slow Down*'s singles had reached the top ten compared to four from *Purple Rain*.

At the AMAs, Prince received ten nominations, and won three: Favorite Pop/Rock Album and Favorite Soul/R&B Album—beating both *Thriller* and

Can't Slow Down in each category—and Favorite Soul/R&B Song for "When Doves Cry." But Richie, with eight nominations, won six, including a pair of video nods for that kitsch monument, "Hello."

It was clear that Prince's peers didn't appreciate his diva turns. At the Brit Awards in London on February 11, Holly Johnson of Frankie Goes to Hollywood introduced him to the stage—by Prince's specific request. "I've never met this person," Johnson announced, "but I've had sex on the phone with him!" A week later, Johnson admitted, "I don't think he was very amused." Two weeks later, on February 26, the Revolution sound-checked for the Grammys, then repaired backstage to a purple-painted trailer while Prince's bodyguard barked at onlookers to quit staring.

The Revolution performed on both the AMAs and the Grammys—lengthy, joyous versions of "Baby, I'm a Star," each finishing off with the bandleader strutting down the hall's aisles and out to a purple limo at the Shrine's door. At the Grammys, Mike Melvoin, the president of NARAS—and Revolution guitarist Wendy Melvoin's father—introduced the band. "Prince looked over at me," Wendy said. "He smiled but he kind of rolled his eyes like, 'Oh my God.' I was slightly embarrassed, but my father was so proud."

Richie's Grammy victory for Album of the Year and a co-win for Producer of the Year, alongside James Anthony Carmichael—they tied with David Foster—were deeply satisfying. "It's heart attack time now," Richie said backstage. "If you knew how many times I've sat out in that audience hearing the names of those other winners, wondering why—I don't want to wonder tonight. I just want to enjoy it."

But even in a year that had been so jam-packed, the Record and Song of the Year categories, which traditionally overlap heavily—they'd averaged 3.8 of the same titles over the previous five years—had only one nominee in common: "What's Love Got to Do with It." (It won in both categories.) But there wasn't one nomination for Prince's "When Doves Cry," the year's biggest *and*, with its missing bass line, most radical hit. As a habit, Mo Ostin, president of Warner Bros., didn't make public pronouncements. So it was quite unusual for him to put his name to a fire-breathing, Grammy-shaming editorial in *Billboard*, which appeared the week of the ceremony:

"Those of us involved in the day-to-day moves of the music business may be like people trying to understand a movie by watching it frame by frame," Ostin wrote. "But it seems that most of the membership of NARAS doesn't even attend the movie until it's in reruns." Noting that "Doves" had been "the year's only platinum hit single," he lashed the awards as "a set of compromised agreements that works against innovative contemporary artists such as Prince."

Prince could console himself with his Oscar. On March 25, he and the Revolution attended the Academy Awards, where *Purple Rain* won Best Original Song Score, beating *The Muppets Take Manhattan* and Kris Kristofferson's *Songwriter* (costarring Willie Nelson). It was the last time the Oscars offered the category.

Oddly, Prince was not among the nominees for Best Original Song. The winner there was Stevie Wonder's "I Just Called to Say I Love You," beating "Against All Odds," "Ghostbusters," "Footloose," and "Let's Hear It for the Boy." Wonder took the award home.

The song came from a Gene Wilder comedy, *The Woman in Red*, for which Wonder had written the soundtrack. (He sat through the movie with help from a sighted assistant.) Motown hadn't wanted him to do it—he still owed them a studio album. "If I don't put a record out, I'll be broke," Wonder admitted in January 1984. Nevertheless, when label exec Jay Lasker heard "I Just Called," he predicted it would be "the biggest single in the history of Stevie Wonder." It stayed at number one pop for three weeks and was the best-selling single of his career.

Wonder didn't sing his own song at the Oscars, though—no nominee did. The Motion Picture Academy decided in 1985 to assign the Best Original Song nominees to different singers than their originators—singers with ties to the film business. Hence, Diana Ross (a Best Actress nominee for *Lady Sings the Blues*, 1972) took on "I Just Called," attempting, and failing, to get the audience to clap along.

For "Against All Odds," they assigned it to Ann Reinking, the star of the musicals *All That Jazz* (1979) and *Annie* (1982). Gregory Peck, the Academy's president, was one of about five people left in America who'd never heard of Phil Collins. The camera caught Collins cringing his way through Reinking's version of his song.

"WE'RE TRYING TO BRING BACK UNITY AGAIN."

On April 20, 1985, Lionel Richie was in the Westwood One radio network's Culver City headquarters, discussing the aims of the charity arm that he, Kenny Rogers, and their shared manager Ken Kragen were aligned with.

Late in 1984, Kragen had received a phone call from Harry Belafonte, who had been watching the Band Aid project in Britain. "Belafonte had said publicly that as a black man he was 'ashamed and embarrassed at seeing a bunch of white English kids doing what black Americans ought to have been doing,'" Bob Geldof wrote.

Kragen had been involved with hunger relief efforts for years; another client, the late Harry Chapin, was an ardent activist in the area who'd enlisted Rogers into the cause. "He felt that what we really needed was to move the people who would ultimately move the bureaucrats," Rogers said of Chapin on Westwood One. "The real key was public awareness."

The obvious model for Belafonte's benefit idea was the Concert for Bangladesh, in 1971—George Harrison's hunger-relief all-star Madison Square Garden show, the live LP of which was the Grammys' Album of the Year in 1973. It had been a financial disaster; the $12 million take was caught in red tape as eight million children starved to death. Kragen suggested instead that they do an American version of Band Aid.

As USA for Africa, Richie, Rogers, Kragen, and Belafonte had joined with some three dozen other performers, under the guidance of producer Quincy Jones, to record the Band Aid answer single, "We Are the World." And now, they were participating in Westwood One's three-hour special, *Radio USA for Africa*.

"We Are the World" was recorded straight after the American Music Awards at A&M Studio, with Quincy Jones and Michael Omartian producing, and was released on March 7, 1985, three months after "Do They Know." Like the singles, the radio special was made entirely on volunteered time. The announcers included anchor Scott Shannon of Z100 in New York, *American Top 40*'s Casey Kasem, and *Soul Train* announcer Sid McCoy.

"It's become a national movement," Kragen said, overstating somewhat. "We've earned $36 million in five weeks. . . . People in the United States need to make up their minds that the elimination of hunger is the number one priority here, and the elimination of homelessness. If we do that, it would be a matter of months, or at least a year or less, I think, that we'll solve the problem of hunger in the United States."

"The sixties" made several appearances. Announcer Scott Muni intoned: "Giving was a big thing back in the sixties. But it seemed like the decade that followed, people just cared about themselves. Now, in the eighties, thinking about one's fellow man [*meaningful pause*] seems to be [*sententious pause*] coming back."

Moments like this abounded. At one point, Casey Kasem read a letter: "I am six years old. I would like to help you raise money. Please let me know what I can do to help. . . . I want kids to have enough to eat. Here is my allowance. [*pause*] Two dollars."

LIONEL RICHIE HAD SIGNED ON TO MAKING AN AMERICAN CHARITY RECord the moment Kragen floated the idea. The initial idea was to bring together Richie and Wonder—two Motown powerhouses still signed to the label would eliminate legal stickiness. But Wonder couldn't commit—he still owed the label a non-soundtrack album—and Quincy Jones did, despite being in the midst of composing the score for *The Color Purple*, the Steven Spielberg–directed adaptation of Alice Walker's novel, which Jones was also coproducing.

Q enlisted his prize client as well. "A few hours later [Jones] called back and said Michael not only wants to participate, he wants to write the song with Lionel," Kragen said.

Lionel and Michael wrote the song in Michael's bedless bedroom at Hayvenhurst—"He just slept on the floor," Richie recalled. At one point early on, Jackson's pet boa constrictor, Muscles, barged in on the session, frightening Michael's guest.

The songwriters listened to national anthems to get the regal feel they were going for. "We didn't want a normal-sounding song," Richie said. "We wanted bombastic, the biggest thing you got." Jones was breathing down their necks. Revising it down to the wire, Richie and Jackson finally finished "We Are the World" and sent cassettes to several of the participants, which Federal Express shipped gratis. Jones added a note: "Leave your ego at the door."

THE CENTRAL MELODIC LINE OF "WE ARE THE WORLD" WAS A REPEATING motif throughout the Westwood One broadcast. It was played on a Fairlight synthesizer; indeed, Fairlight was one of the program's sponsors. When Carl Wilson appeared, he plugged the upcoming Beach Boys album—Brian Wilson was "all over the place on it," Carl assured everyone—it was, he said, made with lots of Fairlights.

Quincy Jones was his usual straight-shooting self when he spoke with Sid McCoy. "This didn't just happen," he began: "Somehow it has become an editorial feeling that if it's a third-world country, it doesn't matter. I can't imagine in my wildest dreams this ever happening to Germany or England or France—I just can't imagine it."

The USA for Africa session had been put together so quickly that there was an ever-present danger of things swerving out of control. "There were so many artists participating in it until no one was allowed into the studio at all, with the exception of the people who were actually working on the recording," Smokey Robinson said. "Whoever you had with you—your mother, your sister, your date, your wife, your husband—no one was allowed in there, no one was allowed in there . . . cameramen, engineers, artists—there had to have been a hundred people in the studio."

Richie had given himself the opening line "so I can get out of the way," he said. Jackson took the first chorus, and he recorded his vocals first, starting at 9:00 p.m., while the AMAs were still happening. Unlike the other singers, he'd provide his own backing vocals and harmonies. When Jackson sang "So let's start giving," the answer to "Giving what?" was obvious: donations, of course. He and Richie knew precisely what they were writing—a song for a telethon.

Jackson didn't take part in the Westwood One special, but one of his self-professed biggest fans did. "USA for Africa is a tremendous private sector initiative that demonstrates the resourcefulness and kindness of the American people," President Ronald Reagan said in a recorded message.

Reagan had done much as president to exacerbate the African famine with his policies, and one of the first things he did when he got into office was cut government subsidies for the needy. So a "tremendous private sector initiative" like USA for Africa, ready to take up the collection hat to help those in need so he could spend all of America's money on the arms race, was just perfect for Reagan. Like many of the other guests on *Radio USA for Africa*, the president also made sure to slip in a plug for his current project: National Volunteer Week.

BOB GELDOF HAD VISITED ETHIOPIA FOR THE FIRST TIME OVER CHRISTmas, a month before the AMA Awards ceremony in LA, courtesy of World Vision, the Christian nonprofit founded in California. On his way, he'd met none other than Mother Teresa at the airport. "She was astonishingly tiny,"

Geldof wrote. "When I went to greet her I found that I towered more than two feet above her." She left him with some advice: "I can do something you can't do and you can do something I can't do. But we both have to do it."

When he'd gotten to Lalibela, someone brought out a tape player blaring "Do They Know It's Christmas": "I looked at the people, ragged and under-nourished and desolated by unnecessary miseries and I looked at the journalists about me just as Bono's voice shouted, 'Tonight, thank God it's them instead of you.'"

At a feeding camp for refugees and the starving, Geldof witnessed a child "shit out his own intestines. He had nothing left inside to evacuate except the torn shreds of his own stomach which had been ripped open by dry grain. I was watching a child die." After witnessing much the same in Sudan, Geldof was incredulous to meet a Sudanese official who told him, flatly, "There is no famine. . . . We have the situation under control." Sudan's Nimeiry regime would be overthrown within months of Geldof's visit.

Geldof was still skittish about how this all might look. Visiting Ethiopia, Geldof forbade any of the photographers on hand to snap him with the starv-ing Ethiopian children. "It will simply be construed as shameful, distasteful and patronizing. You can take pictures of me in the camp. You can take pictures of the kids. But not the two together. This is my trip and anybody who is not pre-pared to agree to my rules can fuck off back to the plane," he said. Naturally, one snapped a side shot anyway.

When Geldof arrived at A&M Studio in January, he was floored by its ostentation, from "guards who checked passes at every other step" to the grotesquely overdone spread in the lounge, "a cornucopia of Hollywood ex-travagance." His mood shifted when he got into the studio's heart.

The sheer star power that walked into the room over the course of a cou-ple of hours was surreal for everybody. Yet the atmosphere was congenial. Now Geldof was talking with . . . Bob Dylan. Then Diana Ross came and sat in Dylan's lap while she and Geldof showed off pictures of their kids. When Springsteen arrived, the room went abuzz over the news that he'd *actually driven himself to the studio* and had *actually parked his own car* (across the street in the lot of a supermarket), and had done so *without any security*.

Quincy Jones had worked with Springsteen when Bruce wrote and played on "Protection," from *Donna Summer*, the album Jones produced right before *Thriller*. Springsteen had, the night before, played the last show on the *Born in the U.S.A.* trek before a month-and-a-half-long break. Then he'd go back out until October, finishing at LA's Memorial Coliseum. Springsteen was an arena rocker now, the biggest around.

In the midst of all this, he was also starting to get serious about someone. Later that spring, on May 13, he'd marry Julianne Phillips, an actress originally from Oregon, following a six-month courtship. Their small ceremony in Lake Oswego, a town of less than forty thousand, would be the site of a feeding frenzy by the emboldened tabloid media: "We got married at midnight, hood-winking the sea of press. The next day, whirlybirds, jammed with tabloid photographers, filled the sky over our reception brunch."

At A&M Studio, Springsteen and Geldof were chatting when Ken Kragen asked Geldof to speak to the group. He sobered the room up: "You see dead bodies lying side by side with the live ones." On Westwood One, Kenny Rogers recalled, "When you see a guy who's been there stand there and tell you, in very graphic terms, what he personally witnessed—and he said, 'This is not third-hand information; I saw this'—how can you not react?"

"IT WAS JUST AN INCREDIBLE THING THAT THEY ALL SHOWED UP," SMOKEY said of the USA for Africa session. "What I was surprised at was the people who *didn't* show up."

Kragen admitted to *Billboard* that he was sore over Prince not contributing to the single. (Sheila E. went, the sole representative of Prince's camp, and sang in the chorus.) "We were disappointed," Kragen said. "We had hoped to have Prince and Michael Jackson sing one line after the other face-to-face at a mike. It would have been classic."

Prince wasn't interested—he didn't like the song, and he wasn't in charge. When his manager, Bob Cavallo, offered Prince to play guitar on the track, Jones retorted: "I don't need him to fucking play guitar!" As it was, Prince's designated line—"But if you just believe, there's no way we can fall"—went to the properly humble Huey Lewis.

Prince's managers begged him to stay in the hotel. Nope—Prince went clubbing. A pair of photographers moved in for pictures, and Prince's bodyguards, Lawrence Gibson and Wally Safford, moved in on them—tearing the film out of one camera and punching another photographer in the eye. Gibson, who'd yanked the film, was released on $6,000 bail; Safford, who threw the punch, was out for $500.

Despite his donating a Jesus story called "4 the Tears in Your Eyes" to the *We Are the World* LP—he'd announced it almost instantly after the fracas—the ensuing brouhaha cost Prince's public perception dearly. He was mocked on *Saturday Night Live*—Billy Crystal, in ill-advised body makeup, fingering his hairy chest through a ruffled collar and howling, "I am *also* the world!" while Hulk Hogan and Mr. T, as the bodyguards, bellowed, "Wanna make something out of it?" as they flung aside cast members imitating Springsteen and Cyndi Lauper.

By the time the tour reached its end at Miami's Orange Bowl in early April, his manager, Steve Fargnoli, announced, "Prince is withdrawing from the live performance scene for an indefinite period of time," adding: "I asked Prince what he planned to do. He told me, 'I'm going to look for the ladder.'"

"The Ladder" was the final song on *Around the World in a Day*, issued on April 22, less than two weeks after the Miami finale. Warner Bros. shipped two and a half million copies to stores, and it sailed to number one. But the album's hard left musical turn, plus the bad publicity over USA for Africa, gave it a strange aftertaste.

"In some ways, [*Purple Rain*] was more detrimental than good," Prince said in 1999. "People's perception of me changed after that, and it pigeonholed me. I saw kids coming to concerts who screamed just because that's where the audience screamed in the movie. That's why I did *Around the World in a Day*, to totally change that." When he showed the psychedelically painted cover art to Jill Jones, who'd appeared in the *Purple Rain* film and sang on *Around the World*, Prince pointed out who each of the figures represented. Then he pointed to the ladder in the middle. It was empty. "I'm up the ladder," he explained. "I'm gone."

"THERE'S AN UNSPOKEN CAMARADERIE IN SHOW BUSINESS AMONG THE people—you know everybody even if you haven't met them," Smokey Robinson told Westwood One. But all the congeniality in the world couldn't make forty-six wildly different voices mesh as one—not immediately. The song's key was too high for many of the men at first. Springsteen, Rogers, Waylon Jennings, and Willie Nelson were asked to lay out. Fine-tuning the mass singalong took hours.

But when the chorus was finished, Jones let everybody hear it. "The first time that they played back the chorus, everyone was just blown away," Lindsey

Buckingham said on Westwood One. "It was really something. . . . Billy Joel and I were standing in the corner, listening to Ray Charles just noodling on the piano, going, 'Oh yeah, that's not something you hear every day.'"

The solos came next. Cyndi Lauper's was the most attention-grabbing—indeed, she was the most disruptive member of the group. At one point, she muttered to Billy Joel, "It sounds like a Pepsi commercial." But when Lauper asked to improvise, Jones gave her the go-ahead: "This is not 'The Rite of Spring.'" On take seven, her tornado wailing had knifed through the song's soft underbelly so audaciously that the studio burst into applause when she finished.

That day, it took several colleagues to save Bob Dylan. He'd laid out of the chorus early on—and in the making-of footage, he's clearly lip-synching in places. After pep talks from Jones and Richie, Dylan asked Wonder to play it for him on the piano. Wonder then *imitated Bob Dylan* to indicate the phrasing. "We were all kind of doing it, and we wanted to make sure we didn't insult anybody," Richie said. With Stevie's prodding, Dylan modulated his way through the chorus, then told Jones to go ahead and erase it if he wanted. Quincy hugged Dylan—no, he didn't want to erase it.

Since Bono had impersonated Bruce Springsteen on "Do They Know It's Christmas?" it was only right that Springsteen imitate himself on the sequel. He'd already taken the top of the second chorus, but nearing the end of the night, Jones asked Bruce to riff on the refrain: "It's like being a cheerleader of the chorus," the producer explained. He got it in one go. The session ended at 8:00 a.m. Jones and Richie were the only principals left in the studio, and they played the whole thing back. Jones realized he still needed an ending, so a day later, Wonder returned to the studio to sing Springsteen's closing volleys back to him. *Now* the song was finished.

"WE ARE THE WORLD" SOLD OUT OF ITS FIRST SHIPMENT OF EIGHT hundred thousand in three days. It moved three million copies by the end of 1985 and spent four weeks at number one.

Near the finish of the Westwood One program, with no preamble, came the announcement: "A letter from Africa." An un-ID'ed speaker intoning, over ominous syn-drums, a poem, swept through with dramatic pauses. Here's how it ends:

WHY?

WHY?

WHY?

HWY? [sic]

—followed, of course, by the piano intro of John Lennon's "Imagine."

When Frank DiLeo accompanied Jackson out of the studio of the USA for Africa session, he told reporters, "Let the song speak for itself. He didn't write for publicity. He wrote to help starving people."

By now, Jackson was planting stories about himself in tabloids such as the *National Enquirer* and *Star*. In 1988, when *The Face* asked DiLeo how much exposure was too much, the manager shrugged: "It's too late anyway. He won't have a normal life even if I stop."

WEMBLEY STADIUM, LONDON, AND JFK STADIUM, PHILADELPHIA

July 13, 1985

SIX DAYS AFTER *RADIO USA FOR AFRICA* SIGNED OFF, THE SAN FRANCISCO concert promoter Bill Graham held a rally to protest President Reagan's impending trip to Bitburg. "He was going to go visit this graveyard in Germany where Nazis supposedly were buried along with American soldiers and other victims of World War II. He was going to lay a wreath on their graves," Graham recalled. "I never thought the President would actually go through with this. I said, 'Come on. You must be kidding. He wouldn't be that stupid.'"

Graham's rally barely made a dent: Reagan laid his wreath on May 5. Graham happened to be in Europe at the same time, staying in Nice, France. The focus of the trip was to discuss the mega-concert-cum-telethon that Bob Geldof wanted to put on. Geldof was insisting that it be held in two cities at once, one in London and the other somewhere on the American East Coast, and broadcast by satellite to every corner of the world.

None of this seemed doable by Graham's lights. In 1983, he'd produced the second US Festival for Steve Wozniak, who'd gone to great lengths to broadcast a Russian rock band playing onstage in Leningrad, live and via satellite, to an

American audience in real time. When Graham was importuned to announce the historic event, he got onstage, looked at the monitors, and said, "This is really being faked from a studio in Southern California." Then he unplugged the connection. Wozniak, furious, fired him.

Graham was born Wulf Wolodia Grajonca to Russian Jewish immigrants in Berlin near the beginning of 1931. His father was killed in an accident two days after he was born. Graham would often claim he had no memory of the first nine years of his life: "My sisters have told me about my childhood," he said. In 1939, his mother sent him and his sister Tolla to an orphanage near Paris. When the Nazis invaded France, he and the other children "retreated in cars and trains, whatever we can."

Through a dangerously circuitous route, he wound up in New York, where a couple from the Bronx adopted him. Little Wolfgang's thick German accent got him beaten up every day. A neighborhood friend helped him practice to get rid of it. He changed his name shortly afterward.

Graham went west to San Francisco, hoping to act. In 1964 he began managing the San Francisco Mime Troupe and worked with the Grateful Dead at the Trips Festival. When the city banned a Mime Troupe show for obscenity in 1965, Graham organized a benefit concert, then two—then began booking concerts full-time. At thirty-five, he'd found his trade.

Graham's personality ran rough from the beginning. He insisted his bands begin on schedule, and he ran around backstage with a clapboard to prompt them. Yelling was endemic to him. In 1968, he opened two clubs, the Fillmore West in San Francisco and the Fillmore East in New York. Both were state-of-the-art facilities—Graham was a fanatic for detail: everything from the sound to the lighting had to be perfect. The Fillmores closed in 1971, enabling Graham to book arenas. By 1981, he was promoting the Rolling Stones' 1981 US tour, the biggest rock road show to date. Graham took a reported 40 percent of the gross.

The day after Reagan visited Bitburg, somebody visited the single-room office of Bill Graham Presents, at Howard and Eleventh Streets, and threw a pair of Molotov cocktails through the windows. Everything was destroyed—the ceiling fell in, and the computer on the desk of Graham's secretary, Jan Simmons, was, she said, "melted flat." On the remaining walls were spray-painted swastikas. There was a million dollars in damage.

Graham spent twenty hours flying back home from Nice, feeling, he said, "like I had been raped emotionally." After arriving, he told a reporter, "This happened a day after Ronald Reagan's visit to Bitburg. I don't think there's any doubt about the connection." He spent fourteen hours telling his girlfriend, Regina Cartwright, about surviving the Holocaust, his sister Tolla starving to death on the roadside as they ran from the Nazis.

"THIS IS, QUITE CATEGORICALLY, THE MOST IMPORTANT CONCERT OF ALL time."

The London promoter Harvey Goldsmith was talking to *Melody Maker*. Live Aid, the name of Geldof's newest music-based African aid initiative, was to be a two-lineup event, linked by satellite in almost exact real time—absolute science fiction even in the tech-obsessed mid-eighties.

Graham was the obvious American promoter. No one in the States matched his status. He had first tried to get them to do it in Stamford, Connecticut—he had a deal on the stadium there. Washington, DC, was too far away; New Jersey's Meadowlands lacked mythical resonance. Philadelphia's history didn't mean much to Geldof, but it did to the United States, and Graham was friendly with Larry Magid, the city's main rock promoter.

Besides, the City of Brotherly Love needed some rehab. On May 13, city police had firebombed the West Philadelphia headquarters of MOVE, a black radical group that had been at odds with the state for years. Over several months, MOVE had built a bunker on their rooftop. The standoff disintegrated, with Mayor Wilson Goode allowing the police to bomb the building. Ramona Africa, one of only two MOVE members to survive the bombing, said, "The whole house shook, but we didn't know what it was. We didn't even know initially that there was a fire." Goode instructed his men to "let the fire burn." Soon the entire block was on fire. Eleven people died, five of them children, and the fire left 250 homeless. The incident was disturbing in every way—not least that a black neighborhood had been firebombed by a black mayor.

BY THE TIME LIVE AID WAS ANNOUNCED JUNE 10, GELDOF AND Goldsmith—as well as the US television producer Mike Mitchell, who'd helped organize the 1984 Summer Olympics in Los Angeles—were hip-deep in preparation. In London, nearly everything was donated—time, talent, supplies, catering. "In England people give their services free," Goldsmith said. "In America they give their services and want to be paid."

Geldof's idea was simple—a "Global Jukebox" where every act was given fifteen minutes to perform: "You had to do hits. You weren't allowed to do anything else." Bono of U2 called Geldof's manner of persuasion "moral blackmail." When Geldof called Pete Townshend, he told the Who guitarist that "one million people would die if [they] didn't perform."

The organizers had little luck with black performers. At announcement time, only four black artists were billed: Stevie Wonder, Billy Ocean, Sade, and Eddie Kendricks and David Ruffin of the Temptations, who were performing with Hall and Oates. (This discounted group members such as Joe Leeway of Thompson Twins and Tony Thompson of the Power Station.)

Geldof, who approached artists directly whenever he could, got assurance on Wonder's behalf from Stevie's friend Keith Harris. After the announcement, Wonder's furious manager, Ewart Abner, rang Geldof, demanding he issue a press release that Stevie was off the bill. Geldof invited them to announce it themselves.

One black act, Run-D.M.C., had actually offered to play, only for one of Graham's employees to turn them down. Graham promptly called Russell Simmons and offered them a slot. Larry Magid opened his Rolodex and nabbed a number of African American stars with Philly ties: the Four Tops, Patti LaBelle, Ashford and Simpson with Teddy Pendergrass.

At one point, Geldof called Ken Kragen to ask after Lionel Richie. Kragen would take until the final week to secure Richie at the end of the American bill, then asked Geldof to keep it quiet. "They were going to see how it panned out," Geldof said. "Right at the last moment, if it was a biggie, they would come in. 'Hey. I'm a *special guest.*'"

FOR GRAHAM AND HIS COHORT, ROCK AND ROLL WAS A REBELLION *AGAINST* television. Even as he perfected rock as a big business, he'd look fondly back to a time when, as he put it, "Rock and roll was the umbilical cord of the alternative society."

"Bill didn't understand that MTV in the mid-eighties was just as important and as dynamic as the Grateful Dead and Jefferson Airplane had been twenty years earlier," said Joshua White, a former Fillmore East staffer who'd become a TV producer.

Geldof was never confused about his venture. "This was going to be a TV show. It wasn't a concert," he later said. Graham, though, insisted otherwise—

that Live Aid was a concert first, and damn the TV crew's schedule. Besides, he didn't really think they could do it. "Assuming it comes off well—and it's hard to say now—it will have the largest viewing audience of any entertainment project that I know of," he said—after JFK Stadium was already secured.

AT 11:30 A.M. SHARP, HALF AN HOUR BEFORE THE CONCERT BEGAN, THE Prince and Princess of Wales arrived at Wembley Stadium. Princess Diana was a twenty-four-year-old rock fan—particularly fond of Phil Collins and Dire Straits—rumored to have roller-skated through Kensington Palace with Duran Duran blasting on her Walkman. Geldof had recently met her and Prince Charles, then thirty-six, at a Dire Straits concert—one of fourteen they were performing at Wembley Arena (one-sixth the size of Wembley Stadium, where Live Aid took place) concurrent with Geldof's show.

Geldof got in around 8:00 a.m. His back was killing him, even beyond nerves. The weather, unusually, was beautiful, and people were leaning out their windows, waving, and shouting good luck to him as he sped by in a donated limo.

Rock had already become part of the royal court thanks to the Prince's Trust charity concerts that Charles convened, but his swinging by with Diana to kick Live Aid off was unprecedented. Outside, as noon approached, scalpers were starting to unload tickets for below face value. (They'd been selling them for fifty pounds each.) "I made my money," one said as he sold his last one for twenty quid. "I just want to get to the show meself." Backstage, Harvey Goldstein told Geldof and the royal couple: "For fuck's sake, you're supposed to be up in the box. It's time to start."

Up in the BBC control room, the prince and princess's change of plans—they were supposed to introduce the show from the stage—initiated a small panic. The producer, Trevor Dann, jotted a variation on the introduction of the BBC Light Programme *Two Way Family Favourites*. The announcer, Richard Skinner, began speaking only to realize he was being broadcast not only on TV but also through the Wembley PA: "It's twelve noon in London, seven a.m. in Philadelphia, and around the world it's time for Live Aid—sixteen hours of live music in aid of famine relief in Africa. Wembley welcomes their Royal Highnesses, the Prince and Princess of Wales."

Charles and Diana sat next to Geldof, Yates, and their daughter Fifi. The row behind them had David Bowie, the members of Queen, George Michael,

Elton John, and Dire Straits' Mark Knopfler. If you wanted a snapshot of Britain's rock firmament as of mid-1985, here it was.

STATUS QUO HAD BROKEN UP A YEAR EARLIER AND "REUNITED" TO PLAY Live Aid. In this way alone, they were the perfect opening band. They kicked things off with "Rockin' All Over the World," a John Fogerty number they'd taken to number three in 1977. Off in the wings, a number of early-arriving rockers were air-guitaring along. After the performance, Geldof told them the worldwide audience was two billion people. "I thought, 'I'm glad you didn't tell me that before,'" Francis Rossi said.

After Status Quo finished, Skinner spoke: "If this isn't the best rock and roll show ever, just look at these headlines." He held up several London dailies—most of them featuring Live Aid on the cover. Unless you were a dying Beatle, pop on the front page was exceedingly rare. There it was, on the *Daily Star*, the *Daily Sun*, the *Daily Mirror*, the *Daily Mail*. These were the tabloids, read by millions, sentimental above all. Of course they went for this great charity story.

"Everybody was crying around me and I thought, 'Christ, what a noise,'" Geldof told the BBC's Janice Long afterward. If he sounded polished, he was—over the four months Live Aid had taken to prepare, Geldof set aside ninety minutes a day for interviews.

GELDOF HAD BARELY SLEPT FOR WEEKS. THE PHONE WOULD RING AT FOUR in the morning—Australia. It would ring in the evening—America. It had been going on ever since he got back from touring with the Boomtown Rats. It was costing him, financially. "You have to pull scams together," he said. "Like changing dollars into pounds but waiting for the dollar rate to fall, so that we'd make extra money on the changeover, maybe four hundred bucks. It's down to that level."

Geldof nonetheless knew how valuable he could be as a hunger advocate outside of politics. "I'm lucky, I don't have to attract votes, so I can argue with Mrs. Thatcher, shout at the guy from Ethiopia, I can say and do exactly what I like," he said. "I don't *mind* being the world's clown, if I'm allowed to do things that are effective."

Sixties and seventies stars dominated the lineup. The postpunk–New Pop axis was effectively neutered. "I take it Bob Geldof didn't like us," Peter Hook of New Order later said. "You felt quite affronted that you weren't asked." Morrissey didn't: "I mean, it's one thing to want to save lives in Ethiopia, but it's another thing to inflict so much torture on the British public," he told *Melody Maker*. Geldof spat back that the Smiths were "just an *awful* band." When a waitress mistook him for a vegetarian, he sneered, "Nah, yer confusing me with Morrissey. Meat might be murder, but veg is *torture*."

Cannily, the Boomtown Rats played third at Wembley—opening would have been presumptuous; prime time, preposterous. They started with "I Don't Like Mondays," and as they played, Geldof wrote, "The pain in my spine vanished. . . . As I began to sing, the preoccupations of the day disappeared." He heightened the drama by holding his fist aloft right after the line, "And the lesson today is how to die"; the band's pause occasioned a huge ovation. (Seventy-two thousand people cheering for that lyric sounds unnerving now.) Alas, during "Rat Trap," Geldof's microphone went out.

The exhilaration of the Rats' moment dissipated in short order. Dressed in black leather, Adam Ant hit the stage for the first time in Britain in three years. He was ready to change his image again—he sang a new song, "Viva La Rock," that nobody knew or liked. "Who the hell's that?" one person shouted. Ant's career never recovered. When it was over, the Prince and Princess of Wales, their duties finished, left the royal box.

WHEN AN ECSTATIC GELDOF TOLD GRAHAM HE'D GOTTEN PRINCE Charles and Princess Diana—actual royalty—to open the show in London, Graham decided that America's equivalent of "royalty" was the leering Hollywood star Jack Nicholson. This was, perhaps, the most "guy" moment of the eighties. Nicholson, a little at sea, introduced the United States to the world, and then introduced Joan Baez, who cast things in stark terms: "Good morning, children of the eighties, and others—this is your Woodstock and it is long overdue."

That, and her long "rap" afterward, was heavy-handed generational self-flattery. "They were waiting for boom-boom rock," Baez said. Her medley of "Amazing Grace" and "We Are the World" may have contained the day's most purely funny moment in Baez's excessively plummy reading of the line "As God has shown us by turning stone to bread."

Backstage, Graham was moving like a dervish, stage-managing as well as producing. "I changed everything from the night before," he boasted. "I didn't like the TV guys at all. . . . I changed their entire script around." It may have been Geldof's event, but Graham felt free to wrong-foot his colleagues for no good reason except that his ego demanded it. And are you surprised to learn that Graham was using a lot of cocaine at this time? He'd always had a wild temper; now, more and more, he was simply belligerent.

When Baez finished, the MTV feed went back to Wembley for another one-song performance. Elvis Costello's troubadour turn—with an electric guitar rather than acoustic—was, in a small way, a masterstroke. Introducing his number as an "old northern English folksong," with the lyrics written on his hand, he launched into the Beatles' "All You Need Is Love" as the stadium sang along. It was a sharp call back to the 1967 *Our World* special when the Beatles had premiered the song: an earlier TV event broadcast live and simultaneously from all corners of the globe.

The vocal microphone at Wembley went out again for Sade. She stayed cool throughout—her backless dress surely helped—but the past year she'd had her eyes opened by attempting to sell to America. "I'm starting to learn expressions like 'crossover,'" she told *Billboard*. "And think the record will cross over naturally, because people are talking about it, and not because of which station it's played on. . . . Maybe they took a bit of convincing, became they couldn't see us comfortably fitting into any of the American radio categories. Since I've been here, I've become aware of how very bracketed all the music is."

BLACK SABBATH HAD GOTTEN ONTO THE LIVE AID BILL, BOTH GRAHAM and Geldof hinted broadly in their memoirs, by threatening to pull out of their merchandising deal with the Graham co-owned Winterland Productions. Graham put them on at 11:00 a.m. "Can you imagine looking at Ozzy Osbourne at eleven in the morning? Following the Four Tops?" he said. Judas Priest followed later in the afternoon. Here, as Joan Baez put it, was the "boom-boom rock and roll."

Three days after Live Aid, *Variety* datelined a report that Don Arden, Sabbath's former manager, was suing Sharon Osbourne, Ozzy's wife and manager, for "allegedly interfering with his management contract" with Sabbath and Lita Ford, the former Runaways bassist who'd been making a name as a heavy metal solo act. The suit alleged that a full original-band reunion was in place, with Sharon taking over as manager, and asked for nearly $12 million total in damages. *Variety* didn't mention that Sharon Osbourne was also Don Arden's daughter.

Also in 1985, a judge decided in favor of Osbourne in a lawsuit alleging that his 1981 song "Suicide Solution" had prompted a nineteen-year-old man to shoot himself. The song, Osbourne explained in court, was about the death of his friend Bon Scott, AC/DC's first vocalist, who'd died of alcohol poisoning—not an incitement to suicide. The capture in August of Richard Ramirez after he'd committed sixteen murders and twenty rapes and assaults, who'd been a major AC/DC fan—in particular, the track "Night Prowler" from 1979's *Highway to Hell*—also became a talking point for the anti-rock brigade led by the PMRC.

The Senate Commerce Committee announced the PMRC-led "porn rock" hearing for September 19, 1985. The music industry barely responded. Only three name musicians went and argued against the PMRC. The first was John Denver, who argued forcefully against any ratings system: "Mr. Chairman, this would approach censorship. And I'll be very clear that I am strongly opposed to censorship of any kind in our society or anywhere else in the world."

Frank Zappa hadn't had such a public forum in years. He'd spent much of the previous decade and change pursuing both the avant-garde audience and the Dr. Demento one, pumping out novelties such as "Valley Girl" (1982), voiced by his fourteen-year-old daughter Moon Unit—Zappa's only ever Top 40 hit. Zappa's official statement took many jabs at the bodies in front of him: "It is my understanding that, in law, First Amendment issues are decided with a preference for the least restrictive alternative. In this context, the PMRC's demands are the equivalent of treating dandruff by decapitation."

Zappa wore a suit and tie, his hair cut short and neat. Dee Snider of Twisted Sister, on the other hand, arrived in full rocker regalia: blue jeans, sleeveless denim vest over a printed black T-shirt, shades, and his lion's mane of blond curls in full flower. Snider took his speech out of his back pocket and began: "I would like to tell the committee a little bit about myself. I am thirty years old. I am married. I have a three-year-old son. I was born and raised a Christian and I still adhere to those principles. Believe it or not, I do not smoke, I do not drink, and I do not do drugs."

He then dismantled the PMRC's accusations against his band, including the idea that the lyrics of "We're Not Gonna Take It" were "violent." That was the video, he explained: "It is no secret that the videos often depict story lines completely unrelated to the lyrics of the song they accompany," Snider testified. "The video 'We're Not Gonna Take It' was simply meant to be a cartoon with human actors playing variations on the Road Runner/Wile E. Coyote theme; each stunt was selected from my extensive personal collection of cartoons."

At JFK, an enthused Rob Halford mentioned the "burst of wild energy" being onstage had given him. As for Ozzy, when someone mentioned "what they're doing for Ethiopia," Osbourne responded, "What's that, a restaurant?"

IF HEAVY METAL WAS UNDERREPRESENTED, HIP-HOP WAS BUT A BLIP ON the Live Aid radar. But even though Run-D.M.C.'s appearance at Live Aid was brief—two songs—in a field where boasting was all, it gave the trio amazing bragging rights. "I stepped on-STAGE / At Live Aid / All the people GAVE / And the poor got PAID," D.M.C. would snarl a year later on "My Adidas."

Live Aid was their first stadium appearance, but this was a rare occasion that Run-D.M.C. weren't headlining a large show. They'd topped the bill of the 1984 Fresh Fest Tour, a twenty-seven-city rap jaunt that kicked off around Labor Day and finished near Christmas. Featuring an all-star rap lineup (Kurtis Blow, Whodini, the Fat Boys, Newcleus), a trio of major break-dancing crews, and corporate sponsorship by Swatch Watch, Fresh Fest grossed $3.5 million and pushed *Run-D.M.C.*, *Fat Boys*, and *Escape*, the second Whodini album, to gold status.

When the writer Nelson George attended the Washington, DC, edition of the Fresh Fest Tour, he was struck by the symbolism: "It was in the same arena the Beatles played in 1964. It was my first time going to a rap show outside New York and it confirmed rap is more than a regional music." They did it again a year later, with much the same result. By the end of '85, Run-D.M.C. would headline the Krush Groove Christmas Party at Madison Square Garden, which sold out in a week and was broadcast to sixty-five cities on closed-circuit TV.

Run-D.M.C. were in commanding form the minute they took the stage at JFK. It was a show of strength that the other song they performed began with Run announcing: "We got a whole lot of rock groups backstage tonight. But D wantch'all to know . . . one thing." D thundered in: "I'm the king of ROCK / There is none HIGHER / Sucker MCs should call me SIRE," as Jam Master Jay scribbled his records into new shapes.

"King of Rock" had tested MTV. The video featured the group breaking into a putative rock museum and trashing the artifacts, such as Michael Jackson's glove. D.M.C. had to explain to the network's brass about "the glove-stepping thing. I had to bring a glove and demonstrate what I did." Eventually, they were playing it nigh nonstop. Cory Robbins, the president of

Profile Records, boasted to *Billboard* that the new album, also called *King of Rock*, featured "lots of rock guitar." The album would also be the label's first ever available on Compact Disc—not to mention the first rap album in the format.

COLLABORATIONS WERE THE RULE OF LIVE AID. ELTON JOHN WOULD SING with Wham!, Tina Turner with Mick Jagger, Hall and Oates with Kendricks and Ruffin. But Phil Collins collaborated the *most*, like the first half of the eighties in microcosm.

Collins's third solo album, *No Jacket Required*, released in February, had debuted at number one in the UK and topped the US chart for seven weeks; the first two singles, the ballad "One More Night" and the up-tempo "Sussudio," were also American number ones. Collins had approached the album in an up mood: "I just said to myself, 'I'd like to try to write some dance songs, try doing something that is different.' Because I'm remarried, and I guess the ballad side of me is not coming out so much."

Collins had met Sting at the Band Aid session, and the latter guested on *Jacket*'s "Long Long Way to Go." Sting spent much of 1985 denying he'd quit his band. But the album he made that year, *The Dream of the Blue Turtles*, was clearly intended as a reset. He'd hired seasoned young jazz players: saxophonist Branford Marsalis, bassist Darryl Jones (who played with Miles Davis), Weather Report drummer Omar Hakim, and keyboardist Kenny Kirkland would be playing the songs Sting had written in the summer of 1984—the kinds of songs that inspired him to tell interviewers such things as "'Children's Crusade' is an appeal to reason."

When Phil and Sting rehearsed, Collins had written down the lyrics of "Every Breath You Take," to refresh himself. Shortly before they went onstage together, Sting told his costar, "By the way, sometimes I mess around with the words." He did so on that day, stranding Collins, who made a similar error on his own song: "I'm so sweaty that my finger slips off the piano key on 'Against All Odds.' It's a real clanger, and I can almost hear eighty thousand people in Wembley wincing."

Next, Collins caught the Concorde to New York, then helicoptered over to Philadelphia to play again—first by himself, then on the drums with Eric Clapton and the reunion of Robert Plant—Collins's mate—and Jimmy Page. "The syllables 'Led' and 'Zep' [were] never uttered," Collins wrote.

IN THE SUMMER OF 1980, BONO VISITED ANTHONY H. WILSON, THE founder of Factory Records, at the headquarters of Granada Television, where Wilson still held his day job as a host. That May, Ian Curtis, the singer for Factory's key band, Joy Division, had committed suicide, and Bono came as a fan paying his respects. "Tony did tell us later that Bono had come to his office in Granada," the band's bassist, Peter Hook, wrote, "saying that Ian was the best of his generation and promising to carry on in his memory and achieve the success he felt Joy Division deserved."

U2's management pushed hard for a prime-time spot at Live Aid. The band had recently finished their first American arena tour, playing to nearly six hundred thousand people, including an appearance at Madison Square Garden that took little more than an hour to sell out. That March, *Rolling Stone* had put them on the cover with the tagline "Band of the Eighties." They were the first act at Wembley to go on during prime time in the States.

As Jack Nicholson began introducing the band from the JFK stage, drummer Larry Mullen Jr. said, "I could see an Irish flag flying. I proudly said, 'It's amazing, we're the only Irish band playing here today.' Geldof was standing behind me and started to splutter. Of course, the Boomtown Rats had played earlier."

U2 opened with "Sunday Bloody Sunday," its martial beat and wailing chorus rousing the audience. The cameras caught a healthy number of the crowd members flying U2 flags—white, of course. The hair, including the Edge's (it was one of the last times he performed publicly without wearing a hat) and especially Bono's, was a fright: puffy, resplendent mullets. Bono would later call his "one of the worst haircuts in the eighties."

During the Edge's solo, Bono directed a cameraman at stage left to aim at the crowd. He then dropped down to the lower staging area, near a lumbering camera dolly the size of a Zamboni. Then he jumped back onto the main stage to finish: "How long must we sing this song?" His bandmates would soon find out, the hard way.

Next up was "Bad." As the Edge's opening riff rang out, Bono sang a few lines of Lou Reed's "Satellite of Love," standing stock-still at the mike for most of the song proper. Then, right before the second chorus's "I'm wide awake," he jumped back down to the camera stage and, his mullet sticking to his sweating chin, motioned for security to let a woman over the stage barrier; then another. Security was slow to catch on, so Bono jumped down from the camera stage—so quickly that it's still startling even after several dozen viewings.

It was staged, of course. Bono told Michka Assayas: "When you're per-forming, you're looking for those moments. . . . So it wasn't just about rescuing the girl from the crowd, because I'm not so sure she needed to be rescued, but I was trying to find an image just to communicate how we all felt on that day. That was an overpowering day. It was a day that made tiny everybody that was in it, and the subject was so much bigger than anyone on the stage. I was not happy with just playing our songs and getting out of there."

On ground level, Bono coaxed a third woman over the fence, held her close, and led her in a short waltz. He clambered back onto the camera stage to find the first two women from the audience, smooched them, and then went back to the main stage to finish the song along with his furious bandmates—who couldn't see their singer *at all* once he'd hit the ground and had no idea where he'd gone. "I'm just glad the cameras didn't show the rest of the band during the whole drama, because we must have looked like the Three Stooges up there: Curly, Larry, and Moe," Edge later said. Bono fin-ished off "Bad" by quoting from "Ruby Tuesday," "Sympathy for the Devil," and "Walk on the Wild Side." If nothing else, he'd snuck Lou Reed and the Velvet Underground into Live Aid; Geldof and Graham certainly weren't going to.

And that was it: because of Bono's shenanigans, "Bad" lasted twelve min-utes, meaning they had no time to play their planned finale, "Pride"—the only U2 song most people knew. "Everyone was very annoyed at me, I mean, *very* annoyed," Bono said. "I was almost fired." U2's manager, Paul McGuinness, one eyewitness said, "was going nuts at the side of the stage."

Bono's confidence was shaken when he left Wembley. "I thought I'd ruined the band's performance," he said. It took a few days for them to learn other-wise. In America, especially, U2 had stolen the show. They did the same for at least one Englishman. "I actually leapt out of my seat," Tony Wilson said, "and [I] said, 'All right, I give in! You did it, you did it for Ian! God bless you.'"

GELDOF HAD SPENT A GOOD AMOUNT OF TIME CHASING DOWN QUEEN. HE got a provisional in-person yes from guitarist Brian May and drummer Roger Taylor. Singer Freddie Mercury still needed to say yes. "We were touring in the Far East at the time," their manager, Jim Beech, said. "He found out where we were staying in Japan and rang us. Then he found out where we were staying in Australia and rang us there. Finally, we got a call from him when we were in New Zealand." Geldof concluded his pitch thusly: "Tell the old faggot it's gonna be the biggest thing that ever happened."*

This was somewhat surprising, given that Geldof refused to let South Africa, the apartheid state, air the concert and the controversy that still roiled over Queen's seven shows at Sun City the previous October. May and Taylor both later admitted that taking that gig had been a mistake. "We're totally against apartheid and all it stands for, but I feel that by going there we did a lot of bridge building," May said. "The only criticism we got was from outside South Africa."

Yet it also wasn't surprising. For more than a decade, Queen were British superstars; their 1984 LP, *The Works*, had yielded four UK hits, three of them top ten. This was a band in which everybody not only wrote songs but also wrote *hit* songs. The competitive atmosphere could be a grind.

They'd also been losing ground in America, where the video for "I Want to Break Free," written by bassist John Deacon, had fomented a backlash. The band members performed in drag, spoofing the UK soap *Coronation Street*. In the States, where nobody knew the show and Mercury's Castro Street "clone" look (at Wembley: short hair, mustache, white muscle T, skintight blue jeans, a studded leather armband resembling a cock ring) apparently took half a decade to sink in, MTV banned "I Want to Break Free," and the British top three hit struggled to forty-five in America. MTV estimated that the United States cared so little for Queen anymore, it could interrupt their set in favor of an interview with the host of *Solid Gold*, Marilyn McCoo.

Queen's show was the polar opposite of U2's: six songs in twenty-two minutes, including two from *The Works*—a mini-career survey featuring songs from three authors (Deacon's songs sat out). May said they'd had "three days' rehearsal, one three-hour session a day, editing the songs down, compressing them all in. . . . Maybe we should always do it like that."

Mercury, in particular, gave the performance of his life, stalking the stage's edge and ruthlessly teasing and commandeering the crowd. Between the second and third songs, he offered an a cappella call-and-response exercise that allowed him to both show off shamelessly for the whole world and nestle

---

* Geldof was joking—however questionably his overly familiar terms might strike modern ears, he was no homophobe. The Boomtown Rats' *In the Long Grass* featured the song "Dave," a song of empathy for a gay friend. Naturally, the Rats' American label forced Geldof to change the words before they'd release it as a single. He did, and it bombed anyway.

seventy-two thousand people to his swarthy bosom. It helped, Taylor said, that Queen's engineer reset the sound mix: "We were louder than anyone else."

"It might only have been fifteen [*sic*] minutes in a sixteen-hour project," *Melody Maker* reported, "but boy did our Fred go for it in some style, reviving the flagging souls down at the very front with his customary strong-arm tactics. . . . Let's just say that if they could do it like this every time then even [we] would be queuing up for the tickets. A guitar solo–free zone. Freddie, what about it?"

ONE OF THE GRAND STUNTS THE LIVE AID ORGANIZERS ATTEMPTED TO stage was a live transatlantic duet—the first ever!—with David Bowie and Mick Jagger. This proved impossible, even given the day's technological feats; Bowie would be in London, Jagger in New York, and hanging between them was a four-second delay that would have driven a billion fans up the wall. They could accomplish that *without* a four-second delay.

In an interview with the BBC's Paul Gambaccini aired later in the evening, Bowie explained why he and Jagger chose to cover Martha and the Vandellas' Motown classic "Dancing in the Street": "Because I wouldn't do one of Mick's and Mick wouldn't do one of mine." Both men sound piss-drunk on their own hubris, like rich tourists demanding their fifth turn at a crowded karaoke bar. The recording's coproducer, Alan Winstanley, later said that, upon hearing the track's blaring, leaden arrangement, "I had my head in my hands, thinking, 'What the fuck is this?'"

And that was before he, or anyone else, had seen the video—their substitute for a transatlantic duet. Jagger's dance moves always had an element of burlesquing himself, but here his pop-eyed mincing toppled over to the purely buffoonish. Bowie played the straight man, somewhat, giving Mick enough "What's *his* damage?" glance-overs to allow himself plausible denial—just not enough of it. They swam, they shimmied, they judo-kicked, they waggled their hips, all in oversized outfits the B-52's wouldn't have been caught with in a fitting room.

That spectacle mercifully over, the BBC cut back to the commentary box. All day long, the phones at Wembley Stadium hadn't been ringing fast enough for Geldof's like. Earlier, following Dire Straits, he'd implored, with genuine agitation, "There is not enough money coming in, and all these people are not playing for their health. They're playing for the good of other peoples' health.

So *get your phone out now and phone up*, and give us the money. . . . In America it's pouring in, in Japan it's pouring in, in Europe it's pouring in. We've got to do it in this country. . . . Bang up people next door and say, 'Have you given money? If you haven't, get on the phone.'"

This time, Geldof was somewhat mollified—a Kuwaiti sheik pledged one million pounds. Geldof's spiel wound around: "Don't go to the pub tonight—please, stay in and give us the money. There are people dying"—the Irishman's fist rattled the table—"*now*, so give me the money!"

He began reading the phone numbers, before Hepworth stepped in: "Shouldn't we give them the address first?"

That was the way it was in the script. But Geldof had had enough.

"No, *fuck* the address, let's get the *numbers*," he said firmly. "'Cause that's how we're gonna get it."

Geldof's word choice produced a small shock wave: it simply didn't do to curse on live TV. But it got people going: "The phones, which had been quiet, began to light up, then glow and ultimately jam," Hepworth wrote. And afterward, the show's performers and comperes began including pleas and directives for viewers to send money far more frequently than they had before then.

WHEN BOWIE, WHO HAD A LONG-STANDING FEAR OF FLYING, WAS HELIcoptered to the grounds, he winced: "I know it's going to run out of petrol!" The chopper landed in a cricket field near the stadium, where a wedding was being held in the pavilion. "The bride looked up and went 'Fuck me, it's David Bowie!' and got her photo taken with him," Live Aid's publicist Bernard Doherty said.

Bowie was adamant about participating in Live Aid. He attended some of the event planning meetings, including one where Geldof screened a short film put together by the Canadian Broadcasting Company (CBC), of starving Ethiopian children overlaid with the Cars' elegiac synth ballad "Drive." Stunned, Bowie volunteered to shorten his set in order to include it during the show's prime time.

He'd finished touring over a year earlier and needed to put a band together quickly. Among the musicians who took the gig was Thomas Dolby, who played synthesizer; the two had met through guitarist Kevin Armstrong, of the Scottish band Prefab Sprout, who also played with Bowie. Like Queen, the band had three days' rehearsal; they started with ten songs and whittled it to the strongest four. (It was five until Bowie saw the "Drive" video.) Bowie was working on a movie, he told MTV's J. J. Jackson backstage—*Labyrinth*, with producer George Lucas and director Jim Henson. "It's a children's movie," he explained as Jackson guffawed.

Jackson was in London while his VJ colleagues were in Philadelphia. "They sent him to Wembley, and they tried to pretend that was special, but we had no real crew there," Mark Goodman later said. "So J. J.'s participation in our broadcast that day was almost nonexistent—when there was news at Wembley, the four of us in Philadelphia were delivering it. We all felt really bad about that. We knew the sun was setting on him, and he knew it too." Jackson was let go from the network in 1987, the same year Mark Goodman and Alan Hunter left, and one year after Nina Blackwood's departure. Martha Quinn stayed on until 1991.

For the Wembley show, Bowie reprised his powder-blue suit from the Serious Moonlight tour and marched out a set that sharply traversed his career in the same way that outing had—beginning with the New Orleans–flavored "TVC15," the glam stomper "Rebel Rebel," and the *Let's Dance* hit "Modern Love." And there was only one song he could have finished with.

"Heroes" hadn't been a real hit either in the UK (number twenty-four) or the United States (where it missed the Hot 100 entirely). But it did well in Europe and was a huge live favorite. At Wembley, the arrangement was more straightforwardly pumping than on record, the beat abetted by R&B-style riffing from saxophonist Clare Hirst, of the all-woman British band the Belle Stars. Bowie sang with an unstrained command that wore the day's overpowering sentiment like a cloak. Delivering theatrical pomp with real feeling had long been Bowie's ace, and he'd seldom sung with such offhand soul, particularly on the second verse ("And we kissed like nothing could fall"). After introducing the Cars video, Bowie left the stage, went into his trailer, shut the door, and broke into tears.

PRIOR TO LIVE AID, THE WHO'S BASSIST, JOHN ENTWISTLE, HAD BEEN saying that the band—which had broken up three years earlier amid a level of acrimony notable even for a rock band—had only rehearsed for a half hour for their reunion. Backstage at Wembley, the BBC's Gambaccini got hold of Roger Daltrey, who was happy to put the rumor to rest—they had rehearsed for *forty* minutes.

In America, the satellite feed conked out multiple times, the first during "My Generation." Either way, the Who were, on that day, a nostalgia act. "They look a bit, erm, doddery," *Smash Hits* noted. The official Live Aid book even threw shade: "Pete Townshend did the splits in mid-air, just like he used to, and it really didn't matter that he fell over, it really didn't, not to seventy-two thousand people at Wembley who roared their approval."

The Who's drummer, Kenney Jones, told *Rolling Stone* that the band wasn't looking to reunite permanently unless Townshend's writing shaped up: "That was the downfall of the Who, really. The songs have not been that wonderful." Entwistle, meanwhile, would tell *Musician* in 1989, "It got to the point where there wouldn't have been a Who with Kenney Jones," with Daltrey adding, "I just never thought he was the right drummer for the Who. From day one."

The reason they were talking to *Musician* in 1989, of course, is that the Who reunited again. It wasn't just the Who. Live Aid's primary musical legacy was this veritable golden parachute, putting the media spotlight back on acts with nothing to contribute to the present day.

ELTON JOHN WENT ON A CHART STREAK, IN 1983–1984, SCORING A TRIO of top five hits. It wasn't like his mid-seventies prime, when he utterly dominated the charts, but nothing was. He'd scaled things down considerably over the years—at his April 1984 world tour kickoff, in Sydney, Australia, *Variety* noted, "Gone are the glasses, light bulb suits and high heels of earlier years. These days John's dynamism and skill, with the help of a purple tuxedo and modest boater, speak for themselves."

Elton was determined to stay in the game. "The States gives me something to work for," he said. "I want that platinum album again, I want that top ten album, yeah." He watched the charts like a hawk. "I've been a fan of Prince since his first album," he said. "I especially like Wham! My favorite single was 'Wake Me Up Before You Go-Go.' It's the nearest anyone has ever come to making an old Motown track."

They met at the Ivor Novello Awards. Elton gave George Michael the award for Songwriter of the Year with a tribute so fulsome that Michael began crying. "That to me was the first real acknowledgement that I'd ever received professionally, the first proper sign from within the industry that what I was doing was actually worthwhile," Michael said. Wham! had met,

Michael said, after he and Andrew Ridgeley had "both just bought *Goodbye Yellow Brick Road.*"

Up on the Wembley stage, Elton, *Melody Maker* reported, "look[ed] like a cross between Tommy Cooper and a Cossack warrior and who beat out the great crashing rhythm of the seminal 'Bennie and the Jets' with the enthusiasm and sheer glee of a two-year old." His singing had begun its long journey into pure brassiness, but the enthusiasm was real. When Elton introduced the two members of Wham!, he did so, conspicuously, by their individual names.

That March, Wham! became the first-ever Western pop group to play in China. "Within a month of coming home we were booking Wham! on a US stadium tour, when previously they were playing small theatres," their manager, Simon Napier-Bell, recalled. Breaking the barrier to China practically made Wham! into pop statesmen. A month before Live Aid, Michael had met the Queen for the first time.

Michael was almost dreamily confident. "My songwriting is getting better all the time," he said. Michael also appeared onstage at Live Aid with a face full of stubble. That was new. A year later, on June 28, 1986, Wham! returned to Wembley for its final show.

ONE OF THE EMOTIONAL HIGH POINTS OF THE DAY DIDN'T AIR ON MTV. It didn't fit the format.

During the seventies, Teddy Pendergrass may have been R&B's ultimate male sex symbol. Six feet tall, warmly handsome, decked out in chest-flaunting designer suits, possessing a gravelly baritone that conveyed torrential feeling even at a whisper, Pendergrass was a singer who got used to having women throw their underwear at him onstage. In the late seventies, he and his management came up with the ultimate sex symbol gimmick: a series of concerts dubbed For Women Only. "When I'm singing," he said in 1978, "I imagine I'm singing to all the women everywhere."

In March of 1982, Pendergrass was driving a new Rolls-Royce when the brakes failed. He crashed into a guardrail and was trapped in the vehicle for forty-five minutes. His companion, Tenika Watson, was a transsexual nightclub performer, but a public outpouring of goodwill overwhelmed the story's potential scandal (Teddy maintained that he was merely giving an acquaintance a ride home). Pendergrass, the paragon of virility, was now paraplegic, mostly paralyzed from the neck down.

He made a lot of progress in two years. In 1984 he recorded his first LP for Asylum Records, *Love Language*. "Hold Me" was a duet with an up-and-comer who'd done a lot of session work since the late seventies named Whitney Houston. Her self-titled debut was released in February 1985; it would be certified platinum a month after Live Aid. *Love Language* itself had gone gold. "It's more sensitive," Pendergrass said. "I don't want to say my [earlier] songs were cavemannish, but the lyrics were more hard-sell, more direct."

Satisfying as the album was, Pendergrass later wrote in his memoir, "composing and recording could never replace the experience of performing onstage. For me, that had always been what it was all about. God, how I missed it: the audience's love, the sense of transcendence, the joy—even the panties." He hadn't been onstage since before the accident.

He appeared at Live Aid alongside compatriots. Nick Ashford and Valerie Simpson were married and had been late-sixties Motown writer-producers, responsible for most of the great Marvin Gaye–Tammi Terrell duets. They became R&B stars on their own in the seventies, their strings-laden arrangements adapting flawlessly to disco. Then, like many peers, their sales tailed off in the eighties. That changed in late 1984 with "Solid," a brassy midtempo salute to their longevity as a couple, and their first R&B number one as artists (number twelve pop).

July 13 was a rough day for Teddy, who'd arrived to JFK in his wheelchair only to find that nothing had been prepared for him, or anyone else in his condition. "I was nervous enough as it was, and every time my chair hit a bump, I felt like crying," he wrote. When he finally got to his trailer—there was no ramp—he found it wasn't air-conditioned: "One result of my injury is that I can't regulate my body temperature. I simply don't sweat, which can result in my becoming dangerously overheated." After some finagling, he was taken to "a tent with several groaning electric fans to 'cool' it down to about eighty-five unbearable degrees."

Taking the stage, Ashford and Simpson went right into their hit, very supper-club professional. With "Solid" finished, the duo brought on their special guest. The crowd's sustained roar buoyed the singer. The song Teddy sang wasn't one of his hits, but an old number Nick and Valerie had written for Diana Ross, "Reach Out and Touch (Somebody's Hand)." It was corny, but both singer and audience were in tears by the end. Backstage, the artists gathered to watch, cheering. When he got home, Pendergrass wrote, "For the first time in three years, I allowed myself to dream."

"MADONNA WILL BE OUT OF THE BUSINESS IN SIX MONTHS," *BILLBOARD*'s Paul Grein boldly predicted to *Time*. But the singer herself had other ideas. "If there were ten rungs on a ladder, I'd say I was on the third rung now," Madonna told the *Los Angeles Times*.

The first two rungs were her first two albums, the third the April 1985 release of *Desperately Seeking Susan*, Madonna's first film. It had been shot the previous fall; Orion Pictures insisted on rushing it out in spring to capitalize on its star's ascendancy. The movie's publicist, Reid Rosefelt, wrote that they "feared that Madonna might be a flash in the pan and they wanted to pop the film out before the interest in the Material Girl dematerialized. . . . Full-blown obscurity could hit Madonna any second!"

Desperately Seeking Susan was nothing of the sexploitation flick that any number of people expected—*Pink Rain*, as one wag put it. The movie got good reviews, and so did Madonna. "This movie is like a return to those simple, straightforward caper comedies Claudette Colbert and Carole Lombard made in the thirties," she said.

The inclusion of a new song, "Into the Groove," for a club scene birthed yet another hit, first as the B side of *Like a Virgin*'s "Angel," then on its own. The addition irked Madonna's costar, Rosanna Arquette; when *Rolling Stone*'s Fred Schruers mentioned that the scene had "become an issue," she replied, "Who's it become an issue with—besides Rosanna?"

Like *A Hard Day's Night* had with the Beatles, *Desperately Seeking Susan* made Madonna respectable to previously skeptical adults. That spring, Madonna's recordings were selling about seventy-five thousand copies per day.

Madonna became a modern Mae West, tailoring her sex appeal to a wide audience while calling her own shots. That included getting in line to be parodied by "Weird Al" Yankovic, who released "Like a Surgeon" ("Cuttin' for the very first time") a month before Live Aid. "It was her idea," Yankovic said. "I didn't even know Madonna. I was flattered. She suggested it to a friend of mine. The title is hers, too."

The first nationwide Madonna tour began while *Susan* was in wide release, and a live show would be the fourth rung of success. Onstage, Madonna simply updated her track show, corralling a live band—including drummer Jonathan Moffet, from the Victory Tour—and putting multiple tiers on the stage to move among. Initially booked into three- to five-thousand-seaters, a number of tour dates had to be rebooked into arenas.

In San Francisco on April 23, concessions were through the roof—one twenty-dollar Madonna T-shirt was selling every six seconds. "She sells more than Springsteen, the Rolling Stones, or Duran Duran," Dell Furano, her merchandiser, told *People*. That same day, *Like a Virgin* was certified four times platinum.

Every stop, Madonna looked out to the crowd and saw hundreds, or thousands, of teenage girls (and, sometimes, their mothers) dressed like her. In Los Angeles, a sixteen-year-old girl told *People*, "Madonna's living out our fantasies. She's able to do something our parents would never let us get away with. The whole slut image. It's usually just the guys who get to do that. But don't quote me. My mother would kill me."

Daughters and mothers alike wanted to kill Madonna's opening act. The Beastie Boys had been a hardcore band and were now recording rap twelve-inches for Rubin and Simmons's Def Jam Records. The credibility this gave them in New York meant zero to the mall kids who'd shown up for an MTV-riffic time. Instead, they got three obnoxious jerks with barely enough material to fill out a short opening slot. The Beasties had to record a new twelve-inch, "She's on It," just to have a third song to perform. The fourth was a cover of T La Rock & Jazzy Jay's "It's Yours."

When the show came to New York, Def Jam's radio promoter, Bill Stephney, told Alan Light, "Ad-Rock ended the show by saying, 'I'm happy to be home, and you know why I love New York? Because it's got the best pussy!' The horror in the audience—these are suburbanites, the bridge-and-tunnel crowd, the pre-soccer moms, and the boos are cascading down, and I'm thinking, *These guys are gonna be something.*"

Like clockwork, the nudes emerged. In 1979, Madonna had posed for a couple of photographers' figure studies. On July 11, a New York Federal Court denied a preliminary injunction disabling *Penthouse* magazine from publishing the nudes. The same day, spokespeople for *Penthouse* and *Playboy* both crowed that each had gotten to the stands first.

But the bombshell was Madonna's response: "I'm not ashamed of anything." She adroitly called the bluff on the scandal right as it left the ground, effectively icing it—and did so while also saying things like "Crucifixes are sexy because there's a naked man on them."

The whiff of scandal was fresh in the air at JFK Stadium when Madonna appeared. Yet she wore it as lightly as she did her mint-green silk frock coat and multiple chains. The weather was hot, and everyone would see her sweat:

"I ain't taking shit off today! You might hold it against me ten years from now." She cavorted exuberantly through "Holiday" and "Into the Groove" before being joined by the Thompson Twins and Nile Rodgers for yet another new one—"Love Makes the World Go Round" would appear a year later, on her third album, *True Blue*, minus the microphone feedback that marred it at Live Aid.

THE LAST PERSON YOU WANT THE MIKE TO GO DEAD ON IS THE LAST PERson on the bill. Especially if it's Paul McCartney, and he hasn't played live in eight years.

McCartney went on after a brief rainfall—the sound became so bad that some BBC technicians wound up broadcasting through the stadium's PA. Worse, for the first eighty seconds of his performance of "Let It Be"—Geldof's request—McCartney's voice was inaudible. (The 2004 DVD release of the concert features a replacement vocal.)

Everyone sang along, of course. Backstage in Philadelphia, the MTV director had the cameras turn to the VJs, then requested they sway to the music. "MTV made matters worse," *Rolling Stone* sniffed, "by constantly segueing from performers to close-up shots of swaying veejays." "I didn't sway, and I stayed off camera," Nina Blackwood recalled. "But he cut from McCartney to the swaying VJs, and the critics just ripped us to shreds."

Backstage in London, as McCartney struggled with his equipment, a number of the day's performers struggled with the finale. Gary Kemp of Spandau Ballet played an unplugged electric guitar in a corner of the Hard Rock Café's dining area; Bowie, at last, took the opening lines. Mid-rehearsal, Geldof, Bowie, Pete Townshend, and Alison Moyet of Yazoo were summoned to help with the finale of "Let It Be." When the song was finished, Townshend and McCartney, Geldof's childhood heroes, lifted Bob onto their shoulders. Geldof heard a struggling Townshend mutter: "Fuck me, he's a heavy bastard."

THE POWER STATION WAS NAMED FOR THE NEW YORK RECORDING STUdio known for its enormous reverb, and the band's self-titled debut album sounded like it had been recorded in an empty volcano, so engulfing was its echo. Their performance at Live Aid made that album sound like Prokofiev by comparison. John Taylor and Andy Taylor look coke-blasted and sound coke-blasteder.

Things had been even rougher before they went on: Andy's amp had blown, forcing him to borrow Jimmy Page's. Bill Graham seized the chance to blow his stack at a member of a younger generation whose musical values he held in contempt. Worse, Graham kept screaming at Taylor after the performance was done. Andy finally snapped, "Why don't you shut up?" That took nerve—he had to face Graham again in less than two and a half hours, for Duran Duran's performance.

They hadn't played together in a year. "The air was acrid with tension," Andy wrote. "In truth, we could barely stand to be in the same room." Duran drummer Roger Taylor, Andy continued, "looked like Death warmed up, almost as if he wasn't there, and you could see the strain of our spirit-sapping lifestyle etched across his face." A year after Live Aid, Roger retired to his farm at age twenty-five, completely burnt out. "I didn't want to end up like Elvis," he said.

Duran Duran opened with "A View to a Kill," their newest single—the James Bond theme. Le Bon was "slid[ing] around the stage as if practicing for his forthcoming tempest-tossed yachting adventure," as Smash Hits put it. Le Bon had gotten serious about yacht racing. He hit the song's final high note with a frog, his voice dying on "With a vie-yoo-ow to a kill!"

A month after Live Aid, finishing the Power Station's US tour, Andy Taylor saw on television that his old band's lead singer's vessel had capsized off the coast of Cornwall. Le Bon and his crew were overboard more than an hour before their rescue. Duran Duran's original lineup, minus Roger Taylor, wouldn't play together again until 1989.

AFTER FLYING OVER ON THE CONCORDE, AS BROADCAST ON THE BBC—a planned interview fell through in a wallfire of static—Phil Collins joined Eric Clapton onstage in Philadelphia. He fit in perfectly. Afterward, Collins would join, as they were billed, Robert Plant and Jimmy Page. He did not fit in perfectly.

This wasn't simply Plant and Page, though. It was also John Paul Jones. Collins hadn't understood that this was going to be a Led Zeppelin reunion. When they asked Collins to rehearse—they already had another drummer, Chic's Tony Thompson, lined up—Phil had to say no. He'd just gotten back home to England after a long American tour. But hey, he'd woodshed on the plane.

The Zeppelin rehearsals were as tense as Duran Duran's. At one point, Plant announced that he refused to sing "Stairway to Heaven," then changed his mind backstage, after being spooked by Queen's performance. Plant wrote the lyrics down for himself—it had been ages. One TV anchor reported being on the train to Philadelphia and seeing an entire car full of Led Zeppelin T-shirts.

The band played "Rock and Roll," "Whole Lotta Love," and "Stairway to Heaven" at Live Aid. "We virtually ruined the whole thing because we sounded so awful," Plant said. "I was hoarse and couldn't sing and Page was out of tune and couldn't hear his guitar." Collins's practice on the Concorde had been for naught—he and Thompson didn't mesh at all.

In January 1986, Page, Plant, Jones, and Thompson gathered in Bath, England, to try to make a Zeppelin reunion happen. But Plant could no longer play second fiddle to Page: "When I reach a conclusion, I immediately react to it. Way back in the old days, this might have taken a week of mutual discussion." He added, "It sounded kind of like David Byrne meets Hüsker Dü"—meaning that it would never, ever get onto American rock radio now living in the past.

MTV's Alan Hunter attempted to talk to the band afterward. Seeing Page and Plant treat Hunter in a nonchalant manner—"being difficult, giving vague, cocky answers to straight questions"—Collins decided to step in. "So I try to come to the rescue by steaming in with answers. Answers to some questions I'm not really qualified to answer."

Collins's two-continent stunt became the day's ready-made punch line. "Phil Collins is on stage again!" *Smash Hits* reported. "Does this man *never* tire?" The official *Live Aid* book couldn't resist: "Nobody would have been surprised if Phil suddenly came on stage again, grabbed Eric Clapton's guitar, and started playing that. He wouldn't have played it as well, of course, but would it necessarily have stopped him? He just didn't think of it."

THE RUMOR AROUND THE 1981 ROLLING STONES TOUR WAS THAT IT would be their last. Mick Jagger was almost forty! That air was even stronger at Live Aid: Keith Richards and Ron Wood appeared with Bob Dylan, but not their fellow Stone.

This was how the great sixties rockers' careers continued—not by progressing musically but by providing a continuing soap opera for fans to follow along in the *Rolling Stone* gossip pages. Are Mick and Keith bickering this month? Will CSNY ever *really* reunite (as they did for a couple of songs in Philadelphia)?

Who's suing whom this week? Wait, that person or group made an album *recently*?

The geezers cut off the new world in kind. When a *Smash Hits* reporter told Jagger he'd recently interviewed Morrissey, Jagger responded, "Morrissey? Who's that?"

Tina Turner canceled a show in upstate New York to make it down. She and Mick performed "State of Shock" as a duet. Along with the finale—an all-hands-on-deck rendition of the MJ-cowritten "We Are the World"—this would be the only real trace of Michael Jackson on Live Aid.

Turner was presently working on her memoir, an as-told-to written by Kurt Loder of *Rolling Stone*, and later of MTV News, that recounted the rough stories of her time with Ike. "I drank a lot of wine," she said. Turner turned down a starring role in Steven Spielberg's movie adaptation of the Alice Walker novel *The Color Purple*, the story of a black woman with an abusive background and life. "Black people can do better than that," she said. "I've lived that life with my husband. I've lived down south in the cotton fields. I don't want to do anything I've done."

ONE PERSON EVEN BILL GRAHAM WOULDN'T DARE TO TRY TO BULLDOZE was Bob Dylan. Graham asked him to drop a song from his set. Dylan refused.

Dylan's guest guitarists wound up there by happenstance. "Bob dropped by on Ronnie [Wood] one night and I was there," Keith Richards told *NME*. "It was a Thursday night, and Saturday night was the gig, right? . . . He comes back downstairs again—'Heeey, they want me to play with the Tom Petty band and I don't know those guys. Would you do it?'"

They opened with "Ballad of Hollis Brown"—which they hadn't rehearsed, and which Wood didn't know. It did not improve from there. Backstage afterward, Dylan told *Rolling Stone* that onstage they "couldn't hear anything," adding, "We had fun rehearsing." The tone and tenor of the performance were caught in a nutshell by *Vanity Fair*'s James Wolcott: "My God, he sounds as if he could go on grinding out this crap *forever*."

As in London, backstage in Philadelphia there was an impromptu gathering of singers to bring the whole thing to an end with "We Are the World." Though Lionel Richie didn't perform at Live Aid, he showed up for the finale. Hey, he was a *special guest*.

As Richie headed to a mike, dozens of others rushed onstage as Dylan finished. The listed headliner looked confused as he whirred around to see who else was joining in. Walking offstage, Dylan passed his manager and said, "Sorry."

IN 2004, TREVOR DANN, THE BBC PRODUCER OF LIVE AID, TOLD MARK Ellen, one of the broadcast's correspondents, "I remember thinking that what might have happened in the sixties had finally come true. We do make a difference. Pop music can change the world. . . . I thought Live Aid was the beginning of a new era. But actually it was the slamming of the door on the old one."

The new era Live Aid portended, though, had more to do with its many visible corporate sponsorships than any world saving, per se. It sealed pop stardom as another facet of modern celebrity—turned it, officially, into a kind of landed gentry. "I just don't think about class any more, you know," Sting told *The Face* shortly before Live Aid. "I've been with the jet set, I've met Lady Diana and Prince Charles and felt equal to them. I do not accept that I'm anything but equal."

ACKNOWLEDGMENTS

ANGELA GUNN, BRITTANY GOMEZ-MATOS AND HER FAMILY, ALEXANDRIA Matos-Pak and her family, Nate Patrin, Paulette Myers-Rich and David Rich, Rahawa Haile and Futurecat, Fiona Birch, Gregory Scott and Caitlin Berry, Mairead Case, Andy Zax and Lisa Jane Persky, Anna Eveslage, Ann Powers and Eric Weisbard, Tricia Romano, Jen Matson and Mike Baehr, Alfred Soto, Ned Raggett and Kate Izquierdo, David Schmader, Tamara Palmer, Maura Johnston, Geeta Dayal, Chris Molanphy, Rod Smith, John Darnielle, Kate Clarke, Annie Zaleski and Matt Wardlaw, Stephen Thomas Erlewine, Raymond Cummings, Joseph McCombs, Dylan Hicks, Peter S. Scholtes, Brett Baldwin, Cecilia Johnson, Mary Lucia, Jim McGuinn, Brian Oake, David Safar, Andrea Swensson, Jay Boller, Duncan Dick, Ryan Dombal, Andrew Flanagan, J. C. Gabel, Jacob Ganz, Keith Harris, Jessica Hopper, J. Edward Keyes, Marcus J. Moore, Piotr Orlov, Keith Phipps, Mark Richardson, Brandon Stosuy, Brad Efford, Michael Tortorello, Sven von Thulen, K. Leander Williams, Briana Younger, the Pop Conference brigade but particularly Kate Koliha, Charles Hughes, and Karen Tongson, JoAnn Olson, Sasha Todryk and Leore Wohl, Esten Staab and Tahsha LePage, Neil Fox and Elaine Marigold Avery, Nola Wick and Evian Rave, Steven Centrific and Jasmine Seuling, every friendly face on every friendly dance floor, P. L. Dean and Rebecca Noran, the staff of the Minnesota Historical Society, Allison Aten of MNHS Press, Jasen Emmons and Elliott Hansen of EMP Museum (now MoPop), Jon Copeland of the Minneapolis Public Library, John Rumble and Kathleen Campbell of the Country Music Hall of Fame and Museum, the staff of the Nashville Public Library, the staff of the Seattle Public Library, the staff of Claddagh Coffee on West Seventh, all of the book's interviewees, Paul Bresnick, and Ben Schafer: Thank you all. And thank you for reading.

NOTES

INTRODUCTION

vii–viii **"American explosion":** Dave Marsh, *The Heart of Rock & Soul: The 1,001 Greatest Singles Ever Made* (Cambridge, MA: Da Capo, 1999; orig. 1989), 94.

ix **"sent us a letter":** Thomas K. Arnold, "Owner Takes Charge at Z-90," *Billboard*, August 25, 1984.

x **as David Hepworth pointed out:** David Hepworth, "The Day TV Changed Forever," *The Word*, no. 21, November 2004.

x **"I've seen the changes go":** "Quincy Jones: Musically Speaking," *Radio & Records*, November 23, 1984.

xi **"Our audience is completely mixed":** James R. Blandford, "Culture Club," *Record Collector*, November 1998.

xi **"Pop just means shit":** Knox Robinson, "Kanye West," *The Fader*, December 2003–January 2004.

xi **"You can divide":** "My '80s: Marco Pirroni," in "80 from the Eighties" insert, *Mojo*, August 2007.

CHAPTER ONE: WPLJ-FM, NEW YORK CITY, AUGUST 7, 1983

Author interview with Larry Berger (August 26, 2016).

1 **"It's eight o'clock":** "Program Director Larry Berger Explains New Format, WPLJ New York | July 1983," Airchexx, https://airchexx.com/program-director-larry-berger-explains-new-format-wplj-new-york-july-1983/. Actual airdate is August 7, 1983, confirmed via email with Berger. All subsequent on-air quotes are from this program.

2 **"Has AOR radio become":** Ed Harrison, "AOR: Where Have the Black Sounds Gone?," *Billboard*, November 15, 1980.

2 **"The twelve-to-twenty-four demos":** Douglas E. Hall, "AOR Nears Crucial Crossroads Demographics: Ad Pressures May Force Fragmentation," *Billboard*, May 22, 1982.

2 **"a soft mid-tempo ballad":** Paul Grein, "Promo Men Lament Fragmentation," *Billboard*, August 15, 1981.

3 **"On the sixties' Top 40 radio":** Jay Cocks, "Rock Hits the Hard Place," *Time*, February 15, 1982.

3 **"The sales of musical product":** "Better Times Aren't Coming," *Trouser Press*, no. 42, September 1979.

3 **"shattered sales records":** Sam Sutherland, "The Music Industry," in *Musician: The Year in Rock, 1981–82*, ed. John Swenson (New York: Delilah Books, 1981).

3 **"We wanted to work":** Paul Grein, "New Chic Game Plan: No Disco," *Billboard*, December 15, 1979.

4 **"One of the reasons":** Paul Grein, "Martin/McCartney 'Tug' Team Scores," *Billboard*, February 26, 1983.

4 **"This is just not a growth industry now":** "What Is Stalling the Record Business," *BusinessWeek*, November 30, 1981.

4 **CBS Records was forced:** Christopher Connelly, "1982 in Review: Who Won, Who Lost," *Rolling Stone*, February 17, 1983.

4 **"The number of albums certified platinum":** Paul Grein, "Gold, Platinum Down in '82," *Billboard*, January 15, 1983.

4 **Record Bar:** Irv Lichtman and Earl Paige, "Dealers Post Modest Yule Gains," *Billboard*, January 8, 1983.

4 **8 percent rise:** "CBS Records '82 Profits Down," *Billboard*, February 19, 1983.

4 **"The record business is not":** Peter Lyle, "Michael Jackson's Monster Smash," *The Telegraph* (London), November 25, 2007, via telegraph.co.uk/culture /3669538/Michael-Jacksons-monster-smash.html.

4 *Off the Wall*: Sylvie Simmons, "No Angel, but No Osmond Either," *Creem*, June 1983.

4 **third-most-added:** Rock Albums & Top Tracks (chart), *Billboard*, December 18, 1982.

4 **"I said at the time":** Lyle, "Michael Jackson's Monster Smash."

5 **"'Beat It' is not just for kids":** Epic Records trade ad, *Radio & Records,* spring 1983.

5 **"about fifty AOR playlists":** "Industry News and Notes: Jackson Gets AOR Airplay," *Rolling Stone*, February 3, 1983.

5 **"If there was a lawn":** Chuck Taylor, "WPLJ 25th Anniversary: New York's Award-Winning Top 40 Turns 25," *Billboard*, December 21, 1996.

5 **"I'm tired of all this 'racist' stuff":** Michael Shore, *The Rolling Stone Book of Rock Video* (New York: Quill/Rolling Stone Press, 1984), 182.

5 **"I had fifteen copies":** Deborah Russell, "Video Kills the Radio Star," *Billboard*, November 1, 1994.

5 **"The average MTV viewer":** Drew Moseley, "Anatomy of a Monopoly," in *The Rock Yearbook, Volume IV*, ed. Al Clark (London: Virgin Books, 1983), 120.

6 **"Yeah, but we can't play this":** Nina Blackwood, Mark Goodman, Alan Hunter, and Martha Quinn, with Gavin Edwards, *VJ* (New York: Atria Books, 2013), 157.

6 **"There was never any sort":** Matthew Billy, episode 03: "I Want My MTV," October 4, 2015, in *Between the Liner Notes*, produced by Matthew Billy, podcast, betweenthelinernotes.com/episodes-1/mtv.

6 **"The only 'Pressure'" and "We've been guaranteed":** "'Billie Jean' Gets Her MTV," *Billboard*, March 26, 1983.

6 **"He showed off moves":** Steve Pond, "Former Motown Stars Return for Birthday Bash," *Rolling Stone*, May 26, 1983.

7 **"That was the greatest":** John Jeremiah Sullivan, *Pulphead: Essays* (New York: Farrar, Straus & Giroux, 2011), 122.

7 **"*Thriller* had already sold":** Shore, *Rolling Stone Book of Rock Video*, 202.

7 **"may end up going as high":** Steve Pond and Kurt Loder, "Summer Sales Surge Gives Record Business a Boost," *Rolling Stone*, September 1, 1983.

8 **Growing up in Chicago:** Marc Fisher, *Something in the Air: Radio, Rock, and the Revolution That Shaped a Generation* (New York: Random House, 2007), 189–192.

8 **"You'd hear twenty minutes":** Bill Flanagan and Jock Baird, "The Failure of Corporate Rock," *Musician*, December 1982.

8 **"In 1977, I felt no regrets":** Jeff Gelb, "Consultant Comparison: Rick Carroll and Lee Abrams," *Radio & Records*, January 28, 1983.

8 **"We're changing from an industrial base":** Bill Holland, "AOR Mainstay WIYY-FM Slips New Music into Mix," *Billboard*, March 12, 1983.

9 **"pointed to an emergence" and "We're de-emphasizing":** "Abrams, Billboard Meets Signal Changes in AOR Programming," *Billboard*, February 5, 1983.

9 **"In their hearts":** Gelb, "Consultant Comparison."

9 **"a group of sinners confessing together" and "We were lulled":** "Abrams, Billboard."

9 **"There's been a reversal":** Christopher Connelly, "Top 40 Knocks AOR off the Charts," *Rolling Stone*, January 19, 1984.

9 **"by and large a lost cause for AOR":** Hall, "AOR Nears Crucial Crossroads Demographics."

12 **"juvenile, dumb, or stoned-out callers":** Eric Weisbard, *Top 40 Democracy: The Rival Mainstreams of American Music* (Chicago: University of Chicago Press, 2014), 220.

12 **"one of the classic stupid moves":** Connelly, "Top 40."

13 **"As the New York City area" and "I want you to take your radio knob":** nycradiofan, "Z100 Z Morning Zoo 'Shannon & The Other One' (scoped) [WHTZ NYC] (08-04-1983)" (air check), YouTube video, 37:55, published February 24, 2013, youtube.com/watch?v=e7dq46SzvWc.

13 **"It's time to wake up!" and "Now! There's a new way to spell hits":** nycradio fan, "WHTZ Z100 New York—Z100's First Day Sign On—Scott Shannon—

Aug 2, 1983" (air check), YouTube video, 00:50, published July 31, 2013, https://www.youtube.com/watch?v=knpP1Cei2UA.

13 **"high energy and fast talk":** Tony Schwartz, "The Wizard of Z100," *New York*, April 2, 1984.

13 **"We just dedicated ourselves":** David Adelson, "The Cash Box Interview: Scott Shannon," *Cash Box*, September 22, 1984.

14 **"I can't blame Lee Abrams":** Connelly, "Top 40."

14 **"In the spring of 1983":** Adelson, "The Cash Box Interview."

CHAPTER TWO: SUPREME COURT, WASHINGTON, DC, JANUARY 17, 1984

Author interviews with Arthur Baker (September 12, 2017) and Tom Silverman (August 4, 2017).

15 **"contributory infringement":** "Home Taping Ruled Legal by High Court," *Radio & Records*, January 20, 1984.

15 **"against sixteen":** Richard L. Gordon, "Broadcasters Benefit from Taping: Sony," *Advertising Age*, December 7, 1981.

15 **"We pay more":** Geoffrey Colvin, "The Crowded New World of TV," *Fortune*, September 17, 1984.

16 **Coalition to Save America's Music:** Is Horowitz, "Music Coalition in Drive for Home Taping Royalty," *Billboard*, April 3, 1982.

16 **"Their goal" and "Our industry sold":** Clinton Heylin, ed., *The Da Capo Book of Rock & Roll Writing* (Cambridge, MA: Da Capo, 1999), 495.

16 **"blank tape sales":** Robert Christgau, "Rock 'n' Roller Coaster: The Music Biz on a Joyride," *Village Voice*, February 7, 1984.

16 **"Time-shifting":** *Sony Corporation of America et al. v. Universal City Studios, Inc. et al.*, US Supreme Court, January 17, 1984, https://www.oyez.org/cases/1982/81-1687.

16 **"risks eroding":** Aric Press, "A Blank Tape for Hollywood," *Newsweek*, January 30, 1984.

16 **"Copyright infringement has traditionally":** Editorial: "Protection," *Cash Box*, March 3, 1984.

16 **"We know that a great percentage":** Anita M. Wilson, "Home Taping Laws Sought," *Cash Box*, April 14, 1984.

16 **"I'm dancing in the streets!":** "Video Merchants Speak Out on High Court Taping Case," *Cash Box*, February 4, 1984.

17 **"One small step for man":** Tom Shales, "I'll Tape Tomorrow," *Washington Post*, January 18, 1984.

17 **"Microprocessors have made possible":** Martin Polon, "Fast Forward: Winter CES," *Billboard*, January 8, 1983.

18 **sixty-six thousand:** "1984 Winter CES Opens in Las Vegas; State of Industry Probed," *Cash Box*, January 14, 1984.

18 **"If Mac's sales":** William D. Marbach, "Reviewing the Mac," *Newsweek*, January 30, 1984.

18 **"The Yuppie work style":** Andrew Hacker, "The Endangered Yuppie," *Success!*, November 1984.

18 **"The Mac team alone":** Stephen Randall, ed., *The Playboy Interviews: Movers and Shakers* (Milwaukie, OR: M Press, 2007), 78.

18 **"an endless cocktail party":** Michael Rogers, "It's the Apple of His Eye," *Newsweek*, January 30, 1984.

18 **"We in the U.S. record industry":** Stan Cornyn, "Japanese Hardware Firms and U.S. Record Companies Should Cooperate for Mutual Benefit," *Variety*, January 11, 1984.

18 **"We can't afford to rely":** Bob Summer, "Buoyant Demand for Records Shown by Mega-Seller Increase; Home Taping Is Chief Danger," *Variety*, January 11, 1984.

19 **"Because the player is digital":** "Digital Audio Builds Toward a Sales Crescendo," *BusinessWeek*, January 30, 1984.

19 **"a marvel":** Summer, "Buoyant Demand for Records."

19 **"Throughout the show":** Paul Terry Shea, "Kodak Shakes Up the Video Industry with Its New 'Camcorder': Combination Camera and VCR Shown at Consumer Show," *Rolling Stone*, March 15, 1984.

19 **"The personal cassette systems":** Steven Dupler, "Break Dance Commotion Grips Portables," *Billboard*, June 9, 1984.

19 **over eight hundred:** "CD Sales Are 70% Pop in U.S., Sez Petrone; Ditto for Titles," *Variety*, March 21, 1984.

19 **RCA announced:** "Pop Title Bowing in CD, LP Formats," *Variety*, January 4, 1984.

19 **"The black disc":** Jim Evans, "The Business Year/UK," in *The Rock Yearbook 1985*, ed. Allan Jones (New York: St. Martin's Press, 1984).

20 **"We should not put emphasis":** Dorian Lynskey, "How the Compact Disc Lost Its Shine," *The Guardian* (Manchester), May 28, 2015, theguardian.com /music/2015/may/28/how-the-compact-disc-lost-its-shine.

20 **"It will be like hearing the tapes":** Gary Marmorstein, *The Label: The Story of Columbia Records* (Cambridge, MA: Da Capo, 2007), 522.

20 **"Do you cut the price":** "CD Lowballing Hits New York," *Billboard*, January 28, 1984.

20 **"We're talking real innovation":** Greg Milner, *Perfecting Sound Forever: An Aural History of Recorded Music* (London: Faber & Faber, 2009), 214.

20 **"could be one of the things":** Sam Sutherland, "Yetnikoff 'Reasonably Optimistic,'" *Billboard*, March 19, 1983.

20 **In September 1983:** Ken Terry, "Disk Biz Consolidation Continues Apace: Labels Struggle for Supremacy," *Variety*, January 11, 1984.

20 **nearly 20 percent in 1983:** Chrissey Iley, "International Dateline: United Kingdom," *Cash Box*, January 14, 1984.

20 **extra-long cassettes:** Drew Moseley, "The U.S. Business Year," in *The Rock Yearbook 1982*, ed. Al Clark (London: Virgin Books, 1981).

21 **selling six-to-four:** Jeffrey Peisch, "Cassettes Now Outselling LPs," *Rolling Stone*, November 24, 1983.

21 **the same ratio at which Nashville:** Anita M. Wilson, "Cassette Sales Increase Say Retailers, Labels," *Cash Box*, January 21, 1984.

21 **only two hundred vinyl titles:** Peisch, "Cassettes Now Outselling LPs."

21 **"too much trouble":** *The Record Producers: Todd Rundgren* (documentary), BBC Radio, 1982.

21 **"Nobody, in my opinion":** *The Record Producers: Glyn Johns* (documentary), BBC Radio, 1982.

21 **"For someone who considers himself a colorist":** Sam Sutherland, "Buckingham into 'High-Tech Folk,'" *Billboard*, August 18, 1984.

22 **"establishes a universal standard":** Radcliffe Joe, "Roland Bows Interface System," *Billboard*, February 19, 1983.

22 **"the lead story":** Jock Baird, "Heat Wave in Anaheim: The Best of N.A.M.M.," *Musician*, April 1984.

22–23 **"allow a complex mix":** Richard J. Ripani, *The New Blue Music: Changes in Rhythm & Blues, 1950–1999* (Jackson: University Press of Mississippi, 2006), 138.

23 **"Since last summer":** Paul Colbert, "In the Moog," *Melody Maker*, February 4, 1984.

23 **"One hundred and twenty-eight":** Mark Jenkins, "For Simple Minds," *Melody Maker*, March 31, 1984.

CHAPTER THREE: *NEWSWEEK*: "BRITAIN ROCKS AMERICA—AGAIN," JANUARY 23, 1984

Author interview with James Miller, by email (August 12–15, 2017).

24 **"The extent of the new":** Jim Miller, "Britain Rocks America—Again," *Newsweek*, January 23, 1984.

25 **"Really, are Boy George":** "Letters," *Newsweek*, February 6, 1984.

25 **"So roll over" and "It is ironic":** Miller, "Britain Rocks America."

26 **"Before I started":** Geoffrey Himes, "Hey Fella . . . You Wanna Step Outside and Say That? Boy George and Culture Club Aren't What They Seem," *Musician*, October 1983.

26 **"What I do is not drag":** doyoureally, "Boy George, Joan Rivers Interview (1983)" (clip from *The Tonight Show*, November 30, 1983), YouTube video, 10:05, published November 1, 2011, youtube.com/watch?v=zZmb_RKzTIY.

26 **"He's built like a boxer":** Eamonn Forde, "A Tale of Two Smash Hits," *The Word*, April 2012.

26 **"You must understand":** Sally Brompton, *Chameleon: The Boy George Story* (Kent, UK: Spellmount, 1984), 124.

26 **"I used to be":** Frank Broughton, ed., *Time Out Interviews, 1968–1998* (New York: Penguin, 1998).

26 **"I thought, if Johnny":** Boy George with Spencer Bright, *Take It Like a Man* (New York: HarperCollins, 1995), 148.

26 **"It seemed like" and "I knew when I met George":** Himes, "Hey Fella."

27 **"I don't believe in":** Roy Trakin, "Sweat & Ice: The New British Dance Romantics—ABC, Thompson Twins, Yaz, Culture Club," *Musician*, March 1983.

27 **"I didn't want to be":** Himes, "Hey Fella."

27 **"Listening these days":** Allan Jones, "The New Pop Tarts," in *The Rock Yearbook 1983*, ed. Al Clark (London: Virgin Books, 1982).

27 **"Whatever happened to the idea":** James Henke, "Middle Class Heroes," *Rolling Stone*, February 2, 1984.

27 **"The [UK] 'rock' press":** Al Clark, ed., *The Rock Yearbook Volume IV* (London: Virgin Books, 1983), 123.

27 **"never necessarily anti-technique":** Clinton Heylin, ed., *The Da Capo Book of Rock & Roll Writing* (Cambridge, MA: Da Capo, 1999), 199.

27 **"The eighties":** James R. Blandford, "Boy George," *Record Collector*, November 1998.

27 **"The way in which punk":** faberandfaber, "Dave Rimmer on *Like Punk Never Happened*," YouTube video, 6:26, published July 20, 2011, youtube.com/watch?v=xoiUVpgxqmU.

28 **"The serious rock press":** John Mendelssohn, "Adam Ant: Sex-Person Without a Cause!," *Creem*, May 1984.

28 **"shifted as many posters":** Al Clark, ed., *The Rock Yearbook 1982* (London: Virgin Books, 1981).

28 **"The greatest skills":** Clark, *Yearbook 1983*.

28 **"Blitz took up the gauntlet":** Jon Savage, "Androgyny: Confused Chromosomes and Camp Followers," *The Face*, June 1983.

28 **"He was like the pied piper":** Prima Elan, "It's Blitz: Birth of the New Romantics," *The Guardian* (Manchester), May 15, 2010.

29 **"the first clubs run for kids":** David Johnson, "63 Dean Street," *The Face*, February 1983.

29 **"There wasn't any need to":** Ian Birch, "New Romantics," in *Smash Hits 1984 Yearbook* (EMAP Publications, November/December 1983).

29 **"hard-edged European disco":** David Johnson, "Spandau Ballet, the Blitz Kids and the Birth of the New Romantics," *The Observer* (London), October 3, 2009.

29 **"We want to be like ABBA":** Robin Denselow, "Acts of the Year: Human League," in Clark, *Yearbook 1983*.

29 **"The problem with having" and "We relied on him":** Paul Lester, "Dare to Be Different," *Mojo*, November 2016.

29 **"At that point":** Ian Birch, "Hysteria?," *Smash Hits*, June 21–July 4, 1984.

30 **"plodding, second-rate *Dare*":** Peter Martin, "Album Reviews: Human League, *Hysteria*," *Smash Hits*, May 10–23, 1984.

30 **"a refugee from the Ramones":** Richard Grabel, "Nobody But Us Humans in Here!," *Creem*, December 1984.

30 **"Even the roadies":** Trakin, "Sweat & Ice."

30 **"You're in the wrong dressing room":** J. D. Considine, "Synth-Pop," *Musician*, August 1982.

30 "So if there's a new British Invasion": Ken Barnes, "The 'New British Invasion'—Is It Already Over?," *Radio & Records*, January 27, 1984.

30 "By early 1983": Simon Reynolds, *Rip It Up and Start Again* (London: Faber & Faber, 2007), 336.

31 "Jon was a staunch Tory": George with Bright, *Take It Like a Man*, 179.

31 Tony Hadley: Michael Hann, "Spandau Ballet: The Sound of Thatcherism," *The Guardian* (Manchester), March 25, 2009.

31 "I certainly wasn't": Rosie Millard, "Gary Kemp on David Bowie, Margaret Thatcher, and Joining the Establishment," *The Spectator* (London), March 23, 2013.

31 Ian Curtis: Luke Bainbridge, "The 10: Right-Wing Rockers," *The Guardian* (Manchester), October 13, 2007.

31 "I've never seen politics": Annene Kaye, "The Man from D.U.R.A.N. D.U.R.A.N.," *Creem*, July 1983.

31 "We had no political agenda": John Taylor, *In the Pleasure Groove* (New York: Dutton Adult, 2012), 188.

31 "the ultimate glossy": Richard Harrington, "Living Up to Video Images," *Washington Post*, February 23, 1984.

31 "Tucker wrote that Simon Le Bon ": Ken Tucker, "Boys on Vid," *Village Voice*, March 20, 1984.

31 "do[ing] things that we frankly": Grabel, "Nobody But Us Humans."

31 "I see no reason why": Neil Tennant, "A Public Figure," *Smash Hits*, January 19–February 1, 1984.

31 "We're poseurs": Henke, "Middle Class Heroes."

32 "two and a half years": Parke Puterbaugh, "Duran Duran: The Little Girls Understand," *Rolling Stone*, May 12, 1983.

32 "To headline shows": J. Taylor, *In the Pleasure Groove*, 107.

32 "jumped on the bandwagon": Henke, "Middle Class Heroes."

32 "We're sort of": Kaye, "The Man."

32 "Talk to Duran Duran": Puterbaugh, "Duran Duran."

32 "We'd go to . . . like, Pittsburgh": Kaye G., "The Man."

32 "Video to us": Henke, "Middle Class Heroes."

32 "In Britain we have": Kaye, "The Man."

32 "I've got two sisters": Judy Wade, "A Salmon Screams," *The Sun*, October 21, 1982.

33 "We're a fucking rock band": J. Taylor, *In the Pleasure Groove*, 178.

33 "I crossed a line": J. Taylor, *In the Pleasure Groove*, 236.

33 "She was tiny": J. Taylor, *In the Pleasure Groove*, 238.

33 "a stunning hybrid": Miller, "Britain Rocks America."

33 "An incredible variety": Freff, "Eurythmics: Anything Goes," *Musician*, November 1983.

33 "I hated it": Kurt Loder, "Eurythmics: Sweet Dreams Come True," *Rolling Stone*, September 29, 1983.

34 "From that minute on": Ian Birch, "Secrets Out!," *Smash Hits*, January 5–18, 1984.

34 **"I had to get rid":** Helen Fitzgerald, Eurythmics booklet, *Melody Maker*, February 11, 1984.

34 **"I dressed up":** Freff, "Eurythmics: Anything Goes."

34 **"Often we had to wait":** Fitzgerald, Eurythmics booklet.

34 **"And he said":** Freff, "Eurythmics: Anything Goes."

34 **"RCA offered":** Fitzgerald, Eurythmics booklet.

34 **"voice was beginning":** "Annie Gets All-Clear on Voice," *Melody Maker*, January 14, 1984.

35 **"prancing around":** "Wally of the Week; Bob Geldof," *Melody Maker*, January 14, 1984.

35 **"Film of Margaret Thatcher":** "Bitz," *Smash Hits*, February 2–15, 1984.

35 **"The sorrow of the IRA Brighton bombing":** Jon Savage, "The Smiths," *Spin*, June 1985.

35 **"Indubitably, Buzzcocks":** Pat Long, *The History of the NME* (London: Anova Books, 2012), 160.

35 **"We're so uncool":** Merle Ginsberg, "The Smiths: Through Being Cool," *Creem*, June 1984.

36 **"Books were always":** Roy Trakin, "The Smiths: This Charming Band Says Goodbye Techno-Bleak, Hello Gladiola," *Musician*, June 1984.

36 **"I find most people":** Savage, "The Smiths."

36 **"I couldn't imagine":** "Morrissey Quotes," in *The Smash Hits Yearbook 1986* (Brentford, UK: EMAP Publications, 1985).

36 **"I can't think of anybody":** "Super Starts: The Smiths," *Rolling Stone*, November 10, 1983.

36 **"We're the most important band":** Ginsberg, "The Smiths."

36 **"Where America's concerned":** Trakin, "The Smiths."

37 **"Einstürzende play hydraulic drills":** Merle Ginsberg, "Heady Metal," *Village Voice*, March 20, 1984.

37 **"Before anyone knew":** Cynthia Rose, "Letter from Britain: Music Hall to Mark '84?," *Creem*, April 1984.

37 **"When the [ICA staff] brought":** Chris Bohn, "Excited by Destruction," *New Musical Express (NME)*, January 14, 1984.

37 **"managed to violently polarize":** Rose, "Letter from Britain."

37 **On May 6, 1983:** Tony Fletcher, *A Light That Never Goes Out: The Enduring Saga of the Smiths* (New York: Crown Archetype, 2012), 259.

38 **"The Peel Sessions of 1978–1981":** Ken Garner, *The Peel Sessions* (London: BBC Books, 2007), 110–111.

38 **"spark an entire regional scene":** David Cavanagh, *Good Night and Good Riddance: How Thirty-Five Years of John Peel Helped to Shape Modern Life* (London: Faber & Faber, 2015), 233.

38 **"a scorching leather-bound version":** Gavin Martin, "Pink and Perky!," *NME*, November 5, 1983.

38 **a hundred thousand quid:** Mark Ward, "Frankie Goes to Hollywood," *Music Collector*, December 1990, zttaat.com/article.php?title=552.

38 more than seventy times: "BBC: Thanks But No Franks," *Smash Hits*, February 2–15, 1984.

38 "And at number six": "Fury over Frankie," *No. 1*, January 21, 1984.

38 "There's no one person": "Frankie Goes from the Airwaves," *Melody Maker*, January 28, 1984.

39 "And if you're thinking": "BBC: Thanks But No Franks."

39 "I hated punk": Simon Reynolds, *Totally Wired* (London: Faber & Faber, 2009), 337.

39 "I remember thinking": Freff, "Trevor Horn: A Studio Wunderkind and His Quiver of Production Arrows," *Musician*, March 1984.

39 "It's like Bob Dylan": Reynolds, *Totally Wired*, 340.

39 "knitting fog": Mick Brown and Howard Rosenberg, "Days of Whine and Poses—Two Diatribes," *Spin*, May 1985.

39–40 "to see if I could do an AOR": Freff, "Trevor Horn."

40 "just threw this out one night": Parke Puterbaugh, "Yes: A Seventies Dinosaur Comes Back to Life," *Rolling Stone*, February 4, 1984.

40 "Anyone can make": Freff, "Trevor Horn."

40 "I'm sure I'm not denigrating it": Richard Buskin, *Inside Tracks* (New York: Avon Books, 1999), 284.

40 "They want to be loved": Brown and Rosenberg, "Days of Whine and Poses."

40 "We used to hate him": Martin, "Pink and Perky!"

41 "People say": Paul Simper, "Frankie Goes to Hollywood," in *The Rock Yearbook 1985*, ed. Allan Jones (New York: St. Martin's Press, 1984).

41 "With 'Relax' we did a complete swerve": Buskin, *Inside Tracks*, 280

41 "I thought, *Thank you, Mike Read*": "A Day to Remember: Holly Johnson," *Smash Hits*, March 15–28, 1984.

CHAPTER FOUR: SUNSET STRIP, HOLLYWOOD, FEBRUARY 25, 1984

Author interviews with Steve Peters (July 2019) and Tom Werman (December 12, 2017).

43 "glutted": Paul Grein, "Werman Keeps Polishing Metal," *Billboard*, June 9, 1984.

43 a mere thirteen days: "The Knack Gets Gold," *Cash Box*, July 21, 1979.

43 only $18,000: Jim McCullough, "Knack Rides Charts with $18,000 Album," *Billboard*, August 4, 1979.

44 "You know, once": Martin Popoff, *The Big Book of Hair Metal* (Minneapolis–St. Paul: Voyageur Press, 2014), 27.

44 "Heavy metal and hard rock": Grein, "Werman Keeps Polishing Metal."

44 Sunday was Heavy Metal Day: Roman Kozak, "Heavy Metal Keeps Banging On," *Billboard*, September 17, 1983.

44 "God decided to pay us": Toby Goldstein, "Attack of the Techno-Tribes: How I (Sort of) Survived the US Festival," *Creem*, September 1983.

44 "Usually it's whoever": Steven Rosen, "Ace of Bass," *Guitar Player*, May 1986.

44 **"Van Halen smacked":** Edouard Dauphin, "Monkeys Pawed My Obelisk," *Creem*, May 1984.

45 **"I sell big smiles":** Ethlie Ann Vare, "Van Halen's Roth: Maybe It's Over," *Billboard*, January 12, 1985.

45 **"was a Dutch resistance fighter":** Debby Miller, "Van Halen's Split Personality," *Rolling Stone*, June 21, 1984.

45 **"He had to walk six miles":** Steve Sutherland, "The Gripes of Roth," *Melody Maker*, April 14, 1984.

45 **"My dad was one":** Jas Obrecht, ed., *Masters of Heavy Metal* (New York: Quill/Guitar Player Books, 1984), 150.

45 **"Alex is better technically":** J. D. Considine, "Eddie Van Halen: The Natural Virtuoso as High School Hero," *Musician*, September 1982.

45 **"Edward played acoustic guitar":** David Lee Roth, *Crazy from the Heat* (New York: Hyperion, 1997), 69.

46 **"New York certainly reflects":** Ian Christe, *Everybody Wants Some: The Van Halen Saga* (New York: Wiley, 2007), 14.

46 **"My family moved around":** "Personal File: David Lee Roth," *Smash Hits*, March 29–April 11, 1984.

46 **"I went to junior high":** Keith Phipps, "Interview: David Lee Roth," *Onion A.V. Club*, June 19, 2002.

46 **"I was on the floor":** Phipps, "Interview: David Lee Roth."

46 **in 2015 told an interviewer:** Chuck Klosterman, "Eddie Van Halen on Surviving Addiction, Why He's Still Making Music and What He Really Thinks of David Lee Roth (and Other Past Van Halen Bandmates)," *Billboard*, June 19, 2015.

46 **"I have no particular":** Dauphin, "Monkeys Pawed My Obelisk."

46 **"upper-middle-class daddies":** Roth, *Crazy from the Heat*, 56.

46 **"a carnal gymnast":** Mikal Gilmore, "Van Halen: The Endless Party," *Rolling Stone*, September 4, 1980.

46 **"Lost denizens":** Gilmore, "Van Halen: The Endless Party."

46 **"I felt the name":** Roth, *Crazy from the Heat*, 61.

46 **"I didn't like the idea":** Gilmore, "Van Halen: The Endless Party."

47 **"The first show I played":** Miller, "Van Halen's Split Personality."

47 **"Around the time we auditioned":** David Wild, "Eddie Van Halen: Balancing Act—the Rolling Stone Interview," *Rolling Stone*, April 6, 1995.

47 **"the hammer-on":** Considine, "Eddie Van Halen."

47 **"They just floored me":** Gilmore, "Van Halen: The Endless Party."

47 **"shimmering arpeggiated figures":** Considine, "Eddie Van Halen."

47 **"I did not take it as flattery":** Klosterman, "Eddie Van Halen on Surviving."

47 **"But you're really articulate":** Miller, "Van Halen's Split Personality."

47 **"You actually listened to him?":** Considine, "Eddie Van Halen."

48 **"The sense of humor":** Nina Blackwood, Mark Goodman, Alan Hunter, and Martha Quinn with Gavin Edwards, *VJ* (New York: Atria Books, 2013), 2.

48 **"While people over twenty years old":** Steve Feinstein, "Tempering the Metal," *Radio & Records*, September 7, 1984.

48 **"AORs are basically chicken":** Earl Paige, "Chains in Heavy Push for Metal," *Billboard*, October 13, 1984.

48 **"The whole reason":** Klosterman, "Eddie Van Halen on Surviving."

48 **"Shut up!":** Miller, "Van Halen's Split Personality."

48 **"Keyboards in our band?":** Rosen, "Ace of Bass."

48 **"I played it for the people":** Fred Bronson, *The Billboard Book of Number 1 Hits*, 5th ed. (New York: Billboard Books, 2003).

48 **"There was some stud":** Dauphin, "Monkeys Pawed My Obelisk."

49 **"'Jump' . . . is not exactly":** J. D. Considine, review of Van Halen's *1984*, *Rolling Stone*, March 1, 1984.

49 **"that Prince clone 'Jump'":** Greg Tate, "Van Halen Survive the Wars," *Village Voice*, April 10, 1984.

49 **"Van Halen's 'Jump' really does belong":** Brian Chin, "Dance Trax," *Billboard*, February 25, 1984.

49 **"The world's Top 40" and "I read reviews":** Sutherland, "The Gripes of Roth."

49 **"a laugh like a gaggle":** Debby Miller, "Quiet Riot: Heavy Metal's Latest Hotshots," *Rolling Stone*, January 19, 1984.

50 **"He finally just said":** Jon Wiederhorn and Kathryn Turman, *Louder Than Hell: The Definitive Oral History of Metal* (New York: It Books, 2013), 155.

50 **"Heavy metal bands":** Kozak, "Heavy Metal Keeps Banging On."

50 **"trying to repeat":** Popoff, *Big Book of Hair Metal*, 71.

50 **"Their own anthems stink":** Ira Robbins, ed., *The Rolling Stone Review: 1985* (New York: Rolling Stone Press/Scribner, 1985).

50 **"Kids don't want":** Bruce D. Rhodewalt, "Def Leppard: Heavy Metal for People Who Think," *Rolling Stone*, July 7, 1983.

51 **"His idea for the band":** Phil Collen with Chris Epting, *Adrenalized: Life, Def Leppard, and Beyond* (New York: Atria Books, 2015), 60.

51 **"There's synthesizer all over":** Grein, "Werman Keeps Polishing Metal."

51 **"Mutt's whole thing was":** Jake Brown, "Mike Shipley: Def Leppard and Mutt Lange w/Thomas Dolby and Corky Cortelyou," *Tape Op*, March/April 2017.

51 **"There are a lot of kids":** Jeffrey Peisch, "Cassettes Now Outselling LPs," *Rolling Stone*, November 24, 1983.

51 **"Britain has always":** Popoff, *Big Book of Hair Metal*, 49.

52 **"I felt he had":** Laura Jackson, *Jon Bon Jovi* (New York: Citadel Press, 2003), 29.

52 **"I think we should go out":** Ray Waddell, "Jon Bon Jovi Talks Loyalty, Universal Music and His 'Personal and Vulnerable' New Album," *Billboard*, November 4, 2016.

52 **"lifted almost wholesale":** Vici MacDonald, "Singles," *Smash Hits*, September 27–October 10, 1984.

52 **"Like Loverboy":** Joe Sasfy, "Bon Jovi: Tempered Heavy Metal," *Washington Post*, March 16, 1984.

52 **"I don't like any of that shit":** Obrecht, *Masters of Heavy Metal*, 135.

52 **"Van Halen, and I'm sure":** Toby Goldstein, "Judas Priest Eaten Alive!," *Creem*, July 1984.

53 **"When I think of heavy metal":** J. D. Considine, "Good, Bad & Ugly: A Field Guide to Heavy Metal for Confused Consumers, Outraged Critics and Wimpy New Wavers," *Musician*, September 1984.

53 **"I couldn't figure out":** Judy Wieder, "Rob Halford: Between Rock and a Hard Place," *The Advocate*, May 12, 1998.

53 **"It's tongue in cheek":** Goldstein, "Judas Priest Eaten Alive!"

53 **"A twenty-foot-high":** J. D. Considine, "Purity & Power: Total, Unswerving Devotion to Heavy Metal Form—Judas Priest and the Scorpions," *Musician*, September 1984.

54 **four semis of stage gear:** Ethlie Ann Vare, "Iron Maiden Pierces Iron Curtain," *Billboard*, October 13, 1984.

54 **"How can a band be pompous":** Tom Harrigan, "Iron Maiden," *Smash Hits*, October 25–November 7, 1984.

54 **"heavy metal bands with punk attitudes":** Sylvie Simmons, "Better Eddie Than Dead: Iron Maiden Tattoos America," *Creem*, October 1983.

54 **"Before, our records":** Adam Sweeting, "Another Perfect Daze," *Melody Maker*, May 14, 1983.

54 **"It's great to be back":** "The New-Look Motörhead," *Melody Maker*, March 17, 1984.

54 **"Ageless, trend-free":** Adam Sweeting, review of Motörhead's *No Remorse*, *Melody Maker*, September 8, 1984.

54 **"the volume was so loud":** John Petkovic, "Lemmy's Legendary 1984 Cleveland Motörhead Show: How a Kid Posed as a Journalist to Meet His Hero," *Cleveland Plain Dealer*, January 21, 2016.

55 **tape traders:** Ian Christe, *Sound of the Beast: The Complete Headbanging History of Heavy Metal* (New York: HarperEntertainment, 2003), 50.

55 **a month on Diamond Head's couch:** David Fricke, "Metallica: Heavy Metal Justice," *Rolling Stone*, January 12, 1989.

55 **"Hetfield felt":** Sylvie Simmons, "The Mojo Interview: Lars Ulrich," *Mojo*, December 2016.

55 **"These labels have already":** Kozak, "Heavy Metal Keeps Banging On."

56 **"Metal Blade's 'speed metal'":** Kim Freeman, "Two Views of Heavy Metal Mania," *Billboard*, October 13, 1984, 78.

56 **"beer and Chinese food":** Paul Brannigan and Ian Winwood, *Birth, School, Metallica, Death* (Cambridge, MA: Da Capo, 2014), 166.

56 **"We were shocked":** "Letters," *Billboard*, August 4, 1984.

57 **"Clearly, any parents":** Mick Farren, "Video: Bringing Too Much Back Home," *Creem*, March 1985.

57 **"A lot of people watch Ted Koppel":** Ethlie Ann Vare, "Rockin' Robot Joins Ranks of Veteran Rockers Y&T," *Billboard*, September 15, 1984.

57 **"look[ed] like the Green Bay Packers":** Charles M. Young, "Heavy Metal: In Defense of Dirtbags and Worthless Puds," *Musician*, September 1984.

58   **"We made a standing offer":** Ethlie Ann Vare, "Twisted Sister's 'Hideous' Road to Success," *Billboard*, September 22, 1984.

58   **"Your image is ridiculous":** Toby Goldstein, "Twisted Sister! Local Heroes in Warpaint Make Good," *Creem*, March 1984.

58   **"particularly surprised":** Dee Snider, *Shut Up and Give Me the Mic: A Memoir* (New York: Gallery Books, 2012), 193.

58   **"We don't want to alienate women":** Vare, "Twisted Sister's 'Hideous' Road."

59   **"*All of my anthems are*":** Snider, *Shut Up and Give Me the Mic*, 237.

59   **"the police were there in force":** Snider, *Shut Up and Give Me the Mic*, 304.

59   **say "fuck" for him:** Snider, *Shut Up and Give Me the Mic*, 305.

59   **"satanical worship":** Maurie Orodenker, "Court Refuses to Allow Osbourne to Do Concert," *Billboard*, February 26, 1983.

59   **"a tray of drinks":** "Mutterings," *Smash Hits*, May 10–23, 1984.

59   **"I'm a Christian guy":** J. Kordosh, "Now It Can Be Told! I Was a Monk for Ozzy Osbourne! My Secret Shame . . . ," *Creem*, June 1984.

59   **"I didn't feel too clever":** "Personal File: Ozzy Osbourne," *Smash Hits*, August 16–29, 1984.

59   **"it was like someone sticking":** Brian Harrigan, "Ozzy Osbourne," *Smash Hits*, October 11–24, 1984.

60   **"It was a full-on fight":** Mary McNamara, "It's Not a Reunion," *Los Angeles Times*, June 22, 1997.

60   **"so intense it seemed":** Tommy Lee, Mick Mars, Vince Neil, Nikki Sixx, and Neil Strauss, *The Dirt: Confessions of the World's Most Notorious Rock 'n' Roll Band* (New York: HarperEntertainment, 2001), 82.

61   **"I'm struck far less":** Steve Perry, "Heavy Metal's Reich 'n' Roll," *City Pages*, November 14, 1984.

61   **"In the same way":** Deborah Frost, "White Noise: How Heavy Metal Rules," *Village Voice*, June 18, 1985.

61   **"Sorry":** Sue Cummings, "Asleep at the Wheel," *Spin*, December 1985.

61   **"looked at each other":** Sylvie Simmons, "New Cosmetic Heavy Metal Show: Mötley Crüe Calling," *Creem*, February 1984.

62   **"we wanted to have ":** Wiederhorn and Turman, *Louder Than Hell*, 138.

62   **"You might as well learn":** Simmons, "New Cosmetic Heavy Metal Show."

62   **"He told everyone":** Phelim O'Neill, "Degeneration X," *Mojo*, September 2015.

62   **Bob Greene:** Bob Greene, "American Beat: Words of Love—from Today's Teenagers, a Different Kind of Fan Mail," *Esquire*, May 1984.

CHAPTER FIVE: SHRINE AUDITORIUM, LOS ANGELES, FEBRUARY 28, 1984

Author interview with Larry Harris (November 2009). All quotes from *The 26th Annual Grammy Awards* (CBS, February 28, 1984), in author's collection.

63   **he'd sold out Red Rocks:** Parke Puterbaugh, "Concert-Biz Blues: Long, Cold Summer," *Rolling Stone*, September 15, 1983.

64 **Jerry Weintraub:** Jordan Riefe, "Jerry Weintraub: How I Snookered Elvis Presley, Saved Sinatra," The Wrap, November 1, 2011, thewrap.com/jerry-weintraub-how-i-snookered-elvis-presley-revived-sinatra-32368/.

64 **near again until 2012:** Nellie Andreeva, "Whitney Houston Tragic Grammys Draw 39.9 Million Viewers, Second Most Watched Ever," Deadline Hollywood, February 13, 2012, deadline.com/2012/02/ratings-rat-race-grammys-sharply-up-in-early-ratings-230237/.

64 **"When disco started to die":** A. D. Amorosi, "Electronic Conductor," Wax Poetics, no. 62 (Summer 2015).

65 **"Why did we take":** Sylvie Simmons, "Give Us a Kiss," Creem, February 1985.

65 **"It felt like an unintentional commentary":** Tim Lawrence, Life and Death on the New York Dance Floor, 1980–1983 (Durham, NC: Duke University Press, 2016), 436.

65 **"The number of cases":** Michael Daly, "AIDS Anxiety," New York, June 20, 1983.

65 **"[He] told us in no uncertain terms":** Eric Marcus, Making Gay History (New York: HarperCollins, 2002), 247.

66 **"We're both in it":** Randy Shilts, And the Band Played On (New York: St. Martin's Press, 1987), 422.

66 **"To me it had always":** Donna Summer, Ordinary Girl (New York: Villard Books, 2013), 192–193.

66 **"Donna . . . really did not like gays":** David Marchese, "Giorgio Moroder: Back to the Future," Spin, May 22, 2013, spin.com/2013/05/avidc-moroder-daft-punk-donna-summer-interview-2013/.

66 **"I was tired and cranky and pregnant":** Summer, Ordinary Girl, 187.

66 **"It takes more than Springsteen's name":** Christopher Connelly, "Rock Radio: A Case of Racism?," Rolling Stone, December 9, 1982.

66 **"I came to find out later":** Summer, Ordinary Girl, 189.

66 **"upset because I was back on top":** Summer, Ordinary Girl, 190.

67 **"got stuck in a mile-long line":** Summer, Ordinary Girl, 192.

67 **"The Police was originally your band":** Charles Doherty, "Stewart Copeland: Policeman on the Beat," DownBeat, May 1984.

67 **"One of the Copelands'":** Brian D. Johnson, "The Police at the Top of Rock," Maclean's, August 15, 1983.

68 **"The police was a catalyst":** Michael Goldberg, "Andy Summers Unmasked," DownBeat, July 1983.

68 **"We played the Last Chance":** Sal Manna, "Police Get Their Bullets," Trouser Press, no. 59 (January 1981).

68 **"It takes two to tango":** Doherty, "Stewart Copeland."

69 **"One aspect of the Police":** Manna, "Police Get Their Bullets."

69 **"a raving capitalist":** Johnson, "The Police at the Top."

69 **"Sting and I would argue":** Vic Garbarini, "I Think If We Came Back . . . ," Revolver, Spring 2000.

69 **"I think the Clash":** Vic Garbarini, "Sting: The Lion in Winter," Musician, June 1983.

69 **"I'm *fifteen* years old":** Dave DiMartino, "Poised on the Brink of Infinity the Police Have 'It' All!," *Creem*, November 1983.

69 **"It's not an easy relationship":** Kristine McKenna, "A Monster Called Sting: The *Rolling Stone* Interview," *Rolling Stone*, September 1, 1983.

69 **"The drums sounded so much better":** Richard Buskin, "Classic Tracks: The Police's 'Every Breath You Take,'" *Sound on Sound*, March 2004.

70 **"both flattered and horrified":** Bill Flanagan, *Written in My Soul: Conversations with Rock's Great Songwriters* (Chicago: Contemporary, 1986), 302.

70 **"I remember calling my manager":** Buskin, "Classic Tracks."

70 **"updated fifties atmosphere":** Andy Summers, "The Cruel Sea," *Musician*, June 1983.

70 **110 CHR stations:** Most Added Records (chart), *Billboard*, June 4, 1983.

70 **of *Radio & Records'* AOR chart:** AOR/Hot Tracks (chart), *Radio & Records*, June 10, 1983

70 **In some shops:** Steve Pond and Kurt Loder, "Summer Sales Surge Gives Record Business a Boost," *Rolling Stone*, September 1, 1983.

70 **"This band *could* end tomorrow":** Garbarini, "Sting."

70 **"FUCK . . . OFF":** Frank Broughton, ed., *Time Out Interviews, 1968–1998* (New York: Penguin, 1998).

71 **"The band were understandably distressed":** Boy George with Spencer Bright, *Take It Like a Man* (New York: HarperCollins, 1995), 226.

71 **Pan Am Games:** "How We Got Here: A Timeline of Performance-Enhancing Drugs in Sports," *Sports Illustrated*, March 11, 2008, si.com/more-sports/2008/03/11/steroid-timeline.

71 **three athletes:** Associated Press, "Swede Loses Silver for Using Steroids," *New York Times*, August 5, 1984.

72 **"that he had provided anabolic steroids":** Michael Janofsky, "Doctor Says He Supplied Steroids to Medalists," *New York Times*, June 20, 1989.

72 **written in eight weeks:** Fred Schruers, *Billy Joel: The Definitive Biography* (New York: Crown Archetype, 2014), 172.

72 **"public songs":** Chris O'Leary, "Let's Dance," Pushing Ahead of the Dame (blog), October 20, 2011, bowiesongs.wordpress.com/2011/10/20/lets-dance/.

72 **"empty, drained, and rotting inside":** Jay Cocks, "David Bowie Rockets Onward," *Time*, July 18, 1983.

72 **"I would never have thought" and "I don't think I would want to":** Chris Bohn, "Merry Christmas Mr. Bowie," *New Musical Express* (*NME*), April 16, 1983.

73 **"Man, it must be fantastic":** *The Record Producers: Nile Rodgers* (BBC Radio documentary, January 1, 2007).

73 **"It didn't really turn out":** O'Leary, "Let's Dance."

74 **"only black musical style":** Nelson George and Mark Rowland, "Michael Jackson's Perfect Universe," *Musician*, July 1984.

74 **"on Michael Jackson albums":** Josef Woodard, "Toto," *Musician*, February 1985.

74 **"a Velveeta-orange leisure suit":** Parke Puterbaugh, review of *Toto IV*, *Rolling Stone*, July 22, 1982.

74 **"the MTV horrific years":** Matt Wardlaw, interview with Steve Lukather (transcript), December 2012, in author's possession.

75 **"shouldn't get a Grammy":** Zack O'Malley Greenburg, *Michael Jackson, Inc.: The Rise, Fall, and Rebirth of a Billion-Dollar Empire* (New York: Atria Books, 2014), 78.

75 **"For the first time in my entire career":** Elisabeth Bumiller, "Michael Jackson, Back in Step," *Washington Post*, February 8, 1984.

75 **"Magazines think":** Richard Harrington, "The Rock Chameleons," *Washington Post*, March 21, 1984.

75 **"preposterous hunting coat":** Michael Oldfield, "It's Alive: Eurythmics, Jahrhundert Hall, Frankfurt," *Melody Maker*, February 18, 1984.

75 **"the still-suffering victim of psychedelia":** James Truman, "Frankenstein's Children," *Village Voice*, February 28, 1984.

76 **"I looked like a groupie":** Bryony Sutherland and Lucy Ellis, *Annie Lennox: The Biography* (London: Omnibus, 2009), 207.

76 **"a second- or third-generation":** Truman, "Frankenstein's Children."

76 **"There had been a lot of talk":** Sutherland and Ellis, *Annie Lennox*, 207.

76 **"He melted":** Brian Mansfield, "How the Grammys Got Annie Lennox to Sing with Hozier," *USA Today*, February 6, 2015.

76 **"90 percent":** "35 Greatest Moments in Rock 'n' Roll Television," *Spin*, August 1990.

77 **"My wife believes":** Rodney Dangerfield, live at D.A.R. Hall (early show; soundboard tape), Washington, DC, March 10, 1984.

77 **"They asked me to leave":** "Personal File: Cyndi Lauper," *Smash Hits*, July 5–18, 1984.

77 **"I'd see her come home":** David Frankel, "Funny Girl," *New York*, December 26, 1983.

77 **"I told the other guys":** Cyndi Lauper, *Cyndi Lauper: A Memoir* (New York: Simon & Schuster, 2012), 64.

77 **"the Crystals with punk hair and Fender guitars":** Gillian G. Gaar, *She's a Rebel: The History of Women in Rock & Roll* (New York: Seal Press, 1992), 329.

77 **"He was trying to pick up another girl":** Gael Love and Glenn O'Brien, "Cyndi Lauper," *Interview*, April 1986.

78 **"a sort of MTV Bernadette Peters":** Laura Fissinger, "Cyndi Lauper Has a Great Personality," *Creem*, May 1984.

78 **"to make a record where":** Steven Dupler, "Cyndi Lauper Pulls No Emotional Punches," *Billboard*, February 16, 1985.

78 **"It was basically":** Gaar, *She's a Rebel*, 330.

78 **"Just a logical thing":** Michael Shore, *The Rolling Stone Book of Rock Video* (New York: Quill/Rolling Stone Press, 1984), 168.

79 **"Oh, Lou, you're such a natural":** Shore, *Rolling Stone Book*, 175.

79 **"You know when I was surprised?":** Love and O'Brien, "Cyndi Lauper."

79   **"In Britain":** Simon Frith, ed., *Facing the Music* (New York: Pantheon, 1988), 209.

79   **"When a man says he's straight":** George with Bright, *Take It Like a Man*, 167.

79   **"Virgin wanted any old press":** George with Bright, *Take It Like a Man*, 175.

80   **Frank DiLeo:** George with Bright, *Take It Like a Man*, 226.

80   **"In America":** James R. Blandford, "Culture Club," *Record Collector*, November 1998, 40.

80   **"There was never any time":** George with Bright, *Take It Like a Man*, 227.

80   **drowned in Marina del Rey:** "Beach Boys Drummer Buried at Sea," UPI, January 5, 1984.

80   **"When you're sixteen":** Michael Goldberg, "Dennis Wilson: The Beach Boy Who Went Overboard," *Rolling Stone*, June 7, 1984.

81   **"would be totally qualified":** Robert Hilburn, "CBS Group President Walter Yetnikoff," *Billboard*, July 21, 1984.

81   **Jackie Wilson:** "R&B Great Jackie Wilson Dead at 49," *Cash Box*, February 4, 1984.

81   **"He performed with the Chicago symphony":** Bill Flanagan, "Herbie Hancock: A Man for All Seasons, Be They Heavy or Lighthearted, Hip Jazz or Hip-Hop, Natural or Digital," *Musician*, January 1985.

82   **"It just went to my core" and "When I did *Head Hunters*":** Rafi Zabor and Vic Garbarini, "Wynton vs. Herbie," *Musician*, March 1985.

82   **"just tryin' to make some money":** Jon Balleras, "Herbie Hancock's Current Choice," *DownBeat*, September 1982.

82   **"One thing about pop music":** Zabor and Garbarini, "Wynton vs. Herbie."

82   **"Columbia wanted him":** David Fricke, "Herbie Can't Dance," *Rolling Stone*, October 25, 1984.

83   **"For people who like 'out' music":** John Diliberto, "Material," *DownBeat*, August 1982.

83   **"I always approach it":** Bob Belden, interview with Bill Laswell from liner notes to Herbie Hancock, *Sound-System* (Columbia, 1984; CD reissue, 1999).

83   **"Those guys had read my mind":** Fricke, "Herbie Can't Dance."

83   **Roger Trilling:** Mark Katz, *Groove Music* (Oxford: Oxford University Press, 2012), 91.

83   **"You're not going to get":** Rusty Cutchin, "The Rhythm Section," *Cash Box*, September 29, 1984.

83   **"They said they wanted to do":** Drew Wheeler, "Herbie Scratches the Surface," *Creem*, January 1984.

84   **a four-second close-up:** Randall Sullivan, *Untouchable: The Strange Life and Tragic Death of Michael Jackson* (New York: Grove, 2012), 96–97.

85   **"The fourth time":** Nancy Collins, "Ricky Martin: The *Rolling Stone* Interview," *Rolling Stone*, August 5, 1999.

86   **"the days when Frank Sinatra":** "Menudo Plays N.Y. in 10-Day Sellout," *Variety*, February 15, 1984.

86   **View-Masters:** "Jackson's 'Thriller' Now with 3-D Pics," *Variety*, April 11, 1984.

87 **He'd give Lewis piggyback rides:** Sullivan, *Untouchable*, 93.

87 **"It's not important to me":** Zafor and Garbarini, "Wynton vs. Herbie."

87–88 **"I don't have him in the band":** A. James Liska, "Wynton & Branford Marsalis: A Common Understanding," *DownBeat*, December 1982.

88 **"obsessed":** Steve Bloom, "The Hottest Lips in America," *Rolling Stone*, November 8, 1984.

88 **Cannonball Adderley's:** "New Faces to Watch: Branford Marsalis," *Cash Box*, April 14, 1984.

88 **"If you don't play":** Bloom, "The Hottest Lips."

88 **"I wore them down":** Phyl Garland, "Blowing Solid Gold," *Black Enterprise*, December 1984.

89 **"I wasn't even thinking":** Zafor and Garbarini, "Wynton vs. Herbie."

89 **"a shot of adrenaline" and "I was on the phone":** Phyl Garland, "All That Jazz," *Black Enterprise*, December 1984.

89 **Branford's list of 1984 favorites:** Year-end package in *Musician*, February 1985.

89 **"When do they give the award for best ass?":** Debby Miller, "The Secret Life of Prince," *Rolling Stone*, April 28, 1983.

90 **"Michael told me when you hear":** Lisa Robinson, "New Again: Janet Jackson," *Interview*, February 1987.

91 **"He's got a long chain":** Harold Conrad, "The Glamorous Life of Al Yankovic," *Spin*, August 1985.

91 **$40,000:** Jack McDonough, "Seminar Panelists Warn: Clip Fees Could Do Harm," *Billboard*, June 9, 1984.

CHAPTER SIX: CASTRO THEATRE, SAN FRANCISCO, APRIL 24, 1984

92 **"how really strange we were":** Jay Cocks, "Rock's Renaissance Man," *Time*, October 27, 1986.

92 **"my slightly removed":** David Byrne, *How Music Works* (San Francisco: McSweeney's, 2012), 45.

92 **"With David it's all or nothing":** Gregory Isola, "Tina Weymouth," *Bass Player*, March 1997.

93 **"Talking Heads still enjoy":** Scott Isler, "Chris & Tina: Talking Heads' Beat Team," *Musician*, August 1984.

93 **"Finally, people can see":** David Adelson, "Filmusic," *Cash Box*, September 15, 1984.

93 **twenty bucks a head; and "We've never seen this before, either":** Jennifer Preissel, "Great Moments—Talking Heads: Dancing in the Aisles," San Francisco International Film Festival (blog), 2006, history.sffs.org/great_moments /great_moments.php?id=13.

93 **the manager was trying:** David Bowman, *This Must Be the Place: The Adventures of Talking Heads in the 20th Century* (New York: HarperCollins, 2001), 271.

93 **In October 1977:** Cocks, "Rock's Renaissance Man."

94 **"The term 'punk' is as offensive":** Theo Cateforis, *Are We Not New Wave: Modern Pop at the Turn of the 1980s* (Ann Arbor: University of Michigan Press, 2011), 25.

94 **still toured in a van:** *End of the Century: The Story of the Ramones*, directed by Jim Fields and Michael Gramaglia (Rhino DVD, 2005).

94–95 **"That was right when Martin Scorsese's":** Isola, "Tina Weymouth."

95 **"punk" (later "metal"):** "Concert Reviews," *Variety*, November 7, 1984.

95 **"It's the spaghetti in the face principle":** Roman Kozak, *This Ain't No Disco: The Story of CBGB* (London: Faber & Faber, 1988), 113.

95 **"took this bottle":** Tony Rettman, *New York Hardcore, 1980–1990* (New York: Bazillion Points, 2014), 193.

95 **"At a time when unemployment":** "Behind the Market's Wild Ride," *Business-Week*, October 25, 1982.

95 **"swelled to about seventy thousand":** Kim Foltz, "The Celebrity Stockbrokers," *Newsweek*, February 6, 1984.

96 **"the only socially commendable form of greed":** Peter Plagens, "Cents and Sensibility: Collecting the '80s," *Artforum*, April 2003.

96 **"A friend of mine set up a meeting":** David Browne, "Tom Wolfe on the Secret to Great Reporting and Why He Never Tried Acid," *Rolling Stone*, May 15, 2018, rollingstone.com/culture/features/tom-wolfe-talks-electric-kool-aid-acid -test-new-journalism-w520345.

96 **"In the early eighties":** Tom Feiling, *Cocaine Nation* (New York: Pegasus Books, 2012), 49.

96 **"It makes a big difference":** Robin Tolleson, "Tina Weymouth: Fresh Designs on Funk Bass," *Guitar Player*, March 1984.

96 **"I decided that making":** Byrne, *How Music Works*, 32.

97 **"David would do anything":** Cocks, "Rock's Renaissance Man."

97 **"Somehow, to us":** Byrne, *How Music Works*, 37.

97 **"We started Talking Heads":** Cocks, "Rock's Renaissance Man."

97 **"only to please Chris":** Isola, "Tina Weymouth."

97 **"Are you guys a feminist band?":** Julian Marszalek, "Tom Tom Club's Chris Frantz on David Byrne, Brian Eno, and Lee 'Scratch' Perry," The Quietus, June 3, 2009, thequietus.com/articles/01782-tom-tom-club-chris-frantz-talking -heads-interview.

97 **"The image we present":** James Wolcott, "A Conservative Impulse in the New Rock Underground," *Village Voice*, August 18, 1975.

97 **"I always felt that":** Christopher Connelly, "Byrne in Love," *Rolling Stone*, October 27, 1983.

98 **"The first time I ever met":** Rick Karr, "Once in a Lifetime," *All Things Considered*, NPR, March 27, 2000, npr.org/2000/03/27/1072131/once-in-a-lifetime.

98 **"We built up":** Byrne, *How Music Works*, 47.

98 **"We raised a stink about it" and "I didn't read those books!":** Scott Isler, "4 Heads, 3 Solo LPs, 1 Band," *Trouser Press*, no. 72 (April 1982).

99 **"When Busta was in the group":** Tolleson, "Tina Weymouth."

99 **"Tom Tom Club was intended":** Isola, "Tina Weymouth."

99 **"We never said":** Isler, "4 Heads."

99 **"because white radio doesn't play us anymore":** Greg Tate, "Talking Heads: Grooves from the Heart of Darkness," *Musician*, September 1983.

99 **"It's nothing but a gospel song":** Rusty Cutchin, "The Rhythm Section," *Cash Box*, October 20, 1984.

100 **"highly stylized" to "completely transparent":** Byrne, *How Music Works*, 50–56.

100 **"It was a very transcendent experience":** Clark Collis, "Talking Heads' Chris Frantz on 25 Years of 'Stop Making Sense' and the Possibility of a Heads Reunion," *Entertainment Weekly*, October 13, 2009.

100–101 **"I freaked out" and "My main idea":** Melissa Locker, "David Byrne and Jonathan Demme on the Making of *Stop Making Sense*," *Time*, July 15, 2014.

101 **moved up to October 1:** "Talking Heads, Byrne Expanding into Film, Television, Theater," *Variety*, September 5, 1984.

101 **"It was a combination":** Lynden Barber, "The Man in the Large Flannel Suit," *Melody Maker*, November 24, 1984.

101 **"The other Heads":** "Talking Heads, Byrne."

101 **"a story about":** Jeffrey Ressner, "Points West," *Cash Box*, January 21, 1984.

102 **edited down from fifty hours of footage:** Scott Tobias, "Christopher Guest on 'Mascots' and Why His Comedies Are Completely Different," *Rolling Stone*, October 14, 2016, https://www.rollingstone.com/movies/movie-features /christopher-guest-on-mascots-and-why-his-comedies-are-completely-different -104133/.

102 **"We tried to make it":** Richard Harrington, "It Took Backbone to Make a Rock Satire That Works," *Washington Post*, April 15, 1984.

102 **"a kind of Greatest Hits of Rock Idiocy":** Adam Sweeting, "Spinal Column," *Melody Maker*, September 15, 1984.

102 **"but how weird is this":** Samuel Graham, "Spinal Tap: Art Astutely Imitates Life in a Heavy Metal Cinematic Send-up," *Musician*, April 1984.

102 **"delightful":** Jon Young, "Indestructible Metal," in *The Rolling Stone Review: 1985*, ed. Ira Robbins (New York: Rolling Stone Press/Scribner, 1985).

102 **"It's not anywhere near":** Sylvie Simmons, "Give Us a Kiss," *Creem*, February 1985.

102 **"We were chased out of theaters":** Nathan Rabin, "Harry Shearer," *The Onion A.V. Club*, April 23, 2003.

103 **"Just by chance":** Alex Cox, *X Films: True Confessions of a Radical Filmmaker* (New York: Soft Skull Press, 2008).

103 **"It has sort of an emblematic quality" and "endlessly imitated":** Nathan Rabin, "Alex Cox," *The Onion A.V. Club*, September 20, 2000.

103 **"If you continue to go":** Debby Miller, "Rock Is Money to Hollywood Ears," *Rolling Stone*, October 27, 1983.

103 **"When the teen market":** David Hinckley, "'Big Chill''s Big Sounds," *Washington Post*, January 2, 1984.

104 **"a rock video in reverse":** Ira Robbins, ed., *The Rolling Stone Review: 1985* (New York: Rolling Stone Press/Scribner, 1985).

104 **"It felt to me":** Fred Bronson, *The Billboard Book of Number 1 Hits*, 5th ed. (New York: Billboard Books, 2003).

104 **"The first video":** Robbins, *Rolling Stone Review*.

105 **"synthesize the rock-funk" and "We got flak":** Nelson George, "Shalamar: A Crossover Success Is Threatened by the Distractions of Fashion," *Musician*, December 1983.

105 **"I think black audiences":** Steve Ivory, "Shalamar Eye Pop Stardom," *Billboard*, November 24, 1984.

105 **"R&B's reigning female vocalist":** Lisa Collins, "This Is Niecy!," *Sepia*, December 1980.

106 **"I sort of looked":** Ethlie Ann Vare, "George Duke Set to 'Do a Job on Myself,'" *Billboard*, August 18, 1984.

106 **"In the sort of church":** Alan Jackson, "Let's Hear It for the Girl," *Melody Maker*, June 9, 1984.

106 **"He has a great awareness":** Peter Holden, "Soundtracks Chart Success," *Cash Box*, May 12, 1984.

106 **"because I had one too many":** J. D. Considine, "The Second Coming of Phil Collins," *Musician*, June 1985.

107 **"match the scenes from the film" and "(Collins does not appear in *Against All Odds*)":** Richard Gold, "Studios & Labels Pan Soundtrack Gold—but Some Fear Genre Overkill," *Variety*, April 18, 1984.

CHAPTER SEVEN: ISLAND RECORDS, LONDON, MAY 8, 1984

Author interviews with Paul Rhodes Trautman (September 21, 2017) and Stephen T. McClellan (August 2015).

108 **Dave Robinson:** Gareth Murphy, *Cowboys and Indies: The Epic History of the Record Industry* (New York: Thomas Dunne Books, 2014), 298–304.

109 **"I started figuring out":** Craig Rosen, "Bob Marley's 'Legend' Lives on at Radio, Retail," *Billboard*, September 4, 1993.

109 **"are profitable even though":** Kip Kirby, "Polygram Digs into Vaults," *Billboard*, November 24, 1984.

109 **"When things were steamrolling along":** Mark Humphrey, "LP Strategy: Old Music, New Profit," *Rolling Stone*, April 28, 1983.

109 **"seeing what's in their own catalog":** Sam Sutherland, "Rhino Records' Archival Mission Gaining Momentum," *Billboard*, July 28, 1984.

110 **"I don't think the majors":** Adam White, "UK Majors Easing Oldie Licensing Limits," *Billboard*, September 22, 1984.

110 **"I've been tripping":** David Stubbs, *Ace Records* (London: Black Dog Publishing, 2007), 94.

110 **"probably the most intelligent re-packager":** Parke Puterbaugh, "Rhino Records: A Little Label with Big Ambitions Puts the Fun Back in Music," *Rolling Stone*, May 10, 1984.

111 **"For the first time in decades":** Humphrey, "LP Strategy."

111 **"to start convincing yourself":** Robert Christgau, "Consumer Guide," *Village Voice*, December 25, 1984.

111 **"teen-directed compilation":** "RCA Steps Up Presley Campaign with Youth-Oriented Strategy," *Variety*, October 24, 1984.

111 **"the loose booty":** Dave Marsh, ed., *The First Rock & Roll Confidential Report* (New York: Pantheon, 1985), 275.

111–112 **His Memphis mansion Graceland:** Laura Sanders, "Sell Me Tender," *Forbes*, February 13, 1984.

112 **Joan Deary:** Sam Sutherland, "Presley Box the Result of Detective Work," *Billboard*, December 8, 1984.

112 **"My contact with white and black audiences":** Peter Holden, "Reggae Gains with Independent Labels at Grass Roots Level," *Cash Box*, August 11, 1984.

112 **"The music is getting out":** Nelson George and Isaac Ferguson, "Jamming in Jamaica," *Black Enterprise*, May 1983.

113 **"The name 'dancehall'":** Kevin O'Brien Chang and Wayne Chen, *Reggae Routes: The Story of Jamaican Music* (Philadelphia: Temple University Press, 1998), 59.

113 **deeply offensive to reggae fans:** Roger Steffens, "Reggae 1984: Fragments of a Fallen Star," *Musician*, February 1984.

113 **"I found out the women":** Roy Trakin, "Yellowman: Reggae's Clown Prince," *Creem*, January 1985.

113 **"A political singer":** John Leland, "Ruben Blades and Willie Colón: The Beat Goes North," *Musician*, December 1984.

114 **"You have to remember":** Pete Hamill, "Hey, It's Ruben Blades," *New York*, August 19, 1985.

114 **"sold somewhere between":** Marsh, *First Rock & Roll Confidential*, 127.

114 **"A lot of the major":** Leland, "Ruben Blades and Willie Colón."

114 **the "rock-oriented record buyer":** Enrique Fernandez, "What's Happening in the Industry?," *Billboard*, September 1, 1984.

114 **"I needed the degree":** John Leland, "Blades Running," *Spin*, September 1985.

114 **"In half, they want me":** Hamill, "Hey, It's Ruben Blades."

115 **"incredible pedal steel guitar solos" and "re-record[ings]":** Phil Freeman, "King Sunny Adé: From Lagos to Hollywood," *Red Bull Music Academy Daily*, July 23, 2014, daily.redbullmusicacademy.com/2014/07/king-sunny-ade-from-lagos-to-hollywood.

116 **"for expenses":** Leo Sacks, "King Sunny Gets Royal Welcome," *Billboard*, February 19, 1983.

116 **"fully integrates electronics":** Randall F. Grass, review of King Sunny Adé's *Synchro System* and Juluka's *Scatterlings*, *Musician*, September 1983.

116 **a standard at the Loft:** Tim Lawrence, *Life and Death on the New York Dance Floor, 1980–1983* (Durham, NC: Duke University Press, 2016), 385.

116 **"Hugh, let's make one":** Michael Goldberg, "Hugh Masekela's Afro–New York Disco," *Rolling Stone*, August 30, 1984.

117 **"Adé strives to compromise":** Don Palmer, "Juju Beat: King Sunny Adé," *DownBeat*, December 1984.

117 **"more reminiscent this time out":** "Concert Reviews," *Variety*, August 29, 1984.

117 **Blackwell took the credit in the trades:** See "Mango Skeds Series of Reggae Albums," *Variety*, November 7, 1984.

CHAPTER EIGHT: THE 13TH ANNUAL INTERNATIONAL COUNTRY MUSIC FAN FAIR, NASHVILLE, JUNE 4–10, 1984

Material accessed from the library of the Country Music Hall of Fame and Museum, Nashville, Tennessee, is indicated below (as CMHOF), as are interview transcripts from the museum's Country Music Foundation Oral History Project.

118 **"Willie was not":** Sharon Allen, "Nashville's Fan Fair Fanfare," *Radio & Records*, June 15, 1984.

118 **"I phoned [manager] Mark Rothbaum":** Tom Roland, *The Billboard Book of Number One Country Hits* (New York: Billboard Books, 1991), 385.

119 **"Do you want to keep working here?":** "Julio at the Universal Amphitheatre: Winning Voice of the '84 Olympics," *Billboard*, August 11, 1984.

120 **"What I always liked to do":** Jim Hatlo, "Willie Nelson," in *Country Musicians*, ed. Jodie Eremo (New York: Grove, 1987), 85.

120 **a chain saw:** Sandy Neese, "Stars' Belongings Up for Bid," *Tennessean Sunday Showcase*, June 3, 1984.

120 **one of only two 45s:** John Lomax III, *Nashville: Music City U.S.A.* (New York: Harry N. Abrams, 1985), 183.

120 **"could set the image of country music":** Kip Kirby, "'Rhinestone': Dolly, How Could You?," *Billboard*, July 7, 1984.

120 **On June 1, the Country Music Hall of Fame and Museum:** Robert K. Oermann, "Dolly Display Adds New Dimension to Hall of Fame Exhibits," *The Tennessean*, May 19, 1984.

120 **"They worked right up":** Robert K. Oermann, "Country Music Museums in Fan Fair Spotlight," *The Tennessean*, June 6, 1984.

121 **"Subsequently Opryland" to "smile back at them":** Miriam Pace, "Rooted in the Country: Music Business Offshoots," *Nashville!*, June 1984.

121 **"reap the harvest":** Mark Zabriskie, "Lucky 13 Sets Fan Fair Crowd Record," *Nashville Banner*, June 9, 1984, via CMHOF.

121 **by 1984 it was overseeing:** Don Rhodes, "Fan Fair Evolved from a Single Club," *Athens Banner-Herald*, June 1984, via CMHOF.

122 **"So many fans were coming in":** Zabriskie, "Lucky 13 Sets."

122 **"If you want to load people on buses":** Rhodes, "Fan Fair Evolved."

122 **660 booths:** Robert K. Oermann, "Fabulous Fan Fair; It's Finally Arrived!," *The Tennessean*, June 4, 1984.

122 **2,000 additional seats were added:** "Strong Demand for Booth Space at Fan Fair," *Amusement Business Weekly*, March 31, 1984, via CMHOF.

122 **Norway, South Africa, England:** "Today's Fan Fair at a Glance," *The Tennessean*, June 6, 1984.

122 **"not-too-well-known" and "Something like Fan Fair":** Roberts, "Country's Stars Do It All for the Fans," *Virginia Pilot*, June 1984, via CMHOF.

122 **"Their first gift":** Robert K. Oermann, "A First in Fan Fair History: Wedding Bells in Booth 431," *The Tennessean*, June 9, 1984.

123 **"My mother is the kind of person":** Bruce Feiler, *Dreaming Out Loud: Garth Brooks, Wynonna Judd, Wade Hayes, and the Changing Face of Nashville* (New York: Harper Perennial, 1999), 144.

123 **"Their background has traditional roots":** Interview with Joe Galante by Paul Kingsbury, November 15, 1985 (OHC125), in the Country Music Foundation Oral History Project, Country Music Hall of Fame and Museum, Nashville, Tennessee.

123 **"One of the chief concerns":** Lomax, *Nashville*, 114.

124 **"I left one company on a Friday":** Interview with Jim Foglesong by John W. Rumble, June 18, 1992 (OHC103-LC), in the Country Music Foundation Oral History Project, Country Music Hall of Fame and Museum, Nashville, Tennessee.

124 **"Western swing":** Bob Allen, *The Blackwell Guide to Recorded Country Music* (Hoboken, NJ: Blackwell, 1994).

124 **"There are young women":** Interview with Jimmy Bowen by Paul Kingsbury, November 27, 1985 (OHC34-LC), in the Country Music Foundation Oral History Project, Country Music Hall of Fame and Museum, Nashville, Tennessee.

124 **"There are no pop":** Interview with Joe Galante, in the Country Music Foundation Oral History Project.

124 **"pop music became very stale":** Interview with Jimmy Bowen, in the Country Music Foundation Oral History Project.

125 **"I'm quick to do things":** Barry Bronson, "Lee Greenwood Pays the Price," *Music City News*, April 1984, via CMHOF.

125 **"Greenwood's repertoire ranges":** David Gates, "Don't Get Above Your Raisin': Ricky Skaggs, Alabama, and Their Contemporaries," in *Country: The Music and the Musicians* (Nashville: Country Music Foundation, 1988).

125 **"Lee is not, certainly":** Interview with Jim Foglesong, in the Country Music Foundation Oral History Project.

125 **"wave of patriotism":** Roland, *Billboard Book*, 379.

126 **"one of the most lucrative songs":** Interview with Jim Foglesong, in the Country Music Foundation Oral History Project.

126 **"This is the ultimate compliment"**: Greg Bailey, "Fans' Ovation Gives Show to Greenwood," *Nashville Banner*, June 5, 1984, via CMHOF.

126 **Barbara Mandrell showed up:** "Fantastic Fan Fair Festival," *CMA Close Up*, July 1984, via CMHOF.

126 **"as though it were a new national anthem"**: Sandy Neese and Robert K. Oermann, "Shining Stars," *The Tennessean*, June 9, 1984.

126 **"For the future"**: Interview with Jimmy Bowen, in the Country Music Foundation Oral History Project.

CHAPTER NINE: WPIX CHANNEL 11, NEW YORK CITY, JUNE 29, 1984

Author interviews with Arthur Baker, Chrissie Dunlap (September 2, 2015), Michael Holman (July 5, 2018), Tom Silverman, and Paul Spangrud (September 24, 2015). Sources from the Adler Hip-Hop Archive, via the Cornell Hip-Hop Collection (digitized at https://rmc.library.cornell.edu/hiphop/adler.php), are marked "via Adler."

128 **"such a phenomenal smash"**: Aaron Fuchs, "Bobby Robinson: Up from the Streets," *Soho News*, December 22, 1981, via Adler.

130 **"To me, it was the first time"**: Kethu Gallu-Badat, "The Host with the Most," *Wax Poetics*, no. 26 (December 2008–January 2009).

131 **"a generic street term"**: David Hinckley, "Grandmaster Flash Set for Court," *New York Daily News*, February 23, 1984, via Adler.

131 **"If you got five pockets"**: Carlo Wolff, "Grapevine," *Goldmine*, June 22, 1984, via Adler.

131 **"glib, show-biz style"**: Lynden Barber, "Flash in the Pan," *Melody Maker*, April 14, 1984.

131 **"We would like to request"**: Western Union Mailgram from Sylvia Robinson to all disc jockeys: "It's Melle Mel Who Stars in 'Beat Street,' not Grandmaster Flash," May 20, 1984, via Adler.

132 **LA Sunshine, had just left the group:** JayQuan, "Interview with L.A. Sunshine" (printout from blog.myspace.com/treacherous 3, March 18, 2007), via Adler.

132 **"Kool said"**: "Hip-Hop Memories," *The Source*, no. 50 (November 1993).

133 **"First rap club was the Language Lab"**: Tim Westwood, "The B & S Team," *Blues & Soul*, no. 469 (October 21–November 3, 1986).

133 **"cannibalizing other crews"**: Gallu-Badat, "The Host with the Most."

133 **"When we get up on it"**: Cameron Crowe, "Joni Mitchell Defends Herself," *Rolling Stone*, July 26, 1979.

134 **"the year when big money"**: "Lucky Breaks," *Melody Maker*, December 22–29, 1984.

134 **"creating obstacles"**: Jeffrey Ressner, "Points West," *Cash Box*, January 28, 1984.

135 **"What they do here that's unique"**: Richard Harrington, "The Wild Style Breaks into Town," *Washington Post*, January 27, 1984.

135 **"I wanted to make sure":** Jeff Chang, *Can't Stop Won't Stop: A History of the Hip-Hop Generation* (New York: St. Martin's Press, 2005), 148.

135 **"twenty-five hundred":** rchecka, "The Big Breakdance Contest Full (Remastered Audio)," filmed WABC-TV, New York, December 17, 1983, YouTube video, 21:38, published December 13, 2011, youtube.com/watch?v=C1flHrhfLbk.

136 **as big as Elvis Presley's "Jailhouse Rock":** Rick Sklar, *Rocking America: How the All-Hit Radio Stations Took Over* (New York: St. Martin's Press, 1984), 190.

136 **"She thought this might be important":** Ron Hart, oral history of *Beat Street* (2014), courtesy of author.

136 **"They didn't want it to be an unrealistic":** Janet Maslin, "At the Movies: Capturing the Hip-Hop Culture," *New York Times*, June 8, 1984.

136 **"prove that blacks can make 'bankable' films":** Amy Virshup, "Harry's Kids," *New York*, March 12, 1984.

136 **"possibly three volumes" and "the epitome of rap records":** Peter Holden, "Belafonte Explains Story Behind 'Beat Street' Project," *Cash Box*, May 19, 1984.

137 **"Two blacks and the token white girl":** "Lucky Breaks."

137 **"It is one of the fastest-made":** Jeff Silberman, "Industry Update: Soundtrack Fever Fueled by Videos," *BAM* (San Francisco), July 13, 1984.

137 **two hundred grand:** Richard Harrington, "'Wild Style': Art to Go," *Washington Post*, January 26, 1984.

137 **"Harry was really disappointed":** Hart, oral history of *Beat Street*.

138 **"The title song":** Rusty Cutchin, "Breakin' Goes Platinum—Sequel Now in Production," *Cash Box*, June 30, 1984.

139 **"the only guy on the rap scene":** Nelson George, *Buppies, B-Boys, Baps & Bohos: Notes on Post-Soul Black Culture* (New York: HarperCollins, 1992), 52.

139 **thirty-five dollars a show:** Ronin Ro, *Raising Hell: The Reign, Ruin, and Redemption of Run-D.M.C. and Jam Master Jay* (New York: Amistad, 2005), 16.

140 **"It's too hard":** Ro, *Raising Hell*, 36.

140 **"We didn't want to do":** Chris Williams, "Key Tracks: Run-D.M.C., 'Rock Box,'" *Red Bull Music Academy Daily*, December 23, 2014, https://daily.redbull musicacademy.com/2014/12/key-tracks-run-dmc-rock-the-box.

140 **"I had a lot of fun, Mom":** Ro, *Raising Hell*, 32.

140 **"Jay knew many drug lords from Queens":** Ro, *Raising Hell*, 59.

141 **"Russell was like, *oh shit*":** Ro, *Raising Hell*, 53.

141 **"Runde MC":** Dan Charnas, liner notes for *Giant Single: The Profile Records Rap Anthology* (Arista/Legacy 2CD, rec. 1981–1996/2012).

141 **"Professional sound system":** Run D.M.C., December 28, 1983, First Avenue & 7th Street Entry Band Files, Minnesota Historical Society.

141 **hung from the ceiling:** Peter S. Scholtes, "First Love," *City Pages*, September 3, 2003.

142 **"Rap albums don't sell":** Ro, *Raising Hell*, 70.

142 **"When punkers tried":** Fred Goodman, review of Run-D.M.C.'s *King of Rock*, *Musician*, April 1985.

142 **$27,000:** Carol Cooper, "Run-D.M.C.: Run for It," *The Face*, November 1984.

143 **"I wanted to stay jazz":** "New Faces to Watch: Shannon," *Cash Box*, February 18, 1984.

144 **"Plans are to release":** RJ Smith, "Shannon Lets It Play," *Creem*, September 1984.

144 **"It presents hip-hop":** "'Graffiti Rock' Tunes In on the Hip-Hop Culture," *New York Times*, June 28, 1984.

144 **Coca-Cola and the US Army:** Gallu-Badat, "The Host with the Most."

145 **"It was forty-five dollars an hour":** Bill Adler and Dan Charnas, *Def Jam Recordings: The First 25 Years of the Last Great Record Label* (New York: Rizzoli, 2010), 28.

145 **"the blackest hip-hop record":** Stacy Gueraseva, *Def Jam, Inc.* (New York: One World, 2005), 33.

146 **"Russ's name was on all these records":** Adler and Charnas, *Def Jam Recordings*, 31.

146 **"It felt like black punk rock":** Nathan Rabin, "Rick Rubin," *The A.V. Club*, January 12, 2005.

146 **"The experience that I had":** Adler and Charnas, *Def Jam Recordings*, 26.

146 **"there were no white people involved":** Rabin, "Rick Rubin."

146 **"twelve rap acts":** "Russell Simmons' Rush Represents Rappers," *Billboard*, September 15, 1984.

147 **"Of course, this is typical":** Adler and Charnas, *Def Jam Recordings*, 44.

147 **"We'd sit around":** Amos Barshad, "Rude Boys: The Birth of the Beastie Boys—an Oral History on the 25th Anniversary of *Licensed to Ill*," *New York*, April 24, 2011.

147 **"We were listening":** Adler and Charnas, *Def Jam Recordings*, 22.

147 **"Not only did we get 'Cooky Puss'":** Alan Light, *The Skills to Pay the Bills: The Story of the Beastie Boys* (New York: Three Rivers Press, 2006), 52.

147 **"American hardcore":** ABC News (Australia), "Beastie Boys' Mike D Talks About MCA, Breaking Up the Band and Almond Milk" (interview), YouTube video, 12:47, published July 10, 2014, youtube.com/watch?v=FN2v7VmvA9I.

147 **"Rick picking up the tab":** Light, *Skills to Pay the Bills*, 54.

148 **"Rick was this larger-than-life character":** Adler and Charnas, *Def Jam Recordings*, 22.

148 **"Russell was talking about":** Ro, *Raising Hell*, 37.

148 **"This guy would be out drinking":** Ro, *Raising Hell*, 90.

148 **"The first time I met 'em" and "They were incredibly deferential":** Light, *Skills to Pay the Bills*, 60.

148 **"every day for, like, two weeks":** Adler and Charnas, *Def Jam Recordings*, 61.

148 **"If you can write a song":** David Hinckley, "Let's Stop Giving Them a Bad Rap," *New York Daily News*, December 27, 1985, via Adler.

149 **"Why don't we just do it ourselves?":** Adler and Charnas, *Def Jam Recordings*, 61.

149 **"He delivers his raps":** John Leland, "L.L. Cool J: B-Boy Wonder," *Music and Sound Output*, November 1985, via Adler.

149 **"I want to make records like Run":** Ro, *Raising Hell*, 94.

149 **"I'd like to play the Meadowlands":** Hinckley, "Let's Stop Giving Them."

CHAPTER TEN: ARROWHEAD STADIUM, KANSAS CITY, MISSOURI, JULY 6, 1984

150 *Rock & Soul* **magazine:** Lisa Robinson, *There Goes Gravity* (New York: River-head, 2014), 164–165.

150 **"Big Nose":** Randall Sullivan, *Untouchable* (New York: Grove Press, 2012), 171.

150 **quoted his horoscope:** Robert E. Johnson, "Michael Jackson: The World's Greatest Entertainer," *Ebony*, May 1984.

151 **"Oh come on, look":** Danny Baker, "The Great Greenland Mystery," *New Musical Express (NME)*, April 4, 1981.

151 **"How big is Michael Jackson?":** Michael Goldberg and Christopher Connelly, "Trouble in Paradise?," *Rolling Stone*, March 15, 1984.

151 **"stopped the presses":** Chuck Conconi, "Personalities," *Washington Post*, January 27, 1984.

151 **eight hundred thousand copies:** "For the Record," *Billboard*, October 6, 1984.

151 **"Although 'Thriller' is no more misogynist":** J. Hoberman, "Scanners: Video to Go," *Village Voice*, April 17, 1984.

151 **"Jackson wore no hat":** Elisabeth Bumiller, "Michael Jackson, Back in Step," *Washington Post*, February 8, 1984.

152 **"All your article":** Letters to the Editor, *Ebony*, March 1983.

152 **the first of many plastic surgeries:** Sullivan, *Untouchable*, 171.

152 **more like Diana Ross's:** Sullivan, *Untouchable*, 216.

152 **"Michael isn't gay":** Jay Cocks, "Why He's a Thriller," *Time*, March 19, 1984.

153 **fake facial hair:** Jermaine Jackson, *You Are Not Alone: Michael Through a Brother's Eyes* (New York: Touchstone/Simon & Schuster, 2011), 227.

153 **Jehovah's Witnesses were:** Dave Marsh, *Trapped: Michael Jackson and the Crossover Dream* (New York: Bantam Books, 1985), 115.

153 **"That would kill him":** Fred Dellar, "The Michael Jackson Story," *Smash Hits*, July 5–18, 1984.

153 **destroy the negatives:** Zack O'Malley Greenburg, *Michael Jackson, Inc.: The Rise, Fall, and Rebirth of a Billion-Dollar Empire* (New York: Atria Books, 2014), 76.

153 **"I'll never do a video":** Marsh, *Trapped*, 117.

154 **"Are you kidding me?":** Jackson, *You Are Not Alone*, 243.

154 **"I found him extremely impressive":** Steve Knopper, *MJ—the Genius of Michael Jackson* (New York: Scribner, 2015), 135.

155 **"My hair gives me":** Shirley Norman, "Don King: World's Greatest Promoter," *Sepia*, March 1981.

155 **pay-per-view audience of over a billion:** Ed Ward, Geoffrey Stokes, and Ken Tucker, *Rock of Ages: The Rolling Stone History of Rock & Roll* (New York: Rolling Stone Press, 1986), 590.

155 **"The wrong *Thriller*":** Greenburg, *Michael Jackson, Inc.*, 84.

155 "get[ting] on a plane": Knopper, *MJ—the Genius*, 135.

155 **$2.10 per album sold:** Goldberg and Connelly, "Trouble in Paradise?"

155 **$20 billion by 1983:** "Coke's Big Marketing Blitz," *BusinessWeek*, May 30, 1983.

155 **"Pepsi Challenge":** Stephen Miller, "Roger Enrico, Pepsi CEO Who Closed Gap with Coke, Dies at 71," *Washington Post*, June 2, 2016.

155 **$750 million:** "Coke's High-Priced Bid for Entertainment," *BusinessWeek*, February 1, 1982.

156 **"Things Go Better with Coca-Cola":** Douglas Wolk, "On Coca-Cola Ads," (presented at Pop Conference, Experience Music Project, Seattle, WA, April 15, 2005), courtesy of author.

156 **Bill Cosby, Julius (Dr. J) Erving:** Pamela Noel, "TV Ad Wars' Newest Weapon," *Ebony*, July 1984.

156 **between $160 and $200 million:** Bryan Burwell, "Super Deals for Superstars," *Black Enterprise*, July 1984.

156 **"This is an area":** Bernice Kanner, "Rock 'n' Roll Marketing," *New York*, May 7, 1984.

156 **"It took me about five years":** Bruce Horowitz, "Matchmaker Was First to Rock Ad World," *Los Angeles Times*, September 10, 1991.

156 **"nervous about getting too close":** Michael Paoletta, "The Billboard Q&A: Jay Coleman," *Billboard*, November 11, 2006.

157 **"the Woodstock generation":** James P. Forkan, "Holdouts on Rock Tie-ins Entering Fold," *Advertising Age*, November 2, 1981.

157 **TDK cassettes in Germany:** "Top Bands Turn to Sponsors," *Melody Maker*, January 28, 1984.

157 **"While the Stones themselves":** "Jovan Tie-in Set for Stones' Tour," *Advertising Age*, August 31, 1981.

157 **"Now the only big":** Kanner, "Rock 'n' Roll Marketing."

157 **"The payoff is down the road":** Steven Dupler, "BASF Searching for 'Bit Parts' on Screen," *Billboard*, June 16, 1984.

158 **"not to communicate with anyone":** Goldberg and Connelly, "Trouble in Paradise?"

158 **"The tour name means":** Video of Jacksons press conference for the Victory Tour, author's collection.

158 **"Tickets are being sold":** "Mutterings," *Smash Hits*, July 5–18, 1984.

158 **"It helps us keep ticket prices down":** Robert Palmer, "The Pop Life: String of Hits for Hall and Oates," *New York Times*, March 16, 1983.

158 **"Nobody talked about Julio Iglesias":** Ira Robbins, ed., *The Rolling Stone Review: 1985* (New York: Rolling Stone Press/Scribner, 1985).

159 **"Who else could have":** Nelson George, "The Rhythm & the Blues: King Speaks Out on Jacksons Tour," *Billboard*, July 14, 1984.

159 **"the Nitro Tour":** Goldberg and Connelly, "Trouble in Paradise?"

159 **more than eighty arrests were made:** Suzanne Daley, "Youth Gangs Rob Fans After Show," *New York Times*, July 24, 1983.

159 **"The Jacksons do not have a history":** Goldberg and Connelly, "Trouble in Paradise?"

159 **"four hundred tickets":** Paul Grein, "Jacksons' Ticket Price: $30," *Billboard*, June 16, 1984.

159 **Rupp's management wanted:** Robbins, *Rolling Stone Review: 1985.*

160 **"If I make all the concessions":** Paul Grein, "Jackson Backlash Seen Building," *Billboard*, July 7, 1984.

160 **Foxboro's board of selectmen:** Marsh, *Trapped*, 238.

160 **75 percent . . . per unsold seat:** Marsh, *Trapped*, 243.

160 **"have got to understand" and "Comments like these":** Miles White, "The Real Business Behind Those Magical Musical Tours," *Black Enterprise*, December 1984.

160 **six records by various Jacksons:** "Top 100 Black Contemporary Singles," *Cash Box*, September 22, 1984.

161 **"Tell Me I'm Not Dreamin'":** David Adelson, "Most Added Single Is Not a Single," *Cash Box*, May 12, 1984.

161 **following Michael's orders:** Greenburg, *Michael Jackson, Inc.*, 88–89.

161 **Some copies of the promo were destroyed:** Nelson George, "The Rhythm & the Blues: Michael—from Jermaine to Jagger," *Billboard*, June 9, 1984.

161 **as an album cut:** Paul Grein, "Chart Beat: Girls Just Want to Have Hits," *Billboard*, June 9, 1984.

161 **committing to sing backup:** Jason Newman, "How 'Somebody's Watching Me' Singer Rockwell Created a Paranoid Pop Classic," *Rolling Stone*, December 7, 2016, rollingstone.com/music/music-features/how-somebodys-watching-me-singer-rockwell-created-a-paranoid-pop-classic-125907/.

161 **shared a lawyer:** Greenburg, *Michael Jackson, Inc.*, 81.

161 **$28 million for four albums:** Jack Egan, "Pop Records Go Boom," *New York*, October 31, 1983, p. 53.

161 **a million copies within a month:** Leo Sacks, "Two Million Units of Jacksons Album Shipped," *Billboard*, July 7, 1984.

161 **"shipped two million":** Sacks, "Two Million Units."

162 **"There's no direction, no fire":** Ian Birch, review of Jacksons' *Victory*, *Smash Hits*, July 19–August 1, 1984.

162 **"What more could you want?":** Robbins, *Rolling Stone Review: 1985.*

162 **"AL-TV":** uhf89, "Harvey Leeds—State of Shock (1080p HD)," September 3, 1984, as part of "AL TV," YouTube video, 4:01, published March 10, 2012, youtube.com/watch?v=eLzVgfOCKkk.

162 **"suggested that Black America":** William H. Penn Sr., "The NAACP Diamond Jubilee Convention," *The Crisis*, August–September 1984.

162 **"Under Mr. Reagan's leadership":** "Excerpts from Convention Speeches," *The Crisis*, July–August 1984.

162–163 **"what America ought to be" and "Don't let Mr. Reagan":** Penn, "The NAACP Diamond Jubilee."

163 **"came from nowhere in 1984":** Matt Bai, "How Gary Hart's Downfall Forever Changed American Politics," *New York Times Magazine*, September 18, 2014.

163 **"There is the liberal":** "Excerpts from Convention Speeches."

163 **"the ideals of family unity":** Penn, "The NAACP Diamond Jubilee."

163 **"for the example that you've given":** Greenburg, *Michael Jackson, Inc.*, 78.

163 **Elvis Presley visiting Richard Nixon:** Nelson George, *Post-Soul Nation* (New York: Viking, 2004), 89.

163 **"as soon as possible":** Paul Grein, "Change in Jacksons Ticket Plan," *Billboard*, July 14, 1984.

163 **"The other day I got a letter":** Marsh, *Trapped*, 246.

163 **"I've always believed you":** "Woman Recalls 1984 Meeting with Michael Jackson," *Dallas News*, May 9, 2012.

164 **The temperature reached:** Paul Grein, "No Violence in K.C.: Jacksons' Tour Starts Smoothly," *Billboard*, July 21, 1984.

164 **refused to air-condition his hotel room:** "Mutterings," *Smash Hits*, July 19–August 1, 1984.

164 **a half million people:** Penn, "The NAACP Diamond Jubilee."

164 **expecting to gross $10 million:** Paul Hohl, "Aftermath of Jacksons' Shows: Kansas City Economy Boosted," *Billboard*, July 21, 1984.

164 **"a carnival":** Nelson George, *Thriller* (Cambridge, MA: Da Capo Press, 2010), 172.

164 **The Glove:** TheMotiondevotion, "Part 2: Jacksons 1984 Victory Tour—Bob Sirott Feature on Chicago TV," YouTube video, 3:41, published March 6, 2013, youtube.com/watch?annotation_id=annotation_846356&feature=iv&src _vid=HNYt9tT1Xys&v=ktdEHLzfCXw.

164 **LJN Toys:** "Making History!," *Record Collector*, March 1999.

164 **one-quarter of the dolls' profits:** Sharon Davis, "Victim of Circumstance," *Blues & Soul*, no. 469 (October 21–November 3, 1986).

164 **"Contrary to popular belief":** Jeffrey Ressner, "Points West," *Cash Box*, March 17, 1984.

164 **$50 million civil suit:** "Making History!"

165 **two hundred pounds of dry ice:** See TheMotiondevotion, "Part 3: Jacksons 1984 Victory Tour—Bob Sirott Feature on Chicago TV," YouTube video, 4:05, published March 6, 2013, youtube.com/watch?annotation_id=annotation _152425325&feature=iv&src_vid=HNYt9tT1Xys&v=_UjAVut8_xM.

165 **losing a million dollars a week:** Knopper, *MJ—the Genius*, 143.

165 **"Each brother had a lawyer":** Philip Manoevre and Sheryl Garratt, "Walking on the Moon," *The Face*, no. 100 (September 1988).

165 **Zoetrope Studios:** Jackson, *You Are Not Alone*, 248.

165 **from 120 to 105:** Knopper, *MJ—the Genius*, 143.

165 **"That's unconstitutional, you know":** Marsh, *Trapped*, 248.

165 **five times the amount:** Knopper, *MJ—the Genius*, 144.

165 **"I don't think the black community":** Paul Hohl, "Kansas City Ready for Jacksons," *Billboard*, July 7, 1984.

165 **"perhaps the oldest and youngest":** twelvehatcher23, "The Jackson's Victory Tour Controversy Is Discussed on ABC Nightline Part 2," aired July 6, 1984, ABC-TV, YouTube video, 8:51, published June 13, 2015, youtube.com/watch ?v=ieGIGfD558M.

166 **"a fireworks display":** Paul Grein, "Jacksons Paint by the Numbers," *Billboard*, July 21, 1984.

166 **"like going to the Ice Capades":** George, *Thriller*, 173.

166 **"Who's Michael Jackson, Mommy?":** Dave Marsh, ed., *The First Rock & Roll Confidential Report* (New York: Pantheon, 1985), 95.

166 **a pair of Jehovah's Witnesses:** Greenburg, *Michael Jackson, Inc.*, 91.

166 **On June 21:** Mark Bego, *On the Road with Michael!* (New York: Pinnacle Books, 1984), 15.

166 **Paula Abdul:** Robinson, *There Goes Gravity*, 172.

166 **"You think you can come back":** Bego, *On the Road with Michael!*, 9.

166 **"So obviously scripted":** Grein, "Jacksons Paint."

167 **"We're gonna give you the old stuff!":** Bego, *On the Road with Michael!*, 10.

167 **"glorified rehearsal":** George, *Thriller*, 173.

167 **"seamless and precise":** Grein, "Jacksons Paint."

167 **"They're buying the *Victory* album" and "a limited financial success":** Hohl, "Aftermath."

167 **"Everyone seemed baffled" and "The Jackson concert":** Marsh, *First Rock & Roll*, 86–87.

CHAPTER ELEVEN: MANN'S CHINESE THEATRE, HOLLYWOOD, JULY 26, 1984

Author interviews with Ted Cohen (April 25, 2016), Kevin Cole (December 26, 2011; September 29, 2015), Daniel Corrigan (September 1, 2015), Andre Cymone (April 25, 2016), Dez Dickerson (April 25, 2016), Chrissie Dunlap, Matt Fink (June 6 and 26, 2016; April 10, 2018), Steve McClellan, Rod Smith (August 30, 2015), and Paul Spangrud. Material accessed from the website PRN Interviews (sites.google.com/site/prninterviews/) is indicated below as "via PRN." Material accessed from the First Avenue Band Files at the Minnesota Historical Society in St. Paul (December 2014) and the cache of oral history transcripts from the Museum of Pop Culture in Seattle are indicated in full.

168 **"It felt like my legs":** "Woman Recalls 1984 Meeting with Michael Jackson," *Dallas News*, May 9, 2012.

168 **320 chauffeured limos:** Dave Marsh, ed., *The First Rock and Roll Confidential Report* (New York: Pantheon, 1985), 87–88.

168 **James Huberty:** Jessica Gresko, "20 Years Later, San Ysidro McDonald's Massacre Remembered," Associated Press, July 18, 2004, web.archive.org/web /20090831002428/http://www.nctimes.com/news/local/article_2ba4343e-7009 -54ce-98df-79a23ff8d0d7.html.

169 **"Understandably, everyone was freaking out":** Jermaine Jackson, *You Are Not Alone: Michael Through a Brother's Eyes* (New York: Touchstone/Simon & Schuster, 2011), 264.

169 **"In Dallas, the humidity":** Ira Robbins, ed., *The Rolling Stone Review: 1985* (New York: Rolling Stone Press/Scribner, 1985).

169 **thunderous ovation:** Ian Christe, *Everybody Wants Some: The Van Halen Saga* (New York: Wiley, 2007), 107.

169 **"That cat is really talented":** Nelson George, "Quincy Jones," *Musician*, September 1982.

169 **"Quite honestly":** John Kenneth Muir, *Music on Film: Purple Rain* (Pompton Plains, NJ: Limelight Editions, 2012), 55.

170 **"He just kind of choked":** Duane Tudahl, *Prince and the Purple Rain Era Studio Sessions—1983 and 1984* (Lanham, MD: Rowman & Littlefield, 2018), 138.

170 **"I didn't really have a record player" and "We basically got":** Bill Adler, "Will the Little Girls Understand," *Rolling Stone*, February 19, 1981.

170 **"The predominance of German" and "To an extent":** Steve Perry, "Ain't No Mountain High Enough: The Politics of Crossover," in *Facing the Music*, ed. Simon Frith (New York: Pantheon, 1988), 79–80.

171 **"Moon . . . chose Prince":** Steve Perry, "Prince, the Early Years: Creating the Minneapolis Myth," *Musician*, August 1986.

171 **Sheila Escovedo:** Sheila E. with Wendy Holden, *The Beat of My Own Drum* (New York: Atria Books, 2014), 146.

172 **"Judging by the [second] album":** Dave Hill, *Prince: A Pop Life* (New York: Harmony Books, 1989), 83.

173 **"copping my licks":** Rick James with David Ritz, *Glow* (New York: Atria Books, 2014), 210.

173 **"She's amazing, she can play":** K. Nicola Dyes, "The Rest of My Life: Gayle Chapman Talks About Events After Prince," The Beautiful Nights Blog, August 5, 2013, beautifulnightschitown.blogspot.com/2013/08/the-rest-of-my-life-gayle-chapman-talks.html.

173 **"There was something about":** Alex Hahn, *Possessed: The Rise and Fall of Prince* (New York: Billboard Books, 2003), 38.

173 **"Nobody knew what was going on":** Adler, "Will the Little Girls."

174 **"Warner Bros., understandably":** Robert Hilburn, "The Renegade Prince," *Los Angeles Times*, November 21, 1982, via PRN.

174 **"The LP might":** Ken Tucker, review of Prince's *Dirty Mind*, *Rolling Stone*, February 19, 1981.

175 **"If you were a black band":** Peter S. Scholtes, "First Love," *City Pages*, September 3, 2003.

175 **"One of the things we learned":** Chris Williams, "Key Tracks: Jimmy Jam on Janet Jackson's *Control*," *Red Bull Daily*, February 26, 2016, daily.redbullmusic academy.com/2016/02/key-tracks-janet-jackson-control.

175 **"Prince is the Minneapolis sound" and "The only thing we intend":** Steven Ivory, "Harris & Lewis: Our Time Has Come," *Billboard*, February 2, 1985.

175 **October 7, 1981:** The Time, October 7, 1981, First Avenue & 7th Street Entry Band Files, Minnesota Historical Society.

176 **"The record industry provides":** Howard Bloom, "Commentary: Breaking the Color Barrier," *Billboard*, August 8, 1981.

176 **"I'd suggest booking him":** Dave Hill, *Prince: A Pop Life* (New York: Harmony Books, 1989) 83.

176 **a significant role in Reagan's 1980 election:** Dominic Sandbrook, *Mad as Hell: The Crisis of the 1970s and the Rise of the Populist Right* (New York: Alfred A. Knopf, 2010), 344–360.

176 **"I also knew the concern":** Craig Endicott, "Television's Watchdog," *Advertising Age*, August 31, 1981.

177 **"in favor of outlawing abortion":** "Planned Parenthood Ads Aborted by Radio," *Advertising Age*, October 26, 1981.

177 **"It was our decision alone":** Richard Ringer, "Massage Parlor Ads Rubbed Out," *Advertising Age*, February 15, 1982.

178 **"Programmers may have a problem":** Leo Sacks, "Out of the Box," *Billboard*, January 8, 1983.

178 **"Finally . . . the one":** Warner Bros. trade ad, *Radio & Records*, spring 1983.

178 **"After seeing him perform":** Martin Keller, "Caught in the Act," *City Pages*, March 23, 1983.

179 **"the curb lane," et al.:** Minnesota Dance Theatre Benefit with Prince, August 3, 1983, First Avenue & 7th Street Entry Band Files, Minnesota Historical Society.

180 **"Almost every night":** Maggie Macpherson, MoPop Oral History transcript, June 6, 1998.

181 **"Music is like a newspaper to him":** Greg Kot, "Twin Cities Tycoon," *Details*, November 1998.

181 **"at least sixteen apparent uses":** Bill Holland and Craig Rosen, "Indecency Action Sparks Radio Call for FCC Guideline," *Billboard*, November 11, 1989.

182 **demoed in 1981:** Tudahl, *Prince and the Purple Rain Era*, 94.

182 **"He loved every one of them":** Muir, *Music on Film*, 45.

182 **"It seemed obvious that we could":** Paul Grein, "Unorthodox 'Prince' of a Film," *Billboard*, June 16, 1984.

182 **"To us, this would still":** Sam Sutherland, "Labels, Studios Get Closer on Soundtracks," *Billboard*, June 30, 1984.

182 **"I jumped in":** Brian Raftery, "Purple Rain: The Oral History," *Spin*, July 2009.

182 **"She jumped into a lake":** Muir, *Music on Film*, 61.

183 **"The studio we worked at":** "New Faces to Watch: Cherrelle," *Cash Box*, June 23, 1984.

183 **"Why pay taxes":** Leo Sacks, "The Rhythm & the Blues: Morris Day Decides to Call Time Out," *Billboard*, August 18, 1984.

184 **"I've got too much money now":** Jon Bream, *Prince: Inside the Purple Reign* (New York: Collier Books, 1984), 94.

184 **"I knew the script":** Aldore Collier, "Ebony Interview with Eddie Murphy," *Ebony*, July 1985.

184 **"Don't feel bad"**: Bream, *Inside*, 93.

184 **"At that point Prince suddenly lost it"**: Tudahl, *Prince and the Purple Rain Era*, 354.

185 **July 4 picnics:** Emily Strohm and Rose Minutaglio, "Growing Up with Prince: Children of Star's Longtime Bodyguard Open Up About His Very Private Life," *People*, April 24, 2016, people.com/celebrity/growing-up-with-prince -children-of-stars-longtime-bodyguard-open-up/.

185 **"The first time I realized what was happening"**: Neva Chonin, "The Artist Formally Known as Prince Plans to Party Until It's 1999," *Tower Pulse*, February 2000, via PRN Interviews.

185 **"It does to me"**: Bream, *Inside*, 94.

185 **the press didn't see it:** J. Kordosh, "Prince's *Purple Rain*: 'Scuse Me While I Get Some Popcorn," *Creem*, September 1984.

185 **"the *Citizen Kane* of rock movies"**: Alan Light, *Let's Go Crazy: Prince and the Making of Purple Rain* (New York: Atria Books, 2014), 178.

186 **"Compared to *Beat Street*"**: Nelson George, "The Rhythm & the Blues; 'Purple Rain' Storms Silver Screen," *Billboard*, July 28, 1984.

186 **He spent much of July:** See Tudahl, *Prince and the Purple Rain Era*, 337–349.

186 **"We've got to go after some of that Duran Duran money"**: Per Nilsen, *Prince—Dance, Music, Sex, Romance: The First Decade* (Richmond Hill, ON: Firefly Books, 1999), 208.

186 **On June 7:** Prince, June 7, 1984, First Avenue & 7th Street Entry Band Files, Minnesota Historical Society.

186–187 **1,616 fans; and "Mr. Stark":** Prince and the Revolution, August 14, 1984, First Avenue & 7th Street Entry Band Files, Minnesota Historical Society.

CHAPTER TWELVE: *MATTER* NO. 9, CHICAGO, ILLINOIS, JULY–AUGUST 1984

Author interviews with Jello Biafra (September 2017), Kevin Cole, Daniel Corrigan, Chrissie Dunlap, Julie Farman (September 2017), Ray Farrell (September 2017), Jefferson Holt (September 2015), Peter Jesperson, Terry Katzman (September 2017), and Stephen T. McClellan. Additional interviews from August–September 2017 conducted by Andrea Swensson (Grant Hart), Mary Lucia (Bob Mould), and Brian Oake (Greg Norton and Henry Rollins) are also utilized unless otherwise specified. The 2017 interviews first appeared on the podcast *Do You Remember? The Life and Legacy of Hüsker Dü*, from The Current (89.3 FM, Minneapolis–St. Paul): stitcher.com/podcast/avidce-public-media/do-you -remember-the-life-and-legacy-of-husker-du/e/52039857.

188 **"Subscribe!":** *Matter*, no. 9 (July–August 1984).

188 **"wanted to start an R.E.M. fanzine"**: Steve Albini, MoPop Oral History transcript, March 27, 2007.

189 **"miles sharper than *Murmur*"** to **"blew their wad with 'Radio Free Europe'"**: "New Matter," *Matter*, no. 9 (July–August 1984).

189 **"[It] was the first time":** Daniel Sinker, ed., *We Owe You Nothing: Punk Planet— the Collected Interviews* (New York: Akashic Books, 1999).

190 **"Anyone stupid enough":** Lee Sustar, "Ruthless and Proud of It," *Matter*, no. 7 (February 1984).

190 **London's Rough Trade shop:** Alex Ogg, *Independence Days* (London: Cherry Red Books, 2009), 194.

190 **"They were a million things":** Sinker, *We Owe You Nothing*.

190 **"That whole axis":** Peter, Effigies interview, *Non Stop Banter*, no. 6 (May/June 1986), dementlieu.com/users/obik/arc/effigies/int_nsb6.html.

190 **"significance [that] has become clear":** Sustar, "Ruthless and Proud of It."

190–191 **"I'd say I'm a lot happier":** Effigies interview, *Druglovers* (1984), dementlieu .com/users/obik/arc/effigies/int_druglovers7.html.

191 **On April 26:** R.E.M., April 26, 1982; September 22, 1982; and May 23, 1983, Minnesota Historical Society (MNHS), St. Paul.

192 **thirty-five rock bands:** Denise Sullivan, *Talk About the Passion: R.E.M.—an Oral History* (New York: Pavilion, 1995).

192 **"Largely, it's just the chemistry":** Mike Mills, "Our Town," *Spin*, July 1985.

192 **"country clubs":** John Platt, ed., *The R.E.M. Companion* (New York: Schirmer Books, 1998), 15.

192 **"We'd take any date":** Jeff Nesin, "R.E.M. on Broadway: Tales of the Oblique," *Creem*, September 1984.

192 **"The early songs":** Platt, *R.E.M. Companion*, 11.

193 **"You can't escape history":** Nesin, "R.E.M. on Broadway."

193 **"saw the first billboard about AIDS":** Christopher Bollen, "Michael Stipe," *Interview*, May 2011.

194 **all the decision-making power:** Anthony DeCurtis, "Introduction," from *R.E.M.: The Rolling Stone Files* (New York: Hyperion, 1995), 6.

194 **"a good, tight little business":** Johnny Black, *Reveal: The Story of R.E.M.* (Lanham, MD: Backbeat Books, 2004), 77.

194 **"the most wretched and abysmal experience of our lives":** Barney Hoskyns, "Bucking for Sainthood," *New Musical Express* (*NME*), April 21, 1984.

194 **"We wanted no lead guitar":** Black, *Reveal*, 76.

194 **"Suggested cuts: ALL":** Review of R.E.M.'s *Murmur*, *CMJ Magazine*, April 11, 1983.

194 **"intelligent, enigmatic":** Steve Pond, review of R.E.M.'s *Murmur*, *Rolling Stone*, May 26, 1983.

195 **"Essentially, we make records":** Platt, *R.E.M. Companion*, 21.

195 **"was mixed and recorded":** Allan Jones, "R.E.M.: Marching Through Georgia with the Pride of the South," *Melody Maker*, June 15, 1985.

195 **"We wanted to record as far as possible":** Platt, *R.E.M. Companion*, 20.

195 **"It's one of the first ones":** Greg Kot, "R.E.M.'s Best Album Side? Band Members Say It's Not 'Automatic,'" *Chicago Reader*, November 27, 1994.

195 **"We did major publicity":** Sullivan, *Talk About the Passion*.

196 **"I think we're making inroads":** Dave Riley, "Hüsker Dü: Will These Guys Be the Year's Top Pop Wimps?," *Matter*, no. 9 (July–August 1984).

197 **Claude Bessy:** Ogg, *Independence Days*, 195.

198 **"After a while, I felt a contact high":** Bob Mould with Michael Azerrad, *See a Little Light: The Trail of Rage and Melody* (Boston: Little, Brown, 2011).

199 **"Black Flag's going to tour a lot":** "Artists Survey of '83," *Trouser Press*, nos. 92–93 (December 1983–January 1984).

199 **"To this day":** Andrew Warde, "Black Flag," *Option*, B Issue (May–June 1985).

200 **"It got to where we would rent a hall":** Sinker, *We Owe You Nothing*.

200 **"We always felt a lot safer":** Greg Ginn, MoPop Oral History transcript, November 20, 1999.

200 **"flaked out, and I just thought":** Warde, "Black Flag."

200 **"My mom was working for Humphrey's":** Henry Rollins, MoPop Oral History transcript, February 24, 1998.

200 **Teen Idles:** Jeff Nelson, MoPop Oral History transcript, November 2, 1998.

200 **"a monster performer":** Bruce Pavitt, *Sub Pop USA: The Subterranean Pop Anthology, 1980–88* (Seattle: Fantagraphics, 2014), 261.

200 **"anti-parent":** Joe Carducci, *Rock and the Pop Narcotic* (Chicago: Redoubt Press, 1990), 112.

200 **sued to get off Unicorn:** John Sippel, "Black Flag Unicorn Pact Subject of Court Dispute," *Billboard*, February 12, 1983.

201 **"first in a series of four LPs":** Pavitt, *Sub Pop USA*, 240.

201 **"vibed out" and "about Greg Ginn":** Stevie Chick, *Spray Paint the Walls: The Story of Black Flag* (Oakland, CA: PM Press, 2009), 283.

201 **"Whenever the band changed":** Greg Ginn, MoPop Oral History transcript, November 20, 1999.

201 **Los Angeles–area reading nights:** Peter Holden, "Points West," *Cash Box*, December 1, 1984.

201 **"raw sewage":** Warde, "Black Flag."

201 **"Make no mistake":** "New Matter."

202 **"was nineteen":** Michael Bonner, "SST Records," *Record Collector*, April 1993.

202 **"The incredible thing":** Ira Robbins, ed., *The Rolling Stone Review: 1985* (New York: Rolling Stone Press/Scribner, 1985).

202 **"the punk answer to *Blonde on Blonde*":** Robbins, *The Rolling Stone Review: 1985*.

202 **Zero Club:** Ian Christe, *Everybody Wants Some: The Van Halen Saga* (New York: Wiley, 2007), 105.

202 **"We liked the Grateful Dead":** Curt Kirkwood, "Under the Influence: Jerry Garcia," *The Fader*, no. 46 (May–June 2007).

203 **"This would only be any good":** "New Matter."

203 **"on mushrooms":** Joe Carducci, MoPop Oral History transcript, August 9, 2010.

203 **"A variety of bands":** Pavitt, *Sub Pop USA*, 267.

203 **"Four people onstage":** *"Last Roundup,"* *Matter*, no. 9 (July–August 1984).

203 **"This is pure spurs":** Pavitt, *Sub Pop USA*, 255.

204 **"The Blasters had a huge influence on us":** John Doe, MoPop Oral History transcription, April 2, 1998.

204 **"Groups like Blondie":** John Doe with Tom DeSavia, eds., *More Fun in the New World: The Unmaking and Legacy of L.A. Punk* (Cambridge, MA: Da Capo Press, 2019), 258–259.

204 **Jane Wiedlin:** Doe and DeSavia, *More Fun in the New World*, 39–41.

205 **"Band 'Z'":** Bob Biggs, "Commentary: Educating A&R Personnel," *Billboard*, July 28, 1984.

205 **"I've got three other friends":** Kristine McKenna, "X: L.A. New Wave Grows Up," *Musician*, June 1982.

205 **"triple, quadruple, octuple":** Doe and DeSavia, *More Fun in the New World*, 261–262.

205 **Cosloy suggested:** Gerard Cosloy, *Conflict*, no. 36 (August–September 1984).

205 **"If you are a Chicano":** Chris Morris, *Los Lobos: Dream in Blue* (Austin: University of Texas Press, 2015), 25–26.

205 **"We were playing in a restaurant":** David Fricke, "Los Lobos' Roots Music," *Rolling Stone*, April 12, 1984.

206 **"We hadn't even got":** Doe and DeSavia, *More Fun in the New World*, 127.

206 **"skirling norteno accordion":** Gene Santoro, "Los Lobos: Hour of the Wolves," *DownBeat*, March 1985.

206 **"We were grooming [the Replacements]":** Jud Cost, Andrew Earles, Matthew Fritch, Matt Hickey, Steve Klinge, Eric T. Miller, David Olson, Hobart Rowland, Matt Ryan, and Jonathan Valania, "A Tale of Twin Cities," *Magnet*, July–August 2005.

206 **Between 1982 and 1986:** Various Hüsker Dü band files, 1982–1986, Minnesota Historical Society (MNHS), St. Paul.

206 **"We're more conscious":** The Replacements/Laughing Stock/19800th Lifetime, December 26, 1984, Minnesota Historical Society (MNHS), St. Paul.

207 **"the greatest thing since the Rolling Stones":** Peter Jesperson, MoPop Oral History interview, September 22, 1998.

207 **"Anything we can do":** The McKenzie Tapes, "Replacements Interview on KJHK—Lawrence, KS (unknown date—1984)," themckenzietapes.com/tapes/2018/11/13/replacements-interview-on-kjhk-lawrence-ks-unknown-date-1984.

207 **fifty-five college radio stations:** Bob Mehr, *Trouble Boys: The True Story of the Replacements* (Cambridge, MA: Da Capo Press, 2016), 143.

208 **"It was pretty overwhelming":** Jesperson, MoPop Oral History interview, September 22, 1998.

CHAPTER THIRTEEN: NEW MUSIC SEMINAR, NEW YORK CITY, AUGUST 6–8, 1984

Author interviews with Arthur Baker, Chrissie Dunlap, Patrick Epstein (September 1, 2015), Michael Holman, Vince Lawrence (January 11, 2013),

Jane Lerner (December 5, 2012), Charles Little II (April 18, 2013), Stephen T. McClellan, and Tom Silverman. Material accessed from the website Madonna: The Warner Bros. Years (mtwy.tumblr.com) is indicated below as "via MTWY."

209 **"the industry's first weekly trade chart":** "Stepping on the Dance Floor," *Cash Box*, January 28, 1984.

210 **"brought the over-mixed 'thump'":** Brian Chin, "Dance Trax," *Billboard,* July 21, 1984.

210 **"cancer":** Al Clark, ed., *The Rock Yearbook Volume IV* (London: Virgin, 1983).

210 **"is not gay music":** Dave Rimmer, "High Energy," *Smash Hits*, June 7–20, 1984.

210 **"technologically brilliant":** Bill Brewster and Frank Broughton, *Last Night a DJ Saved My Life: The History of the Disc Jockey—Updated and Revised Edition* (New York: Grove Press, 2006; orig. 1999), 216.

210 **"Pete Burns had actually":** Richard Buskin, *Inside Tracks* (New York: Avon, 1999), 232.

210 **"weaves a touching tale":** Keith Zimmerman, "New Releases," *Gavin Report*, December 7, 1984.

210 **"This English trio":** Ron Fell, "Albums of the Week," *Gavin Report*, December 21, 1984.

211 **"New Music Week":** Fred Goodman, "4,000 Expected at 'Mainstream' '84 New Music Seminar," *Billboard*, August 11, 1984.

211 **"Most of our DJs":** "DJs Advance Dance by Exploring Format Frontiers," *Billboard*, June 19, 1982.

212 **"all the DJs from those rock clubs":** Tim Lawrence, *Life and Death on the New York Dance Floor, 1980–1983* (Durham, NC: Duke University Press, 2016), 283.

212 **"making some substantial neighborhood noise":** Brian Chin, "Dance Trax," *Billboard*, June 9, 1984.

212 **"Many veterans of the new wave":** Mark Josephson, "Commentary: Keeping Pace with Change," *Billboard*, August 4, 1984.

213 **the first New York club to install:** Michael Shore, *The Rolling Stone Book of Rock Video* (New York: Quill/Rolling Stone Press, 1984), 74.

213 **"System installers":** Stephanie Shepherd, "Video Clubs Diversify Images," *Billboard*, August 11, 1984.

213 **"provides four floors":** Ken Terry, "Rockamerica Video Seminar Capsulizes State of Business," *Variety*, August 15, 1984.

214 **"When we do something":** Rusty Cutchin, "Indies Look to Past, Future of 12-inch Market," *Cash Box*, May 26, 1984.

214 **"leave the lion's share":** Fred Goodman, "At New Music Seminar—Indies Stand Up to Majors," *Billboard*, August 18, 1984.

214 **"Some of the NMS people":** Ken Barnes, "New Music Seminar: Bridging a Gap," *Radio & Records*, August 24, 1984.

214 **"Admittedly, we don't":** Joel Denver, "The Future of Pop Radio? Fabulous!!!," *Radio & Records*, August 24, 1984.

214 **"As long as hit radio":** Leo Sacks, "Radio Panelists Urge End to 'Old-Line Prejudices,'" *Billboard*, August 18, 1984.

215 **"It was crazy":** Knox Robinson, "Return to New York," *The Fader*, no. 15 (March–April 2003).

216 **"the first Top 40 pop single":** Brian Chin, "Dance '84: Urban Fusions Cross-Multiply Pop Impact—This Year's Bigger, Better Beat," *Billboard*, August 11, 1984.

216 **"We get on fine":** "Working Holiday," *No. 1*, February 4, 1984, via MTWY.

216 **"We both started to move":** Christopher Connelly, "Madonna Goes All the Way," *Rolling Stone*, November 22, 1984.

216 **"We have a very volatile relationship":** Rick Sky, Madonna interview transcription, February 1984, via MTWY.

216 **"Saturday nights at the Roxy":** Glenn Albin, "Madonna," *Interview*, April 1984, via MTWY.

216 **"the co-opting of the dance scene":** "The Rhythm Section," *Cash Box*, January 14, 1984.

216 **"He already had a sound":** Seymour Stein with Gareth Murphy, *Siren Song: My Life in Music* (New York: St. Martin's Press, 2018), 207–219.

217 **International Conference on Consumer Electronics:** Moira McCormick, "1,000 Expected at Chicago Meet," *Billboard*, May 26, 1984.

217 **"The Use of Computers in Music Education":** "Economic Recovery Spurs Growth of '84 NAMM Expo," *Music Trades*, May 1984.

217 **La Mere Vipere:** Roman Kozak, *This Ain't No Disco: The Story of CBGB* (London: Faber & Faber, 1988), 110.

217 **"about a hundred copies a month":** Moira McCormick, "Five New 'Trax' Due from Chicago Retailer's Label," *Billboard*, June 9, 1984.

217 **Medusa's:** Jacob Arnold, "Medusa's: Chicago's Missing Link," Resident Advisor, September 4, 2013, residentadvisor.net/feature.aspx?1917.

218 *Music Video 60*: Moira McCormick, "Teen Video Show a Chicago Hit," *Billboard*, June 9, 1984.

218 **WFBN (channel 66):** Moira McCormick, "Music Video Hours Pared at Chicago's WFBN-TV," *Billboard*, July 14, 1984.

218 **"A lot of accounts are selling":** Moira McCormick, "Chicago Wholesaler Notes White-to-Black Crossover," *Billboard*, September 8, 1984.

218 **"I just loved that record":** Jacob Arnold, "Vince Lawrence, House's Architect," Gridface, January 19, 2010, https://www.gridface.com/vince-lawrence/.

219 **"It's that shit you be playing":** Dorian Lynskey, "The House That Frankie Knuckles Built," *The Guardian* (Manchester), October 13, 2011, theguardian.com/music/2011/oct/13/frankie-knuckles-your-love.

219 **preempt him by announcing on-air:** Jonathan Fleming, *What Kind of House Party Is This?* (Slough, Berkshire, UK: MIY Publishing, 1995), 219.

219 **"I'd extend the drum break":** Jesse Saunders, MoPop Oral History transcript, August 17, 2001.

220 **January 1, 1984:** Moira McCormick, "New Chicago Pressing Plant Targets Local Acts," *Billboard*, February 11, 1984.

220 **"If a guy brought in a tape":** Sean Bidder, *Pump Up the Volume* (London: Channel 4 Books, 2001), 33.

220 **"It was the revolution, man":** Bidder, *Pump Up the Volume*, 30.

221 **"I'm working the rock clubs":** 243sd, "Letterman: James Brown Jul 12 1982," on *Late Night with David Letterman* (NBC), July 12, 1982, YouTube video, 41:25, published April 19, 2018, youtube.com/watch?v=nWWQuzZe2LM.

222 **finished in two days, video included:** Vikki Tobak and Sophie de Rakoff, "Afrika Bambaataa and His Nation," *Beat Down*, December 1992, via Adler.

222 **"If we'd just put it out":** "Unusual Approach Set for 'Unity,'" *Billboard*, July 28, 1984.

222 **"a contemporary artist":** James Brown with Bruce Tucker, *The Godfather of Soul* (Boston: Ticknor and Fields, 1986).

222 **"funk grooves have finally":** Nelson George, "James Brown's Bag Still Sounds Brand New," *Billboard*, September 22, 1984.

222 **"teens . . . regarded JB":** Cynthia Rose, "Letter from Britain: Are Hits Legit?," *Creem*, October 1984.

222 **"I got too far ahead":** Daddy Cool, "In Conversation with James Brown: Kitchener, Ontario, July 11th, 1984," *Soul Survivor* (UK) 1, no. 1 (1985).

223 **"Bambaataa always came":** Nelson George and Alan Leeds, eds., *The James Brown Reader* (New York: Plume Books, 2008), 181.

223 **"I used to be in the Black Spades" and "I thought *Zulu*":** Ian Pye, "We Have to Shape Our Own Destiny," *Melody Maker*, June 11, 1983.

223 **"Bambaataa played everything":** Lawrence, *Life and Death*, 158.

223 **"Flash and Bambaataa":** Bill Brewster, "Author and Experimental Musician David Toop on Hip-Hop's First Decade," Red Bull Music Academy, June 2001, daily.redbullmusicacademy.com/2018/03/david-toop-interview.

223 **"For years there were rumors":** Dave Wedge, "Afrika Bambaataa Allegedly Molested Young Men for Decades. Why Are the Accusations Only Coming Out Now?," *Noisey*, October 16, 2016, noisey.vice.com/en_us/article/8xx5yp/afrika-bambaataa-sexual-abuse-zulu-nation-ron-savage-hassan-campbell.

223 **Bambaataa denied all charges:** Daniel Kreps, "Zulu Nation Apologizes to Alleged Afrika Bambaataa Abuse Victims," *Rolling Stone*, June 1, 2016, rollingstone.com/music/music-news/zulu-nation-apologizes-to-alleged-afrika-bambaataa-abuse-victims-32589/.

224 **"Hip-hop's something":** Lawrence, *Life and Death*, 177.

224 **"I want to make this record":** Winston C. Robinson Jr., "Big Bam Boom Speaks About . . . ," *Rockamerica Magazine*, April 1985, 12, via Adler.

224 **"If you're going to steal":** Rusty Cutchin, "New Music Seminar Brings Vets, Newcomers to N.Y.," *Cash Box*, August 18, 1984.

224 **"Tickets would be":** Goodman, "At New Music Seminar."

225 **"That's more people":** Gavin Martin, "James Brown (and Afrika Bambaataa): Sex Machine Today," *New Musical Express* (NME), September 1, 1984.

225 **"responsibility of an artist":** Dave Marsh, ed., *The First Rock & Roll Confidential Report* (New York: Pantheon, 1985), 33–34.

225 **"Do the splits, James":** Martin, "James Brown."

225 *three* **splits:** Shawn Setaro, "Tom Silverman on the New Music Seminar Past and Present, the Future of the Industry, and More," Forbes.com, June 8, 2015, forbes.com/sites/shawnsetaro/2015/06/08/tom-silverman-on-the-new-music-seminar-past-and-present-the-future-of-the-industry-and-more/3/#c62f8d7112b6.

225 **"I like to get into":** Tom Vickers, "A Journey to the Center of Parliament/Funkadelic," *Rolling Stone*, August 26, 1976.

225 **on average 850,000 apiece:** Emmett George, "Parliament/Funkadelic," *Sepia*, June 1978.

225 **"The only thing":** George and Leeds, *James Brown Reader*, 183.

226 **"about fifteen to seventeen albums":** John Morthland, "Putting on the Atomic Dog: George Clinton Cries 'Woof,'" *Creem*, July 1983.

226 **"vials of cocaine":** "Rock Musicians Busted for Drugs," UPI, August 20, 1981, upi.com/Archives/1981/08/20/Rock-musicians-busted-for-drugs/2631367128000/.

226 **already having trouble with his Capitol deal:** George Clinton with Ben Greenman, *Brothas Be, Yo Like George, Ain't That Funkin' Kinda Hard on You?* (New York: Atria Books, 2014), 241–242.

226 **A** *New York Times* **feature:** Bill Flanagan, "Peter Wolf: Funk and the Chill Factor," *Musician*, August 1984.

226 **"the easiest person":** Julie Panebianco, "Michael Jonzun's Space Shake," *Musician*, July 1984.

227 **"selling about two hundred thousand":** Steve Ivory, "'Bubblegum' Jacksons Link Sticks to the New Edition," *Billboard*, October 27, 1984.

CHAPTER FOURTEEN: MEMORIAL COLISEUM, LOS ANGELES, AUGUST 12, 1984

228 **"anti-Olympian actions":** Rebecca R. Ruiz, "A Secret Soviet Doping Plan, Decades Old, Echoes in Rio," *New York Times*, August 13, 2016.

228 **"an evil empire":** Sean Wilentz, *The Age of Reagan: A History, 1974–2008* (New York: Harper Perennial, 2008), 162–163.

228 **"If a Third World War":** Peter C. Newman, "Is World War III Inevitable?," *Maclean's*, February 15, 1982.

229 **"intercept and destroy":** Linda McQuaig, "The Ultimate Weapons Race," *Maclean's*, April 4, 1983.

229 **"Chernenko was always":** Kenneth Reich, *Making It Happen: Peter Ueberroth and the 1984 Olympics* (Santa Barbara, CA: Capra Press, 1986), 209.

229 **"directly or indirectly":** "Peter Ueberroth's Olympic Glory," *Success!*, January 1985.

229 **"no-frill Games":** Jerry Kirshenbaum, "The 1984 Olympics," *Sports Illustrated*, July 17, 1984.

229 **"basically the Southern California Olympics":** "Behind the Success of the 1984 Summer Olympics," *CBS This Morning*, CBS-TV, July 26, 2014, YouTube video, 4:07, published July 26, 2014, youtube.com/watch?v=piBv6J8LcUs. The sportswriter is Geoff Foster of the *Wall Street Journal*.

230 **$225 million from ABC:** "Peter Ueberroth's Olympic Glory."

230 **"I don't think you can light the torch":** Reich, *Making It Happen*, 191.

230 **"Operation Hammer":** Kevin M. Kruse and Julian E. Zelizer, *Fault Lines: A History of the United States Since 1974* (New York: W. W. Norton, 2019), 198.

230 **Jim McKay extolled:** Javier Saborido Teira, "Los Angeles 1984 Olympic Games—Opening Ceremony," YouTube video, 3:16:09, youtube.com/watch?v=ZiW5_vblQu8.

230 **"After this summer":** Nelson George, *Post-Soul Nation* (New York: Viking, 2004), 91.

231 **"God only knows what the 2.5 billion people":** Kruse and Zelizer, *Fault Lines*, 127.

231 **"Gee, when I used to go":** Dave Zimmer, "Olympics '84: Where's the Music?," *BAM* (San Francisco), July 27, 1984.

232 **James's heroin addiction:** Joel Selvin, "A Thinner Etta James Fills Out New Album," *San Francisco Chronicle*, Sunday, June 22, 2003.

232 **"singing low and sultry":** Etta James with David Ritz, *Rage to Survive: The Etta James Story* (New York: Villard Books, 1995), 242.

232 **On June 20, 1984:** "Little Richard Sues over 1959 Contract Waiving Royalties," *Variety*, June 27, 1984.

232 **$114 million:** Associated Press (AP), "Star People," *Ocala (FL) Star-Banner*, August 17, 1984, via Google News.

232 **"All that a black person":** "Label Exec Sues Little Richard re: Remarks on Radio," *Variety*, October 3, 1984.

232 **dismissed in federal court:** "Little Richard Lawsuit Draws Court Dismissal," *Variety*, December 5, 1984.

232 **settled privately in 1986:** Sam Sutherland and Irv Lichtman, "Inside Track," *Billboard*, May 17, 1986.

233 **"There are pirates all around":** David Adelson, "Death of Big Mama Thornton Stirs Friend's Sorrow, Anger," *Cash Box*, August 11, 1984.

233 **August 25 issue:** Paul Grein, "Six of Top 10 Album Slots Go to Black Artists," *Billboard*, August 25, 1984.

234 **"upswing in contemporary R&B ballads":** Harry Weinger, "Widening World of Crossover Sparks Black Radio Resurgence," *Billboard*, June 16, 1984.

234 **"all subliminal suggestion about oral sex":** Marc Fisher, *Something in the Air: Radio, Rock, and the Revolution That Shaped a Generation* (New York: Random House, 2007), 208.

234 **November 1977:** Eric Harvey, "The Quiet Storm," Pitchfork, May 15, 2012, pitchfork.com/features/underscore/8822-the-quiet-storm/.

234 **fifteen-song playlist:** *The Quiet Storm*, WHUR/Washington—Sample Music Hour (sidebar), *Radio & Records*, July 20, 1984.

234 **"Inner City officials do stress":** Walt Love, "Happy New Year," *Radio & Records*, January 6, 1984.

234 **"I'm proud of the fact":** Joel Dreyfuss, "Motown's $10 Million Gamble," *Black Enterprise*, July 1981.

235 **"There were quite a few white folks":** Paul Grein, "Midnight Star's 'Freak' Success," *Billboard*, February 11, 1984.

235 **number three A/C label:** Top Adult Contemporary (charts), *Billboard*, December 22, 1984.

235 **"I deliberately set out":** "Marvin Gaye Returns Single, Free & Sexy," *Jet*, November 29, 1982.

235 **"came to Radio City":** David Ritz, *Divided Soul: The Life of Marvin Gaye* (Cambridge, MA: Da Capo, 1985), 319.

236 **"My son, my poor son":** Ritz, *Divided Soul*, 329.

236 **"He kicked me everywhere":** "'I Pulled the Trigger,'" *Washington Post*, April 9, 1984.

236 **"I still felt sorry for him":** Ritz, *Divided Soul*, 339.

236 **"Ah, shit":** Justin Tinsley, "The Players' Anthem: When Marvin Gaye Sang 'The Star-Spangled Banner' at the 1983 All-Star Game," The Undefeated, February 13, 2018, theundefeated.com/features/marvin-gaye-the-star-spangled -banner-1983-nba-all-star-game-players-anthem/.

236 **"If Marvin Sr. were here":** AP, "Tribute to Marvin Gaye," *Washington Post*, April 6, 1984.

237 **hooked on cocaine:** Craig McLean, "Smokey Robinson Interview: 'God Saved Me from Cocaine,'" *The Telegraph* (London), September 4, 2014, telegraph.co .uk/culture/music/rockandpopfeatures/11077737/Smokey-Robinson-interview -God-saved-me-from-cocaine.html.

237 **"I think that there is, uh":** Steve Pond, "Lionel Richie: The Pot of Gold in the Middle of the Road," *Rolling Stone*, March 3, 1983.

237 **"What they didn't realize":** Robert E. Johnson, "Will Superstardom Spoil Lionel Richie," *Ebony*, January 1985.

237 **Booker T. Washington:** "Lionel Richie Makes First Album Without Commodores," *Jet*, November 15, 1982.

237 **"Lionel does":** Pond, "Lionel Richie."

237 **"That's a clever sister":** A. Peter Bailey, "Lionel and Brenda Richie's Endless Love," *Essence*, April 1984.

238 **"had had a heart attack":** David Foster with Pablo F. Fenjves, *Hitman* (New York: Pocket Books, 2008), 104.

238 **"The thing was to pick":** Sharon Davis, *Lionel Richie—Hello* (London: Equinox Books, 2009), 42.

238 **"as sentimental and courtly":** Nelson George, *Buppies, B-Boys, Baps & Bohos* (New York: HarperCollins, 2002), 201.

238 **"With 'Three Times a Lady'":** Davis, *Lionel Richie—Hello*, 42.

238 **receiving at least one platinum album:** "(December RIAA Certifications) Rogers Sets Platinum Album Record," *Billboard*, January 12, 1985.

238   "The Commodores have done": Davis, *Lionel Richie*, 55.

239   "not just country songs but countrypolitan ones": Al Clark, ed., *The Rock Yearbook Volume IV* (London: Virgin Books, 1983), 108.

239   "I feel like I've opened": Lionel Richie cover story, *Sepia*, September 1981.

239   *Endless Love*: Davis, *Lionel Richie*, 57.

239   "I considered myself a quarterback": "Lionel Richie Tells Why He Really Quit the Commodores," *Jet*, February 21, 1983.

239   "I thought I could keep": Pond, "Lionel Richie."

239   "more of a blow": Davis, *Lionel Richie*, 64.

239   "The greatest thing": "Commodores Keepin' on Without Lionel Richie," *Jet*, August 29, 1983.

239   "to make sure": Pond, "Lionel Richie."

239   "the musical equivalent": Ira Robbins, ed., *The Rolling Stone Review: 1985* (New York: Rolling Stone Press/Scribner, 1985).

239   "We're seeing breakdance appeal": Weinger, "Widening World."

240   "Nice choreography": Michael Shore, *The Rolling Stone Book of Rock Video* (New York: Quill/Rolling Stone Press, 1984), 150.

240   "vile": Dessa Fox, "Goodbye to 'Hello,'" *Melody Maker*, March 31, 1984.

240   "energetic, loose, mobile": Rob Hoerburger, "Talent in Action: Lionel Richie and Tina Turner, Uniondale, N.Y.," *Billboard*, June 16, 1984.

240   faster than the record: Paul Grein, "Talent in Action: Lionel Richie," *Billboard*, October 13, 1984.

240   "We heard that stations were saying" and "It's a great country record": Kip Kirby, "Lionel Richie's Reach Extending to Nashville," *Billboard*, July 28, 1984.

241   "The Gatlins walked out": Greg Bailey, "Richie Is a Stunner in Concert," *Nashville Banner*, May 23, 1984.

241   "drew applause when he spoke": Robert K. Oermann, "Partying with Lionel & Tina; Prince & Princess of Soul Give It Their All," *The Tennessean*, May 23, 1984.

241   "If Democratic presidential hopeful": Bailey, "Richie Is a Stunner."

241–242   "And now, to give voice" and subsequent closing performance quotes: Lucivaldo Oliveira da Silva, "Lionel Richie—Abertura Olimpiadas 1984 (240p_H.264-AAC)," YouTube video, 9:44, published September 4, 2012, youtube.com/watch?v=3zj7C3GRj7s&t=117s.

242   "only entertainer to appear": John Sippel, "Inside Track," *Billboard*, July 28, 1984.

242   jump 84 percent: "First Half VCR Sales Jump," *Billboard*, August 4, 1984.

242   according to NARM: "NARM Figures Show Increase of 17% in January–July Sales," *Billboard*, October 6, 1984.

242   "largely evaporated": Subrata N. Chakravarty, "Lost Bearings," *Forbes*, August 13, 1984.

243   "We were the group of kids": Ricki Harris, "The Story of Cuba Gooding Jr.'s 1984 Olympic Break Dancing Performance," ABC News, August 19, 2016, abcnews.go.com/Entertainment/story-cuba-gooding-jrs-1984-olympic-break-dancing/story?id=41493572.

243 **The stage cost half a million:** Frank Litsky, "A Striking Closing Ceremony," *New York Times*, August 13, 1984.

243 **"I left the house":** Alex Pappademas, "Lionel Richie Wants to Teach You to Be a Real American Idol," *New York Times*, March 8, 2018.

243 **assault and battery:** "Richie's Wife Arrested in Assault," *Los Angeles Times*, June 29, 1988.

CHAPTER FIFTEEN: RADIO CITY MUSIC HALL, NEW YORK CITY, SEPTEMBER 14, 1984

Author interviews with Chrissie Dunlap, Patrick Epstein, and Stephen T. McClellan. Material accessed from the website Madonna: The Warner Bros. Years (mtwy.tumblr.com) is indicated below as "via MTWY."

244 **"an industry in search of an identity":** Adam Sweeting, "The French Collection," *Melody Maker*, October 27, 1984.

244 **That February:** Laura Foti, "MTV, Labels Talk Payments," *Billboard*, February 11, 1984.

244 **"There are no provisions":** Allan Jones, ed., *The Rock Yearbook 1985* (New York: St. Martin's Press, 1984).

244 **"co-conspirators":** Faye Zuckerman and Kip Kirby, "Lawsuit Challenges MTV Deals," *Billboard*, September 29, 1984.

244 **Ted Turner:** "Good News, Bad News for Turner's Cable TV," *BusinessWeek*, June 14, 1982.

244 **moved the date up, to October 26:** Steven Dupler, "Turner Moves Up Music Bow," *Billboard*, September 8, 1984.

245 *Night Tracks:* Michael Shore, *The Rolling Stone Book of Rock Video* (New York: Quill/Rolling Stone Press, 1984), 203.

245 **"If he says he's going to do it":** Kip Kirby, "It's Turner's Turn for Cable Rocker," *Billboard*, August 18, 1984.

245 **Festival International du Video Clip de Saint-Tropez:** James Melanson, "St. Tropez Music Video Festival Fails to Generate Much Action," *Variety*, October 17, 1984.

245 **"huge white motor-yacht":** Sweeting, "The French Collection."

245 **"about 41 percent":** John Craft, "Cable Television: Coming of Age," *Billboard* insert, December 15, 1984.

246 **Of a dozen likely new shows:** Laura Foti, "Music Picks Up Steam on TV," *Billboard*, March 5, 1983.

246 **Dick Ebersol's:** James Andrew Miller and Tom Shales, *Live from New York: The Complete, Uncensored History of 'Saturday Night Live' as Told by Its Stars, Writers, and Guests* (New York: Back Bay Books, 2015), 250.

246 **rumors ran that NBC was looking:** Christopher Connelly, "Random Notes—'Friday Night Video': A Hit," *Rolling Stone*, September 15, 1983.

246 **"scribbled [a] note":** Peter J. Boyer, "Guiding No. 1: The Man Who Programs NBC," *New York Times*, April 19, 1988.

246 **"*Miami Vice* is about colors":** John Leonard, "Evil Under the Sun," *New York*, October 8, 1984.

246 **"There is a fascinating amount":** Richard Zoglin, "Video: Cool Cops, Hot Show," *Time*, September 16, 1985.

247 **"I said that even though we were going to fight":** Cyndi Lauper with Jancee Dunn, *Cyndi Lauper: A Memoir* (New York: Atria Books, 2012), 134.

247 **McMahon brought his son:** Stephen Randall, ed., *The Playboy Interviews: Movers and Shakers* (Milwaukie, OR: M Press, 2007), 325.

247 **"I'm gonna take over this business":** Hulk Hogan with Marc Dagostino, *My Life Outside the Ring* (New York: St. Martin's Press, 2009), 101.

247 **"A wrestler might do anything":** Bruce Rubenstein, "Can Hometown Wrestling Survive the Onslaught from the East?," *City Pages* (Minneapolis–St. Paul), March 27, 1985.

248 **"had the highest twenty-four-hour rating":** Shore, *Rolling Stone Book of Rock Video*, 182.

248 **a million dollars a week:** Jake Austen, *TV a-Go-Go* (Chicago: Chicago Review Press, 2005), 194.

248 **"featuring cel animation":** Mark Rowland, "Music Industry News," *Musician*, May 1984.

248 **60 percent of the stock:** "MTV Stock Sale Blocked in 11 States," *Cash Box*, September 15, 1984.

248 **"MTV's definitely a bad influence":** Erik Hedegaard, "Ted Turner Takes on MTV," *Rolling Stone*, October 25, 1984.

248 **"prohibited from losing":** Tony Seideman, "Rough Start for Turner's Music Channel," *Billboard*, November 17, 1984.

248 **twelve-million-viewer base:** Tony Seideman, "Discovery Network Thinks Big," *Billboard*, December 1, 1984.

248 **"We were the faces":** Nina Blackwood, Mark Goodman, Alan Hunter, and Martha Quinn, with Gavin Edwards, *VJ* (New York: Atria Books, 2013), 229–230.

248 **"five hundred cases of Hawaiian Punch":** Gregory Dobrin, "Audio/Video," *Cash Box*, July 21, 1984.

249 **"I'd like to explain my decision":** Joe Jackson, "Commentary—Video Clips: A Personal View," *Billboard*, June 16, 1984.

249 **"We see the awards show":** Laura Foti, "Awards Show to Kick Off MTV Deal with Ohlmeyer," *Billboard*, January 21, 1984.

249 **"prowled about the stage":** Robert Hilburn, "Madonna Takes Total Control," *Los Angeles Times Calendar*, November 11, 1984.

249 **"her career was over":** Andrew Morton, *Madonna* (New York: St. Martin's Press, 2001), 123.

250 **"immodest":** Mark Bego, interview with Madonna on the set of *Desperately Seeking Susan*, September 1984, via MTWY.

250 **"He never wanted me to be":** "Working Holiday," *No. 1*, February 4, 1984, via MTWY.

250 **"From when I was very young":** Jeffrey Ferry, "The Glamourous Life," *The Face*, February 1985, via MTWY.

250 **"We had to start calling her Mom" and "enjoyed athletics":** "Madonna—Born to Be a Winner," *Seventeen*, April 1985, via MTWY.

250 **"When I was growing up":** Glenn Albin, "Madonna," *Interview*, April 1984, via MTWY.

250 **"He's the one who really inspired me":** Ferry, "The Glamourous Life."

250 **"my introduction to glamour and sophistication":** Christopher Connelly, "Madonna Goes All the Way," *Rolling Stone*, November 22, 1984.

250 **four-year scholarship:** Pete Bishop, "Madonna: Real Life Music Video," *Pittsburgh Press*, May 1985, via MTWY.

251 **"You got paid ten dollars":** "Meet Madonna, Multimedia Star," *Glamour*, February 1985, via MTWY.

251 **"I was just too smart for that":** Sandy Robertson, Madonna interview for *Sounds*, March 12, 1983, via MTWY.

251 **"He stuck a guitar in my hand":** Connelly, "Madonna Goes All the Way."

251 **"He was a lifesaver":** Connelly, "Madonna Goes All the Way."

251 **"It didn't have a bathtub":** "Meet Madonna."

252 **"He took me around to record companies":** Neil Tennant, "Madonna," *Star Hits*, February 1984, via MTWY.

252 **"Many are surprised":** "Madonna: Virgin Pop," *Island*, October 1983, via MTWY.

252 **Billboard's Nelson George:** Nelson George, "The Rhythm & the Blues: 'Breakin': Leading Chart Surprise," *Billboard*, August 4, 1984.

252 **"You get paid thousands of dollars":** Tennant, "Madonna."

252 **"I guess that means I'm ugly":** Gael Love and Glenn O'Brien, "Cyndi Lauper," *Interview*, April 1986.

253 **"I'm desperate to start":** "Working Holiday."

253 **"Art and music can never be too permissive":** "Madonna," *No. 1*, March 24, 1984, via MTWY.

253 **"None of the dancing":** Bego, interview with Madonna, 1984.

253 **"a constant presence backstage":** Jermaine Jackson, *You Are Not Alone: Michael, Through a Brother's Eyes* (New York: Touchstone/Simon & Schuster, 2011), 268.

254 **"When there was a 6 a.m. call":** Allan Metz and Carol Benson, eds., *The Madonna Companion* (New York: Schirmer, 1999), 107.

254 **"The very first night I met her":** Nile Rodgers, MoPop Oral History transcript, February 13, 2003.

255 **"felt like she was at a bar mitzvah":** Toby Goldstein, "Inside the MTV Awards: The Media Glitz," *Creem*, January 1985.

255 **"The MTV Video Music Awards":** Billy Altman, "Video: The Guillotine, Please," *Creem*, January 1985.

255 **"because no one ever does it":** Rusty Cutchin, "East Coastings," *Cash Box*, September 29, 1984.

255 **$600:** Ian Christe, *Everybody Wants Some: The Van Halen Saga* (New York: Wiley, 2007), 101.

255 **"I feel absolutely no responsibility":** Steve Sutherland, "The Gripes of Roth," *Melody Maker*, April 14, 1984.

256 **"a loss of focus":** Rod Stewart, *Rod: The Autobiography* (New York: Crown Archetype, 2012), 269.

256 ***Entertainment This Week:*** Faye Zuckerman, "Music Monitor," *Billboard*, July 28, 1984.

256 **only to announce in December of '84:** Mark Gleeson, "Rod Stewart Signs for S. Africa Tour as Others Cancel," *Variety*, December 19, 1984.

256 **"Stewart, perhaps":** Goldstein, "Inside the MTV Awards."

256 **"giggling-church-boys routine":** Cutchin, "East Coastings."

256 **"God, I hate those damn things":** Charles Shaar Murray, "David Bowie: Sermon from the Savoy," *New Musical Express* (*NME*), September 29, 1984.

256 **"among the least-loved":** Chris O'Leary, *Ashes to Ashes: The Songs of David Bowie, 1976–2016* (London: Repeater Books, 2019), 201–202.

256 **"I wanted to keep my hand in":** Murray, "David Bowie: Sermon from the Savoy."

257 **"I wish I'd thought of this in '74":** Charles Shaar Murray, "David Bowie: The Byronic Man," *The Face*, October 1984.

257 **"Ottawa was the fourteenth":** Kurt Loder, "Sole Survivor," *Rolling Stone*, no. 432 (October 11, 1984).

257 **she paid him back for it two years later:** Fred Bronson, *The Billboard Book of Number 1 Hits,* 5th ed. (New York: Billboard Books, 2003).

257 **"She was on food stamps":** Tina Turner with Kurt Loder, *I, Tina* (New York: William Morrow, 1986; reprint, It Books, 2010), 199.

258 **"I *am* rock and roll":** Mark Rowland, "Tina Turner," *Musician*, September 1984.

258 **"Because I don't want to go to church":** Mark Rowland, "Mega Woman Conquers the World," *Musician*, October 1986.

258 **"You have to fire everybody":** Rowland, "Mega Woman."

258 **"Synthesizers always sounded good":** Dave Hill, "Heaven 17: Definitive Synthpop—A British Groove Thang Even Tina Turner Could Love," *Musician*, January 1985.

259 **an EMI executive had tried cutting her out of the deal:** Christian John Wikane, "The Story of a Soul Survivor: *Private Dancer* at 25," PopMatters, November 24, 2009, popmatters.com/feature/116661-the-story-of-a-soul-survivor-private-dancer-at-25/P1/.

259 **"They all came down":** Turner and Loder, *I, Tina*, 232.

259 **"Look, there's no point":** Hill, "Heaven 17."

259 **"When Tina Turner's name came up":** David Fricke, "Jeff Beck: Number One with a Slow Bullet," *Musician*, May 1985.

260 **"I hate it, it's just not my kind of song":** Brian Chin, "Tina Turner Is Competition for Everybody," *Billboard*, February 2, 1985.

260 **Alan Clark and guitarist Hal Lindes:** Rob Hoerberger, "Talent in Action," *Billboard*, June 16, 1984.

260 **"It was real hard being on stage":** Lynn Norment, "Tina Turner: Sizzling at 45," *Ebony*, May 1985.

260 **"Oh, is *that* how it sounds":** Chin, "Tina Turner."

260 **Grace Slick of Jefferson Starship:** Christopher Connelly, "Behind the Scenes at MTV's First Annual Video Awards," *Rolling Stone*, October 25, 1984.

260 **Paul Kantner:** Paul Liberatore, "Lib at Large: Mickey Thomas and the Mutinous Jefferson Starship," *Marin (CA) Independent Journal*, May 18, 2012, web .archive.org/web/20180910015432/https://www.marinij.com/2012/05/18/lib -at-large-mickey-thomas-and-the-mutinous-jefferson-starship/.

261 **"First time I saw it" and "None of us like organs":** Jeff Nesin, "Whopping & Bopping with ZZ Top," *Creem*, September 1983.

261 **accidentally shot in the abdomen:** "ZZ Top Guitarist Shoots Himself by Accident," *Variety*, December 19, 1984.

261–262 **"The heaviness of the synthesizers":** Joe Bosso, "Billy Gibbons Talks ZZ Top: The Complete Studio Albums (1970–1990)," Music Radar, June 3, 2013, musicradar.com/news/guitars/billy-gibbons-talks-zz-top-the-complete-studio -albums-1970-1990-575728.

262 **outsold every other act on Warner Bros.:** Kurt Loder, "ZZ Top: The Boys Just Wanna Have Fun," *Rolling Stone*, April 12, 1984.

262 **custom Nudie suits:** Benniken, "ZZ Top—Sharp Dressed Man 1984 MTV VMA's," YouTube video, 3:57, published September 5, 2018, youtube.com/watch ?v=nhodVTERDeo.

262 **"a bit of a step for him":** Brian Chin, "Dance Trax," *Billboard*, July 14, 1984.

262 **August 29:** Ira Robbins, ed., *The Rolling Stone Review: 1985* (New York: Rolling Stone Press/Scribner, 1985).

262 **the producers of *Ghostbusters* . . . admitted:** "Who Ya Gonna Call? Ghostbusters Exclusive! Inside Story of a Comedy Classic," *Premiere*, June 2004.

263 **"We got a major apology":** Joel Selvin, *Smart Ass: The Music Journalism of Joel Selvin* (Kassel, Germany: Parthenon Books, 2011), 343.

263 **"The offensive part":** Teri Vanhorn, "Ray Parker Jr. Suing Huey Lewis over 'Ghostbusters' Comments," MTV News, March 23, 2001, mtv.com/news /1442126/ray-parker-jr-suing-huey-lewis-over-ghostbusters-comment/.

263 **"if Randy Newman could sing an eensy bit better":** J. Kordosh, review of Huey Lewis & the News' *Sports*, *Creem*, February 1984.

263 **"We could barely draw":** Paul Grein, "Huey Lewis Makes Concert News," *Billboard*, July 7, 1984.

264 **"effectively provided":** Mark Evans and Philip Hayward, eds., *Sounding Funny: Sound and Comedy Cinema* (Sheffield, UK: Equinox, 2016), 104.

264 **"the consummate riff burglar of his generation":** Ken Barnes, "45 Revelations," *Creem*, October 1984.

264 **Davis offered him an artist deal:** Clive Davis with Anthony DeCurtis, *The Soundtrack of My Life* (New York: Simon & Schuster, 2013), 259.

264 **"Not because the song":** Davis and DeCurtis, *Soundtrack of My Life*, 261.

264 **"A number of stations":** Tony Seideman, "Hancock Stars at MTV Awards," *Billboard*, September 29, 1984.

265 **"In less than a year":** Steve Perry, "Views from the Ladder," *City Pages* (Minneapolis–St. Paul), May 8, 1985.

265 **"pretty funny":** "Maybe She's Good," *Record*, March 1985.

CHAPTER SIXTEEN: CIVIC ARENA, PITTSBURGH, SEPTEMBER 21, 1984

Some materials related to this show were accessed via brucebase.wikidot .com/gig:1984-09-22-civic-arena-pittsburgh-pa.

266 **January 23, 1984:** Associated Press (AP), "Confessions of a Hoax," *Washington Post*, January 25, 1984.

266 **"We wanted to precipitate":** "Crass 'KGB Tape' Hoax," *Sounds*, January 28, 1984.

266 **"Soviet active measures":** AP, "Confessions."

266–267 **"I don't think there is a major record company":** Peter Jones, "British Retailer Convicted in Obscenity Case," *Billboard*, September 15, 1984.

267 **"Voting for her was like buying":** Julie Burchill, "Burchill on Thatcher," *The Face*, no. 100 (September 1988).

267 **"I cannot produce jobs":** David North, "A Conversation with the Iron Lady," *Maclean's*, October 10, 1983.

267 **"sent anonymously a copy":** Arthur Scargill, "'We Could Surrender—or Stand and Fight,'" *The Guardian* (Manchester), March 6, 2009.

268 **"incapacitating":** Gareth Peirce, "How They Rewrote the Law at Orgreave," *The Guardian* (Manchester), August 12, 1985.

268 **"spotted these three old ladies":** Roy Wilkinson, "Test Dept. on the Front Line of the Miners' Strike, 1984," *Mojo*, October 2015.

268 **As Thatcher requested Botha withdraw from Namibia:** "Apartheid 'Unacceptable,' Thatcher Tells Botha," *Washington Post*, June 3, 1984.

268 **The Special AKA—earlier:** Steve Lake, "One More Change in a Black & White World," *Melody Maker*, June 2, 1984.

269 **"the British government":** Elvis Costello, *Unfaithful Music & Disappearing Ink* (New York: Blue Rider Press, 2015), 392.

269 **One was "Shipbuilding":** Robert Sandall, "The Lasting Legacy of 'Shipbuilding,'" *The Telegraph* (London), April 5, 2007.

269 **"three-piece-suit-with-watch-and-chain arrangements":** Greil Marcus, *In the Fascist Bathroom: Punk in Pop Music, 1977–1992* (Cambridge, MA: Harvard University Press, 2001; orig., 1993), 258.

269 **"Congratulations!":** Elvis Costello, liner notes to *Goodbye Cruel World* (Rykodisc reissue, 1995; orig., 1984).

269 **Costello would later acknowledge:** Bill Flanagan, "The Last Elvis Costello Interview You'll Ever Need to Read," *Musician*, March 1986.

269 **"A lot of the hit records":** Costello, *Unfaithful Music*, 437.

270 **"add[ed] to the blacks' leverage":** "Black Miners Drive a Wedge into Apartheid," *BusinessWeek*, May 2, 1983.

270 **so-called free state:** Alexis de Veaux, "Black South Africa: One Day Soon," *Essence*, July 1983.

270 **"honorary white person":** Nelson George, "The Rhythm & the Blues," *Billboard*, January 5, 1985.

270 **"The last place for a boycott":** Aaron Latham, "Ronstadt in Sun City," *Rolling Stone*, July 7, 1983.

271 **"Rough Trade had a constitution":** Neil Taylor, *Document and Eyewitness: An Intimate History of Rough Trade* (London: Orion, 2012), 275.

271 **Heidi Berg:** Peter Ames Carlin, *Homeward Bound: The Life of Paul Simon* (New York: Henry Holt, 2016), 277–281.

271 **drove all the way to Harrison's studio:** Scott Cohen and Glenn O'Brien, "Sounds Like the Talking Heads," *Spin*, June 1985.

272 **Mike Love:** Mike Love with James S. Hirsch, *Good Vibrations—My Life as a Beach Boy* (New York: Blue Rider Press, 2016), 301–308.

272 **arrested in Dallas:** Ira Robbins, ed., *The Rolling Stone Review: 1985* (New York: Rolling Stone Press/Scribner, 1985).

272 **Neil Young:** Bill Flanagan, "The Real Neil Young Stands Up," *Musician*, November 1985.

273 **"The Recovery Cheers the GOP":** *BusinessWeek*, November 28, 1983.

273 **"Conservative free-market economists":** Kevin M. Kruse and Julian E. Zelizer, *Fault Lines: A History of the United States Since 1974* (New York: W. W. Norton, 2019), 136.

273 **"As deregulation takes hold":** "Deregulating America," *BusinessWeek*, November 28, 1983.

274 **"In sum, the president has":** Michael Kramer, "Thinking About Reagan," *New York*, November 21, 1983.

274 **"He has a tendency":** Lewis Lapham, "Reagan's New America," *Maclean's*, January 26, 1982.

274 **"I said, 'Bruce'":** Fred Goodman, "The Rolling Stone Interview: Walter Yetnikoff," *Rolling Stone*, December 15, 1988.

274 **"That whole *Nebraska* album":** Jeff Burger, ed., *Springsteen on Springsteen* (Chicago: Chicago Review Press, 2014), 134.

275 **"Nobody But Springsteen Can Tell Stories Like These":** Clinton Heylin, *E Street Shuffle: The Glory Days of Bruce Springsteen & the E Street Band* (New York: Viking, 2012), 259.

275 **"One of the things that happens":** Heylin, *E Street Shuffle*, 265.

275 **"I think it originally started":** Jon Bream, "Bruce Springsteen: Rock and Roll Glory Days!," *Creem*, January 1985.

276 **"It was a protest song":** Bruce Springsteen, *Born to Run* (New York: Simon & Schuster, 2016), 314.

276 **"He left and he didn't come back" and "One of the things":** Kurt Loder, "The *Rolling Stone* Interview: Bruce Springsteen," *Rolling Stone*, December 6, 1984.

277 **"The subversiveness of the Top 40 radio":** Burger, *Springsteen on Springsteen*, 228.

277 **"to get as close as possible" and "When I was growing up":** Dave Herman, "Interview from the Vault: Bruce Springsteen, 1978," *Paste*, March 9, 2012, pastemagazine.com/articles/2012/03/from-the-vault-bruce-springsteen-1978 .html.

277 **"I have seen rock and roll future":** Jon Landau, "Growing Young with Rock and Roll," *Real Paper*, May 22, 1974.

277–278 **"I think what he was actually saying" and "What frightened me about it":** Herman, "Interview from the Vault."

278 **"a summer-long monopoly":** Paul Grein, "Chartbeat: 'Footloose' Gets Serious Competition," *Billboard*, June 16, 1984.

278 **"Jon [Landau] had been bothering me":** Bill Flanagan, *Written in My Soul: Rock's Great Songwriters Talk About Creating Their Music* (Chicago: Contemporary, 1986), 159.

279 **"When he's not bellowing":** Robert Christgau, *Christgau's Record Guide: The '80s* (Boston: Ticknor & Fields, 1990), 247.

279 **Van Zandt left the band:** Peter Ames Carlin, *Bruce* (New York: Touchstone Books, 2013), 309.

279 **"I got the job about four weeks":** Christopher Phillips, "The Nils Lofgren Interview," *Backstreets*, no. 74 (Spring–Summer 2002).

279 **"As the first woman in the band":** Springsteen, *Born to Run*, 323.

279 **"He's been running up and down":** Leo Sacks, "Springsteen Fans in Pilgrimage to St. Paul," *Billboard*, July 14, 1984.

280 **"He's abandoned":** Mary Arkansas, "Nervous Breakdown: Dancing in the Light," *City Pages*, July 11, 1984.

280 **"I was a big fan":** Carlin, *Bruce*, 301.

280 **"We took a lot of different":** Loder, "The *Rolling Stone* Interview."

280 **"ruffled a few feathers":** David Adelson, "L.A. Radio Scrambles to Tell Listeners Who's 'The Boss,'" *Cash Box*, November 10, 1984.

280 **"I would have regretted terribly":** Christopher Phillips and Louis P. Masur, eds., *Talk About a Dream: The Essential Interviews of Bruce Springsteen* (London: Bloomsbury, 2014), 255.

281 **"I'm registered, yeah":** Loder, "The *Rolling Stone* Interview."

281 **"That was something":** Phillips & Masur, *Talk About a Dream*, 309.

281 *National Review*: Michael Daddino, "Right of the Dial: The National Review Contra (and Pro) Sixties Rock" (presentation at Pop Conference, Seattle, April 2007), Medium, published December 24, 2017, medium.com/@epicharmus /right-of-the-dial-the-national-review-contra-and-pro-sixties-rock-99c907 b32431.

281 **Weinberg . . . had invited both:** Carlin, *Bruce*, 317.

281 **"In other words":** Dave Marsh, ed., *The First Rock and Roll Confidential Report* (New York: Pantheon, 1985), 64.

282 **"All that we've done":** Ronald Reagan, "Remarks at a Reagan-Bush Rally in Hammonton, New Jersey," Ronald Reagan Presidential Library and Museum, September 19, 1984, reaganlibrary.gov/research/speeches/91984c.

282 **"It was part of a shopping list":** Carlin, *Bruce*, 318.

282 **"Republicans at that time":** Burger, *Springsteen on Springsteen*, 275.

282 **"a Republican Party intent":** Springsteen, *Born to Run*, 315.

282 *Post-Gazette***:** Tim Ziaukas, "Arena Crowd Relates with Fervor to Springsteen's Hard-Times Message," *Pittsburgh Post-Gazette*, September 21, 1984.

282 **"Bruce may have been born to run":** Marsh, *First Rock and Roll Confidential*, 66.

283 **"the national security police":** "Kuti Court Cases," *Melody Maker*, September 22, 1984.

283 **"Kafkaesque":** Randall Grass, "Fela: Rebel on Ice," *Spin*, May 1985.

283 **"They know that my going to America":** Jim Miller, "Rocking All the Way to Jail," *Newsweek*, July 15, 1985.

283 **the Kalakuta Republic:** Vivien Goldman, "The Rascal Republic Takes Over the World," *New Musical Express* (*NME*), October 8, 1980.

283 **"dance craze":** Peter Shapiro, "The Primer: Fela Kuti," *The Wire*, no. 234 (August 2003).

284 **"That should be put in your contract":** Peter Shapiro, "Invisible Jukebox: Bill Laswell," *The Wire*, no. 193 (March 2000).

284 **"for more info":** Kent Zimmerman, "The Album Chart: Analysis," *Gavin Report*, March 8, 1985.

CHAPTER SEVENTEEN: EMI RECORDS, NEW YORK CITY, NOVEMBER 13, 1984

Author interviews: Arthur Baker, Larry Berger.

285 **"worrying":** Lou Gramm with Scott Pitoniak, *Juke Box Hero: My Five Decades in Rock and Roll* (Chicago: Triumph Books, 2013), 111.

285 **"fluffy":** Fred Bronson, *The Billboard Book of Number 1 Hits*, 5th ed. (New York: Billboard Books, 2003).

285–286 **"I certainly want to retain the rock image" and "I enjoy the anonymity":** Paul Grein, "Foreigner Still Loyal to Records," *Billboard*, January 26, 1985.

286 **"We've had number one albums":** Bronson, *Billboard Book of Number 1*.

286 **"something nobody would expect me to do":** Freff, "Trevor Horn: A Studio Wunderkind and His Quiver of Production Arrows," *Musician*, March 1984.

286 **keeping his eye on them:** Gramm and Pitoniak, *Juke Box Hero*, 110.

286 **"What do you mean":** Matt Wardlaw, Mick Jones interview transcript, February 25, 2013, courtesy of author.

287 **two more than "State of Shock":** Dave Sholin, "Top Forty: Analysis," *Gavin Report*, November 30, 1984.

287 **"I'm being generous":** Gramm and Pitoniak, *Juke Box Hero*, 116.

287 **"Halfway through the song":** Ahmet Ertegun et al., *"What'd I Say": The Atlantic Story—50 Years of Music* (New York: Welcome Rain, 2001), 390–391.

287 **"Stadium rock is a phenomenon":** Al Clark, ed., *The Rock Yearbook 1982* (London: Virgin Books, 1981).

288 **"I wanted to have a really high-end":** Mr. Carty, "Castles Burning: The Herbie Herbert Interview," 2001, web.archive.org/web/20111023190513/http://members.cox.net/mrcarty/page11.html.

288 **"We were told":** Tim Jones, "Raised on Journey," *Record Collector*, March 1999.

288 **TV ads for Budweiser:** See Louise Long, "Journey Budweiser Commercial #1," YouTube video, 1:05, published June 25, 2009, youtube.com/watch?v=zklTW7Q0ElU.

288 **"nothing wrong with being commercial":** Jones, "Raised on Journey."

288 **"I regret to announce":** Greil Marcus, *In the Fascist Bathroom* (Cambridge, MA: Harvard University Press, 1993), 204–205.

288 **"cigar-chomping manager":** Dave Marsh, "American Grandstand: Shoot at Your Own Risk," *Record*, February 1983.

288 **"predominance of synthesizers":** Leo Sacks, "Out of the Box," *Billboard*, February 5, 1983.

289 **"Let's get this straight":** Kevin Knapp, "Night Ranger Want to Meet Your Sister Too!," *Creem*, September 1984.

289 **"Later, we got all these calls about it":** Carolyn Jones, "Night Rangers Revisit 'Sister Christian' and San Rafael," *San Francisco Chronicle*, November 11, 2005.

290 **"The feedback confused me":** Danny Seraphine with Adam Mitchell, *Street Player: My Chicago Story* (New York: Wiley, 2011), 201.

290 **threatening to break Foster's legs:** Seraphine and Mitchell, *Street Player*, 207.

290 **"Madison Avenue approach to rock and roll":** Jay Cocks, "Rock Hits the Hard Place," *Time*, February 15, 1982.

291 **In 1984, the RIAA estimated:** Larry E. Wacholtz, *Inside Country Music* (New York: Billboard Publications, 1984), 43.

291 **"A big star'll average":** Bill Flanagan and Jock Baird, "The Failure of Corporate Rock," *Musician*, December 1982.

291 **from a 3.3 share up to a 3.9:** "Good News for Top 40 Format: KIIS, Z-100 Top Spring Ratings," *Billboard*, July 21, 1984.

291 **"You can't be an all-teen station and survive":** "What's Next for Top 40 Stations?," *Billboard*, August 4, 1984.

291 **"stampede toward Top 40":** Thomas K. Arnold, "Format Panel Raps 'Stampede' of Changes," *Billboard*, September 29, 1984.

291 **"One week in L.A.":** Russell Reid, "CHR Inspires Big Seminar at NAB/NRBA Convention," *Cash Box*, September 29, 1984.

291 **"The only silly moments":** "Talent in Action," *Billboard*, September 22, 1984.

292 **"I think you have to be excellent":** Bronson, *Billboard Book of Number 1*.

292 **"Hiring the Network guys"**: Stan Cornyn with Paul Scanlon, *Exploding: The Highs, Hits, Hype, Heroes, and Hustlers of the Warner Music Group* (New York: It Books, 2002), 318–319.

292 **"found no evidence of payola"**: Bill Holland, "House Subcommittee Drops Payola Probe," *Billboard*, September 29, 1984.

292 **"Okay, do your act"**: Jan Hoffman, "Howard Stern Just Won't Shut Up," *New York*, November 18, 1985.

292 **"Yesterday on NBC Radio"**: Dan O'Day, "Howard Stern: The Art of Outrage," *Radio & Records*, March 23, 1984.

293 **"Stern would joke about AIDS"**: Hoffman, "Howard Stern."

293 **"You're never too old to rock and roll"**: WSHE-FM, Ft. Lauderdale-Miami, advertisement in *Spin*, no. 1 (1985).

293 **"I targeted 'dog FM stations'"**: Fred Jacobs, "The State of Classic Rock Is . . . ," Jacobs Media (blog), September 6, 2013, jacobsmedia.com/the -state-of-classic-rock-is/.

293 **"Top 40 stations . . . began"**: "Super Chart (A Countdown of the Top 43 AOR Songs)," in *Radio & Records: The AOR Story* (1978).

293 **"I've always been proud"**: J. D. Considine, "Robert Plant: Life in a Lighter Zeppelin," *Musician*, December 1983.

294 **"The Baby Boomers are riding"**: "Baby Boomers Push for Power," *Business-Week*, July 2, 1984.

294 **"*Astral Weeks* is the kind of album"**: Happy Traum, "Van Morrison: In Conversation," *Rolling Stone*, July 9, 1970.

294 **Warner Bros. announced:** William K. Knoedelseder Jr., "Turnaround After 2 Years of Setbacks: Warner Bros. Records Plays a Happier Tune," *Los Angeles Times*, February 14, 1985.

294 **Morrison was incensed:** David Wild, "A Conversation with Van Morrison," *Rolling Stone*, August 9, 1990.

294 **"I don't think they maliciously said"**: James Henke, "Bonnie Raitt: The Rolling Stone Interview," *Rolling Stone*, May 3, 1990.

294 **"You could be indoors for months"**: Paul Williams, *Bob Dylan—Performing Artist: The Middle Years, 1974–1986* (San Francisco: Underwood-Miller, 1992), 262.

295 **from $24,500:** Dennis McNally, *A Long Strange Trip* (New York: Three Rivers Press, 2001), 547.

295 **Shakedown Street:** David Gans and Blair Jackson, *This Is All a Dream We Dreamed: An Oral History of the Grateful Dead* (New York: Flatiron Books, 2015).

295 **"If somebody can find a use"**: Sandy Troy, *Captain Trips: A Biography of Jerry Garcia* (New York: Thunder's Mouth, 1994), 201.

295 **"There's no bass"**: David Browne, *So Many Roads: The Life and Times of the Grateful Dead* (Cambridge, MA: Da Capo, 2015), 308.

295 **Joan Baez:** Browne, *So Many Roads*, 304.

295 **"Hunter sang 'Touch of Grey'"**: Gans and Jackson, *This Is All a Dream*.

295 **On Halloween:** Grateful Dead Live at Berkeley Community Theater on 1984-10-31, archive.org/details/gd1984-10-31.145613.aud.lamarre.berger.flac24/gd1984-10-31s2t01.flac.

296 **"Hey, Jerry, you're on stage!":** Bill Kreutzmann with Benjy Eisen, *Deal: My Three Decades of Drumming, Dreams, and Drugs with the Grateful Dead* (New York: St. Martin's Griffin, 2015).

296 **"God, wouldn't it have been nice":** Robert Greenfield, *Dark Star: An Oral Biography of Jerry Garcia* (New York: William Morrow, 1996), 204.

296 **David Crosby:** David Crosby, as told to Todd Gold: "The Happy Lazarus of Rock 'n' Roll," *People*, April 27, 1987.

296 **"He did this on his own":** Alex Williams, "Who Was the Real Lou Reed?," *New York Times*, October 31, 2015.

296 **Robert Quine:** Jason Gross, "Robert Quine Interview," *Perfect Sound Forever*, November 1997, furious.com/perfect/quine.html.

297 **"He's even making a video":** Scott Isler, "Lou Reed: A Reluctant Legend Doffs His Mask—Briefly," *Musician*, October 1984.

297 **"Irving's the kind of guy":** Fred Goodman, "The Rolling Stone Interview: Walter Yetnikoff," *Rolling Stone*, December 15, 1988.

297 **"They had no sense of history":** Paul Grein, "Former Eagle Flies to MCA," *Billboard*, July 14, 1984.

297 **"California rock":** Christopher Connelly, "1982 in Review: Who Won, Who Lost," *Rolling Stone*, February 17, 1983.

298 **"They said it wasn't":** Grein, "Former Eagle."

298 **"So concrete, so androgynous" and "You mean about me being perceived as [*sneers*] a balladeer?":** Jock Baird, "Glenn Frey's Benign Dictatorship," *Musician*, October 1984.

298 **"I was a little leery":** Marc Eliot, *To the Limit—the Untold Story of the Eagles* (Boston: Little, Brown, 2009), 214.

298 **"I saw this brand new":** Timothy White, "Don Henley: Beauty and the Beast," *Musician*, March 1985.

299 **"I think if the Eagles were to fart in a bag":** Grein, "Former Eagle."

299 **"Ten years ago":** Christopher Connelly, "Christine McVie," *Rolling Stone*, June 7, 1984.

299 **"I had seen it coming, and denied it":** Mick Fleetwood with Stephen Davis, *Fleetwood: My Life and Adventures in Fleetwood Mac* (New York: William Morrow, 1990), 257.

299 **"overexposure through video":** Michael Shore, *The Rolling Stone Book of Rock Video* (New York: Quill/Rolling Stone Press, 1984), 149.

299 **"depict[ed] Squier cavorting":** Paul Grein, "Squier; I Was Clipped by Clip," *Billboard*, November 24, 1984.

299 **"I think it confused people":** Paul Grein, "Squier: I Was Clipped by Clip," *Billboard*, November 24, 1984.

300 **"[Giraldo] started fooling around":** Pat Benatar with Patsi Bale Cox, *Between a Heart and a Rock Place: A Memoir* (New York: HarperCollins, 2010), 142.

300 "We were a 'rock' band": Benatar and Cox, *Between a Heart*, 143.

300 "They wanted it to be a guarded secret": Benatar and Cox, *Between a Heart*, 157.

300 "How are you doing this?": Benatar and Cox, *Between a Heart*, 161.

300 "I want to congratulate Jim Kerr": "Mutterings," *Smash Hits*, August 30–September 12, 1984.

301 "The doctors [had] told him": Charles M. Young, "The Pretenders Change Diapers and Wrestle Death to a Draw," *Musician*, March 1984.

301 "I suppose people could feel sorry for me": Gary Graff, "A Pretender Bender? Here Comes the Brood," *Creem*, August 1984.

301 "a triumph of art over adversity": Kurt Loder, review of Pretenders' *Learning to Crawl*, *Rolling Stone*, February 18, 1984.

301 "Hynde summarized her band's faceless vigor": Richard Cook, "Chrissie Hynde: Rock and Roll Face," *New York Rocker*, no. 57 (May 1984).

301 "About as interesting as a road map of Belgium": Steve Lake, "Private Lives," *Melody Maker*, July 28, 1984.

301 "They don't like to be called Hall & Oates": Roy Trakin, "Daryl Hall and John Oates: A Coupla White Guys Sittin' Around Talking," *Creem*, April 1985.

302 "If we have a cause or a crusade" and "We're musicians who are using": Al Clark, ed., *The Rock Yearbook Volume IV* (London: Virgin, 1983), 96.

303 "Am I gonna be saddled": Kurt Loder, "David Bowie: Straight Time," *Rolling Stone*, May 12, 1983.

303 "What constitutes a challenge": Vic Garbarini, "Mick Jagger: Sympathy for the Dybbuk," *Musician*, December 1983.

303 "He's got a problem with his attitude": Vic Garbarini, "Keith Richards: The Heart of the Stones," *Musician*, December 1983.

304 "He asked me, 'What did you think?'": Lawrence Grobel, *Above the Line: Conversations About the Movies* (Cambridge, MA: Da Capo Press, 2000), 341.

304 "merely the crumbs of the Lennon revival": Colin Irwin, review of John Lennon and Yoko Ono's *Milk and Honey*, *Melody Maker*, January 28, 1984.

304 On January 15: Keith Badman, *The Beatles After the Breakup—1970–2000: A Day-to-Day Diary* (Baltimore: Omnibus, 1999), 329–330.

304 "It's appalling to have to buy back": Frank Broughton, ed., *Time Out Interviews, 1968–1998* (New York: Penguin, 1998).

305 "Beatle suit": "Saturday Night Live Season 10 Episode 08 on December 8, 1984 with Host Ringo Starr and Musical Guest Herbie Hancock," SNL, nbc.com/saturday-night-live/season-10/episode/8-ringo-starr-with-herbie-hancock-64811.

305 Ringo Starr . . . refused to play drums: Nick DeRiso, "Inside Paul McCartney's Career-Turning Stumble on 'Give My Regards to Broad Street,'" Ultimate Classic Rock, October 22, 2015, ultimateclassicrock.com/paul-mccartney-give-my-regards/.

305 *Billboard* shamed McCartney: Paul Grein, "'Broad Street' Is McCartney's Folly," *Billboard*, November 3, 1984.

305 On October 15: Badman, *Beatles After the Breakup*, 340.

305 "The twenty-one-year-old Julian Lennon": Mark Ellen, review of Julian Lennon's *Valotte*, *Smash Hits*, October 25–November 7, 1984.

305 "Thank God!": Badman, *Beatles After the Breakup*, 345.

CHAPTER EIGHTEEN: SARM STUDIOS, LONDON, NOVEMBER 25, 1984

The 1984 *Smash Hits* readers' poll (*Smash Hits*, December 20, 1984–January 2, 1985) is quoted throughout.

306 "a light drinker": Rob Fitzpatrick, "The Artists Formerly Known as Swoon," *The Word*, November 2004.

307 "got violently ill on the salmon mousse": John Taylor, *In the Pleasure Groove* (New York: Dutton Adult, 2012), 247.

307 "the absolute acme": J. Taylor, *In the Pleasure Groove*, 252.

308 "It's not the something extra": *MTV Rockumentary: George Michael—Music, Money, Love, Faith* (1989).

308 "The teacher ordered me": Fred Bronson, *The Billboard Book of Number 1 Hits*, 5th ed. (New York: Billboard Books, 2003).

308 "I think it's brilliant" and "I think May": Neil Tennant, "The Beach Boys," *Smash Hits*, May 24–June 6, 1984.

309 "I like to have a line or two": Ian Birch, "'We're No Con!,'" *Smash Hits*, September 27–October 10, 1984.

309 paid his airfare from France: "Bitz," *Smash Hits*, September 13–26, 1984.

309 "A lot of people" and "If a bunch of ugly bastards": Birch, "'We're No Con!'"

309 "A blowtorch couldn't separate us now": Boy George with Spencer Bright, *Take It Like a Man* (New York: HarperCollins, 1995), 254.

310 "a family sized Coca-Cola bottle": George and Bright, *Take It Like a Man*, 238.

310 "because I think it's a mistake": Sylvie Simmons, "Hey There, Georgie Boy," *Creem*, April 1985.

310 "Being a pop star" and "Frankie's for kids": Peter Martin, ". . . More War!," *Smash Hits*, September 27–October 10, 1984.

310 "George was more interested": James R. Blandford, "Boy George," *Record Collector*, November 1998.

311 "to kill them off completely": Simon Reynolds, *Totally Wired* (New York: Faber & Faber, 2009), 334.

311 "I know a lot of people think" and "agreed to do literally": Ethlie Ann Vare, "Frankie Satisfies Stateside Curiosity," *Billboard*, December 22, 1984.

311 "It will be very difficult to push": Marci McDonald, "An Encore for the Oldest President," *Maclean's*, November 19, 1984.

311 FRANKIE SAY SHIT THE POLITICIAN: David Keeps and David Sprague, "Frankie in America," *Smash Hits*, December 6–19, 1984.

312 **"Frankie Goes to Hollywood is supposed to be a rock band":** Laura Weber, "Caught in the Act: Frankie Goes to Hollywood," *City Pages*, November 28, 1984, Minnesota Historical Society (MNHS), St. Paul.

312 **"came across like Elvis Costello":** Jon Bream, "Controversial British Group Has Form, Not Substance," *Minneapolis Star & Tribune*, November 27, 1984, Minnesota Historical Society (MNHS), St. Paul.

312 **"Suddenly, people were looking to Frankie":** Mick Brown and Howard Rosenberg, "Days of Whine and Poses—Two Diatribes," *Spin*, May 1985.

312 **"I think it's garbage, total garbage":** TheBestOfVoxPop, "Mick Jagger: On Frankie Goes to Hollywood (Interview—1985)," YouTube video, 0:38, published August 28, 2013, youtube.com/watch?v=NYDhjuq08Fg&feature=youtu.be.

312 **"The Big Music":** Rob Hughes, "The Return of the Big Music," *Classic Rock*, June 13, 2014, loudersound.com/features/the-return-of-the-big-music.

312 **"We don't have blues scales":** Jim Green, "U2: The Pluck of the Irish," *Trouser Press*, no. 71 (March 1982).

312 **"If we stay in small clubs":** John Jobling, *U2—The Definitive Biography* (New York: Thomas Dunne Books, 2014), 104.

312 **"I never bought into the cliché":** Michka Assayas, *Bono in Conversation* (New York: Riverhead Books, 2005), 282.

313 **"quickly took things over":** Neil McCormack, "The Unbelievable Book," *Hot Press*, December 3, 1987, hotpress.com/music/the-unbelievable-book-1488562.

313 **"Usually they would say":** Assayas, *Bono in Conversation*, 282.

313 **"We actually had run out of cash":** Neil McCormick, Bono, the Edge, Adam Clayton, and Larry Mullen Jr., *U2 by U2* (New York: It Books, 2009), 130.

313 **"It's very hip to knock America":** Kevin Knapp, "U2 in America: Pop Morality vs. the Irish Way," *Creem*, September 1983.

313 **"They were devoted to the idea":** Adam Block, "Bono Bites Back," *Mother Jones*, May 1, 1989.

313 **"Bono kept saying":** Bill Flanagan, *U2 at the End of the World* (New York: Delta, 1996), 45.

314 **"click track":** McCormick et al., *U2 by U2*, 135.

314 **"complexity to the emotion":** Jeffrey Ressner, "Brian Eno on Synths, CDs, and Spiritual Gospel Music," *Cash Box*, March 24, 1984.

314 **"clearly with the intention":** McCormick et al., *U2 by U2*, 148.

314 **"Once I'd met Bono":** Helen Fitzgerald, "The Life of Brian," *Melody Maker*, September 29, 1984.

315 **"When your friend becomes a junkie":** Gavin Martin, "We Build the Positive," *New Musical Express* (NME), October 27, 1984.

315 **"And I, like an idiot":** McCormick et al., *U2 by U2*, 151.

315 **"When that stupid river":** Jobling, *U2—The Definitive Biography*, 120.

315 **"It was originally meant" and "pompous, signifying delusions of grandeur":** Martin, "We Build."

315 **"pop colors":** Jobling, *U2—The Definitive Biography*, 132.

315 **"We were really trying to be":** McCormick et al., *U2 by U2*, 159.

316 **"I don't wanna play rock music":** Adam Sweeting, "The Style Council: My Ever Changing Moods," *Melody Maker*, March 24, 1984.

316 **"jazz for people who don't like jazz":** "Concert Reviews," *Variety*, May 16, 1984.

316 **"it isn't Paul Weller":** Sweeting, "The Style Council."

316 **"She's not only doing her job badly":** Richard Holmes, "Paul Weller Style Council TV Interview from 1984 Earsay," YouTube video, 8:45, published January 25, 2017, youtube.com/watch?time_continue=8&v=G6KOZNj344s.

316 **"*All of Wham!, that is*":** Adam Sweeting, "Pit-Head Ballet," *Melody Maker*, September 15, 1984.

317 **"Go for fucking what?":** Alexis Petridis, "Talented and Unique: George Michael Took a Singular Path to Stardom," *The Guardian* (Manchester), December 26, 2016, theguardian.com/music/2016/dec/26/george-michael-talented-success-wham-artist-singer-teen-idol.

317 **"It was almost entirely breakdancing":** Bill Brewster, "The Original Punks: Mark Cotgrove, AKA Snowboy, on the Soul Mafia and the UK Jazz Dance Scene," Red Bull Music Academy, 2005, published January 10, 2019, daily.redbullmusicacademy.com/2019/01/mark-cotgrove-interview.

317 **"*Eden* came along":** Ian Wade, "From Eden with Love: Everything But the Girl Interviewed," *The Quietus*, June 19, 2012, thequietus.com/articles/09091-everything-but-the-girl-interview.

317 **"Her marriage had broken":** Colin Irwin, "The Jewel in the Crown," *Melody Maker*, December 15, 1984.

317 **"Charming she is":** Ian Pye, "African & White," *Melody Maker*, February 18, 1984.

318 **"because they considered" and "That's just chauvinism":** Irwin, "The Jewel in the Crown."

318 **"making and selling one-offs":** "Shrink Rap: Sade," *Melody Maker*, May 26, 1984.

318 **"Sure. And I can write songs, too":** Jessica Berens, "Sade," *Spin*, May 1985.

318 **"Doing the small set":** Pye, "African & White."

318 **"We tried quite a few drummers":** Jon Young, "The Genesis Autodiscography," *Trouser Press*, March 1982.

318 **"Younger fans who would never dream":** Ray Fox-Cumming, "Genesis: Not Poor but Bankrupt," *Disc*, January 19, 1974, thegenesisarchive.co.uk/interview-genesis-not-poor-but-bankrupt-disc-19th-january/.

319 **"I remember I felt":** Young, "The Genesis Autodiscography."

319 **"We're channeling our individual songs":** Robert Payes, "Phil Collins," *Trouser Press*, June 1981.

319 **Roland TR-808s:** J. D. Considine, "The Second Coming of Phil Collins," *Musician*, June 1985.

319 **"This is a record!":** Phil Collins with Craig McLean, *Not Dead Yet: The Memoir* (New York: Crown Archetype, 2016), 161.

319 **"More producers and engineers"**: Greg Milner, *Perfecting Sound Forever* (London: Faber & Faber, 2009), 166.

319 **Even Neil Young**: Steven Dupler, "Neil Young Purchases Digital System From Sony," *Billboard*, August 25, 1984.

319 **"It sounds like synthesized drums"**: Bill Milkowski, "Phil Collins: Genesis of a Drummer," *DownBeat*, July 1984.

320 **"Basically, it's the 'In the Air Tonight' sound"**: Considine, "The Second Coming."

320 **"We used to call it the facehugger" and "If the first one"**: Danny Eccleston, "Against All Odds," *Mojo*, December 2015.

320 **"By the time February 1984 rolls around"**: Collins and McLean, *Not Dead Yet*, 184–185.

321 **"a rock cut with Phil Collins' style"**: "Record Reviews: Singles," *Variety*, November 21, 1984.

321 **"was banned, effectively"**: Barbara Pepe, "Bob Geldof: Back to Boomtown," *Spin*, September 1985.

321 **"A new lot of people"**: Tom Hibbert, "What Went Wrong?," *Smash Hits*, June 7–20, 1984.

321 **"silly"**: Fred Schruers, "Bob Geldof: Conscience, Irritant, 'Minor' Pop Star, and (Oh Yeah) Boomtown Rat," *Musician*, August 1985.

322 **issued a warning that twenty-two African nations**: Shona McKay, "The Terrible Face of Famine," *Maclean's*, November 19, 1984.

322 **only about 43 percent**: Reuters, "Ethiopia Sets Plan to Combat Drought," *Washington Post*, October 5, 1984.

322 **"Once again it was the media"**: Peter Gill, *Famine & Foreigners: Ethiopia Since Live Aid* (Oxford: Oxford University Press, 2010), 42.

322 **"There were about ten thousand people there"**: David Fricke, "Bob Geldof: The Man Who Wouldn't Take No for an Answer," *Rolling Stone*, August 15, 1985.

323 **"Ethiopia. Everyone who visits"**: Bob Geldof, *Is That It? The Autobiography* (New York: Grove, 1987), 217.

323 **"I said, 'Piss off'"**: Barry McIlheney, "Feed the World," *Melody Maker*, December 8, 1984.

323 **"[We] had to be brutal"**: Lori Majewski, "The Making of Band Aid: Secrets and Stories from the Star-Studded Session," *Rolling Stone*, November 25, 2014, rollingstone.com/music/music-news/the-making-of-band-aid-secrets-and -stories-from-the-star-studded-session-172815/.

324 **"I'd like to say hi"**: Geldof, *Is That It?*, 230.

324 **"Geldof just says, 'Start here'"**: Collins and McLean, *Not Dead Yet*, 196.

324 **"Who's there?"**: Majewski, "The Making of Band Aid."

324 **"It was as if everybody"**: George and Bright, *Take It Like a Man*, 257.

325 **"Everybody was just totally out of it"**: Jobling, *U2—The Definitive Biography*, 136.

325 **"didn't seem a very big deal":** Peter Martin, "A Year in the Life of Wham!," in *The Smash Hits Yearbook 1986* (Brentford, UK: EMAP Publications, 1985).

325 **"to hide how scruffy":** Andy Taylor, *Wild Boy—My Life in Duran Duran* (New York: Grand Central Publishing, 2008), 210.

326 **"suddenly nobody want[ed] to sing":** McIlheney, "Feed the World."

326 **"Do I have to sing that?":** Geldof, *Is That It?*, 228.

326 **"Right up until the last minute":** McIlheney, "Feed the World."

326 **"This is not about what you want":** Majewski, "The Making of Band Aid."

326 **"I knew I was there":** McCormick et al., *U2 by U2*, 158.

327 **"[It's] not saying":** Majewski, "The Making of Band Aid."

327 **"kind of did an impersonation":** McCormick et al., *U2 by U2*, 158.

327 **"Well, Bob":** Jobling, *U2—The Definitive Biography*, 136.

327 **"Today proved once and for all":** Peter Martin, "The Single for Ethiopia," *Smash Hits*, December 6–19, 1984.

327 **"To realize what made *Smash Hits* special":** Mark Frith, ed., *The Best of Smash Hits: The '80s* (London: Sphere, 2006), 3.

327 **"The Bobby O influence":** Chris Heath, *Pet Shop Boys, Literally* (Cambridge, MA: Da Capo Press, 1990), 56–57.

CHAPTER NINETEEN: WESTWOOD ONE, CULVER CITY, CALIFORNIA, APRIL 20, 1985

Author interviews with Susan A. Baker (July 2019) and Chrissie Dunlap, Steve Peters, and Tom Werman. A number of quotes are taken from *Radio USA for Africa* (Westwood One Radio Network special, April 20, 1985), via spreaker.com/show/the-raydio-show.

328 **"The number of platinum albums":** Paul Grein, "Big Jumps in Platinum, Gold," *Billboard*, January 12, 1985.

328 **"Record/tape retailers spelled Christmas":** Fred Goodman and Earl Paige, "Catalog Sales Make Dealers Merry—Cassettes, CDs Also Contribute to Holiday Surge," *Billboard*, January 12, 1985.

328 **$299.95:** "Overview," *Billboard*, December 22, 1984.

328 **between thirteen and fifteen dollars:** Is Horowitz, "CD Back Orders Vex Labels," *Billboard*, December 22, 1984.

328 **"It seemed there were a lot of kids":** Goodman and Paige, "Catalog Sales."

329 **less than six weeks:** John Sippel, "Droz: WEA's '84 Sales Will Show 35% Hike," *Billboard*, December 15, 1984.

329 **"When Madonna's newest":** Peter Holden, "Retailers Look Back on Prosperity," *Cash Box*, December 29, 1984.

329 **"Epic just wanted to certify":** Paul Grein, "106 Multiple Platinums Kick Off RIAA Award," *Billboard*, December 15, 1984.

329 **"Let's hope it won't":** "Editorial: Platinum Alone Is Not Enough," *Billboard*, December 8, 1984.

329 **"toastmaster general of the immoral majority":** fasterpdiddy, "12/31/1984 MTV 4th Annual New Year's Eve Rock and Roll Ball—Drunk DLR Clips," YouTube video, 13:31, published March 5, 2019, youtube.com/watch?v =Ncb8oalNStk.

330 **"Let's pretend you and I were managers":** Billy Altman, "David Lee Roth: & the Gleeby Shall Rock," *Creem*, April 1985.

330 **"I've heard some great music":** Ethlie Ann Vare, "Van Halen's Roth: Maybe It's Over," *Billboard*, January 12, 1985.

330 **"At first the *Crazy*":** David Wild, "Eddie Van Halen: Balancing Act—the Rolling Stone Interview," *Rolling Stone*, April 6, 1995.

330 **"Well, guys":** Ian Christe, *Everybody Wants Some: The Van Halen Saga* (New York: Wiley, 2007), 115.

330 **"I felt like I'd put up" and "We jammed":** Wild, "Eddie Van Halen."

330 **"shut the door on everything":** G. R. Anderson Jr., "I Hate 1984: Van Halen's '1984'—the Working Dirtball's California Dreams" (printout), CityPages.com, March 31, 2004, from author's collection.

331 **"A nurse who lived nearby":** Phil Collen with Chris Epting, *Adrenalized: Life, Def Leppard, and Beyond* (New York: Atria Books, 2015), 100.

331 **"Their look seems tailor-made":** Richard Fantina, "Hanoi Rocks Not Chinese," *Creem*, August 1984.

331 **on $2,000 bail:** "Mötley Crüe Frontman Accused of Manslaughter in Fatal Auto Accident," *Variety*, December 12, 1984.

331 **"Our drummer died":** Martin Popoff, *The Big Book of Hair Metal* (Stillwater, MN: Voyageur Press, 2014), 81.

332 **That July:** Sue Cummings, "Asleep at the Wheel," *Spin*, December 1985.

333 **early-sixties Dion hits:** Zack O'Malley Greenburg, *Michael Jackson, Inc.* (New York: Atria Books, 2014), 98.

333 **spent 1981 trying:** Irv Lichtman, "ATV Music on Sales Block," *Billboard*, October 13, 1984.

333 **$20 million bid:** Randall Sullivan, *Untouchable* (New York: Grove Press, 2012), 103.

333 **Holmes à Court was asking $60 million:** Lichtman, "ATV Music."

333 **"Michael Jackson appears":** "Inside Track," *Billboard*, December 22, 1984.

333 **May 1985:** Sullivan, *Untouchable*, 103–104.

334 **some $8 million . . . mild heart attack:** Steve Knopper, *MJ—The Genius of Michael Jackson* (New York: Scribner, 2015), 148.

334 **"spending 1984 giving":** Rusty Cutchin, "'Victory' Was a Real Show Off Stage Too: Tour Is Over, Battles Remain," *Cash Box*, December 15, 1984.

334 **"biggest-selling record of all time":** Robert J. McNamara, "Prince Dominates Sales," *Rolling Stone*, October 11, 1984.

334 **Warner Home Video:** Tony Seideman, "Holiday Sales Seen Capping Video Boom," *Billboard*, November 10, 1984.

334 **"You know . . . for five years":** David Keeps, "Chaka Khan," *Smash Hits*, November 8–21, 1984.

334 **1.7 million tickets:** Sarah Dupuis and Erik Myers, "*Purple Rain* by the Numbers," *Spin*, July 2009.

334 **less than ten hours:** "Prince Concert Dates Set D.C. Ticket Sales Record," *Billboard*, October 13, 1984.

334 **twenty dollars apiece:** Nelson George, "Prince, Frankie Go to Town," *Billboard*, November 10, 1984.

335 **"I'm supportive of the arts":** "Governor Rudy Perpich: Pop Music Quickly Becomes Focus," *Billboard*, August 25, 1984.

335 ***Billboard* had totted up 1984's top artists:** "Overview."

336 **"I've never met this person":** Chris Heath, "The Frankie Goes to Hollywood Story," *The Smash Hits Yearbook 1986* (Brentford, UK: EMAP Publications, 1985).

336 **Prince's bodyguard barked at onlookers:** Dee Snider, *Shut Up and Give Me the Mic: A Memoir* (New York: Gallery Books, 2012), 317.

336 **"Prince looked over at me":** Jon Bream and Chris Riemenschneider with Jim Meyer, "Prince: An Oral History," *Star Tribune* (Minneapolis–St. Paul), March 14, 2004.

336 **"It's heart attack time now":** Thomas O'Neil, *The Grammys for the Record* (London: Penguin, 1993), 390–391.

336 **"Those of us involved":** Mo Ostin, "What Do the Grammys Represent?," *Billboard*, February 23, 1985.

337 **"If I don't put a record out":** Richard Harrington, "Stevie Wonder: The Goal Achieved," *Washington Post*, January 14, 1984.

337 **"the biggest single in the history of Stevie Wonder":** Fred Bronson, *The Billboard Book of Number 1 Hits*, 5th ed. (New York: Billboard Books, 2003).

338 **"Belafonte had said publicly":** Bob Geldof, *Is That It? The Autobiography* (London: Weidenfeld & Nicholson, 1986), 257.

338 **the Concert for Bangladesh:** Richard Harrington, "The Greatest Show on Earth, Tomorrow," *Washington Post*, July 12, 1985.

339 **"A few hours later":** Sharon Davis, *Lionel Richie—Hello* (London: Equinox, 2009), 94.

339 **"He just slept on the floor":** Gavin Edwards, "Billboard Legend of Live Honoree Lionel Richie Remembers His Time with the Rolling Stones, Frank Sinatra and Michael Jackson (and His Snake)," *Billboard*, November 14, 2014, billboard.com/articles/news/6319722/lionel-richie-billboard-legend-of-live-honoree-remembers-michael-jackson-frank-sinatra-rolling-stones.

339 **"We didn't want a normal-sounding song":** Brian Mansfield, "'We Are the World' at 30: 12 Tales You Might Not Know," *USA Today*, January 27, 2015, usatoday.com/story/life/music/2015/01/27/we-are-the-world-30th-anniversary/22395455/.

339 **"Leave your ego at the door":** Davis, *Lionel Richie*, 95.

340 **Bob Geldof [quotes]:** Geldof, *Is That It?*, 240–259.

342 **"We got married at midnight":** Bruce Springsteen, *Born to Run* (New York: Simon & Schuster, 2016), 331.

342 **"You see dead bodies":** Gavin Edwards, "'We Are the World': A Minute-by-Minute Breakdown," *Rolling Stone*, March 6, 2020, rollingstone.com/music/music-features/we-are-the-world-a-minute-by-minute-breakdown-54619/.

342 **"We were disappointed":** Paul Grein, "First Three Stars Pledge Tracks to Africa Album," *Billboard*, February 16, 1985.

342 **"I don't need him":** Edwards, "'We Are the World.'"

342 **Prince's bodyguards:** Carol McGraw, "Prince's Bodyguards Held," *Los Angeles Times*, January 30, 1985.

343 *Saturday Night Live*: marman51212, "I Am Also the World" (segment) in "Hulk Hogan and Mr. T host SNL," *Saturday Night Live*, aired March 30, 1985, YouTube video, 20:28, published October 18, 2013, youtube.com/watch?v=74fFSVN-GkQ.

343 **"Prince is withdrawing":** Cox News Service, "Prince Says He'll Quit Stage After Concert in Orange Bowl," *Minneapolis Star & Tribune*, April 4, 1985.

343 **"In some ways":** Bream et al., "Prince: An Oral History."

343 **"I'm up the ladder":** Chris Heath, "The Extraordinary Ordinary Life of the Artist Formerly Known as Prince," *GQ*, December 2016.

344 **"It sounds like a Pepsi commercial":** Jordan Runtagh, "Flashback: Music Stars Record 'We Are the World' on January 28, 1985," *Rolling Stone*, January 28, 2019, rollingstone.com/music/music-news/we-are-the-world-record-usa-africa-785832/.

344 **"This is not 'The Rite of Spring'":** Edwards, "'We Are the World.'"

344 **"We were all kind of doing it":** Mansfield, "'We Are the World' at 30."

344 **"It's like being a cheerleader of the chorus":** Edwards, "'We Are the World.'"

345 **"Let the song speak for itself":** "Michael Jackson and Lionel Richie's Song Earns Millions for Africa's Famine Victims," *Jet*, April 8, 1985.

345 **"It's too late anyway":** Philip Manoevre and Sheryl Garratt, "Walking on the Moon," *The Face*, no. 100 (September 1988).

CHAPTER TWENTY: WEMBLEY STADIUM, LONDON, AND JFK STADIUM, PHILADELPHIA, JULY 13, 1985

A complete recording of the Live Aid audio, sourced from the BBC and MTV, is quoted throughout this chapter. Material accessed from the website Madonna: The Warner Bros. Years (mtwy.tumblr.com) is indicated below as "via MTWY."

346 **"He was going to visit this graveyard":** Bill Graham with Robert Greenfield, *Bill Graham Presents: My Life Inside Rock and Out* (Cambridge, MA: Da Capo Press, 2004; orig., 1990), 453.

347 **"This is really being faked":** John Glatt, *Rage & Roll: Bill Graham and the Selling of Rock* (New York: Birch Lane Press, 1993), 208.

347 **"My sisters have told me":** Docs&Interviews on MV, "Bill Graham—Interview—8/4/1974—KQED (Official)," YouTube video, 25:10, published September 25, 2014, youtube.com/watch?v=eVeuDS0n3XI&feature=emb_title.

347 **a reported 40 percent:** Al Clark, ed., *The Rock Yearbook 1983* (London: Virgin Books, 1982).

347 **"melted flat":** Graham with Greenfield, *Bill Graham Presents*, 456.

347 **"like I had been raped emotionally":** Graham with Greenfield, *Bill Graham Presents*, 458.

348 **"happened a day after":** Glatt, *Rage & Roll*, 220.

348 **fourteen hours:** Glatt, *Rage & Roll*, 218.

348 **"This is, quite categorically":** "Band Aid Live!," *Melody Maker*, June 15, 1985.

348 **"The whole house shook":** Cherri Gregg, "Survivor Remembers Bombing of Philadelphia Headquarters," CBS Philly, May 13, 2013, philadelphia.cbslocal.com/2013/05/13/survivor-remembers-bombing-of-philadelphia-headquarters/.

348 **"let the fire burn":** Gene Demby, "I'm from Philly. 30 Years Later, I'm Still Trying to Make Sense of the MOVE Bombing," NPR, May 13, 2015, npr.org/sections/codeswitch/2015/05/13/406243272/im-from-philly-30-years-later-im-still-trying-to-make-sense-of-the-move-bombing.

348 **"In England people give their services free":** Michael Goldberg, "Live Aid 1985: The Day the World Rocked," *Rolling Stone*, August 16, 1985.

349 **"You had to do hits":** Graham with Greenfield, *Bill Graham Presents*, 467.

349 **"moral blackmail":** David Fricke, "Bob Geldof: The Man Who Wouldn't Take No for an Answer," *Rolling Stone*, August 15, 1985.

349 **with black performers:** Roger Catlin, "USA for Africa: Five Years, $106 Million," *Hartford (CT) Courant*, April 15, 1990.

349 **Ewart Abner:** Bob Geldof, *Is That It? The Autobiography* (London: Weidenfeld & Nicholson, 1986), 280.

349 **"They were going to see how it panned out":** Graham with Greenfield, *Bill Graham Presents*, 470–471.

349 **"Rock and roll was the umbilical cord":** Joe Smith, "Off the Record Interview with Bill Graham, 1988-05-09," loc.gov/item/jsmith000024/.

349 **"Bill didn't understand that MTV":** Glatt, *Rage & Roll*, 224.

349 **"This was going to be a TV show":** Graham with Greenfield, *Bill Graham Presents*, 467.

350 **"Assuming it comes off well":** Glatt, *Rage & Roll*, 223.

350 **roller-skated through Kensington Palace:** "Live Aid R.I.P.," *The Word*, November 2004.

350 **"I made my money":** Leslie Berman and Rosemary Passantino, "London Calling," *Village Voice*, July 23, 1985.

350 **"For fuck's sake":** Geldof, *Is That It?*, 300.

350 **Trevor Dann:** Mark Ellen, "The Longest Day," *The Word*, November 2004.

351 **air-guitaring along:** Ian Cranna, ed., *The Rock Yearbook 1986* (New York: St. Martin's Press, 1985), 36.

351 **"I thought, 'I'm glad'":** Carl Wilkinson, "Live Aid in Their Own Words," *The Guardian* (Manchester), October 16, 2004, theguardian.com/music/2004/oct/17/popandrock5.

351 **"Everybody was crying around me":** Geldof, *Is That It?*, 293.

351 **"You have to pull scams together":** Fricke, "Bob Geldof."

351 **"I'm lucky, I don't have to attract votes":** Frank Broughton, ed., *Time Out Interviews, 1968–1998* (London: Penguin, 1998), 176.

351 **"I take it Bob Geldof didn't like us":** "80 from the Eighties," insert from *Mojo*, August 2007.

352 **"I mean, it's one thing":** "The Morrissey Inquisition," *Melody Maker*, March 16, 1985.

352 **"just an *awful* band":** Broughton, *Time Out Interviews*.

352 **"The pain in my spine vanished":** Geldof, *Is That It?*, 303.

352 **"Who the hell's that?":** "Saturday 13th July 1985: The Greatest Show on Earth," *Smash Hits*, July 17, 1985.

352 **"They were waiting for boom-boom rock":** Bill Barol, "Rock Around the World," *Newsweek*, July 22, 1985.

352 **"I changed everything":** Graham with Greenfield, *Bill Graham Presents*, 474.

353 **"I'm starting to learn expressions":** Ethlie Ann Vare, "Sade Faces Tough U.S. Sell Despite Success in U.K.," *Billboard*, February 16, 1985.

353 **"Can you imagine looking":** Graham with Greenfield, *Bill Graham Presents*, 469.

353 **"allegedly interfering":** "Sabbath Mgr. Sues Osbourne Family," *Variety*, July 17, 1985.

354 **"Night Prowler":** Linda Martin and Kerry Segrave, *Anti-Rock: The Opposition to Rock 'n' Roll* (Cambridge, MA: Da Capo Press, 1993), 282.

354 **"Mr. Chairman, this would approach censorship":** guyjohn59, "John Denver at PMRC Hearings," September 19, 1985, YouTube video, 7:38, published June 21, 2010, youtube.com/watch?v=VgSjjD6rRu4.

354 **"It is my understanding":** Clinton Heylin, ed., *The Da Capo Book of Rock & Roll Writing* (Cambridge, MA: Da Capo Press, 1999), 502.

354 **"I would like to tell the committee":** Dee Snider, *Shut Up and Give Me the Mic: A Memoir* (New York: Gallery, 2012), 341–348.

355 **"what they're doing for Ethiopia":** Lyndsey Parker, "An Oral History of Live Aid: The Ones Who Made a Brighter Day, 30 Years Ago," Yahoo! Entertainment, July 10, 2015, yahoo.com/music/an-oral-history-of-live-aid-the-ones-who-made-a-123778461786.html.

355 **"It was in the same arena":** "Hip-Hop Memories," *The Source*, no. 50 (November 1993).

355 **sold out in a week:** David Hinckley, "Let's Stop Giving Them a Bad Rap," *New York Daily News*, December 27, 1985, via Adler Archive.

355 **"the glove-stepping thing":** Ronin Ro, *Raising Hell* (New York: Amistad Press, 2005), 109.

356 **"lots of rock guitar":** Kim Freeman, "Profile Label Seeking New Music Mix," *Billboard*, January 12, 1985.

356 **"I just said to myself":** J. D. Considine, "The Second Coming of Phil Collins," *Musician*, June 1985.

356 **"'Children's Crusade' is an appeal to reason":** Timothy White, "Sting II," *Spin*, July 1985.

356 **"By the way":** Phil Collins with Craig McLean, *Not Dead Yet: The Memoir* (New York: Archetype, 2016), 208.

356 **"The syllables 'Led' and 'Zep'":** Collins and McLean, *Not Dead Yet*, 204.

357 **"Tony did tell us later":** Peter Hook, *Substance: Inside New Order* (New York: Dey Street, 2017), 14.

357 **"I could see an Irish flag":** Neil McCormick, Bono, the Edge, Adam Clayton, and Larry Mullen Jr., *U2 by U2* (New York: It Books, 2009), 160.

357 **"one of the worst haircuts in the eighties":** John Jobling, *U2—the Definitive Biography* (New York: Thomas Dunne Books, 2014), 132.

358 **"When you're performing":** Michka Assayas, *Bono in Conversation* (New York: Riverhead, 2005), 210.

358 **"I'm just glad the cameras":** McCormick et al., *U2 by U2*, 160.

358 **"Everyone was very annoyed":** Assayas, *Bono in Conversation*, 210–211.

358 **"was going nuts":** Jobling, *U2—the Definitive Biography*, 144.

358 **"I thought I'd ruined":** Assayas, *Bono in Conversation*, 211.

358 **"I actually leapt":** Simon Reynolds, *Totally Wired* (London: Faber & Faber, 2009), 71.

358 **"We were touring in the Far East":** Peter Hillmore, William McGuire, and Bob Geldof, *Live Aid: The Greatest Show on Earth* (London: Sedgwick & Jackson, 1985).

359 **"Tell the old faggot":** David Thomas, "Their Britannic Majesties Request," *Mojo*, August 1999.

359 **"We're totally against apartheid":** William Shaw, "Queen," *Smash Hits*, March 26–April 8, 1986.

359 **Marilyn McCoo:** Minute-by-minute review of the MTV "Live Aid" live broadcast on July 13, 1985, liveaid.free.fr/rewind/mtv/index.html?fbclid=I wAR1LhWw6pva_AFvBW_3u0cd11o4tWFI-cnYvO3x3J48CC9N_fMJRz QmRHKA.

359 **"three days' rehearsal":** Mark Ellen, "It's 12 O'Clock in London," *The Word*, November 2004.

360 **"We were louder":** Thomas, "Their Britannic Majesties Request."

360 **"It might have only been":** Barry McIlheney and Carol Clerk, "The Greatest Show on Earth; Live Aid, July 13, 1985," *Melody Maker*, July 20, 1985.

360 **"Because I wouldn't do":** Ellen, "It's 12."

360 **"I had my head in my hands":** Chris O'Leary, *Ashes to Ashes: The Songs of David Bowie, 1976–2016* (London: Repeater Books, 2019), 234.

361 **"The phones, which had been quiet":** David Hepworth, "The Day TV Changed Forever," *The Word*, November 2004.

361 **"I know it's going to run out of petrol!":** Cranna, *The Rock Yearbook 1986*, 36.

361 **"The bride looked up":** Bernard Doherty, "All So Terribly English," *The Word*, November 2004.

362 **"It's a children's movie":** LiveAidWizard, "MTV Interview—David Bowie & Thomas Dolby (MTV—Live Aid 7/13/1985)," YouTube video, 3:11, published July 10, 2016, youtu.be/k0fcyS1boKM.

362 **"They sent him to Wembley":** Nina Blackwood, Mark Goodman, Alan Hunter, and Martha Quinn, with Gavin Edwards, *VJ* (New York: Atria Books, 2013), 248.

363 **"They look a bit":** "Saturday 13th July 1985."

363 **"Pete Townshend did the splits":** Hillmore et al., *Live Aid.*

363 **"That was the downfall of the Who":** Goldberg, "Live Aid."

363 **"It got to the point":** Charles M. Young, "Who's Back," *Musician*, July 1989.

363 **"Gone are the glasses":** "Concert Reviews: Elton John (Ent. Ctr., Sydney)," *Variety*, March 28, 1984.

363 **"The States give me":** Joe Smith, "Off the Record Interview with Elton John, 1986-10-19," hdl.loc.gov/loc.mbrsrs/mbrsjoesmith.1835722.

363 **"I've been a fan of Prince":** Ron Fell, "Elton John: Off the Road and Ready for '85," *Gavin Report*, December 21, 1984.

363 **"That to me was the first":** Peter Martin, "A Year in the Life of Wham!," in *The Smash Hits Yearbook 1986* (Brentford, UK: EMAP Publications, 1985).

364 **"both just bought":** Joe Smith, "Off the Record Interview with George Michael, 1986-11-10," hdl.loc.gov/loc.mbrsrs/mbrsjoesmith.1835742.

364 **"look[ed] like a cross":** McIlheney and Clerk, "The Greatest Show on Earth."

364 **"Within a month of coming home":** Pat Gilbert, "Wham! Play China, 1985," *Mojo*, September 2015.

364 **"My songwriting":** Cranna, *The Rock Yearbook 1986.*

364 **"When I'm singing":** Bill Lane, "Teddy Pendergrass Sings for Women Only," *Sepia*, December 1978.

364 **Tenika Watson:** Tim Purtell, "Encore: The Trials of Teddy Pendergrass," *Entertainment Weekly*, March 18, 1994.

365 **"It's more sensitive":** Rusty Cutchin, "The Rhythm Section," *Cash Box*, June 9, 1984.

365 **"composing and recording":** Teddy Pendergrass and Patricia Romanowski, *Truly Blessed* (New York: G. P. Putnam's Sons, 1998), 270–271.

365 **"I was nervous enough":** Pendergrass and Romanowski, *Truly Blessed*, 271–272.

365 **"For the first time":** Pendergrass and Romanowski, *Truly Blessed*, 273.

366 **"Madonna will be out of the business":** "These Big Girls Don't Cry," *Time*, March 4, 1985, via MTWY.

366 **"If there were ten rungs":** Robert Hilburn, "Madonna Takes Total Control," *Los Angeles Times*, November 11, 1984.

366 **"feared that Madonna might":** Reid Rosefelt, "My Life as a Blog: Taking Madonna to the Amadeus Party and Other Tales of Madge's Early Days," Moviemaker.com, February 28, 2011, moviemaker.com/archives/blogs/blog-my-life-as-a-blog/my-life-as-a-blog-taking-madonna-to-the-amadeus-party-and-other-tales-of-ma/.

366 *Pink Rain:* Michael London, "Strong-Willed Women Behind 'Seeking Susan,'" *Los Angeles Times*, April 2, 1985, via MTWY.

366 **"This movie is like" and "become an issue":** Fred Schruers, "Lucky Stars," *Rolling Stone*, May 9, 1985.

366 **seventy-five thousand copies per day:** Carl Arrington, "Madonna," *People*, March 11, 1985.

366 **"It was her idea":** Harold Conrad, "The Glamorous Life of Al Yankovic," *Spin*, August 1985.

367 **"She sells more than Springsteen" and "Madonna's living out":** *People*, May 13, 1985, via MTWY.

367 **"Ad-Rock ended the show":** Alan Light, *The Skills to Pay the Bills: The Story of the Beastie Boys* (New York: Three Rivers Press, 2006), 64.

367 **On July 11:** "Injunction Denied, Penthouse to Print Nudes of Madonna," *Variety*, July 17, 1985.

367 **"I'm not ashamed of anything":** Stephanie Mansfield, "Madonna's Photo Finish," *Washington Post*, July 11, 1985.

367 **"Crucifixes are sexy":** Scott Cohen, "Confessions of a Madonna," *Spin*, May 1985.

368 **"MTV made matters worse":** Blackwood et al., *VJ*, 249–250.

368 **"Fuck me, he's a heavy bastard":** Geldof, *Is That It?*, 310.

369 **"Why don't you shut up?":** Andy Taylor, *Wild Boy—My Life in Duran Duran* (New York: Grand Central Publishing, 2008), 215.

369 **"The air was acrid":** A. Taylor, *Wild Boy*, 4.

369 **"I didn't want to end up like Elvis":** Rob Fitzpatrick, "The Artists Formerly Known as Swoon," *The Word*, November 2004.

369 **"slid[ing] around the stage":** "Saturday 13th July 1985."

370 **"We virtually ruined the whole thing":** Tom Hibbert, "Robert Plant: Guilty!," *Q*, March 1988.

370 **"When I reach a conclusion":** David Fricke, "Robert Plant: The Rolling Stone Interview," *Rolling Stone*, March 24, 1988.

370 **"being difficult, giving vague":** Collins and McLean, *Not Dead Yet*, 214.

370 **"Phil Collins is on stage again!":** "Saturday 13th July 1985."

370 **"Nobody would have been surprised":** Hillmore et al., *Live Aid*.

371 **"Morrissey? Who's that?":** Tom Hibbert, "If You Don't Know Who This Bloke Is, Ask Your Parents," *Smash Hits*, February 14, 1985.

371 **"I drank a lot of wine":** Brian D. Johnson, "The Comeback Queen of Rock'n'Roll," *Maclean's*, July 22, 1985.

371 **"Bob dropped by on Ronnie":** Mat Snow, Keith Richards feature, *New Musical Express (NME)*, February 22, 1986.

371 **"couldn't hear anything":** Goldberg, "Live Aid."

371 **"My God, he sounds":** James Wolcott, "Dylan Beyond Thunderdome," *Vanity Fair*, October 1985.

372 **"Sorry":** Geldof, *Is That It?*, 312.

372 **"I remember thinking that":** Ellen, "The Longest Day."

372 **"I just don't think":** "Timeline," *The Face*, no. 100 (September 1988).

INDEX